The Light and the Dark Mabdelore Winter

The Trilogy

"An epic tale of Witches, Daemons, Angels, Gods and Goddesses, spanning across space and time."

By

David M Martin

This book is dedicated to my wife Moira, my soul mate, who constantly encourages me, and believes in me when others doubt.

Acknowledgments

A number of people have supported me in the writing of Mabdelore Winter, The Trilogy.

I would like to thank:

My wife Moira, for her constant support and encouragement.

Antonio Lopez, and his team for the calm and confident way they managed the progression of the book through to publication.

Heidi Adams, for her kind and helpful comments throughout and for her review of the book contents.

Mike Ross for his relentless editing of the manuscript.

"...whether we like it or not, and no matter where we may travel in the multiverse, all sentient creatures know that there is good and there is evil, all know the difference and all are free to choose which path to follow."

- **Master Takeo Daichi Kanaka**

Contents

Prologue

Walim Winter and Sopa Allarn grew up on farms and met at a local farmers' show when they were teenagers. They married in their late teens and initially lived with Walim's parents but then moved to Blant when Sopa's father died and Sopa inherited the farm.

Walim and Sopa had been married for ten years and still, Sopa had not conceived. They desperately wanted a baby and so visited medics, experts in herbal medicines, local sears and also witches. They attended church every week and prayed every night before going to sleep, but nothing made any difference. Eventually, they came to accept that, for whatever reason, it wasn't going to happen.

It was late on a cold autumn night when the local Priest knocked on their door and asked if he could speak to them about a private matter. The Priest explained that an infant girl had been found in the church wrapped in a silk cloak. A message was left saying that the child's name was Mabdelore and Mr and Mrs Winter had agreed to adopt her. The Priest said he discussed the matter with his superior, who instructed him to prepare the necessary adoption forms, take them to Mr and Mrs Winter for signing and then lodge them with the authorities.

Walim looked at Sopa and then asked the Priest where the child was. The Priest said the child was at his house, and his wife was looking after her until the forms were signed. Sopa asked to see the forms which he produced together with a pencil, he pointed to the signature box. Sopa looked at Walim, took the pencil and signed her name in the box. She then handed the pencil to Walim, who did the same.

Walim and Sopa followed the Priest on their horse and trapped to the rectory. The Priest's wife brought the child, still wrapped in silk and handed her to Sopa. She told Sopa that the child's name was Mabdelore, now Mabdelore Winter. Sopa and Walim, from first sight, were besotted with Mabdelore, her shock of blonde hair, her pale white skin and her blacker-than-black eyes. Sopa said she was the most beautiful thing she had ever seen. Mabdelore Winter looked up at her mother and smiled her biggest smile.

Takeo Daichi Kanaka, even as a young man, was a world-class swordsman and a recognised expert on swords and swordsmanship. He was also a gifted martial arts student with powerful psychic abilities, all of which made him a very formidable warrior. He had participated in a number of battles over the years in support of the military but had come to realise that there was nothing skilful, elegant or satisfying about war. The butchery associated with mass killing was not for him, it turned his stomach. One-to-one combat, however, was different; pitting your skills against an equally gifted opponent, especially when swordplay was involved, could be skilful, elegant and in many ways beautiful to behold.

He left the military for a position as Head of a martial arts school, which he developed into the largest, most successful school in the Northern region. It was through his success in that role that he was offered the position of Principal of the Guild of Sorcerers (the GOS). Kanaka wanted to move to the Southern region, that was where the real seats of power resided. The Palace and the four magic schools were located there in relatively close proximity to each other. Outside of the Southern region, the habitable areas were sparse and largely agricultural in nature and were regarded by many as backwaters. He also knew that a combination of magic and martial skills was needed to create the very best warriors, and he dreamed of being or creating the perfect warrior. He, therefore, accepted the offer without question.

Kanaka understood that his main task would be to turnaround the poor performance of the GOS. To do that he needed to attract the very best talent into the Guild. In fact, when he took up his new position, he found the role difficult mainly because there was an inordinate amount of paperwork to get through on a daily basis. He was a warrior, not an administrator. After five years in the post, he was coming to the conclusion that he should look for another, perhaps more hands-on, role. But then he was involved in an interview with a young girl who was applying to become a student of the Guild. Everything changed.

Book One

The Bane of the Dark Prince

Chapter One: The Guild of Sorcerers

Mabdelore Winter, or Mab as she was known as a child, had a mop of curly blonde hair as an infant. This changed to a silky black by the time she was six or seven years old. Her eyes, however, didn't change. They were deep black orbs which, against her pale skin, could be quite disconcerting.

Mab's parents had a small holding with goats, pigs and chickens and also two large allotments where they were able to grow a variety of vegetables. The farm was located just outside the village of Blant, where Mab went to school. The farmhouse was large and sprawling, but several of the outbuildings were dilapidated and the living accommodation was difficult to heat during the winter months. They would often resort to living in one room when the weather was particularly harsh. The family was reasonably self-sufficient with regard to food, but money was tight and they could not afford the finer things that some other families enjoyed. Mab, however, could not have been happier. Her parents, Walim and Sopa, adored her and Mab knew that she was loved, so nothing else mattered. At school, she was by all accounts a shy, rather introverted child who was clearly very bright but did not like to contribute to class discussions. It was when she entered senior school at the age of fifteen she came to the attention of the Guild of Sorcerers.

The Guild Masters, at that time, visited schools in order to identify latent talent that could aspire to become student members of the Guild. On the morning of their visit, Mab arrived late to school. Her walk from home to school took her through a stretch of dense woodland known as Bluebell Wood, which in the spring and summer months was vibrant with life. As she walked, small animals would often follow her and birds often swoop low around her; she had grown used to this but thought it strange that it only happened when she was on her own. On this beautiful summer morning, she wandered off her usual path, engrossed by the wildflowers, and so arrived at school almost an hour late.

Mab rushed through the main entrance and along the long corridor to her classroom, but no one was there. Ms Elder, who was the Deputy Headmistress, saw her and called out, 'Mab, late again! You are supposed to be in the back playground. Go now!' Mab dropped her bag in fright but quickly recovered and made her way, panting, to the back of the school. She saw her classmates standing in four widely spaced lines before three figures, one dressed in a long black and gold robe and the other two with grey, less ornate robes. Mab's eyes nearly popped out of her head when she saw the largest dog she had ever seen lying on the ground beside the three strangers!

Mab caught sight of her friends Izzy, Mel and Gord standing in the back row and rushed to join them while avoiding the look of disapproval on Ms Elm's face. Mab whispered to Mel, 'What's going on?'

'They are from the GOS; look at that dog!' replied Mel.

'Yes, it's as big as a donkey! But what do they want with us?' said Mab.

'I'm not sure, I think it's an inspection,' replied Mel.

Ms Elm then stepped forward and said, 'Children, we are honoured today by a visit from the esteemed Guild of Sorcerers. Every year, the GOS visits schools in our region to assess stage three children for potential studentships with the Guild. Being a very small school, we have never had any studentships awarded.' Ms Elm looked disappointedly at the GOS representatives before adding, 'In any case, Master Boe will now explain the work of the Guild and the opportunities for studentships.'

Master Boe, in a soft melodic voice, said, 'Thank you, Ms Elm, as you say, this is a very small school and the latent abilities we seek are rare, so please do not be disappointed with regard to studentships; there is always hope that a diamond may be found amid the dross.' Ms Elm gave him an icy look but said nothing.

'I think he means we are the dross?' said Gord.

'I don't like him,' said Izzy as she switched places with Gord and stood next to Mab.

'You don't like anyone other than Mab,' said Gord.

'What is dross?' said Izzy, whispering closely into Mab's ear.

'I don't know, I don't think it's anything bad,' replied Mab, smiling at Izzy. Mab's face suddenly flushed with anger; she had just remembered the meaning of 'dross.' The big dog stood up.

Master Boe, glancing down at the dog, said, 'This is Meldran. Please don't be afraid. He will not harm you. As Ms Elm said, we are from the Guild of Sorcerers. The Guild is one of the great schools of Magic and we are constantly on the look-out for young boys and girls who have the potential to study at our school. Gho and Zak are students of the Guild and will walk around; you don't have to do anything other than stand still, try to clear your mind and answer any questions as best you can. Gho, Zak, please continue.'

The two students started to walk slowly along the lines, sometimes stopping for a few seconds before moving on. Meldran started walking slowly to the back row, with Master Boe following. Meldran stopped at the end of the row and stared directly at Mab. She had her head down but could feel the weight of his stare. Mab lifted her chin and turned cold eyes toward him. Meldran flinched as if he had been physically struck, dropped his head with a low whine and took several steps backward. Master Boe walked towards Mab and said, 'Who are you?'

'I'm Mab,' said Mab in a matter-of-fact tone. Mab looked at Meldran, smiled warmly and said, 'Meldran, I'm sorry if I scared you.' Meldran loped towards her and snuggled in. Mab laughed and rubbed his huge head behind the ears.

Ms Elm approached and said, 'Is there a problem, Master Boe?'

Master Boe said, 'A problem? No, Ms Elm, I think not. But there is something here that I don't understand. I would like you to bring Mab to the Guild for a formal interview and assessment. I would also like her parents to attend. Could that be arranged?'

Ms Elm replied, 'Well, yes, of course, but I will first need to speak to Mab's parents.'

Master Boe said, 'Please do so.' Master Boe turned to look once again at Mab with Meldran, who was behaving like a puppy, wagging his huge tail vigorously and looking at Mab with big, round eyes. 'Extraordinary.' said Master Boe, whispering to himself. Master Boe thanked Ms Elm and left with his students and Meldran in tow. Ms Elm dismissed the assembly.

Gord, Izzy and Mel gathered around Mab. 'Mab, what just happened? Are you in trouble?' asked Izzy.

'I don't know, I was really worried that I scared Meldran,' replied Mab.

'How could you scare that thing? I was terrified when it walked towards us!' said Mel.

'But what did you do?' asked Gord, looking at Mab.

'I didn't do anything, I just looked at him,' replied Mab.

'We best get back to the class, or we will all be in trouble!' said Izzy.

When Mab returned home that evening her parents already knew what had happened. Ms Elm had gone to see them earlier in the afternoon to discuss the meeting with the Guild. They said Ms Elm was very excited as the school had never had a studentship from the Guild, and she was hoping that Mab would be their first. Mab said she didn't want to go to the Guild as she would miss her friends in the village. 'I know, but you'll make new friends at the Guild, and you will be able to come back home at the end of term or at weekends if you like,' said Sopa.

'What exactly happened?' asked Walim.

'I really don't know, Dad. I didn't do anything. I think it was something to do with the big dog, Meldran, he seemed to like me,' replied Mab.

'Well, they haven't offered you anything yet, so let's just see what happens; we are going to visit the Guild on the day after tomorrow,' said Walim.

The GOS was by far the oldest of the four magic schools, the other three being the School of Psych and Sorcery, The Academy of Magic and the Occult, and the Guild of Witches and Warlocks. The GOS was regarded as traditional, stuffy even, and somewhat old-fashioned. This was reflected in a year-on-year fall in student numbers, with young talent preferring the more modern facilities and teaching methods offered by the other schools. There was also a noticeable decline in the performance of the GOS in the annual competitions hosted by the Prince Royal. This was a source of some personal embarrassment to Master Kanaka, the GOS Principal. The Annual Meeting of Magic School Principals was held shortly before the yearly competition and was hosted by Prince Sollgar, the Prince Royal.

Master Kanaka's day started with preparations for the monthly meeting of GOS Masters. Kanaka was not an administrator. In fact, he loathed the business side of running the Guild and delegated much of that to Master Paull and his young Administrative Assistant, Jon. Kanaka was fundamentally a warrior who was somewhat frustrated in his role as Principal of the GOS, which was largely that of a figurehead. He had a passion for swords and was a recognised expert in that subject. Indeed, his collection of swords was second to none, even that held by the Palace.

Kanaka's Assistant Jon was taking him through the agenda for the day and the various papers submitted by the masters. 'The masters have all submitted their usual updates on individual disciplines,' said Jon.

'Yes, this all looks fine. Has Paull detailed the progress and financial situation regarding studentships?' replied Kanaka.

'Yes, Master Paull has submitted a paper on that subject, and I will remind him regarding the need for detail,' said Jon.

'What about Boe? Has he submitted a paper on the latest round of talent searches?' asked Kanaka.

'Yes, Master Boe has submitted an update on that, he also requests your presence at a meeting with a young girl and her parents in that regard,' replied Jon.

Kanaka asked, 'He wants me to be present at the meeting?'

Jon replied, 'Yes, sir, he was quite insistent.'

Kanaka replied, 'Did he say why?'

Jon said, 'No, sir, but…'

Kanaka replied, 'But what?'

Jon said, 'Gho, a friend of mine, said this young girl just looked at Meldran and he backed away whining and the next minute, he was behaving like a puppy around her?'

Kanaka replied, 'That is strange. When is the meeting?'

Jon said, 'Sir, it's this afternoon immediately following the monthly… I know, but Master Boe was insistent.'

Walim, Sopa and Mab arrived at the Guild mid-afternoon, as agreed with Master Boe. They had never been to the Guild before and were overawed by the scale and age of the buildings. It was as big as the Royal Palace and much older. It was castle-like in appearance, with many towers and turrets and enormous oak doors. They were first led into the Great Hall, a huge space with enormous tapestries and oil paintings depicting scenes from battles with great wizards and witches of the past.

'This is magnificent, the size of this room, the paintings...' said Sopa. Just then, a tall, thin student arrived carrying a silver tray with tea, coffee and warm muffins. She wore a grey hooded robe with black braiding. 'I could get used to this!' said Sopa.

The student smiled and said, 'Hello, Mr and Mrs Winter. My name is Mona and I will be looking after you today. You must be Mab?'

Mab nodded a *yes* and Sopa said, 'Thank you very much, Mona.'

Mona sat down, poured the hot drinks and said, 'I'll come back in half an hour or so and take you to Master Kanaka's office for the interview and assessment.'

Mab said, 'I thought I would be seeing Master Boe?'

Mona replied, 'Master Boe will also be present. There is nothing to worry about, Mab, just relax and answer any questions they ask. The masters just want to take a closer look at you. I'll see you later!'

Mona returned as promised and shepherded them through long corridors of cold stone and marble, eventually arriving at the bottom of a spiral staircase. The stone treads had been worn down through the ages and the walls were covered with strange geometric shapes. Mab started to feel somewhat uncomfortable as the party climbed the steps, but at the top, the stairway opened into a large hallway and her uneasiness faded. Mona approached a huge oak door and knocked twice. The door was opened by Master Boe who greeted them warmly and led them into a large office which was lined by overloaded bookshelves on every wall. They were seated at the opposite side of the table to four masters of the guild. The Principal wore a robe which was stunning in its simplicity, fine black silk with thin gold braiding. The other masters donned heavier robes which had thick gold braiding. All of the masters wore their gold pendants of office.

'Mr and Mrs Winter, Mabdelore, welcome to the Guild. I am Master Kanaka, the school Principal. Mab, you have already met Master Boe and on my right, we have Masters Ochran and Lamm. You were invited here today by Master Boe following his recent school visit. Master Boe, please continue,' said Kanaka.

Master Boe said, 'Mr and Mrs Winter, I understand you adopted Mab when she was very young?'

Sopa replied, 'Yes, Master Boe. She was only a baby; Walim and I could not have children of our own.'

Master Boe said, 'I assume you have no contact with her real parents?'

Mab glared at him and said, 'They are my real parents.' Boe felt a darkness descend over his eyes as if he was about to lose consciousness.

Walim said, 'Mab, Master Boe meant no offence.'

The light started to come back into Boe's vision, and he recovered his composure. Boe said, 'Apologies, Mab, indeed my words were clumsy. Of course, I meant your biological parents.'

Walim said, 'No, there are no records of her biological parents. From what we understand, there was a fire shortly after she was born, and many birth records were destroyed.'

Boe said, 'Mab, could you tell us a bit about you, your hobbies, what you like doing, any special friends that you may have?'

Mab replied, 'I go to school, but it's a bit boring. I like walking in the forest, looking at the flowers and the animals.'

Lamm said, 'What kind of animals do you see in the forest?'

Mab replied, 'I see squirrels, small deer, badgers and lots of birds. I love big Brown Owl, that's what I call him, he hoots especially for me!'

Lamm said, 'I also love animals; do you sneak up to get close to any of them?'

Mab replied, 'No, I don't sneak, they come to see me when I'm walking.'

Lamm asked, 'Do they talk to you?'

Mab replied, 'No, but I know what they are thinking when they are happy or sad or scared.'

Lamm asked, 'Are there any animals that you are afraid of?'

Mab said, 'No.'

Ochran said, 'What about your friends?'

Mab replied, 'I have friends at school, Izzy, Gord and Mel. Izzy is my best friend. We live on a farm; I don't have many friends who live nearby.'

Sopa said, 'The farm is some way from the centre of the village.'

Ochran asked, 'Do you have any special friends?'

Mab replied, 'I used to have a special friend when I was very young.'

Sopa said, 'She was an imaginary friend, Mab. What was her name again?'

Mab, somewhat embarrassed, replied, 'Her name was Uri, but she is gone now.'

Ochran asked, 'When did she go?'

Mab, with a degree of irritation in her voice, replied, 'I don't remember.'

Kanaka intervened, 'That's fine, Mab. We would now like to do some simple tests. Walim, Sopa, could you please wait outside? I hope you don't mind. It's just that having parents present can distract the student and affect the outcomes. The tests will only take thirty minutes or so. Mona will look after you in the meantime.' Mona arrived and took Walim and Sopa back to the Great Hall.

Master Boe said, 'Mab, we want to test how you react to particular circumstances; please don't be afraid, we do these tests with all of our students. As you may know, we all have magic to a greater or lesser degree and there are different types of magic. Much of the magic taught in schools is Craft, that is, know-how or knowledge, for example, how to make healing potions or how to construct a spell or an enchantment. There is another magic that cannot be taught. Although we can teach a student how to control and direct it, it is this magic that we are testing today. Do you understand?'

Mab replied, 'I think so, what do you want me to do?'

Boe said, 'You don't have to do anything; just sit still. If you feel uncomfortable in any way, let us know immediately. Close your eyes if you wish.'

The four masters arranged their chairs in a horse-shoe shoe shape around Mab. Lamm closed his eyes and his mind linked with Mab. 'Hello, Mab, it's Master Lamm. How are you feeling?'

Mab replied, 'Oh! I didn't expect that; I'm feeling fine, Master Lamm.'

Lamm said, 'Is this what it is like when you talk to animals?'

Mab replied, 'No, animals don't talk, but I know how they feel, and I can ask them to do things.'

Lamm said, 'Can you make them do things that they don't want to do?'

Mab replied, 'I would never do that.'

Lamm asked, 'But could you?'

Mab replied, 'I don't know, but I wouldn't do it.'

Lamm said, 'Do you mind if I try to make you do something? This is part of the test, but I need your permission.'

Mab replied, 'Yes, what should I do?'

Lamm said, 'Just relax. I will try to make you stand up. You need to resist and remain seated.'

Mab initially felt a slight niggle at the edge of her consciousness that made her think she should stand up. The feeling gradually increased in intensity, she began to feel uneasy, the presence in her mind, she should not have let him in, a feeling of panic ensued. 'No!' her mind shutters came down instantly and locked in place.

Master Lamm, his forehead beaded with sweat, gasped, 'Mab, I apologise. I perhaps took the test a bit too far. How are you feeling?'

Mab replied, 'No, Master Lamm, it was my fault. I've never had someone do that to me before.'

Kanaka was smiling and said, 'Mab, you certainly passed that test, I think Master Lamm only just got out in time!'

Lamm said nothing, he was looking at Mab with a wry but warm smile on his face. Ochran said, 'Mab, if you are feeling fine, then I would like to proceed with the second test.'

Mab asked, 'Do I have to let you into my mind?'

Ochran smiled and replied, 'No, this is not a mind test. It involves actions on inanimate objects, not living creatures.'

Ochran opened his right hand and a ball of fire appeared. He then held his left hand up, palm facing outwards and a pen from Master Kanaka's desk flew into his grasp. Mab gasped in astonishment and said, 'How did you do that!'

Ochran replied, 'You should think about it in the same way you mind link with animals. Reach out with your mind and will object to come to you. Don't concentrate your mind, like screwing up your eyes, you need to be calm, relaxed but also focussed.' Ochran returned the pen to the desk and said, 'Your turn now.'

Mab sat back, closed her eyes and tried to relax. She lifted her hand, but she couldn't seem to get any reaction. Ochran said, 'Mab, you are trying too hard, relax, clear your mind. Look down, keep your eyes closed and think of nothing. Now, slowly raise your head and focus.' Mab first opened her left-hand palm up and concentrated on forming a ball of fire. After a few moments, she could feel it, she opened her eyes and saw a small, intensely bright ball of white flame hovering above her palm. She closed her eyes and reached out to the desk, willing the pen to come to her. There was a loud scraping, squealing sound. She opened her eyes to find that the desk, with everything on it, had moved across the floor.

Kanaka said, 'Ochran, in fairness, she did bring the pen!' and smiling at Mab said, 'There are another two tests, but we will dispense with those. We have sufficient information to reach a decision on your future young lady.'

Mab replied, 'I'm sorry about the desk, Master Kanaka.'

Kanaka beamed at her and said, 'Mab, you don't have to worry about that. Mona will now take you back to your Parents, but I'd like to see you all before you leave. Mona will collect you and your parents shortly and bring you back here.'

When Mona and Mab left the room, Kanaka looked at the other masters and said, 'Comments!'

Boe said, 'She is an extraordinarily powerful psychic, when I referred to her 'real parents,' I almost lost consciousness. I don't think she understands how powerful she is, and it seems clear that she can't control it.'

Lamm said, 'Yes, I agree. We can teach her how to control her powers, at least the ones we have tested today, but they are extraordinary. When I was mind-linking with her, I tried to probe further, but she was closed, and I mean closed; she could not be coerced. When that mind shutter came down, I only just escaped!'

Ochran said, 'I think that is a key point, she is an extraordinary talent, we can teach her control, but it could be dangerous.'

Kanaka said, 'Yes, but she is gifted and clearly willing to learn. In my view, we need to do everything we can to convince her to take up a studentship with us rather than with another school. Do you concur?'

'Aye,' said the three masters.

Mona returned with Mab and her parents. Boe thanked Mab and her parents for attending the interview and explained that the formal process would be for the Guild to write to them and the school with the outcome of the interview and details of the studentship, should an offer be made. Boe then asked if they had any questions. Walim asked when they would hear back from the Guild and expressed concerns regarding the tuition fees and living expenses. Boe looked at Kanaka. Kanaka looked at Walim and said, 'Let me say first that we were most impressed by Mab, she is a real credit to you. The Guild will be making an offer to Mab, and you will receive this in writing within the next week or so.' Mab looked at Master Kanaka and smiled; she had tears in her eyes.

Sopa said, 'Master Kanaka that is truly wonderful news! But can I ask you about the fees? At present, our income barely covers our outgoings. If Mab is to attend the Guild, then we will need to raise the funds.'

Walim said, 'I can do extra hours in the evening and, if needed, increase our loan.'

Mab said, 'No, Dad, I don't want you to do that!'

Kanaka said, 'Let me explain. In the case of Mab, we will be offering a full studentship. This means that all her fees will be waived, including tuition, food, accommodation, books, and equipment and travel expenses. In effect, there will be no fees.'

Sopa said, 'Master Kanaka that is very generous of you and the Guild. Thank you so much!' As they stood up to leave, Mab ran to Master Kanaka and gave him a big thank-you hug.

Kanaka said, 'Mab, we are looking forward to seeing you at the start of the new term as a fully signed-up student of the Guild of Sorcerers. Congratulations!'

Chapter Two: Fresher's Week

Walim dropped Mab, together with her belongings, off at the Guild on the first day of term, making use of his pony and trap. Mab was so excited, especially as Izzy had also been offered a place at the Guild to study craft and lore. Master Boe had gone back to the school to have further discussions with Ms Elm and to carry out more thorough checks on the rest of the students and selected Izzy. Mab eventually spotted Izzy at lunch break in the Great Hall and, following the welcome speeches, rushed over to sit by her side and said, 'Izzy, I heard you had been offered a place! What subjects are you studying?'

'I'm studying lore, potions and spells this year,' replied Izzy.

'I'm studying lore, psycho-kinetics and mind control,' said Mab.

'Those are the senior disciplines. Does that mean you will be working as an adept with the military?' asked Izzy.

Mab replied, 'I hope not. Let's meet up tonight after school, my room is in Sapphire Block. Where are you staying?'

Izzy said, 'I'm in Emerald, room 21, on the second floor.'

Mab replied, 'I'll come to you tonight. See you later.'

Izzy said, 'Mab, it's so good to see you.'

Mab smiled at her warmly. Mab made her way to the first of her classes, which was with Masters Lamm and Toker. She knew Master Lamm from her first visit to the Guild, but Master Toker was something of a surprise. She was a youngish woman and wore a beautiful blue robe, and had piercing blue eyes. Mab went straight to the front row and took a seat. Master Lamm glanced her way and smiled. He then explained that the lesson today concerned mind control and coercion and that all present in the class had shown promise in this field of study. The lesson would focus on both theory and practice, how to connect and communicate with another, how to enter another's mind, how to coerce another and also how to protect yourself against unwanted mind connections and melds.

As he was speaking, Mab felt something brush against her consciousness, yes there it was again, it was the woman master. She was scanning minds around the room. So soft, delicate, almost imperceptible. Mab turned and looked at her. She immediately locked with Mab's eyes for a few seconds and then smiled. Mab brought the shutters down; Master Toker's smile widened.

Master Lamm reminded the class that mind-melding and coercion required consent, other than in competitions or for the purposes of learning. If consent was not given, then the practice was unlawful. He then introduced Master Toker, who worked as part of the Prince Royal's team of adepts and was a visiting Master of the Guild; her specialism was in mind reading and coercion. Master Toker said, 'First, let me say how happy I am to see you all here today. I know you are all happy to be here because I have been shallowly scanning your minds as you were listening to Master Lamm; please raise your hand if you were aware of the mind scanning.'

Two hands were raised, and the students were asked to come to the front of the class. Master Toker invited the students to explain what they had experienced. The first student was a young boy of a similar age to Mab. He said, 'My name is Doni. I felt a strange, soothing feeling in my mind, but I didn't know what it was. It felt wrong, but I didn't know what to do and then it disappeared.'

Toker replied, 'Yes, Doni, what you described is very typical of what others experience. The soothing feeling is to make you relax, so it is easier to collect thoughts, it is a soporific layer that is placed down before entering another's mind. To delve deeply into another's mind, the soporific layer has to be stronger, much stronger than what you experienced.'

The second student was also a boy but somewhat older than Doni. Mab thought he was probably 16 or 17 years old. He said, 'Hello, my name is Axel. I started to feel a bit sleepy, but I could tell there was something else going on. Memories from my past started to come into my thoughts unbidden. I didn't know what was happening, but then, as Doni said, it just disappeared.'

Toker replied, 'Axel, I delved a bit deeper with you being more mature than some of the others. The unbidden memories were due to the mind reading process where the mind is stimulated, you could say prodded, by the reader's mind. In the case of Coercion, the prodding is much more severe and can cause brain bleed, even death if the reader is strong enough. In view of this it is essential that you are able to recognise when someone is trying to enter your mind and to prevent or expel the attacker.'

Master Toker turned and looked directly at Mab and said, 'You, young lady, what is your name?'

'My name is Mab,' replied Mab. Master Toker explained that she would demonstrate with Mab how to expel a reader from her mind.

'Mab, I would like you to relax while I carry out a shallow scan. I will then ask you to expel me. Ready?' said Toker.

'Yes,' said Mab. Mab felt the soporific effect on her mind beginning to develop. Master Toker started to probe deeper. Mab started to feel uncomfortable, so she pushed gently back, but Master Toker pushed harder and deeper still. Mab started to panic, *it's a mistake*, she was in too deep, *stop, stop, stop*, but Master Toker wouldn't stop. Mab tried to grab hold of the probe with her mind, *slippery… too slippery*. It slowed, but she couldn't stop it or expel it. She had no control of what happened next, it was not a conscious action but something instinctive, an auto-reaction rather than a deliberate action. A tsunami of power welled up from deep within her, it raced up through her chest and outward from her forehead, severing the mind link and driving the probe backwards. Mab looked down. Master Toker had collapsed to the floor; blood was running from her nose and ears.

Master Lamm mind linked with Mab and said, 'Mab, are you okay? Or are you injured? I think Master Toker has fainted?'

Mab, sweating, replied, 'I think, I'm alright. She didn't faint.' The school Medics were called, and they took Master Toker to the clinic for prompt treatment before transferring her to the Infirmary at the Royal Palace.

In the evening, Mab made her way to Emerald Block to meet up with Izzy. She rapped on room 21, Izzy opened the door and had a wide smile on her face. She also had a couple of friends with her who were preparing a meal with drinks for four. Mab started to sob with relief, Izzy rushed to her and hugged her tightly and then cuddled her softly until she had recovered. Izzy then introduced Mab to Cat and Charly, her new roommates. Mab explained what had happened. Cat said she was sure everything would be alright as the masters were always responsible in these situations not the students. Charly concurred and said, 'No need to worry about it, Mab, here, have a nice goblet of chilled white wine.'

Mab had never tasted wine before, so she took a really large gulp and said, 'Oh, I do like this!' Izzy, Cat and Charly rolled around with laughter.

Charly and Cat laid out the food, which consisted of various local breads and cheeses, cooked meats, pickled vegetables and boiled eggs. Mid-meal, a scratching sound was heard at the door. Izzy said, "I think there's someone at the door.' The girls froze into silence, more scratching at the door.

'Answer it, Izzy,' whispered Cat. Izzy crept silently over to the door, slowly turned the handle and pulled the door quickly inwards. In rushed a huge shaggy dog, which made a beeline for Mab.

'Meldran!' screamed Mab. She threw her arms around Meldran's huge neck and kissed him on his head and face. Meldran was, in turn, licking Mab's face ferociously; he was also enjoying being pampered by the other girls who were hugging him and giving him pieces of chicken, which he wolfed down in an instant.

'So this is where you are!' said Master Boe, who was standing in the doorway. 'I heard what happened today and I just wanted to check that you were ok. I went to your room first, but then I asked Meldran to find you.'

'I'm fine, Master Boe. I was a bit upset, but I'm feeling better now,' said Mab.

'That's good to hear, we will talk more about it tomorrow. Meldran will stay with you tonight, anyway. I'm not sure I could prise him away from you at present!' said Master Boe.

Mab, after another goblet of wine, fell into a deep sleep on the floor, hugging Meldran.

Kanaka paced the floor of his office in silence. It was clear to Lamm and Boe that Kanaka was worried about the incident with Mab, but they knew it was better to remain silent until the Principal had thought things through. 'Lamm, to be clear, are you saying Toker went too far with the mind probe?' asked Kanaka.

Lamm replied, 'I was monitoring the situation closely, and, in my opinion, she went too far. The purpose of the exercise was for Toker to carry out a shallow mind scan and for her to flag to Mab when to expel the probe from her mind. However, although Toker's initial scan was shallow, she then delved much deeper to the point where Mab could not expel the probe.'

'You say she went too deep, I need you to be precise. How deep did she go?' asked Kanaka.

Lamm paused and, took a deep breath and said, 'In my estimation, the probe penetrated to the limit of the third level before being expelled.'

'What, are you sure?' cried Kanaka.

Master Lamm paused and once again took a deep breath before saying, 'Master Kanaka, I am positive. Had the probe not been expelled when it was, Mab could have suffered a serious brain injury.'

Boe asked, 'Why did Toker delve deeper? Was it her intent to damage or kill Mab?'

Kanaka said, 'Yes, that is indeed the question. Lamm, what are your thoughts on this?'

Lamm replied, 'I can only speculate, but having had time to reflect on this there can only be two reasons. The first is that Toker intended to kill or injure Mab, but for what purpose? The second is that she found something interesting when doing the shallow scan and so delved deeper without permission and with no regard for Mab's safety.'

Kanaka said, 'The latter would be a breach of code and practice and merit a significant sanction. So, whatever Toker found must have been extremely interesting. Lamm, you have carried out shallow scans on Mab's mind without incident.'

Lamm replied, 'Well, I wouldn't say without incident, but you have to remember that Toker is regarded as extremely adept in the area of coercion and mind melding. She also has much practical experience in the military, whereas I am merely a teacher.'

Kanaka said, 'I wouldn't say you were merely a teacher, Lamm! But yes, our focus is on linking and melding rather than coercion.'

Lamm replied, 'The other important question is how the mind probe was eventually expelled?'

Kanaka said, 'What is your view.'

Lamm replied, 'I have no idea, but it was not retracted by Toker, that much is clear.'

Kanaka said, 'We will discuss this further with Mab tomorrow. I don't need to remind you that Toker is not only a Palace adept, she is a favourite of the Prince. There is a political context to this so let's keep things tight at present. My understanding is that Toker is in intensive care but stable and expected to recover. Boe, I trust you have left someone with Mab tonight?'

Boe replied, 'Yes, Mab is with three friends. Meldran is also with her, so her safety is assured.'

When Mab awoke in the morning, Meldran was sleeping on the bed and she was still on the floor but hugging Izzy. Mab untangled herself from Izzy and decided to walk back to Sapphire Block with Meldran. It was a cold early autumn morning and the fresh chill in the air helped her to clear her head and think more calmly about what had happened with Master Toker. Her worst fear was that she could be expelled from the GOS, particularly if Toker was seriously injured. But she couldn't understand why Toker would try to hurt her. Neither did she understand what she did to protect herself from the mind probe. The reality is that she didn't understand anything or do anything, but would anyone believe her?

As she approached Sapphire Block, Meldran suddenly stopped. A stooped hooded figure stepped out from the shadow of a great oak tree. Meldran moved between Mab and the figure. 'I mean your ward no harm, but I bring a warning,' said the mysterious figure, looking first at Meldran and then at Mab. The voice was high-pitched, wavering and throaty like that of an old crone.

'What warning? Who are you?' asked Mab.

'I am a seer. Hear me, child. They seek high magic to bend to their own dark purposes. To them, you are both a boon and a bane. Who or what you are, or what you will become, I know nought, but beware, for it is not merely your life that is at stake but your very soul.'

With that, the figure stepped back into shadow and vanished. Meldran ran a few paces forward but then stopped and looked back at Mab, who immediately understood that pursuit would be fruitless.

Mab got back to her room, showered and prepared for her usual morning session on meditation and mind space. She reached the lecture room to find Master Lamm and several other students already there. 'Good morning, Mab. Could you wait behind following this session? We want to have a chat with you regarding the incident yesterday?' said Master Lamm. Mab was expecting this, but even so, it made her feel uneasy; they would have questions, but she had no answers.

'Yes, Master Lamm,' was her only response. She kept her head down and sat at the back of the room rather than her normal front-row position. Why she did this, she couldn't rationalise, but she felt let down by the school in some way and she missed her Mum and Dad. She knew she was feeling sorry for herself, but things were getting difficult here. Perhaps she should go home and forget about the GOS, work on the farm, and walk in the forest like before. She came out of her reverie to find Master Lamm standing beside her and the other students looking back to see what was happening.

Lamm reached down and took her hand. Mab looked up at him, she had tears in her eyes. Lamm said, 'Mab, let's find your seat.'

He led Mab down the aisle to her usual seat at the front of the room and said, 'This is your seat; this is where you belong.'

'Thank you, Master Lamm,' said Mab with the tears now running down her cheeks. There was spontaneous applause from all the students in the room. Lamm smiled and asked for silence before commencing the lesson.

Lamm said, 'The mind is powerful, much more powerful than most people imagine. The mind, in fact, defines reality; without the mind, there can be no reality. Consciousness and the nature of reality are therefore inextricably linked and through this mechanism, your mind can influence the nature of the world around you. Certain thoughts, words, and gestures used in isolation or in concert can have a significant effect on reality. As you know, within the study of magic and the occult arts, there are various disciplines that result in a degree of specialism. In this very Guild, we are organised on the basis of disciplines, with each Master specialising in a particular area of endeavour. However, this division is an illusion; there is only one discipline and that relates to the power of the mind.'

'Master, what of the magic possessed by daemons and spirits?' asked Axel.

Lamm replied, 'That is a good and important question, Axel. The magic you refer to is known as High Magic and this can be dark or light depending on the nature of the wielder. High magic cannot be learned or taught. It is the magic of another, higher realm. However, the magic we teach is powerful, and that power is dependent on the power of the mind, its capacity and strength of will. You can improve your mind through exercise. One such exercise is the mind palace. I want you to build a mind palace. This is a house in your mind, start with a small house with two or three rooms. Visualise the house and every day add more objects to the house. When the rooms are furnished, add another room and continue. This enables you to strengthen and expand your mind. Also, and of prime importance, you must practice meditation every evening for at least an hour. Meditation helps you to relax your mind and to understand your inner self. In time this will be extended into mind space. Mind-space is a virtual plane, we think it lies between our physical world and other planes of existence. This is only for advanced students, but I want to introduce you to the subject. For now, just before you finish a meditation session, I want you to focus on the darkness before your closed eyes; think of moving forward through it and eventually beyond it, for this is the pathway to mind space.'

When the lesson finished and the rest of the students departed, Master Lamm and Mab made their way back to the Great Hall and the Principal's office. Kanaka and Boe were having coffee and discussing preliminary arrangements for the end-of-year house games. Kanaka welcomed Mab with a warm smile, nodded for her to take a seat and said, 'Mab, how are you? It's understandable that you would be upset by what happened to Toker, but you are not responsible. Anyway, I heard this morning that she is now out of intensive care and feeling much better. Most likely, she will be discharged sometime soon.'

Mab replied, 'Yes, I was upset by the whole thing, but I am feeling better, especially now I know Master Toker is recovering.'

Master Boe poured hot coffee for Mab and Lamm and said, 'Mab when accidents happen, we have to do an investigation to find out what went wrong and how to prevent it happening again. So, we would like you to tell us in your own words what you think happened. Do you think Master Toker fainted? That would certainly explain the head injury?'

Lamm said nothing and waited for Mab to respond. Mab said, 'I've been thinking about this ever since it happened. The truth is I don't really know what happened to Master Toker, but I do know she tried to hurt me. I know this may be difficult for you to believe. I tried so hard to expel the mind probe, but she was very skilled and wouldn't stop. I trusted her and let her in too deep. She didn't faint, but I didn't consciously do anything to hurt her.'

Kanaka looked thoughtful before saying, 'Mab, has anything like this happened before?'

Mab hesitated before saying, 'When I was a child, I think 7 or 8 years old, I was being bullied by an older boy. The bullying didn't bother me too much and I used to get my own back by humiliating him in front of the other girls in his class. But it was starting to get out of hand, escalating, until one morning, he hit me on the head with a garden spade in the school playground. It should have killed me, at least that's what people said, but instead, he ended up in a coma for three months with brain trauma. I was also taken to the hospital, but they only found a deep cut and bruising to my head. He never came back to our school, his brain injury was too serious for normal schooling. I don't know what happened to him, but, as with Master Toker, I didn't consciously do anything.'

Master Kanaka looked pensive and said, 'When you say you didn't consciously do anything, does that mean that you were not aware of what was happening?' Mab paused for a long moment and said, 'No, in the case of Master Toker's mind probe, I was aware of a well of power from somewhere deep within me, it flowed upwards and outwards. I wasn't in control of it, but I felt calm and knew immediately the probe was being expelled. I think if Master Toker had been less skilled, she would have been seriously injured.'

'Mab, what makes you say that?' asked Master Lamm.

'Her reaction, the speed and precision, she shrank back away from it; her mind only caught the backwash,' replied Mab.

Master Kanaka said, 'Mab, you have given us much to think about and I want to emphasise to you that this accident is of Toker's making, she is culpable, not you. However, there is a political aspect to this that needs to be handled with care so please do not repeat anything discussed here today until matters are resolved with the Palace. Boe, we need to review and increase security presence in and around the school, we don't yet know the motivations of Toker, but we have sufficient evidence to assume they are malign.'

Mab said, 'Master Kanaka, there is something else. When I returned to my room early this morning, a stranger stepped in front of me on the path just before Sapphire Block. He was hooded but seemed from his voice to be very old. Meldran didn't think he was a threat, but the stranger said he had come to warn me that my life and soul were at risk.'

Kanaka was visibly disturbed by this and said, 'This illustrates the need for heightened security in and around the Guild. Boe, do you have any idea who this stranger could be?'

Boe said, 'I will look into the matter, but as you know, we often have 'heretics' who rail against the magic schools in different ways and preach their particular view of the world on the street corners. Some of them possess remarkable skills. Do you think this stranger could in some way be related to the incident with Toker?'

Kanaka replied, 'It seems too much of a coincidence. Even in the best of times, I do not like coincidences. Mab, you also need to take extra care, as a precautionary measure, please make sure you are accompanied when you walk in the grounds. Boe, could you look into finding accommodation for Mab and her friends in the main building? Would that be ok for you and your friends Mab?'

Mab replied, 'Yes, I think they would absolutely love that!'

Kanaka nodded to Master Boe, who left with Mab to make the necessary arrangements. Kanaka said, 'Lamm, something is afoot here, and we need to get to the bottom of it. I sense a subtle hand at work, and I think it relates to the Palace. Toker knows something about Mab. I suspect it is related to the high magic but there must be something else?'

Lamm said, 'It could be the degree of high magic involved. Mab seems to possess it to an extraordinary level, and I am not sure we, or she, have yet seen the limit of it.'

Kanaka replied, 'Agreed, but even so, the palace has adepts who have trained for many years and developed truly extraordinary powers. There must be something more.'

Lamm replied, 'Perhaps we are overthinking it. If the Palace was behind this and Toker felt Mab was, or could in the future be, some kind of threat, it follows that they would either try to eliminate her or persuade her to join their ranks.'

Kanaka stood up, walked to the office window and stared out over the rolling fields and hills that surrounded the Guild. He then turned to Master Lamm and said, 'I received a mind message this morning from the Palace. They asked that Mab visit the Palace to discuss the incident with Toker. Of course, I refused. I received another message in reply saying they intend to visit the Guild to discuss the hosting of the annual competition and will take that opportunity to meet Mab. They assured me that no blame is being attributed to Mab in relation to the Toker incident and in fact, they wished to reassure Mab in that regard.'

'When will they be visiting us?' said Lamm.

'Early next month, the delegation will be led by Master Ansek, their new Principal of Magic,' replied Kanaka.

Lamm said, 'So soon. Have you met Ansek?'

Kanaka replied, 'No, but I've heard of him. He trained at the Academy and progressed quickly up through the military ranks. I understand that he is heavy on discipline and quite ruthless.'

'What happened to old Master Pendleton?' asked Lamm.

Kanaka replied, 'I don't know, but my guess is that he fell out of favour with the Prince regarding the ever-increasing military control over the magic schools.'

Lamm asked, 'Do you think that is the real reason for their visit next week?'

Kanaka replied, 'It will be on their agenda, but no, the visit has something to do with Mab and the Toker incident. They have been spooked. You talk to Boe and make the necessary arrangements to host the visit. We will need a meeting space, a formal dinner in the evening and a tour of the Guild the following morning.'

Lamm said, 'Yes Master Kanaka.'

Mab took Izzy, Cat and Charly to see their new room. It was situated at the top of the Northwest turret in the main building. They climbed a stone spiral staircase to the first floor, entered through a heavy oak door and climbed a much narrower spiral staircase to the turret room. Mab lifted the latch lever and pushed with her shoulder and the large door swung open slowly but surprisingly easily. The turret room was originally designed to accommodate visiting dignitaries, but the furnishings had been laid out with beds, desks, chairs, and two very large leather sofas. The stone floor was covered in places with thick pile rugs and there was a very large and luxurious toilet bathroom suite and a small kitchen area. Best of all, each desk was set against a turret window, offering spectacular views over the surrounding countryside.

'Mab, this is fabulous!' said Izzy. Cat and Charly were looking around in astonishment. The walls were decorated with fine tapestries, and the roof was covered with runes and patterns that looked like stars and constellations.

Boe entered the room, panting after climbing the stairs and said, 'I hope you girls like your new room?'

'Yes!' they replied as one.

Boe, looking at Mab, said, 'My room is the one across the corridor at the bottom of the stairs. I share my room with Meldran. I'll leave you to settle in, but if you need anything, please let me know.'

As Boe started to leave, Mab said, 'Master Boe, thank you for this. Thanks for looking after me so well.'

Boe paused, smiled warmly and bowed before saying, 'Mab, sincerely, it is my honour and pleasure to do so.' Mab and her friends were astonished, a master bowing to a student! Master's only bow to a superior, never to students and certainly not to a junior student. Mab bowed deeply and brought the palms of her hands together in a gesture of esteem and respect. Boe's smile widened, and he thought to himself, yes, this, indeed is the daughter I never had. Mab seemed to understand, she walked over and hugged him. As Boe made his way down the stairs, he felt tears coming to his eyes; that hadn't happened to him for many years.

Chapter Three: Visit from the Palace

Mab watched the palace delegation arrive from her turret window. She wondered for a moment if the Prince would be there but quickly dismissed the idea. No, he would send his adepts to remind the Guild who was really in charge. She was also wondering if they intended to make an example of her due to the Toker incident and what they would actually do to her. Mab had been meditating and mind-training hard over the recent weeks, she had come to realise that she really was 'different.' It wasn't about the learning, the knowledge or the craft; it was just her. Since the incident with Toker, she was beginning to discover herself, her strength and confidence were growing at an exponential rate. It was as if Toker's mind probe had caused something within her to be released.

The delegation started to assemble in the Minor Hall within the main building. There was a huge oak table that could have comfortably seated fifty people. However, the delegation numbered only twenty, mostly adepts and military personnel. Principal Ansek was readily recognised by his beautiful gold braided cloak of black silk, beneath which he wore a black unadorned uniform and black leather boots. As with all the military, he was an accomplished psychic and had very strong powers of coercion. Ansek wore no medals or insignia other than the Prince's single clenched white fist on both lapels.

Kanaka watched Ansek enter the hall and thought him to be remarkably young for such a senior position, or perhaps it was just me getting old, he mused. Then he noticed Toker, she was wearing a blue uniform, which indicated her military adept Coercer status. Ansek's first-line team were all adepts and veterans of many conflicts. They sported both medals and insignia; the uniforms were of different colours, each specific to their particular discipline. Guild senior students were acting as servers, moving around the delegation with drinks and platters of meats and fruit. When the food and drinks activity started to diminish, Master Kanaka called the delegation to order and asked that everyone take their seats. Ansek sat at the head of the table, but the rest of his delegation stood to attention behind him despite the number of empty chairs. It was unnerving. Kanaka had known this would be a difficult meeting, but for the first time, he realised it could also be short and very dangerous. He glanced sideways at Lamm, Ochran and Boe and saw understanding on their faces. Ansek, picking up on Kanaka's sideward glance, said, 'My team is all high adepts of the Palace; they represent our key disciplines of Coercion, Mind Control and Psychokinesis. Of course, you know Master Toker, the others will introduce themselves properly later in the evening.'

Kanaka thought to himself, *he is making the point that if things go badly wrong, he thinks they have more firepower*. Kanaka said, 'Master Ansek, thank you for visiting the Guild. You and your delegation are most welcome. For our part, I represent the Guild as Principal, Master Lamm, Master Ochran, and Master Boe. We can, of course, make other masters and senior students available to support the meeting as and if required.'

Master Kanaka then invited Master Ansek to take the meeting through the proposed agenda. It was the Palace that had called this meeting, but if there was an agenda, Kanaka had not seen it. Ansek stared at Kanaka and said nothing for almost 30 seconds. Kanaka simply returned the stare with a smile of anticipation on his face and also said nothing. Ansek then spoke in a deep, steady voice, 'Kanaka, the reasons we are here are first to discuss funding for this institution, secondly to host the annual competition, and thirdly to discuss the injury sustained by Master Toker. I want to emphasise that times are tough. We need to be sure our funding is generating value, and my understanding is that the performance of the Guild has been less than satisfactory in recent years.'

Kanaka replied, 'Master Ansek, as you know, our previous discussions have been with Master Pendleton, and I can assure you that he was satisfied with the costs incurred and value generated by the Guild. Competitions are important for the Military, of course, we understand that, but private donations and long-standing scholarships also fund us. The Military funding is some 20% of our funding, so it is very important to us, but competitions are not the prime metric against which we judge ourselves.'

Ansek replied, 'Kanaka, to be candid, in my view, there are too many schools. I also warn you that there is a strong argument that all four schools should be brought under the management of the

Military. That is not my view, but we need to demonstrate value for the money we give you. Forgive me for expressing this in simple terms, but if our funding is 20% of your total revenue then I would expect you to win at least 20% of the competitions and provide the Military with 20% of your best students. Alternatively, perhaps through the fundamental research work you do here, you can offer the Military something else: new ways of doing things, new powers, and different types of magic.'

Kanaka replied, 'Master Ansek, I will certainly think about what you have said, and I thank you for being so candid. Master Boe will send details of our most recent financial statements to the Palace to confirm the funding situation, and I will think about some additional metrics to help address your other concerns. Can I ask you if you have already discussed this with Master Pendleton?'

Ansek said, 'That will be fine, Kanaka. However, it would be difficult for me to discuss this with Pendleton. I'm afraid he is dead.' There was some muted laughter from the delegation.

'When and how did he die?' asked Kanaka.

'He died some months ago. I killed him,' said Ansek in a matter-of-fact tone. Kanaka wasn't entirely sure he had heard him correctly.

'You killed him? Can I ask why you killed him?' said Kanaka.

Ansek replied, 'Kanaka, things have changed at the Palace. The Prince is doing things differently; there are pressures at that level that you would not understand. The Prince expects results, so I expect results. Pendleton was very old school and couldn't change; I tried to convince him, but he resisted and, unfortunately, he died, it was not my intent to kill him.'

Kanaka said, 'How did you say he died?'

Ansek replied, 'I didn't say. Kanaka, we are somewhat tired after the journey this morning. Can I suggest that we break now and have our further discussions over dinner tonight?'

Kanaka, still somewhat shocked, said, 'Yes, of course, forgive me.'

As Ansek was getting up to leave, he moved closer to Kanaka and said, 'Kanaka, I want to work with you and the Guild more closely. I am proposing that this year you host the competition, in spite of the rather poor performance in previous years. But I want the Guild to step up a gear and get results; it's all about the results.'

Kanaka replied, 'Well, that at least is good news. I will give serious thought to the points you have made.'

As Ansek walked away, he said, 'For the dinner tonight, could you have the student Mabdelore Winter attend? I would like to meet her and give Toker an opportunity to discuss face-to-face what went wrong.'

Boe led the delegation off to rooms provided for them in Opal Block, and Lamm escorted Ansek to a turret room in the Guild's main building. Kanaka had hoped to avoid involving Mab, but they would sense her presence, and under the circumstances, it would be difficult to avoid. Kanaka asked Ochran to warn Mab regarding the delegation of adepts and to make sure she wore something suitable for the dinner. Ochran made his way to Mab's room in the north-west turret. However, when he arrived, Lamm was already there talking with Mab. Ochran nodded to Lamm and said, 'Mab, Master Kanaka asked me to talk to you about the delegation and the dinner tonight.'

Mab replied, 'Yes, Master Ochran, Master Lamm was just explaining what went on today.'

Lamm said, 'I've just dropped off Ansek and thought I best warn Mab about the dinner. I think the main thing is to be on your guard regarding mind scans or even attacks. The delegation has a number of extremely competent psychics, including, of course, Toker. Regarding the incident with Toker, I suggest you say you don't know what happened and stick to that if questioned.'

Ochran said, 'Yes, I agree with Master Lamm. On more practical matters, what will you be wearing tonight?'

Mab replied, 'I don't know. The only really nice thing I have of my own is the cloak that I was wrapped in as a child. But I will borrow something from Izzy or Charly. They have some nice dresses.'

Ochran said, 'Fine, but let me know in good time if there is a problem and we will find you something suitable. The dinner is at the eight in the Great Hall, so arrive a bit early for pre-dinner drinks.'

'Wow, pre-dinner drinks!' said Mab. Lamm and Ochran laughed. They just couldn't imagine Mab, knowing her background, at a formal dinner with all of pomp, circumstance and finery.

Later that evening, Mab's friends had her trying all sorts of evening dresses, but they settled for Izzy's long, close-fitting white sequined dress. Charly had washed and platted Mab's hair, which flowed like a river of silk down to the small part of her back. Mab retrieved her childhood cloak from the linen bag at the bottom of her luggage crate. She couldn't remember when she had last seen it and was not expecting it to be in good condition. However, when she pulled it from the bag, Charly, Cat and Izzy gasped in amazement. The cloak was whiter than white and entirely unblemished. It seemed to be made from the very finest silk. There were no visible strands or stitches. There were patterns and symbols within the fabric, just visible, that changed shape with movement. It was strange because the shapes seemed to match the white hue of the dress perfectly. Cat grabbed hold of the cloak and put it over Mab's shoulders, fastening it loosely with the silver neck chain. She then pulled Mab's hair out and draped it down the cloak. The three friends stood staring at Mab with their mouths open. Izzy said, 'Mab, you look so beautiful, as do the dress and cloak, your pale skin, your lovely black eyes, and your silky hair.'

Charly said, 'Be careful, Mab, I think Izzy is falling in love with you!' Cat and Charly burst out laughing, but Izzy just smiled warmly at Mab and then looked down as her face turned bright red.

The guests had all assembled in the Great Hall and were having pre-dinner drinks when Mab arrived. Ansek saw her first and said to Kanaka, 'Who is that?'

Kanaka looked, his eyes widened, and said, 'That is Mabdelore Winter. You requested her attendance.'

'Really, she is stunning, not what I expected,' replied Ansek. He watched Mab as she walked across the floor, she was remarkable. The way she walked, her face, and those eyes were extraordinary. Just then, Mab turned and looked directly at him, he only just held her gaze before she looked elsewhere. Master Boe walked to meet Mab to simply shepherd her towards Lamm and Ochran, but when he reached her, she put her arm around his and they walked together like father and daughter. Boe beamed with pleasure as he approached Lamm and Ochran, who clapped their hands together in applause.

'Don't you scrub up well!' said Ochran.

Mab smiled and said, 'I got a lot of help!' The gong sounded and Kanaka asked everyone to take their seats.

Kanaka intercepted Mab and asked her and Master Boe to sit to his left at the head of the table, with Ochran and Lamm to his right. Ansek sat at the opposite head of the table with his adepts on either side of him.

Ansek said, 'Forgive me, Master Kanaka, but before we start, do you think you could introduce us formally to the young woman sitting to your left?'

Kanaka said, 'Yes, of course. Everyone, this is Mabdelore Winter. She wasn't present at the meeting earlier today, but Master Ansek asked to meet her, and we thought she could do it with a good dinner!'

Mab, already sipping an ice-cold goblet of wine, said, 'Yes, Master Kanaka, you are right!'

Everyone laughed. Ansek replied, 'It is very nice to meet you. Could you tell us a bit about yourself? STANDING UP!'

The psychic coercion in the command was immense; some of the adepts and masters felt themselves starting to stand, and they were on the periphery of the attack, which was directed at Mab. Mab saw the attack coming, but a strange thing happened. For her, time seemed to slow down, or perhaps she was speeding up, but Ansek's voice command from her perspective was stretched over at least 30 seconds. The coercive power was effectively nulled, and she had time to think about her next action. She decided to pretend nothing had happened. Mab waited a few moments, took another sip of her wine, turned slowly to Ansek, stood up and said, 'Why, of course, Master Ansek. My name is Mabdelore, although I prefer Mab. I am a junior student, but I am working hard to improve my skills. I've never been to anything this grand before, so thank you, Master Ansek and Master Kanaka, for inviting me.'

Ansek was incredulous; he had directed his full coercive power at her, focusing on only two words and she didn't feel or even acknowledge it. She didn't even put down her goblet of wine! Master Toker said, 'Mab, no, thank you. We wish you well with your studies and hopefully, I will see you again in class when I have fully recovered from my fainting episode. Now, Master Ansek and Master Kanaka, if you are both agreeable, I suggest we enjoy dinner!'

Mab loved every minute of the ten-course dinner. She also consumed huge quantities of wine, which didn't seem to have any effect on her. Ansek watched Mab intently throughout. He marvelled at the smooth motion of her hands as she picked up utensils, the way her hand found the wine goblet even though she wasn't looking at it, and the way she collected grapes from the fruit platter one-handed when he needed both. These were small things, but they confirmed to him that there was something about this girl that he did not understand. She also seemed familiar with the obsidian eyes and the paler-than-pale skin; it was as if he had seen her before in a previous life. Kanaka was watching Ansek watching Mab, he caught his eye and Ansek gave him an uncharacteristic smile. Kanaka turned to Mab and said, 'Mab, I don't know where you put all that food and wine!'

Mab, eating some more bread pudding, replied, 'It's so good, Master Kanaka. Do you mind if I take some back for my friends?'

Kanaka, laughing, said, 'Of course not, take as much as you like.'

Kanaka stood up and said, 'If we are all finished, and I think we are, after-dinner drinks are being served in the Minor Hall.' He turned to Mab and said, 'Stay close to Boe and Lamm.'

The guests walked through the archway to the Minor hall. The long table was full of drinks of every description, from fine wines to local ales and special liquors. Master Kanaka said, 'I would like to take this opportunity to thank Master Ansek and his team of adepts for their friendship and continued support of our Guild and also for the pleasure of their company this evening. If you could all fill your goblets, I propose a toast to the Prince.' Everyone filled a goblet of their choice and then Ansek said, 'Master Kanaka, I would like to thank you and the Guild for this wonderful evening. To be frank, I had developed a somewhat dim view of the guild, but on coming here, I realise now that I was entirely mistaken in that view. It gives me great pleasure to announce that I would like the Guild to host the annual competition and I wish you every success. So, everyone, please raise your goblets. The toast is *The Prince and the Guild!*'

'The Prince and the Guild!' cried all.

The delegation split up into smaller groups, with the Guild masters engaging with the adepts and sampling the various drinks. Kanaka walked over to Ansek, shook his hand and said, 'Ansek, thank you for your support and endorsement. You have my word that we will work hard to improve performance and achieve the results that you need.'

In the meantime, Mab found a cardboard box and filled it with leftover food and wine from the dining table in the Great Hall. She started to make her way through to the Minor Hall when she heard a scream of pain. She rushed into the Hall to see Boe lying on the floor, he was writhing in agony. Lamm and Ochran were kneeling beside him with Kanaka shouting for Medics; Ansek and his adepts were looking on, uncertain how to help.

Mab walked quickly across the floor towards Boe. As she walked, her cloak billowed behind her as if she was walking against a strong breeze. She made eye contact with Master Boe and saw the agony on his face. Then she saw black flames licking and whipping around him, her eyes followed the flames back to the source. They were being projected by a Palace adept, but he was removed from the others, standing in the shadow of a great stone column. The other Masters, including Ansek, seemed to be completely unaware of his presence and also unaware of the black flames torturing Master Boe. Mab walked between Boe and the adept, she was immediately engulfed in the black flames but felt no pain. Boe was now in Mab's shadow, free of the flames and the Medics were arriving.

The adept increased the ferocity of his attack on Mab and, laughing, said, 'Another human to flay and burn, I think I will enjoy burning you even more than your petty Master. Perhaps I will burn all of your petty Masters. You know not who I am, child, I will drink your soul.'

Mab opened her arms slowly as if in welcome and, facing him, said, 'Daemon, I name you Cham. Get from my sight or I will slay you where you stand.'

The adept staggered backwards, clawing at his face as if he was being attacked by a swarm of wasps before dropping to the floor where he lay still. Ansek, saw the stranger drop to the floor and ran past Mab to give aid. Mab turned and ran after the Medics who were taking Master Boe to the Guild Hospital. Kanaka joined Ansek and said, 'What is this, Ansek? Answer me!'

Ansek looked up at Kanaka and said, 'Kanaka, believe me when I say that I have never seen this person before. He is dressed as a Palace Adept, but he is unknown to me. It would have been good to have him alive, but he is quite dead. It appears to me that your so-called 'junior student' has slain him, albeit with good cause.'

Kanaka replied, 'Ansek, yes, I do believe you. When Mab stepped in front of him, Boe seemed to have recovered. I detected a psychic exchange between the stranger and Mab, but it lacked definition.'

Ansek said, 'You were focusing on Boe at the time. I saw Mab enter the room and watched her as she approached. There was an enormous amount of psychic energy, but it was one way from the stranger to Boe and then to Mab. I picked up on it when I saw Mab switch her gaze from Boe to the stranger. It was only then that I saw him; he was attacking Boe, but Mab walked quite deliberately between them and into the line of fire. The stranger was laughing initially, but whatever he was doing seemed to have no effect on Mab. She then said something to him that had a devastating and terminal effect.'

Master Lamm, together with Adept Tanya, approached Kanaka and Ansek. Adept Tanya said, 'Sir, apologies for interrupting, but I recognise the stranger. I do not know his name, but he is a member of the Prince's personal guard. I have seen him on a few occasions in the Palace.'

Ansek replied, 'Tanya, please find out all you can about this stranger and report back to me. This needs to be treated with the utmost secrecy; go, discuss this with no one.'

Kanaka said to Lamm 'How is Boe?'

Lamm replied, 'He is comfortable, he was able to protect himself to some extent, but he has suffered significant skin burns and has whip-like lacerations on his torso and shoulders. The Medics are looking after him and Mab hasn't left his side.'

Ansek said, 'How is Mab?'

Lamm replied, 'She is worried about Boe, but otherwise seems fine. She asked me to collect a box of food and wine that she left behind… and, if I wouldn't mind, take it to her room.' Ansek and Kanaka looked at each other and, in spite of the sombre occasion, couldn't stop themselves from laughing.

Chapter Four: Adepts and Daemons

Ansek had dismissed his entourage with instructions to return to the palace first thing in the morning and discuss what happened with no one. Kanaka had a very high degree of confidence that Ansek's instructions would be followed to the letter. Kanaka and Ansek returned to Kanaka's office. They were each sipping a strong liqueur, which was distilled on the Guild grounds. Ansek said, 'I would like to confide in you, Kanaka, but what I am about to say must not be repeated. Do I have your word on this?'

Kanaka replied, 'Yes, of course, provided the secrecy does no harm to the Guild.'

Ansek, in a low whisper, said, 'The Prince has changed and not for the better, he surrounds himself with priests and mystics. His personal guard is now made up largely of such people; they are strange but powerful.'

'Powerful in what sense?' asked Kanaka.

'Not in the military sense or in relation to the overt magic disciplines that we follow. They dabble in the occult, the spirit worlds. It is said that they commune with creatures and beings that inhabit other planes of existence. It sounds somewhat far-fetched, but the changes are real and after what happened tonight, I am beginning to give this some credence,' said Ansek. 'I have come across shamans and hermits who tread a different path from the one we follow. Some of these possess skills, but those I have met have been harmless and usually wish to be left alone in order to specialise in a narrow field of endeavour. Why do you think the incident tonight relates to the Occult?' asked Kanaka. Ansek replied, 'As I said earlier, the stranger was laughing when he was torturing Boe and attacked Mab. This is not normal, it is malevolent. I am a soldier and have killed many people, but I can honestly say that I have never found any joy in doing it. Also, I don't know what Mab said to the stranger, but I didn't detect any psychic energy flowing from Mab. It was as if the words themselves killed him, which doesn't make any sense.'

Kanaka said, 'I intend to speak to Mab first thing in the morning about the incident together with Lamm. I wonder if you could delay your departure and sit in on the discussion. Only Mab knows what actually happened, but I don't want to put her under any pressure or indicate that she was in any way responsible. In my assessment, she saved Boe's life and for that alone, I am enormously in her debt.'

Ansek replied, 'Thank you, Kanaka. I would very much like to hear Mab's account of what happened. The stranger was from the Palace, and Mab may help us understand why and how he attacked Boe. There is something else that I feel you should know, it concerns Toker. Firstly, I hope you will forgive me for testing young Mab tonight, but Toker had painted a rather different picture of her. I was under the impression that Mab was an accomplished but arrogant student who launched a surprise attack on a trusting mentor. I had thought to teach her a lesson. Of course, I was entirely wrong; she is, in fact, the most remarkable and endearing student I have ever come across. However, you should understand that Toker is not only an adept under my authority, she is also a favourite of the Prince and a member of his Personal Guard.'

Kanaka said, 'You mean Toker would know or at least should have recognised the stranger?'

Ansek replied, 'Precisely, but please understand that my authority over her is limited. I suspect there is much that she knows and much that I don't know.'

Mab left the clinic late and made her way back to her room. Her roommates were waiting for her and had the table prepared for a late supper of sweets, savouries and wine from the box left by Master Lamm. They asked about Master Boe, and Mab explained that he had been attacked by a stranger and was being treated for weals and burns on his face and body. The stranger was dead, but no one knows exactly what happened.

'Who he was?' asked Izzy.

Mab replied, 'He was dressed as a Palace Adept, but none of the other adepts recognised him. He must have sneaked in past security. I left Meldran at the clinic with Master Boe just in case there are others.'

'You think there could be others sneaking around the campus?' asked Charly.

'It wouldn't be hard to get past our security, so we need to be fully prepared for tall, dark, strange, perhaps handsome men snooping around,' said Cat, smiling.

'Cat, you are incorrigible,' said Izzy.

'In… what?' replied Cat.

'Right, you lot shut up and pass me some wine, cheese, bread and cake,' said Mab.

The next morning, following the first period on craft and potions, Lamm went with Mab to visit Boe. Mab was happy to see that he was sitting up in bed drinking through a straw. His face had raw surface flay wounds, which were left to the open air, but the others must have been much deeper and so were covered with a light bandage. She kissed him gingerly on the cheek between the bandages, and he smiled. He signed that he could not speak very well due to the burn injuries around his mouth. Lamm asked him if he was in a lot of pain, and Boe nodded his head as negative, he then asked Boe if he recognised the attacker. Boe once again indicated a negative. He then asked him if he had spoken to the stranger, Boe indicated in the positive. Lamm then said, 'Boe, did he give you any idea what he wanted?'

Boe nodded in the affirmative and then nodded toward Mab. 'He wanted Mab?' asked Lamm. Boe nodded in the affirmative again.

Mab said, 'Master Boe, did he say why he wanted me?' Boe, with tears welling up, responded in the negative. Lamm and Mab left Boe to finish his breakfast and made their way to Master Kanaka's office.

When they entered the room, Mab was surprised to see that Ansek was there and having coffee with Kanaka. Ansek was dressed in a white shirt, brown leather waistcoat, light slacks and sandals. Mab thought the informal clothes made him look even younger than when she last saw him. Kanaka was also dressed informally in a loose-fitting black samue style top, baggy trousers and light shoes. Kanaka said, 'Lamm, Mab, please join us. You both know Master Ansek, he agreed to stay for another night so we could have further discussions regarding the annual competition. I also asked him to sit in on this discussion in view of the stranger's possible links to the Palace.'

Lamm and Mab sat down, and Mab poured two fresh coffees. She then topped up the other two cups whilst receiving nods of gratitude. Lamm explained that he and Mab had just been to visit Boe and that he indicated the stranger had come specifically for Mab. Mab added that, most probably, the stranger had approached Master Boe when he was on his own and asked how to find her, when Boe refused, the stranger resorted to force. Ansek said, 'Mab, do you know that for sure or are you surmising.'

Mab replied, 'We know for sure that the stranger was trying to find me, Master Boe was definitive on that.'

'Do you know why he was trying to find you?' asked Ansek.

Mab replied, 'No, but I don't think he was anxious to be my friend.'

Ansek laughed and said, 'Yes, Mab, I think we can all agree on that.'

Kanaka said, 'Mab, we don't want to put you under any pressure, but can you explain to us what actually happened step by step?'

Mab replied, 'I can try, but I am not sure I fully understand it myself. As you know, when the dinner finished, everyone made their way to the Minor Hall for drinks. I thought I would gather up some of the leftovers and take them back for my roommates. I was packing stuff away when I heard a scream of pain from Master Boe. I knew it was Master Boe, so I ran into the Minor Hall and saw him writhing in pain on the floor. Master Lamm was kneeling beside him, and you, Master Kanaka, were calling for Medics.

'At first, I didn't understand what was happening, but then I saw the black flames. Master Boe was engulfed in them, especially around his face and head, but they were also whipping around his upper body. I didn't understand why no one else seemed to see them or feel them. The flames were being produced by what looked like an adept. I thought the only way to help Master Boe was to block or stop the flames, so I walked between the adept and Master Boe. I felt the flames immediately; they were repulsive, but the pain went away within a few seconds, and I realised that I had stopped them from reaching Master Boe.'

Ansek asked, 'Mab, you described the flames as 'repulsive', that's a strange word to use?'

'Yes, it made me want to vomit. I live on a farm at home, and the smell was like that of an animal that had been dead for a while. It was sweet but nauseating,' replied Mab.

Ansek asked, 'Did the adept say anything to you?'

Mab paused before she answered, 'No, he did not.'

Ansek replied, 'Mab, are you sure? I saw you exchange words with him.'

Kanaka put his hand on Mab's arm and said, 'Mab, if you don't want to talk about this, then don't worry. There is no blame here. We are only trying to understand what happened so we can be better prepared if anything else occurs. Would you like to leave it for a bit, perhaps until Master Boe recovers?'

Mab looked at Ansek and said, 'Master Ansek, I did not exchange words with the adept; that was not possible. However, I did exchange words with the creature that inhabited his body.' Ansek stared at Mab, comprehension dawning on his face.

Kanaka said, 'Mab, are you saying another being possessed the adept?'

Mab replied, 'Yes, when I first looked at the adept, I thought he looked wrong, so I looked deeper, and I saw the daemon looking back at me.'

Ansek said, 'Mab, what did this daemon say to you?'

'It threatened me.' replied Mab.

'What form did the threat take?' said Kanaka.

'It said it would drink my soul.' replied Mab.

'How did you respond?' said Ansek.

Mab replied, 'I threatened it and it left the body of the adept, however, the adept died. The creature was ancient and powerful; it was embedded deeply into the adept's mind.'

'Can I ask as to the nature of the threat you made to expel the creature?' said Kanaka.

Mab paused to think and then replied, 'The only way I can express it to you is that as I looked into the adept and saw the daemon, the daemon looked into me and saw me. It was afraid, it reeked of fear. I'm very sorry for the adept, but I had to stop the creature, there was no other way.'

Ansek said, 'Mab, Master Kanaka and I discussed the death of the adept earlier this morning. You did what you had to do and in doing so, you saved the life of a Guild Master. For that alone, we are in your debt. Our main concern now is your safety, so we need to speak openly here in this place. However, what is discussed here must go no further. I trust we are all agreed on that?'

All nodded in agreement and replied, 'Aye.'

Kanaka said, 'I'm sorry to say this, Ansek, but the Palace seems to be at the root of this unhealthy interest in Mab. From what you have said, both Toker and the adept are members of the Prince's personal guard.'

Lamm said, 'I agree, however, the key question is why the interest in Mab.'

Ansek replied, 'You are both right about what you say. However, this is not simply an interest. It is clear to me that the Palace sees Mab as a threat and is intent on removing that threat. Mab, you are a gifted student. Can you think of any reason why the Palace would consider you to be a threat?'

Mab hesitated and then said, 'I'm not sure. Since I started studying at the Guild, I have discovered a lot about myself, especially through meditation techniques. I am only a junior student, but I already know that I am a powerful witch and I feel myself getting stronger every day. It's as if I had removed the stopper from a bottle; it's coming from within me, not because I am practicing, although I am doing that as well.'

Ansek laughed and said, 'Mab, I expect you may well be improving faster than your peers, but I don't think that would be a threat to the Palace.'

Mab replied, 'Master Ansek, that's not what I meant. I can't explain it, but the magic is different.'

Kanaka said, 'Mab, I think what you are saying is that the Palace could see you as a threat because of the nature of the powers you possess rather than the degree or quantum of power.'

'Thank you, Master Kanaka. Yes, I think that is what I was trying to say,' replied Mab.

Lamm said, 'Master Ansek, how do you think this daemon creature got into the adept? Could the Palace be making use of these creatures in some way?'

Ansek replied, 'Lamm, you have said what I feared to say. The Prince's personal guard and the priests and mystics that surround them may well be experimenting with the use of these creatures. If Mab is able to detect and expel them, she would certainly be a threat to their plans. It may be that Toker detected this when scanning Mab and sought to get to the root of the matter.'

Kanaka replied, 'Ansek, what of the other schools? Are we the only ones who suspect the goings on at the Palace?'

Ansek replied, 'That I don't know, but we have a council meeting of the schools soon. Perhaps that will help to shed light on the situation. I will carry out my own investigations at the Palace. Perhaps you could try to find out, discretely, if any of the other schools know anything. We can compare notes when we next meet, which I guess will be the council meeting.'

Kanaka looked at Lamm and said, 'We need to once again ratchet up campus security and review how we can better protect Mab. With immediate effect, no visitors will be on campus without my approval. If what we suspect is true, then we should expect further attacks on the Guild, particularly on Mab.'

Mab returned to her room and found senior student Gho waiting for her at the bottom of the turret room stairs. 'Gho, what are you doing here?' said Mab.

'I wanted to talk to you about the inter-house games, it's only a few weeks away and I have to put a team together for Sapphire. I know you are living here now, but you are still affiliated with Sapphire House. How about it?' replied Gho.

'How about what?' said Mab.

'How about you joining the team; we've only won the competition once before and that was long before I was born,' replied Gho.

'I don't know anything about it, what would I have to do?' said Mab.

'There are four different games: mind ball, weightlifting, flame ball throwing and mind control. We are having a practice session soon. I'll let you know,' replied Gho as he walked off down the corridor.

As Mab climbed the stairs to her room, she opened her hand, and a small silver ball of fire appeared hovering above her palm; at least I can do that, she thought. She threw herself into bed with the intention of getting to Master Lamm's session on meditation, but she slept through most of the day and was woken by Izzy and Cat returning in the early evening. Izzy said, 'Mab, I hear you are on the Sapphire House team.'

'I'm thinking about it,' replied Mab.

'You are definitely on the team; the posters are all over the campus,' said Cat.

'Oh no,' said Mab with a groan.

Gho had arranged the practice session at the sports field for early the following week. The Sapphire team consisted of Gho, Tam, Mona and Mab, with Mab being the junior student as required under the rules of the competition. Gho explained to Mab that this session was to meet each other and agree on a strategy for the two team events. The other events were done on an individual basis. Tam said, 'The team events are mind-ball and weightlifting. In mind-ball, two teams compete to get a large ball through a horizontal hoop; 15 minutes of play are allowed in each direction and the highest score wins. In weightlifting, each team has to work in concert to lift ever-increasing weights and hold the weight above the ground for at least 15 seconds.'

Gho said, 'Mind-ball is about grasping and moving the ball with your mind to put it through the opposing team's hoop. Players can play in defence of their hoop or attack the opposition hoop. The key is having the strength to hold onto the ball and the speed to prevent the opposition from reacting in time. Tam and I will be the strikers, our job is to put the ball through the opposition's hoop. Mona, you and Mab will be the defenders, your main job is to prevent the ball from being put through our hoop. Remember, you can't enter the field, but you can go anywhere else you like. The normal approach is to have two players on each side of the field, one striker and one defender. So, Mona and I will be on one side, with Mab and Tam on the other side.'

Tam, pointing at a pile of stone slabs, said, 'These are the weights; each round stone slab is identical and weighs, roughly speaking, the weight of a fat man. The competition starts with two slabs, so we need to be able to lift at least that. The team doing the lifting can ask for any number of slabs to be added to the pile, but if they ask for more than one slab to be added and the weight is not held for 15 seconds and at least 12 inches above the ground, they are automatically disqualified.' Tam moved one slab at a time and arranged Gho, Mona and Mab around the pile. Tam was diametrically opposite Gho and Mab was diametrically opposite Mona. Tam said, 'When I say, focus your minds and slowly lift the stones. Ok, Relax, focus and now lift.' The slabs lifted slowly, although it took some practice to coordinate the movement in order to keep them together and level.

Mab asked, 'Tam, how many stones do you think we would need to lift to win the event'?

'That's a good question. Last year, the winning lift was nine stones. Should we have a go at that?' replied Tam, looking at the others.

'Why not? Let's have a go,' said Mona.

Tam and Gho moved slab after slab onto the pile until it stood nine high. Everyone took their positions around the pile. 'Remember, we have to hold it for 15 seconds, ready, lift!' said Gho.

At first, the pile didn't move, but then it started to rise. Tam said, 'Hold, everyone, hold, hold, hold and lower.'

Gho punched the air and shouted, 'Yes! Yes! We did it!.'

Tam said, 'Is everyone alright?'

Mona replied, 'Yes, but it was hard, really hard.'

'Mab, how about you.' said Tam.

Mab replied, 'Yes, I'm fine, I think we should be in with a good chance on this event!'

Gho said, 'Let's have a go at mind-ball. We will use one hoop. Mab and Mona, you try to stop Tam and I from putting the ball through the hoop.' Gho threw the ball up into the air; Tam caught it with his mind and raced it towards the hoop. Mab ripped it from his grasp and threw it to the far end of the pitch, but Gho grabbed it and threw it back to Tam, who had moved it much closer to the hoop. Tam threw the ball downwards at great speed, but Mab punched it away again. Gho caught it again and set it on a course toward the hoop, but this time, the ball followed a zig-zag path. Mona signalled to Mab that it was moving too fast for her. Mab pushed a large volume of air around the ball away from the hoop and the ball went with it. Tam, however, plucked the ball from the air and threw it at enormous speed directly at the hoop, but it stopped dead in the air just before going through. Gho and Tam tried to push and pull it, but it would not move even by the smallest amount. Gho gave up, looked at Mab with a wry smile on his face and said, 'Mab, you are not allowed to stop the ball. It must always remain in motion.'

'Oh okay, I didn't know that,' replied Mab.

Just as Mab released her grip on the ball, Tam pushed it through the hoop and cried, 'Yes! Yes! It's a strike!!' Mab, Mona and Gho howled with laughter.

Gho said, 'That's great, guys. I think we will need further practice on the mind-ball, so I'll set up another session on that. Let's not worry too much about the weightlifting. I think we can do our own individual preparation for that.'

As Mab and Mona made their way back to their rooms, Mona said, 'Mab, thanks for your help with the weights. It was just too heavy for me, I could feel you supporting me.'

Mab replied, 'Don't mention it; anyway, it's a team effort, so it's within the rules to help each other. We have a good chance of winning in the weights, but not sure about the mind-ball! I think that's a real team skill and needs a lot of practice. We don't have much time to prepare for the House games, but we do for the inter-school competition.'

Mona replied, 'Yes, but the inter-school competition has different events. It is more martial in nature because it is under the control of the Palace. Injuries are common and we have even had some deaths. Anyway, you won't be taking part as junior students are not permitted. It is usually only senior students and adepts that are allowed to enter the competition.'

'I didn't know that. Is mind-ball included?' asked Mab.

Mona replied, 'No, it's not included, although weightlifting and fireball are included as individual events. The high-level events are on free-style combat, both individually and in teams, where the objective is to make your opponent submit. Usually, the weaker contestants yield before any damage is done. There are also coercion events where you have to control animals and make them do stuff, such as shepherding sheep and driving cattle. The House games are usually good fun, but the interschool competition is scary. I think if the masters had a choice, they wouldn't allow the Guild to participate.'

'Why don't they have a choice?' asked Mab.

'It's all to do with the funding, the Palace provides a lot of funding to the magic schools and so they call the shots. The money comes from the military budget, so their main interest is on finding new adept recruits,' said Mona.

Chapter Five: Visit to the Palace

Kanaka arrived at the Royal Palace tired. It was a ten-hour walk from the Guild, but that was what he did, it was a ritual, a validation he performed ever since he was appointed as Principal. However, since the episode with Master Boe, he had not slept properly, and he hadn't heard anything from Ansek, which was worrying.

He mused that on previous visits, he had always enjoyed travelling to and from the Palace, but he seldom enjoyed his stay. The Palace was, of course, magnificent; a sprawling edifice of stone walls, cloistered courtyards and grand halls. The walls were draped with huge tapestries depicting seminal battles and great leaders dating back into antiquity. *However,* thought Kanaka, *the Guild was older still and it predated all of this.* Indeed, many of the artefacts on display in the Palace were, in fact, looted from conquest and subjugation of other, now forgotten, regions and cultures; history is always penned by the victors, never the losers.

When Kanaka checked in at the palace reception, he was told that the other Principals had already arrived and were at lunch in the mess hall. Kanaka dropped his backpack off in his room, had a quick shower and change then made his way to the mess room. When he arrived, he recognised Masters Sirak (Principal of the School of Psych and Sorcery) and Master Jessam (Principal of the School of Witches and Warlocks) but not the other Master.

'Kanaka, good you see you again. I guess your walk gets harder every year or is it you that gets weaker every year?' said Sirak, smiling warmly.

Kanaka laughed, nodded to Jessam, and said, 'Good to see you too, Sirak; I think it's a bit of both!' As Kanaka sat down, he looked at the other Master and said, 'I don't think we have met, is Master Gould unable to attend?'

The Master said, 'Pleased to meet you, Master Kanaka. I am Anara Birrio, the recently appointed Master of the new Academy of the Occult. The Academy of Magic and the Occult has been restructured and renamed to better serve the needs of the Palace.' 'I see, but what of Master Gould?' replied Kanaka.

Birrio said, 'I had hoped to have his support and council during the transition, but unfortunately, he suffered a severe brain haemorrhage, which we think was due to the stress of the ongoing changes.'

'He's dead?' asked Kanaka.

'I'm afraid so,' said Birrio.

Kanaka stared at her incredulously; he was just about to reply when Ansek arrived and said, 'Sorry to be so late, but I was tied up with other business. You must be Birrio. Congratulations on your appointment.'

'Thank you, Ansek,' replied Birrio.

Ansek said, 'Kanaka, I had hoped to catch up with you over lunch?' The other three masters explained that they had already eaten and excused themselves. Kanaka and Ansek picked up some food and drinks and made their way to a secluded table. Ansek said, 'Birrio was an adept in the Prince's Personal Guard. The Palace has essentially taken over the Academy, which is now dedicated to all matters occult. This could be the first step in all four magic schools coming under Palace governance.'

Kanaka replied, 'Ansek, it is as you suspected, but what can we do?'

Ansek said, 'That's what we need to figure out. I suspect Gould was killed to make way for Birrio, but killing Gould would not be easy and we only have Birrio's word that Gould is dead. Birrio was a very good adept, but I would not put her in the same category as Gould.'

Kanaka said 'Perhaps Birrio is not Birrio, if you get my meaning?'

Ansek replied, 'Yes, but how would we know?'

Kanaka said, 'I'll mind message Lamm, he can link to Mab; she may be able to advise.'

Ansek said, 'Tanya told me that the adept who attacked Boe and Mab was known as Arfet and confirmed that he was of the Prince's Personal Guard. When Mab confronted him, she mentioned an attar of decay but also that she could see the daemon within him.'

Kanaka replied, 'Yes, but Mab could also see the black flames and we could not. We need to find a way of identifying the presence of these creatures. I was unable to contact Gould, and now I know why, but Sirak and Jessam have no knowledge of these events. If I get anything sensible back from Lamm, I will let you know, but now I think I'll get a couple of hours of sleep before the meeting and dinner tonight.'

Ansek replied, 'Yes, you do look tired, Kanaka and we will need our wits about us tonight.'

Kanaka messaged Lamm while walking back to his room. In reply, Lamm said he would talk to Mab and get back to him. However, Lamm said he had been doing his own research into possession and it seems that a daemon could only enter a host with permission or otherwise if the host was of feeble mind or will. It could only be expelled against its will by a priest or celestial being. It may be that the Palace Adepts had found a means by which a daemon could enter a host without permission. Kanaka thanked him for the information and then fell into a deep sleep.

Kanaka woke in good time for the council meeting and dinner. He had another shower to freshen up and changed into his formal dress which consisted of a robe and trouser suit of black silk with fine gold braiding and soft leather lace-up boots. He wore the Guild's ancient golden neck chain and medallion around his neck, which signified that he was the Guild Principal. He also shaved and oiled his head with balsam, as was the custom of his ancestors.

Lamm's mind messaged him as he was preparing to leave his room. He had spoken to Mab and she had first detected the daemon by the flames, but the smell was unmistakable. She said she could see the daemon clearly and suggested you rest your gaze on the face of the host for several seconds and then try to look within. She said it was similar in some ways to a mind scan. Kanaka thanked him once again and then made his way to the council meeting.

As he entered the meeting room, he saw that the other three Principals and Ansek were already there. He took his usual seat between Sirak and Jessam but noted that Birrio was seated next to Ansek on the Palace side of the table. The meeting room was appropriately small, with a thick horseshoe-shaped table occupying much of the space. The Prince would usually sit at the top of the horse shoe with the Principals down the left leg and any Palace representatives down the right leg. Not for the first time, Kanaka thought this meeting was going to be difficult. They sat in silence until finally, the Prince arrived with a party of three, all were dressed in black robes, all stood up and sat down again when the Prince had taken his seat. It was then that Kanaka noticed the smell. It was subtle, but once recognised, it seemed to get stronger. Kanaka glanced across at Ansek. Yes, he had also picked-up on it.

The Prince said, 'Principals, welcome back to the Palace. This will be a short but important meeting. First, however, some introductions. On my left, we have Masters Jessam, Kanaka and Sirak from The Guild of Witches and Sorcerers, The Guild of Sorcerers and The School of Psych and Sorcery, respectively. On my right, we have Masters Ansek and Birrio from the Palace Military and the Academy of the Occult, respectively. Also, on my right, we have Master Toker and Adepts Mago and Amay. Ansek, from what you tell me, Kanaka will be hosting the annual competition this year?'

Ansek replied, 'Yes, my Prince, the preparations are underway as we speak.'

The Prince looked at Kanaka and said, 'Kanaka?'

Kanaka replied, 'Yes, Prince, Master Ansek and I are progressing the matter.'

The Prince paused for almost 30 seconds and then said, 'Very well, but you should know that for subsequent years, I intend that the annual competitions be held here at the Palace. But more of that in a few minutes.'

Kanaka replied, 'That would be a significant change from custom, but I don't necessarily see it as a problem for the Guild. I am, however, somewhat concerned regarding the change in the status of the Academy.'

The Prince stared at Kanaka as if he had just committed treason and said, 'We are engaged in a restructuring exercise. The first step in that was to bring the Academy under the direct control of the Palace Military. The Academy will focus on the Occult as that is an area of great interest and importance to me, particularly in relation to my personal guard. The Academy is now part of the Palace military, financially and with regard to curriculum. Master Birrio is the new Principal and she will report to Master Toker, who has been appointed as Head of my Personal Guard.'

Kanaka replied, 'Yes, Prince, but I would have thought that if there was to be a restructuring, then we, as Principals of the schools, would have been consulted?'

The Prince said, 'Well clearly you thought wrong, Kanaka. If we look to make changes in relation to the GOS then rest assured, we will consult you at that time. Now, with regard to the annual competition, there may be five entries. This is because the four schools will be competing, as usual, but an additional team will be put forward by my Personal Guard. In future competitions, we may merge the Academy and Palace teams, but let's see how things go on this occasion. In terms of funding, all will remain the same for the three remaining independent schools at present, depending on the outcomes of the restructuring process, which is ongoing. Any questions on that direct them to Ansek. Does anyone want to raise anything else before we have dinner?'

Kanaka said, 'Yes, I would. Recently, an assassin attempted to kill a Guild Master and one of my students. Fortunately, he did not succeed. The assassin was dressed exactly like one of your personal guards.'

The Prince replied, 'Kanaka, just because he was dressed as a Palace Adept does not mean that he was, in fact, of the Palace.'

'His name was Arfet; he was known to Master Toker,' replied Kanaka.

Toker replied, 'Master Kanaka, I found out about this only recently. Arfet was suffering from extreme stress and depression, for which he was under strong medication. I fear he stopped taking the medication with tragic results. I would like to emphasise that he was not part of the Palace group and should not have been present at the event. I have to say that you should look into your own security arrangements, as he should never have been allowed access to the campus. However, we can be thankful that Master Boe and young Mab were uninjured, so please pass our apologies to them both.'

The Prince said, 'Tragic indeed, please also pass on my apologies. Kanaka, this student of yours, 'Mab,' this is the second time I have heard her name mentioned. Is she particularly gifted?'

Kanaka replied, 'Mab is one of our junior students, she works hard and learns fast.' The Prince said, 'Ansek, have you met her? If so, what is your assessment.'

Ansek replied, 'My Prince, I concur with Kanaka, she works very hard and is, in some ways, quite remarkable.'

The Prince, laughing, said, 'I think you may have taken a shine to her, Ansek. What say you?'

Ansek replied, 'I think you may be correct, my Prince, but it seems everyone who meets her takes a shine to her.'

The Prince said, 'Kanaka, I would like to meet this Mab. Could you make it happen, please?'

Kanaka replied, 'Certainly, Prince, you will meet her at the competition, although as a junior student, she will not be competing.'

The Prince replied, 'Kanaka, if she has sufficient skills, then she should compete, based upon your judgement, of course.'

Kanaka replied, 'Thank you, Prince, I will discuss it with her.'

The Prince stood up and said, 'I suggest we continue our discussions at dinner.'

Everyone stood up and followed the Prince into the dining hall reception room, where military students were serving fine sparkling wines, aperitifs and canapes. Kanaka was standing close to Birrio and was attuned to the sickly sweet attar she was exuding. Toker appeared normal but the two Adepts Amay and Mago had gone. Toker said she had dismissed them as they were uncomfortable in formal settings but wanted them to at least meet the school Principals.

Ansek looked at the Prince and said, 'My Prince, if I may ask, why do you feel your personal guard should compete in the annual competition?'

The Prince replied, 'Why not? I need my personal guard to be the best they can be. The annual competition will help them to achieve that goal. I am sure the schools are not afraid of some additional competition. Sirak, Jessam, what say you?'

Sirak said, 'I have always regarded the Military as benefiting from the outcomes of the magic schools rather than competing with them. On the basis that the Palace Personal Guard is largely made up of graduates from the four magic schools, then I don't see how their involvement would help to drive further improvement.'

Jessam said, 'I concur with that assessment unless, of course, the Palace intends to source graduates from far-flung places or engage practitioners with radically different approaches to that of our magic schools?' Kanaka said nothing but rested his eyes gently on Birrio as her attention was on Jessam. Ever so slowly, he deepened his gaze behind her facial skin, then behind her eyes and then it came into focus, a blackness, a foul presence that dominated her very being.

The stench suddenly grew much stronger. Kanaka withdrew his gaze and realised that Birrio was staring directly at him with a sickening smile on her face. Kanaka gagged and only just managed to keep the contents of his stomach from pouring onto the floor of the Palace dining room.

The Prince looked at Kanaka and said, 'Kanaka, would you like some water? Are you feeling unwell?'

Kanaka replied, 'Yes, I will have some water. I think I may be dehydrated after my journey here.'

The Prince said, 'Please take a seat. Dinner is about to be served.'

The Prince sat at the head of the table with Jessam, Sirak and Kanaka on his left and Ansek, Toker and Birrio on his right. When all were seated and the meal was underway, Ansek said, 'My Prince, returning to the points made earlier by Sirak and Jessam, is the Palace looking into procuring graduates from other schools or seeking new sources of magic that are not part of the current curriculum?'

The Prince replied, 'Ansek, it would be remiss of me not to do that. Remember, the purpose of the military is to defend our homeland and defeat those who seek to harm us at any cost.'

Ansek replied, 'Are you able to share anything further on the new schools and new approaches? I am sure the Principals would be keen to understand developments in these areas and perhaps make their own contributions?'

The Prince replied, 'Yes, we are certainly looking into new approaches, this work is being led by Toker. In relation to the schools, as I said earlier, there will be no immediate further changes, but the restructuring project is an ongoing project.'

Kanaka looked at Toker and said, 'Master Toker, who is the person sitting to your right?'

There was complete silence in the room. Birrio replied in her slow, soft, monotone voice, 'I am Master Birrio, Principal of the Academy of the Occult and Member of the Princes' Personal Guard. You shall address me as such.'

Toker said, 'Master Kanaka, Birrio represents a significant step forward in our plans to strengthen military capability. We have been able to harness powers we could only dream of previously by seeking alliances with other planes.'

Jessam said, 'What do you mean other planes? Are you saying Birrio is from another plane of existence?'

Kanaka replied, 'Jessam, Birrio is not from another plane, it is the creature that possesses her who is from another plane.'

Sirak said, 'Toker, have you gone completely mad? What is the nature of this creature?'

Toker replied, 'The being is from another plane. We were able to establish communications with them through mind-space. They cannot exist in our plane without a willing host body; our Adepts and Priests were able to devise a process to enable the passage. When in our plane, they are far more powerful than our best adepts.'

Kanaka asked, 'Was Birrio willing to give up her body and soul to this creature?'

Toker replied, 'Kanaka, Birrio is a military officer and follows orders even if the consequence is death. This process has nothing to do with souls or any other such superstitious nonsense. We have identified powerful allies who are ready and willing to help us should we be in need, just as we recruit skilled Guild graduates when needed.'

The Prince said, 'Kanaka, Jessam, Sirak, perhaps you see these initiatives as a threat to your roles and contributions to the Palace. However, the facts are as Toker states. These creatures are powerful; we can make use of them within the military, and they are willing, eager even, to support us. From what I understand, their plane is a dreadful dismal place to exist, they require nothing else of us other than to live in peace.'

Kanaka looked across the table at Birrio and said, 'Daemon, what is your name?'

Birrio replied in her characteristic drawl, 'Kanaka, as I said before, my name is Birrio.'

Kanaka said, 'What is the nature of the place you came from?'

Birrio replied, 'You would call it a prison, a living hell. I am forever in the debt of the Prince and Master Toker for giving me the opportunity to exist on this plane.'

Kanaka said, 'What is your daemon name?'

Birrio replied, 'Of that, I will not speak.'

The Prince said, 'Kanaka, enough! We have now shared this military knowledge with the Principals. I remind you that you are bound by the confidentiality agreement. This will go no further or the consequences will be dire, if not terminal.'

The dinner continued with small talk, the guests having much to think about and being reticent to make further contributions for fear of attracting retribution from the Prince. Ansek and Kanaka left separately and at different times, but both returned to Ansek's quarters in the Palace to share thoughts. Ansek produced a strong fine liquor which had a pungent odour of mint and said, 'This should help to take the smell away.'

Ansek finished pouring the liquor and said, 'I have to say, Kanaka. I was surprised by your candour and equally surprised by their candour!'

Kanaka replied, 'Yes, I was also surprised by their candour. As for my own reaction, I saw the daemon, it was staring back at me from across the table.'

Ansek said, 'You saw it? How?'

Kanaka replied, 'Lamm spoke to Mab, she explained to him how she was able to see the daemon in the Adept. It is similar to a shallow mind scan, rest your gaze lightly on their face for a few moments and then look deeper just behind the eyes, but you need to fine-focus.'

Ansek said, 'What exactly did you see?'

Kanaka replied 'It was vile, malevolent, its very presence was wrong in every sense of that word. I do not believe Birrio would have willingly given up her life and soul for that thing. Mab said the daemon she saw was old and powerful and that was also my impression. It's difficult to articulate, but I had the feeling that I was looking at something ancient and fundamentally evil.'

Ansek said, 'If these creatures can be harnessed for use in battle, then should we not make use of them? That at least is the argument put forward by the Prince and Toker.'

Kanaka replied, 'Ansek, they are deluded if they believe that. These daemons cannot be trusted or harnessed. Their only wish is to escape a prison that has held them for centuries, or even millennia, and feed on the souls of the innocent, our souls in our plane.'

Ansek said, 'Do we know how to kill them if needs must?'

Kanaka replied, 'I am not sure they can be killed. Mab was able to expel one of them, but that may not be the same as killing it. We need to find out more from the priesthood, perhaps, when expelled, it returns to its plane of origin. I have always regarded demonology as religious mysticism, but it appears I was wrong. I would have thought that the Prince would not give permission for these creatures to be brought over if they could not be killed.'

Ansek said, 'The other concern I have is how many of these creatures have already been brought over. To date, we are aware of only four, the one slain by Mab, Adepts Mago and Amay and, of course, Birrio. I will tackle Toker on this issue, you focus on how to expel or, preferably, kill them. Kanaka, there is something else. When we went to dinner, the smell receded, no doubt because Mago and Amay did not attend. I was not sitting close to Birrio although I still detected her foul attar to my right. However, there was also a heavily perfumed smell to my left with a subtle undercurrent of the attar.'

Kanaka replied, 'You mean The Prince? If he has been taken by a daemon then this is a very grave matter indeed. It could mean that Toker has been colluding with the priests and daemons against the Prince. Ansek, take great care if you plan to face scan the Prince, if he has been taken, the daemon will know that you can see him.'

Ansek said, 'Yes, it is grave and alarming, be assured I will not face-scan him until I know how to kill the daemon within. Kanaka, you need to keep Mab away from the Prince. She has piqued his interest and I suspect it is not only because she has the ability to expel daemons but, as we suspected, something to do with her witch powers.'

Kanaka replied, 'Yes, I agree. He won't have an opportunity to see her until the competition, so I will need to manage things at that time to minimise her exposure to him. Anyway, it's getting late, and I will be up and out early for the long walk back to the Guild. Thanks, keep in close contact.' Kanaka and Ansek shook hands and Kanaka made his way back to his room.

Chapter Six: The Lost Library

Mab had been busy over the period leading up to the House games. She had found a secret working space in one of the many libraries on the Guild campus. The small library was within the main Guild building on the lower basement floor directly below the Great Hall. This was where some of the oldest Guild books were kept. The walls were lined with bookcases which were stacked floor to ceiling with books of every conceivable size and shape. Halfway up one of the walls there was a gallery set back, which supported a small oak table and two chairs. Access to the gallery was via a beautifully ornate oak ladder, which perfectly matched the table and chairs. One of the chairs was made from stiff oxblood leather stretched over an oak frame, this was intended for detailed work at the table. The other was a large, comfy sofa-type chair for relaxing and easy reading.

However, Mab did not go there to read books; the lost library, as she called it, was a place of peace and absolute silence. She would often meditate for several hours at a time, sometimes exploring mind-space and other times looking within, seeking to understand herself. She would place a large cushion from the comfy chair on top of the table and sit there cross-legged enjoying the silence and comforting smell of the old books. It was through her contemplation and meditation that Mab came to realise that she was different. Her powers had increased at an extraordinary rate to the point where she was almost afraid of her capabilities. She had awoken from a deep meditation on one occasion to find herself floating above the table albeit still cross-legged; she remained quite still and slowly lowered herself down to the cushion. Mab also realised that her witch senses had developed apace: she could sense the presence of other living creatures before hearing or smelling them; when in the lost library, she had thought to find references to demonology and her senses directed her eyes to several books, which she retrieved with a simple hand-gesture. She had even practiced remote mind scanning with Izzy and Charly, who were happy to participate. Cat had refused on the basis that Mab would be shocked by what she might find.

Even so, Mab remained confused. She was certainly different, but why was she so different? Who was she really? The question she had to confront, who were her biological parents and would this knowledge help to explain who she was? Of course, Mab knew the answer to the latter was a definitive 'Yes' but did not want to think about the former; her parents were Sopa and Walim and that was that.

Mab still attended her classes but had come to realise that her powers were implicit within her. They could not be learned, only discovered. Moreover, the skills that her peers and masters had learned and practiced constantly were but a pale shadow of her powers. Mab had, therefore, started to hide her powers in an attempt to fit in, to avoid being singled out. In that way, she could have a reasonably normal life at school and keep her close friends.

When the morning of the house games arrived, there was great excitement around the Guild campus. There were stalls selling all kinds of foods, drinks, curiosities and also genuine antiques. The local farming community had brought their prize-winning animals to show them off; there was a pig race and a falconry show where the birds swooped low over the heads of the spectators to catch a fresh meat lure being dragged by volunteer children. It was a clear, sunny day. The playing fields were arranged as four rectangular shaped areas to the North side of the Guild green. The vendor stalls were set out in the two cross-corridors between the playing areas, and the animal show areas were on the South side of the green to allow easy access for the farmers.

Mab donned her blue Sapphire House tunic and made her way to the playing fields; she wished her Mum and dad were here to see this, they would just love it, she thought. Then she caught sight of Gho, Tam and Mona on field 4. They were warming up by passing a practice ball to each other. She ran over, immediately grabbed the ball and passed it quickly to Mona; Gho then called them together for a pre-match talk. He said, 'We are up against House Opal in the first round; they are a very good team, in fact, they have won the event more times than any of the other houses. Mona, Mab, remember that you are defending, your job is to keep the ball out of our basket and feed it to Tam and myself to strike.'

The first game played was House Emerald v House Amber on field 3. Izzy, Charly and Cat were there to support Emerald. Mab ran over to them and as expected, they had brought a second breakfast of rustic bread, cheeses, fresh fruit and even a pitcher of ale. As they tucked into the second breakfast, Mab got the opportunity to watch her first real mind-ball game. It was fast and furious, must faster than she had envisaged. She was about to sample the ale when Tam called out to her; they were about to start on field 4.

Mab ran across to field 4 and took up her position close to her team's basket and on the opposite side of the field to Mona. Tam was to her right but much farther up the field and close to House Opal's basket. The referee threw the ball into the field and there was an immediate tussle for the ball, which was won by the Opal striker Dia, who immediately launched the ball at tremendous speed towards the Sapphire hoop. It looked as if the ball was going well over and out of the field, but at the last second, Dia drove it downwards. Mab slapped it across the field to Mona just before it went through the hoop. Mona caught it and fired it up the side of the field to Gho, who launched it towards the Opal hoop. As it approached the hoop, Tam rammed it home before his opposite number could react.

The final score was 3-1 in favour of Sapphire House. When Tam had scored the second hoop for Sapphire Mab decided to let Opal score just to even things up a bit. Mab and Mona were somewhat magnanimous in victory, but Gho and Tam were truly ecstatic. Amber defeated Emerald in their contest and so the final game between Sapphire and Amber took place early in the afternoon. Sapphire won the match 2-1, but this time, the Amber striker, Jamal, was too fast even for Mab.

The weight-lifting event was also won by Sapphire due to Mab supplying just enough lifting power to win at each stage of the game. Following the victory and allowing a suitable period of time for Gho and Tam to bask in glory, Mab ran off to find Izzy and the rest of her friends. She found Izzy, Charly and Cat watching the falconry display. The birds were awesome, although Mab didn't like seeing them in captivity. She took a swig of ale and did a gentle mind scan of the birds and found that they seemed to be happy, content and definitely well-fed. In fact, she was thinking they were a bit over-fed when her senses picked up on something wrong.

Mab turned her head quickly and focused on a horse; she ran towards the horse enclosure, closely followed by Izzy. She saw a heavy horse running fast in a zig-zag pattern, constantly changing direction, it was covered in sweat and breathing heavily. Three senior students were leaning on the enclosure fence, drinking ale and laughing. Izzy ran around the enclosure fence towards them, shouting, 'Stop! Stop! Stop!'

Mab bounded straight over the fence with blinding speed and mid-air, made a gesture with her hand. The horse stopped and stood still, shivering and panting; Mab landed only a few feet from the horse and put her hands out, palms up. The horse walked slowly towards her, and she gently placed her palms on the horse's cheeks and kissed him on the nose. She turned her head and rested her cheek on his nose and caressed him with her mind. She felt and absorbed his pain, he became calm, almost serene. Mab stayed gently holding him for almost ten minutes, she had tears in her eyes as she led him to the far end of the enclosure and tethered him next to a pile of fresh hay and a water trough.

Mab turned to look, with tearful but baleful eyes, across the enclosure at the senior students; she saw that Izzy and Master Lamm had been talking to them and were now walking toward her. Master Lamm was shocked to see how this had affected Mab, he said quickly, 'Mab, I have spoken to them, and they are sorry for any distress this may have caused.'

Mab replied, 'Sorry, I think not.'

Lamm said, 'Mab, come with me now, I assure you they will apologise.'

Mab, with tears once again forming in her eyes, said, 'He has a big heart, his loyalty, his devotion, they are not worthy. I will not permit them to treat him in this way.' Lamm was aghast and only now did he recognise the seriousness and the danger. He turned and started to walk back to the students, and, to his horror, they started laughing again; he ran towards them, expecting an imminent attack from Mab. However, it was too late, Mab had already stripped them of their psychic powers. Mab turned to Izzy, and they walked together back to their room.

Mab missed the presentations which were carried out by Master Kanaka, but Gho and Tam came to see her the following morning sporting two silver cups one for mind-ball and the other for weightlifting. Gho proudly pointed out the House Sapphire inscriptions on both cups, together with the four names of the winning team. He also explained that House Amber won the flame ball throwing event, but the mind control event was cancelled due to some incident with senior students mistreating a horse. Master Lamm also came to see her later the next day and said, 'Mab, I wanted to apologise to you for yesterday. I know you were very upset with the way the students had treated the horse. They have apologised to me once again and this time, it was sincere.'

Mab replied, 'There is no need for you to apologise to me, Master Lamm.'

Lamm said, 'Following the incident, the students appear to have lost their psychic abilities. Do you know how that could have happened?'

Mab replied, 'Yes, I will not permit the torture of innocent creatures.'

Lamm said, 'You removed their powers?'

Mab replied, 'I have blocked their powers.'

Lamm said, 'I see, and are you able to remove the block?'

Mab replied, 'Yes, but I will not. You did not feel the fear, the hurt, the fatigue, the incomprehension. They are alive, they should reflect on their good fortune.'

'Very well, I understand,' said Lamm.

When Lamm left, Mab made her way to the Clinic to see Boe. He was asleep when she entered the room, so she sat beside his bed and waited for him to awaken. Boe must have sensed her presence as he woke only a few minutes later. When he saw Mab, he smiled warmly. 'You look a lot better, Master Boe,' said Mab.

Boe replied, 'I do feel a lot better; the deep burns are now healing, and they have taken all the bandages off. My beautiful face will, however, bear the scars for some time to come.'

Mab laughed and said, 'Yes, well, I am sure your beautiful face will eventually heal. In any case, war wounds can be quite attractive to some women, you know.'

Boe went into a fit of laughter and said, 'Mab, don't make me laugh. It hurts! Anyway, what's this I hear about you rescuing a horse from some students who should know better?'

Mab explained what had happened. Boe said, 'Yes, Mab, they did a very bad thing, no question about that. But there is something I think you should know. Not everyone is like you, they don't have the same understanding or the insight that you possess. Neither do they hold to the same standards with regard to the treatment of animals or, indeed, other people. You see and feel things that others do not and yet you judge them by your standards. What they did was wrong by any measure, and you were right to intervene. However, by removing their psych abilities, you have effectively destroyed their future, everything they had worked for over the past decade. You have taught them a lesson they will never forget, that's for sure, but perhaps you could help them to improve their understanding that power must always be tempered by responsibility.'

Mab paused in thought and then said, 'Yes, I see what you mean. I suppose there is always hope that people will eventually do the right thing. Thank you, Master Boe.'

Boe replied, 'Mab, you should go and see Master Lamm, he was quite upset following his discussion with you; he greatly values your opinion and holds you in the highest regard, as do I.'

Mab kissed Boe on the cheek and said, 'I'll go and see Master Lamm now.'

Mab sent Lamm a mind message and asked to speak face to face. He replied immediately and said he was on his way to her room. When Mab got back to her room, Master Lamm was already there waiting. Mab said, 'I've just come from Master Boe he looks so much better.'

Lamm replied, 'Yes, he will be discharged fairly soon I would have thought.'

Mab said, 'I wanted to talk to you about the three students. Master Boe has given me a different perspective on the situation. If you wish, I will remove the psych block, but first, I want to speak to them.'

Lamm replied, 'I am sure that could be arranged; where and when?' Mab asked Lamm to send them to the horse enclosure first thing tomorrow morning.

Mab woke later than usual. She had breakfast with Izzy, Charly and Cat and then made her way to the horse enclosure. She could see the three senior students waiting for her to arrive. As she approached, she could sense their hostility. As senior students, they probably didn't expect to be confronted by a junior student, especially one of Mab's diminutive proportions. Mab asked their names. 'Tili,' the stocky female on the right growled, 'Birto,' and this is my brother, 'Annti,' said the tallest of the three.

Annti nodded and said, 'Master Lamm told us that your name is Mabdelore and that although you are only a junior student, we should tread carefully and do whatever you ask.' Mab stared at them in silence, waiting.

Birto, with his head down, said, 'Mabdelore, I would like to apologise for our behaviour and the way we treated Hercules, the horse. The truth is we had too much ale and couldn't handle it; because of our stupidity, Hercules suffered needlessly. Master Lamm has told us of your love of animals, you were right to stop us. We have disgraced ourselves and the Guild.'

Mab replied, 'You called him Hercules?'

Birto said, 'Yes, Hercules is my uncle's horse, he lets us bring him to the games every year, although I don't think that will continue.'

Mab said, 'Horses have their own names, but they are smells, not words.' Mab looked directly at Annti, who looked down in shame, and then at Tili, but she stared straight back, still with a scowl on her face. 'What do you wish to say, Tili?' asked Mab.

'I am a senior student; you are a junior student! What right do you have to tell me what to do or how to treat an animal?'

Mab replied, 'So you are not sorry for the way you treated Hercules?'

Tili said, 'Yes, I am sorry, it was wrong.'

Mab replied, 'Then why does it matter who points out that you were wrong?'

Tili said, 'I don't know! Yes, alright, it doesn't matter.'

'Is there anything else you want to ask me before I leave,' said Mab. No one said anything. 'Good, I have removed the psych blocks. Now, would you like to thank me,' said Mab.

All three, with heads still bowed, said, 'Thank you, Mabdelore,' in a rather nervous, out-of-sync way.

'One last thing,' said Mab, 'don't do it again!' She transformed into a huge Saber-Cat and let out a horrendous roar with saliva and spittle spraying in every direction before transforming back. The three students were thrown backwards with the power of the giant cat's roar, the two males losing control of their bladders.

Mab decided to make her way back to the lost library to meditate before having lunch with her friends. As she made her way down the staircase, she knew something was different; someone had been here very recently. Her senses picked up the small changes in temperature and smell. Someone was in there; she opened the door but waited outside. 'Hello Mab,' said Kanaka.

Mab walked in and looked up to see Kanaka sitting on the comfy chair up in the gallery. She climbed the ladder and said, 'Master Kanaka, this is my special place. How did you know?'

Kanaka replied, 'I didn't know, but this was also my special place when I was a student here many, many years ago; it's so peaceful. Also, there are many books kept here that are not what you might call mainstream reading, so I have come to do some research. What do you do when you are here?'

Mab replied, 'I usually put that big cushion on the table, climb on top and meditate.'

Kanaka said, 'It's good that you are here, I have been meaning to speak to you on a very important matter.'

Mab replied, 'Oh, it's not about three students and a horse, is it?'

Kanaka laughed and said, 'That sounds like the beginning of a very good joke, which you can tell me later! No, what I want to talk about is my recent visit to the Palace for the Council Meeting. It seems that the Palace Priests and Adepts are dabbling in daemonology. The adept that you confronted is but one of a number. We don't know the precise number that is possessed by spirits. The use of these daemons is for military applications, the work is being led by Master Toker under the authority of the Prince. The Palace is in denial regarding the incident with Master Boe, but we know that the adept was sent, we assume, by the Palace and most probably under orders from Toker to either capture or kill you. As you know, the reason, we believe, has to do with the nature of your magic. Also, the Palace now has confirmation that you have the ability to expel these daemons. The Palace has asked, on several occasions, for you to visit, and I have consistently refused as it would put you in great danger; this is also Master Ansek's view. The Prince expects to meet you when he attends the Annual Competition and he has given his consent for you to participate in the events even though you are, strictly speaking, a junior student. You should also know that the Palace will most likely be fielding their own team in this year's competition, we assume some of the adepts will be hosting daemons. Mab, you must never agree to visit the Palace on your own and you must not participate in the annual competition. Your life is at stake, and I am not sure we have the capability to adequately protect you against the forces arrayed against us.'

Mab was silent for a few moments and then said, 'Master Kanaka, these creatures are malevolent spirits, they are of the Abyss. Such creatures are fundamentally evil and cannot be trusted or controlled. If Master Toker thinks she is leading them she is very much mistaken. For my part I have no wish to compete in the competition or visit the Palace. But, evil must be combatted and I will not abrogate my responsibilities in that regard.'

Kanaka replied, 'Yes, none of us will shirk from what must be done. But what must be done is not yet clear. What I cannot understand is that, according to Toker, the host adepts have willingly given up their bodies to these daemons.'

Mab said, 'The Palace Priests may have discovered a way of enabling the creatures to inhabit the host in the absence of consent. Perhaps the mind of the host is first dulled by coercion or seriously injured. Even so, it is still difficult to imagine giving up body and soul to such creatures.'

Kanaka hesitated for a few moments before saying, 'Mab, Ansek thinks the Prince may also be a host. He is not certain, but it could help explain things. A direct order from the Prince must be obeyed, at least, that is what a military adept would believe.' They sat in silent thought for several minutes.

Then Kanaka said, 'Well, are you going to tell me the one about three students and a horse?'

Mab laughed and replied, 'No, Master Kanaka, I suggest you ask Master Boe or Master Lamm about that one!'

Kanaka said, 'Very well, I'll be sure to do that. Anyway, I have the books I need, so I will leave you, in our special place, to your meditations.'

Mab entered into a state of deep meditation, her mind relaxed and roaming without focus. Her body was floating several feet above the tabletop in the full lotus position without volition. She had been in that state for exactly one hour when she focussed her mind on the entrance to mind space, her body lowered slowly onto the cushioned table. A door blacker than the surrounding black appeared in the centre of her vison, she moved towards it, using her mind to force it open and moving into mind space. Mab had already realised that mind-space was, in fact, a different plane of existence but most probably an interface layer between other more physical planes of existence. She had thought that it might be possible to travel through this interface layer into more substantive worlds, but how that could be accomplished while her physical body remained on her own plane, she didn't know.

It was strange, she was flying, without corporal form, through what appeared to be endless space, she had just flown further than any of her previous sorties when she saw a distant light. She flew faster and, although she had no physical terms of reference, felt that she was covering immense distances. The light was a Sun and there was a system of planets. She flew faster, still past the outer planets and headed for the third, the one that she sensed could be habitable. She flew down through the atmosphere and thick cloud formations and landed in the middle of what appeared to be a small town, very like her own hometown. The people were human, but there were marked differences. The men appeared to be much larger and more heavily built, they had thick black hair on both their heads and faces. The women were much smaller than the men and their skins were a beautiful olive colour. Their hair was black and typically tied back or worn in a ponytail, their eyes a deep, earthy brown colour. There was a bustling market that was centred on the village square and surrounding streets. Mab floated upward and flew slowly along, heading for the square, she noticed what seemed to be a church at the far end. The church didn't have a steeple or spire, but it was a grand stone building, priests in robes were welcoming the locals within.

Mab moved towards the entrance, but just as she was about to cross the threshold, an old priest looked up directly at her, pointed and shouted a string of words of which she understood only two, 'Daemon! Daemon!' Several other priests came running, pointed their staffs upwards towards Mab and started to chant. Mab decided to stay where she was rather than enter the church, the words of the chant were incomprehensible, but Mab's senses began to twitch. She was beginning to feel uncomfortable, beginning to sweat profusely.

She tried to pull away but found that she couldn't, she was trapped. She lifted her right hand, palm facing the wall of the church, and let off a psychic blast, the force partially demolished the wall above the church entrance but also propelled her backwards. The falling masonry struck several of the priests and interrupted their chanting.

Mab flew upwards at great speed and left the solar system within a few minutes. She hung motionless in deep space, taking time to calm herself before entering back into a deep meditative state. The mind-space door opened, and she moved back into her body; according to the library clock, she had been away less than thirty minutes. Mab slept on the comfy chair for just over two hours before making her way back to her room.

Izzy, Charly and Cat were preparing lunch of bread, cheeses, fresh fruit and hot mint tea. Charly said, 'Mab, you are just in time to pour the tea.'

Mab made her way over to the table to help out. Izzy said, 'Mab, did you hear about the senior students who were attacked by a tiger this morning?'

Mab replied, 'Attacked by a tiger, were they injured?'

Charly, winking at Izzy, said, 'No, they were just shaken up a bit, they used their witch powers to scare it off.' Mab replied, 'They scared it off?'

Cat said, 'Yes, it appears this particular tiger was a bit of a scaredy-cat and ran off with its tail between its legs.'

Mab turned to look at them and they all burst out laughing. Mab grabbed a pillow from her bed and started beating Cat with it. Izzy and Charly joined in, the pillow fight was in full tilt when Master Lamm said, 'I hope I'm not interrupting anything important.'

Izzy replied, 'Oh no, Master Lamm, we were just testing the quality of the pillows.'

Charly said, 'Master Lamm, would you like to join us for mint tea.'

Lamm replied, 'No, I just dropped by to thank you, Mab, for your help with the senior students. They seem to have learned a valuable lesson that they won't easily forget!'

Mab replied, 'I have also learned from this experience, from you and Master Boe.'

Lamm said, 'Perhaps I will join you,' and took a seat.

They tucked into lunch, with Mab eating huge quantities of bread and cheese, while Charly recounted the story of the three students and the timid tiger, much to Master Lamm's amusement. Master Lamm, when he stopped laughing, said, 'Mab, you are taking this teasing in very good spirit, and I'm pleased to see that you haven't lost your appetite.'

Mab replied, 'Master Lamm, there is something I need to discuss with you. Do you have a few minutes now?'

Lamm replied, 'Yes, of course. I'm free for the rest of the day.'

Izzy, Charly and Cat had a tutorial and were getting up to leave. When they left the room, Mab poured Lamm and herself a fresh cup of mint tea and said, 'This morning, following my meditation session, I entered into mind space.'

Lamm replied, 'Mab, you shouldn't have done that; it can be very dangerous.'

Mab said, 'What I wanted to know is if I go into mind-space and get killed, will my physical body on this plane also die or will I simply wake up?'

Lamm replied, 'We don't really know the answer to that. If the death is quick and clean, there should be minimal mind trauma, and I suspect you would simply wake up. However, if the death is protracted, for example, being burned alive, then it may be that the mind trauma would be too great, and your physical body would die. We have not put that to the test for obvious reasons. Our exploration of mind-space is minimal; we only discovered it a year or so ago and our primary use is for large meetings. You and I have a direct mind link for messaging, but if we need to meet as a large, geographically diverse group, then mind space is perfect. We think it is simply an interface, a division, between different planes and in theory, we should be able to pass through it into other planes, but I suspect the distances involved would be enormous.'

Mab said, 'Yes, Master Lamm, the distances are enormous, but it is possible to travel at great speed. I did some exploring this morning. It is not an interface, it is actually another plane of existence.'

Lamm replied, 'You did some exploring? You travelled through mind-space!'

Mab said, 'Yes, but there is too much to explain, you need to see it yourself. Would you be willing to travel with me?'

Lamm said, 'Yes, of course. When do you suggest?'

Mab replied, 'How about early tomorrow morning? We should meet in the main building basement library. Do you think Master Kanaka would be interested?'

Lamm said, 'Yes, he may well be interested, I will let him know what we are planning.'

The following morning, Mab met Lamm and Kanaka in the lost library. Mab brought the comfy chair cushion down to the floor with a gesture. Kanaka and Lamm brought their meditation mats. They bolted the library door from the inside and took their positions on the floor. Kanaka and Lamm quickly went into a meditative state and entered into mind space. A short time later, Mab arrived. Mab said, 'Now follow me, we must stay together in tight formation.' Mab started to move away, but it took some time for Kanaka and Lamm to get going. Mab said, 'Move forward with your mind, imagine you are moving inwards to do a mind scan.' Kanaka and Lamm then started moving forward and Mab gradually increased the speed until they were rocketing through mind-space. She pointed to the light in the distance, accelerated into the solar system and then stopped. The three spirits hung in space.

Lamm said, 'Mab, you were right. This is another plane, and this solar system is not unlike our own.'

Kanaka said, 'Truly astonishing!'

Mab replied, 'Master Kanaka, it gets better, the third planet is inhabited. Yesterday, I went down to the surface and flew slowly through a village thronged with people. The people are not like us in appearance, but they are human. I flew close to a church and tried to enter, but the priests, although they couldn't see me, detected my presence and used some kind of magic chant to restrain me. I couldn't understand the language, but they did use the word 'Daemon.' They thought I was a Daemon.'

Kanaka said, 'Mab, lead-on.'

The three plummeted towards the planet and surface slimmed across an ocean until they approached land. Mab led them to the small town she had visited previously, they moved slowly, floating just above the red-tiled roofs and looking at the people moving below. They were probably at a similar stage of development to our civilisation, thought Kanaka. Then a huge roar went up, they soared upwards expecting an attack, but then realised the sound was coming from a stadium. They changed course and landed on the rough wooden roof structure of the stadium.

They saw huge warriors dressed in full armour, they were fighting with each other using great swords and what looked like pitchforks. One of the warriors had been very seriously injured, he was on the ground writhing in pain; blood was flowing from a deep gash that almost completely severed his right shoulder and arm. Kanaka realised the crowd was roaring in appreciation and said, 'This is a competition, a battle to the death between two opposing sides for the purposes of entertainment.'

Lamm replied, 'We also have competitions, but the weapons being used here and the injuries they cause it is barbaric and horrific.'

Mab said, 'It looks as if it's all over for the blues. No, look, the red team are killing the wounded!'

The four members of the red team that remained standing received a standing ovation from the crowd as they walked off the field. Lamm wanted to move on, but Kanaka wanted to stay a bit longer and said, 'This gives us a real insight into their culture. They are extremely warlike, but it is curious that they fight with such crude weapons. Does this mean that they have no mind powers?'

Mab said, 'The priests have mind powers, but I suspect they are quite limited.'

Lamm pointed and said, 'The villagers are pouring onto the field, but only women and children.'

Kanaka said, 'Surely they are not going to make them fight to the death!'

As they watched, the entrance gates were closed locking the villagers in the combat field. Smaller gates were opened, and large cat-like beasts ran upwards from their cages onto the combat field. 'Lions!' cried Lamm. The women and children were screaming in terror, but then one of the women stood up and started singing. Slowly, the others joined in, holding their children close to them so they couldn't see the approaching lions. Mab flew slowly forward so she was hovering horizontally directly above the field. She spread her arms outwards, and the lions stopped and lay down. The crowd fell silent, the villagers continued to sing. Mab returned to the stadium roof. The lions were being shepherded back into their cages, but then more warriors were brought onto the field and started to slaughter the villagers to great applause from the crowd.

Kanaka said, 'We cannot interfere further here, Mab, better a quick clean death by the sword. At least you have given them that mercy.'

A voice from behind said, 'You have spoiled my fun.' They turned to see a huge, armoured warrior staring at them.

Kanaka said, 'You can see us? Who are you?'

The warrior replied, 'It is you who will answer my questions.'

Mab said, 'You are a daemon in the guise of a villager. You really stink.'

The daemon laughed and said, 'Yes, I am and what are you, child, if I may ask.'

Mab replied, 'You will know who I am in good time, Baymon.'

The daemon's eyes widened when he heard his name and he moved slowly backwards. Kanaka said, 'Mab, Lamm, we should leave.'

The daemon launched a blistering psychic attack, Lamm took the brunt of it and dropped to the roof unconscious. Kanaka responded with an equally ferocious psychic blast that drove the daemon backward. Mab raised her right arm, opened her hand and then clenched her fist. The daemon dropped to his knees, clutching at its throat. Mab walked towards the demon and said, 'Baymon, leave this body and return to whence you came.'

Mab could see the daemon was fighting to remain and she said with some force, 'Baymon, leave him!' The warrior's body dropped onto the roof of the stadium, but he was alive and free of the daemon. Kanaka lifted the warrior gently to his feet. The warrior looked around wildly as he felt his body being lifted up, tears flowing down his face. He could no longer see his savours, but he bowed deeply in all four directions, then dropped to his knees and brought his palms together on his chest.

Kanaka said, 'Mab, I think he is praying, thanking you for releasing him from that foul creature.'

Mab said, 'Master Lamm has disappeared we need to go back.'

Mab and Kanaka flew upwards, first towards the Sun and then out to the edge of the solar system. They hung in space for several minutes before moving back through their mind-space door and awakening in the lost library. Kanaka was first to wake from his meditative state and he found Lamm on his side and breathing strongly. He used smelling salts to help bring him around. When Mab awoke, Kanaka said, 'Mab, he's coming round now.'

Mab replied, 'Hopefully he hasn't been injured.'

Lamm recovered quickly and, surprisingly, remembered everything up to the point when the daemon attacked. Mab said, 'I'm sorry, Master Lamm, I should have expelled the daemon immediately, but I had hoped to extract information from it.'

Lamm said, 'Look on the bright side, we now know that being killed in mind-space doesn't necessarily mean our physical bodies die.'

Mab replied, 'Yes, true, but you have a very strong mind, Master Lamm. I suspect the average person would not survive or would be seriously damaged.'

Kanaka said, 'Mab, what information did you seek to extract from the daemon?'

Mab replied, 'Why would anyone willingly allow a daemon to take control of their body and soul? I had hoped to find the answer to that question from the daemon. We could communicate directly with the daemon but not with the villagers as we don't understand their language.'

Lamm said, 'Mab, on your first visit there, you said the priests referred to you as a daemon. So, they clearly have experience of dealing with daemons, but from their perspective what is the difference between a daemon and one of us?'

Mab replied, 'When a daemon possesses a person, the mind of that person is caged. The daemon sees, speaks and feels through the person who becomes a mere spectator to what is now the daemon's life. Daemons are entirely of the spirit world, they are immortal and have no body. They are parasitic beings who feed on fear and superstition, they grow stronger through the suffering of others. That is why the daemon was present at the stadium, to relish the slaughter of innocent men, women, children and animals. There may be many daemons in that place, most likely, it is they who are responsible for organising the competitions.'

Lamm said, 'It could be that the daemons from that plane are finding their way, perhaps assisted by the Palace, into our plane through mind-space.'

Kanaka said, 'Mab, what you have shown us today is nothing short of astonishing. You were right to allow us to witness it ourselves because, even coming from you, I would have struggled to believe it. What Master Lamm has just said worries me, the Palace is clearly in league with these creatures, whatever their origin. Also, you knew the name of the daemon, you called it Baymon? How did you know that and how were you able to expel it?'

Mab replied, 'I can't really explain it, Master Kanaka, when I look at a daemon, I just know its name. It's like when you look at a colour you know immediately that it is red or green. A daemon will never willingly tell you its name because that is the key to expelling it. The daemon that attacked Master Boe left the host because it was afraid. However, Baymon was not afraid and was determined not to leave the warrior's body, so I had to use its name twice in order to expel it. Master Lamm could well be correct with regard to the source of the daemons. But, there may be other sources of daemons in mind-space. It is said that all daemons originate from the Abyss. Perhaps the Palace has found a way of releasing them and bringing them directly to our plane or via mind-space? I think there is only one way of finding out.'

Kanaka said, 'What would that be?'

'We need to capture one,' replied Mab.

'How would we do that?' asked Master Kanaka.

Mab replied, 'Master Toker has a few, she wouldn't miss one.'

Kanaka put his arm around Mab and, with a wry smile on his face, said, 'I'm sure she wouldn't. Lamm, I've been meaning to ask you, have you heard the one about three students and a horse?'

Chapter Seven: Masters and Daemons

The organising of the Annual Competition involved almost everyone on the campus. The four-quarter fields were converted into two large arenas, each with tiered seating and a fabric roof that protected from wind and rain. A huge number of wooden huts for vendors were constructed around the two large stadiums, creating the impression of a small town growing up around the two larger buildings.

The building enclosures were decorated with thousands of coloured lights and each stadium had five huge flagpoles. The first flag was that for the Palace, which was rectangular with a black dragon and four clenched white fists on a yellow background; the second was that for the GOS, which was rectangular with a blue cross and four blue lion rampant figures on a white background; the third was that for the SOPS which was rectangular with two yellow crescent moons and twelve white stars on a black background; the fourth was for the AOMO (now the Academy of the Occult) which was rectangular with two diagonal yellow stripes and four yellow sunbursts on a green background. The fifth was that for the GOWW which was rectangular with two white rampant unicorns on a blue background.

Additional accommodation for the two-day event was provided by Guild students doubling up, allowing Amber House to be devoted to visiting competitors. Mab, Izzy, Charly and Cat were moved to a converted room in the loft space above Boe's room; this was accessed by means of a secret stairway that spiralled from the entrance vestibule to Boe's room up to the loft space. The new room was a huge space with many roof lights and other feature windows. The move was done to free up their turret room for dignitaries or other important persons and to provide increased security for Mab. Also, with Boe being discharged from the clinic, he was able to bring Meldran back to the Guild from his brother's farm, where he was residing until he recovered. The horse and other animal enclosures were increased in size to cope with additional sheep, cattle and horses for use in the competition.

Ansek arrived at the guild two days early, at the request of Kanaka, to inspect the preparations for the annual competition and he was clearly very pleased with the progress that had been made. They were in Kanaka's office, sharing a particularly good bottle of red wine and canapés before having dinner. Ansek said, 'I am now fairly sure that the Prince is not a host. I suspect this is a military project of limited scale and the Prince is giving Toker rather too much autonomy with regard to the use of daemons.'

Kanaka said, 'Do you know how it is accomplished, how the daemon is summoned and how the possession is carried out?'

Ansek replied, 'No, I don't. I have heard rumours that the Priests are involved and that those possessed are typically soldiers who have been seriously injured or otherwise have low or no quality of life. It is said that the daemon is able to restore and share, the body and so significantly improve their lives, but I have no real evidence of this.'

Kanaka said, 'I ask because Mab wants us to capture one for interrogation.'

Ansek replied, 'Capture a daemon? She must be out of her mind!'

Kanaka said, 'A lot has happened since we last met and we can discuss that over dinner tonight. I have invited Mab and Masters Boe, Lamm, Ochran and Paull. There will be a small ceremony where we will appoint Mab as an Honorary Master of the Guild. She is unaware of this, but please be assured that it is thoroughly deserved. Frankly, for her to be classed as a junior student is ridiculous, especially when her skills exceed that of anyone in the Guild; it is an absurdity that we need to correct.'

Ansek replied, 'She has improved that much?'

Kanaka said, 'She is a phenomenon; indeed, I am not sure that word is entirely adequate. I will present her with the gold medallion, would you be willing to present her with her robe?'

Ansek replied, 'Yes, of course, I would be honoured to do so.'

Mab and her roommates were busy arranging things in their newly appointed suite, as Charly had decided to call it when she received a mind message from Lamm to attend an informal dinner that evening with Masters Kanaka and Ansek. Lamm said, 'It's important, so you must attend and wear something smart, perhaps a nice frock?'

Mab messaged back, 'Fine food and wine, can't wait. I don't have a frock. I was thinking jeans and rubber boots.' She didn't expect a reply and didn't get one.

Mab said to her roommates, 'I'm going out for a really nice dinner tonight with fine food and wine. You lot are not invited, but the first person willing to lend me a nice dress will receive generous leftovers from the dinner.'

Izzy said, 'Who will be at the dinner?"

Mab replied, 'Master Kanaka and Master Ansek. It needs to be something smart, and it shouldn't be the same as the dress I borrowed last time. I wouldn't want them to think I have a limited wardrobe.' This resulted in hoots of laughter.

Cat, pulling a dress from a cupboard, said, 'Mab, you haven't got a wardrobe! This small black dress is smart, but without being too over the top, try it.' It fitted Mab perfectly. Izzy produced a fine white silk shawl and hung it over her shoulders, but Mab wanted to wear her white cloak and Cat's black shoes. Charly told Mab to sit down. She brushed her hair and applied scented oils and continued the process until it looked like a slab of polished obsidian.

Mab made her way down the stairs and met Master Boe in the vestibule coming out of his room dressed in full regalia. Mab said, 'Master Boe, are you going to the dinner with Master Kanaka?'

Boe smiled warmly and said, 'Oh yes, this is the most important dinner of the year.'

Mab replied, 'I was told it was informal, do you think I look alright or should I change into something else?'

Boe said, 'Goodness no, Mab, you look beautiful as always.'

Mab put her arm around his and said, 'You always say such nice things, Master Boe. Let's go!'

When Boe and Mab arrived at the Hall, Mab saw that the Guild Senior Masters and Master Ansek, were all there and, like Master Boe, wearing full Guild regalia. They were standing in a group drinking wine from ceremonial silver goblets.

As Mab and Boe approached, Master Lamm walked towards them, holding two goblets of wine and said, 'You will need these for the toast.'

Master Kanaka turned to greet Mab and said, 'We are gathered here for a very special and solemn occasion. That occasion is the acceptance of a new Master into the Guild of Sorcerers. This new Master position will be both honorary and emeritus; I am the nominee and all present have seconded the nomination.'

Mab was looking around the hall to see if the new master was about to make a dramatic entrance when Master Kanaka approached her and hung a gold chain and medallion around her neck. She looked down in astonishment. Master Kanaka, smiling, said, 'Could everyone, except Mab, raise their goblets for the toast? To Mabdelore Winter, Master of the Guild of Sorcerers!'

Following the toast, everyone gave a hearty applause. Then Master Ansek walked towards her carrying a large box and said, 'Mab, many congratulations on your new appointment. Please accept your robes of office; tradition requires that you don these now.'

Mab opened the box and removed the robe, it was black silk with a fleecy lining and a large hood that could be pulled over to fully cover the face. It had to braid around the cuffs, collars and hood. She put it on and found that it was not only a great fit but it was also surprisingly light and warm. Mab said, 'I'm not just surprised by this. I'm astonished and quite lost for words. I would like to say that I have grown to love the Guild, it is my new home, and to be given this great honour and responsibility is humbling. Thank you, masters, for your support, for your confidence in me and most of all, your friendship, which I treasure above all else.' All participated in another round of hearty applause.

'Now, please be seated for dinner,' said Kanaka.

The ceremonial goblets were removed and the waiters replaced these with wine and liquor goblets, which were rapidly filled. The large oak table was laid out with silver cutlery and chargers before the kitchen staff started to bring out the first of the six courses. Kanaka turned to Mab and said, 'Mab, your position is honorary, so that means we don't really expect you to do any teaching unless you want to, but you will now have free food and accommodation and also a stipend from the Guild for life. Paul will explain the financial details to you, but I think this will give you the security you need to stay here at the Guild as long as you wish.'

Mab replied, 'So, what do you expect me to do if not teach?'

Kanaka said, 'Continue to improve your skills and knowledge to benefit both yourself and the Guild. That is the reason I nominated you as Guild Master. I want you to use your knowledge and research to improve the capability of the Guild, both its students and its masters. Understand that an honorary and emeritus position is a full Guild Master appointment and more; it is of the highest order that can be granted, and you are fully deserving of it.'

Mab said, 'Thank you again, Master Kanaka. I will do my very best.'

Ansek said, 'Mab, how do you do that?'

Mab replied, 'Do what?'

Ansek said, 'It's the way you eat, use your cutlery, pick up your wine goblet. It's so smooth as if the knife moves into your hand rather than you picking it up; it is quite mesmerising.'

Mab said, 'I'm not consciously doing anything, maybe the cutlery has taken a liking to me?'

Ansek replied, 'I have to say that wouldn't surprise me at all. Anyway, I hear you want to capture a daemon?'

Kanaka said, 'Mab, I explained our concerns regarding the source of the daemons and how they are able to take possession of the adepts. Ansek is of the opinion that the hosts could be willing, as they are often soldiers who have been seriously injured. What about the source, Ansek, any ideas?'

Ansek replied, 'No, I'm afraid not. I suspect the Priests have found a way of calling them if that is the correct term, and then enabling them to enter into the host. I have to say though, I cannot imagine how you think you will be able to capture one!'

Mab said, 'Master Kanaka, have you had time to discuss our recent visit to foreign parts with Master Ansek?'

Kanaka replied, 'No, Mab, I have not yet discussed our findings from that trip.'

Mab said, 'Master Ansek, to answer your question, the truth is that we have already captured a daemon.' Everyone at the table stopped talking and looked at Mab.

Ansek said, 'You have captured a daemon and brought it here?' Kanaka was staring at Mab askance.

Mab, sipping her wine and looking at Ansek, replied, 'Yes, it is here.'

Ansek replied, 'Where is it!?'

Mab said, 'I'm looking at it.'

Ansek replied, 'Are you out of your mind!'

Mab said, 'Master Ansek, I know you can see and hear me, stay strong, you will be free soon. Daemon, you have made a grave error in coming here. I speak not of banishment; look into me now and see your death.'

The daemon looked intently at Mab and quailed; it tried to stand but found it was completely immobilised. It stopped struggling and, in a slavering drooling voice, said, 'Fools, all of you! Ansek is already dead; this is my body. You think you can expel me with your ridiculous conjuring? You will release me, else I will feast on your souls before this day is finished.'

Mab said, 'Masters, Ansek has been possessed by a daemon. It is vile. Every utterance from its foul mouth is lies and deceit. But its miserable life is about to end unless, of course, it cooperates. Master Kanaka, we need to do what must be done and quickly. Is there a dungeon or prison cell-type space where we can take Ansek?'

Kanaka replied, 'Yes, the dungeon entrance is at the basement level. Can you keep him restrained until we get there?'

Mab said, 'Yes, but we must all go now!'

The masters walked as a group from the Hall and down to the basement level. Kanaka led them past the Lost Library and along a very narrow single-file passageway, which terminated at a small circular hall with a large stone slab in the middle of the floor. Kanaka raised his left hand, the stone slab groaned and then moved slowly sideways to reveal a square opening, which was the only entrance to the dungeon. Kanaka lowered himself down through the opening and sent four fireballs into the space, these took up positions at the corners of the dungeon. Mab lowered Ansek, still immobilised on the chair, down through the opening and was followed by the rest of the masters.

The dungeon was dark and damp, the floor was puddled in places with groundwater and there was a strong smell of fungus and decay. The walls and floor of the dungeon had large iron restraint rings, with heavy iron link chains attached, anchored deep into the thick stone walls. Mab turned to Ansek and, with a hand gesture, lifted him from the chair and pushed him against the wall. Lamm and Ochran attached the wrist and ankle restraints to all four of Ansek's limbs and then moved away. Mab released Ansek and his body dropped to the floor in a sitting position. Kanaka closed the entrance slab and sent another four additional fireballs upwards to increase the light levels. Mab said, 'Masters, the daemon can only escape this dungeon by moving the stone slab; we must prevent it from leaving of its own accord, so be ready.' Mab then turned to face Ansek and said, 'Daemon, I name you Amaymon, brother of Baymon whom I banished. Know this, Amaymon, I will destroy you utterly unless you tell me what I must know.'

When the daemon heard its name spoken, it writhed on the floor and pulled ferociously against its restraints. The iron wrist and ankle bands cut deep into Ansek's flesh, and bright red blood ran down his forearms. The daemon drooled, saliva running from its mouth and said, 'I will tell you nothing, child of a slut.'

Mab walked forward, elevated his Ansek's body and clamped her hands on either side of his head. An argent silver light shimmered around her hands and she said, 'Amaymon, leave him!' The daemon released a blood-curdling scream and flew from Ansek's body, which went limp on the floor. The stone slab groaned but was held in position by the Masters.

Boe went to Ansek and said, 'He is alive, breathing strongly but unconscious.'

Mab could see Amaymon hovering as a black shadow at the roof-wall corner. She said, 'Amaymon, come here.'

The daemon lowered itself to the floor close to Mab and said in a soft, pleading voice, 'I did not harm the body; I could have slain him, but I did not. Did you know my brother?'

Mab said, 'Be silent! You will speak when you have permission. Who summoned you?' Amaymon said, 'I was summoned by another of my kind.' White flame beamed from Mab's hand and wrapped around the daemon's head. Amaymon screamed in agony.

Mab said, 'I asked a question. You will answer.'

Amaymon gasped, 'I was summoned by Mahazael, the Prince, the Prince.'

Mab released him and said, 'How were you able to possess Ansek?'

Amaymon said, 'I will answer, but first, you must promise not to kill me.'

Mab replied, 'I promise that if you do not answer, your long life will end here in this place.'

Amaymon said nothing.

Mab grabbed hold of the daemon, pulled it towards her and then slammed it backwards hard into the wall; a whip of light lashed Amaymon's face. It screamed in pain and changed into an amorphous mass of black. A ball of white flame punched a hole through the mass and brought another agonising scream from Amaymon; it changed back to a human shape.

Amaymon cried out, 'I will answer, I will answer, please stop.'

Mab replied, 'I will ask the question again, but I will not ask you a third time. How were you able to possess Ansek?'

Amaymon replied, 'It is a procedure which I do not understand. The human is brought to a state of near-death by means of a certain poison. There is a precise moment when it is possible to enter the mind and body without consent; the person is then resuscitated.'

Mab said, 'Who carried out the procedure?'

Amaymon replied, 'It was carried out by Priests and Medics working under the supervision of Toker.'

Mab said, 'Masters, do any of you wish to question this creature further?'

Kanaka said, 'This Mahazael is a daemon like you and it has possessed Prince Sollgar?'

Amaymon replied, 'Yes, but Mahazael is not like me, he is a spirit, Ruler, whereas I am but a follower.'

Kanaka asked, 'Are there other rulers?'

Amaymon replied, 'There are only four rulers but many followers.'

Lamm said, 'From where did this ruler summon you?'

Amaymon replied, 'I was with my brother when I was summoned.'

Lamm said, 'You were at the Stadium participating in the games?'

Amaymon replied, 'Yes, the lions hadn't been sufficiently starved, so we used pikes and swords. It was joyous, but I would have preferred to see the lions tearing off limbs.'

Lamm fought hard to keep his composure and then said, 'I had thought you daemons were of the Abyss. Is that where your brother has returned?'

Amaymon replied, 'I don't know, we can only remain in other planes for a short time outside of a living host. If we cannot find another host, then we are pulled back to our own domain. My brother may have found a suitable child, it is easy to gain consent from a child.'

Lamm asked 'Where is the Abyss?'

Amaymon laughed and said, 'The Abyss is everywhere, it is known by many names: the Warp, the Immaterial, the Hades, the Hell, the Sheol, the Gehenna, the Tartarus. It lies between the planes, it is a realm of chaos and disorder inhabited by unspeakable creatures. Yes, you consider me and my kind to be evil, but you have no conception of the evil that resides there. I have now answered all of your questions, release me as promised.'

Mab, looking at Master Boe, said, 'How is Ansek?'

Boe replied, 'He is stable and will be fine when we get him to the medics.'

Mab said, 'Master Kanaka, I think this creature has told us everything we wanted to know. Do you agree?'

Kanaka said, 'Yes, but what do you intend to do with it?'

Mab said, 'I will not slay it, I gave my word. Let me discuss the matter further with it and I will join you shortly to finish dinner?' Mab restrained Amaymon while the masters left the dungeon with Ansek.

Amaymon said, 'You promised to release me if I answered your questions!'

Mab said, 'No, I did not. I promised that I would slay you if you did not answer my questions. If I release you now, where would you go?'

Amaymon replied, 'I would go to my Ruler and do as I am told.'

Mab said, 'At least in that you are truthful, however, I cannot allow you to return to the Palace. You will, therefore, remain here until we have removed the rest of your kind from our plane.'

Amaymon said, 'If you leave me here, I will perish and return to the Abyss. You will never remove my kind from this plane, the Ruler is too strong.'

Mab replied, 'I give you another promise, if I see you again on this plane, I will slay you, Amaymon.' Mab flew up through the dungeon entrance hole and pushed back the slab. She used a narrow beam of light on the slab edges and melted the stone, melding and fusing it with the stone, forming the dungeon roof. She knew the demon did not have the strength to break out of the dungeon. She mused on the fact that Amaymon was now the prisoner and Ansek was free.

Mab arrived back at the Grand Hall to find that everything had been cleared away. Kanaka and Lamm were sitting in a sofa chair drinking fruit liquor. Kanaka said, 'Boe and Ochran have taken Ansek to the clinic and will return here as soon as he is comfortable. The kitchen is preparing some fresh food for us.'

Lamm poured some liquor for Mab and pulled a sofa chair closer for her to use. Mab said, 'I sealed Amaymon in the dungeon; he will eventually die and return to the Abyss.'

When Boe and Ochran arrived back, the kitchen staff had reset the table and were bringing out platters of meats, fruits and vegetables. Boe said, 'Master Paull has retired for the evening as he was feeling unwell, I think it was the dampness in the dungeon, he has trouble with his lungs. I will visit him in the morning to check on his condition. Ansek, however, is recovering well. Mab, he sends you his regards and gratitude for freeing him from the daemon. He is anxious to talk to you, but I think it best to leave it until tomorrow morning, give him time to rest and gather his thoughts.' Mab nodded her assent as she poured a goblet of wine and reached for a thick crust of bread.

Kanaka said, 'So we now know that this ruler Mahazael is responsible for bringing the demons into our plane and that he has taken the Prince's body. We also know how the possession is carried out. The host is brought to a near-death state, the daemon enters the host, who is then resuscitated. We also know that the Abyss is, in fact, the space between planes, but we don't know how to enter it or if we would survive on entering it.'

Lamm said, 'This Mahazael seems to be the head of the serpent, but we don't know its capability or how many daemons it has brought over into our plane already.'

Mab replied, 'Ansek is perhaps best placed to answer that.'

Boe said, 'Please correct me if I am wrong, from what I have heard, these daemons feed on fear and violence. Think of the way Amaymon described the killing of women and children as 'Joyous.' It made me shudder. The question in my mind is, why do they wish to populate our plane? We are, relatively speaking, of course, a peaceful, non-violent society.'

There was silence for a few moments, then Mab said, 'Could it be that they are drawn to our plane for that very reason, more souls to corrupt? I have a feeling that the society we visited was, in fact, peaceful and caring, but it was under strict martial law enforced by the daemons. I was struck by the people in the arena singing even as they were being hacked to pieces by the warriors, some of whom we know were daemon hosts.'

Kanaka said, 'So, the daemon's ideal is to have a peaceful, moral, non-violent society over which they can rule with harsh laws and inflict terrible punishments on the innocent with impunity?'

Boe said, 'Yes, I see it now; they want to change or supplant the leadership, not change the society.'

Mab said, 'In our case, the leadership will be gathered here for the annual competition. The daemons will also be here in some numbers together with their Ruler. From their perspective, it could be a good opportunity to do some 'supplanting' or even eliminating.'

Kanaka replied, 'My thoughts exactly, we should visit Ansek first thing in the morning.' Mab returned to the 'suite' late, but her roommates were still up waiting for her; the dining table was set out, ready for the food to arrive. She had brought the usual box of leftover food together with two bottles of wine and a bottle of fruit liquor. When she walked in dressed in full master regalia, she received whistles and gasps of surprise and astonishment.

Mab bowed low, with an exaggerated swing of her arm, and said, 'I got a promotion, Master Mab at your disposal!'

Izzy lifted the medallion and gave it a close inspection while Charly was running her hands over the robe. Cat took the box from Mab and started sharing the food and pouring the wine and liquor.

Cat passed the full wine goblets around; Izzy was now wearing the medallion and Charly the robe. They raised their goblets and Cat said, 'To Master Mab, bringer of good food and wine!' There was a scratching at the door.

Mab said, 'I know who that is!' as she ran to the door and pulled it open. Meldran rushed into the room, bowling Mab over and sat on top of her, licking her face. Izzy, Charly and Cat grabbed Meldran and hugged him tightly.

Izzy said, 'Don't worry Meldran, we've got plenty of food to go round, no need to eat Mab.'

Kanaka, Lamm, Ochran and Boe were already at Ansek's bedside when Mab arrived at the clinic early the following morning. Kanaka was explaining what had happened and that Amaymon was being held in the Dungeon but would most likely die and return to the Abyss.

Ansek said, 'Mab, it's good to see you. You saved my life; you saved me from a living hell. No words are sufficient to thank you.'

Mab said, 'The daemon was in complete control of your mind and body?'

Ansek replied, 'Yes, I was conscious, and I could see and hear, but the Daemon was in complete control. The link between my mind and my body was no longer present, the daemon even had access to my memories. It has no morals and no compassion. It fears you greatly; for the first time in its existence, it feared for its life.'

Kanaka said, 'Ansek, can you explain how the possession is carried out?'

Ansek replied, 'I don't know the details, but I do know that I was poisoned. Toker invited me to her room for what she said would be a private conversation regarding the Prince, so of course, I accepted. I had some wine and started to feel woozy, I thought I was just tired, but by the time I realised the wine had been poisoned, it was too late. I woke several times but couldn't move, I knew I was strapped down on a stone slab in the Palace somewhere. The last time I tried to wake I found that I couldn't move, open my eyes or speak. The daemon told me its name was Amaymon and that my body was now its body; it said it would allow me to see and hear but nothing else. I tried to fight back, but it was simply impossible; I could only watch and listen and Amaymon could have removed even that from me. Of course, it only allowed me to keep those senses so it could enjoy my horror and revulsion at the unspeakable acts it carried out. That is all I know of the process; I was not present when the other possessions were carried out.'

Lamm asked, 'What of the numbers? How many daemons have been called and taken possession of adepts?'

Ansek replied, 'I don't know the precise number but, an estimate, around thirty daemons brought over and, yes, most of these will be hosted by skilled adepts. The daemon will have access to their host's skills and, of course, supplement that with their own vile knowledge and practices. Kanaka, have you thought about cancelling the competition? We can only play along with this charade for so long.'

Kanaka said, 'It's too late to cancel and in any case, that would simply give the Palace time to bring even more daemons into play. No, the competition must go ahead, and we must defeat whatever they bring against us.'

Chapter Eight: The Annual Competition

The delegates, competitors, visitors and vendors started to arrive early on the first morning of the competition. The Guild was bustling with activity when the Palace delegation arrived. The Prince and the elite from his personal guard took up their reserved places in the North Stadium, where refreshments were awaiting them. A raised dais had been constructed at a central position in each stadium to accommodate the Palace delegates and the Masters of the four schools. Competitors were shepherded to the Guild gymnasium block, where facilities for changing and washing were available, together with storage for clothes and weapons.

Ansek, Jessam and Sirak were with Kanaka discussing recent events. Jessam said, 'If the Palace is fielding Adepts who host daemons, then surely that infringes competition rules?'

Ansek replied, 'Probably, but it is something of a moot point. The Prince himself is host to a daemon, so he is hardly likely to agree with our interpretation of the rules.'

Kanaka said, 'Jessam, please understand that this competition is a charade. What is likely to happen here is that the daemon-assisted team from the Palace will seriously injure or kill a number of our students. The daemons relish slaughter, in that context, there are no rules. We could have cancelled the competition, but that would simply delayed the inevitable conflict with the Palace. We cannot allow ourselves to be ruled over by monsters who have no place in our plane of existence.'

Sirak replied, 'Kanaka, I agree with your assessment, but I will not allow my students to be wantonly slaughtered in this competition or any other. We, all four of us, and our masters must intervene if the situation you describe comes to pass.'

Ansek said, 'Then you must go now and talk to your own masters and students. You need to warn them to be on their guard and to signal if they are in difficulty, at which point we will intervene.'

When the competition got underway, Mab, Izzy, Charly and Cat were browsing the vendor stalls, looking for bargains while chewing their way through crusty fruit scones and drinking cool lemon water. The sun was beating down, Mab had left her formal robes back at the 'suite' and wore shorts and a light silk blouse. When they eventually entered the North Stadium, it was crammed full of spectators cheering their particular champion. The first events in the competition were weight-lifting and fireball.

The weight-lifting event involved four lifting stations. Competitors waited in four lines beside each lifting station. The starting lift was set at four standard stone circles, which weeded out a great many would-be competitors. For GOS, only Gho was able to satisfy the minimum requirement of a 4-stone lift. Mab cheered him on but realised that he was struggling just to qualify. The next competitor, from SOPS, asked for the lift to be set to 6-stones and he accomplished that albeit with a struggle. Gho knew he simply could not lift that sort of weight and so dropped out. The final involved only four competitors, two from SOPS, one from GOWW and the other an adept from the Palace. The first competitor, from GOWW, asked for a 7-stone lift, which he had only just accomplished. The second competitor from SOPS asked for an 8-stone lift, but he failed to hold the weight and was disqualified. The third competitor, from the Palace, asked for a 10-stone lift which he accomplished albeit with some difficulty; the remaining competitors dropped out. Mancha, the Palace adept, therefore, won the open weight-lifting competition. The Palace flag was raised on the scoreboards in both stadiums. The Prince rose to his feet and applauded Mancha, who bowed graciously.

The next individual event was a flame ball. This called for competitors to conjure a fireball with the strength to blast a hole in various targets at different distances. The targets consisted of tree trunks of three diameters, stone slabs of three thicknesses, and iron slabs of three thicknesses. These were arranged at short, medium and long distances, the easiest target being a slim tree trunk positioned at the short distance and the most difficult being a thick iron slab at the longest distance. The first competitor, GOWW, chose to start the competition with the thickest tree trunk at a medium distance. She conjured and concentrated the fireball, raised her arm and threw it will all her might. The tree trunk only partially shattered; she let out a shriek of frustration and was disqualified from the competition. The second competitor, from SOPS, chose the thick tree trunk at the shortest distance. He launched his fireball and successfully severed the trunk, so remaining in competition. The third competitor, from the Palace, chose the thick stone slab at medium distance. He conjured a black fireball, which seemed to squirm in his hands, he raised his arm and launched the fireball, which struck the slab with devastating force but only just penetrated through the stone. Following inspection and some discussion, the throw was accepted and the Palace guests roared their approval.

There was a short pause in the proceedings as the remaining competitors appeared to have dropped out but without advising the referee. Finally, the referee announced that there was, in fact, one remaining entry from the GOS. A diminutive figure, a young girl wearing shorts, sandals, sunshades, and a cap, walked into the arena; the crowd thought it was a joke and so cheered. Mab chose the iron plate at the furthest distance, when the referee announced this, the crowd went wild with laughter. Mab walked forward and performed an elaborate deep bow, which brought further cheers and laughter. She then placed her arms, bent in front of her chest, palms facing each other, and closed her eyes. A silver ball appeared, small at first, but it started to grow; it became so bright that it couldn't be looked at directly. Mab then cupped her hands as though concentrating on the ball then stretched her arms forward and released it. It launched from her hands at an astonishing speed, but Mab then moved her right hand, figures pointing outwards, back towards her chest, the ball elongated mid-flight into the shape of a spear, she rotated her hand quickly and the spear of light started to spin about its axis. The spear struck the iron plate, imparting a staggering amount of energy, the impact zone turned to a plasma and the spinning effect drove the spear through the iron like a knife through butter. The crowd leaped to their feet, the applause was deafening. The referee looked questioningly at the remaining Palace competitor, who shook his head in response.

The Prince rose to his feet and gave a slow handclap. Mab walked towards the dais, removed her sunshades and stared up at the Prince, she remained silent, her piercing black orbs holding the Prince's gaze. The Prince sat down. Mab moved several paces to the right and bowed to Master Kanaka, who stood and applauded, the crowd roared their approval. The GOS flag was raised on the scoreboards in both stadiums. Mab made her way back to the North stand and returned the cap and sunshades to Cat with thanks. They then made their way back to the vendor stalls to have a late lunch and continue the search for bargains.

When Mab and her roommates returned to the suite, she received a mind message from Lamm to meet in Kanaka's office as soon as possible. Mab changed into her formal master's robe and made her way to Kanaka's office. Ansek, Lamm and Ochran were already there and helping themselves to snacks and cold drinks. Ansek said, 'Mab, congratulations on your fireball, or should I say missile! You certainly gave the Prince something to think about!'

Kanaka said, 'Yes, that was very well done, Mab, it gave us and the students a real boost. We are meeting here to discuss what might happen tomorrow in the freestyle combat events. Frankly, we think the Palace will take the opportunity to seriously injure or kill the leadership of the three independent schools. Their aim being to supplant us with daemon hosts, we cannot allow that to happen.'

Mab replied, 'The daemon Mahazael occupies the Prince's body. I saw it today for the first time; it is ancient and extraordinarily powerful. Amaymon did not reveal its true nature; Mahazael is one of the four Princes of the Abyss, the Ruler of the Element Earth, and second only to Lucifer. It is extraordinary that it is present here on this plane, we need to understand what it wants or seeks. We may be able to expel it, but the Prince is unlikely to survive. I do not think such a being can be slain.'

Ansek said, 'We had assumed the motive was purely subjugation of our people; you are saying that this would not be sufficient motive for such a creature to come to our plane?'

Mab replied, 'Yes, I think there has to be something else.'

Lamm said, 'Perhaps it's you, Mab? Could it be that your presence here is a broader threat to their ambitions not only on this plane but throughout mind-space? It may be that they mean to eradicate that threat before it gets out of hand?'

Mab replied, 'You mean it has come specifically to kill me?'

Kanaka said, 'Yes Mab, I think Lamm is correct. You are the real threat to them, so they have sent a Prince to deal with you as others could not. If you participate in the competition tomorrow, you will be their target. If the Adepts don't kill you, Mahazael will come for you. I have warned all the masters that tomorrow is likely to result in injury for many and death for some. All are ready to intervene to protect their students and fellow masters.'

Mab replied, 'Yes, and as we discussed, Master Kanaka, I will not participate in the competition, but I will act to protect myself and the slaughter of innocent people.'

Kanaka said, 'So we agreed, if one intervenes, we all intervene?'

All present said, 'Aye.'

Mab returned to the suite to find the table being laid out for dinner. Izzy was busy preparing fish and vegetables while Charly and Cat were arguing about the wine. 'No, Cat, there's no point in asking Mab's opinion; she will drink anything. This red wine is supposed to complement fish dishes. Why do we always have to have white wine?' said Charly.

Mab replied, 'Why don't we have both?'

Cat said, 'Trust you to come up with that solution!'

By the time Mab had changed and showered, the food had been laid out and they all sat down to tuck in. Mab complimented Izzy on the cooking and Charly and Cat on their choice of wines. Mab decided to have a goblet of each in order to check if they were both appropriate for the fish dish, which she happily confirmed. Following the meal, Mab said, 'I need to speak to you about something very important. The competition tomorrow will be dangerous. We are expecting the Palace to use the open combat sessions to injure or kill as many senior students and masters as possible. What you and many others don't know is that many of the adepts, and the Prince himself, are not what they seem. They are no longer human, their bodies have been possessed by powerful daemons who wish to supplant the current leadership of the magic schools. I am telling you this because if things go badly wrong tomorrow, you need to escape from this place, go back to your families and have no further dealings with the magic schools. You must keep this knowledge to yourselves; otherwise, there will be general panic and many more will die as a consequence.'

Izzy, with tears running down her face, said, 'You want us to run away and leave you behind? That's not going to happen, Mab.'

Mab put her arm around Izzy and said, 'Izzy, it may not come to that, we have all the masters and senior students from three schools on our side. If all-out war happens, then we are ready to do what must be done. If we fail then I, and many others, will be finished. I will not allow my body to be taken by a daemon; I want you to promise me now that if I fall, you will leave this place.' Charly and Cat were now crying and threw their arms around Izzy and Mab.

'Mab, if you fall, we will take you with us, we will never leave you alone,' said Cat.

Mab, also now with tears in her eyes, replied, 'Yes, please take me with you if you can, but you must go. Anyway, it's not even started yet, and they will find that I am not very easy to kill.'

Charly said, 'If you get hurt, you could transform into something and escape!'

Mab replied, 'What, you mean the scaredy-cat? I guess I could outrun them?' They were now laughing and crying at the same time.

Mab said, 'I'm off to bed now. I think I'm going to need my sleep tonight.'

Mab woke early the following morning and dressed in her soft black leather booties and baggy black linen trousers with a white silk blouse. She decided not to wear her formal master's robe but donned her white silk cape and golden Guild medallion. As she passed Master Boe's room, the door opened and Meldran rushed out. Master Boe's head then popped out, he said, 'Good morning, Mab, could you take Meldran out with you?'

Mab replied, 'Good morning, Master Boe, of course, I'd love his company!' Mab walked through the Great Hall and out past the quadrangles, heading for the sports fields and the stadiums. It was a fresh morning with a little chill in the air, offering the promise of a dry but hot afternoon. The vendors had arrived early and were already setting out their stalls for the day.

Mab made her way over to the animal enclosure and was leaning on the top bar looking at the horses when Meldran gave a low growl. She turned and was astonished to see a huge white wolf not ten paces from her, even so, the horses remained calm and Meldran decided to lie down! She started to walk towards the wolf when it mind-linked with her, 'She Witch, I bring you a message. The future of all life on this plane hangs in the balance. Even if all around you fall, you alone must not despair. Old…'

Meldran leapt up and growled ferociously. The wolf turned suddenly and loped away towards the forest treeline. The horses were spooked and rushed towards the Mab as if for protection. Mab looked across the enclosure and saw the Prince looking back at her. He looked young to be a Prince, he was dressed in casual clothes with a loose-fitting yellow shirt, baggy black trousers and sturdy walking boots. Even from that distance, however, Mab could sense the dark presence lurking inside the young man. Mab told Meldran to wait, and she walked slowly around the enclosure towards the Prince; he was following her every step, and he was smiling. 'Mabdelore Winter, I presume,' said the Prince in a deep, gravelly voice.

Mab replied, 'Mahazael, I presume.'

Mahazael said, 'Yes, that is so.'

Mab replied, 'What do you want?'

Mahazael said, 'I want everything.'

Mab replied, 'You cannot have everything.'

Mahazael said, 'I can and I will; you and your masters will kneel before me this day.'

Mab replied, 'I promise you that will not happen.'

Mahazael said, 'Then you will all die, and I will find another use for your bodies. Let me explain something to you. I have existed for millennia, even before humans walked on this plane, and I am immortal. I cannot be killed, think about that. I will take everything and there is nothing you can do to stop me.'

Mab replied, 'You may be immortal, but, nevertheless, we will try with our every breath and sinew, whatever the cost, to save our friends and families from you and your kind.'

Mahazael said, 'Wonderful, I look forward to that! But alas, I must go, breakfast awaits.'

Mab said, 'Before you leave, I would like to congratulate you on one thing, however.'

'Yes?' said Mahazael.

Mab, laughing as she walked away, replied, 'You don't stink quite as bad as you used to, have you introduced a new personal hygiene initiative?'

Mab, called Meldran and made her way back to the suite for a light breakfast and then went straight to the lost library to meditate. She woke with a clear, focussed mind and made her way to the South

Stadium for the individual combat event. Kanaka, Jessam, Sirak and Ansek were seated on the opposite side of the field from the Princes' dais. The masters and senior students from the three magic schools were seated behind them. Mab went to join Lamm, Ochran and Boe. The Palace adepts were arrayed behind the Princes' dais; Toker was sitting to the right of the Prince.

Many of the visitors that attended the previous day had been turned away; notices had been posted that attendance at the combat events was by invitation only. Mab noticed on her morning walk that only a very few vendors were setting up stalls.

The referees entered the field and announced two competitors from each of the schools. The GOS put forward Gho and Mona; the SOPS put forward two senior students, Amla and Coran; the GOWW also put forward two senior students, Reni and Bers. The Palace put forward two Adepts chosen from the Prince's personal guard, Mago and Goap. Mab stared across at Mago and Goap, she could see the daemons hanging behind the face-façades of the two students. It made her retch in disgust. Lamm said, 'Mab, are you alright? Do you need some water?'

Mab replied, 'No, Master Lamm, I am fine.' The first four bouts took place simultaneously on the four quadrants of the field. Mona was drawn against Mago, Gho against Bers, Alma against Goap and Reni against Corin. It was clear from the outset that the Palace Adepts were intent on causing serious injury. Mona stood little chance against Mago, who knocked her off her feet within the first few seconds of the bout. As she got to her feet, Mago hit her with a fireball, she screamed in pain but attacked with a psychic blast, which Mago barely registered. Mago retaliated with a whip of black light, which lashed Mona on the cheek and then coiled around her neck. Mona couldn't speak and dropped to her knees; the referee did not intervene.

Master Boe leapt over the barrier and into the quadrant, followed by Meldran. Boe blasted Mago backward, causing him to release his grip on Mona. Meldran leapt at Mago and brought him to the ground, but Mago blasted him off and got to his feet. Meldran hit and demolished the barrier, letting out of yelp of pain. Boe was leaning over Mona, cradling her head, when Mago lifted a sharp spar of wood from the broken barrier and launched it at Boe's back, but it didn't reach the target. At that very moment, Mab was in mid-flight, she saw the missile approaching Boe and batted it off course, she then spun in the air as she approached Mago, bringing her short sword around at an astonishing speed, striking Mago on the neck and decapitating him. The head flew into an adjacent quadrant and the body dropped to the ground with blood spraying from the severed neck. Mab ran to Meldran, who was seriously hurt, a piece of wood had pierced his leg, Mab pulled it free and tried to cauterise the wound, which had been bleeding badly. Medics arrived and took Mona and Meldran off the field.

The other bouts were stopped, but too late for Alma, who was killed by Goap. Her body was covered in wounds, cuts and burns. The masters approached the Prince's dais. Kanaka said, 'This competition is over, we will not expose any more of our students to you and the rest of your filth. You are a disgrace to everything that we hold dear. You will leave our school now and take your tawdry bunch with you.'

The Prince replied, 'Kanaka, you disappoint me. We have not yet had a team competition. I couldn't possibly leave before that. I will now field my Adepts and you and your tawdry bunch will try to defend yourselves. I've been so looking forward to this!'

Toker let out a shriek as blood started to run from her nose and ears. She put her hands to her head, screamed and fell to the ground. The Prince turned to look at her and then looked down at Mab and said, 'Mabdelore Winter, I am forced to like you even though I must destroy you. However, I have a special friend who will make good use of your body. Let the competition begin!' With that, the battle commenced. The Palace fielded roughly twenty adepts, all of whom hosted daemons. The three magic schools fielded the four Principals (including Ansek), each with three masters and three senior students. The teams were, therefore, balanced in terms of numbers, but the magic schools relied heavily on the masters as the students were no match for the adepts.

Mab struck the first blow, and the psychic blast hammered into the nearest Adept, Goap, with force so great that his limbs were torn from his body. Mab was scything through the Adepts with blinding speed, firing out psychic bursts of energy together with balls and beams of white flame. She paused, suddenly, everything was in slow motion and she spun around in time to see a black spear almost on her. She threw her head backwards and towards the ground, arching her back to an absurd degree, her head just touching the ground; the spear grazed her chest as it passed and buried itself in the stomach of an Adept. Mab recoiled back and threw a ball of white flame, which she stretched into a spear, straight back at the Prince, but he had vanished. In the same movement, she pulled her short sword from its scabbard and spun low, severing the leg of a nearby Adept and then decapitated him as he fell to the ground.

Kanaka found himself in a protracted contest with a huge, Adept warrior who just wouldn't go down. He had tried everything, but he didn't have enough firepower, then he remembered what Mab did to Mago and so launched a psychic blast but then followed that up with a high round-house kick. The warrior dropped to the ground and Kanaka despatched him with a flame ball to the head, which consumed his entire face, including much of the skull structure.

The fighting went on into the early afternoon. It was a short but hard-won battle. The magic schools prevailed. Kanaka, Lamm and Mab remained standing together with Jessam, Sirak, one other master and students Gho and Tam. The dead included Ochran, Ansek and all of the senior students, with the exception of Gho and Tam. The adepts were all slain. The eight that remained standing turned to face the dais, but the Prince was gone. Mab leapt up onto the dais and screamed, 'Mahazael!, Mahazael! Coward! Coward!'

But there was no response. Kanaka said, 'Mab, it has fled back to the Palace. Come, we have done enough for one day. But I take no joy in this victory. Many good people have died, on both sides, because of these daemons.'

Mab said, 'Yes, I sense that it has fled; we live to fight another day. But that day must be soon else wise Mahazael will use the time to once again strengthen his daemon horde.'

Kanaka replied, 'Yes, that is certain; but let us rest today and discuss tomorrow.'

Mab could see Kanaka was totally exhausted and said, 'Agreed, we need to rest and gather our thoughts.' Medics arrived and started to remove the bodies.

Mab made her way back to the suite to find Izzy, Charly and Cat waiting. They rushed to her and threw their arms around each other for a group hug. Izzy said, 'Mab, we were worried sick about you. What happened? Are we safe?'

Mab replied, 'Yes, we are safe, we won the battle, but the Prince escaped. Many were killed on both sides. Masters Ochran and Ansek are dead.' There was silence for a few minutes.

Izzy said, 'Mab, you need to soak in the bath. Come on, let's go. Charly, Cat, could you prepare dinner with plenty of wine for our warrior.'

Charly said, 'Mab, I'll bring you a nice goblet of warm red when you get into the bath.' It was only when she stripped to get into the bath that Mab understood how close the Prince had come to killing her. There was a long weal along her chest from the top of her tummy to just below her neck. It had bled a little during the battle but seemed to have healed over. Her hair, face and neck were filthy with dust, grime and spatters of blood. With help from Izzy, she slowly lowered herself into the hot bath and then submerged completely. When she came up for breath Izzy helped her to wash. Charly arrived with the promised goblet of red wine and passed it to Izzy, who gave it to Mab and kissed her on the cheek. Mab sighed her thanks and then burst into tears.

Izzy held her tightly until she stopped sobbing and said, 'Mab, good people died today to protect their families and friends. What they and you did will save the lives of countless people now and in the future. These daemons must be stopped. Otherwise, our future will be chains and slavery, not only for us but our children and their children's children.'

Mab replied, 'Izzy, yes, you are right; it's just the deaths, the masters and students.'

Following dinner, Mab went into a deep sleep and woke early the following morning. She was stiff and sore but managed to pull on some fresh casual clothes and also donned her Masters' robe to protect her from the early morning chill. She knocked on Boe's door, but there was no response. She walked out to the stadium area and saw that the dead and the detritus of the battle had been cleared away and the ground surface raked over. It looked as if nothing had happened, she felt tears coming to her eyes again for Ochran and Ansek and the students she didn't really know. She turned to go and found herself once more looking into the cold blue eyes of a great white wolf. The wolf mind messaged, 'She Witch, the battle is won, but the war is yet to come. Mahazael has returned to the Palace and even now makes preparations for your arrival.'

Mab replied, 'Who are you and what do you want?'

The wolf replied, 'I am a friend and a messenger.'

Mab replied, 'Then give me your message.'

The wolf said, 'My master would have you slay this Mahazael, banishment is not sufficient.'

Mab replied, 'The creature is immortal, it cannot be slain.'

The wolf said, 'It would have you believe that it cannot be slain, but this is a lie.'

Mab replied, 'Then tell me how it can be slain.'

The wolf said, 'A daemon can be killed by rending; it needs to be torn or hacked apart or contained and incinerated such that it can no longer agglomerate its form. Mahazael is, however, a powerful daemon, its death will only be delivered by many cuts.'

Mab said, 'Who is your master?' But with that, the wolf turned and loped off.

Mab started to make her way back to the suite for breakfast but received a mind message from Lamm to say coffee and breakfast in Kanaka's office. When she arrived, Kanaka, Lamm, Boe and Paull were already there. The atmosphere was sombre. Kanaka said, 'We won the battle, but we also suffered great losses. Sirak and Jessam have returned to their schools and taken their dead with them. But we need to decide on a forward plan of action.'

Mab was cradling a mug of steaming hot coffee in her hands while helping herself to various pastries. Lamm watched her for a few moments, smiled warmly and said, 'The ones with the chocolate in the middle are my favourite.' Mab looked up at him, tears came to her eyes, and she said, 'Yes, Master Lamm, mine too.' Everyone was silent for several minutes, lost in their own thoughts. Then Mab said, 'I will go to the Palace and slay Mahazael, the head needs to be cut from the serpent. I haven't been there before, so I will need a map.'

Kanaka looked at her and this time, tears came to his eyes, he said, 'Mab, you won't need a map. I have been there on many occasions.'

'Me too,' said Lamm, Boe and Paull.

Kanaka said, 'Masters Boe and Paull, you need to remain here to look after the Guild. If we fail in this endeavour, then the future of this Guild is in your hands. The libraries need to be protected and, if necessary, moved to secure locations.'

Mab said, 'Master Kanaka, I should go alone. If I fail, you can make the necessary arrangements to protect the Guild.'

Lamm said, 'Mab, Master Kanaka and I will be going with you. We will get you to Mahazael and help as much as we can to protect you from his cohorts. Gho and Tam will also come to support as much as they can.'

Mab beamed at Kanaka and Lamm and said, 'Thank you, but I don't want you to risk your lives for me.'

Kanaka replied, 'Mab, it is you who are risking your life for everyone else. I want you to know that I am eternally grateful for what you did yesterday. There is no one in this Guild who would not gladly give their life to protect you.'

There was silence for a few moments, then Mab said, 'Then we are decided. When do we leave?'

Kanaka said, 'We need to strike quickly, a surprise attack, we leave at midnight and arrive at the Palace with first light. Five horses will be made ready with provisions for the journey. We will meet at the animal enclosures.'

Mab, after collecting some of the breakfast pastries, made her way back to the suite. Charly was preparing breakfast and so Mab passed her the bag of pastries. 'Oh lovely! Have you already had breakfast, or is that a silly question?' asked Charly.

Mab smiled and said, 'I had a very light breakfast, more of a starter course.'

Izzy and Cat chuckled and Charly said, 'Second breakfast coming up, you deserve it!'

Izzy pulled Mab's blouse up to look at the weal and said, 'That's healing nicely, but you need to rest, Mab! After the second breakfast, why don't you go back to bed for a bit?'

Mab said, 'Yes, I'll do that, but there is something I need to tell you and it must not be repeated. I will be leaving the Guild tonight. If all goes to plan I'll be back tomorrow night.'

Charly said, 'Mab, you are not fit enough to leave the Guild! You need more time to rest and recuperate.'

'Where are you going?' said Cat.

Mab replied, 'I can't tell you where I'm going and you must not discuss this with anyone.'

Izzy started crying and said, 'The Palace, you're going there, and you won't come back. Mab, please don't go, please, please. We can go away together, all three of us, to my parent's house and stay there.'

Mab went to Izzy, hugged her and said, 'Izzy, I must go, but I'm not going alone. I want nothing more than to come back here to you, but the Prince has to be stopped or everything will change.'

'But I love you, Mab, I can't bear it,' whispered Izzy.

Mab kissed Izzy softly on the forehead and on the lips and whispered, 'And I love you, Izzy.' Cat looked over at Charly and raised her eyebrows a few times, Charly smiled back.

Chapter Nine: The Daemon Prince

Mab slept until almost midnight, then slipped out of the suite unseen and made her way to the meeting point. She wore her master's robe and carried a small package, left for her by Izzy, in the inner pocket. Kanaka, Lamm, Gho and Tam were already there. Kanaka said, 'We set off now, move quietly and slowly, the horses have padded shoes, no speaking unless absolutely necessary. We make two stops, the first midway and the second when we are close to the Palace.' Kanaka wheeled his mount around and set a comfortable pace, leaving from the rear entrance to the Guild and lifting his hand, but not slowing, to the gate guard as the posse passed through.

The path rapidly changed into a track which was unsuitable for carts but perfect for the horses. It was clear to everyone that Kanaka knew every twist and turn in the route, even in the limited moonlight. The brush started to give way to small trees and before long, they were riding through dense forest tracks, the horse hoofs were further silenced by the soft pine-needle overlay. The smell of the forest was refreshing and invigorating, it seemed to lift the spirits of the horses and the posse alike. The cloud cleared and they were bathed in moonlight, there was a sharp chill in the air, they could see their breath, and the horses were snorting steam. At that moment, Mab thought they were on a magical journey; if only she could do this with Izzy. She was snapped out of her reverie when Kanaka called a halt. The track was blocked by a large white wolf; there was a pack behind him, and there was still more in the forest around the track; strangely, the horses were not spooked.

Mab walked her mount forward and said to Kanaka and Lamm, 'I know this wolf; he means no harm to us.'

The wolf mind-linked with the three Masters simultaneously and said, 'I and my brethren have come to assist the She-Witch in her quest.'

Mab said, 'Who sent you?'

The wolf replied, 'Of her, I do not speak.'

Mab replied, 'The quest is dangerous, you and your pack could be killed.'

The wolf replied, 'She-Witch, we do this at our own volition. The filth that infests the Palace must be cleansed not only for humankind but for all species.'

Mab replied, 'What is your name?'

The wolf replied, 'I have many names, you may call me Amarok.'

Mab dismounted and walked towards Amarok. She knelt on one knee in front of him, bowed her head and said, 'Amarok, your assistance is sorely needed and much welcomed. I will never forget this act of friendship and kinship.'

The wolves howled in pleasure. Amarok stared into her black orb eyes and said, 'You speak the truth, She-Witch and are worthy of the pack. Continue your journey. We range far and wide. If there is danger, we will deal with it. If we cannot deal with it, we will alert you.'

With that, Amarok loped off into the forest and the pack followed. Kanaka looked at Mab and said, 'We seem to have signed up some potent allies.'

Mab replied, 'Yes, at least we don't have to worry about the journey. The wolves will have our back.'

The posse rode on for a while before Kanaka called a halt at what he thought was roughly the halfway point. They dismounted Gho and Tam looked after the horses while the masters prepared a light breakfast. Mab unwrapped the package Izzy left for her. It contained two chocolate-filled pastries and also a silver necklace with 'Mab' and 'Izzy' engraved on a heart-shaped pendant. The heart was inlaid with precious stones. There was a handwritten note which read, 'Mab, I had two of these made some time ago when we were at school together. I always wear mine, but I was too scared to give you yours until last night. Love you forever, come back to me. Izzy.' Mab's eyes filled up. She pulled down her robe and put the necklace on, pushing the heart-shaped pendant down the inside of her blouse. Kanaka looked at her and said, 'Mab, that's beautiful. Is it from someone close to you?'

Mab replied, 'Yes, Master Kanaka, it's from Izzy.'

Kanaka said, 'Close relationships change you, make you care more, worry more?'

'Yes, I'm only now beginning to understand that,' said Mab. Kanak. 'I also have something silver for you, it is a very special artefact that has been with the Guild for centuries but never used. I am hoping that you will find a use for it today.'

Kanaka went to his horse and removed a scabbard wrapped in hessian. He sat close to Mab and unwrapped it. The scabbard was of a black metal inlaid with silver runes along its full length. The hilt was golden and grooved to prevent slip in combat, the pommel was a short stocky bar of white gold and the guard's two silver bars worked to sharp points. Kanaka slowly pulled the sword from the scabbard. Mab gasped when she saw the blade, which was double-edged. It was straight and covered in runes, which were only slightly darker than the surrounding silver. There were no other grooves or markings. Kanaka handed the sword pommel first to Mab, who said, 'Master Kanaka, I have never seen such a blade.'

Kanaka said, 'There has never been such a blade. Be careful; the edges are as sharp as razors; the technology to make such a thing is unknown to us today. It is a named blade and belonged to Master Yam, who was the founder of the Guild many centuries ago. Legend says that it was once owned by an Angel who gave it to a great hero of the past.'

Mab's eyes widened. 'Its name is Durandal. It is sentient!' said Mab.

Kanaka replied, 'What, the sword speaks to you!'

Mab replied, 'Speaks no, but it imparts thoughts and emotions.'

Mab stood up and cut the air with the sword. She could feel the hilt moving, adjusting, correcting, in her hand. She continued the practice until her movements blurred, then spun in the air and brought the blade down hard against the nearest tree. The blade howled in pleasure and sliced through the tree as if it wasn't there. She held the sword point-up and said, 'Durandal, we go to slay daemons. We do this to free our plane from slavery and despair now and in the future. I beg you to aid me in this quest.'

The sword hilt pulsed in her hand. Mab said, 'Master Kanaka, we have another powerful ally.'

'Then, back to horse!' replied Kanaka. The posse rode on clear of the forest and into the flatlands beyond, they slowed to a walk whenever they came across signs of battle. Amarok and his pack had been hard-pressed, there were many dead soldiers to be found along the way, most probably scouts sent by the Prince. Adepts were amongst the dead, and some were wolves.

They arrived in close proximity to the Palace, as planned, just before first light. They dismounted, had a light breakfast, and prepared for battle. The masters packed their robes away and all donned rustic farmworker clothes. Kanaka said, 'Gho, Tam, we three masters will lead and you will follow to protect our backs. If one of us falls, you will take their place. The Palace building is of a similar size to the Guild, but the Prince will either be in his office or in the throne room. The office is on the floor above the throne room and looks out over the Northern approach to the Palace. We will tether the horses here and approach the Palace from the South, entering through the goods and servants portal. This will also be guarded but not as heavily as the alternative approaches. Also, the Prince is arrogant beyond measure, he will not be expecting us to respond so quickly and in such small numbers. I want to emphasise that the sole objective of this mission is, as Mab so eloquently described, to cut the head from the serpent or, in simple terms, to kill the Prince and the daemon within. So, this is a stealth campaign until we confront the Prince, at which point we do everything in our power to kill him, even at the cost of our own lives. Are we all agreed?'

'Aye,' said all.

They pulled the horses back into thicker cover and long-tethered them so they could access grass and water. They watched and waited until a train of horse-drawn carts appeared on the track headed for the south portal, they then sprung from cover and joined a group of stragglers walking behind the carts. They engaged the strangers in banter so the guards would assume it was a single party associated with the goods delivery. They walked through without challenge. Kanaka whispered, 'I didn't expect it to be that easy; we need to be wary that it could be a trap.'

Lamm whispered back, 'No, I think it is as you said, they are expecting us to build an army in the coming months and then lay siege to the Palace. A small group sneaking into the Palace would, in their view, of course, be complete madness.' Kanaka looked over at Mab with a wry smile; Mab struggled to keep a straight face. Gho and Tam played their part superbly, they looked like a couple of lazy teenagers who wanted to be somewhere else and do anything else other than what they were doing at that moment.

The large group entered through the service door, but Kanaka veered to the left and led his team along a very long, narrow and winding corridor which was set within the thickness of the Palace walls. They stopped when they came to a stairway, Kanaka whispered, 'This stairway allows access to every floor in the Palace other than the turret rooms. The access doors from this stairway are usually locked, but I have these.'

Kanaka displayed a set of keys and lock picks and said, 'We will go to the throne room first, which is on the floor above. If he's not there, we will go to the office on the next floor. We leave all the doors unlocked and escape down this stairway the same way we came in. Understood?' All nodded in agreement. Kanaka led the group silently up the first flight of the heavy stone stairs to the first access door. As expected, it was locked. Kanaka tried his selection of keys, but none was suitable. He then used two lock picks working in tandem and was able to defeat the lock. They waited and listened for a few moments, then Kanaka slowly opened the door. He could see the main entrance at the far end of the hall. The large doors were guarded but only on the outside. Kanaka signed for everyone else to stay and he would look into the throne room. With that, Kanaka slipped out, closed the door behind him, and made his way to the entrance to the throne room. He listened briefly and then slowly opened the door, popped his head into the room and then quickly made his way back to the access door and the stairwell. Kanaka whispered, 'No one there; let's make our way up to the office.' The second access door was also locked, but Kanaka once more made use of his lock picks and successfully defeated the lock.

Kanaka slowly opened the door and looked out. The office had two guards at the door and every minute or so, someone would either ascend or descend the main stairway. Kanaka whispered to Mab, 'Could you kill them silently with your mind, the way you killed Toker?' Mab nodded affirmatively.

Kanaka whispered, 'We go as a group; Mab will lead and kill the guards and anyone else that sees us. Gho and Tam will drag the bodies into the office and ensure the doors remain closed until we are ready to make our escape. Understood?' All nodded in agreement. Mab opened the door slowly and peeked out; then, she opened it completely and walked towards the office door. As she approached, the guards turned to look but then put their hands to their heads, dropped to their knees and then lay prone on the floor.

Kanaka arrived, opened the door to the office, and walked straight in. Mab and Lamm followed. The prince, who was at his desk with two acolytes, looked up and said, 'Good morning, I trust this is not a friendly visit.' Kanaka blasted the acolyte nearest him, who fell to the floor unconscious. Lamm did the same to the remaining acolyte.

Mab reached out and ripped the huge oak desk away from the prince, sliding it across the floor to the other side of the room. 'We have come to end your miserable life,' said Mab.

The prince leapt into the air, moving with blinding speed, he ran up the wall to his left and unhooked a huge black broadsword. Guards were trying to break the door down, but Gho and Tam were holding them back. Kanaka hit the prince with a powerful psychic blast, but he barely acknowledged it. Mab struck him with a concentrated fireball, which knocked him back against the wall but didn't appear to slow him down. Lamm was firing everything he had in an attempt to at least drain the prince of energy. The prince attacked Mab directly, swinging the huge sword as if it had no weight. Mab was staggered by the speed at which he was moving, and his sword was even faster. The prince was driving the three of them back but manoeuvring to get closer to the door. Mab realised that if he got close to Gho and Tam, he could slay them with a single stroke and soldiers would then pour into the room. Mab concentrated and then released an enormous psychic blast that hit the Prince square in the chest. He flew backwards under the power of the impact and hammered into the stone wall. The magnitude of the force cracked and displaced the heavy stones, but he quickly recovered and attacked again with similar vigour, albeit showing signs of pain.

A black whip lashed out and wrapped around Lamm's neck. He was pulled from his feet and his head rammed against the wall. Lamm fell to the floor unconscious. The prince once again ran directly at Mab, swinging the broadsword with blinding speed. But then he veered to the side and hit Kanaka with a black fireball, which knocked him to the floor. He then turned once more to face Mab. Mab felt Durandal pulse against her hip, she put her hand towards the hilt and the sword moved to meet it, as soon as she grasped the hilt, the sword swept from the scabbard of its own volition.

Mab moved to meet the prince, Durandal, moving at lightning speed. Mab brought Durandal down on the prince's broadsword, which bit deep into the blade. Mab pulled back, ducked low and swept Durandal across the Prince's legs. The sword sliced through armour, muscle and bone alike. The prince screamed in pain; black, stinking blood poured from the wounds. As Mab came up she saw the downward stroke from the broadsword coming and spun to the right, but the edge of the broadsword cut into her arm. The prince staggered backwards against the wall for support and raised the broadsword up for protection, but Durandal sliced downwards, severing the broadsword blade and the prince's sword arm alike. The heavily armoured arm and the broken sword blade clattered to the floor.

Mab backed off and then stepped slowly towards the Prince, but suddenly, she felt weak and light-headed. She realised the broadsword was a fell blade, the cut on her arm throbbed, she had been poisoned. She dropped to her knees, still holding Durandal and trying to cleanse the poison from her system. The prince laughed and said, 'You didn't really think you could kill me. I told you I am immortal.' Gho and Tam rushed to her side, but the door to the office was forced open. Amarok and the wolf pack loped into the room.

Mab used the last of her strength to look up at the prince and raise her sword arm. She pointed Durandal at the prince, who laughed again, but Mab released Durandal, who flew towards him, piercing his chest and burying itself in the stone wall. Mahazael screamed in pain and tried to leave the prince's body but quickly realised that Durandal held him fast. Mab's head dropped slowly to the floor, she put her hand inside her shirt and held Izzy's pendant. Then a voice in her mind said, 'She-Witch, it is I, Amarok. You are in dire need; you must summon your Mother.'

My mother? thought Mab.

'Your first and oldest friend,' said Amarok.

Mab turned her head slightly, the room was full of wolf's legs and whispered to herself. 'Uri, I am dying, I summon thee.'

A spot of light immediately appeared in the centre of the room. Gho and Tam helped Kanaka and Lamm to the wall, which was well away from the light. The wolves also backed away, only Amarok remained by Mab's side. The light intensified and the spot elongated to create a vertical cut in the air. A beautiful young woman stepped through the cut and looked around the room. She wore a silver cloak of the finest silk, her hair was long and black, her skin pale, and her eyes were piercing black orbs. None could hold her gaze. Amarok bowed his head and backed away. Mahazael laughed and said, 'What, this is your mother; I will feast on her soul also.'

The woman ignored Mahazael and walked to Mab, crouched, and placed her hand on her head. Mab's body was engulfed in silver light. She felt energy flowing into her like a fresh mountain stream, the stench of poison and puss was replaced with that of pine needles and fresh grass. The wound on her arm expelled the poison, which flowed down her arm and was boiled off by the light. 'Rise up, daughter,' said the woman.

Mab stood up and felt better than she had at any time in her life and said, 'Uri, my mother?'

Uri smiled warmly and said, 'Yes, and you Mabdelore, are my likeness in every way.'

When Uri smiled Mab felt wonderful, warm, safe, happy, and loved, all at the same time, Mab said, 'But why did you leave me? Who is my father?'

Uri said, 'Mabdelore, you were created human. I am not. I am both woman and man, mother and father. Your parents are good people, and this time and place was best and safest for you.'

Uri put her arms around Mab, held her tightly, kissed her on the head and whispered, 'I cannot stay on this plane for long; it is not possible, but of that, we will speak later. You are the greatest gift of my life, and I love you more than anything that is or has been. I will come to you, I promise.'

Uri then turned slowly and looked at the Prince. Mahazael laughed and said, 'You cannot harm me, witch. I am a Prince of the Abyss.'

Uri said, 'You, Prince of Filth, will be silent whilst I consider what punishment is merited.'

'Who are you?' spat Mahazael.

Uri said, 'You do not recognise me?'

Mahazael stared at her first in incomprehension and then, as realisation dawned, fear, an emotion he had never before experienced. Mahazael said, 'I did not know she was your daughter otherwise, I would not have dared…'

Uri said, 'Is that fear I smell? Surely a Prince of Filth cannot know fear?'

'I fear you, Uriel,' replied Mahazael.

'Wisdom indeed,' replied Uriel as she reached out, plucked a great silver sword from the air and said, 'I see you have already met my sword, Durandal; this is his brother Eurandal.'

The sword flew from Uriel's hand and plunged through the skull of the prince and, like Durandal, buried itself up to the hilt in the stone wall. Mahazael screamed in agony. Uriel then turned to Amarok and, pointing at Mahazael, said, 'Amarok, rend this filth unto its death.'

Amarok leapt at the Prince and ripped his throat out. The swords continued to support the head and body and ensured Mahazael could not escape. Black, stinking blood gushed from the torn throat; the rest of the wolf pack then attacked. The wolves ravaged the body, tearing off lumps of flesh and muscle and cracking bones. Amarok's powerful jaws crushed what was left of the skull and tore the prince's black heart from his chest. Many of the wolves had swallowed the foul blood and were regurgitating it onto the floor. 'Enough, the daemon is no more,' said Uriel.

The wolves ran from the Palace and made their way back to the forest, only Amarok remained, his mouth and fur covered in black, foul-smelling blood. Uriel walked back to Mab's side and said, 'It breaks my heart to leave you once more, but leave I must. As promised, we will speak soon.' Uriel hugged Mab tightly, kissed her on both cheeks and vanished.

Kanaka and Lamm were still sitting propped against the wall, but they looked much better than Mab had feared. Gho and Tam helped them to their feet. Kanaka said, 'Mab, let's leave this place. I can't bear the stench much longer.'

Mab replied, 'Agreed, as planned, we go out the way we came in, let's go.'

Before leaving the room, Mab looked back for the swords, but they were gone. She thought Uriel must have taken them; at least she didn't have to worry about getting Durandal back to its own plane. The group made their way slowly down the hidden staircase, along the long, narrow corridor and out through the servant's entrance. *Strangely, there were very few soldiers or adepts to be seen, the death of Mahaziel must have had significant repercussions*, thought Kanaka.

Amarok led them out through the South gate, which was unguarded, back across the flat lands and into the cover of the forest. The horses were safe and had been protected by the pack. Kanaka said, 'It looks like we are safe enough here, and there are no signs of pursuit. I suggest we rest here before starting on the journey back to the Guild?'

Mab looked at Amarok and said, 'Are we being pursued? Do you sense any danger?'

Amarok bowed and said, 'No, Mabdelore, many have fled the Palace and the rest of my pack are not far from this location. This place is safe; I will scout the area while you rest.'

Mab nodded and said, 'Yes, Master Kanaka, we should rest for a while.' Gho and Tam searched through what was left of the provisions and produced some crusty bread, fruit and slices of cold meat. They ate in silence, each thinking about what had happened, what they had witnessed and how close they had come to death.

Mab walked to her horse and removed a small package from her saddlebag. She produced a bottle of fruit liquor and a set of small, nested cups, which she placed on the forest floor. She poured a generous helping of the strong liquor into the five cups and said, 'Master Kanaka, could you propose the toast?'

Kanaka smiled warmly and said, 'Mab, you always come prepared! To the Guild, Long Life and Happiness.'

All lifted their cups and said, 'The Guild, Long life and Happiness.'

Chapter Ten: The Home Coming

The journey back from the Palace was uneventful, although Amarok and the wolf pack were never far from them; they only departed when they reached the safety of the Guild. They rode through the main entrance and were met by the Guards who made arrangements for the horses to be stabled and fed. Kanaka said, 'Masters, we meet in my office first thing in the morning to bring Boe and Paull up to date. Gho and Tam, you are excused from the meeting, but thank you for everything. Your courage is an inspiration to all students of the Guild and will not go unrecognised or unrewarded.'

'Thank you, Master Kanaka,' replied Gho and Tam.

Mab made her way back to the suite and, as she climbed the stairs, she heard the voices of her roommates and bounded up the remaining steps. Charly and Cat were preparing the table for supper, they ran to hug her. Mab said, 'Where's Izzy?'

Cat said, 'Her parents arrived this afternoon and took her home. They heard about what happened in the competition. Izzy was frantically worrying about you and didn't want to leave. But her parents insisted and said that when you return, you should go to their house to see Izzy and stay as long as you like. Izzy's parents have two or three large houses. They have gone to their place in the mountains, Izzy said you knew where it was?'

Mab said, 'I've never been there, but yes, I know where it is. I would go now, but I have a Masters meeting in the morning; I'll leave immediately after that.'

Charly said, 'Let's have some supper and you can tell us what happened.' Mab explained that the mission had been successful in that the Prince and Mahazael were dead, but she couldn't go into any detail as she first had to attend the briefing in the morning. With that, she went for a long soak in the bath and then to bed.

Mab arose early in the morning, donned her formal master's robe and went for a walk around the campus. When she reached Kanaka's office, Lamm, Paull and Boe were already there and having a light breakfast. Kanaka said, 'The good news is that Mahazael is dead. Mab would have killed it had she not been cut and poisoned by the fell blade of the prince. However, her mother, Uri, turned up and promptly slayed it. We can be fairly sure the daemon prince is dead as she had Amarok, the wolf, and his pack rip the body to pieces. I have to say, Mab, your mother is quite something, astonishingly beautiful and enormously powerful.'

Mab replied, 'Yes, I remembered her as 'Uri,' an old, I thought, imaginary friend. She used to mind-speak to me when I was very young, although I had come to think that I must have been dreaming. I had completely forgotten about her; it was Amarok who reminded me and asked that I call on her for help. Thankfully, she answered the summons.'

Boe asked, 'And she is definitely your mother?'

Mab replied, 'Yes, although I'm not sure if she is my mother in the biological sense. It was Amarok who told me she was my mother.'

Boe said, 'Amarok, that is certainly a name of myth and legend, although I have not heard of the name Uri. You must take after your mother, Mab, as she also seems to be a most powerful witch.'

Mab replied, 'Yes, I guess so. The most amazing thing is she looks just like me, although she is quite a bit taller!'

Paull said, 'She healed you during the battle?'

Mab replied, 'Yes, by driving out the poison. I think I would have died.'

Lamm said, 'It was the most extraordinary thing I have ever witnessed. She told Mahazael that he was the 'Prince of Filth' and to be silent! He was very afraid of her, but he referred to her as Uriel, not Uri.'

Boe stared at Lamm in disbelief and said, 'Lamm, are you sure her name was Uriel?'

Lamm replied, 'Yes, that was the name Mahazael used. Is it a name you recognise?'

Boe looked at Mab and said, 'Uriel is an Archangel, the Angel of Wisdom and the Bringer of Light. One of the most powerful beings in the Universe!'

Kanaka said, 'Mab, this explains why the Palace was so afraid of you. The powers you possess are celestial and anathema to the Abyss.'

Paull said, 'With the death of Mahazael, can we assume that the daemons he brought into our plane will now return to the Abyss?'

Kanaka replied, 'We strongly suspect that to be the case, but we don't know for sure. I will contact Jessam and Sirak; we need to make a concerted effort to root out any remaining daemons.'

Mab said, 'Master Kanaka, I intend to travel to the Mountains tomorrow to visit friends and family. I hope you can spare me for a few days?'

Kanaka replied, 'Mab, of course, take whatever time you need. In any case, the term break is now upon us, so if anyone is leaving the campus, be careful and advise your students to be careful. The Palace is in disarray. I have already heard reports of soldiers resorting to criminal activities in order to make a living.'

Mab said, 'We need to decide what to do regarding the adjacent plane. The people there are enslaved, we must do what we can to help them. In any case, it is likely that daemons from that plane are crossing over to us; it would be best to fight them there rather than here?'

Kanaka replied, 'Mab, you visit your friends and family. Let me know when you intend to get back. I will arrange for Jessam and Sirak to be here and we can then discuss what to do, but I think we should travel as a group to the other plane.'

Mab asked the stables to prepare a horse and provisions for several days and then returned to the suite to pack. Charly and Cat had prepared food for her journey and also helped her pack a saddlebag with clothes. When she returned to the stables, Master Kanaka was waiting by her horse. Kanaka said, 'I asked the stables to prepare White Lady, she is stronger and faster than any of the others.'

Mab hugged and thanked Kanaka. Kanaka said, 'Now that Durandal has been reunited with his brother, I have another sword for you. This is a two-handed katana-style sword, it has been in my family for many generations. Its name is Dawn-Breaker, and you will need practice in its use. The blade is silver and the single cutting edge is forged using a rare element that is harder than diamond. I want you to accept this as a gift from me and the Guild.'

Mab pulled it from the sheath and said, 'It is extraordinary, beautiful. Thank you so much, Master Kanaka.'

Kanaka replied, 'Take care on the road. There are many villains abroad.'

Mab turned Lady and rode fast towards the mountains. She spoke to Lady as she rode, telling her about the journey ahead when they would stop, the danger of bandits and when she may have to run very fast. The tracks were surprisingly quiet. She saw a few walkers but didn't stop to talk to them. The mountain village where Izzy's parents lived was Cetha; many wealthy people had second homes in the mountains due to the climate during the summer months, which could be very oppressive in the lowlands. Mab was pleased she had brought her robe as there was beginning to be a real chill in the air. She pulled it from one of the saddle bags and manoeuvred herself into it, pulling the generous hood over her head. Soon, she saw a sign for Cetha and followed it off the main track along a downward trail sheltered from the icy winds being just below the main ridge line. The scenery was beautiful. Mab could understand why Izzy liked to come here. As she came around the next bend in the trail, she could see the village ahead, but something was wrong. There were fires, smoke and noise.

Mab jolted Lady straight into a gallop and thundered along the trail and into the main street of the village. There were soldiers wandering around, some of the small vendor sheds had been burned, and windows on houses had been boarded up. Mab slowed Lady to a trot and made her way along the main street and off to the right immediately past the vendor sheds where Izzy's parent house was located. Mab recognised the house immediately, it was very grand and in a slightly elevated position, but some of the windows had been broken. Mab heard noises from the back of the house and so rode Lady up the entrance path and around to the rear of the property. Mab was appalled by what she saw; an elderly man and woman were tied to wooden posts and soldiers were taking turns to fire arrows at them; they were laughing and drinking heavily. Then Mab saw Izzy, she was also tied to a post, she was almost naked and had been badly beaten. Her body was covered in bruises, her face and hair were caked in blood.

Mab pushed Lady on towards the soldiers, one of them shouted, 'Lads, look what we have here, get her off that nag.'

Izzy looked up and cried out to Mab. Mab, incandescent with rage, leapt from Lady and landed close to the soldier nearest Izzy.

As Mab hit the ground, the soldier's skin started to peel from his body he screamed in agony. Mab walked towards Izzy and as her bindings fell away, she collapsed into Mab's arms. Mab carried Izzy away from the soldiers and wrapped her in her master's robe.

Then she turned back to the soldiers, the first was still screaming as the flesh and muscle continued to peel from his body, and the others found that they could not move. Mab, pointing at the first soldier who was writhing on the ground in a pool of his own blood, said, 'You will all die in this way.' Mab went to Izzy's parents, many arrow wounds had punctured their bodies; they were dead. They were old, frail and had lost too much blood. Mab lifted them both, took them inside the house and laid them on the floor. She then went to Izzy and physically carried her into the house. Mab helped her to wash in a hot bath and then left her to go back to the soldiers.

The first soldier was dead, a clean white skeleton surrounded by gore, flesh, muscle and organs lay on the ground. The four remaining soldiers were terrified. Mab said, 'I will spare you the agony of your friend.'

Three of the soldiers let out cries of pain and fell to the ground, clutching their heads, blood streaming from their noses, ears and eyes. The remaining soldier was the youngest of the group. To him, Mab said, 'You will go into the village and tell everyone you see that this village is now under the protection of the Guild of Sorcerers. Soldiers wearing military uniforms are not permitted in the village, all visitors must report to this house and register, yobbish loutish behaviour is not permitted. You will ensure people understand and follow these rules and report any breaches to me immediately. Do you understand?'

'Yes, Master,' said the young soldier. Mab incinerated the bodies of the dead in a blaze of white flame until no trace of them remained.

Izzy, dressed in casual but warm clothes and came searching for Mab. They embraced for a long time before Mab said, 'Are you ok? Do you want to stay here or should we go to my parents' house for a while?'

Izzy said, 'I would like us to stay here. My Mom and Dad would like that. I told them all about you, how we loved each other and wanted to live together. They were so looking forward to meeting you.'

Mab replied, 'Yes, you are right, Izzy, this should be our first home together. It's not too far from the Guild, so we can travel back in term time when we get the chance. I will ask Master Kanaka for our own room at the Guild. I'm sure that can be arranged.'

In the days that followed, Mab explained to Izzy all that had come to pass with the Palace, the Daemon Prince and meeting her mother. She also took Izzy on a visit to Blant. Mab's parents were thrilled to meet Izzy and even more thrilled that Mab had become a Master of the Guild of Sorcerers.

Chapter Eleven: In Search of Witches and Daemons

Kanaka, Jessam and Sirak sat around the meeting table in the Minor Hall of the Guild, waiting for the others to arrive. Kanaka said 'Mab, and her partner Izzy, are travelling in from their summer home in the mountains. They should be here imminently, Lamm has gone to greet them. Boe and Paull will not be attending, they have Guild business matters to attend to. As discussed, the daemon Mahazael was slain by Mab and her mother. We think the daemons that Mahaziel summoned to our plane have consequently been banished back to the Abyss, but we are unsure. The purpose of this discussion is to agree on what can and must be done to ensure we are free of these creatures now and in the future.'

Jessam replied, 'Kanaka, is it true that Mab is now a Guild Master? I have to say that I was somewhat taken aback by that news. I would expect someone, even of Mab's capabilities, to achieve that status only after many years of study and practice and yet she has only been with the Guild for a few months.'

Kanaka replied, 'Jessam, I would agree with what you say for anyone else other than Mab. She is extraordinary in every sense of the word. She possesses the high magic to the level I did not believe possible, her powers are also celestial in origin. Boe thinks her mother is the Archangel Uriel. The daemon Mahazael referred to Mab's mother as Uriel shortly before she skewered him through the head with a sword she plucked from nowhere. Can I, therefore, council you to choose your words carefully with Mab, she looks and sometimes behaves like a young student, but she is very much not what she seems.'

'Understood,' replied Jessam.

Lamm walked into the Hall and said, 'Apologies, Mab will be here shortly she and Izzy are just dropping their things off in their new accommodation.'

Kanaka replied, 'Where is her new accommodation?'

Lamm replied, 'Boe has converted their suite into three bedrooms, one a large double for Mab and Izzy and the other two smaller rooms for Charly and Cat. There is also a generous shared living and dining area. They all seem very happy with the new arrangements.'

Jessam said, 'Perhaps you could remind her to...'

Mab walked into the Hall and said, 'You can remind me yourself, Master Jessam.' Mab didn't have time to change and so wore casual clothes, a light blouse, heavy denim trousers and leather boots. She had a sheen of sweat on her face and arms from the journey.

Kanaka said, 'It's good to see you, Mab. How was your short break?' as he poured a cold lemon water drink for her.

Mab replied, 'Thank you, Master Kanaka. Izzy's parents are dead, killed by rogue soldiers. Fortunately, I got there in time to save Izzy. It was, as you said, the military is in disarray. We left to see my parents soon after the burying of Izzy's. My mom and dad were fine, there was no sign of any soldiers in their village. I have put both villages under the protection of the Guild.'

Jessam said, 'Under the protection of the Guild? What does that mean exactly? Mab stared at him for several seconds and then said, 'What did you want to remind me of?' Jessam's face drained of colour, he was having difficulty breathing, sweating profusely, his head throbbed, darkness started to descend he was beginning to lose consciousness.

Kanaka said, 'Mab, Lamm told me what had happened, I was so sorry to hear about Izzy's parents. Master Jessam wanted to remind you of his invitation to visit the School of Psych and Sorcery, but clearly, you have had more pressing matters to attend to.'

Mab turned back to Jessam and said, 'Thank you, Master Jessam. I hadn't forgotten, but with everything that has happened, I just didn't get the opportunity. But we would love to visit the school.'

Jessam felt as if the sun had suddenly appeared after a long absence, as if he was being bathed in wellness, happiness and good fortune. He smiled warmly at Mab and said, 'Mab, we would be very honoured to receive you and your partner Izzy. Please accept my condolences for the death of your partner's parents.' Mab beamed at him. Jessam stared back with big, round eyes like a smitten child.

Kanaka said, 'As I was saying earlier, Jessam, with Mab now being a Guild Master, I expect her to visit all of the magic schools and help us to gather and spread knowledge and expertise. We need to work together, now more than ever.'

Lamm replied, 'As a first step, should we not go back to the Palace? This was the origin of the problem, and we have no way of knowing what is happening there at present?'

Mab said, 'Yes, I agree, we cut the head off the snake, but there must be others involved and accountable. What of the Academy and Birrio?'

Sirak replied, 'An interesting question, Mab. I didn't see Birrio at the competition and from your question, I assume she was not at the Palace?'

Kanaka said, 'We don't know if she was there or not. Our prime objective was to slay Mahazael and in that, we were successful. I am now thinking that we should go to the Academy first and, depending on what we find there, go on to the Palace.'

Mab replied, 'Master Kanaka, I agree with that. However, we should not forget the adjacent planes. We know that at least one of these is a potential source for daemons coming over to our own plane and that the people there are enslaved and in need of our help.'

Jessam, looking at Mab's askance, said, 'You have travelled to other planes?'

Kanaka replied, 'Yes Jessam, Mab has discovered astonishing things in mind-space which she has shared with Lamm and I. Frankly, I wouldn't have believed it had I not experienced it first-hand. I agree with your concerns, Mab. We must address the issue of the adjacent plane and help those poor people. However, first let us resolve as far as possible the issues at hand, the Academy and the Palace. Following that, we should travel with Jessam and Sirak to the adjacent plane and consider what we can do, should do and must do.'

Mab said, 'Yes, I agree, Master Kanaka.'

Kanaka said, 'I propose we five leave at first light tomorrow for the Academy and we arrive there unannounced. What say you?'

All said, 'Aye.'

Kanaka asked Lamm to make the necessary arrangements with the stables for horses and provisions. Mab made her way back to the refurbished suite. Izzy, Charly and Cat were having coffee and fruit scones. Mab said, 'I hope you've saved something for me?'

Cat replied, 'Oh, of course, Master Mab, or whatever you call yourself nowadays, I will fetch it immediately.'

Mab replied, 'Excellent, be quick about it. Is a simple bow and curtsey too much to ask?' Charly grabbed Mab from behind and wrestled her to the floor. Cat and Izzy joined in and between them, pinned Mab down.

Charly said, 'So our great warrior has been conquered by three beautiful, young female students.'

Cat said, 'Turn into the scaredy-cat and we will let you up.' Mab's form began to change and suddenly, the three girls were holding onto a giant Saber-Cat. The beast turned its massive face to Cat and its huge tongue licked her face from chin to forehead, leaving a wide trail of saliva; it promptly turned back into Mab, who was laughing her head off. Cat said, 'Mab, that was gross! I'm going for a shower.'

Mab called out, 'What about my scones and coffee? I think you forgot to bow and curtsey?'

Charly, still laughing, said, 'I'll get your coffee and scones.'

Izzy put her arms around Mab and said, 'I like you as a giant Saber-Cat. I could get used to it. You could wander around the campus with me on your back?'

Mab replied, 'It's back to work for me, I'm afraid. We are going to the Academy and then on to the Palace. I'll be away for a few days, maybe a week, depending on what we find.'

Izzy said, 'That is bad news, when do you leave?'

Mab replied, 'First light tomorrow but I need to get some sword practice in. I'll do a couple of hours after I get my scones and coffee, of course.'

Izzy said, 'Are you expecting trouble?'

Mab replied, 'I'm not sure. I think there is more to this than we currently know. Five of us are going, all masters, so we are well prepared.'

Mab arrived at the playing fields late in the afternoon. She wore a tight-fitting sports top and slacks. She carried Dawn-Breaker at her back and could readily unsheathe the blade with either hand. Mab stood still, calming her mind and then launched into Lamu, which was regarded as one of the most advanced and difficult sword Kata's.

She executed the moves perfectly but added her own modifications, passing the sword between her hands in mid-air, making much more use of holding the sword single-handed for greater reach, and combining the sword actions with her own lethal kicks, punches and chops. She performed the Kata ten times, resting for only two minutes between each. When she completed the final Kata, she was drenched in sweat but breathing normally. She threw Dawn-Breaker up into the air, caught it on the way down and slid it into the scabbard in one smooth movement.

The sound of applause surprised her, she turned to see Kanaka, Sirak and Jessam at the other side of the field and made her way to them. Mab said, 'I am sorry, Master Kanaka, I made certain changes to the Kata to better fit my fighting style.'

Kanaka replied, 'Yes, I noticed, but you performed the Kata moves perfectly. I think the modifications enhanced the Kata, made it more real.'

Sirak said, 'Can I have a look at your sword? It is a magnificent weapon.'

Mab unsheathed Dawn-Breaker in an instant, the movement of arm and sword was a blur. She then handed the sword to Sirak slowly and hilt first. Sirak held the sword up, out and then looked down at the blade and said, 'It is truly magnificent, a most fitting weapon for someone with your skill.'

Mab replied, 'Dawn-Breaker was a gift from Master Kanaka and the Guild. I try to honour the sword whenever I practice.' Kanaka beamed at Mab.

Mab made her way back to the suite, showered and went to bed. She awoke early, kissed Izzy and made her way to the stables. Lady was waiting and had already been saddled with provisions packed. Mab threw on her small saddle bag and nodded to Jessam and Sirak. Lamm and Kanaka were already mounted and walking their horses around the field; Mab walked Lady into the field and joined them.

Kanaka said, 'Good morning, Mab!'

Mab nodded to Kanaka and Lamm and said, 'How long will it take to get to the Academy?'

Lamm said, 'I reckon three hours if we spare the horses. But from there to the Palace could be five hours, I would have thought.'

Mab replied, 'I guess we will be staying in the Academy tonight. Most probably, there will be pre-dinner drinks followed by what, say, nine or ten courses?'

Kanaka laughed and said, 'Yes, I am sure Birrio will be the perfect 'host,' if you pardon the pun.'

Jessam said, as he and Sirak caught up with Kanaka, 'I see your jokes haven't improved Kanaka.'

Kanaka replied, 'No, I guess you are right, Jessam. Let's get moving, Mab is anxious to get there in time for pre-dinner drinks!' as he spurred his horse into a brisk canter.

The Academy lay South and East of the Palace and only slightly North of the Guild. The landscape to the East was less inviting than that of the North as it consisted of open flat planes and rocky hills with a paucity of tree cover, although there was a covering of thick yellow gorse. The terrain was good going for the horses, but the posse felt somewhat exposed. After almost two hours, they came to a halt by a small tarn and secured the horses on long ties with access to water. They sat silently, eating dried fruits and meats and drinking fruit juice. Kanaka was about to speak when the horses spooked. Kanaka signed for silence, he and Lamm moved around to the right, Sirak and Jessam to the left and Mab took the middle. They moved slowly toward the horses; Mab stood up quickly and called out, 'Wolves, they want the horses!' The group ran to the horses, and Mab soothed and settled them. It was a very large pack, and they quickly surrounded the masters.

The pack leader slowly approached. Mab thought about killing him, but she did not like harming animals. She linked minds with the alpha male and tried to dissuade him from attacking, but he had the killing lust upon him. All he thought about was ripping a horse open, feasting on the organs and drinking the rich, warm blood. One of the wolfs towards the back of the pack let out a yelp of pain, the alpha male turned and looked back only to see the largest wolf he had ever seen walking calmly towards him through the pack; as he passed, the adjacent wolfs lay down. When he at last reached the alpha male, he also lay down in submission.

Amarok bowed slowly to Mab and, speaking to all five Masters, said, 'Mabdelore, I thank you for sparing my brother and his pack. He was not aware of who you are. I ask for your forbearance; I will ensure this does not happen again.'

Mab walked towards Amarok and knelt down in front of him, embraced him and said, 'Amarok, you are like a brother to me, and you have saved my life. Forbearance is given gladly, for I have always loved the Wolf above all other creatures.'

Amarok replied, 'High-one, with those words, you honour me and wolf-kind greatly.'

Mab said, 'Address the Pack now. Explain who I am and my love for the Wolf.'

'Yes, of course,' said Amarok, as he started to howl at the Pack. The whole pack started to howl their appreciation.

Mab said to Amarok, 'Go now, ask the pack to stay in the shadows and to watch our backs while we cross this land. We travel to the Academy and then, depending on what we find, on to the Palace.'

Amarok replied, 'High-One, the pack will do what it can to deal with renegade soldiers and their like. However, with the demise of the Palace there are many dangers in these parts, renegade soldiers being the least. I speak of Daemons and Black Witches.'

Mab said, 'You have seen these with your own eyes?'

Amarok replied, 'I found a daemon in my own pack. I had to slay the wolf to banish the daemon. In doing so, I obtained certain information. Black Witches summoned the daemon, but the intended host died during the possession process. The pack was near the Academy, the daemon entered the wolf rather than return to the Abyss.'

Mab turned to Kanaka and said, 'Master Kanaka, did you hear Amarok's words?'

Kanaka replied, 'Yes, Mab, this is very worrying.'

Mab said, 'Amarok, what do you know of these Black Witches?'

Amarok replied, 'I know only what I have heard, high-one. It is said that there are two covens, one at the Academy and the other at the Palace.'

Mab said, 'I wish you and the pack well and know that we stand ready to assist wolf-kind whenever there is a need.' Amarok turned and loped off through the gorse, with the pack following silently.

Kanaka said, 'Who are these Black Witches?'

Jessam replied, 'It may be that they are students or adepts who have been schooled in black arts by the daemons.'

Lamm said, 'I heard stories of Black Witches long before we discovered the daemon problem. Is it not more likely that these witches are responsible for bringing Mahazael over into our plane and the contagion has spread from that?'

Sirak replied, 'Yes, Lamm, I suspect you are correct, but we will only know when we get to question one of them.'

Kanaka said, 'To horse everyone, we will find the answers at the Academy.'

The posse picked up speed and reached the Academy in less than an hour. They stopped and dismounted in a sheltered cutting to the West of the Academy. Jessam said, 'I think we should just ride in and ask for Birrio. I don't see why we should do anything covert?'

Kanaka said, 'There is an appealing simplicity in that course of action. But I would prefer that one of us rides in first.'

Mab said, 'Master Kanaka, I will go in first and message Master Lamm if all seems normal.'

Lamm replied, 'No, I think we should do it the other way around. Mab, they would recognise you immediately. I wouldn't be surprised if they had wanted posters of you all over campus! I suggest that I go in as a representative of the Guild to establish and renew contacts. If all is well, I will message Mab. If you don't hear from me, then you should assume all is not well.'

Kanaka said, 'Yes Lamm, I agree.'

Lamm mounted and made his way towards the Academy at a slow canter. The main entrance to the campus was on the North side via a tunnel that ran through the ground floor of the main building. This left the façade of the main building exposed to attack from outside of the campus. The Academy was, however, a modern facility, and, unlike the castle-like structures of the Palace and the Guild, it was not designed for warfare or siege. Nevertheless, the entrance tunnel had robust gates on the interior and exterior sides of the main building. Lamm reached the exterior gate and told the Guards that he was a Master of the Guild and here to re-establish contact with Master Birrio, or whoever was now the Principal of the Academy. The Guards called on an acolyte to stable Lamm's horse and take him to the reception area. Lamm was escorted to the reception area, which he recognised from previous visits, and told to wait. Lamm messaged Mab about progress so far. Eventually, a senior student arrived and said, 'I understand you have come to see our Principal. Do you have an appointment?'

Lamm said, 'I am Master Lamm of the GOS. I do not have an appointment. I wish to see Master Birrio, or whoever is the Principal, on a matter of urgency. I have been here many times before and I am not used to being kept waiting.'

The student replied, 'Master Lamm, apologies, I did not realise you were a Guild Master. There have been many changes since you were here last, some of which we are still struggling with. Please follow me. I will take you to the Principal immediately.'

Lamm followed the student and quickly realised that there had indeed been many changes. It was as if anything relating to the history of the Academy had been removed. Portraits of previous principals, statues, busts and tapestries depicting great heroes or battles had been taken down. In some places, they had been replaced with drawings and paintings with strange, seemingly meaningless shapes and colours. In other places, the wall markings denoted the absence of the original artwork, which, Lamm thought, was in some ways more insightful than where it had been replaced by 'modern art.'

The student said, 'Master Lamm, my name is Afla, and our Principal is High Priestess Luticia. It is custom to bow in her presence.' Lamm messaged Mab with an update.

'Wait here, please,' said Afla.

Afla knocked on the heavy double doors and went into the room, after several minutes, she returned and bid Lamm to enter. The room was huge, but the furnishings were minimalist. There were no rugs on the floor or tapestries on the walls. The only redeeming features were the huge fireplace, the floor-to-ceiling windows that bathed the room in light, and the extraordinary, vaulted ceiling, which had been painted by true artists and depicted historical battle scenes, heroes of the past, mythical beasts and other monsters. The High Priestess was a large woman who, incongruously, sat behind a small writing desk in the far corner of the room. As he walked toward her, Lamm felt his senses jarring; it was as if a drunken architect had mixed up the dimensions of the room and its contents. The High Priestess stood up as Lamm approached and said, 'Master

Lamm, I am very pleased to meet you. My name is Luticia and I am the High Priestess of the Academy. Please take a seat.'

Lamm noticed that she seemed to be 'heavy-boned' rather than fat. She had her personal armour and weapons hanging on the wall beside the desk. Luticia noticed his gaze and said, 'Yes, although I am a High Priestess, I am also an accomplished warrior. Why have you come here today, Master Lamm?'

Lamm said, 'I have come for several reasons. The first is to understand what changes have been made here at the Academy, the second is to meet the new Principal and the third is to determine whether the Academy has conspired with the Palace to bring daemonic creatures into our world.'

Luticia replied, 'I look forward to having cordial relationships with the various magic schools. However, with regard to the changes I have made here and our current and ongoing activities I do not consider this any of your business. Do I instruct the Guild Masters in what they should and should not be doing?'

Lamm replied, 'The Palace sits above the schools and it funds, at least partially, their activities. However, the Palace is in disarray with the killing of the Prince and the Archdaemon that controlled him. We will not permit any more of these creatures to enter this plane.'

Luticia said 'When you say we will not permit. Who exactly are you referring to?'

Lamm replied, 'I am referring to the magic schools. I had hoped to include the Academy in that, but let me be clear. The three independent schools will not permit these daemonic activities to continue. We did not go to the trouble of slaying Mahazael only to see you summon more of these foul creatures.'

Luticia said, 'You slayed Mahazael, that is ridiculous. Such a being cannot be slain merely banished.'

Lamm replied, 'I was there; it was rended unto it's death.'

Luticia said, 'I see, so you conspired in the murder of the Prince?'

Lamm said, 'I will bandy words with you no longer. Are you with us or against us? Think carefully before you answer.'

Luticia replied, 'We will be continuing our activities, including daemonology, and I will not stand for any interference from you or the Guild. You are a fool to come here alone. You are under arrest for conspiring in the murder of the Prince by your own admission and will be sentenced to death.'

Lamm messaged Mab and said to Luticia, 'Yes, I would be a fool to come here on my own. I assure you I am not a fool.'

A commotion was heard outside, explosions, shouting. Afla's high-pitched scream, and then the doors were ripped off their hinges. A huge Saber-Cat leapt into the room and let out an ear-bursting roar of pure rage. Luticia stood up and staggered backwards, almost tripping over her chair while reaching for her sword. Lamm sat perfectly still with a smile on his face. The giant cat walked towards Luticia whose sword looked ridiculous in relation to the size of the cat. Then the cat reared up on its hind legs and transformed into a rather small girl who said, 'Hello, my name is Mab. Put the sword down.'

Luticia said, 'I think not, child' and ran straight at Mab, skilfully swinging her broadsword. Mab thought about blasting her out of the window. But then she said, 'At last, some real sword practice!' Lamm, still with a smile on his face, turned his seat around to watch the battle and shouted, 'Be careful, Luticia, she uses both hands.'

Mab shouted back, 'Master Lamm, you are supposed to be on my side!' Mab pulled Dawn-Breaker from its scabbard in a blindingly fast motion, leapt upwards, somersaulted over the top of Luticia and smacked her on the back of the head with the flat of her sword. Luticia recovered her composure and approached Mab slowly and carefully, holding her broadsword one-handed. In her left hand, she held a short knife close to her side. Mab knew immediately the knife was poisoned; she slammed Luticia hard against the wall and ripped the knife from her grasp. The knife flew across the room and buried itself in the opposite wall. Mab said as she sheathed Dawn-Breaker, 'I don't like poisoned blades, the sword practice is over.'

Luticia threw her broadsword to the floor and said, 'As you wish, child.'

Just then, Kanaka, Sirak and Jessam entered the room and made their way over to Lamm. Kanaka said, 'What's going on here?'

Lamm replied, 'Mab is having some sport with Luticia, the new Principal of the Academy.'

Kanaka said, 'Mab, please try not to kill her.' Luticia launched a huge fireball at Mab's head.

As the fireball approached, Mab curled up on the floor like a child with her hands on her head and then, as the fireball passed over, looked up with a big smile on her face and said, 'Hi everyone.' Kanaka and Lamm went into a fit of laughter.

Mab leapt to her feet and walked towards Luticia, but she disappeared and reappeared at the other side of the room, launching another fireball, which Mab redirected through one of the windows. Mab walked towards her once more, but Luticia disappeared again and reappeared on the opposite side of the room. This time, she launched a powerful psychic blast at Mab and followed it up with a knife throw. Mab deflected the psychic blast and she stopped the knife in mid-air only a short distance from her head, she noted that it was the poisoned blade. Luticia must have removed it from the wall. The knife dropped to the floor and Mab walked towards Luticia, but she once again vanished. Mab, more than a little annoyed, focussed her senses around the room, time slowed and then she saw her translating, a silhouette moving at great speed.

Mab roared, 'Enough!' as she grabbed her mid-flight and slammed her against the nearest wall and then upwards, ramming her head against the ceiling.

Mab held Luticia up against the ceiling as she walked over to Kanaka and said, 'I had hoped to have some fun, but I don't think that's in her vocabulary.'

Kanaka, laughing, said, 'Don't worry, Mab, we'll find you someone else to play with.'

Mab sat on the desk close to Lamm and lowered Luticia down from the ceiling, but not to the floor, and pulled her towards the group. Luticia's nose was broken and she was also bleeding profusely from a cut in her head. Lamm stood up and said, 'Mab, put her on this chair.' Mab put her on the chair and said, 'Luticia, you will answer the questions put to you by the masters.'

Luticia looked up at Mab and said, 'Who are you?'

Mab replied, 'I'm a Master of the GOS. Who are you?'

Luticia said, 'I'm the High Priestess of this Academy.'

Kanaka said, 'Please tell me what happened to Master Gould and Master Birrio?'

Luticia snapped, 'I will tell you nothing.'

Mab said, 'If you refuse to answer our questions, then you are of no value to us. We will strip you of what little powers you have, and you can make a living out on the streets.'

Luticia replied, 'You cannot strip me of my powers, I am a high Priestess.'

Mab said, 'It is already done. Master Kanaka, she is useless to us. I am sure we can find others here who will be more willing to help.'

Luticia started to cry and said, 'Please, please I will tell you anything you want to know, please restore my powers, please help me, please.'

Mab said, 'When you have answered all of our questions fully and completely, then we will decide whether to return your powers.'

Kanaka said, 'Masters Gould and Birrio, where are they?'

Luticia replied, 'Gould was imprisoned, Birrio lost her daemon and is now an adept of the Palace.'

Kanaka said, 'Where is Gould now?'

Luticia replied, 'In the basement cells.'

Jessam said, 'Sirak and I will find him.'

Kanaka said, 'Tell me, Luticia, how is it that you came to be the Principal of this Academy.'

Luticia replied, 'We were a small coven but started to grow rapidly with the forming of the Academy. Many students drop out of the Academy because they wish only to learn practical magic and not broader occult philosophies. And, frankly, many students could not afford the school fees and so came to us to work and learn. We, in our coven, have no fees, but we generate income by offering help and support to others, including the Academy. We have benefited from the knowledge of the Academy as they have benefited from our knowledge. We have long understood the nature of mind-space and through that knowledge, we were able to summon the great daemon Mahazael into this plane from his abode in the Abyss. Mahazael appointed Birrio as Master of the Academy, but with Mahazael returning to the Abyss, the daemons that were brought here through his summoning have now also returned to the Abyss. I am the most powerful witch in this region and therefore, I assumed the leadership role here.'

Lamm said, 'As I told you, Mahazael has not returned to the Abyss, the creature is dead.'

Luticia replied, 'And as I told you, Mahazael cannot be killed. He is immortal.'

Kanaka said, 'I'm afraid not, it was ripped apart. Mab killed it with a little help from her mother.'

Luticia stared at Mab in horror, Mab smiled back at her. 'You killed a Prince of Hades?' said Luticia.

'Prince of Filth,' replied Mab, still smiling.

Kanaka said, 'How many adepts or witches here currently host daemons and were these hosts forced to accept the possession.'

Luticia said, 'No Witches were offered as daemon hosts. Toker and Birrio selected the required hosts from adepts under the control of the Palace. We carried out the rite here on only a few occasions using students, perhaps four or five times. The rite to bring Mahazael over was carried out at the Palace with the prince as the host. The selected students and the prince were, of course, unwilling hosts, but we developed a plant-based poison to bring the host body close to death, in that condition, consent to the possession is not required.'

Kanaka said, 'Yes, we know about that. I want you to close all gates in and out of this campus and gather together the witches, and students of the Academy. I want them to line up in the square outside in three groups. I want this done now.'

Luticia replied, 'Yes, that can be done. I will send students to round everyone up and instruct the Guards to close the campus and then I will return here.'

Lamm said, 'I will go with you.'

As Luticia and Lamm made their way out, Sirak and Jessam returned. Jessam said, 'Bad news, Gould is dead and has been so for some time.'

Luticia and Lamm returned promptly to advise that runners had gone out to make the necessary arrangements. Sirak, looking at Luticia, said, 'Master Gould is dead, he lies in his cell chained to a wall.'

Luticia replied, 'I didn't know, I have only recently taken up this office. It was Birrio who deposed and imprisoned Gould.'

Kanaka said, 'Yes, but you could have released him but chose not to.'

Luticia replied, 'Yes, that is true. I would have released him eventually, but I have had too many other things to deal with over recent weeks.'

Mab said, 'Is there any food in this place?'

Luticia replied, 'Apologies, yes, of course. Afla is across the corridor, I will ask her to arrange it.'

Mab added, 'And some good quality wine.'

Kanaka, winking at Lamm, said, 'Mab, do you think it's safe to eat, it could be poisoned?'

Mab replied, 'Don't worry, I'll make her eat some first.' Kanaka and Lamm stifled their laughter.

The food arrived promptly. It consisted of a variety of meats, fish, fresh fruit, rustic breads and several bottles of wine. Mab put a selection of the food on a small plate, poured a half goblet of wine, handed them to Luticia and said, 'Eat and drink this, quickly.'

Luticia understood the intent and quickly ate and drank what she had been given. 'That's good enough for me!' said Mab as she helped herself. Mab, after tasting the wine, said, 'Luticia, this wine is particularly good. Do you think I could take a few bottles of this back to the Guild, or better still, could you send them by courier?'

Luticia replied, 'I'm pleased you like it. I'll send you a few cases. We have a very large vineyard.' Kanaka looked at the other masters and rolled his eyes.

Afla entered the room and said, 'High Priestess Luticia, your instructions have been carried out. You can commence the inspection now if you wish.'

Luticia said, 'Thank you, Afla, we will be with you shortly.'

When Afla left the room, Mab said, 'Luticia, you are indeed a powerful witch. I sense that your powers are already returning. However, I give you a grim warning. Do not attempt to harm our company or frustrate our work here. You have a second chance, an opportunity to work with us, not against us. Please take it, if you do not, then you and many others here will be ended.'

Kanaka nodded and said, 'Just so.'

Luticia looked at Mab, then looked deeper and said, 'Who are you, and why are you here?'

Mab replied, 'I am Mabdelore Winter, Master of the Guild of Sorcerers, I am helping to rid this plane of daemons.'

Luticia walked the masters around the student group first. Kanaka stopped in front of a tall, gangly student and asked him his name. The student replied, 'Sir, my name is Pann. I am an advanced student witch.'

Luticia said, 'Is there a problem here, Master Kanaka?'

Kanaka said, 'Mab, could you take a look?' Mab walked forward, stared for a few moments at Pann and said, 'Daemon, look at me! I name you Egym. You will leave this body or I will slay you where you stand.'

Pann cried out in pain and collapsed to the ground. Lamm helped Pann to stand, the boy was crying with relief. He looked at Mab and said, 'Thank you, Master, thank you for giving me back my body and life.'

Lamm said, 'Luticia, he will need complete rest for at least a week.' The inspection of the students found only one other host and Mab expelled the daemon with ease.

Luticia, pointing to the second group, said, 'These are our witches. We no longer use the title Master, we have junior and senior witches. The senior witches are on the front row and the junior witches on the second.'

The masters walked slowly along the rows, but then three of the senior witches stepped out and blocked the group. The middle witch said, 'We will not tolerate this inspection. This is our academy; what right do you have to come here and make us stand in line as if we are children?'

Another said, 'We are many and you are few. You will leave our Academy immediately.'

The rest of the senior witches cheered and hurled more insults at the masters. Kanaka looked at Luticia and said, 'This is getting out of hand. I strongly suggest that you calm them down. Otherwise, people are going to get hurt and it won't be us.'

Luticia called for silence and said, 'Please listen to me. These are the masters of the other three schools. They have slain the great daemon Mahazael. Their mission is to rid this plane of daemons and of those who support daemons. It is true that we have worked with the Palace in demonology, but that is now ended. We will no longer be known as black witches but simply Witches and we will work for the good, not the evil. You say they are few and we are many, that is true, but in this case, the few will defeat the many. If you wish to remain a black witch, then I must ask you to leave the Academy.'

The middle witch, Melsa, said, 'Luticia, we are, and will remain, black witches. If you wish to leave the Academy, then please do so, but we will not be leaving.'

Mab said, 'You are correct, you will not be leaving.'

Luticia looked pleadingly at Mab and said, 'Please, Mabdelore, they do not understand. Master Kanaka, please can you intervene?'

Kanaka looked down and shook his head. Luticia walked towards the middle witch and said, 'Melsa, you are a fool. She will slay all of you, not just you three. Everyone will die.' Melsa laughed and said, 'She will slay all of us? I think you must have lost your mind, Luticia. Or perhaps you have a more material interest in colluding with these so-called masters. Let us put them to the test. Three black witches against three masters, full combat!'

The crowd roared their approval and chanted, 'Combat! Combat! Combat!'

Kanaka said, 'What would be the rules of this combat?'

Melsa said, 'It will be fight to the death, no military weapons except long or short swords.'

Kanaka said, 'And what if we win?'

Melsa replied, 'You will not win, but if you do, then Luticia will have her way.'

Kanaka said, 'Very well, give us a moment to decide on our team.'

Melsa, pointing at Mab, replied, 'It has to include that bitch, she is mine.'

The masters went into a huddle. Kanaka whispered, 'The witches will major on powers rather than weapons. I suspect Melsa is a powerful witch, perhaps stronger than Luticia. Mab, I think you need to be in the team and take-on Melsa. I'm happy to be the second member. Jessam/Sirak, what about one of you as the third?'

Jessam said, 'Yes, I'm happy to be the third. However, you are right regarding the witches focussing on powers rather than weapons, and some witches are extraordinarily powerful.'

Mab said, 'Master Kanaka, in terms of our approach. We need to convince the rest of the witches that they should align with us rather than remain black witches. I was going to suggest that I fight all three of them just to get the message across that black witchcraft is not as strong as white witchcraft. I am guessing that you won't agree to that?'

Kanaka replied, 'You guess right, Mab, these witches are an unknown. If you are unlucky and get injured, then we would be unable to assist. However, I see the point you are making we do need to convince others that our way is not only right but also stronger.'

Mab said, 'So, what I propose is that I lead the attack on the three. You and Jessam stay a bit further back, to my left and right. I will be the tip of the arrow. You fire from a distance and only get close-up if I get injured or get into difficulty?'

Kanaka said, 'Jessam, your views?'

Jessam replied, 'Yes, I think what Mab proposes makes sense. However, if the arrow formation gets broken during combat then we make the best of the situation as it arises.'

Kanaka turned to Melsa and said, 'Our team includes me, Master Jessam and Master Mabdelore.'

Luticia led the group to the combat hall. It was a huge space located in the sports complex. It had a removable roof and extremely thick stone walls. The single entrance and exit door was also of heavy stone but was moved by a gear mechanism. Once the competitors were inside the combat hall, they were effectively sealed in. The walls were two stories high and then tiered back to accommodate seating for the spectators. It was a full house, the crowd roared as the witches entered the Hall and jeered when the masters appeared. The three witches stood together in the centre of the Hall. Mab walked forward and stood only a few paces away, facing them. Jessam was some ten paces behind to her left and Kanaka the same to her right. Melsa looked down at Mab and said, 'Are you ready to meet your maker child?'

Mab smiled and said, 'I have already met my maker and I'm looking forward to seeing her again.'

Luticia said, 'This combat is to the death. When the bell rings, the combat will commence. The combat will stop when all members of the losing team are dead. If you accept the rules, say Aye.'

Melsa said, 'Aye.'

Mab said, 'Aye.' Luticia walked back to the entrance door and locked the competitors in the combat hall.

The bell rang. Time slowed for Mab; the instant the bell stopped ringing, she was airborne with Dawn-Breaker in her right hand. She saw Melsa beginning to move, but it was too late, thought Mab as she spun in mid-air and swept Dawn-Breaker through Melsa's neck. She then reversed the leap, landed back in her original position and sheathed Dawn-Breaker. No one had time to react. The decapitation took less than one second. The Hall was silent, the spectators stunned, as Melsa's head hit the ground amid a fountain of blood.

The two remaining witches, Sati and Fora, recovered their composure, Sati fired a powerful flame ball directly at Mab's head and then vanished. Mab dropped to the ground cross-legged and watched in slow time as Sati translated. Fora sent something through the ground towards her, it looked like a black snake. Mab levitated fast, turned and sent an enormous psychic blast at Sati. The blast hit Sati like a thunderbolt, the entire structure rocked seismically. Sati slammed against the stone wall and was killed instantly. Mab looked down and could see the black snake squirming below, she incinerated it with a beam of white flame and remained hovering in full lotus position. The crowd remained strangely silent.

Mab looked down at Fora, the youngest of the three witches, she was crying and shaking with fear. Mab levitated Fora, pulled her closer and said, 'Fora, do you want to continue with this combat?'

Fora said, 'No, but the rules are the losing side must all be killed. I don't want to die. I have a child. But I am a black witch and must accept my fate or all respect for us will be lost.'

Mab replied, 'Fora, I am also a witch. We are the same, but you choose darkness and despair, whereas I choose light and hope. Join us, reject the dark and the evil. Help us cleanse this plane of filth, if not for you, for your child.'

Fora said, 'I would take that opportunity gladly, but it is not allowed.'

Mab replied, 'It is allowed.' as she lowered herself and Fora to the ground. Mab opened her arms and said, 'Fora, come to me.'

Fora, tears still flowing down her face, walked to Mab, who embraced her. The crowd roared their approval and chanted, 'The White Witch! The White Witch! The White Witch!'

Mab whispered in Fora's ear, 'I think we will be great friends.'

Luticia opened the Hall door and walked towards Mab, who was still holding Fora. Mab said, 'Fora and I are now good friends. No harm is to come to her.'

Luticia said, 'Mab, thank you. Of course, no harm will come to her.'

Mab turned around to see Masters Kanaka and Jessam walking towards her. Kanaka said, 'I had thought you would leave one of them for us to deal with but I can see now that was never going to happen! Luticia, could you arrange for us to talk to all of the witches early tomorrow morning? We have to make clear the changes we expect to happen and how we see the future of the Academy. Perhaps we could all have dinner tonight to prepare?'

Luticia said, 'Yes, Master Kanaka, I will make the necessary arrangements.' Luticia arranged rooms for the Masters in one of the student accommodation blocks. Mab had time to shower and settle into her room when there was a knock at the door. It was Kanaka and Lamm.

Kanaka said, 'We thought to go for a stroll around the campus before dinner, would you like to join us?'

Mab replied, 'Good idea.'

A large market had been set up in the Academy main square with many vendor stalls selling foodstuffs, wines, wood carvings, jewellery and other arts and crafts type items. Mab spotted a beautiful ring set, two identical gold rings sprinkled with small diamonds, sapphires and emeralds. She tried one on her finger, it fitted perfectly. Mab bought the set and convinced the vendor to throw in a large soft toy bear.

Lamm said, 'Expensive, but you wouldn't get that quality anywhere else. I assume for you and Izzy?'

Mab replied, 'Yes, she'll love these, the bear is for Fora's child.'

As they walked through the market, people were beginning to recognise them and spoke in hushed but respectful tones. Kanaka said, 'We should make our way back now, pre-dinner drinks, Mab!' As they started to walk back some commotion broke out at the far side of the square. Kanaka changed direction in order to get a better view of what was happening. A group of witches were having an argument with two priests. The priests were saying Fora should have fought to the death and that she had brought shame on the Academy.

Mab realised that Fora was part of the group, she had her child with her, a girl 4 or 5 years old, and had her head bowed as if in shame. Kanaka led Lamm and Mab through the gathered crowd, who began to realise who they were and parted to let them pass. The first Priest said, 'You are not welcome here.'

Mab ignored him and walked towards Fora, who lifted her head and smiled in relief. Mab kissed her on the cheek, bent down and said, 'What's your name, little one? You must be a Princess.'

Fora said, 'Her name is Pip. Pip say Hello to Mab.'

Pip said, 'Hello, Mab, I'm going to be a Princess when I grow up.'

Mab laughed and, handing the soft toy bear to her, said, 'I think you are already a Prince. Here is a special present just for you.'

Kanaka said, 'Mab, could you take a look at these.'

Mab turned, looked at the Priests and said, 'The older one is possessed by a daemon, the younger one is clean.'

The crowd gasped, as did Fora. Mab turned to Fora and, pointing at the older Priest, said, 'This is what must be cleansed. The Priest is still in there, but this daemon filth has imprisoned him and taken control of his body and his life. Put Pip behind you, she shouldn't see this.'

The old priest said, 'Don't listen to this foolish child. You all know me, but who is she?'

Mab said, 'I name you Egin. You will answer my questions. Otherwise, I will rend you unto your death.'

The old priest staggered backwards and started to claw at his face. Mab said, 'Where have you come from and who summoned you?' A beam of light from Mab's right hand engulfed the Priest's head.

The Priest screamed in agony and said, 'I came from another plane. I was summoned by the black witches of the Palace.'

Mab said, 'Egin, leave this body and return to the Abyss.'

The old Priest dropped to the floor and was supported by his younger acolyte. Kanaka bent down to examine him and said, 'Yes, I think he will recover.'

The old Priest was helped to his feet. He was crying with relief, he looked at Mab and said, 'Thank you, great one, for freeing me. I owe you my life and more.'

The crowd cheered. Mab said to the crowd, 'You must not allow these daemons to infest your community. For the hosts, it is a living hell. We masters can see these daemons, but you cannot. However, if you notice changes in someone, their behaviour, their personality, their beliefs, then report it to Luticia or Fora or someone else that you trust.'

Mab kissed Fora and little Pip goodbye then joined Kanaka and Lamm, who were making their way back to meet Luticia. When they arrived at the dining hall, Luticia, Sirak and Jessam were already there; junior witches were serving canapes, wine and fruit juice. Kanaka described what had occurred in the market with the Priests and said, 'Luticia, we need to rid the Academy of these parasites. We can show you how to recognise them, so you can lock them in a cell or dungeon, but at this time, only Mab is able to expel them.'

Mab said, 'Master Kanaka, it may be that the Priests could perform an exorcism. Luticia, you should speak to them about that. In any case, if the hosts are locked up, then I could visit the Academy periodically to expel the daemons. I expect we will have the same issues when we visit the Palace.'

Luticia said, 'Yes, my first priority will be to cleanse the Academy of these creatures. I think we should change the name of the Academy to 'The Academy of White Witches' and fully expunge the links that have developed with the occult.'

Kanaka replied, 'An excellent idea, Luticia.'

The bell rang for dinner to be served and the group took their seats. Sirak said to Mab, 'Mab, I hope you don't mind me asking, but when the witches vanish and reappear in a different location, you seem to be able to track them. Is that what you are doing?'

Mab replied, 'I'm not sure what the witches think they are doing, but yes, I can see them translating from one position to another.'

Luticia said, 'Really, that is strange. When I vanish and reappear in a different location, it is instantaneous.'

Mab replied, 'For you, it appears to be instantaneous, but in fact, you are actually moving very quickly from one place to another.'

Luticia said, 'Mab, I was sorry for Melsa, but I have to say that sword stroke was unbelievably fast. I have never seen anyone move like that.'

Kanaka, winking at the other Masters, said, 'Yes, it was fast, although the swordsmanship was a bit sloppy.' Mab looked up at him and everyone, including Kanaka, started laughing.

Lamm said, 'I am now going to tell you the one about The Horse, The Three Students and the Scaredy-Cat.'

Mab groaned as Lamm recited the story, much to everyone's amusement. When the laughing had subsided, Luticia said, 'Mab, can I ask how you are able to remove a witch's powers.'

Mab replied, 'There is a certain part of the brain that is responsible for powers. If this is prodded, it goes into shock. However, the effect wears off naturally in a few days. It is possible to kill someone by using the same technique but with greater energy in the prod. You recovered quickly because you have strong powers.'

Kanaka said, 'Luticia, about tomorrow, we need to explain to the witches that we will not accept the presence of daemons in the Academy or, indeed, on this plane. We should also announce the change in direction away from the occult and black witchcraft. I think your suggested new name for the Academy is excellent, but that is for you to decide. You may want to restructure the organisation. Some may find themselves to be square pegs in round holes.'

Luticia replied, 'Yes, Master Kanaka, I fully understand.'

The dinner was sumptuous, even Mab was quite full and didn't feel the need to take anything back to her room. She retired earlier than usual but needed the sleep. When Mab left the room, Luticia said, 'Master Kanaka, I hope you don't mind me asking, but who is Mab? Her powers are truly extraordinary.'

Kanaka replied, 'Luticia, in all candour I do not feel comfortable discussing that subject. It is not a secret, Jessam and Sirak know the story, but only four living people, and Amarok the Wolf, can bear witness to the truth of Mab's origins. What I can tell you is that Mab's powers are more extraordinary than you could possibly imagine. Fortunately, she is slow to anger, quick to forgive and has a very good sense of humour. But, mark these words, being around great power is dangerous, it must always be treated with respect. She is human and can react badly if slighted or if her friends and family are threatened. When you attacked Mab, she saw something in you, a goodness that she liked. Otherwise, you would surely be dead.'

Luticia replied, 'Yes, I realised fairly quickly that she was, in fact, playing with me. But I have to say this experience has shown me what I already knew but couldn't accept; we have been wrong all these years. We must now strive to do good and abandon the teachings of the occult and daemonology. With the demise of the Palace, we have an opportunity for a new start.'

Kanaka said, 'If you explain that tomorrow to the rest of the coven, then you will have taken the first of many steps on the road to recovery.'

Mab awoke early the next morning and decided to go for a brisk walk around the campus before breakfast. She donned her white silk cloak, although when she ventured outdoors, there was something of a chill in the air. Grin and bear it, she thought. She spotted Lamm and ran to catch up with him. He said, 'Good morning, Mab. Did you sleep well?'

Mab replied, 'Yes, Master Lamm, I was really tired last night but feel much better this morning. Do you think we will be setting off for the Palace soon?'

Lamm said, 'I expect so. I guess it depends on the reaction from the witch coven. Luticia needs to get them on board with the new direction. I think they are beginning to see the light, especially after your lesson in combat yesterday.'

Mab and Lamm made their way back for breakfast and noticed that the witches were beginning to assemble in the Square and that a dais had been erected. When they reached the dining hall the other masters were already there together with Luticia and had finished eating. Lamm said, 'The Coven is assembling now in the square, Mab and I will have a quick breakfast and catch up with you.'

The witches were assembled on four rows of seats facing the dais. When Mab and Lamm arrived, Luticia was in full flow, explaining the new direction and the need to cleanse the Academy of Daemons. The Masters were sat on the dais behind Luticia, two seats were free for Lamm and Mab. However, as Mab walked onto the dais, all eyes turned to her. Mab took the seat next to Master

Kanaka. When Luticia had finished describing the new direction, she said, 'That, in a nutshell, is what we want to achieve, but we want to hear your views. You are the Coven and the backbone of this Academy. Please let us know what you think.' There was silence.

Then, a Witch on the front row raised her hand. It was Fora, she said, 'We all know that working with the occult and daemonology is wrong. But we had to obey the leadership and direction set by the Palace. I want to be on the side of good, not evil. Yesterday, we saw the power of the White Witch and we saw her cast out daemons. The light was stronger than the dark, the good triumphed over evil. I wholeheartedly support the new direction and I thank those here who have made it possible.' The Coven applauded enthusiastically.

Another witch put her hand up and said, 'What does the White Witch say of the new direction?'

Luticia, looked back at Mab, who stood up, walked to the lectern and said, 'I say that Fora is correct, this is a simple choice between good and evil. All of you would, I am sure, choose good over evil. However, good is easily recognised, but evil is not because it is rooted in lies, deception and despair. The new direction will free you of evil. The four magic schools will work much more closely together; this is a commitment that the four Principals have made. I look forward to visiting this Academy much more often than previously and supporting the new curriculum.'

The Coven gave Mab a standing ovation. Luticia said, 'The detail is still to be worked out, but we are thinking that a possible new name of the Academy could be 'The Academy of White Witches,' any views?'

The Coven rose to their feet once more and roared their approval. Luticia said, 'That seems to be popular! Thank you all for attending this morning, this meeting of the Coven is now dissolved.'

Kanaka said, 'Luticia, I regret that we must now move on to the Palace.'

Luticia said, 'I would come with you, but there is so much to be done here.'

Kanaka replied, 'Thank you for the offer, but I agree that you are best placed here to consolidate the transition away from the dark to the light if you understand my meaning. We will leave immediately and keep you informed of our findings.'

Chapter Twelve: Return to the Palace

The posse rode hard from the Academy and headed West and then North towards the Palace. Every so often, Kanaka noticed one or more wolves running parallel to them, but they didn't approach the track or the horses. After three hours, Kanaka called a halt close to a stream and just before the trail entered Deeping Forest. The horses were tethered and the masters retrieved provisions from their saddle bags. Sirak said, 'Kanaka, how do you propose we enter the Palace?'

Kanaka replied, 'It depends on what we find when we get there. If there is heavy security, then I thought we would do as we did on our last visit, enter through the South gate and use the service corridor to access the main areas of the Palace.'

Lamm said, 'Who would be the natural successor to the Prince?'

Jessam replied, 'The Prince didn't take a wife. I guess the worst-case scenario is that the military is in charge, but they may not be that organised; the Palace could be ransacked for all we know. I understand there are deserters roaming the area looking for work.'

Kanaka said, 'Mab, you look pensive. What do you think we will find?'

Mab looked up and said, 'I don't know what we will find, but I feel something is wrong. It's at the edge of my consciousness, I just can't grab hold of it.'

Kanaka said, 'I think we should push ahead. If you think something is wrong, we need to find out what it is and quickly. To horse everyone!'

The masters mounted up and set off into the forest apace. They had been riding hard for about an hour when Mab called a halt and dismounted. She levitated upwards over the top of the tallest trees and rotated slowly, looking in all directions and then dropped to the ground. She looked at Kanaka and said, 'Ansek once told me that the Palace military would not fear a single witch no matter how powerful.'

Kanaka replied, 'Yes, I remember that discussion.'

Mab said, 'Jessam said earlier that he had seen soldiers roaming the countryside. I also saw soldiers in the village where Izzy and I made our new home.'

Kanaka said, 'I'm not following you, Mab. What's your point?'

Mab replied, 'How many soldiers does the Palace have?'

Sirak said, 'My understanding is that they have around 500 men, including the Adepts.'

Mab replied, 'I guess that would take a lot of organising, lines and layers of command?'

Sirak said, 'Yes, absolutely.'

Mab asked, 'If your School had been infiltrated and a master killed, what would you do?'

Sirak said, 'I would try to find those responsible.'

Mab replied, 'Yes, but what would you do?'

Sirak said, 'I would send out scouts and spies.'

'Precisely,' said Mab.

Kanaka looked at Mab and said, 'What you are saying is that the Palace is unlikely to be in disarray due to military command and that the soldiers we are seeing roaming around are actually scouts and spies.'

Mab replied, 'Yes, disguised as deserters, layabouts and drunks.'

Lamm said, 'When we arrive at the Palace, we should therefore expect a trap?'

Mab replied, 'Yes, by now, they almost certainly know who we are and they may even know where we are. But the most important question is, where are the soldiers?'

Kanaka said, 'The Guild!?'

Mab replied, 'That is my fear. I tried to far sense, but the distance is too great.'

Amarok leapt from the tree cover onto the trail and mind-messaged the masters. 'High-one, the Palace army arrived at the walls of the Guild this morning. The masters have locked the gates against them, but I fear they will not resist for long.'

Kanaka said, 'We need to get back to the Guild!'

Mab said, 'Master Kanaka, you and I should return to the Guild. Masters Jessam, Sirak and Lamm, you should continue to the Palace.

I suspect the Palace will only have a handful of soldiers, with the vast bulk of the military being arrayed against the Guild.'

Kanaka replied, 'Yes, I agree. Jessam, Sirak, Lamm go to the Palace. The mission has changed. You must destroy it, burn it to the ground. Ensure that you also destroy everything concerning the military, particularly the accommodation blocks and the armoury.'

Jessam said, 'Understood, between us, we need to destroy their military capability.'

Mab said, 'Master Kanaka, dismount, we must make haste.'

Kanaka leapt from his mount and said, 'What do you have in mind?'

Mab grabbed his hand and closed her eyes; two huge white eagles soared skywards. Kanaka said, 'My word, this is fun but really scary; at this rate, we should reach the Guild in less than 20 minutes.'

Mab replied, 'My guess is that they are either discussing terms with Masters Boe and Paull or they have breached the gates and are rampaging through the Guild. Smoke, I smell smoke! Faster Master Kanaka!'

The eagles were flying high but then plummeted towards the Guild. As they looked down, they saw that the gates had been breached and were ablaze; ant-sized soldiers were running all over the campus. The battle Commander had held back much of his forces, which were arrayed in lines outside the Gates, and sent his shock troops in first to kill as many as possible and sow the seeds of despair. Mab said, 'Master Kanaka, I must get Izzy to safety first and then I will go to the North Wall and attack the lines of soldiers not already committed.'

Kanaka replied, 'I will look for Boe and Paull but also kill as many soldiers as I can within the Campus.' Mab and Kanaka landed on the sports fields and changed back to human form.

They both ran towards the main building, Mab bounded up the stairs towards Boe's room. Soldiers were everywhere but now seemed to be preoccupied with looting. When she reached the entrance to Boe's room she realised that the room had been ransacked. She opened the lower door to the suite and took the steps two at a time.

Izzy and Charly were lying on the floor, they had been put to the sword. Izzy had a huge bruise on her forehead. She must have been knocked unconscious by the sword pommel and then killed. Mab dropped to her knees, sobbing. She lifted Izzy gently and put her on their bed and kissed her on the lips, tears streaming down her face. She then stood up and let out a terrible cry of sheer anguish, the skies darkened, thunderclaps shook the Guild buildings, lightning bolts streaked across the sky.

Kanaka lost count of the soldiers he had slain before he discovered that Boe and Paull were being held under house arrest by the Palace Commander and his adepts in the Grand Hall. Kanaka walked straight in and said, 'I don't know who you are, but you will release my masters immediately and remove all of your soldiers from this Guild.'

The Commander looked up, laughed and said, 'Oh really? This facility is now under military control as an adjunct to the Palace. You and your so-called masters will be put to death for treason. They are in the basement cells where they belong and that's where you are going until we get around to hanging you.'

Kanaka said, 'I see you now, daemon; you and your kind will be purged from this plane now that Mahazael, your Prince of Filth, has been destroyed.'

The Commander replied, 'The great Lord has merely gone back to the Abyss.'

Kanaka said, 'No, he was rended to his death. I am pleased to say that I was there to witness it.'

The Commander replied, 'The great Lord is immortal. None have the power to slay him.'

Lightning bolts suddenly flashed across the sky, the thunderclap that followed was as if God had looked down on the planet and severed a mountain in half with a great sword. Kanaka said, 'She who slayed Mahazael is now here, in this very building.' The doors to the Grand Hall were blasted inwards and a giant Saber-Cat padded into the room. It was a sight that Kanaka hoped never to see again. The cat's face and neck were covered in blood, and pieces of flesh hung from its enormous teeth. Its huge claws, which were also covered in blood and gore, clattered on the stone floor as it approached Kanaka.

Kanaka looked into the watery eyes of the Cat, saw its pain, and whispered, 'Mab, I'm so sorry,' tears flowed from his eyes.

The Commander said, 'Adepts, kill this fool and bring me the skin of the cat.' But there was no response from the adepts, they were immobilised. The Commander tried to draw his sword, but he also was immobilised. The Saber-Cat reared up and transformed into a young woman, her mouth, face and hands covered in blood. The tracks of her tears were evident on both cheeks. Mab said 'Master Kanaka, they killed Izzy and Charly.'

Kanaka bowed his head and said, 'I thought as much. Mab, there will be a time to mourn, but this is not it.'

Mab replied, 'This is the time for retribution. I will start with this filth.'

Mab looked at the Commander and said, 'You will not be expelled but rended to your death by burning. And, know this daemon, I will kill everyone under your command. Even now, your Palace is being razed to the ground.'

The Commander was lifted off the floor and slammed back into the wall. Mab pinned him to the wall with a beam of light from her left hand and incinerated him with flame from her right hand. The daemon screamed in agony as it died. Mab also incinerated the six adepts where they stood, there was no mercy. Mab said, 'Master Kanaka you find Boe and Paull. I will go to the North Wall.'

Kanaka could find no appropriate words, so nodded and said nothing. Mab ran to the North Wall overlooking the soldiers held in reserve. It looked as if they were preparing to enter the campus. She jumped up onto the ramparts and cried out, 'Hear me, soldiers of the Palace!'

Many looked up at her, pointing, others shouted out, 'The White Witch has come.'

Flame balls, arrows and spears were launched at her, but the few missiles that reached her bounced off her sheen of shimmering power. She cried out to them, 'Soldiers and Adepts, go back to your homes. Your daemon commander is rended. All that awaits you here is death.'

Mab stretched out her arms and let out a shriek of pain as her body started to expand and gain mass. Her features changed; her arms became wings and her face extended outwards and upwards as the transformation progressed. The Soldiers and Adepts started to panic, but then they stilled and stared up, mesmerised by the creature looking down at them. The enormous silver dragon roared in fury, sucked in an astonishing volume of air and released an apotheosis of utter destruction which blasted down on the ranks below. As the dragon lifted his huge head large swathes of all living things were consumed in the silver flame. The force of the blast cut deep into the ground, forming enormous furrows of death. The great dragon roared once more, took to the air and flew to the North, towards the Palace.

Mab mind messaged Lamm, 'Master Lamm, I will arrive at the Palace soon. Please ensure all friends and allies are off the campus and well clear of the buildings.'

Lamm replied, 'Mab, we have only just entered the Palace. There are some soldiers here, but we can handle them.'

Mab said, 'The mission has changed, forget about the soldiers. In less than 30 minutes, the Palace will be rubble, and everyone therein will be dead.'

Lamm replied, 'Understood, I will message you when it's done.'

Lamm, Sirak and Jessam were in the Palace service corridor. Lamm whispered to them, 'There is a change of plan. Mab is on her way here now. We need to get out of the Palace and warn friendlies to do the same. We should forget about the soldiers and adepts.'

Jessam said, 'What! How are we supposed to do that?'

Lamm replied, 'We spread-out, avoid the soldiers and adepts, tell everyone that there is an imminent attack, they need to leave the Campus and take shelter in the forest. Jessam, you go to the top floor, I'll do the second floor and Sirak, you do the ground floor. Whatever happens, make sure you are out of this place in 15 minutes.'

Sirak said, 'This is crazy! We will never get everyone out in time.'

Lamm replied, 'Sirak, we don't know what has happened at the Guild. But I know Mab, she is coming here to destroy this place and I don't think she cares who is in it. So, let's do the best we can and then get out!'

The Palace was, in fact, relatively free of soldiers and adepts these being committed to the attack on the Guild. Most of the Palace staff were administrators and the bulk of the rest were contractors or vendors. The masters screamed at them to leave, and they did, a panic ensued, but people were pouring out of the building, even the guards took the warning seriously and ran towards the tree line. Lamm released horses and other animals from the peripheral barns that were closest to the Palace. The masters met outside the Palace South entrance. Lamm messaged Mab, 'Mab, most people are now out of the Palace. We don't know if there are hostiles in amongst them but, in any case, there are very few soldiers and adepts here. I guess pretty much all the soldiers are at the Guild. Are you alright, Mab?'

Mab replied, 'No, Master Lamm, I am not alright. I was too late. They killed Izzy and Charly.'

Lamm said, 'Mab, I am so sorry… is the battle at the Guild still underway?'

Mab replied, 'No, the battle is over. The soldiers and adepts are all dead, the masters are finishing off the stragglers. I am here now, over the palace.'

A huge roar erupted from the skies; all eyes looked up. The huge silver dragon landed on top of the South wall, which started to crumble under its weight. A blast of red and white flame demolished part of the Palace roof, the dragon leapt upwards, beating its wings and hovering while sweeping its massive head, causing devastation in all directions. The ancient hard stone of the Palace could not tolerate dragon fire and was blasted apart on contact. The dragon was also ripping the stone apart using powerful claws and using its tail to wreck anything else around it. Lamm thought the fury and destruction was a catharsis for Mab, for the pain of losing her partner and her friend. The Palace was destroyed in less than an hour. The great dragon rested atop the pile of rubble for a while and then vomited up a green liquid which liquefied the stone. The dragon sprayed the entire demolition with acid, not resting until even the shapes of the Palace stones were unrecognisable. It then let out a final roar and transformed into a young, blood-spattered woman.

Lamm ran from the forest towards Mab as she made her way down the mountain of rubble. As he got closer, he could see that she was covered in dried blood and, when closer still, that she was sobbing. Lamm threw his arms around her and held her tight, Mab buried her face in his shoulder until she recovered her composure. Sirak and Jessam reached them, but Lamm signed, 'Do not say anything.'

They walked back to the forest, and Sirak led them to the horses. Amarok and some of his pack were there waiting for them to return. Amarok bowed and said, 'High-One, I thank you for what you have done here and at the Academy. You have freed many and cleansed our plane. We, and many others, are forever in your debt.'

'Amarok, you owe me no debt,' replied Mab.

Amarok bowed once more and said, 'We will escort you back to the Guild.'

Lamm said, 'Mab, you should eat something first; you must be exhausted.'

Mab replied, 'I am exhausted, but I will rest and eat in the saddle. I am anxious to return to the Guild.'

Lamm said, 'Fine, mount-up!' Lamm passed Mab a hip flask of strong liquor. Mab took a big gulp, passed it back and nudged her horse into a fast canter.

The posse rode in silence through the forest for nearly two hours until Mab suddenly stopped. Amarok bounded onto the trail and stood beside Lady. The trees ahead rustled, but there was no wind. Mab strained her witch senses but could detect nothing, she looked to Amarok. But Amarok bowed his head low and didn't move or respond.

Then, a young woman came from the forest and wandered onto the trail. She was being followed through the forest by a veritable menagerie of animals and birds. Mab leapt from her horse and said, 'Everyone dismount and bend the knee.' Mab and the masters knelt beside Amarok and waited for the woman to approach.

'Daughter, what are you doing down there? Come to me.'

Mab ran into the arms of her mother and sobbed. 'I have lost Izzy. They killed her, put her to the sword.'

Uriel replied, 'Hush, my child, she was but sleeping, she is now awoken.'

Mab sobbed and said, 'No, she is dead, Charly too. I found them.'

Uriel replied, 'Did I not say she has awoken?'

Mab stared up at her mother and whispered, 'She lives?'

Uriel said, 'She lives and waits for your return. So, no more tears, please.'

'But…'

'And no more buts!'

Mab dropped to her knees and looked up at her mother, sobbing her heart out and trying to thank her at the same time. Uriel looked down on her daughter, her blood-spattered face, her filthy matted hair, the tears mixed with the blood running down her cheeks. A single teardrop appeared in the corner of her eye. It dropped from her face and hit Mab on the forehead. Mab was immediately engulfed in a silver light; it burned her clean, renewed her, and filled her inside with love and hope for the future. Her mother lifted her up, hugged her and said, 'Mabdelore, I am so proud of you; you have freed this plane of evil and accomplished everything I had hoped for. You need to rest now; you have done more than enough. I will visit you again soon.' Uriel kissed Mab on the forehead and vanished.

Mab turned and walked back to the masters who were still kneeling and said, 'She's gone. You can get up now.' The masters stared at Mab in amazement.

Lamm said, 'Mab, you are glowing. Your skin and hair, you look amazing!'

Mab replied, 'I feel amazing! Let's get back to the Guild!' Amarok loped back into the forest and the posse continued the journey.

As they approached the Guild, they could see that the main structural damage was to the North Wall Gates. The land in front of the gates was scorched and deeply furrowed. Lamm guessed the reason but said nothing. Mab pushed her horse into a gallop, she thundered past the Guards and rode on to the stables. Mab ran towards the main building and up the stairs to towards the suite. She burst into the room, but no one was there. She walked back down the stairs and met Boe, she threw her arms around him. Boe said, 'Mab, it's great to see you again, I was so worried about you.'

Mab said, 'Master Boe, have you seen Izzy?'

Boe replied, 'Yes, she is in the Great Hall helping with the clean-up.' Mab rushed down the stairs and into the Great Hall. Izzy turned and saw her. They ran towards each other, hugged tightly and kissed each other franticly.

Mab said, 'The last time I saw you, you looked dead!'

Izzy said, 'It's strange. Soldiers burst into our room and killed Charly, I saw them do it! They must have knocked me out, but Charly found me on the bed and woke me up!'

Mab said, 'Where is Charly?'

Izzy said, 'I'm not sure, she was here earlier, but she's fine.'

Mab said, 'What about Cat?'

Izzy said, 'Cat was lucky, she went back home to see her parents just before the army arrived. I haven't seen her since, but she should be fine. What have you done to your hair!'

Mab replied, 'Nothing, what do you mean?'

Izzy reached over Mab's shoulder, pulled her hair forward and said, 'Look, it's silver and absolutely beautiful. I love it. And your skin, you look as if you've been to a health spa. I thought you were off fighting to save us!'

Mab said, 'I tried to do a bit of fighting, but it's just too hard. So, I decided to take a short holiday at a spa. I hope you don't mind?'

Mab received a mind message from Lamm, 'Mab, Kanaka wants a masters meeting first thing tomorrow morning.'

Mab looked at Izzy and said, 'Looks like I have the rest of the night off. How about a nice dinner, a bottle or two of fine wine and then off to bed!'

Izzy replied, 'Perfect!'

Chapter Thirteen: Battles in Mind-Space

Mab awoke early, donned her master's robe and went for her usual walk around the campus. The Guild was surprisingly intact; most of the military activity had been in the main building. Ironically, Mab's roommates would have been safer in the student accommodation, which was untouched. The soldiers were more interested in the masters and the staff than the students. Mab strolled to the Northern Gates. She nodded to the Guards and walked outside to view the location where Palace's main force had been assembled. The furrows were cut deep into the ground, everything was scorched black. Only a few signs remained of the many soldiers that had met their deaths there. The dragon fire was all-consuming, the ground in that area would be dead for many years. 'It had to be done, we had no choice,' said Kanaka.

Mab turned to see Master Kanaka walking towards her. Mab replied, 'True, but so many deaths.'

Kanaka said, 'How is Izzy?'

Mab replied, 'She is fine, we are fine. I was so relieved when my mother told me she was alive.'

Kanaka said, 'Yes, Lamm told me about your mother's second visit.'

Mab replied, 'She was pleased with what we had done, cleansing the daemons and destroying the Palace.'

Kanaka said, 'Then we are surely on the side of the good. How about some breakfast and hot coffee?'

Kanaka and Mab walked back through the campus, into the main building and up the stairs to Kanaka's office. The other masters were already there, including Masters Boe and Paull. They were helping themselves to cold meats, bread, pastries and hot coffee. Mab asked, 'How many of ours were killed?'

Boe replied, 'Surprisingly few. The only deaths we know of are two junior students who just happened to get in the way. We had thought Izzy and Charly had been killed for much the same reason, seasoned soldiers rushing into a master's room expecting to find valuables but being disappointed and killing out of sheer frustration. However, they made a miraculous recovery, I understand, with the help of your mother.'

Mab replied, 'Yes, my mother intervened.'

Paull said, 'The rooms in the main building have been ransacked, but fortunately, they were not interested in the libraries. I don't believe they had time to remove anything of great value. So, most of the restoration work, other than the gates of course, will be in cleaning up. If the soldiers outside the campus had been committed to the battle, then the situation would have been very different.'

Kanaka looked at Lamm and said, 'What about your mission to the Palace?'

Lamm replied, 'It went as well as could be expected. We got most people out before Mab arrived and obliterated the Palace.'

Kanaka replied, 'So it would take some time for it to be repaired and restored to a working facility?'

There was laughter around the table. Sirak said, 'I think it is difficult to describe in physical terms what Lamm meant when he used the word obliterate. But it is safe to say that nothing remains of the Palace and nothing will be built on that site ever again.'

Kanaka looked questioningly at Mab, who had a sheepish expression on her face and replied, 'I was a tad angry at the time. I may have gone a little bit too far.' Lamm, Sirak and Jessam struggled to stifle their laughter.

Kanaka said, 'In view of that I think we can be confident that we have virtually eliminated the daemon problem, but we do need to remain vigilant. There may still be hosts, human or animal, that we haven't detected, but these should be isolated instances. The Palace and the Academy, as the root sources of this filth, have been dealt with. All that remains now is the adjacent plane or planes. These represent a threat of spirits making use of mind-space to travel here to our plane, leading to a recurrence of the problem.'

Jessam said, 'Do we know that these spirits or daemons are able to travel here from the adjacent planes? I had thought the Palace sourced the daemons from the Abyss?'

Kanaka replied, 'We don't know for sure, but I think it is probable. After all, we can travel to the adjacent planes essentially as spirits. Mab, what is your view?'

Mab replied, 'Master Kanaka, I think it is very likely that a daemon could cross over into our plane, but it would need to enter an animal or perhaps a child initially until it could find a way of possessing an adult. Also, it would need assistance to possess an adult, and we have removed much of the needed assistance here.'

Kanaka said, 'So you think there is minimal risk?'

Mab replied, 'I think we should intervene in the adjacent plane to help the people there, to save them from slavery. However, if we do intervene the daemons may decide to attack us here on this plane in ways we cannot at present foresee.'

Lamm said, 'Yes, I agree with that Mab. If we intervene directly, then we will draw attention to ourselves and that may precipitate retaliation. However, could we work with the priests, or witches, in that plane and help them to expel or kill the daemons?'

Sirak replied, 'I think that would be a much better and safer approach rather than us launching a direct attack.'

Mab said, 'I agree. The priests on our nearest plane can detect spirits, they detected me even though they couldn't see me. Maybe we could mind-message them or communicate in writing? Do we have any language experts in the Guild or the other Schools?'

Jessam replied, 'Yes, we do. I suggest Master Uvren. He has a very broad knowledge of languages and linguistics.'

Kanaka said, 'Mab, is there any way we could become visible when on another plane? When your mother appears, we can all see her?'

Mab replied, 'I think we could be partially visible by wrapping in a protective skin of power. People would be able to see our shape and human form, but without any detail, it might scare them. My mother is not human, when she appears, she is actually here. She has no physical body, at least in the way we understand it.'

Sirak replied, 'An outline shape is better than nothing. Would you be able to teach us how to develop a skin of power?'

Mab said, 'Yes, it's easy.'

Kanaka laughed and said, 'Mab, easy for you doesn't mean we will be able to do it. Do we need to practice?'

Mab replied, 'No, you don't need to practice. Anyway, if you can't do it, then I can do it for you.'

Kanaka said, 'Great, so we will go into mind-space first thing tomorrow morning. Jessam, I know it's not essential, but it would make sense if you could ask Uvren to come here so we are all physically in the same place.'

Jessam replied, 'Yes, of course.'

Kanaka said, 'Boe, could you arrange for medics to be on-hand monitoring our bodies while we are in mind-space? We will be in the basement library. The medical team needs to remain in the library with the door bolted from the inside. We may be away for several hours of real-time.'

Boe replied, 'Yes, Master Kanaka. I assume you will wish Paull and I to remain here holding the fort as usual?'

Kanaka replied, 'I'm afraid so. When this whole thing is over we should all be able to use mind-space safely and enjoy visiting other places and cultures. But, I fear that is some way off at present.'

Boe replied, 'Understood, I will go now and make the necessary arrangements.'

Mab said, 'Let me show you how to create a skin of power. If you could all stand up?' The masters all stood around the table.

Mab said, 'For tomorrow, the skin of power doesn't need to be strong. The purpose is only to make us visible to humans in the adjacent plane. However, if you are strong enough, the skin will protect you from fire and, to a degree, from physical blows. But it is unlikely to protect you from sword cuts, knife stabs, arrows or lances. Now, stretch your arms out in front of you, palms up. Now, make a ball of fire appear in each hand. Slowly raise both arms above your head, pointing at the sky. Now imagine the fire in your hands is like water. Let it run down your arms and flow over your whole body as if you are having a shower. Now, simply hold it there and walk around a bit. Excellent, l told you it was easy!'

The masters looked at each other as they walked around Kanaka's office. Jessam said, 'Mab, why are the colours all different, reds, greens, yellows, blues?'

Mab replied, 'I don't know, I guess it's just a reflection of your particular magic and personality.'

Mab turned to Kanaka and said, 'Master Kanaka, I was thinking of doing some sword practice this afternoon. Are you available?'

Kanaka replied, 'Yes, provided you promise not to kill me.'

Mab smiled and said, 'Great, I'll meet you in the sports field at midday.'

Mab made her way back to the suite in time for an early lunch. Cat had returned to the Campus. She, Izzy and Charly were preparing the food. Cat ran to Mab, hugged her and said, 'Look at your hair, it's fabulous! I hear you have been busy saving us from the evil hordes.'

Mab replied, 'Yes, we are safe, but many had to die.'

Izzy frowned at Cat and said, 'Mab, come and sit down.'

Cat started crying and said, 'Sorry, Mab, I didn't mean to be flippant. I know that you have all been through hell and back. I'm just so glad we are back together again.'

Charly hugged Cat and said, 'Group hug required!' Izzy and Mab joined Charly and Cat for the group hug.

Mab made her way to the sports fields after lunch. Kanaka was just completing one of the most advanced sword kata's. She applauded and leapt over the fence and into the field. Kanaka said, 'What do you have in mind.'

Mab replied, 'Open combat, we use the wooden practice swords and only strike at the body?'

Kanaka said, 'Great.' They stood several metres apart, bowed to each other and held their practice swords double-handed. A student spotted them and ran off to tell all his friends; soon a large crowd had assembled to watch the battle. Kanaka and Mab approached each other slowly, sliding their feet across the ground. Kanaka suddenly leapt forward and delivered three blindingly fast double-handed vertical sword strokes. Mab retreated backwards but then ducked low and delivered a single-handed swipe which narrowly missed Kanaka's legs. She then ran at Kanaka using the sword single-handed and slicing vertically, blindingly fast. Kanaka backed away, blocking each of the strikes and then leapt to the side and sliced horizontally at Mab's waist. Mab leapt into the air, somersaulted over the blade and sliced down at Kanaka's shoulder, but Kanaka hit the ground and rolled to safety.

They were both sweating with the exertion but once more approached each other. This time, Mab attacked double-handed, delivering four vertical slicing strokes and side-kicking Kanaka backwards. Kanaka continued the backward momentum, spun and brought his sword around single-handed with arm at full stretch in a sweeping horizontal slicing action. Mab only just saw it coming and arched backwards as the blade hissed past just above her chest. She flipped back up and leapt to Kanaka's left, delivering a horizontal slice at his waist, which narrowly missed, as she rolled onto the ground and returned to her feet. They were smiling as they slowly approached each other again. Mab started to say something, but Kanaka attacked with two vicious vertical slices. Following the second slice, Mab ran in close and shoulder-charged Kanaka, knocking him to the ground, but Kanaka rolled across the ground and leapt back to his feet. Mab ran at him, slicing vertically and then somersaulted over him, twisting in the air and slicing at Kanaka's back, the blow missed but only by a fraction. She dropped her sword, jumped on Kanaka's back and clumsily wrestled him to the ground. The audience roared with laughter.

They were both laughing and sweating profusely. Mab said, 'Master Kanaka, that's the best sword practice I have ever had. You make it so difficult for an attacker, your stance, the way you hold your sword, and the way you flow between defence and attack. I had hoped to practice some special moves I had been developing, but it wasn't possible with you. You are too good.'

Kanaka replied, 'That's the benefit of practicing with someone at your own level, and remember, I am a master swordsman. You find that the more elaborate moves you like doing on your own or with a student just don't work with someone who is equally skilled. I really enjoyed that, we should do it more often.'

Mab replied, 'Yes, please.'

As he walked off, Kanaka said, 'See you in the Library first thing in the morning, have breakfast first.'

The following morning, Mab had breakfast with Izzy. They had been up late the previous evening celebrating their reunion. Charly and Cat were sleeping late. Mab had already explained what was happening regarding the trip into mind-space and reassured Izzy that they were not expecting any problems.

When Mab arrived at the lost library, Masters Kanaka, Sirak, Jessam and Boe were already there together with three medics. Kanaka said, 'Good morning, Mab; Lamm has gone to find Master Uvren. He arrived late last night and doesn't know his way around our campus. I suggest that we wait until we enter mind-space and then you talk us through the mission and lead the way. I'm still a bit stiff following our sword practice last night, so go easy. I suppose you are feeling a bit stiff, too. Any aches and pains?'

Mab, smiling, replied, 'No, Master Kanaka, I'm feeling great, no aches and pains at all.' Kanaka rolled his eyes.

Lamm arrived with Uvren, who looked ancient. He was hunched, wore thick lens spectacles and his face looked like wrinkled leather. Jessam introduced Uvren to everyone before Kanaka said, 'We will now enter mind-space. When we are all assembled, Mab will lead the mission, which is to make contact with the priests and or witches on the adjacent plane. Master Boe has a team of medics who will remain in this room and look after us while we are away.'

The masters settled themselves down onto mats or cushions and took up their particular meditation positions. Mab was the last to appear in mind-space, she said, 'We are now going to travel to another plane of existence. The inhabitants will not be able to see us, but they can hear us. When I first visited, the priests were able to detect but not see me. When we arrive at the village, we will hover over a busy public area to give Master Uvren an opportunity to make sense of the language. We will also try to mind-message one of the priests. We know there are daemons on this plane, they will be able to see and hear us. We don't want to engage with them unless we must. Remember, the objective is to find a way to communicate with the priests. We leave now, so stay close together in tight formation. To move forward, use your mind, imagine you are trying to look inside someone who is backing away from you. Once we are all moving together, I will gradually increase the speed.'

Mab started to move forward with Kanaka and Lamm. Sirak and Jessam didn't take long to master the technique, although Master Uvren was a bit slower. Mab led the arrow formation, with Kanaka and Lamm behind her and behind them were Sirak, Uvren and Jessam. Mab gradually increased speed until they were rocketing through mind-space at an astonishing rate. Mab slowed up as they approached the solar system, brought the group to a stop and said, 'This is the solar system, it's similar to ours. We are going to the third planet.'

Jessam said, 'I could stay here forever. It's just beautiful.'

Sirak said, 'It is astonishing.'

Uvren said, 'Can I open my eyes now?'

Mab laughed and said, 'Yes, Master Uvren, you will need them as we descend to the planet. Is everyone ready?'

All replied, 'Aye.' Mab initially followed the same trajectory as on her previous visit. Still, they flew together, hugging the surface of an ocean and veered off landward, following a deep valley to arrive at the town. Mab increased their elevation to give a birds-eye view of the town. The marketplace below once again thrummed with activity, and they could also see the church and the Stadium.

Mab said, 'It might be best if we split up. I will go with Masters Jessam and Sirak to the church to see if we can mind-message or communicate in some other way. Masters Kanaka, Lamm and Uvren, can you hover low over the marketplace and try to understand the language? If anything goes wrong, return to this elevated position and wait.'

Kanaka, Lamm and Uvren descended to a hovering position just above the market. Kanaka said, 'I don't understand a word. What do you make of it, Uvren?'

Uvren said, 'I can understand some of the words. It resembles an old Hebrani language. If you can tell me what you want to say, I think I may be able to make myself understood. I would need more time to do a full mapping between our languages, but it could be done.'

Kanaka said, 'Lamm, could you mind-message Mab to let her know that Uvren may be able to communicate with the Priests.' Lamm sent the mind-message and received a reply back asking them to go to the church.

Mab, Jessam and Sirak initially hovered over the church, simply observing. Then, the doors opened, and people streamed out into the square. The masters descended so they could look inside without actually entering the church. The church had pews arranged on both sides of a central aisle, which stretched to the dais at the rear wall.

The windows were beautifully ornate and made up of many pieces of coloured translucent stone. There was a large round window on the rear wall above the dais, which wonderfully illuminated the space below.

When the congregation had vacated the church, Mab, followed by Sirak and Jessam, moved inside but floated up almost to the apex of the roof. Four Priests in full dress robes were moving through the church, picking up books. The dais area displayed many gold ornaments, including candlesticks, plates and goblets. The walls were decorated with what were presumably great heroes of the past. But then Jessam, in a low whisper, said, 'Mab, come and see this.'

Mab followed Jessam across the church. He was pointing to a painting which depicted the figure of a slender woman with silver hair and eyes of black orbs. The figure wore a white cape and held a large golden sword in her right hand. It was the image of both Mab and her mother. Mab whispered, 'Wait here, I'm going to let them see me; when Uvren gets here, ask him to join me.'

Mab floated to the rear of the church and down onto the Dais. She then made herself partially visible by forming a silver skin of power around her and walked down onto the aisle. One of the Priests turned and saw her. He let out a cry of astonishment and dropped to his knees. The others looked and saw Mab walking up the aisle towards them. They all dropped to their knees. Mab scanned them and then tried to mind-link with what she thought was the more senior priest, but without success. Just then, a Priestess entered the church from a side alcove door, she had a young girl, perhaps 7 or 8 years old. When she saw Mab, she also dropped to her knees, but the child remained standing, staring at Mab. Mab scanned both her and the child and then tried to mind-link. The child understood her! Mab mind-messaged, 'What is your name, child?'

The child replied, 'My name is Dassi, how can you speak to me in my head?'

Mab replied, 'Dassi, ask your mother and the other priests to stand up. I have an important message for them.'

Dassi turned to her Mother and repeated what Mab had said. Her mother and the priests stood up. Mab mind-messaged, 'Dassi, you must repeat what I say to your Mother and the other Priests in your own language. Can you do that for me?'

Dassi replied, 'Yes, I can do that.'

Mab said, 'We have come here to help free this plane of daemons and tyrants to free you and your children from torture, slavery and death. I came here previously and found many soldiers had been possessed by evil spirits. We have come to cleanse you of this evil but need your help and cooperation.'

Dassi repeated the words back to her mother and the priests. The priests talked with Dassi for some time before Dassi mind-messaged Mab. 'They want to know who you are. We have always been troubled by evil spirits, but we did not know that these spirits had possessed soldiers. We live in difficult times, many of us are sacrificed to the sword or the lions. We are also punished and put to death for our beliefs.'

Mab lifted her hand and a beam of intense bright light illuminated the painting of her Mother. She mind-messaged Dassi, 'This is my mother.' All dropped to their knees again. Mab said, 'Tell the Priests that many evil spirits reside in the population here. They have infected the military and also the leadership and government. They feed off your fear and pain. This is the reason they hold these mass killings, which they refer to as games. We have freed our plane of these creatures and now we wish to help you free your own plane. We would need to discuss this with your leadership. Do you have any others who could help in addition to the priesthood?'

Dassi relayed Mab's words to the priests and responded, 'The priests say that they would welcome your help. They have special priests who study magic and sometimes they remove daemons from animals, badly behaved children or crops. There is also a prophet who is said to be able to cast out daemons from adults, but he has been imprisoned. The priests suggest they arrange a meeting of the Councilium, and you explain your plans to them. The meeting could be arranged quickly if you wait here?'

Mab said, 'What is the Councilium?'

Dassi replied, 'It is the people who rule us. The priests, public office bearers and soldiers.'

Mab replied, 'We would be willing to meet with the priests and the administrators but not the military. We will wait here for a short time. Go now.' The Priests and Dassi ran from the church.

Mab removed her skin and floated upwards to the masters. Kanaka said, 'Mab, Uvren is able to decipher some of the words. But I see that you were mind-messaging the child.'

Mab replied, 'Yes, I couldn't link with the adults. They have gone to fetch their leaders. They call them the Councilium. I agreed to wait for a short time and on the basis that no military is involved. I think you should all hover above the door then they won't see you when they enter, and if something goes wrong, you will be able to attack them from behind if necessary. Master Uvren, please listen to everything they say to each other and let Master Lamm know if it's something I should be worried about.'

The Councilium gathered outside the church and then slowly walked through the door towards the Dais. The priests held long golden staffs and the others donned elaborate robes of office. The priestess and her daughter, Dassi, were present but none of the other priests at the earlier meeting were there. Mab floated down and created a silver skin of power around her. Dassi pointed as she approached, the priests turned and gasped when they saw her. The Priests looked at each other; one of them dropped to his knees and others seemed to be in a panic, they were talking over each other, clearly unsure how to react. The senior administrator slammed his staff on the floor, cried for silence and told the kneeling priest to get up off the floor at once. The administrator looked in disgust at the priest and said, 'I don't know, and I don't care, who this charlatan is, but the military will be here soon. All we need to do is keep her talking.'

The administrator looked at the priestess and said, 'Tell your daughter to ask this thing who she is, where she comes from and what she expects us to do.'

Lamm mind-messaged Mab, 'Uvren says the military are on their way.'

Mab looked at Dassi, smiled and said, 'Dassi, could you take your mother's hand and sit down on a pew halfway back, please? You can call out the words from back there.'

Dassi looked at her mother, her eyes silently imparting urgency. She took her hand, held it tightly, and started walking towards the doors. She stopped midway between the dais and the main doors and pulled her mother down onto the pew. Dassi's mother knew something bad was going to happen, so she went along with it even when the administrator told her to stop. The large entrance doors then slammed shut and the ancient lock mechanism grinded round to the double lock position. The smaller alcove door then slammed shut and the two internal bolts rammed home into the lock position. The Administrator shouted into Mab's face, 'What is the meaning of this!'

Mab mind-messaged Lamm, 'The administrator is a host.' The Administrator noticed the movement above the doors and then looked back to Mab.

Mab said, 'Dassi, could you tell the priests that this administrator has been possessed by a daemon.'

The Priests backed away from the Administrator, who said, 'This is completely ridiculous!' Mab raised her hands and two beams of light engulfed the administrator's head. He screamed in agony.

Mab said, 'Daemon, I name you Egitt. You will leave this body.'

The Administrator shrieked in pain and fell to the floor. Mab spun quickly and sent two wide beams of light towards Dassi and her mother, both were covered with a silver skin of light protecting them from daemon attack. Mab elevated them and drew them to her and dissolved the skin of light.

Mab said to Dassi, 'I hope I didn't frighten you. The daemon that came out of the administrator may have tried to possess you.'

Dassi replied, 'We both feel fine.'

The priests were helping the administrator to his feet. He was crying with the joy of being released. He, with Dassi translating, said, 'Thank you, thank you for my life and my sanity. Please tell me who you are?'

Mab said, 'I am Mabdelore, Master of the Guild of Sorcerers. You have an image of my mother on your wall over there.' Mab illuminated the painting, and they all dropped to their knees. Mab told them to rise up and asked Dassi to continue the translation. Mab said, 'We have come to help free you of these creatures. Priests, are you able to carry out exorcisms?'

A priest said, 'My name is Ogan. I am the Head Priest. This is Padwa. He is the administrator and is responsible for all financial matters, but we both report to the military. You must understand that we are not a free people, we live under martial law. We have exorcism rites, but these are seldom if ever, used. We are able to detect spirits but not if they are hidden in a human body.'

Padwa said, 'High-one, I must warn you that the military are even now on their way here. They will attempt to kill you. Perhaps you should leave now, I could not live with myself if you were hurt?'

There was a crashing sound at the church doors. The military was using a battering ram to knock the doors inward. Mab said, 'There is no need to worry, Padwa.' Mab turned, looked up at the masters and then unlocked and opened the doors. The soldiers were using the trunk of a small tree to pummel the doors. Mab thought they would have been there for many hours longer if she hadn't opened the doors for them.

Some twenty or so soldiers ran into the church, swords drawn, their eyes franticly looking around for the enemy and then settling on the young woman standing next to the administrator. Mab said, 'Please, do come in and close the door behind you. Dassi, could you and your mother come closer for the translation.'

The soldiers fanned out around the pews closest to the doors and two senior officers walked towards Mab with an escort of four behind them. The first senior officer said, 'I am Major Kassa. This is Major Obiala, gesturing to the second Senior Officer. You will tell me who you are and what you are doing here.'

Mab replied, 'No, I don't think I will do that. I have already told Padwa and Ogan who I am and why I am here. However, I did want to speak to the military. Do you speak for them?'

Kassa said, 'It is you who will answer my questions.'

Mab replied, 'I don't think so.'

Kassa said, 'You are under arrest.' The lock mechanism on the church doors ground its way around into the locked position.

Mab, using a coercion inflection, said, 'Kneel!' Kassa and Obiala slowly dropped to their knees. The soldiers raised their swords and attacked, but the masters felled them all with psychic blasts before they reached the dais.

Mab said, 'Priests, these officers both host daemons; the soldiers all appear to be clean.' She asked the Priests to carry out an exorcism and said, 'The daemon's names are Loupa and Tartha. You should be able to expel them using these names and carry out the rite in the name of my mother, Uriel. It would take you a very long time to extract the name of a daemon and the process would be extremely traumatic for the host. So, if a daemon refuses to give you its name, then, unfortunately, the most humane action is to kill the host.'

The Priests said prayers over each of the officers and then recited the exorcism rites, naming the daemons and commanding them to leave in the name of the Archangel Uriel. Both exorcisms were successful. The officers were very weak as they had been imprisoned by the daemons for a long time, but they thanked the Priests profusely for freeing them.

Kanaka floated down to the dais and said, 'Mab, we should ask them to work together, the priests, the administrator and the military officers should develop a plan as to how we proceed. The officers will most probably know who else in the leadership is infected. We will return in two or three days to review the plan with them.'

Mab replied, 'Yes, Master Kanaka, I will ask Dassi to put that to them. Hopefully, Master Uvren will be able to make more sense of the language in that time.'

Kanaka said, 'I am very confident that we will. He was actually following and understanding the translation by Dassi. I think it was the speed and dialect rather than the meaning of the words that he was finding difficult.'

Mab mind-messaged Dassi and asked her to explain to the priests, the administrator and the military officers what Kanaka wanted them to do. She then thanked them all and said they would return to the church in three days. Kanaka said, 'Mab, we should go now.' Mab unlocked and opened the church doors, floated upwards and slowly out into the square.

Kanaka said, 'The same formation as before, Mab, lead on.'

Mab flew over the market, which was still thronging with people, then steeply upwards, rapidly gaining elevation through the cloud belt, the upper atmosphere and out into the solar system. She stopped at the edge of the solar system. Master Uvren asked if they could stay there for a while just to gaze at the planets. Kanaka said, 'It is beautifully serene. We will pause for a few minutes.'

A voice said, 'Yes, and it is ours.'

Kanaka said, 'Show yourself.' A huge face appeared before them. It looked like that of a goat but with vicious red eyes and huge black horns. Red steam gushed from its mouth and nostrils. Kanaka said, 'Who or what are you?'

The creature said, 'I am the brother of Mahazael, who was slain by Uriel.'

Mab said, 'You are Samael.'

Samael said, 'And you are the witch, Mabdelore. Know that there is balance in the multiverse. The death of my brother has damaged this balance and it is being damaged further by your presence here. This is our realm, you will leave this place and never return otherwise, your life and soul will be forfeit.' The face then vanished.

Kanaka said, 'Everyone, leave mind-space now.'

Mab woke to find the other masters were being checked by the medics, who were asking all to drink as much water as possible. Mab started to rise but felt stiff and surprisingly tired. Kanaka looked at her and said, 'It seems we have been away most of the day; it's dinner and bed for me. Everyone, can we meet first thing in the morning to discuss?'

The masters all nodded wearily and started to make their way out of the library. Mab walked with Lamm, making her way back to the suite. Lamm said, 'This balance thing, do you think there is anything in that?'

Mab replied, 'It's a good question, I don't know.'

Lamm said, 'Do you remember when we were on our way to the Palace, and you said that you thought something was wrong, but you just couldn't grab hold of it?'

Mab said, 'Yes.'

Lamm replied, 'Well, I feel like that now. It's like an itch that I can't scratch, something obvious, but I can't quite see it.'

Mab stopped, looked at Lamm and said, 'Can you talk about it?'

Lamm replied, 'Yes when you think back to the death of Mahazael. It was a Prince of Hell, probably millions of years old, one of only four such beings. That's a huge loss for 'evil kind' if you see what I mean. But it seems to have been accepted without consequence?'

Mab said, 'Yes, I do see what you mean. If there was a balance, the loss of Mahazael really would tilt the scales but nothing has happened. Let's sleep on it and talk about it tomorrow morning. Would you like to join us for dinner tonight?'

Lamm replied, 'Thanks for the offer, but no, a quick snack and then bed for me. I'll make up for it with a huge breakfast tomorrow morning!'

Mab made her way to the suite and found Izzy, Charly and Cat relaxing with a bottle of red wine. Izzy jumped up, ran to Mab, hugged her and said, 'How did your trip go? Did you get a friendly reception?'

Mab replied, 'Mixed, I'd say. We got a few of the leaders on our side but we are giving them some space to come up with a plan they think will work.'

Izzy said, 'You look tired, sit down I'll pour you a goblet of wine. We have already eaten, but I'll get you some fruit, bread and cheese.'

Mab replied wearily, 'That would be great, Izzy, but I think I'll have a shower and an early night.'

Izzy looked concerned and said, 'Are you feeling all right?'

Mab replied, 'It's something Lamm said to me. I can't stop thinking about it. My senses are telling me that something is wrong, something important that I've missed. Izzy, first thing tomorrow, I want you, Charly and Cat to leave the Guild. Go somewhere safe until I contact you. Tell no one that you are leaving or where you are going. Don't go to our house in the mountains. When I think it is safe, I will come and find you.'

Cat said, 'Izzy, we can go to my parent's house.'

Charly said, 'Mab, are we in danger?'

Mab replied, 'My senses tell me that there is great danger. But I don't know what it is or when it will happen. Promise me that you three will leave first thing in the morning.'

Izzy said, 'Yes, we will pack now and leave at first light.'

Mab said, 'Izzy, you pack. I'll have my shower and we'll take a goblet of wine to bed with us. It may help me sleep.'

Chapter Fourteen: The Balance and the Foreboding

Mab and Izzy woke early. Charly and Cat were already up with saddle bags packed and ready to go. Breakfast was laid out on the dining table, together with hot coffee. Mab was hungry so she tucked in while the girls were preparing to leave. Mab walked with them to the stables, dawn was only just rising, so there were no stable hands around to help ready the horses. Mab said, 'Izzy, take lady. She will look after you.'

Charly and Cat found their own horses and saddled up. Mab hugged and kissed Izzy and whispered, 'It won't be long until we're together again. If I know that you are safe, I can keep myself safe more easily.'

As they rode off, Mab reached out with her senses and said, 'Amarok!'

Amarok replied, 'I hear you, high-one.'

Mab said, 'My partner Izzy and her two friends are travelling from the Guild Westward. Could you ask your brethren to watch over them?'

Amarok replied, 'Yes, it will be done. Do you expect danger?'

Mab replied, 'I sense that something is wrong, but I cannot yet grasp the nature of the threat.'

Amarok replied, 'That is strange indeed, for I have sensed the same thing. An inexplicable foreboding.'

Mab said, 'Yes, that is a good way of describing it. We must stay alert and exercise caution until the threat is manifest. Thank you, Amarok.'

Mab went for a long, slow walk around the campus. The air was cool and refreshing, but she was glad she had donned her master's robe to keep her cosy. She wanted to speak to her mother but that had to be reserved for emergencies, life or death situations. She had to face and solve her own problems. She felt much better knowing that Izzy and their roommates had gone to a safe place. Samael's words kept coming back to her 'The balance… further damaged by your presence here…' Was this true? What balance? Why should there be a balance? Was our intervention in the other plane the right thing to do?

Lamm's words. The itch that can't be scratched, thought Mab. The consequences of killing Mahazael. Why have there been none? And then it came to her, it was her mother that killed Mahazael or at least delivered the fatal blow. Would it not be her that would bear the consequences? Mab started to worry for her mother, but then she brought her palms together in front of her chest, fingers pointing up in the prayer position and said,

'No, I was fully responsible for the attack and for the killing of Mahazael, not my mother. If there are consequences, I will face them. There can be no balance in the fight against evil, and slavery is a great evil.'

'My daughter in whom I am well pleased,' said a voice behind her. Mab spun around and threw out her witch senses, but there was no one there.

The masters assembled in Kanaka's office. Mab went straight for the breakfast platters closely followed by Lamm. Kanaka said, 'Help yourselves.' Mab sat down to a plate filled with pastries, cold meats, a selection of fruits and a large mug of hot coffee. Kanaka said, 'I can see everyone is hungry after the long session yesterday. Let me try to summarise what I think we achieved. Firstly, we made contact with the Head Priest, Ogan, and the Chief Administrator, Padwa. The latter was possessed by a daemon, which Mab expelled. We were also visited by two senior officers from the military, Kassa and Obiala. Both hosted daemons which the priests exorcised, but this was only possible because Mab provided them with the daemon's names. This is good progress because we now have a group made up of senior priests, military officers and the chief administrator, all of whom want to work with us to free their people. We left them the task of developing a plan of attack. We agreed to return in three days to review the plan with them and take the first steps. On the negative side, however, on our return journey, we stopped for a few minutes to take in the scenery. We were confronted by a daemon ruler, Samael, who said it was the brother of Mahazael. It told us not to come back otherwise, our lives and souls would be forfeit. It was a fearsome sight. It also alluded to Mab and her mother upsetting 'the balance' unless you tell us otherwise, Mab, we have no idea what that means. Comments?'

There was silence until Jessam said, 'I think we made an extraordinary degree of progress. The daemon ruler was certainly a very nasty surprise, but what else would we expect? The adjacent plane appears to be rife with the creatures, far more so than our plane. We had a ruler here, so should we not expect to find one, or more, there?'

Sirak said, 'I agree with that Jessam. However, I wonder if we are only seeing part of a much bigger picture. How many planes are there? How does the battle between good and evil play out across the planes? Is there some kind of balance or agreement between the good and the evil over territory?'

Kanaka said, 'Mab, what is your view on this balance question?'

Mab replied, 'I don't know if there is a balance, nor do I care. The word of a daemon means nothing, it could be true or half-true but is most probably a lie; however, whether true or untrue it is irrelevant. We have successfully freed ourselves from a future of slavery under these vile creatures, but the people on our adjacent plane are already enslaved and have been for generations. I cannot allow that to stand under any circumstances, I will not abandon them.' There was a long silence, and then Mab said, 'Masters, I must share something with you. But first, Master Lamm, could you repeat what you said to me last night about an itch that you couldn't scratch?'

Lamm said, 'Yes, Mab, of course. I was explaining to Mab that I have felt for some time that there was something wrong, something that I couldn't articulate, regarding the death of Mahazael. An itch that I couldn't quite scratch. But it came to me when we met his brother on our return journey yesterday. The gist of what I asked Mab was when you consider that Mahazael was a prince of hell, one of only four rulers, probably millions of years old, it is surprising that there haven't been any proportional consequences following its death at our hands.'

Kanaka looked pensive and said, 'Yes, it is obvious now you have said it.'

Mab said, 'This morning, I sent my partner Izzy and our roommates away to stay in the mountains until I advised them that it was safe to return to the Guild. Since my discussion with Master

Lamm, my witch senses have been screaming at me. We are likely to be attacked, but I don't know the nature of the attack or when it is likely to occur and that worries me. It suggests the attack will not originate from this plane. I mind-messaged Amarok this morning just after Izzy left and asked him to watch over her on the road, which he agreed to do. But he also has a feeling of foreboding which he cannot interpret.'

Kanaka said, 'I think all we can do is increase the level of security around the campus. But, if we are attacked from the adjacent plane, it will be by daemon spirits, not humans. The humans there have not reached our level of development with respect to mind-space and sorcery. The spirits will travel through mind space in the same way we travelled to them.'

Mab replied, 'Yes, I think that is correct, Master Kanaka. However, it is not the same. A daemon would need to leave its host and then have a limited amount of time before it was dragged back to the Abyss. The question is, would a daemon, with a host on the adjacent plane, have sufficient time to travel here, attack the Guild and then return to its host?'

Boe said, 'Mab, I think the answer to your question would depend on what you mean by 'attack the Guild.' Let's postulate that the daemons would not travel here in great numbers due to the process of leaving their host and re-entering the same or another host being non-trivial. Also, the fact that they know they are currently under attack, with a number of their brethren already sent back to the Abyss. Now assume this small number of daemons have sufficient time to travel from the adjacent plane to the Guild. What scenario involves two or three enemy agents arriving, entering a facility, completing a specific task in a very short space of time, followed by rapid extraction?'

Kanaka said, 'Assassination.'

Boe replied, 'Precisely.'

Jessam said, 'I suspect these assassins won't be your 'run of the mill' daemon. Most probably specialists, perhaps, literally, coming straight from hell?'

Mab replied, 'Target's?'

Jessam said, 'Mab, you've got to be joking! We are the targets with you at the top of the list.'

Mab, with a wry smile on her face, said, 'Yes, I was joking.'

Sirak said, 'What do we do?'

Mab replied, 'We wait for them to arrive and then kill them.'

Kanaka beamed at Mab and said, 'Well, that's that problem sorted!'

Sirak said, 'We bait them, lay a trap?'

Boe said, 'How reliable are our new friends in the adjacent plane? Can they be trusted?'

Mab replied, 'We don't know. They seem to be on board, but we have no way of knowing if our discussions have leaked out to the daemon leadership. Perhaps we will walk into a trap when we next visit.'

Boe said, 'I think they will attack your physical body, preferably when you are in mind-space and can't do anything to defend yourself.'

Kanaka said, 'I think this comes back to security. We need tight security around our physical bodies when we are in mind-space and as much warning as possible if there is an attack. Perhaps, as Sirak suggests, we lay a trap. If we assume the details of our next visit have leaked, the assassins are likely to attack when we are in mind-space. So, we send two or three masters only. The rest remain locked in the Library to protect our physical bodies.'

Mab said, 'I need to go in order to identify the daemons and help the priests expel them. So, I propose that Master Kanaka, Master Uvren and I go on the visit with the rest of you protecting the library and the Guild?'

Boe said, 'I think that is the best option. We should plan on several layers of security to ensure we have time to wake you if there is a serious attack.'

Kanaka said, 'Boe, could you and Lamm develop a security plan for our next visit? Focus on what is needed here at the Guild. Mab and I will think about what we want to achieve on the mission. Uvren, you should continue developing your understanding of their language.'

Jessam said, 'Sirak and I are travelling back home immediately after this meeting, but we will return here tomorrow evening. Can I suggest we review the arrangements over dinner tomorrow night?'

Kanaka said, 'Yes, that would be perfect.'

Mab returned to the now empty suite, climbed back into bed and slept through the rest of the morning. She woke, had a couple of pastries and a mug of hot coffee and snatched up Dawn-Breaker on her way out, heading for the playing fields. As she approached, she suddenly ran full-tilt towards the boundary fence, dived high into the air, somersaulted over the fence, drew Dawn-Breaker and cut three vertical strokes in the air before hitting the ground running. She stopped in the middle of the sports field, legs relaxed with a slight bend of the knees, her right hand pointing forward and her left hand holding Dawn-Breaker horizontally over her head. She then slowed her breathing and launched into Lamu, the sword Kata. Her moves were the very definition of precision. At times, Dawn-Breaker was moving so fast that the blade could not be seen and at other times, it was moving slowly with perfect poise and position before she launched into the next set of moves. The final sequence brought her to a stop in precisely the same position as when she started the Kata. She held the position perfectly still for two minutes, her heart rate and breathing slow, and then sheathed Dawn-Breaker and relaxed, albeit saturated with sweat.

'High one, I am here,' said Amarok. Mab turned and saw the great white wolf waiting near the horse enclosure and walked towards him.

Mab said, 'Is Izzy in trouble?'

Amarok replied, 'No, High-one, your partner and friends are safe. You need not worry for them, but I have disturbing news from elsewhere.'

Mab waited until she reached Amarok and said, 'Tell me.'

Amarok said, 'Masters Jessam and Sirak are both dead.'

Mab was too shocked to speak. Then she said, 'Amarok, wait. Let me message Masters Lamm and Kanaka. I would rather your message be heard by more than I.'

Mab mind-messaged Lamm, 'Please come to the horse enclosure and bring Master Kanaka. It is important.'

A few minutes later, Kanaka and Lamm appeared, walking quickly towards the enclosure. Mab said, 'Amarok has disturbing news.'

Amarok said, 'Masters Jessam and Sirak are dead.'

Mab said, 'Do we know for sure that they are dead?'

Amarok replied, 'Yes, High-One. I have not seen myself, but the pack leader speaks the truth. The killing was witnessed by a scout who was lucky to escape with her life. The scout took the pack leader to the scene, and he confirmed the two dead were Jessam and Sirak. The pack leader was present when we returned to the Palace and recognised the two masters by their scent.'

Lamm said, 'Do we know how they were killed?'

Amarok replied, 'The scout saw the two riders approaching and so hid in the undergrowth. She then heard and smelled the horses go into a panic. She was downwind, so she knew she was not responsible. But then she picked up another smell that she didn't recognise, she described it as meat that had been left in the sun for many days, but much worse. She lifted her eyes above the undergrowth. The horses had bolted. The masters were doing battle with a dark shadow, it had yellow slits for eyes and large fangs but otherwise, its body was amorphous. The masters were attacking it with fire and psychic energy blasts, but the creature was largely unaffected. The scout said the presence of the creature made her feel weak and it withered the vegetation. The masters were weakened to the point where they could stand no longer. They were then bitten and sucked dry by the creature. I am sorry, but you must know this, the scout said the masters died screaming in agony, as though their very souls had been sucked from them. The scout broke cover and ran. The creature came after her, but her initial sprint put sufficient distance between them for her to recover her strength. She is known for her speed; she ran like the wind and reached the great Deeping forest which the creature would not enter.'

Kanaka said, 'So this is the assassin. What could this creature be? Is it a type of daemon? I have carried out some research in this area, but I haven't come across anything that matches that description.'

Lamm said, 'Mab, perhaps your mother would know?'

Amarok said, 'High-One, there is no need to contact your mother. I know what it is. It is the answer to my foreboding; without question, it is a Dread Lord.'

Kanaka asked, 'A Dread Lord, what is that?'

Amarok said, 'It is a creature from the very bowels of Hell. It should not be here, it feeds on the souls of the damned and carries with it disease and pestilence.'

Mab said, 'Amarok, can it be killed?'

Amarok replied, 'High-One, I do not know. It is beyond my ken, but unless it is stopped, it will devour everything. It will take the life and soul of every living thing on this plane.'

Mab said, 'Amarok, we will consider our options. Keep in touch.' Amarok loped off and was soon out of sight.

Mab said, 'We must hunt this thing down and kill it.'

Kanaka said, 'We don't know if we can kill it.'

Mab said, 'We can try.'

Kanaka said, 'Then we should go now. We will follow in the tracks of Jessam and Sirak until we find them and it.' The stables made horses available for them. They rode for around one hour and quickly found the scene of the battle. It was evident that the masters had run off the trail to reach cover but without success. The vegetation in the area had died back, and there were scorch marks on bushes and shrubs. The two masters were lying only a short distance apart. The bodies were dried husks and the expressions on their faces were horrible to behold. It was clear that they had died in the utmost agony.

Lamm said, 'Mab, do your witch senses reveal anything.'

Mab reached out with her senses and said, 'Yes, the creature is still here. It is moving close to the forest line. Follow me.'

They rode off the trail and towards the forest and then hugged the tree line. Mab pointed and said, 'There, do you see it?'

Kanaka said, 'Yes, a dark shadow against the green of the forest. Amarok said it would not enter the forest, so stay close to the treeline, engage with it and retreat into the forest if needed.'

Mab said, 'Let's go, get it.'

They moved into a canter and got as close as they dared before dismounting and leading the horses into the forest and tethering them. The masters ran along the treeline to get closer to the creature. Kanaka launched a fireball at it to get its attention. The Dread Lord turned and moved towards them. It was a truly horrifying sight. They soon picked up the stench that exuded from it. Kanaka remained where he was, Lamm moved further ahead and stopped closer to the tree line. Mab donned her silver skin of power and moved forward to meet it; she tried to mind-meld with it, but it didn't seem to be aware. She kept walking, the creature moved backwards. Mab stopped and the creature then stopped. The Dread Lord seemed to be studying her. It then looked around as if it was expecting to be attacked. It raised a giant claw and a wisp of black smoke meandered towards Mab, who stood perfectly still. The smoke approached her shimmering protective skin and then reared back. The creature lowered his claw and the smoke disappeared. It then moved slowly towards Mab, its yellow slits following the slightest movement.

Mab gagged at the stench coming from the creature, she reached back and unsheathed Dawn-Breaker. The Dread Lord swiped a huge claw at Mab's head, but she dropped down and spun inwards, bringing Dawn-Breaker down with lightning speed on the claw, but it passed straight through as if it wasn't there. She immediately leapt away from the creature. Kanaka and Lamm launched fireballs and psychic blasts at the creature to draw its attention away from Mab. The fireballs had minimal effect and the psychic blasts had no effect. However, it had the desired result in that the creature turned away from Mab and moved towards them. Mab sheathed Dawn-Bringer and fired a missile of white light at its head. The missile went straight through, but the creature howled in pain. It once again turned towards Mab, who raised both her hands, palms facing outward and launched a torrent of silver flame at the creature's head, the Dread Lord howled in pain. Mab created an inferno of silver flame around the creature. She continually increased the intensity and so temperature of the inferno. The Dread Lord howled in an agony that it had never known possible; it thrashed around trying to escape, but the argent flame was too strong. It collapsed to the ground, but Mab did not relent, instead she pulled the inferno closer, tighter, compressing the flames and hugely increasing the burn temperature. It became like a small sun, so bright that it could not be looked upon. But Mab was still not satisfied; she compacted the colossal ball of energy, driving it further into the creature until every molecule of its being was consumed. Then, she dropped her arms and fell to her knees with exhaustion. Kanaka and Lamm rushed from the cover of the trees and found her kneeling on the still-smoking ground. Little remained of the Dread Lord other than a slick of a black tar-like substance.

Lamm went to get the horses while Kanaka sat with Mab on the scorched, now lifeless soil. Kanaka, hearing Lamm returning, shouted, 'Lamm, bring some provisions and the wine from my saddlebag.'

Lamm appeared a few minutes later with bread, cheese, fruit and a bottle of red wine, which they shared. Mab started to recover when she had something to eat, the wine really helped. She said, 'Thanks, I had no energy left. I'm beginning to feel better now.'

Kanaka went to look at the solidified remains of the Dread Lord, he gave it a few kicks and said, 'Do you think it's dead?' Mab and Lamm burst out laughing.

Mab said, 'Don't make me laugh, I'm too tired!'

Lamm said, 'Let's have another round of that wine before we go.'

Kanaka said, 'An excellent suggestion.'

The three Masters sat in silence and finished their provisions. Lamm broke the silence by saying, 'What should we do about Jessam and Sirak?'

Kanaka replied, 'I will instruct our people to recover the remains and return them to the schools. The schools will make the necessary arrangements for the burial ceremonies.'

Kanaka then looked at Mab and said, 'Mab, only if you are ready should we get to horse?'

Mab replied, 'Yes, Master Kanaka, I am looking forward to an early night.'

Kanaka said, 'Early nights are becoming more frequent these days or am I just getting old.'

Lamm said, 'I think both of those are correct Master Kanaka.'

Kanaka looked at Mab and rolled his eyes. Mab stifled her laughter and mind messaged Amarok, 'Amarok, we have just encountered the Dread Lord, it has been slain albeit with some difficulty. Could you thank the female wolf who witnessed the deaths of Masters Jessam and Sirak and provided us with much needed information? Better still, I would like to thank her personally at a convenient time for her and you.'

Amarok replied, 'High-One, I am pleased that you have vanquished the creature. I will gladly bring Sheva to meet you. You do her a great honour which will be appreciated by all wolf-kind.' When they arrived back at the Guild Mab went directly to the suite, ate a huge volume of cheese, bread and dried fruit washed down with a large goblet of red wine and went to bed.

Mab woke the next morning, had some pastries and hot coffee for breakfast and then went for her usual walk around the campus. Most students were back in school and studying hard. The masters would also be busy teaching, although a lot of the practical lessons were taught by advanced students. Mab thought about Jessam and Sirak, who were Principals of their schools, and how sorely they would be missed by their families. Then she thought about Izzy and wondered what she was doing.

Amarok said, 'High-One, I have brought Sheva as requested.' Mab turned and saw Amarok and Sheva standing close to the horse enclosure. She walked towards them. Sheva was almost as tall as Amarok although much leaner and less muscled. Amarok bowed as Mab approached, Sheva looked nervously at Amarok and quickly followed his example. Mab knelt down in front of Sheva and mind-messaged Amarok to translate 'Sheva, I want to thank you for your bravery yesterday. Many more would have died if you hadn't escaped from the Dread Lord and passed the information to your pack leader. It was your great speed that saved you and many others from a terrible death.'

Mab cupped Sheva's head in her hands and allowed a silver skin of energy to wash over the wolf's body which cleansed, strengthened and renewed her. The wolf moaned in pleasure. Mab then kissed Sheva on the nose and hugged her.'

Amarok said, 'High-One, Sheva thanks you for this great honour. She says she will never forget this moment or your love and kindness.'

Mab smiled warmly at Sheva and looking at Amarok, said, 'Amarok, do you know how this Dread Lord could pass into our plane?'

Amarok replied, 'It would need to have been released by one of the rulers. However, such creatures cannot be controlled or directed. It would be attracted to powerful beings who would satisfy its hunger more than those with no powers. Jessam and Sirak would shine like bright stars amongst the common people of this area. If it hadn't come across the two masters it would most probably have found its way to the closest school which would be the Guild.'

Mab said, 'The masters and I travelled to an adjacent plane recently, one that is enslaved by daemons. We are trying to free the people there. However, on the return journey we were confronted by a ruler, its name is Samael, a bother of Mahazael. It spoke of there being a balance of power and that my presence on that plane was damaging the balance. Do you know anything of this balance?'

Amarok replied, 'On the other plane, was there mention of a great prophet?'

Mab said, 'Yes, one of the Priests mentioned a prophet who had been imprisoned for troublemaking. Is this of any relevance to our mission to free the people there?'

Amarok said, 'Did you meet this prophet?'

Mab replied, 'No, should we free him first?'

Amarok replied, 'High-One, no, you must not meet him or interfere with his imprisonment or his execution. You must discuss this with your mother, much may be at stake.'

Mab said, 'What is at stake?'

Amarok replied, 'High-One, there is a constant battle, you may consider it to be a balance, between good and evil. Certain people, and events, can have a crucial effect on the future and the balance of power; the prophet is such a person.'

Mab replied, 'Why has my mother not told me this?'

Amarok said, 'High-One, you will have to ask her that question. However, you have said before that we are friends so I will speak openly what is in my mind. You are the daughter of Uriel, you will come into your true powers soon and then you will understand your reason for existing and your role in the balance of things. Everyday your powers grow stronger, only yesterday you slew a Dread Lord one of the most fearsome beings in the Universe. You have a destiny to fulfil, and it is greater than being a Guild Master, but I think you already know this truth.'

Mab said, 'Yes Amarok, but what is my destiny?'

'Daughter, your destiny is unknown even to me. However, my hope is that you will be a handmaiden of the host, helping in the battle against evil across space and time,' said Uriel.

Amarok bowed and backed away. Mab turned to find her mother walking towards her. She was wearing casual clothes, a light blouse, denim trousers and black leather boots. Her silver hair was blowing across her face, she looked like a young fresh-faced farm girl but there was a palpable aura of power around her. Uriel embraced Mab and said, 'This is the purpose for which you, and I, were created. You have not yet reached the zenith of your powers, but that time is coming soon.'

Mab said, 'What will happen to me then?'

Uriel replied, 'You will have no need of your earthly body, you will become a spirit, you may go wherever you wish and appear however you wish. You will become as I, an immortal. But, you will have responsibilities. You understand humans, their hopes and aspirations, their emotions, the meaning of their short lives. You will be tasked with the protection of the good and the punishment of the evil. The Dread Lord was released onto this plane by the rulers, it could have consumed every soul in this world had you not slain it.'

Mab said, 'Samael told me that my presence on the adjacent plane threatened the balance. I was intending to go back there tomorrow morning to free more enslaved people. What should I do?'

Uriel said, 'That plane is sensitive because of the Prophet. I will meet you at the church. Yes, I know the church, and I know you have been there. I have been there many times; you may have seen my portrait?'

Mab simply stared at her. Uriel grabbed hold of Mab and hugging her tightly said, 'You look worried Mab, there is no need. I will see you tomorrow, best if you come alone.'

Uriel turned to Amarok and said, 'Thank you for all your help, you are a true friend,' and then she vanished.

Mab mind-messaged Lamm, 'Mother wants me to go with her tomorrow to the adjacent plane. It seems to be more complicated than we thought. Can we discuss?'

Lamm replied, 'Kanaka is up to his eyes in work; let me get back to you.'

Mab made her way back to the suite to have a late lunch. Lamm mind-messaged her and said, 'Dinner in his office tonight.' Mab had lunch and slept for another five or six hours before making her way to Kanaka's office. She still felt weary from her battle with the Dread Lord, it drained her resources far more than she had realised. She knocked and entered Kanaka's office; she saw his desk was covered with papers. Masters Paull and Lamm were seated at the table, which, Mab was pleased to see, was also covered with food. She took a seat next to Lamm.

Kanaka said, 'Paull, I give up. Why don't you just take this stuff away and come back with something that I can sign-off?'

Paull said, 'Yes, of course Master Kanaka. Let's have our dinner now, I will do the work tonight and you can sign-it off tomorrow morning.'

Kanaka walked over, sat opposite Mab and said, 'That's great, I'm glad I got that stuff sorted out.'

Lamm smiled over at Paull who rolled his eyes in response. Mab smiled warmly at Kanaka and said, 'Master Kanaka, you work too hard. Let's do some sword practice tomorrow?'

Kanaka said, 'Now that's the best suggestion I've had all day.'

Paull rolled his eyes once more. Mab laughed and said, 'The sports field, mid-day, real swords.'

Kanaka looked at Mab and replied, 'That's fighting talk young lady, I'll be there.'

The masters started to fill their plates and wine goblets. Lamm said, 'We had intended to visit the adjacent plane first thing tomorrow. But with the death of Jessam and Sirak and the intervention of Mab's mother we need to rethink the plan. Mab could you update us on your thinking following your mothers visit.'

Mab said, 'The situation in the other plane is complicated. I get the feeling that the daemons think they are in charge but in fact they are being led down a particular path by the Angels. For example, when we were there previously, they mentioned a Prophet who was imprisoned for fomenting unrest. My first thought was that we should free him, but it appears that we must not interfere with his imprisonment or imminent execution. So, there are things going on that we do not understand. My mother wants to meet me there tomorrow, hopefully I will find out more.'

Kanaka replied, 'It sounds like there is already a plan and your mother is worried that we go in there and mess things-up. It makes sense for you to go alone; meet your mother there and let us know how she thinks we should deal with the daemon problem.'

Mab said, 'Yes I'll do that Master Kanaka.'

Lamm said, 'Did your mother say anything about Samael?'

Mab replied, 'No, Master Lamm, she seemed uninterested in Samael and was more concerned about the Prophet.'

Kanaka said, 'We are dealing with beings who think, and plan, in terms of millennia rather than years. We can only be guided by Mab's mother with regard to what we can or can't do in the adjacent planes. In any case, let's enjoy our meal and talk more about this tomorrow when Mab returns.'

After dinner, Mab returned to the suite and went straight to bed. She thought about Izzy and wondered what she was doing. She decided she would go and see her soon, stay a couple of days and then travel back to the Guild with her.

Chapter Fifteen: The Angel and the Prophet

Mab woke early, had a light breakfast, donned her robe and made her way to the Lost Library. She was getting comfy on her cushion when her mother appeared. Uriel said, 'Come, give me your hand.' Mab went to her mother's side and took her hand. Uriel said, 'Now, do as I do. See the door to mind-space, move forward through the door, now see the church in your mind, focus on it, now, with me, pull yourself to it.'

Mab materialised inside the church, still holding her mother's hand. Mab said, 'So I am really here, my body is actually here?'

Uriel said, 'Yes, but you have to think of your mind and body as one. Let's do some practice while we are waiting for your friends to arrive. I want you to travel, in the same way you travelled here, up to the apex of the roof.'

Mab thought for a moment and then followed the same procedure. She vanished and then reappeared floating at the Apex of the roof. Uriel said, 'Very good, now I want you to stay where you are, keep your eyes on me, and vanish. You move into mind-space but stay focused on your current position.' Mab followed the same procedure, but this time, as she moved into mind-space, she remained focused on looking at her mother. Her body vanished, but her mind was still present. Uriel said, 'Very good, the Priests are coming, so I will join you up there.'

Uriel vanished and reappeared beside Mab and whispered to her, 'You need to keep practicing; there are many subtleties that you will only learn through doing.'

The doors to the church opened and a group of six Priests, the Administrator, two military Officers and a young girl walked in. The group waited in silence. Mab materialised on the dais, the priests knelt, the administrator bowed his head, but the officers simply stared. Mab mind-linked with Dassi and said, 'Good morning, I trust you are all well?'

Padwa looked at Mab, she could see pleading in his eyes as he glanced at the Officers and said, 'No High One, we are not well.'

Mab looked at the Officers and realised they were not Kassa and Obiala. It was difficult to see their faces as they were in full military uniform. One of the Officers looked directly at Mab and said, 'We have already met. I am Samael. You have disregarded my warning.'

Mab replied, 'Yes, I see you, Samael and this is your colleague Loupa, so soon returned from the Abyss? Or, perhaps you managed to survive as a rat or snake or something else equally appropriate?'

Samael replied, 'You will be silent in my presence, witch, I warned you that I would have your life and your soul.'

There was a flash of blinding light behind Mab as Uriel appeared dressed in silver, her huge white wings spreading across the full width of the church. None could look upon her countenance; the priests dropped and lay prone on the floor. Samael shrieked in pain and backed away from her light. Loupa fled from his host body, which dropped to the floor. Her voice was like thunder. 'You dare threaten my daughter!'

The skies grew dark, bolts of lightning forked over and around the church. Samael said, 'Great one, I did not know...'

'Silence!' commanded Uriel. A bolt of lightning blasted through the roof of the church and struck Samael in the chest, propelling it backwards and slamming its body against the church doors. Uriel folded her wings and floated towards him. Samael was twisting and turning its head, trying to avoid her light, which it could not endure. Uriel looked down upon it and said, 'I should rend you now for your insolence. There will be no more attacks on my daughter and there will be no more daemons or other beasts from Hades released onto her home plane, which is under my protection. You will swear on this now. But, beware, Samael, if you break your vow to me, I will pursue you and slay you, even if I have to drag you from the very bowels of the Abyss. Speak now!'

Samael, writhing in pain, replied, 'I so swear, my vow is given and will not be broken.'

Uriel said, 'Leave this body and return to where you belong.' The daemon Samael fled the body of the soldier who slumped to the floor, injured but still alive. Mab told the priests to rise and seek medical help for the two soldiers. Uriel took Mab's hand and said, 'Make yourself unseen, and come with me.'

Uriel and Mab vanished and flew from the church and across the village towards the foothills of the mountains. Mab could see a large crowd of people; they were shouting, and some were crying. Many soldiers were there; a man had been nailed to a wooden cross. Uriel stopped some distance from the scene. Mab said, 'Mother, we have to stop this!'

Uriel replied, 'Look closer, he is the great Prophet.'

Mab looked closer and said, 'I don't understand, is he possessed by an Angel?'

Uriel said, 'No, he is filled with the power of the holy spirit. Through his death and resurrection, he will save many souls, his life story will endure for millennia. This had to happen before any intervention in this plane.'

Mab continued to watch in silence until Uriel said, 'Time for you to go home, or perhaps you will visit your partner Izzy?'

Mab's face blushed and she said, 'I will go to the Guild first; I have sword practice with Master Kanaka this afternoon. Following that, I will visit Izzy and bring her back to the Guild. Do you think the daemon Samael will keep its word?'

Uriel said, 'Yes, it will keep its word. I suggest you do not make any further interventions in this plane at present. I will let you know when it is safe to do so. However, there are many other tasks that I have for you in time and space. Your powers are developing apace, perhaps in a few years you may even earn your wings!'

Mab replied, 'Wings, you mean I could be an Angel?'

Uriel smiled and said, 'Mab, you are already far more powerful than most Angels, but then you are my daughter. We shall see, perhaps I should give you a set of little wings to practice with?'

'No, thank you!' replied Mab, laughing.

Uriel moved closer to Mab, smiled warmly, and said, 'I must stay here for a while, and you must go. I will see you soon.'

Mab smiled back, vanished and reappeared in the suite at the Guild. She lay on her bed and slept for several hours. When Mab woke, she realised that she was late for sword practice, so she vanished and reappeared on the sports field to find Kanaka practicing a sword Kata. He had clearly been there for some time, as he was dripping with sweat. Mab said, 'Master Kanaka, sorry. I fell asleep.'

Kanaka replied, 'Don't worry, Mab, I guess you have had a very busy morning. Why don't we have a late lunch together in my office?'

Mab replied, 'That would be great. I haven't eaten since breakfast. Should I message Lamm and ask him to join us?'

Kanaka said, 'Yes, good idea, ask him to round up Boe and Paull if they are available.' Mab messaged Lamm and he replied in the affirmative.

Kanaka and Mab walked to the kitchen area in the main building. Kanaka asked the staff to prepare lunch for the five masters in his office. Mab had a hot coffee while Kanaka took a quick shower. The lunch and the rest of the masters arrived promptly. Kanaka said, 'Just to make you all aware, the School of Psych and Sorcery and the Guild of Witches and Warlocks have appointed new Principals. Masters Hanney and Taggar, respectively. Good choices in my opinion, but clearly they do not have the experience of Masters Sirak and Jessam. Lamm, I had thought you might be interested, but I was told that you did not apply?'

Lamm replied, 'No, I did not apply. I am content with my role here at the Guild for at least the next few years.'

Kanaka nodded, turned to Mab, and said, 'Can you bring us up to date with your visit to the adjacent plane this morning?'

Mab said, 'Yes, Master Kanaka, as you know, I went with my mother to meet the priests at the church. She intended to leave the discussion with the Priests and the Administrator to me, but one of the soldiers was host to Samael and another was host to Loupa, who, if you remember, I expelled on our last visit. As you know, Samael told me not to visit the adjacent plane again or my life and soul would be forfeit. Unfortunately, it repeated the threat without realising my mother was present in the church. As you can imagine, she reacted badly. Samael was permitted to live only on the basis that it made a solemn oath that our plane would remain free of daemons and other creatures from the Abyss. Samael swore the oath, and my mother allowed it to escape back to the Abyss.'

Lamm asked, 'Can Samael be trusted to keep its oath?'

Mab replied, 'In normal circumstances, no, but it made the oath to Uriel, an Archangel, who told it if the oath was broken, she would drag him from the Abyss and slay him. Samael was terrified, I am sure that it will not break the oath.'

Kanaka said, 'This is great news! It means we, on this plane, are safe and can get our lives back to normal. Mab, you must thank your mother on behalf of all of us for her intervention.'

Mab replied, 'I will, Master Kanaka. She also explained the reason for caution in the adjacent plane. You may remember a mention of a Prophet? We witnessed his execution. He was nailed to a wooden cross and killed as punishment for, in their view, insurrection. But when I looked at him closely, he was infused with celestial power. My mother said the story of this man's life, death and resurrection would change the course of history and be recited for millennia. She said we must not take any further action in that plane until she advises otherwise.'

Boe smiled warmly and said, 'And what of you, Mab, did your Mother talk of your beginnings or your future?'

Mab replied, 'Yes, Master Boe, she told me that my powers would continue to grow apace and that I would be helping her with various tasks across space and time. She hinted that if I work hard, I may be able to get my wings! Can you imagine that, me an Angel?!'

Boe said, 'Mab, we think you are already an Angel!'

Kanaka said, 'I hope this doesn't mean you will be leaving us, Mab?'

Mab replied, 'Master Kanaka, how could you even think that? This is my home, I will always remain a Master of the Guild of Sorcerers.'

Kanaka, with a wry smile on his face, replied, 'Yes, and think of all the free sword practice. If you keep it up, one of these days you will be as good as me.'

Mab smiled warmly at Kanaka and said, 'Yes, Master Kanaka.'

Book Two

Goddess of War

Chapter Sixteen: City of the Future

Mab and her adopted mother Uriel hovered in mind-space above a busy street in a huge city. Uriel explained that this was the beginning of the third millennium following Mab's birth. Mab said, 'There are so many people here, they all seem to be going somewhere, but in different directions. The lights and buildings are beautiful, but the noise is relentless, and the air is filthy.'

Uriel said, 'This is the age of the machine. They have developed machines for almost everything, but these machines are driven by fuels which produce noxious gases when burned.'

Mab asked, 'Why do they need these machines?'

Uriel replied, 'They don't need them, but there is avarice here the like of which you could not comprehend, which brings me to the reason we are here.'

Uriel and Mab flew upwards to the top of a nearby building and materialised on the roof. Uriel said, 'There is in this building a very rich and evil man who is responsible for the enslavement of thousands to chemical substances.'

Mab replied, 'What kind of substances?'

Uriel replied, 'They are chemicals that are usually injected into the blood. People become addicted to them and are so enslaved to those who own or control the chemicals. The timeline suggests that if we don't act now, the person involved will become too powerful. As with others of his ilk, he surrounds himself with warrior guards who use projectile and explosive weapons. However, more recently, he has engaged the services of a powerful black witch, but we don't know who that is.'

Mab reached out with her senses and said, 'There is so much interference. Wait, yes, I think I have found her. Whatever you have in mind, we should do it now.'

Uriel replied, 'Take me to her.'

Uriel and Mab materialised in an office room on the tenth floor of the building. There was a young woman standing with her back to the door, looking out the window. She turned and said, 'Hello, how can I help you?'

Mab looked closely at the woman, she was young and quite beautiful. Mab said, 'You will tell me who you are and what you do here.'

The woman said, 'My name is Rhiannon and I am a witch protector to Mr John Haskins, the President of this Corporation.'

Mab replied, 'We wish to speak to your master now, by that I mean immediately.'

Rhiannon replied, 'That will not be possible.'

Mab turned to her mother and said, 'He must be around here somewhere. It shouldn't take long to find him.'

Uriel, Mab and Rhiannon vanished and materialised on the top of the building. Uriel said to Rhiannon, 'This is my daughter Mabdelore, it would take less than two seconds for her to end your life. Do you want to live or die?'

Rhiannon said, 'I think it is you who will die.' She launched a psychic attack on Uriel, who merely smiled back at her. Mab vanished, reappeared behind Rhiannon and slammed the hilt of her sword, Dawn-Breaker, into her head.'

Uriel said, 'Immobilise her, we need to find Haskins.' Mab did as she was instructed, a few minutes later, they were back in Rhiannon's office.

Mab said, 'Why don't we split up and look for him?'

Uriel replied, 'Yes, but mind message me if you find him first.' Mab left the room, turned left and walked along a long corridor, the walls of which were lined with images of what she assumed were powerful businesspeople. She heard voices coming from behind a set of large double doors. Mab figured it must be a meeting room of sorts, so she vanished into mind space and floated into the room. There was a large table with around twenty people seated.

At the head of the table sat Haskins, Rhiannon's master; the others around the table referred to him as Mr Haskins. Mab sensed the second witch just in time; she was sitting alone in a dark corner of the room and her eyes locked with Mab's. Mab messaged her mother who appeared beside her in mind space. The witch in the corner stood up, Mab materialised and dropped down onto the table with a thump. There were shouts and cries of astonishment around the table. Mab shouted in a strong, coercer mode, 'Silence!' There was silence.

Mab pointed at the witch in the corner and said, 'You come here!' The witch walked slowly towards Mab, who reached out with her mind and slammed her backwards hard into the wall. The witch lifted her left hand, a number of darts flew at astonishing speed towards Mab, but as they approached, time slowed. Mab side-stepped, stopped the darts mid-flight and said, 'My mother wishes to speak with you.'

Uriel materialised beside Mab, she was glowing with a silver light which only Mab could look upon. Uriel asked, 'Do you know who I am?'

The black witch replied, 'No, but I know you are a high-one.' Shots rang out. Mab turned, saw the projectiles approaching and slapped them to the floor. She sent a psychic pulse outward that rendered all others in the room unconscious.

Uriel said, 'Your name?'

The witch replied, 'Morgana.'

Uriel replied, 'Yes, I thought I recognised the features. I met one of your line many years ago. Morgana, you and your acolyte Rhiannon have assisted Haskins in the enslavement of young people. Many lives have been ruined, many have died and many remain addicted and exploited. We have come here today to remedy the situation. Do you understand?'

Morgana said, 'No, I do not understand. I have vowed to protect my master and I am innocent of any crime.'

Uriel replied, 'You have protected Haskins, supported him in his corrupt business dealings and killed on his behalf. You are far from innocent. I would kill you now, but killing humans is anathema to me.'

Morgana replied, 'What then do you propose?'

Uriel looked at Mab. Mab lifted the unconscious Haskins off the floor and propelled him at great speed through the nearest floor-to-ceiling toughened glass window, where he dropped ten floors to his death. Mab looked at Morgana and said, 'Your vow is now dissolved. Would you like to follow him?'

Morgana looked at Uriel and said, 'Now I understand why you brought her. Will Rhiannon and I be permitted to leave?'

Uriel replied, 'I will give you a last chance to turn from the dark and embrace the light. You and Rhiannon may leave, but I warn you, if you disappoint me, Mabdelore will take your lives.'

The three vanished and appeared on the rooftop beside Rhiannon. Mab released Rhiannon and said, 'We will be watching, go now and do not return here.'

The witches translated and left Uriel and Mab alone. Uriel said, 'Mab, thank you once again for your help. I must leave now, but I wanted to let you know that the adjacent plane can now be cleansed if you are willing.'

Mab replied, 'Yes, the people there are desperate for our help. Has the issue with the Prophet been resolved?'

Uriel said, 'Yes, it is accomplished. You may now intervene, but beware, do not engage with daemon rulers, especially Samael. Summon me if necessary.' With that, Uriel vanished.

Mab sat on the parapet wall at the edge of the building's roof. Her legs hung over the side, child-like, as she looked down on the scene below. The machines were everywhere, roaring, hooting and belching fumes. The people appeared to be corralled at the sides of the machine space; Mab was astonished at their numbers and the way they walked around each other in seemingly every direction. She made herself unseen, floated down and moved along just above head height with the main flow of people. The sun was going down, but the artificial light from the machines and buildings seemed to get brighter. She studied the people; none seemed to be carrying weapons, although she thought that small projectile weapons could be easily concealed about their person. The people were dressed in many different types of clothes, she thought that if she dispensed with Dawn-Breaker, she wouldn't look too out of place. Mab returned to the top of the Haskins building and concealed her sword in a drainage downpipe. She then materialised in a doorway in the busy street below and joined the crowd in walking in a positive way, as if she were going somewhere important.

She was amazed at the smells, some enticing, others noxious, but the place was so alive. Mab heard loud music coming from a place across the road. She saw people crossing, the machines had stopped to let them pass, so she ran after them. Mab walked into the building and found lots of people drinking and talking. A young man came up to her and said, 'Would you like a drink?' Mab understood what he was saying, but could only reply directly by mind message. She hesitated, the young man said, 'Don't worry, no problem!' and turned to walk away.

Mab said, 'I would love some wine.'

The young man stopped, spun around and said, 'How did you do that!'

Mab replied, 'I can't speak your language, but I have learned to communicate using my mind. I hope I didn't scare you. What's your name?'

The man said, 'My name is Alexei, what's yours?'

Mab replied, 'Mabdelore, but you can call me Mab.'

Alexei said, 'Mab, this mind thing is amazing, but it will take a bit of getting used to!'

Mab replied, 'I've just arrived here. I'd love to try the food and drinks, but I don't have any of the local currency.'

Alexei said, 'No problem, let's get you a nice glass of wine and some food. Follow me.'

Alexei led Mab to a table at the very back of the club and close to a raised area that was roped off from the main dining space. Alexei said, 'What would you like?'

Mab replied, 'I eat anything, get me the same as you plus some wine.'

Alexei laughed and said, 'At last, a girl who knows what she wants!' Alexei called the waiter and ordered two extra-large veg-burgers with the full works and two large glasses of dry white wine.

When the food arrived, Mab's eyes nearly popped out of her head. The amount of food on her plate was staggering even by her measures. She thanked Alexei again and tucked in. Alexei explained to Mab that this was a club restaurant where people could eat and watch a show at the same time. Some nights they had singing and dancing, on other nights special acts like magicians or martial arts shows. Mab said, 'When you say martial arts, do you mean fighting to the death?'

Alexei laughed and said, 'No, not to the death. The fights are refereed. I shouldn't tell you this, but in the basement area here, they sometimes have cage-fights. These often end in someone being seriously injured. I've never seen anyone die, but it could easily happen.'

Mab said, 'So they are not allowed to use weapons, swords, for example?'

Alexei laughed again and replied, 'Mab, I think you are the strangest girl I have ever met. There is a cage fight on tonight if you are interested. There is no entrance fee, but you are expected to bet.'

Mab replied, 'Can anyone fight?'

Alexei said, 'There is an open invitation to anyone who wants to fight after the main event. Usually there are three or four bouts and people can place cash bets.'

Mab replied, 'Alexei, I'd love to see it. Could you get me in?'

Alexei said, 'Yes, if that's your thing. The main event starts in less than an hour, most of the people here will be going downstairs to watch the fights, the music upstairs hides the noises from below.'

Mab replied, 'Alexei, that meal was fantastic. Thanks so much,' as she leaned over and kissed him on the cheek.

Alexei said, 'I'll get you another drink!'

The restaurant began to thin out as people either left or made their way down a concealed narrow staircase at the back of the room. A live band was assembling on the roped-off area in the dining room. Alexei led Mab down the stairs. The basement room was large but dingy. The cage was in the centre of the room and consisted of four steel mesh walls, there was no roof, and only one steel mesh door to enter or exit the cage. The seating was basic wooden planks but tiered upwards away from the cage on all four sides. Alexei and Mab sat together on the back row, which offered a good, uninterrupted view of the cage.

The two competitors were already in the cage and limbering up. Alexei said, 'Mab, this can be very bloody. If you want to leave at any time, just let me know.'

Mab smiled at Alexei and said, 'Yes, don't worry, I'll let you know. So, the winner is basically the one left standing?'

Alexei replied, 'Yes, that's right, although just because someone is on the floor doesn't mean they can't be attacked.'

Mab said, 'The big guy looks incredibly strong. I don't think I have ever seen anyone with muscle development like that!'

Alexei replied, 'He is the current champion and a real street fighter. The smaller guy is the challenger. He is a martial arts expert.'

Mab said, 'What's a street fighter?'

Alexei replied, 'It means he has no particular fighting style but has a lot of experience and uses many unconventional, if not illegal, moves. Who do you think will win?'

Mab said, 'I'll let you know in a few minutes.'

The host was short, fat and bald, and appropriately named 'Fats.' He also owned the restaurant, which was called 'Fat Joe's.' Fats asked everyone to take their seats, although no one seemed to take any notice. He then announced the reigning champion as Demetri 'The Hammer' and the challenger as Wang Lei Ivanov who was an ex-full contact karate champion. Fats said betting would cease 30 seconds after first contact. Mab looked at Alexei and said, 'Get ready to place your bet.' Fats sent the competitors to opposite corners of the cage, made his way out and locked the cage door. He then walked to a large copper bell and hammer that hung from the floor above. He struck the bell once and the fight commenced.

The two competitors circled each other Wang Lei attacked with a flurry of high kicks which Demetri easily avoided without contact. Mab said, 'Alexei, I think Demetri will win.'

Alexei ran down the steps to the betting desk and placed a sizeable sum on Demetri to win. When he returned, he said, 'I bet a fair amount on Demetri, the odds were 1 to 2, which means if he wins, I get my stake back plus 50%.'

Mab smiled and turned back to watch the fight. Wang Lei launched another attack on Demetri using a rapid series of roundhouse and straight kicks which drove him back into a corner. Wang Lei moved in with another high roundhouse kick but overreached. As his foot hit the floor, his left side and back were exposed. He realised his error but compounded it by performing an off-balance reverse roundhouse kick. In doing so he protected his side and back but opened his front and crucially brought his head within reach of Demetri who moved forward as Wang Lei's left foot sailed past his face. Demetri's fist hit him between the eyes like a lump hammer, Wang Lei went down but as he fell Demetri grabbed his left arm at the wrist pulling it upwards and swinging him around, he then dropped with his full weight on the elbow joint which made a sickening snapping sound as it shattered.

The crowd cheered, fortunately Wang Lei was already unconscious. Demetri stood up, grabbed him by his hair knot and dragged him across the floor. He then threw him like a rag doll into his corner of the cage and kicked him hard in the groin. Mab stared at Demetri and looked more closely to see if he was hosting a daemon, but she could find no trace. Wang Lei was taken out of the cage on a stretcher, still unconscious. Fats told the crowd that Wang Lei was on his way to a medical facility. Alexei collected his winnings from the betting desk and said, 'Mab, how about another drink?'

Mab replied, 'Let's stay a bit longer, this is really interesting.'

Fats held Demetri's arm up and pronounced him the winner of the championship bout. He then asked if anyone else would like to compete against Demetri informally for sport. There were no takers. Fats said, 'Come now, surely there must be someone who wishes to pit his skills against the Champion. Demetri promises that he will go easy on you!'

Demetri laughed. Still, there were no takers. But then a young woman at the back of the room shouted, 'I will take him on, and I promise not to hurt him too much.' The crowd roared with laughter.

Alexei said, 'Mab, I hope you are joking, there is no way you are going in there with that animal.'

Mab replied, 'Alexei, put all your money on me to win.' She then stood up and walked down towards the cage. The Host, Demetri and the crowd were still laughing. Mab ran towards the cage, leapt high into the air, somersaulted over the top of the cage wall and landed on her feet in the ready position. The crowd went silent; Demetri stopped laughing.

Demetri raised his arms outwards and dropped them as if he were resigned to participating in a ridiculous charade. Fats brought them together and asked Mab her name. He then looked at Demetri and said, 'Don't kill her, rough her up, break a few of her bones, but I don't want a death on my hands.'

Demetri nodded and Mab smiled. The host told them to go to their corners. He then exited, locked the cage door and rang the bell. Mab walked to the centre of the floor. Demetri held his arms out as if he didn't want to compete and was turning and looking to the crowd for support.

Mab said, in his head, 'Demetri, are you ready?'

Demetri spun towards her and said, 'What is this trickery?'

Mab ran towards him, leapt up and kicked him in the chest three times in quick succession, knocking him back into his corner. She then walked back to the centre of the floor. The crowd went wild, the betting desk was being overwhelmed as the odds were suddenly being recalculated and recast. Mab saw Alexei at the front of the melee, clutching his betting slip. Demetri approached her more cautiously, then suddenly feigned to the left but launched a straight kick with his right foot. Mab was much too fast, she spun away from the kick, leapt to her left and punched him, with psychically enhanced might, on his right temple. The punch hit Demetri like a freight train, his head snapped over to his left shoulder and he dropped to the floor, barely remaining conscious.

He struggled to his feet and backed away. *Playing for recovery time,* Mab thought. Mab circled him and was about to launch a new attack when her witch senses alarmed; something was wrong with his stance, his posture. She backed off and scanned him more closely. Then she saw it, a dagger, ultrathin, concealed in his right sleeve. It was a melee weapon that could be used to deliver a fatal blow but leave little trace, often the victim was unaware of the wound and the damage to their internal organs. Mab said, 'I will say this only once. Put the dagger on the floor.'

Demetri grimaced and said, 'Come and get it bitch.'

Mab moved towards him, Demetri pulled out the dagger with his left hand, Mab veered to his right but then changed direction, parried his knife hand with her right arm and punched him in the centre of his chest with her left fist. The punch, to the onlookers, looked like a simple jab. Demetri didn't even flinch, but in fact it was a blow of horrendous proportions. The energy transfer was focused on penetration of the chest wall rather than pushing the body backwards. Demetri's rib cage was shattered, and his heart was pierced with many of the bone fragments. He was dead before his head hit the floor. Mab picked up the dagger and held it high for the crowd to see. The crowd stood and roared their approval.

Fats hurried into the cage and held Mab's hand up as the winner of the bout. Mab said nothing but walked out of the cage and waited at the betting desk for Alexei to collect his winnings. Alexei was ecstatic, he had placed his bet well before first contact when the odds were very much in favour of Demetri.

Mab said, 'Alexei, could you take me somewhere else where we can eat and drink?'

Alexei replied, 'Yes, Mab, I know a great restaurant and night club within walking distance. Let's go!'

Alexei took Mab to an extremely plush nightclub; he had to bribe the doorman and the concierge to find them a good table. There was a live music show with dancers and singers. Alexei ordered for Mab and asked the waiter to bring a selection of fine white wines for Mab to try, but of course, she liked all of them; the food was delicious, although more heavily spiced than she was used to. Alexei said, 'Mab, I hope you don't mind me asking, but where did you learn to fight like that?'

Mab replied, 'I was taught warrior skills by Master Kanaka. I am now head of a warrior school.'

Alexei replied 'I guess that explains it. I hope Demetri learns his lesson; I can't believe he was carrying a weapon.' Mab said 'It's a bit late for learning lessons, he is dead.'

Alexei replied, 'Dead! Are you sure?'

Mab said, 'Yes, quite sure.'

Alexei said, 'You may be questioned by the Police.'

Mab said 'Police, who is that?'

Alexei laughed and said, 'Don't worry, I guess Fats will deal with it.'

Alexei added, 'Where will you stay tonight. You are very welcome to come to my home. It's not far from here.'

Mab replied, 'Thank you, Alexei, but I will travel back tonight, my partner will be waiting for me. Are you married?'

Alexei said, 'No, I'm not married. I live with my girlfriend, but she is working away from home at present. Do you have a long journey ahead of you?'

Mab replied, 'No, not really. It is long in distance but short in time if you see what I mean.'

Mab stood up and said, 'Alexei, thanks for tonight. I have really enjoyed this evening with you, but I must go now. You stay here and finish the wine, if I eat or drink any more, I think I may explode!'

Alexei replied, 'Will I see you again?'

Mab bent down, kissed him on the cheek and said, 'Next time I'm here, I will come and find you.' Mab walked out of the restaurant into the darkness, vanished, and reappeared on top of the Haskin's building. She had just collected Dawn-Breaker when her witch's senses twitched, she levitated high into the air and looked down.

Morgana and Rhiannon were on the other side of the roof, concealed behind a ventilation machine. They were talking to a third person. Mab made herself unseen, floated down and listened to the conversation. Morgana said, 'We are happy to carry on supporting the business under your leadership. Your father was assassinated by professionals, but that doesn't mean the business has to fold.'

Haskins Junior replied, 'But can you protect me and my board from these assassins.'

Morgana replied, 'We can try, but don't forget the other services we provide in procuring customers and moving the product.'

Haskins replied, 'For which you are well paid. But unless you can provide me with protection you are not much use to me.'

Rhiannon said, 'We didn't expect an attack of that nature. We will not make that mistake again.'

Mab said, 'I think you have just made that mistake again!'

Rhiannon spun around fast only to catch a fleeting glimpse of Dawn-Breaker as it sliced her head from her shoulders. A fountain of blood sprayed upwards, and the head fell to the concrete floor with a dull thud. Morgana screamed and vanished. Mab sheathed Dawn-Breaker grabbed hold of Haskins Junior and threw him off the building. She then looked around for Morgana without success and decided to return home.

Mab materialised on the Guild sports field and made her way to the suite above Master Boe's room in the main building. She was still feeling somewhat bloated but took the stairs two at a time. As she opened the door to the suite, she saw Charly and Cat preparing a late meal, Izzy ran to her and hugged her tightly.

Cat turned around and said, 'Another boring day at the office Mab? Don't worry we have a couple of bottles of your favourite wine not to mention Charly's gourmet food.'

Mab replied, 'Great, I can't wait….'

Mab went to see Kanaka first thing the following morning. She found him and Paull up to their ears in paperwork.

Kanaka looked up and said, 'Mab please come in. Paull and I were just finishing up here.' Mab looked knowingly at Paull and smiled.

Paull said, 'Master Kanaka, I will take this away, redo the figures as discussed and bring it back late afternoon for you to approve?'

Kanaka replied, 'Paull, that's perfect, see you later. Mab would you like some coffee?'

Paull walked past Mab, winked and said, 'He didn't offer me any coffee.' He then quickened his departure.

Mab laughed and said, 'Master Kanaka, all work and no play. Do you need some sword practice?'

Kanaka said, 'That would be great, how about first thing tomorrow morning?'

Mab replied, 'Real swords, full armour?'

Kanaka said, 'Yes, could you let the students know, it would be good for them to watch and learn. Perhaps ask them to do a written critique as part of their studies?'

Mab replied, 'That's a good idea. Leave it with me.'

Kanaka sat at the table, poured two coffees and said, 'Well how are things. What have you been up to recently?' Mab tasted the coffee, as usual it was bitter but wonderful.

Mab replied, 'I've never mentioned it before, but my strongest and fondest memory of the Guild is your coffee. I can't explain it but just sitting here with you drinking coffee makes me feel at home.'

Kanaka replied, 'That's a lovely thing to say. I hope you will always feel this is your home. How are things going with your mother?'

Mab said, 'That's what I wanted to talk to you about. She told me that we can now intervene in the adjacent plane.'

Kanaka replied, 'What about the Prophet issue?'

Mab said, 'That is now resolved, he is dead but he has become a martyr, and his death is bringing about change. I think we should now help them to end generations of slavery.'

Kanaka replied, 'Yes, we cannot abandon them. We should raise this at the Council meeting, Lamm will be with us and I think we should be able to convince Taggar and Luticia.'

Mab said, 'When is the next meeting?'

Kanaka replied, 'It was yesterday, you missed it. Don't worry we all know that you are often needed elsewhere. I will ask for an extraordinary meeting of the Council to be held as soon as possible.'

Mab said, 'My mother took me to another plane yesterday. It was far in the future, the buildings were huge towers made from artificial stone and there were so many people. The food was very different to ours, lots of mixed ingredients and they eat huge amounts of it. I entered a fighting competition, for a bit of fun really, but the warriors are huge. The degree of muscle development is staggering. It is an age where machines are used for everything, but the fuel used by the machines pollutes the air and makes it difficult to breath. It was very strange. We went there to kill an evil man, involved in slavery, and the two witches that protected him. I should really go back there to finish the job. I wondered if you would like to come with me. I'm sure you would find it interesting?'

Kanaka replied, 'It sounds fascinating. I'd love to get a glimpse of the future! Let me know when you want to go. In the meantime, I'll get the Council together to discuss the adjacent plane.'

Mab left Kanaka and went to the lost library to meditate. She climbed the ladder to the viewing gallery, removed the cushion from the sofa and placed it on the table. She sat there for a few minutes sending out her witch senses around the campus. She found Izzy and Charly, they were in a potions class with Master Ethan who was explaining how to use a deadly plant for medicinal purposes. Mab's witch powers were still growing at an extraordinary rate, she could now mind link and mind read humans and animals alike and understand their thoughts. This rendered speech unnecessary, moreover she was looking and listening to Master Ethan through Charly who was unaware of Mab's presence in her mind.

Mab reached out still further to the village of Blant and her mother. She was feeding the pigs, she saw the pigs through her mother's eyes. She withdrew and reached out still further, she thought of Alexei and she found him. He had only just awoken and was preparing coffee. Strange, his partner was there with him. Alexei took a cup of coffee to her as she sat-up in bed. Mab looked at her more closely, it was Morgana. Mab withdrew from Alexei and entered Morgana's mind. Morgana was immediately aware of her presence.

Mab said, 'You have some explaining to do. I will return to the roof top of the Haskins building in exactly 24hrs. Be there with Alexei and understand that you cannot hide from me. I could crush your mind now, but I do not wish to end your life.' Mab withdrew and cast her mind to the church in the adjacent plane, nothing. She thought of Dassi the young girl who helped her communicate with the Priests. She found her. She was crying, her mother was holding her tightly. They were in a dark place, Mab entered her mother's mind, she was also crying. Mab saw through her eyes, they were in a large prison, the floor was soil and pebbles, the walls were of heavy cut stone with iron-bar gates, guards were everywhere. Mab's blood ran cold with realisation. She disappeared and materialised in the suite, startling Cat. She pulled on her white cloak and buckled Dawn-Breaker on her back. Mab said, 'Sorry Cat, I must go,' and vanished.

Mab materialised on top of the Stadium roof, in Yehuda, on the adjacent plane and took in the scene below. The crowds were beginning to gather for the warrior battles and the slaughter of the innocent. Mab focussed on Dassi and her mother Satta, she entered Satta's mind and said, 'Hold Dassi tightly, do not let her go.' Mab then focussed her mind and pulled them to her through mind space. They materialised on the roof beside her, still crying and holding each other tightly.

Mab, in their minds, said, 'You are safe. I will take you to my home where you will remain until we cleanse this place of these evil creatures.'

Dassi and Satta were still in shock but threw their arms around Mab, held her tightly, and sobbed in thanks. Mab, with Dassi and Satta vanished and materialised on the Guild sports field. Mab mind linked with Kanaka and said, 'I have rescued Dassi and her mother, Priestess Satta, from the adjacent plane. They were in the holding cells at the stadium waiting to be killed. I'm taking them to Master Boe to see if he can find them some emergency accommodation.'

Kanaka replied, 'Mab, Boe is with me now, bring them to my office.'

Mab walked with Satta and Dassi to Kanaka's office. She knocked once and walked in to find Boe and Kanaka waiting for them. Mab introduced Satta and Dassi and explained what had happened. Kanaka said, 'Mab, I've asked the kitchen to bring up some food. They look terrible, do you know how long they were held in the cells.'

Mab asked Satta, who replied, 'Dassi and I were imprisoned two days ago. We were due to be executed this morning. I was hoping it would be by the sword.'

Mab replied, 'Master Kanaka has asked for some food to be brought here for you.'

Boe stood-up and said he would go and arrange accommodation for them. Mab said, 'They have been in the holding cells for two days!'

Kanaka frowned and said, 'We need to end this slaughter. I'll ask Master Uvren if he would be able to spend some time here to teach them our language.'

Mab replied, 'Yes, Satta will be a great help to us with our plans for the adjacent plane. She knows all the key people not to mention the geography and layouts of the facilities.'

The kitchen staff arrived with platters of cold meats, fruit and vegetables, chilled fruit juice, wine and water. Mab said to Satta, 'This food is for you and Dassi, please eat and drink.' Satta and Dassi tucked into the food and drank copious amounts of fruit juice and water. Kanaka poured himself and Mab a goblet of wine and passed the bottle to Satta, who declined with a warm smile.

Mab said, 'Master Kanaka, I found the witch I was looking for. I have told her to meet me at a certain location tomorrow morning. Would you be able to accompany me?'

Kanaka replied, 'Absolutely, I've been looking forward to it!'

Mab said, 'Don't get your hopes up, it's different but I most definitely wouldn't want to live there! How about we depart shortly after our sword practice session?'

Kanaka replied, 'Yes, a quick shower and then we leave. What's the climate like?'

Mab said, 'It's fairly warm, you don't need a coat but wear long trousers, proper shoes and a long-sleeved top, you will fit-in better.'

Boe returned and said, 'I have a ground floor family room, number 36, in Amber for them. The kitchen has stocked the cold-cupboard and I've asked one of the students, in room 37, to make sure they know how to get to the dining room for breakfast, lunch and dinner.'

Mab said, 'Thank you, Master Boe. I will take them over there and make sure they are settled in. The student in room 37, what is his name?'

Boe replied, 'His name is Tobbi. Mab, take care, the young students are in awe of you. So be gentle.'

Mab looked at Kanaka and then back to Boe and said, 'Whatever do you mean Master Boe. I am the gentlest person I know.'

Kanaka laughed and replied, 'Of course you are Mab. It's just that not many of the people you know, the ones that are still alive that is, fall into the gentle category.'

Boe could not contain himself any longer and burst out laughing. Mab laughed and said, 'You are going to pay for that tomorrow Master Kanaka!'

Mab said to Satta, 'Master Boe has arranged a place for you to stay until it is safe for you to return home.'

Satta stood-up, brought her hands together in front of her chest and replied, 'Please tell the masters that we cannot thank them enough for their generosity. This is a beautiful place with good kind people.'

Mab relayed that to Kanaka and Boe and then led Satta and Dassi through the guild building pointing out the Great and Minor Halls and the dining areas where they should go for lunch and dinner. She walked with them around the campus lanes, which were surrounded by beautiful garden areas. Students would stand to one side and bow as Mab walked past. Mab passed Sapphire House and told Satta and Dassi that she used to live there. Eventually they arrived at Amber House. Mab led them to their room which had a very spacious living area with a separate kitchen and bathroom and two bedrooms. Mab checked the cold cupboard and found that it was fully stocked with bread, water, milk and fruits. The clothes cupboard had been stocked with what Boe thought was appropriate. Mab sat down on the sofa with Satta and Dassi and explained that they should make themselves at home and that it was perfectly safe to walk around the campus. She explained that Master Uvren could speak their language and he would be visiting soon. Mab then took them to the door of the adjacent room and knocked hard twice. The door opened and a young student stared at Mab in disbelief and dropped to his knees.

Mab said, 'You must be Tobbi, please stand-up.'

Mab explained that Satta and Dassi could not speak their language and that he should try to help them find their way around the campus. Mab put her hand on Tobbi's shoulder and said, 'Would you be able to do that for me and let me know if there are any problems?'

Tobbi replied nervously, 'Yes, Master. I will look after them.'

Mab smiled at him warmly and said, 'Tobbi, Master Kanaka and I will be doing sword practice first thing tomorrow morning. You are very welcome to come and watch. Bring your friends if you wish.'

Tobbi gushed with gratitude and said, 'Yes, Master, it is a great honour. Thank you so much.'

Mab explained to Satta and Dassi that Tobbi would help them to find their way around and they should knock on his door if they needed anything.

The following morning Mab met with Master Kanaka on the sports field for their practice session. On this occasion however there was a large crowd of students gathered to watch and learn. Kanaka and Mab wore armoured jackets of thick leather which protected their necks, shoulders and torso's. They stood only a short distance apart and bowed to each other. Kanaka launched a blistering attack on Mab consisting of four vertical sword slices and a low long-reach horizontal slice which almost made contact. Mab however had not yet drawn Dawn-Breaker she was moving back, twisting, turning and spinning at an extraordinary speed avoiding Kanaka's blade. Kanaka continued to press his attack. Mab was about to reach for Dawn-Breaker when Kanaka ran straight at her with another rapid combination of sword swipes. Mab initially moved back but then moved forward and launched herself into a high somersault over Kanaka, as she spun in the air she swept Dawn-Breaker from the scabbard and twisted delivering a diagonal swipe down Kanaka's back. Kanaka however dived forward and rolled to his feet; Dawn-Breaker came within a hair's-width of his back armour. Mab attacked him immediately; her moves were a blur, Dawn-Breaker was moving so quickly the blade could not be seen. Kanaka was moving backwards rapidly and parrying on instinct, he had never seen anyone move with that speed, he then threw himself flat to the ground underneath Dawn-Breaker and kicked Mab's legs from under her.

Mab hit the ground but rolled rapidly away from Kanaka and leapt back to her feet. She sheathed Dawn-Breaker, walked to Kanaka and embraced him. The crowd roared their approval and applauded vigorously. Mab said, 'I didn't see that coming.'

Kanaka replied, 'You were moving so fast, I barely saw you and didn't see anything of your sword!'

Mab said, 'Quick shower, see you here later.'

Kanaka addressed the students, 'I'd like you to consider the different styles of swordsmanship displayed here today. Make written notes on the moves, tactics and their effectiveness. Master Winter will discuss these with you in class. Thank you for coming.' More applause from the audience.

Mab made her way back to the suite and found Izzy and Charly having a late breakfast. Mab said, 'I'll have a quick shower then I am leaving for the City with Master Kanaka to meet Morgana, the witch that escaped.'

Izzy replied, 'Are you going to kill her?'

Mab said, 'I'll try to avoid it, if possible.'

Charly said, 'We'll leave you some pastries, and the coffee is still hot. We have classes this morning.' Mab barely had time to drink the coffee and eat a pastry before she was out the door and on her way to meet Kanaka. She wore a short leather jacket, tight-fitting sports trousers and light boots. Dawn-Breaker was strapped to her back. Kanaka was waiting for her. He wore a long-sleeved sports top with a black leather waistcoat, baggy black trousers and soft leather boots. He also had his sword strapped to his back.

As Mab approached, he said, 'Should we have met in the library?'

Mab replied, 'No, travel has become a lot easier these days! I wanted to talk to you about this and some other things.'

Kanaka said, 'Is something worrying you?'

Mab replied, 'As you know my psychic and other powers have been growing ever since I came to the Guild and particularly since I was attacked by Master Toker.'

Kanaka said, 'Yes, that's good isn't it?'

Mab replied, 'It is good, but I'm scared. I had thought it would plateau-out but the rate seems to be increasing even faster than before. I feel that I could do terrible things, that I am becoming something that's not entirely human.'

Kanaka said, 'Is this something that Uriel could advise?'

Mab replied, 'I don't think my mother realises what is happening to me and I don't feel I can discuss it with her.'

Kanaka said, 'Perhaps it is your destiny? If you have the power to do terrible things, then you also have the power to do great things, either way it is your choice. From the first day I met you I always believed that you would do great things, and you have.'

Mab replied, 'Thank you Master Kanaka. I feel a bit better now. Let's go and see what the future holds. It could be a trap, so be prepared!' Mab put her arm around Kanaka and focussed on the Haskins building roof.

It was around mid-day when they materialised on the roof of the Haskins building. Kanaka said, 'We are really here!?'

Mab smiled, reached out with her witch senses and located Morgana and Alexei, they were in a restaurant on the opposite side of the street below. Mab replied, 'Yes, we are really here. The witch and her partner are in an eating place on the block across the street.' She walked to the edge of the building and pointed.

Kanaka looked down and said, 'The machines, are they carriages?'

Mab replied, 'Yes, they don't seem to have horses or any other animals.'

Kanaka said, 'Maybe they have eaten all the animals! I see what you mean about the pollution, the air is foul.'

Mab said, 'I'll take us to them. I suspect Morgana wants to meet in a public place because she thinks that would prevent me from killing her.'

Kanaka laughed and said, 'She clearly doesn't know you very well then?'

Mab said, 'It's best if we leave our swords here otherwise we will attract attention.'

Mab slid the two swords into the drainage pipe and put her arm around Kanaka. Mab and Kanaka materialised in the shadows close to the restaurant. They walked in together. A waiter approached and asked if they had a reservation. Mab turned her head towards Morgana and using a command inflection said, 'We are with them. Take us there now!'

The waiter did as he was told. Morgana, startled, turned to look at Mab as she approached. Mab said, to all in their minds, 'Good evening. Alexei, Morgana. This is Master Kanaka.' Mab sat beside Alexei and Kanaka beside Morgana.

Morgana, pointing to the Haskins building rooftop, said, 'I thought you wanted to meet up there?'

Mab replied, 'This is much more civilised and we are hungry, are we not Master Kanaka?'

Kanaka said, 'Yes Mab, hungry and thirsty.'

Mab looked at Alexei and said, 'I assume you have coins. Could you order food and drinks for us?'

Alexei said, 'Yes Mab of course. I'll order a selection and we can share.' Alexei summoned a waiter and explained the food order.

Mab said, 'Morgana, tell us about yourself.'

Morgana said, 'What if I don't want to tell you about myself.'

Mab replied, 'My mother told you that if you continued to support Haskins then I would take your life, and yet here you are alive and well.'

Morgana said, 'I live because I escaped from you. My acolyte was not as fortunate.'

Mab replied, 'Morgana, you cannot escape from me. In any case it seems that you are pregnant, I wouldn't feel comfortable killing the unborn.'

Alexei said, 'Pregnant!?'

Mab, looking at Morgana, replied, 'Yes Alexei, it looks like you will be a father soon.'

The food started to arrive, Mab turned to Kanaka and said, 'Think volume rather than quality.'

The food consisted of many platters of meats, seafood and vegetables. Small pots of spices and sauces were placed in the centre of the table. Two bottles of white wine arrived with ice buckets, together with two bottles of fine red wine. Kanaka looked at Mab and said, 'I'm beginning to like this place!'

Mab asked Alexei, 'Do you know if there is any sword fighting going on anywhere?'

Alexei laughed and replied, 'No, we don't have sword fighting. However, Fats was asking if you would be willing to compete again?'

Mab said, 'I don't think so, not today anyway. I'd love to take Master Kanaka to see a fight though. Is that possible?' Mab poured Kanaka a large glass of white wine and did the same for herself.

Alexia said, 'Yes there will be a fight on tonight. When we've finished here we could take a walk round to the club.'

Mab said, 'Morgana, I will spare your life for the sake of the unborn child. But you must first promise me that you will not engage in the enslaving of people using chemical substances.'

Alexei said, 'Morgana, what does Mab mean, have you been dealing in drugs?'

Morgana replied, 'I work for Mr Haskins and now Mr Haskins Junior. My job is to protect and offer advice. I personally do not get involved in drugs, but it is a lucrative part of their business.'

Mab said, 'I'm surprised he survived the fall?'

Morgana replied, 'What fall?'

Mab said, 'After I killed Rhiannon, I threw Haskins Junior off the top of the building.'

Kanaka laughed and said, 'Mab, you are nothing if not effective!'

Alexei said, 'It was on the news. Haskins and his son were both killed by falling from the top of Haskins tower.'

Morgana looked at Mab and said, 'I know it was wrong, I give you my word that I will not engage in drug trafficking again.'

Mab replied, 'Accepted, but this is your last chance.'

Morgana said, 'Understood.'

The waiters cleared the table and brought a wide selection of desserts. Kanaka spooned something ice-cold into his mouth and said, 'Mab, you have to try this!'

Mab followed his example and said, 'Alexei, what is this!'

Alexei laughed and said, 'We call it ice-cream. You have the vanilla flavour, but there are many different types. See, in this bowl there is the chocolate flavour.'

Kanaka and Mab plunged their spoons into the bowls. Morgana laughed and said, 'You two are like a couple of kids. Usually, they are the ones fighting over the ice-cream.'

Mab replied, 'Is the recipe for this ice-cream a secret. Would the owner be willing to part with it?'

Morgana and Alexei went into fits of laughter. Morgana said, 'No, Mab, it is not a secret. If you allow Alexei and I to visit, then I will make some for you.'

Mab, with a serious expression on her face, looked at Kanaka and said, 'Morgana will teach us how to make the ice-cream.'

Alexei said, 'If you want to see some fighting, we have to leave now?'

Mab spooned the last of the ice-cream into her mouth and replied, 'Yes, please.'

Alexei paid the bill and led the group to Fat Joes Night Club. Alexei ordered drinks at the bar. Mab and Morgana had red wine. Alexei ordered generous measures of a fine malt whisky for himself and Kanaka. Kanaka lifted the glass, sniffed the contents and took a sip.

He looked at Mab at said, 'This is fabulous. I'd like to take a bottle of this back home if possible.'

Mab relayed Kanaka's request to Alexei and Morgana. Alexei replied, 'Yes, I'll get a couple of bottles for you to take with you. But now we need to go downstairs.'

The group of four sat at the back of the room in the highest tier. Fats saw them and came running up the stairs. He said, 'Mab, it's great to see you again. Will you be fighting tonight?'

Mab replied, 'No, not tonight, Fats, but maybe soon.'

Fats said, 'No problem. You are always welcome here. Alexei, free drinks for you guys all night, ok?'

Alexei said, 'Great thanks, Fats.'

Fats looked at Kanaka and said, 'What about you, sir? Will you be fighting tonight?'

Mab replied, 'This is Master Kanaka, he doesn't speak your language, but no, he will not be fighting tonight unless, of course, it involves swords.'

Fats said, 'Interesting idea, but no, we don't do swords here. Master Kanaka has the look of a samurai about him. There is a martial arts school in the city that teaches traditional samurai warrior fighting techniques, and apparently it is really taking off with office workers!'

Alexei said, 'Could you give us the details, Fats. Perhaps later, before we leave?'

Fats replied, 'Yes, I'll meet you upstairs later.' Fats ran back down to the betting desk. Mab relayed the information about the warrior's fighting techniques to Kanaka.

Fats welcomed everyone to the fight night and said, 'Tonight, we have two acknowledged experts in the martial arts. As many of you know, the reigning cage-fight champion, Demetri, The Hammer, was defeated a few nights ago in an unofficial bout by an unknown female fighter known as *Baby Face Mab*.' Morgana and Alexei burst into fits of uncontrolled laughter. Mab looked at Alexei, which made him laugh even harder. Mab turned to Kanaka and explained why the others were laughing. He also burst into fits of laughter. Many turned around to see what was going on at the back of the room.

Fats then said, 'Baby Face Mab is here tonight, please, Mab, stand up.'

Mab reluctantly got slowly to her feet, the audience applauded vigorously, and her friends laughed even harder.

Fats said, 'The winner of the official fight here tonight will be recognised as the new cage fight champion. As usual, all betting will end 30 seconds after first contact.'

Fats entered the cage and announced the fighters.

'In the red corner, we have Master Ichiro Yamamoto, who is an ex-world free-style karate champion. In the blue corner, Phillippe Barbeau, who is ex-military and holds an eighth-degree black belt in Krav Maga.'

Mab said, 'Alexei, will you be betting?'

Alexei replied, 'Who do you think will win?'

Mab asked Kanaka, who shrugged his shoulders.

Mab said to Alexei, 'Go to the desk, but don't place your bet until I tell you. I'll raise my left hand for red and my right for blue.'

Fats exited, locked the cage door and sounded the bell. Barbeau circled Yamamoto, feigning and testing his reactions. Kanaka turned to Mab and said, The Blue will win. Mab stood up and raised her right arm. Alexei put a large sum on Barbeau to win and rushed back to his seat. Mab explained the betting process to Kanaka. Yamamoto suddenly launched a flurry of punches at Barbeau, one of which connected with his chin, but Barbeau grabbed hold of Yamamoto's lower arm, pulled him forward and kicked him with precision in the kidney area, under the rib cage, and then leapt backwards.

Kanaka said, 'That must have hurt!'

The blow had clearly affected Yamamoto, who slowed considerably. Barbeau attacked Yamamoto with kicks to his lower body, the ankles, knees and groin. He took another punch from Yamamoto but moved inside and delivered several hard punches to Yamamoto's ribs and stomach. He then used his shoulder to push Yamamoto backwards, turned and punched him in the throat. Yamamoto dropped to the floor, and as he fell, Barbeau kicked him in the groin.

Kanaka looked at Mab and said, 'He's a good fighter but not a warrior.'

Mab replied, 'Yes, sloppy in places, and he didn't need the last kick.'

Alexei made his way to the betting desk to collect his winnings.

Fats unlocked the cage, and his assistants helped Yamamoto to his feet. Medics were onhand to give immediate treatment. Fats said, 'It gives me great pleasure to announce that Phillippe Barbeau is our new cage fight champion! The formal competition is over, and Phillippe is still fresh and willing. Would anyone like to try their luck with Phillippe? Baby Face? How about a friendly sparring session?'

Mab said to Alexei, 'Let's go upstairs and order some of those free drinks we were promised?' Alexei led the group upstairs and ordered another round of wine and whisky.

Kanaka asked Mab if Alexei could arrange a visit to the Swordsmanship School. Mab looked at Alexei, thought for a few seconds and then said to Kanaka, 'I think I know how to solve this language problem. Let me try something.'

Mab's mind linked with Kanaka and Alexei and said to Alexei, 'Master Kanaka asks if you could arrange a visit to the Swordsmanship School sometime soon?'

Alexei replied, 'Yes, of course. I'll give them a ring first thing tomorrow morning to arrange the visit.'

Kanaka said, 'Mab, I understood that! Why does he have to give them a ring? Is it their custom or a payment?'

Alexei said, 'No, Master Kanaka, ring as in ringing a bell. We use electronic communication devices to talk to each other. Let me show you.'

Alexei took his mobile phone from a pocket and said, 'I'll use this to ring Morgana.' He tapped his phone a few times, and a ringing sound came from Morgana. Morgana took her phone from her pocket, answered and passed her phone to Kanaka, who held it to his ear. Kanaka heard Alexei talking on the phone and passed it to Mab, who held it to her ear.

Kanaka said, 'I couldn't understand what you were saying on the device.'

Mab said, 'Master Kanaka, that's because previously it was going through me from mind to mind, but the device is unable to translate the language. I wonder how it works.' Mab held the phone flat in the palm of her right hand and made the smallest of gestures with her left hand. The phone started to disassemble each component, moving apart as if the phone was being blown apart in slow motion. A large sphere of small component parts hovered in the air before her.

Kanaka looked at Mab and said, 'Yes, I think I understand it now.'

Mab laughed, said, 'Yes, I know what you mean!'

She then clenched the fingers of her left hand, and the component parts flew together at enormous speed.

Mab handed the reassembled phone back to Morgana and said, 'Best check if it still works!'

Morgana pushed a few buttons and said, 'Yes, it still works.'

Fats arrived with Phillippe and said, 'Do you mind if we join you?'

Alexei replied, 'No, of course not, pull over some chairs.'

Fats introduced everyone and said, 'Mab, do you think you would be willing to go into the cage with Phillippe. It would be a real crowd puller and it would be very lucrative even if you lost.'

Mab laughed and replied, 'Fats, I wouldn't lose. But no, unlike Demetri, Phillippe is an accomplished fighter, and I may have to hurt him.'

Phillippe went into fits of laughter, thinking it was a joke and he was being set up. But no one else laughed. He then said 'Look, Baby Face, you may have been lucky with Demetri, but I can guarantee that you would not last 10 seconds with me in the cage.'

Morgana said, 'If I may give you some advice Phillippe. You are the new cage fight champion, be content with that.'

Fats said, 'Phillippe was trained in the military and is unbeaten in one-to-one contests. He has even taken on a bear in the cage using only his combat knife. Remember that Phillippe, you cut him up real bad!'

Kanaka groaned and dropped his head into his hands. Mab turned baleful eyes on Fats, and blood started to trickle from his nose.

She then looked at Phillippe and said, 'You come with me.' The group stood up and followed Mab downstairs to the cage. There was no audience.

Phillippe said to Morgana, 'I don't understand what just happened.'

Morgana replied, 'Are you familiar with the phrase Be Careful What You Wish For?'

Phillippe replied, 'Don't make me laugh.'

Mab walked straight into the cage and waited. Phillippe entered and started to limber up. Mab watched him in silence with a grim smile on her face. Fats hit the bell.

Phillippe approached Mab and said, 'Ok, let's do this!' and immediately launched a vicious kick at Mab's groin, but she spun to the side. He then moved forward, throwing punches and kicks, but Mab was much too fast. Phillippe, becoming frustrated, feigned a punch with his left hand but kicked with his right foot. Mab moved forward between the punch and the kick, leapt into the air and head-butted him between the eyes. He fell backwards, hit the floor hard, but rolled and got back to his feet. He was shaken, his nose was broken, and blood was pouring down over his mouth and chin.

Mab moved towards him, but he rushed her, grabbing hold, trying to get a bear-hug lock. He was astonished to find that Mab was enormously strong; she put her right palm on his chest, pushed him away and delivered a powerful back-handed slap to his left cheek. His head snapped around, and he dropped to his knees. Mab backed off and waited for him to recover. He struggled to his feet; his face was swollen out of all recognition. He reached behind, inside his shirt, and pulled out a combat knife which had been concealed at the back of his trousers. He moved towards her, slicing the knife through the air at full stretch. Mab allowed him to come closer, and he brought the knife down in a diagonal arc aimed at the left side of Mab's neck. Mab caught his right arm by the wrist and twisted it around. He has groaned with pain; Mab brought her left hand down at blinding speed, shattering his elbow joint. The damage was such that the lower arm almost separated at the elbow.

Phillippe screamed in agony and dropped to his knees.

Mab backed off and waited.

Fats ran to open the door to the cage, but found he could not open it.

Phillippe got back to his feet using his left hand to support his lower right arm. He looked at Mab and said, 'I'm finished.'

Mab replied, 'I'm not.' She walked towards him, quickly moved to his left and kicked him on the outside of his left knee; the ligaments ripped apart as the joint dislocated. He once more screamed in agony and fell to the floor.

Mab looked down at him and said, 'Tell me again about the bear.'

Phillippe, on his back and struggling to speak, said, 'It was a few years ago. It was just a stunt; Fats drugged the bear, and I killed it in the cage. I had it skinned and made into a rug made for my home.'

Mab lifted her foot and held it over his face. She then slammed it down with enormous force and crushed his skull.

Mab walked out of the cage and said to Fats, 'If I hear of any other animals being maltreated, I will have your life. Do you understand?'

Fats, shaking, said, 'Yes, Mab. It will never happen again.'

Mab said to Kanaka, 'Let's go and finish our drinks.'

The group made their way back upstairs.

Morgana said, 'Mab, Alexei and I have had enough excitement tonight; we will make our way home. How do we contact you?'

Mab replied, 'I'll contact you in a few days. Hopefully, we can visit the school of swordsmanship and then perhaps you could spend a few days with us?'

Morgana said, 'Yes, I am very much looking forward to that.'

Mab and Kanaka sat together and finished their drinks.

Mab said, 'Master Kanaka, what are your thoughts regarding Morgana?'

Kanaka smiled and replied, 'Have you been reading my mind?'

Mab looked at him and said, 'No, but I can see that you also have some reservations?'

Kanaka replied, 'What do we know of her background? Where did she study?'

Mab said, 'Yes, we know very little about her. There is something else lacking, it's as if she is acting, role playing.'

Kanaka replied, 'Gathering information?'

Mab replied, 'Yes, that too. We need to remember that she is a black witch. My senses tell me that the witches of this machine age are weak, but Morgana is old, and she is very clever.'

Kanaka replied, 'She doesn't look old?' Mab said

'I would say she is probably around 350 years old and likely to live until at least her 1000th year.'

Kanaka replied, 'How do you know?'

Mab said, 'I can see the cells of her body and the condition of the bone structure. Morgana is either naturally aging very slowly or she is using her powers to rejuvenate her cells, strengthen her bones and repair her organs.'

Kanaka replied, 'Maybe we should think again regarding her visiting our plane?'

Mab said, 'I agree. Let's take a closer look at her on our next visit. I've been reluctant to do a deep scan as she will be aware and I don't want her to be an enemy, we've got enough of those!'

Kanaka said, 'Let's pick up the liquor and the swords, and make our way home.' Mab nodded, Kanaka went to the bar and retrieved two bottles of fine malt whisky, which Alexei had left for him. Mab put her arm on his shoulder, and they vanished and materialised on the roof of the Haskins building. Mab retrieved their swords from the drainage pipe.

Kanaka said, 'I have to admit there is a certain beauty to the city at night, especially the lights in the buildings and on the transport machines.'

Mab nodded and put her arm around Kanaka. They vanished and materialised on the Guild sports field.

Mab said, 'Master Kanaka, what about the Council Meeting?'

Kanaka replied, 'I asked Jon to arrange it, so let me talk to him. I'll get back to you either tonight or first thing in the morning.'

Chapter Seventeen: Agent Provocateur

Mab spent what was left of the evening with Izzy, drinking wine and telling her about the city. Charly and Cat were at a birthday celebration with Gho and some of his friends, and would be sleeping over.

Mab said, 'You should have gone with them. I would have come to you.'

Izzy replied, 'I know, but I knew you would be tired and thought you would prefer a quiet night in?'

Mab said, 'Yes, you are right, I am tired.'

There was a knock at the door. Izzy opened it, and it was Kanaka.

Kanaka walked into the room and said, 'Mab, I brought a bottle of that liquor over for Boe and thought I'd drop in to let you know that the extraordinary council meeting is tomorrow mid-morning.

Lamm, Luticia and Taggar will be traveling here first thing. We thought it best to have a face-to-face, and we will need to have Satta at the meeting. I'm assuming you will be able to do your mind-to-mind translation?'

Mab replied, 'Yes, no problem. I'll bring Satta with me to the meeting. Thank you, Master Kanaka.'

Mab slept late the following morning and awoke with a start.

Izzy said, 'I thought you had an important meeting this morning? I have a class, so got to go, see you later!'

Mab leapt out of bed, had a quick shower and some coffee. She donned her robe and made her way to Amber House to collect Satta and Dassi. She knocked on the door, but there was no answer. She reached out with her witch senses and located Satta; she was in the Guild dining area. Mab entered her mind and looked through her eyes to see Master Uvren. She then made her way to the main building and found Satta, Dassi and Uvren having coffee together. Satta and Dassi started to rise, but Mab signaled them to stay seated and sat down beside them.

Mab said, 'Master Uvren, thank you for working with Satta and Dassi. It is very much appreciated.'

Uvren replied, 'Mab, it's my pleasure. It is nice to meet people who speak what to us is a forgotten language. Satta and Dassi are quick learners.'

Mab said, 'I must take Satta with me now to the council meeting. We are discussing whether we now need to intervene in the adjacent plane. I will bring her back here in a couple of hours.'

Uvren replied, 'Yes, of course I will continue with Dassi and await your return.'

Mab walked with Satta to Kanaka's office, knocked once and walked in. The other masters were already there.

Lamm walked to Mab, embraced her and said, 'How are you?'

Mab kissed him on the cheek and replied, 'I'm all the better for seeing you again, Master Lamm.'

Luticia also embraced Mab and said, 'It's lovely to see you again, Mab.'

Master Taggar said, 'I'm very pleased to meet you, Winter. I'm Taggar, Principal of the Guild of Witches and Warlocks.'

Mab replied, 'I'm pleased to meet you, Master Taggar.'

Kanaka said, 'This is Satta, she is a High Priestess in the Yehuda region, which is on the adjacent plane. As chairman of the council, I have called this extraordinary meeting, on the advice of Mab, to discuss whether we should intervene on the adjacent plane to free the people there from enslavement by daemons.'

Mab entered Satta's mind and said, 'Satta, I will stay in your mind during this meeting. You will be able to understand everything that is said, and ask questions mind-to-mind through me.'

Mab said to all, 'Satta doesn't yet speak our language, so she will communicate with us mind-to-mind.'

Kanaka said, 'Mab, could you first give us your perspective on this issue?'

Mab replied, 'Yes, of course, Master Kanaka. As most of you know, the plane adjacent to ours has been enslaved by daemons. This has been the case there for generations, such that the people have come to accept the situation as normal. We became involved in this following the discovery that our own plane was falling under the control of daemons. The Palace was rife with daemon hosts; the Prince himself was under the control of a daemon ruler. We have cleansed our own plane, and I feel we must do the same in the adjacent plane. The people there must be set free. Until recently, we did not have permission to intervene, but the situation has changed, and we are now permitted.'

Taggar said, 'I am somewhat confused by this, as I myself have never encountered even one of these daemons. However, if I accept what Winter, as an advisor to this Council, says as truth, our plane is now free of these creatures. Any intervention in another plane, which is a decision for this council and no one else, is likely to be fraught with risk.'

There was a brief silence before Lamm said, 'Master Taggar, I must ask you not to address Master Winter by her surname. It demonstrates a disrespect which is entirely inappropriate for someone who has saved this plane, us and our children, from the slavery being experienced elsewhere. Everyone around this table, other than you, has first-hand experience in battling daemons. Your predecessor was killed by a creature from the Abyss, released onto this plane by a daemon ruler, which no one other than Mab had the power to stop. If she had not succeeded in slaying the creature, none of us would be alive today. Mab has already made the decision to intervene in the adjacent plane. She is asking for our support, not our permission. I consider it an honour to be asked, the full resources of my school will be made available to her, and I will be fighting by her side to free Satta's people.'

Kanaka said, 'Taggar, I feel somewhat responsible for your lack of understanding of Mab's role. Yes, she is an advisor to the Council, a Master of this Guild and Head of our Warrior School, but she sits above the Council; she is not subservient to it. This Guild will be supporting Mab and Satta to free the people of Yehuda.'

Luticia said, 'The White Witch is greatly loved by the Academy; it will be an honour to serve her in any way we can.'

Taggar replied, 'I accept that I do not have knowledge of the previous conflicts, but entering into a war with the adjacent plane is a significant step. However, if it is the view of the council that we should support Master Winter in this endeavour, then the resources of my Guild will be made available. Master Winter, I apologise if my clumsy words caused any offence.'

Mab said, 'I have brought Satta here this morning to assist us in preparing a plan of attack. She has knowledge of the government and leadership in the Yehuda region. My feeling is that we need a two-pronged approach. Cut the head from the snake, whoever that may be, and free as many leaders as possible.'

Satta said, 'There are a number of leaders, many of them Legionnaires, but the most senior is Cassius, Commander of Legions, he is of Rome. Above him, theoretically, there are regional politicians and administrators, but they fear the commander. Below the commander, there are legion commanders who are of the region but trained to be ruthless warriors who care little for their own people.'

Kanaka asked, 'Satta, who is responsible for the killings at the stadium?'

Satta replied, 'Legion Commander Chanoch is directly responsible, but Commander of Legions Cassius is often present to witness the atrocities.'

Lamm asked, 'How many legion commanders are there?'

Satta replied, 'There are four, Chanoch, Mordechai, Fishel and Lieber. Chanoch and Fishel are truly evil, whereas Mordechai and Lieber are more political and seldom attend the Games.'

Taggar said, 'The Games?'

Mab replied, 'The killing of men, women, children and animals purely for entertainment. The more horrific the killings, the greater the enjoyment. When we last visited Yehuda, I was a different person, and my mother was present. This time they will know the consequences of shedding the blood of the innocent.'

Satta, tears running down her face, looked at Mab and said, 'Thank you, high-one, for everything that you have done and will do for me, my family and my people.'

Mab put her arms around Satta and hugged her.

Kanaka said, 'It sounds as if Chanoch and Fishel should be primary targets, but Cassius is the head of the snake. If we could find an opportunity where these were together in one place?'

Mab replied, 'Yes, if we could get them in one place, that would be perfect. Cassius may be hosting a ruler; his death would release many of his subordinates and result in general chaos, which would make things easier for us.'

Lamm said, 'Perhaps Satta could help by sketching out some rudimentary maps so we can locate the targets?'

Satta replied, 'The games are held monthly, although Cassius is not always in attendance. I would need to go back for the maps.'

Mab said, 'Where are the maps located?'

Satta replied, 'I have a map of the Yehuda region and the various villages in my home.'

Mab put her arm around Satta, pulled her close and said, 'Show me your home.'

Satta closed her eyes and thought of her home. When she opened her eyes, she was in her home, standing beside Mab. Satta went to a cabinet in the corner of the room and removed two large canvas tapestries.

Mab and Satta materialised back in Kanaka's office; Satta placed the tapestries on the table. Mab said, 'How long were we gone?'

Kanaka replied, 'Only a few minutes.'

Mab said, 'As we thought, time seems to be moving at the same pace here as on the adjacent plane.'

Luticia asked, 'You have just been to the other plane and returned?!'

Mab replied, 'Yes, I can take a few people with me, but any more than three could be dangerous.'

Taggar said, 'Three is hardly enough to fight a battle.'

Lamm said, 'Mab discovered the adjacent plane by flying through mind-space. It is safer for us to leave our physical bodies here and fight the battle with our minds.'

Kanaka said, 'Satta, could you explain what's on these maps?' Satta opened the first map and, pointing at the stadium, said, 'This is the stadium, in the Moriah district, where the games are held. It is a circular arena, the dignitaries always sit together on the dais, which is on the opposite side to the warrior entrance. The cells, for people and animals, are also on the side opposite to the dais but located underground. This is where Dassi and I were imprisoned before being rescued by Master Mabdelore.'

Satta pointed to a large structure some distance from the stadium and said, 'This is where the Administrator is located.'

Mab asked, 'Is Padwa still the Administrator?'

Satta replied, 'Yes, as far as I am aware, although he may have been taken by a daemon once more.'

Kanaka asked, 'Which buildings house the legionnaires and the legion commanders?'

Satta pointed to two buildings adjacent to each other, located roughly halfway between the stadium and the church and said, 'The larger building is where the legionnaires live, you will see that there are various exercise areas there for legionnaires and horses. The smaller building is in an elevated position and looks over the village, and this is the home of the legion commanders when they are in the area, either for military matters or attending the Games.'

Lamm asked, 'Where does the commander of legions stay when in the Village?'

Satta replied, 'I am not sure, but I think in the same house as the legion commanders.'

Kanaka said, 'Satta, when the Games, or some other special event, are being held, I assume there would be a reception or dinner for dignitaries. Where would that be held and who would host the event?'

Satta replied, 'Yes, the formal receptions and dinners are always organised by the Administrator and held in the administration building. The commander of legions would typically, but not always, host the event depending on the importance of the occasion.'

Mab said, 'Perhaps we should get the commander on his own, as we did with the Prince. It will be hard enough to kill it if it is a ruler, but if it is surrounded by many adepts, it makes things even more difficult. Ideally, we should aim to kill the creature at the legion commander's home and then proceed to the administration building.'

Kanaka said, 'Satta, when is the next big event?'

Satta replied, 'There is a marriage ceremony, the daughter of Fishel, which takes place three days before the end of the month. The first day will be the ceremony, the second will be the feasting and the third day the Games which will be especially horrific and cruel.'

Mab said, 'Then we will attend uninvited on the evening of the second day and do a return visit early on the third day.'

Kanaka replied, 'A small team, an in-and-out assassination on the second night and then a more public display on the third day, making use of the Games?'

Mab smiled and said, 'Yes, Master Kanaka.'

Taggar said, 'Yes, it is a good plan. But we must also consider contingencies and sensitivities. What if there is more than one of these rulers present? What do we do if the commander is not there? What if the wedding is cancelled?'

Kanaka replied, 'Yes, Taggar, those are valid questions. We have time to hone the current plan and develop contingencies.'

Mab said, 'We need the plan to be flexible and dynamic, things are almost never as expected. If the plan fails entirely, then as a last resort, I will hunt the commander and kill him.'

Tagger replied, 'But what if you are killed?'

Mab said, 'Then you return here to safety, and the people of Yehuda continue to live in slavery. This is not complicated, Taggar, we either ignore their plight or we try our best to help them.'

Kanaka said, 'Mab, we will do some more work on scenarios and contingencies. However, the plan as discussed has been agreed upon. We leave on the evening of the second night, the primary objective is to assassinate the Commander, Chanoch and Fishel.'

Master's what say you?

'Aye,' said all. Mab left with Satta. Kanaka signalled to Lamm, Luticia and Taggar to stay behind. Kanaka rested his head in his hands for a few moments. He then said, 'I have had this discussion with others, so please don't take what I am about to say the wrong way. Lamm and I have known Mab since she joined the Guild as a student. She has become a very dear friend and a surrogate daughter to Master Boe. She was appointed a Master of the Guild within a few months of joining. Her powers are extraordinary and continue to grow at an exponential rate. She is also the daughter of the Archangel Uriel. Please, be respectful and be very careful what you say to her. Fortunately, she has matured a lot over recent months, otherwise you Taggar would be dead; and believe me, she could kill you with a thought.'

Taggar replied, 'Surely I am entitled to express my opinion.'

Lamm said, 'Of course you can express your opinion, but you must do it respectfully, you almost accused her of being a liar.'

Luticia said, 'She is celestial, that is wonderful and explains many things. It is a great honour to have her here amongst us. When you told me her mother helped to slay Mahazael, now I understand. Uriel is said to be one of the most powerful beings in the Universe. This is truly extraordinary.'

Kanaka said, 'Yes, it is, and it may be that she will leave us at some point, hopefully in the very distant future. But we all need to be aware when she is present. Choose your words carefully, show respect, remember who she is and know that she is not what she seems. I must ask you to treat everything I have said here in the strictest confidence. Now, we four should work together on the contingencies around the plan and think specifically about the primary objective, who does what and where. If we need Satta's input, we can ask Mab or Uvren to help.'

Mab left Satta with Uvren and Dassi in the dining area and then made her way to the lost library. She reached out to Boe and said, 'Master Boe, could you help me?'

Boe replied, immediately 'Mab, is something wrong? What can I do to help?'

Mab said, 'Could you interrupt the Council meeting and ask Master Kanaka to come with you urgently to the lost library. Don't mention me. Make an excuse, some books were damaged or similar. He must come with you alone. I will explain when you bring him here.'

Boe replied, 'I'm on my way.' Boe knocked on Kanaka's office door, walked in and said, 'Master Kanaka, valuable books have been damaged! Ancient manuscripts! I have the two culprits in my room. I insist that you come with me now to discipline them.'

Kanaka looked at Boe, who was clearly very upset, and said, 'Masters, please excuse me, I must attend to this.' Boe stormed out of the room, still apparently seething in anger and made his way down the stairs, Kanaka following behind. Boe turned to Kanaka and gestured for him to be silent. He then led him down another flight of stairs and into the lost library.

Mab whispered 'Master Boe, thank you. Close and lock the door.'

Mab said, 'Master Kanaka, Master Boe, what do you know of Taggar?'

Kanaka said, 'He was a Master of the Guild of Witches and Warlocks under Jessam. I did think at the time that it was a strange appointment as he has had little involvement in our recent struggles with the Palace and the Academy.'

Boe said, 'I remember him as a student, so I suspect he has been with the Guild of Witches and Warlocks for most of his career. However, his skills are more administrative than magical.'

Kanaka said, 'Mab, I know Taggar was rude and difficult earlier, but I had put that down to his lack of knowledge. Is there something else?'

Mab replied, 'Yes, I'm afraid so. I moved gently into his mind during the meeting; he was not aware of my presence. I collected some of his recent thoughts; he has been in communication with a daemon, one we have met before, Amaymon. I reached out with my witch senses and located Amaymon, he is in Yehuda.'

Boe asked, 'Mab, your witch senses reach that far!?'

Mab replied, 'Yes, it worries me, Master Boe. My powers, they keep increasing. I fear they are changing me into something else, not human.'

Boe wrapped his arms around Mab, hugged her tightly and said, 'You will always be human no matter how powerful you become. And, your appearance has not altered one jot, other than the silver hair of course!'

Kanaka said, 'Mab, what do you suggest we do with Taggar?'

Mab replied, 'I had thought about killing him, but now we know that he is passing information to the enemy, I think we should make use of him. We develop two plans, one disinformation and the other that is the real plan. We need to keep the real plan secret, perhaps we can work on that separately?'

Kanaka replied, 'Yes, we can bring Lamm and Luticia into our confidence when the plans are confirmed.'

Mab said, 'I will remain here for a few hours to meditate.'

Boe returned to his rooms and Kanaka to the Council meeting.

Kanaka took his seat in the Council meeting and said, 'Students tearing pages from ancient manuscripts rather than copying the words. In my day, it would have been a flogging! Where did you get to with the plan?'

Lamm said, 'The attack will take place around the marriage ceremony of Fishel's daughter. The ceremony will be held in the village church on day one, and the feasting will commence on day two. Cassius, Chanoch, and perhaps Mordechai and Lieber will return to the house late in the evening of day 2 following the formal dinner. Fishel is not expected to return to the house; most likely, he will remain local with his family. We think the primary objective should be to kill Cassius, and the secondary objective should be to kill Chanoch. Mordechai and Lieber will only be killed if they intervene. The assassination team will be led by Mab and include Kanaka, me and Luticia. We will arrive at the house in the early hours of the third day. Taggar and Boe will remain in the library with Medics on hand to look after our physical bodies. The assassination team will complete the two objectives and return to the Guild immediately. Later that morning, the team, plus Taggar and Satta, will return to Yehuda to complete the remaining objectives, kill Fishel, intervene in the Games, if they proceed as planned, and kill or expel as many daemons as possible. The latter may require the support of the Priesthood.'

Kanaka said, 'That sounds good to me. Let's work separately on the detail and the risks and come together again next week to finalise and agree it with Mab?'

Chapter Eighteen: A Lesson in Swordsmanship

Mab searched for and found Alexei; he was running but didn't seem to be moving forward. Mab thought he may be in danger, but then he turned his head, and Mab saw there were others also running, but not moving forward. She realised they were running on a machine with a moving floor!'

Mab said, 'Why don't you run outside?'

Alexei grabbed the bar in front of him and said, 'Mab, you scared me!'

Mab replied, 'Sorry. Have you arranged the visit to the swordsmanship school yet?'

Alexei said, 'Yes, it's this afternoon, in a couple of hours. If you can't make it, then I'll cancel and rearrange.'

Mab replied, 'Where do we meet?'

Alexei said, 'Outside of Fat Joes?'

Mab replied, 'Great, see you later.'

Mab reached out to Kanaka 'Sorry for the short notice. Visit to the City in two hours?'

Kanaka replied, 'The School of Swordsmanship?'

Mab said, 'Yes!'

Kanaka replied, 'Too good to miss. I'll meet you on the sports field.'

When Kanaka arrived at the sports field, Mab was waiting. She was holding a sword in her hand. As he approached, she bowed and held it out to him. Kanaka smiled and said, 'What is this?'

Mab replied, 'Master Kanaka, I cannot repay you for everything you have done for me, but please honour me by accepting this gift.'

Kanaka took hold of the sword, which seemed to float, there being no discernible weight. The scabbard was a sheath of fine black bone inlaid with obsidian symbols, which were only visible under certain light conditions. Kanaka, turning the scabbard in his hands, whispered to Mab 'Where did you get this?'

Mab replied, 'I did a lot of research and reached out with my witch senses. It is a sentient blade and wants to be found. It was entombed with an emperor from an ancient civilisation.'

Kanaka grasped the hilt and pulled the sword only one-third out of the sheath. He gasped at the quality of the blade, and it was extraordinarily thin; the single cutting edge was the finest he had ever seen.

Mab said, 'Her name is Onimaru, Slayer of Daemons. Master Kanaka, we have many daemons that need slaying.'

Kanaka pulled Onimaru fully from the sheath and held it point upwards. The blade seemed to emit a satisfied hum, like a tuning fork, as if it were somehow connected to an invisible twin. He sliced her through the air, the blade shrieked as if with pleasure. Kanaka said, 'The blade is so fine. It resonates at different frequencies depending on the speed through the air.' He held the sword double-handed, ran forward and delivered three rapid vertical slices. At high speed, the blade moved from a shriek to complete silence. Kanaka said, 'One cannot own such a sword, but must trust it completely.'

Onimaru pulsed in Kanaka's hand as he sheathed the blade. Kanaka looked at Mab and said, 'Mab, this is much more than a gift, it is a treasure. I can't thank you enough.'

Mab replied, 'I'm looking forward to seeing you and her in action!'

Mab and Kanaka appeared on the rooftop of the Haskins building and looked down on the street below for an appropriate place to materialise. Mab said, 'Let's keep our swords with us this time, but under our robes.'

Kanaka replied, 'Yes, I don't want to let this one out of my sight!'

Mab, pointing down to the street, said, 'Wait a few seconds, we will move to that shaded alley.'

When the crowd had thinned out enough, Mab and Kanaka appeared in the alley and crossed the road to Fat Joes. Mab saw Alexei waiting for them.

Alexei said, 'I love the outfits, they make you look like a couple of priests!'

Mab replied, 'Nice to see you, Alexei. Will Morgana be joining us?'

Alexei replied, 'She is working away from home for a few days.'

Mab said, 'What sort of work does she do?'

Alexei replied, 'She doesn't talk about it, but I know she works for some very important businesspeople, I think advising them on security. Anyway, we must go now if you want to visit the school of swordsmanship. My car is parked just around the corner.' Mab and Kanaka followed Alexei to his car. Alexei opened the rear door, Mab got in and shuffled over to let Kanaka join her. Alexei got in the front and started the engine. Kanaka looked askance at Mab.

Mab said, 'Alexei, what do we have to do?'

Alexei said, 'You don't have to do anything. Are you telling me you have never been in a car before?!'

Mab replied, 'Of course not. I mean when we arrive at the school.'

Mab grinned at Kanaka. Alexia said, 'The Master will show you around the facility. I told him that you had some experience with swords and were thinking about taking some advanced lessons. I had to say that otherwise he wouldn't see you.'

Alexei pulled the car out and gunned it along the highway. Kanaka looked distinctly uncomfortable, but Mab was smiling, looking out the window and pointing at almost everything along the route. They eventually pulled into a large parking area.

Alexei pointed and said, 'There it is.'

The building was much older than those in the centre of the city. It was an enormous stone monolith; the school of swordsmanship was on the second floor. Alexei led the way; they entered through large glass doors into the fencing hall. Kanaka noted that different styles of swordsmanship were practiced in the school. Alexei signed all three of them in at the reception desk and said to the receptionist.

'I'm Alexei Oblonsky, Master Okada is expecting me and my two guests.' After a short wait, Okada arrived and looked very surprised to see the two strangers wearing monk-like robes. Okada introduced himself. Alexei explained that Kanaka and Mab understood the language but only to a basic level.

Okada said, 'This is the finest swordsmanship school in the region. Our students have won many competitions not only nationally but internationally.'

Okada led them to the sword room, which contained quite literally thousands of swords of every type and description. One entire wall was devoted to single-edge blades. Kanaka walked straight to that, his eyes looking in every direction. Okada said, 'I thought you had the look of the samurai about you. This is, in fact, our most popular sport. Are you interested in learning more?'

Kanaka said to Alexei, 'Is it possible for me to handle the blades?'

Alexei asked Okada who consented. Kanaka walked slowly along the wall of swords and stopped near the end. He lifted a rather plain-looking sword, held it in the horizontal position and partially withdrew the blade. He then fully withdrew the blade, made three rapid slices in the air and returned it to the scabbard in one fluid motion.

Okada said, 'You chose one of the best swords, and I see that you have considerable skill.'

Kanaka said, 'In my country I am a Master Swordsman. My colleague and I are visiting the city and thought it would be interesting to visit this School.'

Okada replied, 'Master Kanaka, you are most welcome. Perhaps you would like to see some of our advanced students in practice, follow me?'

Okada led them to a separate room off the main hall. The room was divided into four fighting areas, all of them occupied by students using wooden swords. Okada said

'These are our most advanced students; they practice every night. This hall is for their exclusive use.'

Kanaka watched but was clearly less than impressed. Master Okada said, 'Would you like to fight?'

Kanaka shook his head and said, 'I would probably hurt one of the students. I would be happy to demonstrate a Kata from my country if that would be of interest?'

Master Okada clapped his hands together hard to attract the attention of the students and said, 'Master Kanaka is a master swordsman from overseas. He is visiting our city and has agreed to demonstrate a Kata. Please clear the fighting areas, sit and observe.'

Okada turned to Kanaka and said, 'Do you wish to borrow my sword?'

Kanaka replied, 'No, that won't be necessary, I will use my own.'

Kanaka looked at Mab and said, 'What do you think I should do?'

Mab replied, 'Lamu, no question.'

Kanaka replied, 'I thought you might say that!'

Lamu is one of the most difficult sword katas, and it replicates the sword wielder battling multiple opponents. The moves must be executed with control and precision, but at blinding speed with interspersed periods of slow deliberation. It is beautiful to watch; when performed correctly, the master and the sword are as one.

Kanaka removed his robe and hitched his sword high on his back in the combat position. He walked to the centre of the four fighting areas and stood perfectly still, slowing his breath and clearing his mind. He then moved his left foot back slowly and carefully, but then his hand moved with blinding speed, releasing Onimaru from the sheath. The sword moved so fast it could only be seen when it stopped in the battle-ready horizontal position above Kanaka's head. The students gasped at what they had just witnessed. Kanaka was as still as a statue. He then launched into a forward attack, delivering four vertical slices followed by a horizontal slice, spinning in mid-air and again landing in the battle-ready position. He snapped Onimaru to the horizontal position, spun quickly and executed a reverse roundhouse high kick, quickly followed by two side high kicks, before diving into a forward roll, leaping into the air, somersaulting, and once again landing in the ready position. The Kata continued for 8 minutes and was executed perfectly. Kanaka finished as he started, but with some aplomb, he threw Onimaru high into the air, caught her as she fell and sheathed her in a single movement. The students leapt to their feet and applauded vigorously. However, when Kanaka pulled his hand away from Onimaru, the sword refused to leave and remained unsheathed. Kanaka turned and looked at Mab.

Mab walked towards Kanaka and scanned the hall searching for the daemon. She found three hosts, one being Okada.

She then looked at Alexei and said, 'Alexei, I hope you are not involved in this?'

Alexei replied, 'I don't understand, what's wrong?' But she knew he was lying, and Mab's black orb eyes told Alexei that she knew he was lying. Mab turned to Okada and said,

'You and your two acolytes will remain here; everyone else can leave.'

Okada laughed and said, 'Excellent, I will deal with you two when the students have left. Igor, Michail, remain here. Everyone else, please leave the Hall.'

Mab turned to Kanaka and said, 'Master Kanaka, I'm keen to see your new sword in action. Would you mind killing this filth pointing at Okada? Master Kanaka smiled and said, 'It will be my pleasure.'

Mab looked at Okada and said, 'It's death by the sword or death by incineration, but either way, you will not be returning to the Abyss.' Mab turned to the students and said, 'You will stay where you are.'

The acolytes tried to move but found they were immobilised. Kanaka walked to the middle of the hall and waited. Okada drew his sword and approached Kanaka. Kanaka bowed, and as he did so, Okada attacked, but Kanaka was ready. Kanaka backed off a few steps, Onimaru resting easily in his hands and parrying the blows from Okada's attack. Kanaka was astonished; it was as if he didn't have to think too much, but of course, he did. Okada was an expert swordsman, and his blade was one of the best he had seen. Kanaka went on the attack rushing Okada delivering powerful vertical strikes with Onimaru, he had intended to switch to a single-handed long reach horizontal slice at Okada's abdomen but in the final vertical slice Onimaru rotated in Kanaka's hand and powered down the length Okada's blade severing the cross-guard together with Okada's sword hand. Kanaka pulled Onimaru back, but she suddenly stabbed forward straight through the centre of Okada's chest. Okada died instantly, and the daemon within screamed in agony as the sword took its life.

Mab walked to the first acolyte and said, 'Boul, leave this body or you will suffer the same fate.'

The daemon Boul fled, and the acolyte's body dropped to the ground. The daemon in the second acolyte needed no persuasion, and it left immediately. The two acolytes recovered quickly, both were crying and thanked Mab and Kanaka profusely. Mab said, 'Leave this place and do not return.'

She then walked to Alexei and said, 'You will tell me everything you know regarding daemons and Morgana. If you lie to me, I will know and I will scour your mind for the truth, your brain will be irreparably damaged.'

Alexei replied, 'I will tell you what I know.'

Mab said, 'Morgana is in Yehuda. What is she doing there?'

Kanaka stared askance at Alexei, who replied, 'I don't know anything about Yehuda, but if Morgana is there, it will be for evil purposes. She consorts with daemons and uses her powers to enslave people either through sheer brutality or by means of narcotics or other addictive substances.'

Mab said, 'Where does she live when not with you?'

Alexei replied, 'I have been there only once. It is an apartment on the top floor of the Haskins building.'

Mab said, 'You will go to Fat Joes now and have no direct contact with anyone, especially Morgana. Go now and wait for us there.'

When Alexei left, Mab said to Kanaka, 'We need to search her apartment. She most probably travelled through mind-space so her body may be there.'

Mab put her arm around Kanaka, and they materialised on the top of the Haskin's building.

Mab and Kanaka entered the building through the rooftop access door. The top floor housed around ten apartments. Mab said, 'We need to check them all, her mind is in Yehuda, so I can't track the body.'

Kanaka said, 'Let's just ask someone.' They walked along the corridor, knocking on doors, and on the fourth attempt, a young woman opened the door. Master Kanaka said,

'We are sorry to bother you. We are visiting a good friend of ours who lives on this floor, but there are no numbers or names on the doors! We are at a loss, can you help us?'

The young woman laughed and said, 'Yes, it is a constant problem, but the building owners will not allow us to change anything. What is your friend's name?'

Kanaka said, 'Morgana, she also is young and beautiful.'

The woman's face lit up and she said, 'Why, thank you! Yes, I know Morgana, it's the second door down on the opposite side.' Kanaka thanked her again, and they made their way to Morgana's apartment.

Mab said, 'I see you still have some skills in dealing with young ladies!'

Kanaka laughed and replied, 'I think she felt sorry for me.'

When they reached the door, Mab said, 'Let me scan the room first.'

She reached out with her senses but detected no danger, and she then unlocked the door with her mind. The apartment was huge, and they searched every room methodically. Mab was looking through papers in the office when Kanaka called her. He had moved a large bookcase aside and found a hidden space. Morgana was lying flat on a bed.

Mab said, 'How did you find this?'

Kanaka pointed to the floor and said, 'Scores on the wood, the bookcase is regularly moved aside.'

Mab said, 'Press the point of your sword slowly into her abdomen until she wakes and then hold it in position.'

Kanaka unsheathed Onimaru and placed the point on Morgana's stomach and slowly pushed. The blade penetrated easily, and blood started to flow. Kanaka could feel the blade trying to drive through her body. Kanaka whispered,

'Slowly, Onimaru, this is no daemon.'

Morgana's eyes suddenly opened, she looked at the sword, her eyes widened, and then she saw Mab. Kanaka said,

'Do not move, if my hand leaves the hilt, this sword will drive through your vitals.'

Mab said, 'What were you doing in Yehuda?'

Morgana replied, 'I was called there by a daemon ruler.'

Mab replied, 'I will ask you only once more, what were you doing in Yehuda?'

Morgana replied, 'I was assisting the ruler in finding suitable hosts for his followers.'

Mab said, 'You were helping daemons enter into unwilling human hosts?'

Morgana did not answer. Mab said, 'I will have your answer.'

Morgana replied, 'Yes. I had no choice. It is not possible to refuse a ruler.'

Mab said, 'What was the name of the ruler?'

Morgana replied, 'Samael.'

Mab said, 'What else did you discuss? What plans have you made with your daemon friends?'

Morgana replied, 'He intends to kill you, Mabdelore.'

Mab said, 'How exactly does he intend to do that?'

Morgana replied, 'Your mother will first be removed, and then the rulers will seek you out and slay you.'

Mab said, 'My mother will be removed? How will that be accomplished?'

Morgana replied, 'I do not know.'

Mab looked at Kanaka, Morgana said, hastily, 'I am with Child.'

Mab replied, 'No, Morgana, you are not with child. You manipulated your cells, thinking you could take me for a fool. Did Samael discuss the 'balance' with you?'

Morgana said nothing.

Mab said, 'My mother believes in the balance between good and evil because it has always been that way. You and Samael know this and seek to use it to your advantage. Yes, Morgana, I know that you have discussed this with Samael; it is transparent to me. However, you have made a grave error. What you and Samael do not understand is that, unlike my mother, I do not believe in the balance, there can be no balance where evil is concerned.'

Morgana replied, 'What then is your intention if you do not believe in a truce that has existed since the beginning of time?'

Mab replied, 'There is no truce. I will slay the three remaining rulers and bring light where there is darkness.'

Mab looked at Kanaka, who pushed Onimaru through Morgana's abdomen. Kanaka said, 'I take no joy in this Mab.'

Mab replied, 'I understand, but she had choices. She chose evil and so had to die. I need to do something; I will meet you on the roof in a few minutes.'

When Kanaka left the room, Mab drew Dawn-Breaker and drove it downwards through Morgana's breastbone and into her heart. She then moved the heavy bookcase back, closing off the entrance to the secret room, and made her way to the rooftop. Mab put her hand on Kanaka's shoulder, and they materialised in a doorway on the street below. They walked in silence to Fat Joes.

Alexei was sitting alone in a far corner of the bar area. Kanaka said to Alexei, 'I need a drink.'

Alexei said, 'How about that single malt you like?'

Kanaka replied, 'Bring a bottle.'

Alexei said, 'Mab, what would you like?'

Mab replied, 'Ice cold white wine, bring a bottle.'

Kanaka looked at Mab and said, 'What do you think is happening?'

Mab replied, 'I don't know for sure, but I suspect Samael intends to break the oath he made to my mother.'

Kanaka said, 'That would only happen if a creature from the Abyss was set loose on our plane.'

Mab replied, 'Yes, exactly. My mother would then descend into hell looking for Samael, and the trap would be sprung.'

Kanaka said, 'Would they be able to imprison your mother in the Abyss?'

Mab replied, 'I don't know, but daemons are not the only things that dwell in that place, and my understanding is that once you are there, it is impossible to escape. I'm sorry about Morgana, but there was no other option.'

Kanaka replied, 'I know. Mab, do you mind if I return this sword to you? It is an extraordinary thing, but I would prefer something more human.'

Mab said, 'Yes, but only if you accept Dawn-Breaker in return.'

Kanaka smiled and said, 'I hoped you would say that.'

Mab leaned over, kissed him on the cheek, and rested her head on his shoulder. Alexei arrived with the drinks and said, 'You guys look tired. Have you had a tough night?'

Kanaka replied, 'We have had a difficult few months.'

Kanaka poured the single malt for Alexei and himself, and then the wine for Mab. They drank the first round in silence.

Mab then looked at Alexei and said, 'Has Morgana been in touch with you?'

Alexei replied, 'No, I have heard nothing. She must still be in that Yehuda place you mentioned earlier.'

Mab said, 'Tell us what you know of daemons.'

Alexei replied, 'I know Morgana has dealings with these creatures. She told me they were powerful allies. She employs them to help with the narcotics business. The students and daemons at the swordsmanship school are, or were, being trained for the same purpose.'

Mab said, 'Morgana must have mentioned some names of people she has met or intended to meet.'

Alexei replied, 'She doesn't really talk much about her work or who she meets. She has never been afraid of anyone, but she fears you, Mab. You need to be careful; I think she may try to kill you or, more likely, get someone else to kill you.'

Mab stared, in thought, at Alexei and said, 'Is there anything else that you want to tell us?'

Alexei hesitated and said, 'No.'

Mab said, 'My advice to you is to go home and stay away from Morgana.'

Alexei stood up and left without looking back.

Mab said, 'He knows more, but we may compromise our own plans if we dig deeper.'

Kanaka poured himself another very large measure of single malt and said, 'The summary of the fake plan is that you, me, Lamm and Luticia wait in the commander's house for him and the other regional commanders to return from the evening dinner, in the early hours of the third day. The intention is to kill Cassius and Chanoch at that time, so achieving the primary objectives.'

Mab said, 'Where will Taggar be?'

Kanaka smiled and said, 'With Boe in the library looking after our bodies!'

Kanaka continued 'The assassination team will then return to the library. Later that morning, the team will travel back to Yehuda with Taggar and Satta in order to kill Fishel, intervene in the games, if they proceed, and free as many daemon hosts as possible. We now need to discuss the real plan.'

Mab replied, 'If they are expecting us to be waiting for them in the commander's house, then we must hit them much earlier, either at the wedding ceremony on day 1 or at the dinner on the evening of day 2.

Kanaka said, 'The wedding ceremony doesn't feel right to me. In any case, I don't think Cassius or the other regional commanders will attend the ceremony, which will most likely be family only.'

Mab replied, 'Yes, you are right. It needs to be at the dinner. The downside is the collateral damage and the risk that there may be more than one ruler present. The upside is that all the key people will be in one place.'

Kanaka said, 'We need to wait until the last minute before killing Taggar.'

Mab replied, 'Yes, just before we leave for Yehuda. I hope Morgana's disappearance doesn't spook them too much.'

Kanaka said, 'I don't think so. From what I understand, narcotics is a dangerous business; people go missing and get killed. In any case, they will be preparing their plan using the information Taggar is passing to them. I don't think they will expect to be attacked at the dinner.'

Mab said, 'We need Satta to describe the administration building layout to us in some detail. We don't know if the targets will be easily recognised, so we have to get into the building early and be able to observe the preparations.'

Kanaka said, 'Might be best if you sit down with Satta and think about how we could best position ourselves to observe and then intervene. But she needs to understand that she cannot share the information with anyone other than you. I guess it's too risky to visit the administration building before the event?'

Mab replied, 'I think it is almost essential. But I will talk to Satta about the risks. Following that, I think we develop the best plan we can with the information available and then adapt if circumstances are not as envisaged.'

Kanaka said, 'I agree. Well, I'll have another large one from this bottle, and I see you have almost finished that bottle of wine. Mab, I think you may be developing an alcohol problem?'

Mab laughed and said, 'Yes, you too.'

They sat in silence for several minutes, then Mab said, 'Do you mind my asking why you have never married?'

Kanaka replied, 'No, I don't mind at all. I just haven't found the right person. I guess I've been too busy with work.'

Mab said, 'What would the right person look like?'

Kanaka replied, 'That's a difficult one. Do you remember Melsa, the witch from the Academy that you decapitated?'

Mab said, 'Yes, of course I remember her.'

Kanaka replied, 'Well, she would have been just perfect for me.'

Mab stared at Kanaka, who burst into fits of laughter. Mab grabbed his hand and said, 'Right, back home, you have clearly had too much to drink!'

This sent Kanaka into another fit of laughter. They materialised on the sports field, arm in arm, both still laughing, and made their way back to the Guild building.

It was early evening when Mab got back to the suite. Cat was there but busy working on an assignment. Mab asked if she knew what Izzy was doing.

Cat replied, 'I'm not sure, I know today was a busy day for her, so I guess she is still in classes.'

Mab said, 'I need to sleep, so ask her to wake me when she gets back.'

Cat replied, 'Will do,' and continued with her work.

Mab slept deeply for several hours before waking with a start.

She stood up, reached out with her witch senses and found Izzy in the medical centre. She mind-melded with her and said, 'Izzy, what's happening. Are you ill?'

Izzy said, 'I was bitten on the leg by a big snake on my way back from class. I feel very weak, light-headed and nauseous. My leg is numb. Charly brought me here.'

Mab said, 'Who is there with you? Look up so I can see. Mab saw Charly sitting at Izzy's bedside and two medics that she didn't recognise preparing medication. Mab vanished and reappeared at Izzy's bedside.

She said to the Medic's, 'I hope for your sake my wife recovers quickly.'

Mab ripped the bed cover off to look at the bite. Charly screamed. Izzy's leg was horribly swollen, and yellow puss leaked from two large puncture wounds.

Mab looked at the Medics and said, 'You will remain where you are.'

Mab placed her hand on Izzy's forehead, which was drenched with beads of sweat. Light poured from Mab's hand, engulfing Izzy's head and slowly running down over her body until she was covered in a skin of silver. Mab said to Izzy, 'Try to relax, the light will drive the poison from your system. Don't worry, you will be fine.'

Mab turned to the two medics and said, 'Which one of you bit my wife?'

The first shapeshifter smiled and said, 'Release me and I will tell you whatever you want to know.'

Mab replied, 'Who are you working for?'

The second shapeshifter said, 'We will tell you nothing.'

Mab said, 'I have asked two questions and I expect two answers; otherwise, you are going to die truly horrible deaths.'

Mab said to Charly, 'Go back to the suite and wait with Cat.' Charly ran from the medical centre. Mab went back to Izzy and removed the skin of light. She looked much better, the swelling had gone down, and the poison had been driven from her body.

Mab shook her gently and said, 'How are you feeling?'

Izzy replied, 'I'm feeling so much better.'

Mab said, 'Can you walk back to the suite. I have some business to attend to here.'

Izzy replied, 'Yes, the fresh air will be good for me.'

Mab said, 'This won't take long.' Mab turned to the medics and said, 'Now, where were we. Yes, I remember.'

Onimaru flashed from the scabbard, decapitating the first shapeshifter. The body slumped to the floor, blood fountaining from the severed neck. Mab then walked to the severed head, lifted her foot and slammed it down, crushing the skull to a red, grey and white pulp against the stone floor.

Mab said, 'Try shapeshifting now!'

Mab approached the second shapeshifter, who was trembling, and said, 'Who are you working for?'

The shapeshifter said, 'We were employed by the daemon ruler Samael to intercede in this plane. We were told to come to this school and kill you and as many of your close friends as possible. You were not here, so we attacked your partner.'

Mab replied, 'So you have failed to kill anyone on this Campus?'

The shapeshifter said, 'Yes, but we have only just arrived, and we are not alone.'

Mab replied, 'How many of you are here?'

The shapeshifter said, 'We were a team of four.'

Mab drew Onimaru, decapitated him and crushed his skull to a pulp.

Mab reached out with her witch senses attuned to shapeshifters. They were in Kanaka's office. Mab vanished and materialised in the far corner of his office behind the shapeshifters. The third shapeshifter said to Kanaka, 'We are not here for you, tell us where she is, and you will be spared.'

Kanaka said, 'I know you intend to kill me. I will tell you how to find her, but first, you must tell me who you are and who sent you. Is that not a reasonable request in return for my life?'

The fourth shapeshifter said, 'Very well. We are assassins, we were hired by the daemon ruler Samael to kill the witch Mabdelore Winter and as many of her friends and family as possible within certain time constraints.'

Kanaka replied, 'I see, but did Samael explain to you why he wanted Mabdelore killed?'

The third shapeshifter said, 'That is of no interest to us. This is purely a business transaction. You will now tell us how to find the witch.'

Kanaka sat back in his chair, pointed and said, 'She is standing over there.'

The two shapeshifters turned around to see Mab at a window, nonchalantly waving to someone on the field below.

Mab turned to face them and said, 'Master Kanaka, have you finished with them?'

Kanaka said, 'Yes, they are all yours.'

Mab said, 'Your two friends are dead. If you give me some valuable information, I may allow you to live. If you have nothing to say, then your life ends here. However, before you answer, I would like you to meet my sword, Onimaru.' Mab drew Onimaru from her sheath with blinding speed. The point of the sword contacted the forehead of the third shapeshifter and stopped dead. Mab held Onimaru in position, and a trickle of blood ran down the shapeshifter's forehead onto the side of his nose.

The shapeshifter felt the power of the sword and said, 'What do you want to know?'

Mab sheathed Onimaru and said, 'Tell me everything you know about the daemons and why they sent you here.'

The shapeshifters reiterated that they had been hired by the daemon ruler Samael to kill Mabdelore Winter and her friends and family. Samael had agreed to release one of their brothers who was being held captive in the Abyss as payment in kind.

Kanaka asked, 'If they are holding your brother captive, why don't you try to rescue him instead of killing innocent people?'

The third shapeshifter said, 'It is easy to enter the Abyss, but none who have entered have ever returned unless released by a ruler or Lucifer himself.'

Kanaka replied, 'If there is a door in, then surely there must be a door out?'

The fourth shapeshifter said, 'My sister's boy was taken to the Abyss in order to coerce his father into killing a nobleman on my home plane. Many attempts were made to rescue him, but none who entered returned. The boy was eventually released, after his father carried out the assassination, and I was there when he returned home. He described the Abyss as a place of darkness and constantly changing geography; it is quite literally chaos. Many are held there in chains, physically manacled to walls or posts, but most wander alone through the carnage, trying to avoid the loathsome creatures that feed on the unwary. It is possible to walk for weeks, months or years in one direction, but because everything is in constant change, there is no way of knowing if progress is being made. In that place, magical powers are nulled unless they are daemonic. The boy told us that there is a Palace where Lucifer and the rulers reside when they are in the Abyss. The Palace is visible everywhere, as if the Abyss is a kind of transparent, distorted toroidal surface with the Palace at the centre. Shape and dimensions within the Abyss make no sense and are in constant flux. The Palace itself is huge, and there are said to be countless dungeons within which valuable prisoners are secured and traded.'

Mab said, 'If I release you, where will you go?'

The third shapeshifter replied, 'We will lie low and take our chances, but you have my word that we will not return to this plane.'

Mab looked at the fourth shapeshifter, who nodded in agreement. Mab said, 'Then you may leave. But know this, you cannot kill me. Samael also knows this; he is playing a game and you are the prize.'

The shapeshifters changed into small black birds and flew from Kanaka's office through an open window.

Kanaka said, 'Mab, these shapeshifters are not from the Abyss; therefore, strictly speaking, Samael has not broken his vow.'

Mab replied, 'Yes, although I'm not sure my mother would see it that way!'

Kanaka said, 'We have two days before the wedding ceremony at Yehuda. I have asked the masters to be here on the evening of the ceremony to confirm the plan. We will wait until we are in the library before killing Taggar. We then brief everyone on the real plan and leave for Yehuda straight away. Hopefully, Satta can identify a location in the administration building where we can hold up until the festivities are underway.'

Mab replied, 'I will go to see her now. Dassi is probably in bed, so Satta should have some free time.'

Mab walked from Kanaka's office across the campus to Amber house and knocked gently on the door.

Satta said, 'Who is it?'

Mab replied, 'Satta, it's Mab. Can I speak to you now, or should I come back tomorrow morning?'

Satta opened the door and invited Mab into her apartment. She brought herbal tea and fruit scones to share.

Mab said, 'Master Kanaka and I have been developing our plans for the attack on the daemons in Yehuda. However, we have discovered that Master Taggar is a traitor and has been feeding information to the daemons. So, it is essential that you keep everything we discuss here secret. Do you understand?'

Satta replied, 'Yes, of course. Does he know that he has been discovered?'

Mab said, 'No, he doesn't. The plan we are developing with Taggar and the other masters will be disinformation. The plan that Master Kanaka and I develop will be the real plan. We have decided that we will attack the daemons at the celebration dinner in the administration building. Taggar, however, thinks the attack will be much later in the evening at the commander's house. What I wanted to discuss with you is the layout of the administration building, we will need to access the building early and preferably be in a location where we are able to view the preparations.'

Satta replied, 'The Grand Hall in the administration building is where the celebration dinner will be held. It was previously used as a theatre, and the lower-level seats and the stage areas were all removed during the so-called restoration. However, the high-level viewing areas remain; these would provide an excellent view of the dinner.'

Mab said, 'Tomorrow morning, could you leave Dassi with Master Uvren and travel with me to the Grand Hall?'

Satta replied, 'Yes, of course. Would we be safe?'

Mab smiled and said, 'Yes, Satta, perfectly safe.'

Mab made her way back across the campus and headed for the lost library. She sat in her usual place and reached out with her witch senses.

Uriel said, 'Mabdelore, how are you, my child?'

Mab replied, 'I am fine. We are preparing to rid Yehuda of daemons, we plan to attack them at a wedding dinner in the administration building.'

Uriel said, 'Will you need my assistance?'

Mab replied, 'No, Mother, that won't be necessary. However, Samael sent hired assassins, shapeshifters, to kill me and anyone close to me. I have dealt with them. Sometime within the next few days, I am expecting another attack, which would result in Samael breaking the vow he swore to you. This will be done to ensure you enter the Abyss, where you will be trapped. The rulers think that without your support, they will be able to hunt me down, torture and kill me.'

Uriel said, 'If Samael breaks his vow to me, I will drag him from the Abyss as promised.'

Mab replied, 'But Mother, it is their intention to trap you in that place.'

Uriel said, 'I will not go back on my word.'

Mab replied, 'Have you been there before?'

Uriel said, 'I went there once, a very long time ago, to speak with Morningstar. He warned me never to return, but I have given my word, so I must.'

Mab replied, 'Mother, you gave your word to a daemon!'

Uriel said, 'It matters not if the receiver was unworthy, my word is given and I am bound by it.'

Mab replied, 'Yes, Mother, I understand. I love you.'

Uriel said, 'And I love you, Mabdelore.'

Mab made her way back to the suite to find Izzy, Charly and Cat waiting for her. Mab went to Izzy, embraced her and said, 'Sorry, it took longer than I thought. There were four of them, two in Master Kanaka's office. How are you feeling?'

Izzy said, 'I'm feeling great, that silver skin has completely rejuvenated me!'

Charly said, 'Mab, how about some supper?'

Mab replied, 'That would be great, and I see you have already started on the wine!'

Charly and Cat brought out platters of different types of bread, cheeses, cold meats and fruit. Mab was hungry and tucked in.

Izzy said, 'What did you do to the shapeshifters.'

Mab replied, 'The two that attacked you are dead. We allowed the others, in Master Kanaka's office, to leave as they had not yet harmed anyone. But we all need to be careful, I think there may be another attack on the Guild in the next few days. So don't go walking around the campus at night or go anywhere on your own.'

Mab stirred late the following morning, showered, dressed and went to the dining area to find Satta. She and Dassi were with Master Uvren, who was seconded to the Guild to help Satta and Dassi with languages.

Uvren said, 'Good morning, Mab. Satta has explained that you want to borrow her for a few hours?'

Mab replied, 'I hope that is alright with you, Master Uvren?'

Uvren said, 'Of course, Dassi and I will be here all morning. But in any case, I will keep her amused until you return.'

Mab thanked Uvren and walked with Satta to the lost library.

Mab mind melded with Satta and said, 'First think of the administration building, then of a spacious but safe location where we can materialise without being seen.'

Satta replied, 'The Grand Hall will not be occupied at this time. In fact, it will most probably be locked up.'

Satta and Mab visualised the hall and materialised there. The hall was huge and boasted two enormous wooden dining tables. The chairs and dining accoutrements were stored in auxiliary rooms along the periphery of the main hall. Satta pointed upwards to the high-level viewing areas.

Mab said, 'Those will not be in use during the dinner?'

Satta replied, 'No, they are never used. They are a remnant of the time when we had music, singing and theatre productions. My grandparents told me of those times, but I have never experienced such events.'

Mab said, 'How do we get up there? Satta led Mab to a door in the far corner of the hall, but it was locked. Mab unlocked it with a thought. The door opened onto a stairway that climbed to the upper level. A waist-height parapet barrier ran the full length of the hall, screening off the upper viewing area from the main hall. There was a door at the far end of the upper-level area. Mab said, 'Where does that lead?'

Satta replied, 'It leads onto the main staircase at the front of the building.'

Mab said, 'I am trying to figure out the best escape route. Are there other exits?'

Satta led Mab back along the corridor and down the stairway. She pointed to a doorway that Mab hadn't noticed. Satta said, 'This door leads to the outside.'

Mab said, 'Is it the same arrangement on the other side of the hall?'

Satta said, 'Exactly the same.'

Mab said, 'Let's go back upstairs.' Satta followed Mab back upstairs to the upper level. Mab asked which parapet post would be closest to the head of the table.

Satta said, 'The dignitaries would usually sit at the far end near the exit door. So, the second parapet post would be closest to the head of the table.

Mab walked there, leaned over the parapet, and said, 'Yes, this is perfect. Let's go to the other side and double check.'

Mab and Satta went back down the stairs, crossed the hall and checked the stairway escape routes and upper-level viewing areas on the other side. It was exactly as Satta had remembered.

Mab said, 'Satta, I think we should get back to the Guild?'

Satta nodded. Mab and Satta materialised in the lost library and made their way back to the dining area to find Uvren and Dassi.

Mab walked upstairs to Kanaka's office. She knocked once and stuck her head round the door. Kanaka was there with Boe and Paull.

Mab said, 'Master Kanaka, sorry to interrupt. Could I see you and Master Boe sometime today?

Kanaka said, 'Yes, of course, let's have lunch here together.'

Mab smiled and said, 'Great, see you later.'

Mab made her way downstairs and out into the fresh air. She was walking across the sports field deep in thought regarding the forthcoming attack in Yehuda when her witch senses twitched. She spun around to see two huge black hounds bounding towards her, pursued by Amarok.

Mab said, 'Amarok, my friend, stand down.'

The first hound leapt at Mab, but she stood quite still and watched bemused as the great beast came through the air towards her. She moved blindingly fast, Onimaru flashed from the scabbard, and the hound's head parted from its body. The second hound stopped and circled Mab, clearly wary and fearful of the sword. Mab returned Onimaru to her sheath and stood passively watching the hound. It ran towards her and leapt, its maw closing on Mab's face.

Mab stepped back, raised her hand slapped the hound's face with the back of her left hand. The impact snapped the hound's head around, it yelped like a puppy and dropped to the ground dead.

Mab said, 'Bad doggy.'

Amarok said, 'High-one, I had hoped to aid you, but I see there was no need.'

Mab said, 'Amarok, I am always in need of good friends. Where did they come from?'

Amarok replied, 'High-one, these are Hell Hounds. They must have been released onto our plane by a ruler.'

Mab said, 'Amarok, say nothing of this to my mother. If she discovers Samael has broken his vow, she will go into the Abyss after him and will be trapped there.'

Amarok replied, 'Yes, high-one, I understand.'

Mab said, 'I was expecting an attack but thought it would be something more serious than a couple of puppies from Hell. Have you seen anything else on your travels?'

Amarok replied, 'No, but my pack and I will watch and warn if anything unusual occurs.'

Mab said, 'Thank you, Amarok.'

Mab continued on her walk around campus and then made her way to Kanaka's office for lunch and a meeting with him and Boe. She knocked once and walked into the office. Lunch was laid out on the table, and Boe and Kanaka were sitting at the desk.

Kanaka said, 'Mab, we were just discussing the plan. Let's eat and talk.'

They sat around the table and started filling their plates. Mab told them about the Hell Hounds.

Kanaka said, 'Do you think that would be sufficient cause for your mother to intervene?'

Mab replied, 'Yes, but she doesn't know about it, and I hope to keep it that way. Satta and I visited the Yehuda this morning, we went to the administration building. The hall is an old theatre which has been extended over the years to form the building as it is now. There are viewing areas high up in the walls which are unused. These overlook the hall and will allow us to arrive early, identify the targets and choose the optimal moment to launch the attack.'

Kanaka said, 'What about escape routes?'

Mab replied, 'We have identified three quite separate routes out of the building. I think that the four of us should travel there together. We stay hidden behind the parapet barrier until the dinner is underway. Initially, we could attack from above and then drop down into the hall to ensure we kill the key targets. If everything goes as expected, we will come together, and I will transport us back to the Guild. If we get separated, for whatever reason, we meet up at the church.'

Kanaka said, 'Do you think the commander is a ruler?'

Mab replied, 'I don't know, but I am hoping Samael is there. I will take great pleasure in slaying him.'

Boe said, 'Mab, please be careful, there may be more than one ruler present.'

Mab replied, 'That is possible, but I would be surprised to find two of them in one place.'

Kanaka said, 'I like it. It's simple and offers us options if circumstances are not as we envisaged.'

Mab replied, 'Satta says the wedding dinners usually start mid-afternoon and finish late evening. The rest of the night is spent drinking in various locations. We need to be in position around lunchtime, and we should eat before we leave. I can't think of anything worse than watching others eat and drink. Master Kanaka, would you like me to kill Taggar?' Kanaka looked at Mab and couldn't help laughing.

Mab, looking puzzled, said, 'It's just I thought you might be a bit squeamish with him being a Master and a Principal?'

Kanaka replied, 'No, Mab, he is a traitor. I will dispatch him just before we leave. Do you think we should take extra provisions? I was thinking a couple of bottles of wine with bread, a selection of cheeses and fruit?'

Boe looked away and covered his mouth, struggling not to laugh. Mab looked thoughtful and said, 'Yes, not sure about the wine though. But then again, why not?'

Kanaka replied, 'Mab, I was joking!'

Boe laughing, said, 'Mab, I think you should take your own provisions, let Master Kanaka and the others fend for themselves!'

Mab smiled warmly at Boe and said, 'Will we be having lunch together before we depart?'

Kanaka replied, 'Yes, we should gather here mid-morning. That is when we confront Taggar.'

Mab said, 'I will numb his psychic powers when he enters the room, but we need to act fast as he will recover quickly.'

Kanaka replied, 'Will we have time to interrogate him?'

Mab replied, 'Yes, we do need to interrogate him. If he tries to communicate with anyone outside of this room, I will remove his powers permanently, but that will result in brain damage. In which case, we could imprison him rather than kill him?'

Kanaka said, 'Mab that would be a better solution. In due course, we could have a full hearing, but until then, he remains in prison and unable to communicate with the enemy. Boe, do you know if he has a family?'

Boe replied, 'Yes, I believe he has a partner and children, at least he has mentioned them previously.'

Kanaka said, 'We imprison him and have a hearing at a suitable point in time; there may be mitigating circumstances that explain his treachery.'

Chapter Nineteen: The Cleansing of Yehuda

Mab woke early in the morning of the planned attack and went for her usual walk around the campus. It was a spring morning, but there was still a sharp chill in the air. The sun was just beginning to rise, and it would be a beautiful day, thought Mab. She heard a wolf howl, but it was in the distance, and it was not a howl of distress.

Amarok said, 'High-one, three heavily armed assassins, professionals, in the shadows close to the main gates.'

Mab replied, 'I will go to them. Are you sure there are only three?'

Amarok replied, 'Yes, smell, sound and sight all agree.'

Mab walked to the main gates and spoke to the Guard. He opened a pass gate and closed and locked it when Mab left the campus. Mab floated upwards, the sun was still low in the sky, but she saw the assassins by their heat signatures. They were sitting down in a hollow, probably having a quick breakfast before mingling with other visitors and sneaking into the Guild disguised as contractors or merchants. Mab floated above them for a few moments and then dropped to the ground only a few steps away from them. The assassins leapt to their feet and drew their swords. Mab noted that they were the single-bladed weapons favoured by Kanaka. They wore sophisticated armour which was articulated around the limbs and joints of the body. Mab reached into their minds and said, 'Impressive.' and then sat down. The assassins looked down at her, unsure how to proceed. Mab looked up at them and said, 'You may sit.' The assassins found themselves sitting down without volition. The lead assassin said, 'Who are you?'

Mab replied, 'It is I who will ask the questions.'

The assassins tried to stand but found they could not move.

Mab said, 'You will tell me where you came from, who sent you and why you are here. If you fail to answer these questions, I will crush your minds.'

The lead assassin said, 'If we give you this information, what will you do with us?'

Mab replied, 'I would need certain assurances from you, but I would allow you to return from whence you came.'

Another assassin said, 'Tell the bitch nothing!'

Mab looked at him, and he started to shake violently, blood ran from his ears and nose. His eyes rolled back in his head, and then he was still; his body remained locked in position for several seconds before slumping to the ground. Mab said, 'I will not ask my questions again.'

The lead assassin said, 'We are from another plane, which is more advanced technologically than this place. We were approached and offered a great deal of currency to kill the witch Mabdelore Winter and anyone else associated with her.'

Mab said, 'I am Mabdelore Winter. What was the currency offered?'

The assassin replied, 'You would not understand. It is a drug, a chemical substance, which is used to control people. For that reason, it is extremely valuable.'

Mab said, 'Who were you dealing with? I want names.'

The assassin replied, 'Our contact is Alexei Oblonsky, but he was working for others.'

Mab replied, 'I want the names of the others.'

The assassin said, 'It is an organisation that is hidden within a respectable company called the Haskins Corporation. It is big business; they own the law and have many politicians working for them.'

Mab said, 'I went to the Haskins building. I killed Haskins, and I threw his son off the top of the building. Are you saying the drug operation is unaffected?'

The assassin stared at Mab and said, 'That was you! I'm not surprised they want you dead. But to answer your question, yes, the operation is unaffected; others simply stepped into the shoes of the guys you killed.'

Mab said, 'How did you get here?'

The assassin looked at his colleague, who shrugged his shoulders and nodded. He then said, 'Oblonsky works for one of the Haskins Executives, his name is Robert Samael. He brought us here and told us we would find you at the Guild of Sorcerers.'

Mab said, 'How do you intend to get home?'

The assassin said, 'He said he would come for us midday at the place he dropped us off.'

Mab said, 'You will be imprisoned here for a few days. I will then return you to your plane. Come with me.' Mab delivered the assassins to the security guards, who relieved them of their weapons and escorted them to the cells. Mab reached out to Amarok and said, 'We have imprisoned two of the assassins, the other is dead. Thank you for the warning, once again, please do not trouble my mother with this incident.'

Amarok replied, 'Understood, I will stay in this area for a few days to keep watch.'

Mab made her way to Kanaka's office. When she entered, Lamm, Taggar and Luticia were already there discussing what they thought was the plan. Kanaka was at his desk, he nodded to Mab and then looked at Taggar. Mab delivered a psychic shock to a particular location on the right temporal lobe of Taggar's brain. Taggar felt the blow, and blood leaked from his nose.

He looked at Mab and screamed, 'What have you done to me!'

Mab replied, 'You will be silent.' Taggar tried to stand but found he could not move from the chair. Mab and Kanaka joined the rest of the masters at the table.

Kanaka said, 'Taggar, we know that you have been in communication with the enemy. You will tell us everything you know, otherwise you will be regarded as a traitor and executed.'

Taggar replied, 'Where is your evidence for these allegations?'

Mab said, 'What did you discuss with Amaymon?'

Taggar looked at Lamm and Luticia and said, 'I am innocent, I have had no contact with the enemy!'

Mab said, 'Taggar, you will answer my question.'

Taggar replied, 'I will answer nothing, you arrogant bitch!' Kanaka said, 'Taggar, we know you have been passing information to Amaymon, but in fact, this was disinformation. We have an alternative plan which we are about to implement. You will be imprisoned here until our return, but we cannot risk you recovering your psychic powers in our absence.'

Kanaka looked at Mab and said, 'It is regrettable but necessary.'

Mab nodded, looked at Taggar and said, 'I have already stunned the psychic area of your brain to prevent you from communicating with your daemon friends. I will now destroy that part of your brain, it will be painful and irreversible, but you will live.'

Taggar said, 'No, please stop, I will tell you what I know. Samael was instrumental in my promotion to principal of the school. In return, he wanted me to provide him with the decisions made at the council. I have been passing information regularly to Amaymon. Samael knows that you intend to attack him. He said that he would kill my whole family if I didn't cooperate.'

Kanaka asked, 'The commander of legions is host to Samael?'

Taggar replied, 'Yes, and he is an extraordinarily powerful daemon.'

Mab said, 'Are there any other daemon rulers present in Yehuda?'

Taggar replied, 'Not to my knowledge.' Kanaka looked at Mab; Mab reached into Taggar's mind and seared the temporal lobe. Taggar cried out and lost consciousness. Kanaka called for security to take him to the cells and asked that the medics look after him. He also arranged for the kitchen to bring lunch.

When the guards left with Taggar, Lamm said, 'What of the new plan?'

Kanaka said, 'We leave imminently. We are going as a group with Mab leading, but not through mind-space. Mab, could you explain the building layout?'

Mab said, 'As you know, Samael thinks the attack will take place late this evening when they return to their house. However, we intend to attack them at the dinner in the administration building. The hall used to be a theatre; we will be concealed in one of the disused high-level viewing areas. We will be able to look down on the guests and identify our targets. The higher ground will give us an initial advantage, but we will need to drop down to complete the task. I intend to drop down immediately and concentrate on killing Cassius, who is host to Samael. There are three exit routes from the building, and I will point these out to you when we get there. If all goes well, we group together in the hall and leave as we arrived. However, if we get separated then then we go our separate ways and meet at the church. The primary objective is to slay Cassius, Chanoch and Fishel. All three of these will be at the dinner and most probably sitting close to each other. Any questions?'

Lamm said, 'Why not use mind space to travel there, would it not be safer?'

Mab replied, 'That is what they are expecting. Samael intercepted us in mind space previously, and daemons are more attuned to the presence of spirits than the presence of humans.'

Luticia said, 'How will we know who to attack?'

Mab replied, 'In simple terms, kill anyone in a legionnaire's uniform or anyone hosting a daemon. But we will have time to choose our targets.'

Kanaka said, 'We finish lunch and leave for Yehuda. If you need anything, then get it now.'

Mab tucked into the last of the food, picked up some leftover pastries and stuffed them into her shoulder bag.'

Lamm, smiling, said, 'What else have you tucked away in there?'

Mab replied, 'Wine, cheeses, fruits and pastries, of course. We may be in need of food, plan for the worst, hope for the best!'

The group of four masters formed a tight circle by facing each other and resting their arms on each other's shoulders. Mab said, 'We now communicate only by mind-meld, so no talking!' She closed her eyes and thought of the viewing position closest to the head of the table in the large hall. They materialised behind the parapet, immediately dropped low and then slowly raised their heads to look down into the dining area. The hall was being prepared. Two large tables had been made into a U-shape by adding an additional small table. Mab said, 'That will be the head of the table where the bride, groom and close family will sit. The dignitaries will no doubt be seated close to that area. I will show you the escape routes, follow me.' Mab, bent low behind the parapet, walked along the viewing area and led the group to the bottom of the stairs at the hall floor level. She pointed and said, 'That door leads into the hall, but the one behind me is an exit. The upper-level door leads to the office areas and the main stairway, but that will be busy, so suggest you don't use that route unless it is your only option. The arrangement is the same on the other side of the hall. All the doors will be locked, so you need to overcome the lock or simply blast the door down to get out.' The group returned to the upper level.

Kanaka said, 'When the fighting starts, it will be chaotic down there. So, remember, if we get separated, meet at the church. No one will be left behind.' They sat in silence for almost an hour, then Kanaka lifted his head up, looked over the parapet and said, 'The table is set and almost ready. I expect the guests will be arriving soon.'

Half an hour later, they heard a commotion below. Lamm popped his head up and said, 'They are streaming in and taking their seats.' The noise level in the hall began to rise significantly. Another half an hour or so passed, and Luticia slowly lifted her head up, looked down and said, 'Everyone is seated. Mab, do you recognise the targets?'

Mab looked down at the table and said, 'Yes, from Satta's memories, Cassius is the one in silver armour seated at the nearest table with his back to us. Chanoch is seated at the same table directly opposite Cassius and facing us. He is wearing a red tunic. Fishel is at the head of the table, also wearing a red military tunic. I guess that's his wife beside him. Most of the military personnel are seated at the far table. Mab turned to Kanaka, smiled and said, 'I will drop down onto the nearest table between Cassius and Chanoch. Master Kanaka, you tackle Fishel, blast him from above, then drop down onto the head of the table. Lamm, Luticia, you focus on the military at the far table. Now would be a good time. What say you? 'Aye,' said all.

Mab leapt over the parapet wall and drew her sword in mid-air. As she approached the table, she delivered a vicious downward swipe at Cassius's head. Mab was moving so fast that Cassius barely had time to react. He leaned to the side, but the chair hampered his movement. Onimaru sliced through the left side of his head and cut through his silver pauldron armour, completely severing his left shoulder and arm. Black, stinking blood sprayed across the table. Mab pulled Onimaru back, but Samael rose up and fled the body, which slumped forward onto the table. Mab spun around, holding Onimaru at full stretch. Chanoch tried to push himself backwards on his chair, but Onimaru sliced through his throat. Chanoch fought for breath as blood was drawn into his lungs. Mab then plunged Onimaru through his chest. The daemon screamed in agony, Mab said, 'Amaymon, this is Onimaru. I warned you that I would have your life!'

Kanaka blasted Fishel off his chair, and Dawn-Breaker took the head from his shoulders. Chaos ensued; people were screaming, trying to escape from the carnage. The bride and groom were on the floor, covered in stinking black blood and couldn't get enough purchase to rise to their feet. Lamm and Luticia were blasting the legionnaires to pieces, legs and arms were strewn across the floor in pools of red. Mab, covered in a silver skin, floated slowly to the centre of the room and cried out, in full coercer mode, 'SILENCE!' Everyone stopped what they were doing and stared up at the silver apparition above them.

Mab said, 'Put your weapons down. Military personnel form a line on this side of the hall. Civilians form a line on the other side of the hall. Do it now or I will burn this place to the ground with you in it!' There was a hushed silence as people made their way to one or the other side of the hall. Mab said, 'Civilians first. You will be released one at a time.' Mab unlocked one of the escape route doors, and all of the civilians were checked as they passed; none were found to be daemon hosts. There were some forty or so legionnaires waiting in line. Kanaka did an inspection, and he found five hosting daemons. Mab told the rest to form a ring around the five and explained that they were possessed by daemons. Mab said, 'You will notice that these legionnaires are the most senior. Commanders Cassius, Chanoch and Fishel all hosted daemons.' Mab sent a beam of light which engulfed one of the five legionnaires and said, 'Oriens, leave this body.' The daemon fled, and the legionnaire's body dropped to the floor. Mab helped him to rise and said, 'Tell your friends here what happened to you.' The legionnaire, crying, explained that he had been drugged, and when he woke, a daemon had taken control of his body and essentially stolen his life. His mind was imprisoned; he could only watch and listen. Mab freed the other four legionnaires, who also thanked her profusely for their freedom, and said, 'We have come here to help rid you of these creatures. You have been enslaved for too long. If you do nothing, your children and your children's children will also be enslaved. Talk to your friends and colleagues, explain what is happening. We intend to kill every daemon on this plane, but unfortunately, not all the hosts will be saved. This is the price of your freedom. Listen carefully, at the games tomorrow, stay away from your leaders. You must gather on the opposite side of the stadium, the side with your own people. Now, go home to your families.'

Mab was disappointed that Samael had escaped back to the Abyss.

Kanaka said, 'Amaymon has been slain, and seven other daemons expelled, one of these being a ruler. This sends a powerful message of hope to the people here. That alone is a significant success.'

Mab reached out with her witch senses and found Padwa in an office on the upper floor. She said, 'Padwa, come to the hall, I must speak with you.'

Padwa replied, 'Yes, High-one, immediately.'

Mab said, 'Padwa, the chief administrator, is on his way here.'

There was a knock at the main entrance to the dining room. Mab unlocked and opened the door. Padwa and Ogan, the Head Priest, walked into the room and were aghast at the carnage. Mab said, 'We have permission from my mother to cleanse this region of daemons. This is the first step in the process.'

Ogan and Padwa bowed deeply to Mab and said, 'High-one, you are most welcome. There will be reprisals, but it is a price that we must pay.'

Mab said, 'Will the games scheduled for tomorrow still go ahead?'

Padwa looked down and said, 'Yes, High-one, I'm afraid they will continue. The preparations are complete, and much money has changed hands. The games are an abomination, the wanton slaughter of innocent people and animals to entertain a feckless leadership.'

Mab replied, 'Will you both be present tomorrow?'

Padwa replied, 'Ogan and I are required to attend; if not, we would be executed.'

Mab said, 'Five of the legionnaires here today were possessed by daemons. I expelled the creatures and told them to stay away from their leaders and stand with the people on the other side of the stadium. I require you and the priesthood to do the same.'

Ogan replied, 'High-one, we will do as you command, but be aware that this slight to the leadership will mean our certain death.'

Mab smiled and said, 'Ogan, nothing in life or death is certain. My understanding is that the military and civilian leaders will all be gathered on or around the dais. Is this correct?'

Ogan replied, 'Yes, High-one, it will be so tomorrow.'

Mab said, 'Then tomorrow, the hand of God will strike a fatal blow and free your people.' Ogan and Padwa dropped to their knees with their hands together in front of their chests in the prayer position.

Mab turned to the masters and said, 'We should return and prepare for tomorrow.' They formed a circle, linked arms and materialised in the lost library.

Kanaka said, 'We stink, so freshen up and back to my office for dinner together in an hour or so.'

Mab made her way to the suite only to find Cat. Mab said, 'Is Izzy around?'

Cat replied, 'No, Izzy and Charly won't be back tonight. They have gone on a group expedition to gather herbs and special roots for potions. Master Ethan is leading the expedition, and they will be camping out tonight and rising at dawn to collect the specimens. What's that horrible smell?'

Mab said, 'It's daemon-polluted blood, I'm covered in it.' Cat screwed her face up and backed off. Mab reached out with her witch senses and found Izzy. She was helping to pitch a tent. Mab said, 'Do you need a hand?'

Izzy laughed and replied, 'No, Mab, we will be fine. How was your day?'

Mab said, 'More of the same, really, kill a few daemons, come back home, drink some wine, search for my wife, go to bed.'

Izzy replied, 'Well, your wife will be back tomorrow around lunchtime, so have some wine and go to bed. See you soon!'

Mab showered, changed and made her way back to Kanaka's office. Kanaka, Lamm, Luticia, Boe and Satta were already there. The food was laid out, although Boe and Satta had already eaten. Kanaka, for the benefit of Boe and Satta, explained what had happened at the administration building.

Boe said, 'In many ways a great success, the administrator, the high priest and some of the military now realise that freedom is within their grasp.'

Satta started to cry and said, 'This is a miracle; It is too good to be true. The Prophet promised that we would be free, and it is happening.'

Mab stared at Satta and said, 'The Prophet said, you would be free?'

Satta replied, 'Yes, he said, the lions would lie down with the lambs and that our freedom was at hand.'

Luticia said, 'The daemon ruler, Samael, what of it?' Mab, still deep in thought, said, 'It has returned to the Abyss. My fear is that my mother will pursue it and become ensnared in that foul place.'

Kanaka replied, 'What if that happens?'

Mab said, 'I will go there and do what I can to free her.' There was silence for a few minutes.

Boe said, 'Let us hope that doesn't happen and focus on tomorrow instead.'

Mab smiled at Boe and replied, 'Yes, Master Boe. We have warned the people to stay away from the leader's side of the stadium. That will minimise the number of deaths and allow us to inflict maximum damage on the daemons.'

Luticia replied, 'My preference would be to attack as soon as possible after the leaders are seated. When we have removed the Leaders, we can then free those in the cells.'

Kanaka replied, 'The question is, how do we attack? Perhaps we simply appear in the middle of the arena and start blasting?'

Mab said, 'I think that could work, but I had in mind a rather grander entrance. Satta, do you or your people know of dragons?' Satta replied, 'Dragons? No, I have never heard that term. What does it mean?'

Lamm said, 'It is a fearsome beast.'

Satta said, 'I cannot imagine anything more fearsome than the lions of the games.'

Kanaka replied, 'Then Satta, you haven't seen a dragon! Mab, it is a somewhat blunt tool, but I have to say it would be effective. I do think, though, that we need to be in the arena to make sure the people are protected from the gladiators and the lions. I suggest Lamm, Luticia and I mix with those in the cells and go with them into the arena. If not, the guards may put everyone in the cells to the sword if an attack is made on the leadership.'

Luticia said, 'Yes, that is a very good point. On that basis, I agree that it would be best to wait until we and the prisoners are in the arena before Mab launches the attack.'

Satta said, 'I am a High Priestess. I must be there with my people. I speak their language. They will listen to me and do as I say.'

Kanaka replied, 'Yes, Satta, I had hoped you would agree to join us. To summarise, we leave first thing tomorrow morning dressed as natives, and we assemble in the lost library. Mab will transfer us to the cells beneath the stadium, and Satta will mingle with and reassure the prisoners. We will be in regular communication with Mab and let her know when we are driven out into the arena. We will then keep everyone away from the dais side of the stadium and provide protection until Mab launches her attack. At that time, we also go into attack mode. Is everyone clear?'

Satta said, 'What of this dragon creature?'

Kanaka replied, 'Satta, do not worry. It is a very friendly dragon unless, of course, you happen to be a daemon.'

Satta and Boe retired for the evening, and Kanaka brought out a bottle of single malt from a cabinet in his room. Kanaka said, 'Mab and I brought this back from the city of the future. It is one of the few redeeming qualities of the place.' He placed four glasses on the table and poured a generous amount of whisky into each glass.

Lamm took a swig, his eyes lit up, and he said, 'This is very nice indeed, strong but creamy. What is it?'

Kanaka replied, 'They call it whisky. It is distilled using a grain that we do not have here.'

Mab, looking at Kanaka, said, 'That reminds me that we have some unfinished business with Alexei. Samael has so far made three attempts to kill me here on this plane. The first was a team of four shapeshifters, two of whom almost succeeded in killing Izzy. I killed those two and released the other two in return for information. The second incident was two hellhounds that attacked me on the sports fields, and they were crazed, and I killed them both. The third was a team of three assassins that Samael brought from the city of the future. I killed one of them; the other two are in the cells below. However, they told me that they worked for Alexei and that he reported to Robert Samael, an executive of the Haskins corporation.'

Kanaka replied, 'So Alexei is one of the key players in the drugs and narcotic business that your mother is trying to eliminate?'

Mab said, 'Precisely, so we need to go back there, kill Alexei and bring down the Haskins Corporation.'

Lamm said, 'It's just as well you two aren't very busy at the moment!'

Mab laughed and said, 'I think you and Luticia would love to see the city of the future. What do you think, Master Kanaka?'

Kanaka replied, 'Absolutely, if you do decide to help us, you may even get to see Baby Face Mab performing in a cage fight!' Mab groaned.

Lamm said, 'It's a deal, I couldn't possibly miss that!'

'Me too,' replied Luticia.

Kanaka said, 'Mab, it looks like we are going there in force next time. For now, though, let's get some sleep; tomorrow will be a difficult day.' Mab made her way back to the suite, and Cat was working at her desk; she looked up and said, 'Would you like something to eat?'

Mab smiled and said, 'No thanks, Cat, I've just eaten and have an early start tomorrow. Good night.'

Mab slept soundly and woke early. She showered, dressed, hitched Onimaru on her back, checked her shoulder bag for provisions, donned her robe and made her way to the lost library. Kanaka, Lamm, Luticia and Satta were already there. Mab said, 'Master Kanaka, I suggest we arrive on the Stadium roof first, just to be sure everything is progressing as expected. I will then transport you four into the cells; I must say, Satta, you have done a good job with the clothes.' Satta smiled, and Kanaka nodded in agreement. The group formed a circle facing each other and linked arms. Mab focused on the stadium roof, they materialised and immediately crouched down. The arena was being prepared for the games. Horses were being used to tow large wooden boards to level out the sandy surface of the arena floor. Vendors were setting up stalls in allotted areas between the tiers of seating. Mab pointed out the betting desks conveniently positioned close to the vendor stalls. The dais had already been constructed and was being dressed in bunting, various banners, flags and plaques relating to the region and to Rome. Mab said, 'I'll have a look in the cells.' Mab moved into mind space and flew from the stadium roof across the arena and down into the cells. She found three large cells, each holding around fifty men, women, and children. There were also many animal cells which included lions, bears, horses and bulls. There was a special cell for Gladiators, and Mab noticed two females sitting together amongst the thirty or so making ready for battle.' Mab returned to the stadium roof and explained what she had seen to the masters.

Kanaka said, 'Do we know which group will enter the arena first?'

Satta replied, 'They usually send the animals in first, then the Gladiators and finally the Lions and the People. Gladiators are used to put any remaining or wounded people to the sword. Following that, the Gladiators receive their share of the betting funds and the prize money set by the leaders. Of course, the Gladiators are slaves, so the money goes to their owners.'

Mab said, 'Master Kanaka, it's Izzy. Something has happened. I need to go to her!'

Kanaka said, 'Mab, transport us to the cells and then go to Izzy. Quickly, everyone links arms.'

The group materialised in the corner of the first cell. Mab immediately vanished, materialised beside Izzy and dropped to her knees. Izzy was dead, a deep sword wound to the neck and a thrust to the stomach. Mab, tears pouring down her face, sent her witch senses out for her mother, but she couldn't locate her. She reached out further, still nothing and then a distant indication, almost imperceptible. 'Your mother is in hell,' laughed a voice behind her.

Mab turned, looked and said, 'You did this?'

The creature replied, 'Why of course, I had to get your attention. Killing your colleagues seems to have worked.'

Mab replied, 'You have killed my partner, the woman I love. You have my attention.' Mab could feel the creature scanning her, trying to move into her mind. She studied its form, human-shaped but with elongated arms and legs. The hands and feet bore long, razor-sharp claws. Its carapace was obsidian black and was both skin and armour. Its head was almost triangular with a sharp, pointed chin. Its black eyes were almost invisible against the carapace.

The creature said, 'What are you?'

Mab replied, 'I am your death, of that you can be sure. What are you?'

Amarok groaned and said, 'High-one, I could not save your partner, the creature was too strong. It is a Balerak, an assassin from hell, sent by Lucifer himself.'

The Balerak said, 'Your wolf friend is correct and surprisingly resilient; he should be dead.'

Mab replied, 'Sloppy work, daemon.'

The Balerak said, 'Now you insult me. I am no mere daemon.'

Mab said, 'You all look the same to me. However, I am short on time, so I think I will now take your life.' The Balerak moved with blinding speed, even with Mab's slow time, two of many darts launched struck her. One on the shoulder, the other on her stomach, the poison was extraordinary virulent and exploded into her body. Mab bent over and groaned, the Balerak laughed and said, 'The poison is utterly deadly, there is no cure. I had hoped to play with you awhile, but I think I will leave you to enjoy a slow death. I must return to my Master.'

Mab stood upright and said, 'I think not.' The Balerak looked back at Mab, astonished, as the darts fell from her body, the poison spraying out of the wounds. Mab sent a whip of light at the Balerak, which wrapped tightly around its neck. The creature struggled wildly; it was enormously strong and tried to pull Mab off her feet, but she remained rooted to the earth. Mab held the whip in one hand and tightened the noose still further. The creature managed to draw a short sword and swiped it downwards onto the whip of light, but the blade simply passed through without effect. Mab smiled grimly at the Balerak as she lifted her other hand, a narrow beam of silver light cut through the creature's legs, severing them just above the knee joints and cauterising the yellow blood. The Balerak screamed in agony. Mab held the creature in the air, pulled it towards her and plunged Onimaru through its chest. The Balerak tried to speak but only coughed up blood. Mab sheathed Onimaru, fire blazed from her hand, incinerating the creature until nothing but ash remained. Mab knelt over Amarok. He had been poisoned, but he was still alive. Mab placed her hand on his side; he was immediately enveloped with silver light, which drove the poison from his body.

Amarok said, 'Thank you, high-one. I thought I would die here. I am sorry for your partner.'

Mab replied, 'Amarok, can you stand?' Amarok got to his feet. Mab said, 'I must go to another plane; many lives are in danger. Would you be able to protect this place until I return?'

Amarok replied, 'Yes, high one. The pack is near, I will summon them.'

Mab said, 'Izzy's friend Charly is not among the dead. Search for her, ensure she gets back safely to the Guild.' Mab vanished and reappeared on the roof of the Stadium in Yehuda.

Satta mingled with the prisoners in the first cell. She spoke in hushed tones, telling them to follow her and her three colleagues when driven into the arena. They didn't have long to wait. The animal show was bloody and sickening, but seeing a bear try to defend itself against three male lions was not entertaining even for the basest of the crowd. The Gladiator battle had ended predictably with the reigning champion Marcus Attilius easily defeating the only two challengers. The crowd chanted 'The Lions! The Lions! The Lions!' The doors to the first cell opened, and the guards forced the prisoners up the ramp and into the arena. Kanaka turned left at the top of the ramp, followed by Lamm, Luticia and Satta. Most of the other prisoners followed Satta. They gathered on the opposite side of the arena from the dais and the dignitaries.

Kanaka, looking at the crowd, said, 'It appears that many took Mab's advice and gathered on this side of the Stadium. Lamm, Luticia, you concentrate on as many lions as you can. Make them lie down. I will use psychic blasts to deter them. If any get too close, use fireballs. Satta, tell your people to stay behind us!' The remaining Gladiators climbed up ladders to get out of the arena, and the guards closed the cell gates. Kanaka saw legionnaires moving around the arena walls, getting into position to release the lions. At a signal from the dais, the legionnaires opened two sets of cages, and the lions ran upwards into the arena. The crowd roared their approval.

Mab said to the Masters 'I am only minutes away.'

Kanaka replied, 'Izzy?'

Mab said, 'She is dead, killed by those from the Abyss.' The master could feel the agony in her voice. The lions approached the group, but many of them started to lie down. The crowd went silent, then a huge shadow passed over the stadium, and a mighty roar blasted out from above. A roar such as this had never been heard on that plane, and it was both awesome and terrifying. The lions ran back to the cage entrances and cowered together, trying in vain to escape from the arena. An enormous silver dragon landed in the middle of the arena with a thud that shook the entire stadium. The great beast roared once more, lowered its head, sucked-in a huge volume of air and blasted a torrent of fire at the dais. The dais was blown apart, and everything and everyone in the path of the dragon's breath was instantly incinerated. The dragon then leapt upwards, beating its huge wings ferociously and sweeping a river of death-flame across the whole length of the stadium on the dais side. The force of the blast alone demolished the entire structure, the dragon's breath melting even the stone. The dragon then started to change shape, its wings shrank back to become outstretched arms, and the head and body shrank to human proportions. The body remained in position, hanging in the air, with legs together and arms outstretched. It was surrounded by a silver light so bright that it could not be looked at directly.

Satta pointed and cried out, 'It is the Prophet, he has returned to save us!' All dropped to their knees. Kanaka signalled the masters to do the same. The silver cross pulsed brighter still and then vanished as did Kanaka, Lamm, Luticia and Satta.

Padwa, the Administrator, stood up and shouted, 'Legionnaires, Gladiators, free all the people in the cells, return the animals to their cages!' In the absence of any other leaders, the legionnaires and gladiators followed his instructions.

The masters found themselves back in the lost library of the Guild. Mab, however, materialised beside Izzy and Amarok. Amarok said, 'High-one, your friend Charly was found. She is well and was escorted back to the Guild by the pack.'

Mab said, 'I will take Izzy to our home in Cetha and lay her beside her parents. The Guild will retrieve the rest of the bodies and notify their families.'

Amarok replied, 'And what then, high-one?'

Mab said, 'I must confront the root of this evil and bring it to an end. Thank you once again for your help, Amarok.' Mab vanished taking Izzy's body with her, and she buried Izzy beside her parents in the floral garden at their home in Cetha. She remained in Cetha for several days before messaging Kanaka that she was returning to the Guild.

Kanaka replied, 'Mab, take more time if you need to. The masters decided not to meet again until your return, so just let me know when and I will arrange the meeting.'

Mab asked Kanaka to arrange the meeting for mid-morning tomorrow, and that she was returning to the Guild this evening.

Kanaka replied, 'Mab, I will be in my office until late this evening if you want to talk. If not, then I'll see you in the morning.'

Mab made the house secure and decided to take a walk around Cetha before returning to the Guild. It was early evening, the light was fading, and she could feel the mountain air beginning to chill. She used to walk this route through the village with Izzy by her side, and tears came to her eyes again. Then she thought of her mother and reached out over vast distances with her witch senses. But this time, she knew where to look and immediately identified the almost imperceptible signature of her mother's life force.

Mab focused on that with all her mental capacity and said, 'I love you; I am coming.' Mab wondered if her mother heard her in that place of desolation and despair. She shivered with the thought and the magnitude of what she would face in the Abyss. She lowered her head, tears now running down her face. It was all too much, too much for one person.

'You are not alone, child,' said a voice from behind her. Mab turned and saw a hooded figure, a youngish man with piercing brown eyes staring at her. She was almost transfixed by those eyes, but his voice and her senses told her he was gentle and posed no threat.

Mab replied, 'I am very much alone in every sense of that word.'

The figure approached her slowly, paused and said, 'It is written that even the darkest places shall know the light, and they that dwell in those places shall be cast into the fire.' The stranger looked up and pointed at the Sun. Mab looked up. The stranger said, 'Mabdelore, you are of the light, fear no evil.' Mab turned to look at him, but he had gone. Mab reached out with her witch senses but could find no trace of him. She sat down on a nearby rock, her hands were shaking, and her skin was bristling with power. The interaction with the stranger had infused her with energy; she slowed her breathing, calmed herself and thought of Kanaka.

Mab materialised in Kanaka's office. He stood and walked towards her with his arms wide. Mab ran to him, he hugged her softly in silence for several minutes before saying, 'Come on, let's multi-task, talk, eat and drink!' Kanaka had clearly expected Mab to arrive, and the table was already laid out with platters of cold meats, cheeses, fruits and seeded breads. He poured wine for them both and also poured some of the single malt whisky he brought from the City.

Kanaka said, 'I guessed you wouldn't have had much to eat recently?'

Mab replied, 'Yes, you were right.' They ate slowly and mostly in silence.

Kanaka said, 'Mab, if at any point you need more time, then take it and message me. You don't have to ask.'

Mab replied, 'Thank you, Master Kanaka. So, you haven't returned to Yehuda?'

Kanaka said, 'No, we thought it best to wait for you. Also, I thought giving them some space for a few days might help us to see what transpires in terms of changes in the leadership. I am hoping that Padwa will be able to exercise more authority over the military.'

Mab replied, 'Yes, I see that. However, we need to go back there and talk with him and Ogan to make sure things are progressing.'

Kanaka replied, 'Absolutely, perhaps we can discuss that tomorrow?'

Mab said, 'Yes, well, thank you for dinner, Master Kanaka, just what I needed, but now I need to get some sleep.'

Kanaka replied, 'Good night, Mab, see you in the morning.' Mab left Kanaka's office; on the way downstairs, she vanished and materialised in her bedroom. She couldn't face talking to Cat and Charly tonight.

Mab slept late; when she awoke, Charly and Cat were waiting with breakfast already prepared. They both hugged her. Charly was crying and said, 'Mab, I'm so sorry. I got separated, completely lost. It took me a long time to find a trail, that's when I realised that I was well away from the camp. The wolf pack found me. Amarok spoke to me in my mind and told me what had happened, that everyone was dead, killed by a vile creature and that the pack would take me back to the Guild.'

Cat, also crying, said, 'What do we do now, Mab, now that Izzy is gone?'

Mab replied, 'We do what is right and good. That's what Izzy would have wanted us to do.'

Cat said, 'But what about the creature?'

Mab replied, 'The creature is dead, but there may be others. You must stay within the Guild campus, no travelling unless I am with you.' Mab had breakfast and then made her way to Kanaka's office for the meeting.

Kanaka, Lamm, Luticia and Satta were already there. Mab walked in and they all stood up, embraced her and offered their sympathies for the loss of Izzy. Mab helped herself to a mug of hot coffee and sat down.

Kanaka said, 'The strike on the Games at Yehuda went as well as could be expected. We can be confident that most, if not all, of the dignitaries, the higher echelon leaders and the local rulers would have been killed in Mab's dragon attack. What we don't know is who has now assumed command. Our hope is that Padwa and Ogan, between them, are now the new leadership. But it may be that the military has assumed command.'

Lamm replied, 'We need to return and discuss the current situation with Padwa.'

Luticia said, 'It could be that there are now no daemons left on that plane?'

Satta said, 'What of the Prophet. It may be that he has returned and will intercede?'

Kanaka replied, 'Satta, what do you mean?'

Satta said, 'When the dragon left, the silver cross appeared; it was the Prophet.'

Mab said, 'Satta, it was me. I was the dragon.'

Satta replied, 'But the silver cross, it was the Prophet.'

Kanaka looked at Mab and said, 'It is true, Mab, when you changed back from the dragon form, you appeared as a silver cross.'

Mab replied, 'That is strange, I have no memory of that. Satta, what did the prophet look like?'

Satta said, 'I saw him only once and from a distance. But he was a young man with piercing eyes, a black moustache and a short cut black beard. He always wore a hooded white linen robe.' Lamm said, 'I thought the Prophet was dead, crucified by the military?'

Mab replied, 'Yes, he was crucified. But he has risen.'

Satta looked at Mab and said, 'Yes, that is what my people and I believe.'

Mab said, 'My mother is imprisoned in the Abyss, trapped there by Lucifer and the three rulers. They await my attempt to rescue her; they plan to kill me, so restoring the balance. My life for that of Mahazael.'

Kanaka said, 'Mab, if you have to go to that place, we will come with you.'

Luticia said, 'Master Kanaka, we could not survive in the Abyss. There are unspeakable creatures there, we would be slain or imprisoned for eternity.'

Mab said, 'Luticia is correct. I must go alone.'

Lamm said, 'Mab, that's not going to happen. I am going with you.' Mab, with tears in her eyes, shook her head and said, 'Thank you, but no. I will go alone. I must free my mother. I may die in the attempt, but they will have to pay a high price for my life.'

Kanaka paused and then replied, 'When do you plan to leave?'

Mab said, 'Immediately after this meeting.'

Kanaka said, 'In your absence, we will travel to Yehuda, meet with Padwa and Ogan and try to consolidate the leadership there.

Mab, I expect you to be back here in the next day or so.' Kanaka had tears in his eyes.

Mab smiled and replied, 'Yes, of course, Master Kanaka.'

Chapter Twenty: The Abyss

Mab flew upwards directly towards the Sun. She created a second skin of silver light to protect her from the searing effects of the hot gases that burst from the star sporadically and without warning. Mab approached as closely as she could tolerate and hung stationary within the flaming corona. She reached into the star with her witch senses, assessing the nature of the gases, the temperatures, pressures and densities of the various layers. The deeper she probed, the higher the temperatures and the denser the materials she encountered. The internal pressures were enormous due to the gravitational forces and the combustion effects. She could see how the star burned lighter gases by fusing them together at the atomic level and, in so doing, created different, more complex elements. The star was both destroyer and creator, and it was, Mab thought, a God. Mab used her psychic powers to contain some of the deep material in the form of a small sphere and slowly pulled it towards her. It took enormous concentration and force to maintain the sphere, but she bound it not only by the force of her mind but also supplemented it using a binding spell, which she swore in the name of her mother. The sphere was the size of a large apple, but the mass and energy contained within were of staggering proportions. Mab could not escape the gravitation pull of the Sun due to the sheer mass of the apple; she reached out, found her mother's life-sign and translated to that location. The time to materialise seemed, to Mab, to be tens of minutes, rather than the usual few seconds, but eventually she appeared. The apple floated in the air within Mab's shoulder bag, pulling in no particular direction.

Mab knew immediately that she was in the Abyss. There was a dim, unchanging light, and everything was grey or black. There was a strong wind blowing constantly and the cries of the damned screamed out seemingly from every direction. She created a ball of light above her head and was relieved to find that her powers appeared to be unaffected by the environment. Mab saw the palace in the distance and started walking towards it. The gravitational pull on the apple was much reduced, but it was still a considerable effort to hold it close to her. Time had no meaning in the Abyss, but she had been walking for what she thought was at least an hour, and getting no closer to the palace. The ball of white light above her head deterred many creeping, slithering, scurrying creatures from approaching too close. Mab was exhausted, and she was beaded with sweat; the effort needed to move the sphere was telling on her.

She stopped, raised her left hand and focused on the palace. A thin beam of light cut through the air but then veered off on a tortuous path and reappeared at the Palace. Mab realised that the Palace was not directly ahead of her; the space in this region was folded or distorted, and she would have to follow her light beam rather than the image of the palace before her. She trudged onwards, periodically firing out a thin beam of light. After what seemed like several hours, she came upon the palace. Mab sat down on a rock to rest before going further. As soon as she sat, a black figure ran toward her. It was skeletal with putrefying flesh hanging from its bones. It let out a high-pitched scream. Mab stood up, and Onimaru shrieked from her scabbard. The sword glowed red, flames licked along the blade, the skeletal creature tried to stop, but Mab swiped Onimaru through its neck and decapitated it. The body clattered onto the rocky ground, and the head flew off into the darkness.

Mab heard a slow handclap from above. She looked up and saw a black shape floating in the air, it had the head of a goat with polished horns of obsidian. Its eyes were blood red, and its nose gushed red steam with every exhalation. It was Samael.

The daemon ruler said, 'Welcome to our palace, Mabdelore, we have been expecting you.' The huge doors of the palace cracked open; Mab sheathed Onimaru and walked in. She felt the presence of her mother, but she sat down to rest before going any further.

Samael said, 'I'm afraid the environment here in our home is not suitable for everyone. This is unfortunate as you will be spending the rest of your life here chained to a wall just like your mother.'

Mab stood up and started to walk once more towards her mother's life-sign. She arrived at two huge ancient doors of oak and iron. Mab dropped to her knees.

Samael laughed loudly and said, 'Oh, this truly exceeds my expectations! Let me open the door for you, Mabdelore!' The huge doors slowly swung open. Mab realised it was a throne room, the floor was of highly polished gnarled granite, and the walls were of heavy iron stone. The entire space had been carved out of solid rock, and the throne itself was monolithic, with the floor giving the impression of having grown up out of the base rock. It was twisted and gnarled as if the very rock itself was warped by the creatures that it was forced to bear. The throne looked vacant, but Mab knew Lucifer was there, unseen. Mab looked to her left and saw her mother chained to the rock wall; she looked terrible, her head was hanging down, and she did not even have the strength to raise it. Mab knew she was being watched and studied, and so she slumped down onto the floor, exhausted.

Samael said, 'Lord, it seems our climate is not suitable for Mabdelore. Should we send her back home?'

Lucifer manifested on the throne, laughed and said, 'I think not. We will keep her here for eternity. Uriel will be released, but not before she witnesses what we have in store for her daughter.'

Mab lifted her head slowly to look at Lucifer. He was surprisingly beautiful, not what she expected; he was indeed a fallen Angel. His face was like Uriel's, and he had long black hair and black eyes; his skin was alabaster white.

Lucifer saw the surprise on her face and said, 'I take many forms, child, as you will discover in due course.'

Mab stood up, with ease, walked towards Lucifer and said, 'I came here to rescue my mother, that was my sole purpose. Had you treated her well and given her back to me freely, all would be well. However, I find that my mother, an Archangel, is chained to a wall and barely able to raise her head. Samael's life is already forfeit for breaking his oath, but I now require your life, Lucifer.'

Samael walked towards the throne, almost doubled over with laughter, and Lucifer merely smiled. Mab leapt into the air, Onimaru in her hand and moving with blinding speed, she spun and brought Onimaru down in a vertical swipe through Samael's head and cut him apart from head to groin. Samael made no sound, and the execution was instantaneous. Mab sheathed Onimaru and stood perfectly still, watching Lucifer.

Lucifer said, 'I see now that I will have to kill you! Your daemon sword will not avail you.' Lucifer rose up and transformed into his true shape, his body was entirely black and reptilian. His head was dragon-like, with red slits for eyes and yellow carious fangs. Enormous black wings unfolded as he plucked a huge black sword from the air. Lucifer launched himself at Mab, but he was much too slow and now too large to adequately manoeuvre within the throne room. Mab dived underneath him and sliced part of his wing off with Onimaru. She then ran to her mother, released her shackles with a thought and helped her to stand. Lucifer changed back to his original human appearance, albeit still holding the huge black sword.

He walked toward them and said, 'I'm sorry, but you both have to die.'

Mab replied, 'I have an important message for you. It is from the Prophet.'

Lucifer stopped and said, 'What do you know of him?' Mab said, 'He told me it is written that even the darkest places shall know the light, and they that dwell in those places shall be cast into the fire. He told me to bring light into the darkness.'

Lucifer laughed and said, 'And did you bring light into the darkness?'

Mab replied, 'Yes, I did.'

Lucifer replied, 'I am wearying of this. If you have brought light into the darkness, where is it?'

Mab, pointing to her shoulder bag, said, 'It's in that bag over there!' Lucifer stared at Mab askance, but Mab simply stared back. Lucifer turned, walked to the door and grabbed the shoulder bag. He found that he couldn't lift it off the floor, he crouched, opened the bag and saw the sphere. He scanned it and staggered backwards, comprehension dawning.

Mab released her powerful containment grip on the sphere, nulled the binding spell and said, 'Let there be light.' Mab and her mother vanished and materialised in the garden at Mab's home in Cetha. Mab held Uriel tightly and enveloped her in silver light, feeding her with raw energy. When she felt her mother responding, she took her into the house, put her to bed and sat by her bedside until she woke the following morning.

Mab made hot coffee and fetched fresh bread and pastries from the local store. She took a breakfast tray to her mother and gently shook her awake.

Uriel opened her eyes and said, 'Mab, you came for me.'

Mab replied, 'Yes, leaving you in that place was not an option. How are you feeling?'

Uriel said, 'I am feeling much better, but I almost died. The Abyss sucked the energy from my body. It will take some time for me to recover fully.'

Mab replied, 'How did they manage to nullify your powers?'

Uriel said, 'They weren't nulled, just very much reduced. That's what happens when you enter the Abyss.'

Mab replied, 'Strange, I didn't experience that. I pretended to be weakened so I could get close to you and the throne.'

Uriel said, 'Mab, what happened. I saw you kneeling on the floor, I don't remember much after that.'

Mab replied, 'I killed Samael and was attacked by Lucifer. I managed to get past him to you. I thought of Izzy and my home, I needed a strong anchor point, and transported us both back here. However, just before we left Lucifer's palace, I released the bindings on an apple-sized sphere of compressed star gases. I thought that would probably kill most of the vile inhabitants of the Abyss.'

Uriel said, 'Compressed star gases! Where did you harvest the gases?'

Mab replied, 'From the core of our sun.'

Uriel said, 'The core, that is astonishing. How did you manage to contain it or even carry it?'

Mab replied, 'It was extremely difficult, but it had to be done. It was the Prophet who suggested it. I was in despair, with you being imprisoned, he came to me. He told me that those who lived in the darkness would be cast into fire; he said I was of the light and should fear no evil. He pointed at the Sun, and that was when the idea came into my mind. I didn't realise how difficult it would be, I nearly died of exhaustion.'

Uriel said, 'Mab, he used those exact words?'

Mab replied, 'What exact words?'

Uriel said, 'You were of the light?'

Mab replied, 'Yes, that is what he said. Does it mean something?'

Uriel replied, 'Yes, it means that you will not be an Angel.'

Mab said, 'Mom, I don't mind. The truth is, I think I already knew that I was not worthy to be an Angel. I am so proud to be your daughter, but we are not the same. I could never be as good and kind as you.'

Uriel put her hand on Mab's cheek and said, 'Yes, we are different. But you mistake my meaning. The Prophet is of the light; there are others who are closer to the light than Angels, but even so are not of the light. We Angels were made by the light, and we are subservient to it. We are the soldiers and messengers of the light. Lucifer Morningstar and his cohort rebelled against the light and so were cast down into darkness.'

Mab replied, 'But what am I? Am I still your daughter?'

Uriel said, 'You are my daughter and always will be. Your destiny will unfold in its own time, but you have already brought light to the darkness of the Abyss, something I did not believe was possible.'

Mab kissed her mother and said, 'I will always be your daughter, that is good enough for me. I have to go back to the Guild; they are waiting for me to return before going to Yehuda.'

Uriel said, 'What is the situation there?'

Mab said, 'We have, I think, broken the power of the daemons. But I suspect there will be chaos there until the local administrator regains control of the military. Will you be able to manage here for a few days?'

Uriel replied, 'Yes, it's just nice to spend time with you and have breakfast in bed!'

Mab said, 'When you are ready, take a shower and go for a walk through the village. You need to get some fresh mountain air; I can still smell that foul place on you. I'll get back as soon as I can.'

Uriel replied, 'Yes, I'll do that. See you soon.'

Mab materialised on the Guild sports field. She walked slowly, enjoying the chilled air blowing in off the mountains and thinking of Izzy.

A voice above her said, 'You have won a battle, not the war.'

Mab replied, 'Azazel, what do you want?'

Azazel replied, 'I have come to tell you that Morningstar lives; your attack on the Abyss failed.'

Mab said, 'I went there to rescue my mother, in that I succeeded. I did not go there to slay Lucifer, but I will be going back there soon to discuss his prospects.'

Azazel replied, 'Is there no limit to your arrogance? Have you no regard for the balance that has lasted millennia?'

Mab said, 'My partner, the woman I love, was killed by an assassin sent here by Morningstar. He will pay for that with his life. The balance is ended, and know this, there is nothing I will not do to end the slavery you and your kind have imposed on the innocent. Now get you from my sight.' Mab mind messaged Kanaka 'Master Kanaka, I have returned to the Campus. I'm a bit weary, can we meet later for lunch?'

Kanaka replied, 'Mab, so pleased to hear from you. Yes, come anytime, lunch in my office is good for me.' Mab made her way to the suite, and Cat and Charly were not there. She reached out with her witch senses, and they were both on campus and in classes. Mab lay on the bed and fell into a deep sleep.

Morningstar said, 'Congratulations, your sphere of sunlight didn't quite kill me, but it was close. I wish to talk with you about the future and how we can co-exist. Azazel told me about the assassin who killed your partner. I sanctioned the attempt on your life but not that of your friends and family.'

Mab replied, 'It was not my intention to kill you; if it were, you would be dead. I hold you responsible for the death of my partner.

I don't see how we can coexist; however, I am not unwilling to discuss the matter.'

Morningstar said, 'I and my two remaining rulers will meet you at a time and place of your choosing.'

Mab replied, 'The rooftop of the Haskins Corporation building, your rulers will know that location, at midnight two days from now.' Mab woke and mind-messaged her mother 'Morningstar wants to meet to discuss how we can coexist. I think it is a trap, but I agreed to meet anyway. He will have his two remaining rulers with him. Midnight two days from now on the rooftop of the Haskins building. Will you be strong enough to attend?'

Uriel messaged back, 'Mab, yes, of course. Do we need anyone else?'

Mab replied, 'No, I don't think so.'

Uriel responded, 'Fine, but they cannot be trusted, so expect the unexpected.'

Mab said, 'We can discuss it further when I get back home, hopefully tomorrow night.' Mab made her way to Kanaka's office and was surprised to see Lamm, Luticia and Satta were also there.

Kanaka said, 'I thought we should have a full meeting in view of your return. But first let's have lunch.'

Mab replied, 'This looks fabulous!' Kanaka had ordered an extra-special buffet in view of Mab's return.

Lamm said, 'Mab, you should come back more often!'

Kanaka laughed and said, 'I thought I would order a special buffet to welcome Mab back from the Abyss. Tuck in, everyone!'

Luticia said, 'Mab, I'm afraid to ask, but what happened? Is your mother safe?' Everyone stopped eating and turned their attention to Mab.

Mab replied, 'Yes, she is safe and recovering at my home in Cetha. They had her chained to a wall, and she was near death. The Abyss sapped her of energy, and she could not defend herself.'

Kanaka said, 'How did you manage to rescue her?' Mab replied, 'I was unaffected by the Abyss. I pretended to be weakened and managed to find and get into Lucifer's palace. Samael and Lucifer were there waiting for me. I killed Samael, cut him from head to crotch with Onimaru, I dodged around Lucifer, got to my mother and translated us both back home to Cetha.'

Satta said, 'You did battle with the evil ones!'

Mab smiled and said, 'Yes, Satta, they are evil, and the Abyss is a place of nightmares. I was very happy to leave and have no wish to go back there. However, there is unfinished business.'

Lamm said, 'You mean Lucifer and the remaining rulers?'

Mab replied, 'Yes, Lucifer wants to have a meeting. I expect it to be a trap. I think many inhabitants of the Abyss would have been killed when the light bomb exploded, but unfortunately, he survived.'

Kanaka said, 'Light Bomb?'

Mab replied, 'I forgot to mention that. I harvested gases from the core of the Sun and bound them in a sphere. I managed to drag it with me into the Abyss, and I have no words to explain how difficult that was! A second or so before we translated out, I released the bindings on the sphere; Lucifer was standing close to it when it exploded. I thought it would kill him and everyone else, but it seems I only partially succeeded.'

Lamm said, 'You succeeded in rescuing your mother; that alone is extraordinary.'

Mab smiled at Lamm and replied, 'Yes, that is what really matters.'

Kanaka said, 'Mab, we decided to wait for your return before travelling to Yehuda. Especially not knowing the location of Samael and the other rulers or the repercussions of our attack on the daemons. Our hope is that Padwa and Ogan are now the local leadership, but the only way of knowing is to go there.'

Mab replied, 'What is the situation with Taggar?'

Kanaka said, 'He is still in the cells. Boe visited him yesterday and said he was in good spirits. The school has been told that he was arrested for treason by order of the Council. His family is, of course, very upset.'

Mab said, 'I think we should set him free on the basis that his powers have been removed and his sponsor, Samael, has been slain. He can do us no harm now, keeping him locked up seems pointless.'

Kanaka replied, 'Yes, Lamm, Luticia, do you agree?' Both nodded in agreement. Kanaka said, 'I will ask Boe to release him and ensure that he has sufficient means to get back home.'

Mab nodded and said, 'So, no time like the present, should we pay Padwa a visit?' All said, 'Aye.'

Chapter Twenty-One: Goddess Bellona

Mab, Kanaka, Lamm, Luticia and Satta formed a circle and linked arms. Mab thought of Padwa, and they materialised beside him. He was in a cell. Padwa, shocked and surprised, said, 'You have returned!'

Kanaka replied, 'What are you doing in this cell?'

Padwa said, 'The Romans have appointed a new commander of legions and are scouring the region for those who killed Cassius, Chanoch and Fishel.'

Kanaka said, 'What, you mean us?'

Mab laughed and said, 'Let's go and find the new commander.' The guards suddenly realised that the cell had filled up with new arrivals and approached cautiously with swords drawn.

Kanaka said, 'Satta, tell them we want to speak to their new commander.'

Mab kicked the cell door, and it flew from its hinges, striking one of the guards. She walked out of the cell and said, 'Follow me.' The other guards lost consciousness and dropped to the floor. Mab walked along a long stone corridor, then stopped and said, 'Padwa, how do we get out of this place?'

Lamm laughed and said, 'Mab, I thought you knew where you were going?'

Padwa said, 'Follow me,' and walked back past the cell, through a thick oak and iron doorway and up a flight of stairs.

Padwa said, 'This is the ground floor of the administration building. I suggest we go to my office on the next floor up, and I will try to contact the commander.' The group proceeded up the main stairway to the second floor, and Padwa led them to his office.

Padwa said, 'Apologies, commander, I did not know you were here.'

The commander replied, 'I passed an order to imprison you pending execution. Why are you not behind bars?'

Padwa said, 'I have brought those who killed your predecessor; they wanted to speak with you.'

The commander stood up and walked towards the group. Mab walked past him, sat on his chair and said, 'Azael, I hope you don't mind.'

The commander replied, 'So, we meet at last. Do you intend to kill me also, or are my two brothers sufficient for your blood lust?'

Mab stood up, walked towards the commander and struck him with the back of her left hand. It was a horrendously powerful blow that whipped his head around and knocked him backwards onto the floor. Mab looked down at him and said, 'You will not speak without my permission.' Mab moved her hand slightly, and Onimaru flashed from its scabbard into her open hand, the blade tip only a few inches from the commander's throat. Azael recognised the nature of the blade and froze. Mab returned Onimaru to her scabbard, reached down, grabbed the commander's tunic, lifted him high into the air and threw him across the room into the chair. Mab said, 'Padwa is in command here. Where is Ogan, speak!'

The commander said, 'Ogan is in the cells. You cannot change the command structure here. I represent Rome, this is a conquered nation and is under the rule of Rome.'

Mab replied, 'You will leave that body and return to the Abyss, otherwise my sword will take your life.' Azael left the Roman legionnaire who collapsed to the floor. Padwa and Luticia helped him back to his feet.

Mab said, 'What is your name?'

The legionnaire replied, 'My name is Lucius Attilius, I am the brother of Marcus Attilius, the champion gladiator.'

Mab said, 'Lucius, how did you come to be possessed by the daemon Azael?'

Lucius, with tears in his eyes, replied, 'I don't know, I awoke one morning and found that I was no longer in control of my body. This creature, Azael, had taken my life. I could only watch as he carried out unspeakable atrocities in my name. Thank you for saving me, goddess.'

Mab smiled and said, 'Lucius, I am no goddess, but you are very charming! I assume you know Padwa?'

Lucius replied, 'I know who he is, but I have been unable to communicate with him. I can only say that I am sorry for all that has happened and assure you that I was a hapless spectator.'

Padwa replied, 'I understand, Lucius, the crimes are not yours, they remain with the daemon Azael.'

Mab said, 'Lucius, you must remain commander of the legions on behalf of Rome until we find a suitable replacement. But we need to ensure that the various legion commanders do not host daemons. In that way, we can be sure that the leadership is free of corruption and the people can live in peace and safety.'

Lucius replied, 'Yes, Goddess, it will be done.'

Mab replied, 'I'm not a Goddess. My name is Mabdelore, you can call me Mab.'

Lucius stared at Mab and said, 'Please, all of you, follow me.' Lucius led the group downstairs, out through the main entrance and into a walled garden area. It was beautiful, an oasis in an otherwise dry dust dust-filled village. It had an irrigation system that allowed a huge variety of colourful flowers and shrubs to thrive. Small stepping-stone paths meandered through the garden. Mab stopped to smell many of the flowers and herbs and so lagged well behind the group. She eventually caught up with Lucius and the others, who were standing outside a small Roman temple. It was a temple in miniature, suitable for only ten or so people to worship. Lucius unlocked the door and said, 'Please, follow me into the temple.'

Kanaka said, 'Lamm, Luticia, could you remain here and keep watch?' Lamm and Luticia nodded. Lucius lit a number of wall-mounted candles; the seats were of stone but with a few soft red cushions scattered around. Mab was admiring the architecture, the massive columns which were clearly too large for such a small building, the barrel roof construction and the enormously thick stone walls. She turned to ask Lucius about the construction, but he was pointing at a huge stone statue above the front dais. Kanaka turned and looked at her, and she knew immediately something was wrong.

Mab walked quickly to join him and said, 'What is it?' Lucius pointed at the statue. Mab looked up and saw her own face looking back at her.

She was holding a whip and a sword; the sword was identical to Onimaru. The name chiselled on the stone was The Goddess Bellona, Goddess of War, Daughter of Jupiter and Juno. Satta said, 'Mabdelore, it is you, there can be no question!'

Mab sat down on the cold stone and stared up at the statue for a while before saying, 'Yes, it is me, but what does it mean?'

Kanaka replied, 'Mab, the Gods and the Angels may have different names in the various religions. Clearly, you are the Goddess Bellona, you must at some point intervene in the affairs of Rome in the past; in much the same way as you have intervened in the affairs of the future city.'

Satta said, 'Yes, Master Kanaka, what you say could be true. From what I know, the Roman Gods seem similar to the Greek Gods, but I have never seen images of either.' Mab looked at Lucius and said, 'Lucius, thank you for showing me this. I assume that as a Roman Goddess, all Romans must do as I command?'

Lucius bowed his head and replied, 'Yes, of course, Goddess Bellona. To disobey you would be a crime under Roman law. The emperor Tiberius himself worships you every day when he rises, I know this as a fact.'

Mab said, 'Lucius, you will work with Padwa, Ogan and Satta to help the people here live in freedom and prosperity. There will be no Games other than for sporting events. There shall be no killing of people or animals. All animals currently in captivity will be returned to where they came. These are my orders. Do you understand?'

Lucius bowed and replied, 'Yes, Goddess.' Mab said, 'Lucius, is your brother a good man?'

Lucius replied, 'Yes, Goddess, he is good at heart, but he has had a very hard life.'

Mab said, 'Bring him and Ogan to me. We will be in Padwa's office.'

Padwa led the group back to his office and ordered food and wine to be brought for his guests. Lucius returned with Ogan and said, 'Apologies, Goddess, my brother does not believe in gods, he refuses to see you.'

Mab said, 'Where is he now?'

Lucius replied, 'Where he is always, in the practice arena.'

Mab said, 'Take me to him.' Lucius said, 'Then let me apologise in advance for his behaviour. He has grown to be a coarse man, he curses often and is, how can I say it, very direct.'

Lucius led the group to a small practice arena, which was some distance from the games stadium. The group watched the gladiators training, and it was clear that the fights were more than mere practice. Even as they watched, some were injured by sword strokes or physical blows. The gladiators were huge, but even amongst these, Marcus Attilius stood out as a warrior of awesome proportions.

Kanaka said, 'Now he is a true warrior!'

Mab said, 'Lucius, tell your brother that Bellona wishes to put him to the test in battle.' Lucius leapt over the barrier wall into the arena and approached his brother. After some discussion, Marcus looked towards Mab and laughed. He then shouted to the gladiators that there would now be a contest gladiator against the Goddess, but it would be very short in duration; there was much laughter in the arena.

Lucius ran back to Mab and said, 'Goddess, please accept my apologies. He is willing to be put to the test, but he expects to kill you within the next few seconds.' Mab looked at Marcus Attilius and his Gladiators and said, 'I wonder if he is fond of cats?' Mab leapt high into the air and transformed into a giant Saber-Cat. She hit the arena floor and let off a deafening roar. The gladiators backed away, swords drawn, as the giant cat padded slowly towards them. Suddenly, the gladiators didn't seem to be so fearsome or awesome; in fact, they now appeared like a group of small, frightened children.

Mab melded her mind with Marcus Attilius and said, 'Now that I have your attention, let me introduce myself. I am Bellona. I have come to test you. Tell your Gladiators to put down their swords and move back to the edge of the arena.' Marcus shouted the order 'Put your swords down and move back!' Marcus watched as the giant cat started to change shape, and within a few seconds, Bellona stood before him. Marcus gazed at her and said, 'It is true, you are the Goddess, please accept my apologies.'

Mab replied, 'Apology accepted. But now you will be tested.'

Marcus said, 'How will I know if I pass the test?'

Mab replied, 'You will be alive; if you fail the test, you will be dead.'

Mab leapt up and kicked Marcus hard in the chest. He fell backwards but rolled and quickly returned to his feet. He launched a vicious attack on Mab, swinging his huge broadsword as if it were weightless. Mab ducked, swayed, dived and jumped to avoid the sword blade, but she did not draw Onimaru. Marcus then pulled his short sword. He swiped with his broadsword, but then caught Mab with the short sword as she spun away. Blood poured from a gash in her arm and dripped onto the ground around her. Mab dropped to her knees, put her arms out and waited for the death blow. Marcus raised his sword but then threw it to the ground and bent down to help Mab to her feet. A voice behind him said, 'Marcus, you have passed the test.' Marcus spun around to see Mab standing and smiling at him. He turned back, but his defeated opponent had vanished.

Marcus walked towards her, dropped to his knees and said, 'Goddess Bellona, please forgive me?'

Mab looked down at him and replied, 'You will be my new commander of legions. Now let us return to Padwa's office, there is much to discuss.'

Mab said, 'The leadership team for this region will be Lucius, who will replace Pilate, the current Governor; Padwa, the Chief Administrator; Ogan and Satta, as the Head Priests; and Marcus, who will be the Commander of Legions. I will talk with Tiberius to formalise matters. It is important that, as the leadership team, you ensure any daemons within the military are identified. Ogan and

Satta have the necessary knowledge to expel these creatures. You need to work together, for and on behalf of the people. Padwa, Lucius, these changes take immediate effect. Is this understood?' All present nodded their agreement.

Kanaka said, 'Can we eat now?'

Mab smiled and said, 'Yes, Master Kanaka.' As she poured herself a goblet of rich red wine.

Chapter Twenty-Two: Love and Redemption

Mab got back to her home in Cetha to find her mother weeding the garden. Mab said, 'This was the last thing I expected you to be doing!'

Uriel hugged her and said, 'These last few days have been the best holiday I could possibly imagine. I had forgotten how much I loved tending the garden, and the flowers here are extraordinary.'

Mab said, 'Yes, Izzy and I put a lot of work into it over the holiday period, but we also have a gardener from the village who drops by to tidy up. How are you feeling?'

Uriel replied, 'I feel great and should return to my duties, but I am reluctant to leave here. After my imprisonment in the Abyss, this is just paradise.'

Mab said, 'Are you sure you are ready for the meeting with Lucifer tomorrow night?'

Uriel replied, 'Yes, absolutely. You must not go to that meeting alone.'

Mab said, 'I am expecting his two remaining rulers to be present, so there will be three of them. I will ask Master Kanaka to join us, and he often brings a valuable human insight to situations. He is also a superb planner and tactician.'

Uriel replied, 'Yes, of course.' Mab looked at her mother and said, 'He helps me get things in context. I have become more powerful than I could imagine. It scares me, what I could do if I lost control.'

Uriel replied, 'Mab, I know. I see it in you, but you are what you are. I know you will always strive to do the right thing.'

Mab said, 'We went back to Yehuda and replaced the leadership team. I will pay a visit to Tiberius, the Roman Emperor, to formalise the changes. Did you know he worships the Goddess Bellona?'

Uriel was silent for a while and then replied, 'Yes, I did know that. You have seen the statue in the Roman temple?' Mab nodded. Uriel said, 'Then you know what you are.'

Mab replied, 'No, Mother, I don't know what I am.' Uriel said, 'You are of the light, a Goddess. You will be known by many names and will be omnipresent, and your mind will reach across space and time. You have been brought into being by the light, for what purpose I do not know.' Mab said, 'I thought I was your daughter?'

Uriel replied, 'Mab, you are my daughter! Angels are created and cannot have children in the human sense. I placed you with your human parents to keep you safe until you reached maturity and to enable you to learn about humanity and good and evil. In that I have succeeded.'

Mab said, 'Have I reached maturity?'

Uriel replied, 'In truth, I do not know. I am not fit to answer to that question, it must come from you, Mabdelore Bellona Winter.'

Mab said, 'Who else knows who I am?'

Uriel replied, 'No one, but your visit to Yehuda may set some hares running. Lucifer already suspects that you are not entirely what you seem; this may be the real reason for the meeting.'

Mab said, 'A test?'

Uriel replied, 'Yes, or perhaps just a closer look. Do not underestimate Lucifer; he was the greatest warrior amongst us. Yes, it was Michael who finally cast him down, but he needed a lot of help in doing it.'

Mab said, 'He is formidable, but he must pay for what he did to you.'

Uriel replied, 'I am well now, fully recovered. We should go to the meeting with an open mind. The truth is that before Lucifer was cast down, he and I were close friends. I wish it could be that way again; I miss the Lucifer I used to know.'

Mab said, 'He killed Izzy, sent an assassin in the night. He will pay dearly for that.' Mab walked to her mother, hugged her and said, 'Mom, you are too forgiving. The Lucifer you used to know doesn't exist, he has been replaced with a monster.'

Uriel said, 'Mab, no one is beyond redemption. I once saved Izzy's life, remember that when you come to your decision regarding Lucifer.'

Mab replied, 'I will never forget that. I will return to the Guild now; see you tomorrow night in the city.'

Mab materialised in Kanaka's office. Lamm, Luticia and Satta were sitting down with Kanaka to have lunch.

Kanaka said, 'Mab, perfect timing!'

Mab replied, 'Great, I need to talk to you about the meeting with Lucifer tomorrow night. I am so hungry, let's eat first.'

Lamm said, 'Mab, did you ask your mother about the statue?'

Mab replied, 'Yes, Master Lamm, she knew. Lucius was correct, I am known as the Goddess Bellona. My mother says I have no biological parents. It seems Angels were created by the light but are not of the light! This means I will not be an Angel, but I kind of knew that already.'

Kanaka said, 'The Romans believe that you are the daughter of Jupiter and Juno. I assume these are ancient Gods?'

Satta, staring in wonder at Mab, said, 'Jupiter is said to be the King of the Gods, and Juno is his wife. Juno is known as Hera by the Greeks, and Jupiter as Zeus. Together with Minerva, known as Athena by the Greeks, and Bellona, Jupiter and Juno rule over all other Gods and demi-Gods. Bellona and Minerva are equivalent in status, although Bellona is Goddess of War, whereas Minerva is Goddess of Warfare, that is, the planning of war.'

Mab said, 'Satta, it seems you know more about me than I do!' Satta smiled, bowed and brought her hands together in the sign of respect and said, 'I only know what I have read of those Gods, I never really believed they existed until I saw the statue of you in the temple.'

Mab said, 'Satta, what do you know of Emperor Tiberius?'

Satta replied, 'He spent his youth in the military, and he uses the threat of the legions to influence the Senate. Even now he prosecutes wars in Germania, although it is said that he fights on too many fronts and refuses to bring more legions from Rome due to his fear of rivals fomenting rebellion.'

Mab asked 'You have met Tiberius?'

Satta replied, 'He has visited Yehuda on many occasions. As a High Priestess, I attended several receptions where he was present, but of course I did not speak with him directly.'

Mab said, 'May I enter your mind? I would like to see him.'

Satta replied, 'Yes, of course, Mab.' Mab entered Satta's mind and saw her memories of meetings with Tiberius. He was younger than she was expecting; she absorbed the memories, withdrew and thanked Satta. When they had finished lunch, Lamm and Luticia gave their apologies and left to travel back to their respective schools and homes.

Mab looked at Satta and said, 'I am not familiar with the custom and protocol of Roman Emperors. What would you advise?'

Kanaka laughed and said, 'Custom and protocol! That's the first time I've heard you mention those words!'

Mab smiled and replied, 'Yes, well, I thought I should at least try to make an effort rather than just blunder in and upset everyone.'

Satta said, 'You are the Goddess Bellona, Tiberius is the one who should be worrying about protocol.'

Mab smiled and said, 'I will leave first thing tomorrow morning. If I need advice, can I contact you?'

Satta nodded and said, 'Of course, if you would excuse me now, I need to attend to Dassi.'

Kanaka said, 'What about this meeting with Lucifer?' Mab explained that her mother would be there, and Lucifer with his two remaining rulers, Azazel and Azael. She said, 'I am worried about my mother, how she will react. She was very close with Lucifer before he was cast down; I, however, mean to slay him and his two rulers.'

Kanaka replied, 'Surely you don't think she would turn against you?'

Mab said, 'No, but she may decide on inaction. She told me Lucifer was their greatest warrior, so I don't know what I will be facing, and of course, the daemon rulers need to be considered. I need you to be there and wield Onimaru, with her and your skills, I won't have to worry about the daemons and can focus on the Angels. I may not need your help, but I would like to have you there just in case things go wrong.'

Kanaka replied, 'Yes, of course, Mab. I will take Onimaru, and you, Dawn-Breaker. Suggest we leave from here. When do you expect to return from your meeting with Tiberius?'

Mab said, 'I would have thought sometime in the afternoon. Perhaps we could have dinner here together and then leave, get there early and do a bit of reconnaissance?'

Kanaka replied, 'Yes, perfect.'

Mab said, 'I haven't seen Master Boe for some time. Is he well?'

Kanaka replied, 'Yes, he has taken time off to progress some research work. I expect him back in a week or so.'

Mab said, 'He didn't mention it, do you know where he went?'

Kanaka replied, 'He has friends in the North, and I think he intended to go there and visit one of the libraries in that area. Other than that, no, I don't really know.'

Mab made her way to the suite, but as she walked, she reached out with her witch senses for Boe. She located him and gently entered his mind. He was in a sitting position. Mab looked through his eyes and saw others in the room. Someone was on the floor unconscious, with a pool of blood under his head. Two others were tied to chairs, and they had been beaten, their faces bruised and stained with blood. Mab realised that Boe was also tied to his chair. Their six captors were dressed in robes, and they appeared to be witches or perhaps warlocks.

Mab vanished, appeared in the middle of the room and said, 'What do you think you are doing?' The lead warlock walked towards Mab and said, 'Who are you?' Mab hit him with a backhanded slap, which propelled him backwards across the room. He slammed against the wall and dropped to the floor unconscious. The other five witches put their hands to their heads, screamed and dropped to the floor, blood running from their noses and ears. The restraints on Master Boe fell from his wrists and arms.

Mab said, 'Master Boe, are you hurt?'

Boe managed to stand up and replied, 'No, Mab, I have been tied to that chair for several hours and taken a bit of a beating, but I will recover.'

Mab said, 'Who are these people?'

Boe replied, 'They are a coven of witches who appear to have been in this area for a very long time. This is my friend Ananda's house, but I fear they have killed him. Could you release the two women, one is his wife and the other his daughter?' The restraints fell from the two women who immediately rushed to Ananda.

Boe said, 'Word got around that a master of the Guild was in the village and staying here with Ananda and his family. There is a very old library not far from here. I have been doing some research there, I expect that is how they found me.'

Mab replied, 'What did they want with you?'

Boe said, 'They were asking me about the white witch and the new Academy of White Witches. I told them the principal was Luticia, but they wanted information on you, your name and background. They mentioned a witch known as Morgana who has disappeared without a trace.'

Mab walked to Ananda and placed her hand on his chest; his body was immediately covered in a silver skin of power. Mab concentrated on his head area and found the bleed in his brain. She broke down the blood cells and removed them. She then restored the damaged areas as best she could, knitted together the skull fractures and restarted his heart.

Boe said, 'Mab, he has been dead for almost an hour and has a severe head injury. There is nothing you can do.'

Mab said, 'He will recover, but he may suffer some memory loss.'

Ananda's wife said, 'It is not possible, he is dead.' But then Ananda stirred and looked around the room, Mab levitated him and gently placed him down on a large sofa chair.

Mab walked to the warlock who was still unconscious and said, 'Get up!' The warlock groaned and struggled to his feet.

Mab said, 'Who are you and what are you doing here?' The warlock looked at his colleagues lying on the floor.

Mab said, 'They are not dead, but they soon will be unless you answer my questions.'

The warlock said, 'I am a coven leader. I wanted to question the Guild master over the demise of the Academy of Magic and the Occult. My understanding is that the Guild of Sorcerers was instrumental in this change, and they killed several of our fellow witches.'

Mab replied, 'Yes, that is correct, the new school is known as the Academy of White Witches.'

The warlock said, 'It is said that it is named thus in honour of a white witch from the Guild who defeated three black witches in combat.'

Mab replied, 'That is correct.'

The warlock asked 'Are you known as the White Witch?'

Mab replied, 'I am known by several names, the White Witch being one of those names. Now you will tell me what you are doing here.'

The warlock said, 'We came here to identify the White Witch, seek her out and kill her.'

Mab turned to the other witches and said, 'Get up!' She then looked at the coven leader and said, 'I should kill you all now for what you have done here.'

Mab looked at Boe and said, 'Master Boe, what would you have me do with these excuses for witches?'

Boe replied, 'Mab, you have restored the life of Ananda. This is all I would have wished that you do.'

Mab led the witches to a small paddock behind the house and said, 'Understand this, if you had injured or killed Master Boe, you would all die very slow and painful deaths. However, fortunately for you, that is not the case, and so I give you options. The first is that I remove your witch powers, if you have any, the second is that I kill all of you now, and the third is that you join the Academy of White

Witches. Your three black witch colleagues from the old Academy chose to do battle. I killed two of them and allowed the other to live.'

The warlock replied, 'What do you know of the witch Morgana?'

Mab said, 'She was given several opportunities to turn away from the dark, but she lied to me and conspired with the forces of darkness to lure the innocent into slavery. She is dead; her death was quick and clean, which was more than she deserved.

Now you must make your decisions.' One of the witches stepped forward and said, 'Master, I would like to travel South to the Academy and become a white witch. Two others joined her. Mab said, 'You have made the right decision, stand behind me.'

The warlock said, 'I choose battle.' Mab looked at the other two witches who were very young and said, 'You have your whole lives before you, do not choose death.'

The youngest laughed and replied, 'It is you who chooses death.' Mab made a gesture with her hand, and they both fell slowly to the ground. Mab looked at the warlock and said, 'They are too young to make such choices.' The warlock launched a fireball at Mab, which simply bounced off her. He then drew his sword. Mab couldn't help but admire the blade, which was curved but extraordinarily flexible. It was double-edged and designed for cutting and slashing only. The warlock ran towards Mab, slicing and swiping in every direction. Mab simply moved back, ducked, spun, twisted and jumped but did not draw Onimaru. Then the warlock overreached. Mab moved in, parried the side of the blade and punched the warlock on the side of the head. He dropped to the ground and lay still. Mab bent down and picked up the sword. She flapped it around, still wondering at the flexibility and whether, on balance, it was good or bad. Then she lifted her knee and snapped the blade into two pieces and threw them to the ground.

Mab went back inside to see Boe and said, 'Master Boe, I will take the witches to Luticia at the Academy. I'm afraid the warlock is dead. I wondered if you would like to spend some time at the Academy with Luticia?'

Boe thought for a few moments and replied, 'Ananda seems to be recovering well following your intervention. Also, I have the information I needed from the library, so it may be best if I travel with you to the Academy. I didn't realise the threat that my presence here could cause to my friend and his family. Give me a few minutes and I will join you outside.' Mab mind messaged Luticia and explained the circumstances with Boe and the witches.

Luticia replied that she was looking forward to her arrival; she would meet her and her party on the square.

Boe wandered outside to find Mab and the five witches waiting for him in the paddock. Two witches were sitting on the ground, and three others were standing over them. He also noticed the warlock who lay dead on the ground. Boe said, 'I hope you're not expecting me to bury him?'

Mab laughed, raised her hand, and a broad beam of flame engulfed the warlock's body; the burn was intense and consumed the body rapidly. One of the witches said, 'Master, we will fetch our horses, they are tethered at the other side of the house.'

Mab replied, 'You won't be needing your horses. Everyone link arms in a circle, that includes you two!' pointing at the two youngsters. The group of seven vanished and reappeared in the middle of the square at the Academy. Boe and the witches were only just realising what had just happened when an enormous cheer went up with cries of 'The White Witch! The White Witch! The White Witch!' The crowd of witches was all dressed in Greys and Whites, with the white robes denoting the more advanced witches. Luticia walked towards the small group, bowed low to Mab and said, 'Mabdelore, Bellona, you honour us with your presence.' Mab walked to Luticia and embraced her. The crowd roared their approval.

Mab whispered to Luticia 'I didn't expect this reception, it's wonderful. Thank you, Luticia.'

Luticia then embraced Master Boe and said, 'You look very tired, Master Boe. I will have someone take you to your room immediately. Mab, we have a dinner arranged, in an hour or so, so we will take the group to their rooms to freshen up.'

A white witch was allocated as a guide to each of the group, with Luticia escorting Mab. As the crowd parted before them, Mab spotted Fora and rushed over to embrace her. Mab had forgotten how beautiful Fora was, and hugged her tightly, kissed her on both cheeks and said, 'How is Pip?' Fora, with tears in her eyes, replied, 'She is fine, I have a child minder looking after her.'

Mab whispered, 'So why the tears?'

Fora said, 'I have missed you, I thought to see more of you.'

Mab looked at Luticia and said, 'I assume Fora will be joining us for dinner?'

Luticia said, 'Yes, of course, Fora, you are very welcome.'

Mab had a quick shower and donned a white witch robe that Luticia had provided. Luticia knocked on her door and led her to a special dining room. Mab was pleased to see that many of the old paintings, which had previously been removed, had been recovered and occupied prominent positions on the walls of rooms and corridors. The paintings were typically of ancient battle scenes, great heroes of the past and previous masters of the Academy.

Luticia asked Mab to sit at the head of the table, but Mab declined and insisted that she be at the head of the table as was normal practice. Mab sat to her right and Boe to her left. Mab noticed that none of the witches chose to sit beside her, which was good because she wanted Fora to sit next to her.

Luticia rapped on the table and said, 'Dinner will be served shortly, but first I wanted formally to thank Mabdelore for visiting us here at the Academy, in the usual witch way.' The witches rapped their knuckles on the table.

Mab said, 'Thank you, Luticia, for the wonderful reception and for welcoming the witches from the North into the Academy.'

Luticia replied, 'Mab, I would like to introduce you to my first line witches. On my right, we have Fora, who, of course, you know, then we have Lak, Sopa, Caro and Afla. For the benefit of everyone else, on my left we have Master Boe of the Guild of Sorcerers and the five newcomers from the north. Perhaps you could introduce yourselves?'

The witch immediately to Boe's left said, 'My name is Sara, I was an advanced witch in the black coven', the next said, 'My name is Puli, I was also an advanced witch in the black coven', the next said, 'My name is Tapp, I was an advanced witch in the black coven'. The final two said their names were Bora and Mita and that they were student witches in the black coven.

Luticia said, 'For newcomers, we operate a buddy system. The person sitting directly opposite you at this table is your Buddy. Their role is to look after you, show you around the campus, make sure that you know your way around and that you follow the rules.'

Sara said, 'So, Fora is my Buddy?'

Fora replied, 'Yes, Sara, exactly.' As they got to know each other, the food started to arrive.

Caro nervously asked 'Luticia, when our guests first arrived, you addressed the White Witch by her full name. I had not heard those names before?'

Luticia laughed, saying, 'Why don't you ask the White Witch yourself? She is sitting there.' Caro's face went bright red, and she stammered, 'I am too afraid to speak to her directly.' Fora leaned over and whispered something in Mab's ear.

Mab stood up and said, 'Please, do not fear me. We are all white witches, sisters, you have nothing to fear. Caro asked about my name. It is Mabdelore Bellona Winter, I am a Master of the Guild of Sorcerers and a White Witch of the Academy.' Luticia added 'You are also the Goddess Bellona.'

Everyone looked at Mab. Boe said, 'Bellona, the Roman Goddess Bellona!?'

Mab sat down and said, 'Yes, Master Boe, it appears to be so.'

Luticia said, 'We found a statue in a Roman temple in Yehuda. It was the very image of Mabdelore, I mean identical down to the sword and the whip.'

Boe said, 'But this is extraordinary, Bellona is the Goddess of War.'

Mab replied, 'Yes, I knew I wasn't good enough to be an Angel!'

Boe laughed and said, 'A Goddess is of far more import than an Angel.'

Mab grimaced and said, 'That will be put to the test tomorrow night.'

Bora said, 'Master Mabdelore, I am only a student, but is it really true that white witches are stronger than black witches?'

Mab replied, 'It depends on the wielder of the magic. Magic is not black or white; it is only the heart of the wielder that creates this distinction. You may ask if love is stronger than hate; at the extremity, all other things being equal, yes, it is. But it depends on the heart and will of those involved. I had to kill a creature from the Abyss, some time ago, it had taken the life of two masters and was making its way to the Guild. It was a Dread-Lord, a fearsome beast from the very bowels of the Abyss. At that time, my powers had not yet developed adequately. It should have killed me, but it didn't. I succeeded in killing it not because I was stronger but because of the power of my will and my belief in good triumphing over evil.' Everyone around the table applauded.

Mita said, 'Master Mabdelore, is it true that you can transform yourself into different animals?'

The senior witches laughed at the idea. Mita went bright red and bowed her head. Mab smiled warmly at Mita and said, 'What do you think, Mita, do you believe it is true?'

Mita looked up and said, 'Yes, I believe it!' Mab looked at Fora and said, 'What do you believe, Fora?'

Fora laughed and said, 'I have heard many tall tales about you, one being that you changed into an enormous tabby cat!'

Everyone around the table burst out laughing. Mab pushed her chair back and walked around the table towards Mita. As she did so, her body started to change shape and a huge saber-cat padded down to meet Mita. There were gasps of astonishment around the table. Mab went into Mita's mind and told her to climb on her back. Mita stepped up on her chair and jumped on the back of the huge cat. Everyone stood up and applauded. The giant cat padded around the table, allowing everyone to touch or stroke it. Mita climbed off and went back to her seat, elated. Mab changed back to her human form and walked back to her seat; she mind melded with Fora and said, *Was the tabby cat big enough for you?*' Fora looked at her with a disapproving expression, but then started to laugh. Mab looked at Luticia and said, 'Luticia, thank you again for the wonderful reception. I have a long journey to make tomorrow, so I will say goodnight, and I thank you again for the wonderful welcome.' Luticia replied, 'Thank you, Mabdelore, you are most welcome, and we look forward to seeing you again soon.'

Mab returned to her room, sat cross-legged on the bed and dropped into a deep meditative state. She came out of the meditation and was about to get into bed when there was a knock at the door. Mab opened the door, and it was Fora. She said, 'Mab, I hope I'm not disturbing you.'

Mab replied, 'No, of course not. Come in, I was just about to get into bed.'

Fora said, 'It's just that you said, something to Master Boe about being tested tomorrow night?'

Mab replied, 'Yes, well, it's nothing to be worried about, I'm sure everything will be fine.'

Fora put her arms around Mab's waist and said, 'But I do worry, Mab, I have missed you so much, I love you.'

Mab pulled her closer and kissed her on the lips. They slept together until dawn. When Mab woke, she dressed, kissed Fora as she was sleeping and then concentrated on the emperor Tiberius.

Mab used Satta's memories and her witch senses to locate Tiberius and transported herself to him, but remained unseen. She was inside a very large tent; Tiberius and his military leaders were in heated discussions around a map, which presumably related to the ongoing battle. Mab left the tent and soared upwards to get a birds-eye view of the battlefield. The Roman legions had bridged across a river which had wide, flat flood plains on both sides at that location. However, the enemy was in the forest. The legions were being drawn into the forest and killed mercilessly. The heads of the dead legionnaires were catapulted back into the legion ranks. Mab noted that the enemy had several small camps rather than one large encampment. People were moving between the camps, runners carrying messages! She thought the camps may represent their different clans, which had come together to repel the Roman invaders. Mab was no tactician, but she could appreciate the methodology; the Romans were most probably used to working on open plains and making use of their tried and tested battle formations. However, this was not possible in dense forests, where one-to-one combat was the only option. It was a war of attrition, and the Romans legions were losing.

Mab returned to the tent. She hovered above the group and then manifested on top of the table in a silver skin of power. Mab said, 'I am Bellona, I come to you, Tiberius, in your time of need.'

Tiberius cried out to his officers, 'Kneel before the Goddess!' All dropped to their knees with their heads bowed.

Mab floated to the floor and said, 'Rise, I wish to look upon you. I see that I am too bright for your eyes, I will dim my presence.'

The intensely bright light surrounding Mab dimmed, and they saw the face of Bellona, Goddess of War. All were silent.

Bellona said, 'Tiberius, you have permission to speak.' Tiberius said, 'Goddess, we are greatly honoured and humbled by your presence.' Bellona said, 'You pray to me every morning without fail. This pleases me, and so I come to save you and your legions. Many good men are losing their lives needlessly. You will pull the legions back across the river, and you cannot defeat the enemy in the forest.'

Tiberius said, 'Goddess, will you aid us in this battle?'

Bellona laughed and said, 'Tiberius, I could kill them all with a thought. They have five encampments in the forest, each around one hundred strong. They have five Commanders, one for each encampment and clan. I now enter the mind of the first commander, whose name is Stefan, and he has lost more men than the other clans. He has ambitions to unite the clans and to rule over them all. He has had many wives, many children, some of whom he has never held or even met. The petty desires and grudges of humans! There is only one thing that unites these clans, do you know what it is?'

Tiberius replied, 'No, Goddess.' Bellona said, 'It is their hatred of Rome. Do you believe they have cause to hate Rome?' Tiberius hesitated and then said, 'Yes, they do have cause. This is not our soil; we are the invaders, but that is the Roman way. We are warriors, we conquer or else our empire will die, albeit slowly.'

Bellona said, 'Tiberius, all empires eventually die, even the Roman Empire. You will move back to this side of the river and claim only the land on this side for Rome. You will relinquish the forest and the lands beyond to the clans.'

Tiberius replied, 'Goddess, if this is your wish, then it will be done.'

Bellona said, 'Do it now.' Mab vanished, floated upwards above the battlefield and watched as the Roman legions started to extricate themselves from the forest and flood plain areas. Mab was surprised how quickly they demobilised and progressed the reconstruction of the camp on the other side of the river. The chain of command was astonishingly efficient and effective.

Mab went back to the tent and found Tiberius arguing with two of his Generals over the wisdom of giving up the land on the forest side of the river.

Tiberius, clearly irritated, said, 'Julius, it matters not what you think. The Goddess has spoken.'

Julius replied, 'Does this goddess have any experience of war!'

Tiberius said, 'This is blasphemy, I will not tolerate it.' Julius drew his sword, but suddenly found that he couldn't move.

Bellona appeared beside Tiberius and said, 'What is the penalty for attempting to take the life of the Emperor?'

Tiberius smiled and said, 'Goddess, it is death by beheading or drowning.' Bellona opened her hand, and Onimaru spun over her shoulder; in one continuous, blindingly fast movement, the head of Julius Agrippa was sliced from his body, and Onimaru was returned to her scabbard.

Bellona said, 'Tiberius, I must leave you now, but I will return at first light tomorrow morning. Do everything you can to prevent the enemy from crossing the river; this should not be difficult for your legions. We will determine this battle tomorrow, but there is another matter that I wish to discuss with you regarding Yehuda and the role of the Roman Governor in that area.

Tiberius replied, 'Yes, Goddess. I await your return.' Mab vanished and appeared in Kanaka's office.

Kanaka said, 'I was just thinking about you. Should I order dinner, or perhaps we should just make our way down to the dining hall?'

Mab replied, 'Yes, let's walk down.' When they got to the dining hall, Satta was there with Master Uvren and Dassi.

Kanaka said, 'May we join you?'

Satta said, 'Yes, of course.'

Mab said, 'Master Uvren, how is the language training coming along?'

Uvren replied, 'Very well indeed. I am fairly proficient in the local Yehuda dialect, and as you may know, Satta and Dassi are now very proficient in our tongue. So, I am most pleased!'

Kanaka said, 'That is excellent news.'

Satta said, 'We were just finishing, so we will leave you to it.'

Uvren added, 'Yes, and I must be making my way back home.'

Kanaka said, 'Master Uvren, thank you again for all your work and for supporting Satta and Dassi.'

Mab and Kanaka ordered their food, and Mab said, 'Perhaps we should leave immediately after we finish eating. We could go to Fat Joe's and have drinks before the meeting with Lucifer?'

Kanaka laughed and replied, 'Mab, we are about to have a confrontation involving some of the most powerful beings in the universe, and you want to have a few drinks before it gets started?'

Mab smiled and said, 'Why not? I bet Lucifer is sipping a fine malt as we speak.'

Kanaka went into a fit of laughter and replied, 'No, I am sure that whatever he is doing, it's not that!'

Mab said, 'Yes, perhaps he has a young daemoness on his lap feeding him grapes as he sips on that fine malt?'

Kanaka, still laughing, replied, 'Well, why don't you ask him when we meet?'

Mab said, 'Master Kanaka, tonight you must focus on the two rulers. The rulers will fear Onimaru; its very presence is anathema to them. They also know that you are a master swordsman, so I would be astonished if they attacked you directly. They will most likely try to support Lucifer in his conflict with me. So, you may find yourself defending my back rather than being in direct combat. I will deal with Lucifer and my mother; do not intervene or get between me and Lucifer. The best outcome for me would be all three are slain, but my mother may have other ideas.'

Kanaka said, 'Understood. However, as I said earlier, I am confused regarding your mother. I am sure she would not aid Lucifer against you.'

Mab replied, 'They are Angels, I am not. I am beginning to suspect that the Angels believe in the balance because it is in their own interest. But, to answer your question, no, I do not think she would overtly aid Lucifer against me. However, I do think that she would like to restore the balance.'

Kanaka finished his meal and said, 'I'll go and get changed; meet you on the sports field.'

Mab was dressed in her usual black boots, tight-fitting black leggings, and a thick leather waistcoat with a white silk shirt. Her silver hair was tied at the back and hung down in a loose ponytail over her robe. Kanaka wore his robe with a leather waistcoat body protector, baggy black trousers and black boots. As he approached, Mab handed Onimaru to him, and Kanaka reciprocated with Dawn-Breaker. The swords were effectively concealed beneath their robes.

Mab put her arm around Kanaka and said, 'Better too early than too late.' They materialised on the roof of the Haskins building to find the others had already arrived and were in discussions. Mab walked to Uriel and hugged her; she could sense that Uriel was tense and worried.

Mab said, 'We are early, would you rather we leave and come back at the agreed time?'

Uriel said, 'Mab, we were just reminiscing about the old days. We can start the meeting early, have a seat.'

A ring of large sofa chairs had been positioned on the roof, each had a side table. Mab said, 'This is impressive, I had thought we would be sitting on the stone.' Mab could feel Lucifer studying her. She turned, stared directly at him, smiled and said, 'I see you have your human body tonight. Did you manage to find that piece of wing I cut from you?' Lucifer smiled back and said, 'No, fortunately, my body regenerates quickly.' Mab said, 'Can you regenerate a new head?' Uriel replied, 'Mab, that was unkind. We are meeting here together to reach a compromise, to find a way of co-existing.' Mab simply stared at her vacantly. Uriel said, 'Everyone, sit down please. Let's do the introductions. Mab, could you introduce yourself and your colleague? Mab said, 'I am Mabdelore Winter, adopted daughter of Uriel, and a Master of the Guild of Sorcerers. My colleague is Master Kanaka, Principal of the Guild of Sorcerers and an acknowledged master swordsman. Master Kanaka, could you introduce Onimaru?

Kanaka raised his arm, and Onimaru flashed from her scabbard, red flame licking along the blade. The two daemons cried out and recoiled. Kanaka sheathed the blade and said, 'Apologies if I upset anyone.'

Uriel glared at Mab, who smiled back. Lucifer said, 'I am Lucifer Morningstar, and my two colleagues are Azazel, Archdaemon Ruler of Air, and Azael, Archdaemon Ruler of Water.'

Mab said, 'Who is now ruling Fire and Earth with the demise of Samael and Mahazael?'

Lucifer replied, 'We suffice.'

Mab said, 'The truth is that you are rulers of nothing. The death of Samael and Mahazael has made no difference to the universe whatsoever, other than freeing a great many innocent people from slavery. Is that not so?' Lucifer said nothing.

Mab stood up, walked to the centre of the ring and said, 'Mother, you said earlier that we have come here to discuss how we can co-exist. I know that is your wish, but it is not my view. The Abyss and its inhabitants are equally vile and must be ended. We, I, cannot coexist with this filth while our people are having their lives stolen from them by daemonic possession, having unspeakable atrocities committed in their name and when generations of innocent men, women and children are being held in slavery.' Mab turned, pointed at Lucifer and said, 'Moreover, I hold you responsible for the murder of my partner Izzy, an innocent young woman who knew only love.' Tears started to run down Mab's face. She bowed her head for a few moments to compose herself, then lifted her head, looked directly at Lucifer and said, 'For that, I will have your life.'

Lucifer stared back at Mab and suddenly realised the magnitude of his error. This was not the daughter of Uriel, but something else entirely.

Lucifer looked at Uriel and said, 'Who is this? What is she!?'

Azazel slavered 'Let me feast on her master as I did with her bitch partner.'

Kanaka leapt forward, Onimaru in his hand, he moved with blinding speed, the sword blade a blur as he spun at full stretch and severed the head from Azazel, a fountain of black, stinking blood sprayed into the air as Azazel's head hit the concrete floor with a dull thud.

Uriel cried, 'No, please stop!' Lucifer rose-up, his face taking on a reptilian form with long yellow fangs and cruel slits for eyes. His arms also changed shape, the hands and fingers elongated and developed razor-sharp hooked claws. The creature reached out and plucked an enormous black blade from the air before launching itself at the diminutive form of Mab. Mab flew upwards and backwards at a steep angle. She raised her right-hand palm outwards and released a psychic blast of power the like of which had never been known. Uriel was on the periphery but was blasted off the top of the building and hung in the air on the opposite side of the street, barely conscious. The wave of power hit Lucifer in the chest like a planet collision, and he was propelled backwards at enormous speed, his back slamming into and demolishing a reinforced concrete wall on the adjacent tower block.

Lucifer started to regain consciousness and managed to extract himself from the debris. His wings had been severely damaged, but he stretched them outwards, screaming in pain as bones reconnected and joints relocated. Lucifer looked up and saw Mab, arms folded, hanging still in the air above the Haskins building. He let out an almighty roar and flew directly at her, sword raised. He brought the blade down in a vertical swipe, intending to split her in two from head to crotch. The blade arrested a few inches above her head. He tried with all his considerable strength to pull the blade free, but it was locked; her hold on the sword was immutable. Mab slowly reached up, grabbed the sword blade and brought her other hand around in a chopping motion, snapping the blade in half. She then moved forward and struck Lucifer with a back-handed blow to his face. His huge head snapped around, and he dropped to the rooftop below, landing badly on the concrete. As he started to rise, Mab looked up and pointed to the sky directly above her, which began to darken. She then clenched her fist, slowly lowered her hand and pointed downwards at Lucifer. Lucifer leapt up into the air, but a bolt of lightning streaked across the sky and then plummeted downwards, striking him on the head. Lucifer was blasted back down to the rooftop; he tried to stand, but another, much more powerful lightning bolt struck him, and he lost consciousness. Mab slowly lowered herself and stood over him, waiting.

Kanaka was still battling with Azael, Mab walked towards them and clenched her fist in front of her chest. Azael dropped to his knees, clutching at his neck. Kanaka drove Onimaru through the daemon's chest, withdrew the blade and then decapitated him before the body hit the floor.

Lucifer started to regain consciousness, and he turned and looked up at Mab. He tried to speak, but Mab kicked him hard in the stomach area, and he rolled across the rooftop.

Uriel was screaming at her, 'Mab, please stop. Please, for me, I am your mother!'

Kanaka looked on with a grim expression on his face but said, nothing. Lucifer was lying face down, smouldering; his body was badly burned, and his wings were damaged. He was clearly in considerable pain. Mab placed her left foot on his back and pressed; Lucifer groaned; she then reached down and ripped the left wing from his body. The wing was huge and took much of the flesh and muscle in his back away. Lucifer howled in agony. Mab then put her right foot on his back and ripped off the right wing. Lucifer was barely conscious, but still howled in agony.

Uriel ran to Kanaka and said, 'Please, Kanaka, please no more.'

Kanaka walked to Mab and said, 'If you intend to kill him, do it now.'

Mab looked at Kanaka and then at her mother. She then bent down and grabbed Lucifer by the hair, and dragged him to the centre of the roof.

Uriel ran to Mab and said, 'Please, no more. He was cast down; he has suffered for an eternity in that place of despair. I was only there for the blink of an eye. It was Azazel who gave the order to kill Izzy, not Lucifer.'

Mab looked down at Lucifer and said, 'I accept Uriel's intervention. You are redeemed.'

Mab placed her hand close to the two great wounds on Lucifer's back, and bright red blood began to flow. She cauterised the blood flow, and the wounds began to heal as they were bathed in silver light.

Lucifer turned his head to look at Mab and said, 'Who are you?'

Mab replied, 'I am the Goddess Bellona, daughter of the old gods, reborn of the Light to protect the innocent. You, Lucifer Morningstar, will take your place with my mother, Uriel and the other Archangels. The balance is ended; you will fight for what is good and right in that there can be no compromise. Do you understand?'

Lucifer said, 'I was cast down; are you saying that I am forgiven?'

Mab replied, 'Redemption, not forgiveness. Morningstar, stand-up.'

Uriel helped Lucifer to stand. Mab took his hands, and a silver skin flowed over Lucifer's body like a wave and then back like a retreating tide. He gasped and groaned. Lucifer was suddenly naked, his strong muscular body was perfection personified as if sculpted from alabaster by a master craftsman; his skin was whiter than fresh snow, and his long black hair flowed like a river over his shoulders.

Mab said, 'Your wings?' Lucifer twitched his shoulder blades, and huge white wings spread outwards to their full span. Mab turned to Uriel and said, 'Behold, Lucifer Morningstar, Archangel and protector of the Innocent.'

Uriel threw her arms around Mab and whispered, 'Thank you for this. It is more than I could have hoped for.'

Lucifer closed his wings and knelt before Mab, and said, 'Goddess Bellona, I thank you for freeing me from the Abyss and for bringing me back into the light.'

Mab said, 'You have my mother to thank.'

Uriel said, 'I will take Lucifer with me now to recuperate.'

Mab nodded and said to Kanaka, 'It's time we were going. But perhaps we should visit Fat Joes first; we have some unfinished business with Alexei.'

Kanaka replied, 'Yes, but it is late, and the local military has arrived. I think we should leave Alexei until another day?'

Mab thought for a few moments and then said, 'Yes, Master Kanaka, you are right.'

Kanaka replied, 'I could do with a drink before I hit the pillow, my office?'

Mab smiled and put her arm around him, and they materialised in Kanaka's office. Kanaka put a bottle of Alexei's single malt on the table with two goblets and poured generous measures. After the first couple of sips, they both reclined back in their chairs.

Mab said, 'Thanks for tonight. I know you don't like using Onimaru, but it was necessary.'

Kanaka replied, 'No problem, the two daemon rulers had to die; they were truly evil. What I can't rationalise, though, is Lucifer. He was supposed to be the personification of evil, and I thought for sure that you would kill him, but it didn't turn out that way.'

Mab replied, 'I thought so too. But, as my mother said, he was cast down into darkness and has been there for countless millennia. In his despair, I think he unconsciously shaped the environment around him; his darkest thoughts became the reality of the Abyss and a prison of his own making. Fundamentally, he was not, and is not, evil, but the creatures that rallied to him and thrive in that place are truly evil.'

Kanaka said, 'What of the other Archangels? Why have they not intervened.'

Mab replied, 'I know little about the Angels other than what my mother has told me. I expect if they need my support, they will make contact.'

Kanaka said, 'Yes, I expect so, but in view of the importance of recent events you would have thought they would have taken some interest?'

Mab replied, 'Perhaps they are busy with other things; the universe is a big place!' Mab finished her drink and said, 'I'll be leaving at dawn tomorrow to go back to Tiberius and his legions. Would you like to come?'

Kanaka replied, 'No, I really do need to get on with some work here. Also, I think I've had enough excitement for one day!'

Mab said, 'Goodnight and thanks again for your help tonight.'

She picked up Onimaru and made her way downstairs and outside to take in the night air. As she walked, her witch senses started to twitch. She stopped and said, 'Do you wish to speak with me?' A figure appeared before her. Mab gasped; he was huge but also astonishingly beautiful. He looked to be of similar stature to Lucifer, although more heavily muscled. He wore military-style golden gauntlets and black leather boots, and a golden chest guard. His white cape was identical to Mab's. His face was without blemish, and he looked as if he had just been carved from pure white granite. His long white hair hung down across his shoulders, and his piercing blue eyes took Mab's breath away.

He said, 'I am Michael.'

Mab thought even his voice was beautiful, as if he was singing rather than speaking. Mab replied, 'I am Mab, very pleased to meet you.'

Michael smiled, bowed and said, 'Goddess Bellona, I have come to thank you for freeing and saving my brother, Lucifer. You have restored him to us, something I did not imagine was possible.'

Mab replied, 'You are very welcome, but I sense there is another reason for your visit?'

Michael said, 'Yes, we have been at war for several decades. Our enemies are legion and powerful in many ways, particularly their psychic abilities. We have been able to prevent them from entering our universe in significant numbers, but they grow stronger while we grow weaker.'

Mab replied, 'When you say we grow weaker, what do you mean?'

Michael said, 'We have five Archangels, although, as you may know, Uriel and Raphael are not entirely suited for warfare. The angel host numbered twenty-eight, but six have been killed. For every Angel lost, we would need to kill thousands of the enemy in order to achieve equity, and this is not sustainable.'

Mab replied, 'And if you cannot hold them back?'

Michael replied, 'They will flow across this universe like a plague, killing every living thing that is not of their genus.'

Mab replied, 'This cannot be permitted. I will assist you and the Angels. I have an urgent task to complete tomorrow but following that I will come to you. May I see the nature of these creatures from your memory?'

Michael said, 'I will send you a memory package tomorrow. This will give you all the information you need. When you come to me, we can discuss how to best deploy you. At present, we are all directly involved in front-line battle, but you may wish to take on a more strategic role.'

Mab replied, 'I am Bellona, Goddess of War. I will be in the front line of the battle.'

Michael smiled, bowed and said, 'Goddess Bellona, I had hoped you would say that!' and with that, he vanished.

Mab thought about going to Fora, but it was late, and she needed some quality sleep; tomorrow would be a long day. She loped up the stairs to the suite, materialised in her bedroom and climbed straight into bed.

Mab woke at first light, showered, dressed and then focussed on Tiberius. She appeared in his command tent. Tiberius and his generals were having breakfast and discussing tactics. When Mab appeared, they stood and dropped one knee to the floor.

Mab said, 'Please be seated. I will join you if I may; it is sometime since my last meal.'

Tiberius made space for her, pushed some platters of food closer and said, 'Goddess, would you prefer wine or water?'

Mab replied, 'Water, thank you, Tiberius.'

Tiberius said, 'We have pulled the legions back to this side of the river as instructed. The enemy has made new encampments along the flood plain on the other bank.'

Mab said, 'Tiberius, history will know you as Tiberius the Great and the Wise. Do you know why?'

Tiberius was taken aback and replied, 'No Goddess, I do not think myself worthy of such a title.'

Mab said, 'You abolished those Games that involve the killing of innocent men, women, children and animals. You made peace with your enemies and, whenever possible, changed them into trading partners. In doing so, Rome becomes the centre of the greatest and richest empire that has ever existed. You understood that you exist to serve the people; poverty was eliminated because you would not stand by and allow families to starve while Rome gets richer. You believed in democracy, supported the senate and listened to the will of the people.'

Tiberius stared at Mab and said, 'I will do all of these things?'

Mab replied, 'Yes, you will be known as the greatest leader of the Roman Empire. Greater by far than your predecessor and greater than all of those that will follow you.'

Tiberius turned to his Generals and said, 'Did you hear the Goddess!'

Mab said, 'In Yehuda, the local governor is Pontius Pilate. You will replace him with Lucius Attilius. Your recently deceased commander of legions, Cassius Quintus, will be replaced by Marcus Attilius, the renowned gladiator. These changes are essential for several reasons that I cannot discuss with you.'

Tiberius replied, 'Goddess, of course it will be done as you command.'

Mab said, 'Excellent. Now let us see if your enemies are willing to talk.'

Tiberius and his three generals led Mab outside and down to the side of the river. Mab could see that the enemy had wisely moved their encampments just inside the forest, but their soldiers were arranged in groups on the flood plain.

Mab said, 'Can you send someone over to arrange a parley?'

One of the Generals replied, 'Whenever we send someone to talk, only their head comes back.'

Mab reached out with her witch senses and found one of their leaders. She entered his mind and said, 'Dieter, do not be afraid. I wish to speak with you and the other leaders. I am a Roman God, and I mean you no harm. Please talk to your fellow leaders, Tiberius wishes to negotiate if you are willing.'

Mab turned to Tiberius and said, 'I have just spoken to one of their leaders and asked if they would be willing to parley. Let's wait to see if they take up the offer.'

One of the Generals said, 'Someone is coming down to the waterline.'

Mab reached out to Dieter and said, 'I see you. I am here with Tiberius and three of his Generals. Are you willing to parley?'

Dieter replied, 'You say you are a Roman God. We have our own Gods. We will talk to you about your surrender and nothing else.'

Mab replied, 'Bring forth your own Gods and your best Champion. When they are defeated, perhaps you will agree to talk?'

Dieter laughed and said, 'Yes, we are happy to bring forward our Champion, and when we win, we will require 100 coins of gold as the prize.'

Mab replied, 'And if you lose?'

Dieter laughed again and said, 'We will not lose, but if we do, we will parley.'

Mab replied, 'Agreed.'

Mab turned to Tiberius and said, 'Our champion against their champion. If they lose, they will parley with us. If they win, you pay them 100 gold coins.'

Tiberius replied, 'Then I hope we win; we don't have 100 gold coins to give them.'

Mab said, 'Don't worry, we will win.'

Tiberius said to his Generals, 'Find our best soldier; we need to win this fight.' A short time later, the alarm was raised, and the enemy was approaching the camp.

Tiberius said to his Generals, 'How did they get across the river!'

Mab replied, 'There must be a submerged Ford downstream. This is their country; they know it much better than you!' Mab smiled as they approached, they were simple people with crude weapons, but they were brave walking into a Roman encampment.

They had their own interpreter who said, 'We have brought our champion; the prize is 100 gold coins. Where is your champion?'

Tiberius replied, 'Where is your champion?'

The interpreter pointed and said, 'He comes now.'

The clan leaders started to laugh as they saw the expressions on the faces of the Romans. Their champion was a giant; he carried a huge hammer in one hand and a short sword in the other.

Tiberius whispered, 'What is that creature?'

The interpreter said, 'This is Alaric, all Clans Champion. He is undefeated.' The generals had brought their proposed champion, but Mab could see the fear in his eyes.

She walked forward and said, 'Alaric, I am very pleased to meet you. I am the Roman Champion. Do not be put off by my diminutive stature!'

The interpreter burst into fits of laughter, so much so that he was struggling to translate Mab's words. When he managed to get the words out the clansmen then burst into fits of laughter.

The interpreter pointed to the legionnaire and said, 'I assume that is your champion.'

Mab replied, 'No, it is me. Ask Alaric if he is ready?' Mab walked forward; Onimaru flashed from her scabbard faster than the eye could see. Suddenly, there was no laughing, only silence.

Mab stood a few paces away from Alaric, Onimaru in her hand, but then she sheathed Onimaru and simply waited for the battle to begin. Alaric roared and ran towards Mab, lifting his huge hammer. Mab launched forward into the air, spun inside between the hammer and the sword and struck the giant with a powerful backhanded blow with her left hand. Alaric's head snapped around, and he fell to the ground. Mab landed on top of him and sat down on his huge chest. He was alive, but the blow had damaged his neck. He was in a lot of pain. Mab placed her hands on his neck, and silver light flowed into him, taking the pain away and restoring the muscle function.

Mab entered his mind and said, 'Alaric, I am sorry. I didn't mean to hurt you. Now rise and go home.'

Alaric stood up, bowed to Mab and then walked away. A roar of applause went up from both the Romans and the Clans.

Dieter walked forward and said, 'You are the Roman God?'

Mab replied, 'I am Bellona.

Now bring forward your Gods.' Dieter shrugged and said, 'Our Gods do not speak to us. Some of us think the Gods do not exist.'

Mab said, 'I am a God, and I exist.'

Dieter turned to the crowd and said, 'Bring forth the bear, God.' A wagon was trundled forward, and a cover was pulled from it to reveal a huge bear in a cage. The bear roared and paced,

Mab was appalled. She turned to Dieter and said, 'How long has this animal been imprisoned?'

Dieter said, 'It has been several years. The bear God is well fed and brings us good fortune.'

Mab replied, 'You will tell me who is responsible for this outrage now.'

Dieter, beginning to realise his error, blurted, 'Our clan witch told us that this was the bear God.'

Mab said, 'Release the bear immediately and bring forth this witch.'

Dieter shouted, 'Release the bear!'

The cage was opened, but the bear would not leave. Mab walked forward and entered the cage. She placed her hand on his huge head and calmed his thoughts, bringing them back to hunting his own food, the smells of the forest, swimming in ice-cold lakes and running free with his mate. She told him to fear and shun humans as they were mortal enemies who laid cunning traps and used deadly weapons against all animals. Mab walked from the cage with the bear walking slowly beside her.

Mab looked at Dieter and said, 'You will tell the Clans that the animals of the forest are not to be caged or harmed. I will return to this place periodically. If I find a single animal in a cage, I will slay all of the clan leaders, including you. Do you understand?'

Dieter stared at her and said, 'Yes, I understand.'

Mab said, 'Where is the witch?' Dieter signalled for a woman to be brought forward.

The woman removed her hood and said, 'I am the clan's witch.'

Mab expected to see an old crone, but this was a young, beautiful woman. Mab said, 'What is your name?'

The witch replied, 'Morgana.'

Mab thought for a moment, then looked at the bear, pointed across the river to the forest and said, 'Go now.' The bear ran and leapt into the river and allowed it to carry him downstream away from the humans.

Mab turned to Morgana and said, 'You will have a long life Morgana and you will not die by my hand. Dieter, remove her from my presence and bring the clan leaders to parley with Tiberius. The interpreter will not be necessary.'

Tiberius hosted the parley in his command tent. The five Clan Leaders were present together with three generals and Mab. The ten sat around a table that was arrayed with food.

Mab said, 'I have created links to your minds. You will hear everything that is said in your own language, so speak freely.' Dieter introduced the Clan Leaders and explained that the forest and plains on the other side of the river have for many centuries been sacred to their culture and that they would defend them to the last man if necessary. He further explained that the lands on this side of the river were also their lands but had never been occupied by them and were of no cultural significance.

Tiberius said, 'Our main interest is in trade; we need grain, timber, iron, cotton, precious stones and many other materials. If you were able to supply such things, we would be prepared to pay in gold, barter with weapons or offer protection against your enemies.'

Dieter replied, 'But what of our sacred lands?'

Tiberius said, 'The boundary of the Roman Empire would be drawn here on this side of the river. There would be no physical boundary, and your people would be able to move freely within and across these lands, but we would have a military presence here, and perhaps this could also be the main market hub for trading purposes?'

Dieter replied, 'Yes, Tiberius, a large trading hub here would be very beneficial to our clans. We have huge reserves of grains harvested from the plains that could easily be transported here, but also many exotic materials from the East that may be of interest to Rome.'

Tiberius said, 'Let us agree to end our war on the basis that the Roman Empire terminates on this side of the river. We will establish a trading post here with military support and I will send trading envoys from Rome to meet your representatives. Each party will bring samples of the goods they wish to trade?' Dieter and his fellow Leaders nodded enthusiastically. Tiberius called for goblets and wine and said, 'Then let us toast our alliance.'

Mab had been nibbling at the remains of breakfast and was the first to drink deeply of the wine before realising that it was poisoned. She turned to the clan Leaders and said, 'Put down the wine.' The Leaders looked at her, immediately understanding the implications.

Mab turned to Tiberius and said, 'What do you think you are doing!'

Tiberius looked askance at Mab and said, 'Goddess, what is wrong?'

The three Generals leapt to their feet and drew their swords but suddenly froze in position.

Mab picked up the goblet in front of Tiberius, sipped the wine and said, 'Your wine is also poisoned; it seems your Generals were planning to kill you and the clan Leaders.'

Tiberius replied, 'I need to know who else was involved in this plot.'

Mab released the generals and, with a coercive command inflection, said, 'Sit down!'

Tiberius said, 'If you tell me who else was involved, you will have a quick death, but if not, you will be burned alive.'

The younger general said, 'Emperor, I have no knowledge of this treason.'

Mab reached over, drank some wine from his goblet and said, 'His wine is also poisoned. I will search his mind.' Mab looked at the young General and mind-melded with him.

She then turned to Tiberius and said, 'He is innocent.' Mab looked at the two older Generals, searched their minds and said, 'These two have colluded with Cassius Quintus, not to kill you but to allow a daemon ruler to possess your body and rule in your place. I had hoped not to burden you with this, but it seems that I must. Cassius Quintus was possessed by the daemon ruler Samael, both host and daemon are now dead by my hand. Several high-ranking Roman legionnaires in Yehuda had also suffered this fate, but the last two daemon rulers were slain by my friend only last night.'

Tiberius said, 'So if I died here of this poison, my body would be taken over by one of these daemon spirits?'

Mab replied, 'It is worse than that. The poison takes you only to near death, and you are then too weak to refuse the daemon. It enters your body, usually with the help of a witch or a priest. You become an observer trapped in a corner of your own mind while the daemon steals your life and performs unspeakable acts of evil in your name.'

Tiberius looked at the two Generals and said, 'Speak now, or you will burn slowly.'

The first General said, 'We took our orders from Cassius Quintus. He instructed us to administer to you a substance that would be given to us by a witch. When we had given you the substance, we should let her know and take further instructions from her. He said the witch potion would make you a much stronger leader.'

Mab said, 'What was the name of this witch.'

The General said, 'I don't know her name. I saw her for the first time when she gave me the substance. I saw her again tonight; you were speaking with her.'

Mab said, 'Morgana.' Dieter said, 'She is our clan witch, but we had no knowledge of this treachery.'

Mab replied, 'Dieter, I know this is not of your doing. But you must drive Morgana from the clans. She is evil and very clever; drive her out, but do not kill her.'

Tiberius said, 'Forgive me, Goddess, but could you not rid us of this witch?'

Mab replied, 'I have already had dealings with Morgana, but many centuries in the future. If I kill her here, now, it could result in unforeseen consequences. The future of this plane and many others would change in an indeterminate way. Morgana must be driven out and shunned but not killed. These two generals are guilty of treason; have the Guards execute them.'

Tiberius bowed and replied, 'It will be done as you command, Goddess.'

Mab stared into space for a few moments and said, 'Emperor Tiberius, Clan Leaders, I am needed elsewhere, but I will return soon.'

Chapter Twenty-Three: Genocide of the Serrat

Mab materialised in the Lost Library at the Guild and entered into a prolonged period of meditation. When she surfaced, she went back to the memory package received from Michael.

The battle with the Serrat had been going on for several decades. The creatures were insectoid in nature and fed on vegetation by preference but would also prey on other creatures in times of famine. The Serrat came in a variety of forms based on their particular functions. They had Queens, Soldiers, Workers, Harvesters, Medics and also Domestics who looked after their hives, cared for the young and secured the eggs. They wore no clothing or armour and used no weapons, but they were ferocious in battle. Their soldiers were difficult to kill due to their sheer size, their hardened carapaces, their extraordinary psychic powers and also their formidable claws, mandibles and acidic fluids, which they sprayed to devastating effect from glands in their mouths.

The Angels had been unable to communicate effectively with the Serrat but gleaned that they were trying to migrate into our universe in very large numbers. Michael's view and fear was that they were akin to locusts on earth that moved from one area to another, stripping the land of all vegetation. In the case of the Serrat, however, they, in countless billions, would move from planet to planet, stripping each world of all living things.

More recently, the Angels had come to realise that the Serrat was at war with a more technologically advanced race known as the Vard. They knew this because a Vard pursuit vehicle passed through into our Universe. The Vard were able to communicate with the Angels. The Vard explained that they were at war with the Serrat and apologised for entering our universe uninvited, but warned the Angels that the Serrat is a pestilence that must be eradicated before they multiply and spread. The Angels asked them to return to their own universe, and they did so.

Mab made her way to the dining area and ordered some food. She attracted a lot of attention and so found a quiet corner where she could relax and think about the memory package sent by Michael. She had almost finished her lunch when Satta and Dassi saw her; they walked over and asked if they could join her.

Mab said, 'Yes, of course, please take a seat. Dassi, how are you?'

Dassi replied, 'I am very well. Thank you, Master Mab.'

Mab smiled and replied, 'Goodness, you really have mastered the language. Well done!'

Satta said, 'Dassi, tell Master Mab what you are doing in your classes.'

Dassi said, 'We are learning about animals and how they have feelings too, just like us, even though we sometimes we don't understand their behaviour.'

Mab looked at Dassi and replied, 'Yes, Dassi, that is very true. Animals must always be respected just because they are not the same as us doesn't mean they are any less important.'

Dassi said, 'If a big dog barks at you, sometimes it means he is afraid or thinks you are going to hurt him.'

Mab stared at Dassi and said, 'You are a very clever young girl!'

Mab turned to Satta and said, 'We need to go back to Yehuda soon. I spoke with Tiberius, and he is formalising the leadership changes we discussed. I will be busy for the next couple of days, but after that, perhaps You, Master Kanaka and I should go to see Lucius and Padwa. I expect that you and Dassi would like to go back home once we are sure it is safe of course.'

Satta replied, 'We would like to return home when it's safe. But I'm not sure we are ready yet.'

Mab said, 'Yes, you have been through a very traumatic experience. Perhaps stay here for now and make a few visits to test the water? If it's not for you then of course we would love you to stay here. Anyway, I must go, see you both soon!' Mab thought of Michael and vanished.

Mab materialised beside Michael, and her witch senses were screaming at her, pounding her mind. She looked down and saw the Angel host attacking a grounded Serrat swarm. The Serrat were grouped around what seemed to be a Queen, and the Angels were blasting the creatures with psychic blasts of energy and fireballs. The Serrat soldiers surrounded the Queen while others clung to her body, sacrificing themselves to protect her from the barrage of fire. They were beautiful multicoloured creatures, some slim with fine iridescent wings, others stooped with very heavy carapaces and large horns on their heads. All had faces that were almost humanoid with big, forward-looking childlike eyes. All could walk upright, but the soldiers seemed to prefer moving on all fours. The soldiers were prodigious fighters, but they only just outnumbered the Angels, who were much too strong for them. The Angel host was moving in for the kill, their golden swords were raised, and they were bearing down on the Queen. Mab felt her pain and fear. She plummeted downwards towards her, cried with all her might and coercive powers, 'Enough!' and launched a tsunami of psychic power that swept the Angel host away from the swarm.

Mab landed with a loud thump on the ground beside the Queen, slowly levitated upwards and moved towards her. The Serrat soldiers seemed to sense that she was not a threat and backed away, allowing her to approach. The Queen, unlike the soldiers, did not have a hard carapace and had suffered severe burns along the top of her soft body. Mab placed her hand on the Queen's head, and a silver skin of power slowly flowed over her body. Mab could feel the Queen groaning softly as her body was healed. She placed her other hand on the Queen's head and slowly, gently started to enter her mind. The Queen's initial reaction was to resist, but Mab stopped to give her time to trust her and then continued until the meld was completed. Mab could see everything; she had access to all the Queens memories from when she was hatched on her home world to her arriving here on this planet. Her species, countless billions of sentient creatures, had been massacred almost to the point of extinction by the Vard machines. Mab shared her pain and intense grief. It was an abomination. Tears flowed down her face. She embraced the Queen, dropped to the ground and turned to look at the Angel host, who had landed some distance behind her. Mab hung her head and breathed heavily; what she had learned, experienced, and witnessed through the memories of the queen, it was almost unbearable. Uriel saw the pain and anger in Mab's eyes.

One of the Angels walked towards her and said, 'What is the meaning of this!'

Mab lifted her head, tears streaming down her face, stepped forward and punched the Angel square in the face. It was a stupendous blow that would have killed any living creature other than the Archangel Gabriel, who dropped to the ground unconscious.

Mab stepped over Gabriel, walked towards the host and cried out, 'I am Bellona. Get on your knees!'

Michael descended and hit the ground between Mab and the host, and he immediately dropped to his knees. The rest of the host followed his example.

Mab said, 'Michael, come to me.'

Michael stood, approached Mab and said, 'Goddess Bellona, you are in pain; what is wrong?'

Mab looked into his eyes and imparted the memories of the Serrat Queen which included attacks made by the Angel host. Michael staggered backwards, trying to comprehend what he was seeing; he then brought his hands to his head and dropped back onto his knees. Uriel rushed to his side; Michael could hardly breath but managed to gasp, 'We are not worthy; we have committed abomination on the innocent, the goddess condemns us.'

Mab turned back to the Queen, mind linked with her and said, 'You and your kind are welcome in our Universe. We will protect you from these machines and their masters. If you are able to contact others of your kind, please tell them to come. We are sorry for what we have done to you and your species. We will now do everything in our power to help you, and you have my word.'

The Queen replied, 'We did not wish to come here, but flowing through the black hole was our only hope of escape. The Vard machines are able to return, but we are not strong enough to flow against the currents in the white star. There are other Serrat Queens, I will message them that this is now a safe place and protected by the Goddess Bellona. Our homes have been destroyed, and our children have been exterminated. This is our last hope, but it is not our home.'

Mab said, 'You will multiply here; there are many suitable planets in this cluster. Then, when it is safe, you will return and repopulate your home worlds.'

The Queen replied, 'But the Vard…'

Mab said, 'There will be no Vard.' She then walked amongst the Serrat, healing wounds and reassuring them that they were safe and could make their home here.

Mab returned to the Angel host and found them all still kneeling in silence. She could see that they were distraught and in despair. Michael's head was hung low, and Uriel and Gabriel knelt beside him. Mab stood waiting and watching.

Michael raised his head and said, 'Goddess, I am responsible for this abomination. I am not worthy of the light; take my life.'

Gabriel said, 'No, we are all responsible.'

Mab mind-linked with all the Angels and said, 'Gabriel is right. We are all responsible. We must now do everything in our power to help the Serrat. We will take this battle to the machines in their world, and we will liberate the remaining Serrat. Now stand up!' The Angels leapt to their feet. Mab levitated Michael, Raphael, Gabriel and Uriel.

The Angel host cheered. Mab then pointed and said, 'The prodigal son.' Lucifer manifested next to Uriel, and the Angels cheered again.

Mab said, 'We will bring light where there was darkness; none will stand before us.' The Angels were ecstatic and roared their approval. Mab said to the Archangels, 'Ensure the Serrat finds suitable shelter here with plentiful supplies of food and water. Prepare for the first battle sortie. I will take us through the white star, our primary objective is to destroy as many Vard machines as possible and the secondary objective to free as many Serrat as possible. We will reassess these objectives following completion of the first sortie. I will return early tomorrow so be ready to leave.' Mab vanished and appeared behind Fora at the Academy.

Fora was in the market square buying vegetables.

Mab said, 'You have to squeeze the ends to check if they are overripe.'

Fora laughed and replied, 'So, the Goddess is an expert on vegetables?'

Mab said, 'Yes, of course. May I join you for dinner?'

Fora replied, 'Yes, you may, but don't be expecting too much. I know you are used to banquets and fine dining.'

Mab whispered in her ear, 'Don't worry, I can eat almost anything!'

The crowd around Fora backed away and bowed their heads. Fora smiled, turned around and hugged Mab. They linked arms and walked around the market together.

Fora said, 'You are drawing a crowd; I've got enough now, so let's go back to my place and have a late supper.' When they arrived at Fora's home Mab was surprised to see that it was a house rather than an apartment and located on the corner of a small, cobbled square. When they entered, the childminder saw Mab, froze and then bowed low.

Fora said, 'Thanks again, Mari. Mab, Mari looks after Pip when I'm working.'

Mab walked towards Mari, hugged her and said, 'I'm very pleased to meet you, Mari; I'm Mab.'

Mari was ecstatic; she glanced excitedly at Fora and said, 'Thank you, White Witch, I mean Mab!' and ran from the house.

Fora checked Pip and said, 'She is sleeping.'

Mab pulled Fora towards her and kissed her passionately.

Fora said, 'Would you prefer food or me, Goddess?'

Mab replied, 'You and a nice bottle of wine, in that order, would be perfect.'

Fora smiled, picked up a bottle of white wine and said, 'Let's get started.'

They woke just before dawn, and Fora whispered, 'Did things go well with your meeting and test?'

Mab replied, 'Yes, everything went as well as could be expected. There is a war beginning against machines from another universe. We strike the first blow today; this is the reason I must leave early. Is everything here good?'

Fora replied, 'Yes, I am busy, and Luticia is always very kind to me.'

Mab looked at her and said, 'What is it? There is something else, tell me!'

Fora paused and then replied, 'My husband was involved with some dangerous people. I think they killed him for not repaying a debt, which I have no knowledge of.' They contacted me some time ago and said, that I now owned the debt. But I heard nothing more from them until a couple of nights ago.'

Mab said, 'What happened a couple of nights ago?'

Fora replied, 'Someone came to the door. He was robed. I didn't see his face, but he said he was an assassin and would take my life if the debt was not paid. I asked him what the debt was for and how much was owed. He said it was an honour debt, it had to be paid in blood, and he would return with my instructions.'

Mab mind-melded with Fora and said, 'Let me see him.' Mab looked at the assassin, oversized walking boots, black armour on his legs and torso, slight changes in the flow of his robe suggesting concealed weapons, and gloved hands. His face was hidden, but the way he moved his head and the movement of the hood were telling.

Mab said, 'It is a Balerak; you must leave here immediately.'

Fora replied, 'A Balerak, what is that?'

Mab replied, 'It is a creature from the Abyss. My wife was killed by a Balerak, and it's not going to happen to you. Quickly and quietly, pack some clothes and get Pip ready to leave.' When Fora and Pip were ready, Mab embraced them both and materialised in the garden of her mountain home in Cetha.

Mab said, 'This is my home. You will be safe here until I return.'

Fora replied, 'Mab, it is beautiful.'

Mab smiled and said, 'There is a village market and store only a few minutes away. Have a look around and make yourself at home. I will let Luticia know that you are here. Nothing will happen, but if you see any sign of a Balerak then hide and shout out my name as loud as you can in your mind. Do not confront it or try to fight it, it will kill you. I will return tonight or early tomorrow morning.' Mab hugged and kissed Fora and said, 'Remember, if anything strange or suspicious happens, call out to me.'

Mab thought about the Serrat Queen and materialised before her. She was deep underground and being attended by her workers and servants.

Mab said, 'This is a good refuge. Is everything to your liking, Queen?'

The Queen replied, 'I can't thank you enough, Goddess. This is the first time in many years that I and my swarm have felt safe.'

Mab replied, 'I am pleased to hear that. Have you been able to contact others of your species?'

The Queen said, 'Yes, but it is a long and difficult journey even to reach the black hole.'

Mab replied, 'I will leave you now. We will help any Serrat swarms we encounter and destroy as many of the Vard machines as we can.'

The Queen said, 'I wish you good luck and a safe return, Goddess.'

Mab materialised beside Michael and said, 'Are we ready?'

Michael replied, 'Almost. We have travelled across the various planes of this Universe in space and time but never ventured beyond. What do you think awaits us?'

Mab said, 'I have no idea. How many Angels are you able to translate?'

Michael replied, 'I could carry three or four.'

Mab thought for a few moments and said, 'We will travel in formation through the White Star, creating a psychic shield with me at the tip. This will also be our battle formation. When it comes to the return journey, we will be able to translate back here, focussing on the Queen. If you and the other Archangels each take three Angels, I will take the others. We have all been in direct contact with the Queen in this place so translating back here will be much less risky than coming back through the blackhole. If we intend to bring Serrat back with us, then clearly, we will need to escort them.'

Michael looked at Mab and said, 'So, the white star is seen as a black hole in the other universe?'

Mab replied, 'Yes, but if we manage to pass through the white star, then travelling back through the black hole should be easier.'

Michael said, 'If we manage to pass through the white star? I thought you had done this sort of thing before?'

Mab smiled and replied, 'No, I've never seen a black hole or been so close to a white star. It's terribly interesting though, don't you think?'

Michael looked down at her and couldn't stop himself from laughing. He then said, 'Yes, Goddess. I will advise the others of the battle formation and the options for the return journey.'

Mab said, 'Michael, I haven't had much to eat recently. Where can I get food and wine?'

Michael pointed to a large mess tent that had been set up and said, 'You will find what you need there.'

Mab walked into the mess tent, grabbed a large wooden plate and filled it with cheese, fruits and rustic bread. She also took a pitcher of wine and made her way to the seating area, where before there was a background drone of chatter and laughter, there was now complete silence. Mab looked up and realised she was the cause of the silence. She looked around and saw Gabriel, Raphael and Uriel sitting together.

Mab walked to them and said, 'Do you mind if I join you.' As she sat down. Gabriel started to rise.

Mab said, 'Gabriel, sit down.' Mab looked at Uriel, smiled, and said, 'Mother, how are you? I wasn't expecting you to be part of this?'

Uriel said, 'Mab, I am fine. I will join my brothers; we all feel the need for atonement and retribution in equal measure.'

Mab smiled and said, 'Yes, the Serrat Queen's memories are too much to bear. When this is over, I will expunge them from my mind perhaps I will then be able to sleep properly.' Mab looked at Gabriel and said, 'Gabriel, I apologise for striking you. I was lost in the memories of the Queen and couldn't cope with anything else. It was not my intent to injure you.' Mab put her hand out to him. Gabriel slowly raised his arm, reached out and clasped Mab's hand in friendship.

Gabriel said, 'Is it true that you are of the old Gods?' Mab replied, 'It seems that I am, and was, Bellona, Goddess of War. At least that is what I have discovered.'

Raphael said, 'But the old Gods were false. There is only one God.'

Mab said, 'God is the light, literally the light, of the universe. The Prophet told me that I was born of the light.'

Gabriel said, 'You spoke to the Prophet after his death?'

Mab replied, 'Yes, he was of the light. It suffused his entire being.'

Raphael said, 'Goddess, when we travel through the white star, will we enter another universe?'

Mab, stuffing some bread and cheese into her mouth, replied, 'I guess so, but we will find out very soon!'

The Angels started to assemble in six groupings. Michael led Geniel, Enediel and Amixiel. Raphael led Azariel, Dirachiel and Scheliel. Gabriel led Amnediel, Barbiel and Ardesiel. Uriel led Neciel, Abdizuel and Jazeriel. Lucifer led Ergediel, Ataliel and Azeruel. Mab led Geliel, Requiel, Abrinael, Aziel, Tagriel, Alheniel and Amnixiel. Michael explained the formation through the white star, with Bellona acting as the point, followed by the five Archangels and then the six Angel battle groups.

He then said, 'When we pass through the white star, we remain in formation until told otherwise. Bellona will lead and coordinate the engagement with the Vard.'

When the formation was established on the ground, Mab mind messaged all and said, 'We are about to enter another universe, a universe where the Serrat are being exterminated. It is an affront to humanity and to the light. We will take the first steps today to end this abomination. We leave now!' Mab leaped into the air and soared upwards, and she could feel the five Archangels spread out behind her, and the Angel host behind them. Mab turned towards the white star and accelerated, constantly checking the host was maintaining formation. When she reached the edge of the star, she raised a psychic shield in front of her and then allowed it to flow back, enveloping the entire formation. She could feel the Angels adding to the strength of the shield as they entered the white star and were buffeted by the material and gas flows belching from the adjacent universe. Mab further strengthened the psychic shield and accelerated, pushing the battle formation through the star and out into the cold darkness beyond. Eventually, they escaped from the gravity well of the black hole and hung in open space, still surrounded by the shield bubble.

Mab mind linked with the Queen and explained that the host had passed through the white star. The queen said that several Serrat swarms had been forced down onto the sixth planet of the Ashada Solar System. Mab studied the image of the Solar System and also gleaned information on the sixth planet. The planet was named Boda and was inhabited sparsely by the Serrat. Meshan, the Serrat Queen, had spent some time there when she was a child learning how to survive in the wild. Boda seemed to be a natural wildlife haven and a place where Serrat could spend leisure time. Mab dissolved the psychic shield and shared the information relating to the solar system with the Archangels.

Mab said to all, 'We will hold the spear point formation until I advise otherwise. We have some distance to cover before we reach Ashada.' Mab rocketed through space, followed by the Archangels and the host. As they approached Ashada Mab could see the solar system was alive with hundreds of Vard spacecraft. The lead craft was of staggering proportions and was clearly coordinating the battle. Mab was astonished by the sheer ferocity of the attack; huge light beams were slicing down into the planet, and powerful missile systems were pummelling the surface. Mab screamed to all, 'Break into the six attack groups, destroy them all! My group to me now!'

Mab veered away from the minor vessels and swept around towards the lead craft. The missile defence system on the Vard mothership detected them and launched a blistering attack. Mab immediately threw up a powerful psychic shield. The Angels flew around the edges of the shield and swiped downward with their golden swords at the huge ship. Their swords cut through the spacecraft's energy shield, but they couldn't get close enough to the hull to do any significant damage. Mab looked across and saw that the Archangels were decimating the smaller vessels. She smiled when she saw Gabriel slice the wing off one of the larger vessels, causing it to tumble down towards the planet. Gabriel felt her stare and turned to look at her. She was smiling directly at him, and his spirits lifted. He felt invigorated, suddenly filled with energy.

Mab's mind linked to her battle group and said, 'The mothership is too heavily protected; I will deal with it alone. I want you to break off and support the Archangels in destroying the other vessels. Go now!' The Angels immediately peeled off and threw themselves into the task of destroying the minor Vard ships. Mab flew towards the Ashada Star.

Michael said, 'Where is the Goddess?'

Amnixiel pointed and said, 'She seeks to destroy the Vard mothership.'

They watched as Mab returned from the Star, her right hand holding a whip of light that trailed behind her and was lost in the depths of the Star.

Mab cried out to the host, 'Get behind me!'

The host scattered, raised their shields and looked on in amazement as Mab raised her right arm and lashed the whip forward towards the Vard mothership. The whip pulled a huge Solar flare from the Star with it, Mab brought it down on the Vard ship. The flare sliced through the Vard vessel like a knife through butter. There was an enormous explosion as the Vard ship tore apart, spouting huge volumes of gases and debris into space. Minor explosions continued to erupt in both halves of the dying vessel, and the remaining myriad of smaller vessels suddenly stopped and hung dead in space.

Mab said, 'Archangels to me. Angels push all the minor vessels into Ashada.' Mab and the Archangels flew forward and entered the Vard mothership. They made their way slowly and cautiously to the front of the vessel, expecting an imminent attack, but nothing happened. At last, they reached the front of the ship and entered a small chamber crammed with electrical devices and illuminated with constantly blinking lights of every conceivable colour. Mab said to no one in particular, 'Do you think this is the control centre for the machine?'

Gabriel said, 'I have seen things like this before. The machine is controlled by an artificial intelligence known as a computer.'

Mab stopped suddenly, turned to Lucifer and said, 'Fora, a Balerak, go there. Question the creature, kill it and return here as soon as you can.'

Lucifer nodded and vanished.

Mab looked at Gabriel and said, 'Can we communicate with this computer brain?'

Gabriel shrugged. Uriel said, 'It's worth a try?' Mab reached out with her senses but couldn't make sense of what she found. There didn't seem to be any thoughts, only an innumerable amount numbers.

Mab said, 'The machine systems are responding to number sequences. These must be the equivalent of instructions in the machine world.'

Uriel said, 'Mab, there is something else up there.' Uriel pointed up to an elevated steel platform. The group floated upwards onto the platform. Mab realised that this was, in fact, the heart of the machine.

Michael said, 'I think this is the controller.' The others moved towards Michael, who was pointing at something.

Uriel, clearly revolted by what she saw, said, 'What is that thing?' The creature was submerged in a yellowish fluid contained in a large transparent vessel. Its head was huge and grossly disproportionate to the rest of its body which was almost humanoid but with withered legs and arms. There were no other discernible human features. No ears, eyes or mouth were visible. Uriel said, 'I have mind linked with the creature.'

She said, 'Who are you?'

The creature replied, 'My name is Rogar. I am a Var Battle Commander.'

Uriel said, 'What are you doing here?'

Rogar replied, 'I came here to destroy the Serrat who have taken up residence on the planet below.'

Mab said, 'Why do you want to destroy them?'

Rogar replied, 'Those are my orders.'

Uriel said, 'Who gave you the orders?'

Rogar replied, 'That information is restricted.'

Mab said, 'We wish to speak to your rulers in order to resolve the situation with the Serrat.'

Rogar did not reply.

Uriel said, 'Can you put us in contact with your rulers?'

Rogar replied, 'No, that information is restricted.'

Michael said, 'This thing has no will of its own. We are wasting our time.'

Mab reached deep into the creature's mind and said, 'Many lives are at risk. If you do not provide me with the information I need, I will extract it, and you will not survive the process.'

Uriel said, 'Mab no!' but Michael said, 'Uriel, please withdraw.'

Uriel stepped back; Mab scoured every fibre of the creature's brain.

Michael said, 'Interesting. We have found the Var home planet. It is known as Varalian. Rogar was the only Var present here today. The other vessels are drones commanded from this mothership. The drone soldiers are known as the Vard, but they are machines, not living creatures.'

Mab said, 'Yes, but that is an interesting distinction. Are these machines not also living creatures?'

Michael shrugged.

Gabriel said, 'Should we dispose of this vessel as with the others?'

Mab replied, 'Yes and then we need to visit the Serrat on the planet below.'

Fora was in tears, pleading with the Balerak, 'I am telling you that I know nothing of this debt. If you explain what it is about, then I will do what I can to honour it.' The Balerak said, 'You will administer this potion to Principal Luticia. It is colourless and tasteless. I suggest you add it to a drink. This will repay the blood debt owed. Otherwise, I will take your child's life and then your life.'

Lucifer focussed on the image of Fora that Mab relayed to him and materialised beside her.

The Balerak dropped to its knees and said, 'My Lord, you honour me with your presence.'

Lucifer said, 'Get up! You are a fool of the highest order; do you know who this is!'

The Balerak, realising that something was very wrong, said, 'I was commissioned to kill the Principal of the Academy of White Witches. This witch will administer the poison. She will come to no harm; the poison is absorbed into the atmosphere immediately following death.'

Lucifer stared at the Balerak and said, 'Answer my question!'

The Balerak started to panic and said, 'I know that she is a witch who has access to my prey; that is sufficient for my purposes.'

Lucifer struck the Balerak across the face knocking it to the floor, and said, 'She is the lover of the Goddess Bellona who lifted me from the Abyss. The Goddess sees everything. She knows you are here and sent me to intercede. You will tell me everything you know on this matter else I will rend it from your mind. Speak!'

The Balerak said, 'Lord, I did not know this witch was favoured by the Goddess, else I would never have accepted the commission. Please let me leave this place, and I will never return.'

Lucifer replied, 'You are trying my patience Balerak!'

The Balerak said, 'I was commissioned by the Warlock Malphador of the Northern Covens. He has ambitions to unite his covens with the Academy, but Principal Luticia needs to be removed before that can happen.' Fora stared in astonishment at Lucifer; she had never seen anyone like him before. She bowed and said, 'Lord, have you come to save me from this creature?'

Lucifer turned and said, 'Yes, I am instructed by the Goddess Bellona. She is mid-battle in another realm, but she will return soon.' Lucifer plucked a great black sword from the air, plunged it through the Balerak's chest and said, 'Your life is forfeit, the Goddess will be advised of the treachery in the North.'

Lucifer, with the Balerak skewered on his sword, vanished and appeared beside Mab on the surface of Boda.

Mab looked at the creature hanging from Lucifer's sword and said, 'What of Fora?'

Lucifer replied, 'She is unharmed and calm; she awaits your return. The Balerak sought to use Fora to administer poison to Principal Luticia. The assassination was sponsored by the Warlock Malphador.'

Mab nodded, smiled and said, 'I suggest you wipe that thing off your sword?'

Lucifer looked down at her with a wry smile on his face and said, 'Yes, perhaps. I thought you may want to take a closer look?'

Mab replied, 'No, but I will take a closer look at Malphador. Thank you, Lucifer. I know the changes have been particularly hard for you, but to see you and your brothers fighting together here was truly magnificent.'

Lucifer smiled and said, 'Yes, I also thought it was magnificent and believe me, Goddess, I am grateful for the changes. I have no wish to return to the Abyss.'

Mab called the host together and said, 'We have won a great victory here today, and we now have knowledge of the Var home world which we will visit on our next sortie. I said to Lucifer a few moments ago how magnificent it was to see the Archangels together with the host fighting side by side to liberate the innocent!'

The Angels roared their approval.

Mab waited until the noise subsided and said, 'Now we will escort the three Serrat Queens and their collectives through the blackhole and into our home universe where they will be safe.'

The Angels once more roared their approval.

Mab reached out with her witch senses and located the three Queens. They had each made a safe refuge deep under the ground by extending pre-existing tunnels. Mab explained to them that she had come at the request of Queen Meshan, who had successfully passed through into our universe, where they would be most welcome. The three Serrat Queens were Gosshan, Tenshan and Cepshan, and they agreed to come to the surface and prepare for the journey ahead. The Queens and their collectives soon started to arrive. Tenshan was the closest, and the Angels watched as they staggered toward them. Mab was appalled; she had expected them to be relatively unscathed, being underground, but she was wrong. Mab ran forward to Tenshan, who was badly burned. The Queen dropped to the ground before Mab, exhausted and in terrible pain. Mab placed her hands gently on her head and poured energy into her; a silver skin of light flowed from Mab's hands over her entire body. The Queen gasped in relief as her wounds and pain were washed away. Mab mind-messaged the Angels to attend to the rest of the collective. The Angels rushed forward and saw to the needs of the Serrat, many of whom suffered from wounds and burns. Gosshan and Cepshan arrived almost at the same time but from different directions. These two collectives had fared somewhat better than Tenshan's but also needed medical help and healing.

Mab mind-linked with the three Queens and said, 'We will travel through the black hole together. I know you and your people are tired, but we must get you to safety; the Vard will be arriving soon.'

The Queens replied, as one, 'We are tired, but we are ready to leave now, Goddess. We are exposed when on the surface.'

Mab messaged the Archangels, 'We leave now!' and launched into the air with the Archangels and the host following. The Serrat Queens took flight together with their collectives. The host fell back to protect the rear of the group while Mab and the Archangels led from the front. Mab accelerated and messaged the Archangels and the Serrat Queens, 'We are approaching the black hole. I will throw up a shield, you add to it and advise the host to make sure the rear is protected as we emerge from the white star.' The group flew at astonishing speed into the edge of the black hole, were swept through it, within their shield bubble, and expelled through the white star into the adjacent universe. Mab headed for the planet where Meshan was waiting.

When they landed, the three Queens went to Meshan, where they linked antennae and performed a strange ritual dance of greeting. The Serrat applauded by rubbing their wings together to create a high-pitched squeal. Mab messaged the Archangels and the Queens 'Queens, this unnamed planet is yours for as long as you wish. Make yourselves and your people safe here. I expect the Var to retaliate, but this is our Universe; we will defend it and you. I will return tomorrow, and the host will remain with you. We need to discuss the likely war with the Var and how to rescue the remaining Serrat.'

Mab then walked to Michael and Gabriel and said, 'We need to decide on battle strategy and objectives tomorrow. We may need to make a pre-emptive strike on the Var home world. I would prefer the battle to be in their universe rather than ours. I'll arrive back here early evening; could you set up a meeting with yourselves, the three Queens and I?'

Gabriel replied, 'Do you wish all of the Archangels to be present?'

Mab replied, 'Yes, I guess so.' Mab thought of Fora, vanished and materialised beside her. Fora was in the back garden of Mab's home in Cetha. She and Pip were weeding and planting new flowers.

Pip jumped up, hugged Mab and said, 'We got flowers from the market!'

Fora hugged and kissed Mab and said, 'It is so beautiful here. Are you hungry? Would you like some food?'

Mab said, 'Why don't we go for a walk around the village? I could do with some fresh air.'

Fora replied, 'Yes, but first have a shower and get changed; otherwise, you will scare the neighbours.' The light was dimming when they walked through the village. Mab took a deep breath and felt the fresh, slightly chilled mountain air, bringing back memories of Izzy.

Fora said, 'What are you thinking?'

Mab replied, 'I was thinking how peaceful it is here and how I would like to stay here with you.'

Fora replied, 'I saw the graves in the back garden, Izzy and her parents.'

Mab, looking down at Pip, said, 'Yes, it was a Balerak with Izzy and Soldiers with her parents.'

Fora replied, 'Do you think it will be safe for us to travel back to the Academy? I'm worried about Pip's schooling, and the Balerak managed to find us here.'

Mab said, 'The reality is that a Balerak will find you wherever you are. They are masters in the art of assassination. Only Lucifer and I have managed to kill one. I have made Luticia aware that this Malphador is trying to assassinate her and that you are safe here with me. I can return you tomorrow morning if you wish, but go straight to Luticia, and perhaps you could take a room in the main building until the situation is resolved?'

Fora replied, 'Yes, I'll talk to Luticia about it tomorrow. It's a shame these creatures from the Abyss can't be used to do good. I expect having a few Baleraks on your side wouldn't do any harm. Lucifer was able to change, and he was their Lord.'

Mab stopped and said, 'Fora, that is worth thinking about!'

Fora replied, 'So I'm not just a pretty face?'

Mab said, 'No, but you do have a spectacularly pretty face! Let's make our way back and have a light supper and some local wine?'

Fora smiled and replied, 'Yes, I'd like that.'

Mab woke early the following morning and mind-messaged Kanaka 'Master Kanaka. I know this is very short notice, but could you arrange an urgent council meeting this morning? I will bring Lamm and Luticia to your office when I arrive, so they don't need to travel. I think Master Boe should be there if he is available.'

Kanaka replied immediately, 'Yes, of course. I'm looking forward to seeing you. I need some sword practice!'

Chapter Twenty-Four: War with the Var

Boe sat calmly at the meeting table in Kanaka's office and said, 'Master Kanaka, pacing up and down on the rug will not make Mab arrive any earlier.'

Kanaka replied, 'She said it was urgent, when have you heard her use that word before?'

Boe replied, 'I don't think I have ever heard her use that word.'

Kanaka said, 'Exactly, something is very wrong!'

Boe replied, 'Is that why you have several bottles of her favourite wine on the table?'

Kanaka simply scowled at Boe, who responded with a wry smile.

Mab materialised in Luticia's office with Fora and Pip. Luticia hugged Mab and Fora and kissed little Pip.

Mab said, 'The Balerak that threatened Fora is dead, but I can only assume Malphador still seeks to have you assassinated. You need to increase the security around the campus. Also, could Fora and Pip have accommodation in the main building until I get the opportunity to visit Malphador?'

Luticia said, 'Yes, of course, I will make sure that happens. Fora, I have to leave with Mab, but could you please instruct Afla to make the arrangements?'

Fora replied, 'Thank you, Luticia.'

Mab kissed Fora and Pip goodbye and vanished, taking Luticia with her.

Mab and Luticia materialised in Kanaka's office.

Mab said, 'I'll get Master Lamm.' Moments later, Lamm appeared beside Mab.

Kanaka said, 'Have a seat. Lunch is on its way, and Mab's favourite wine is on the table. Mab, you asked for this extraordinary meeting to discuss an urgent matter; could you give us a quick summary.'

Mab replied, 'Yes, Master Kanaka. As you know, Uriel, my mother, is an Archangel. There are four Archangels, five including Lucifer, and more than twenty Angels.

Boe replied, 'The Angel host was thought to number twenty-eight?'

Mab replied, 'Yes, Master Boe, but some have been killed. This brings me to the reason for calling this meeting. The Angels have, for decades, been fighting a war to prevent an alien species from entering our universe. But the creatures they are fighting, known as the Serrat, are, in fact, fleeing from another species known as the Var, who have driven the Serrat almost to the brink of extinction. Billions of Serrat have been brutely slain. Their last hope was to escape into our universe. But the Angels waged war on them, based on false information given to them by the Var, and have killed thousands of Serrat over recent years.'

Mab hung her head, breathed deeply and said, 'The Serrat are beautiful, multi-colored, highly intelligent creatures. They have highly developed psychic capabilities but are peaceful and not suited to warfare. The Angels are now protecting the Serrat that we brought to safety. However, to rescue them, we destroyed many war vessels, known as the Vard, and also a Var mothership. We are expecting retaliation, and it will be soon.'

The Masters were silent in thought. Lamm said, 'What is the relationship between the Var and the Vard?'

Mab replied, 'The Var is the real enemy. We have only seen one Var, and he was the controller of a mothership. He was linked directly to the ship controls. Basically, a head submerged in a tank of yellow fluid. Whether all Var look like that, we don't know, but I suspect not. The Vard are war machines that are controlled by the mothership. All the war vessels are equipped with potent weapon systems and protective shields.'

Kanaka said, 'What do we know of the Var, their numbers and capability?'

Mab replied, 'Very little. We were on a rescue mission to save a species from extinction. An extinction that we aided. I didn't think about the consequences too much.'

Boe said, 'Do we know where the Var are located and how they enter our universe?'

Mab replied, 'Yes, their home planet is Varalian. I gleaned this from the mind of the Var Commander. They entered our universe in the same way the Serrat did. They travelled through a hole created by a massive star in our universe; the star, in effect, created a tunnel between the two universes. The Vard machines are able to travel through the tunnel by creating an energy field that acts as a shield. The Serrat created a psychic shield and this is also how the Angels and I were able to pass through.'

Kanaka said, 'Is this the only way to pass between the two universes?'

Mab replied, 'I can't be sure about that, but it is the only way the Var and the Serrat know.'

Lamm said, 'Could the tunnel be closed?'

Mab said, 'I hadn't thought of that, but I would be surprised; white stars are the most massive of stars. Anything we do would be fairly insignificant.'

Kanaka said, 'Is the line of travel through the star always the same?'

Mab replied, 'Yes, there is a pathway that is far less turbulent than other potential routes. So, we will know precisely where the Var and the Vard will enter our universe, but I have to say that I had thought to take the war to them rather than have it in our own universe?'

Kanaka replied, 'I think it is both of those. We know where the Var home world is located, so we attack them there with convincing force and seek to destroy as many of their critical assets as possible. A few reconnaissance visits may be necessary. We then retreat back to our own universe but with our main force waiting in ambush as they emerge from the star.'

Boe replied, 'This is all on the basis that war is inevitable. It may be that an agreement with the Var could be negotiated. If we accepted all of the Serrat into our Universe, does that solve the problem for the Var?'

Mab replied, 'Possibly, it is worth a discussion. However, the Serrat are not of our universe and wish at some point to return to their home worlds. Also, we destroyed the Var and Vard vessels in their universe, so my feeling is that we are already at war with them. To ask for negotiations now may be taken as a sign of weakness.'

Kanaka said, 'Mab, I agree with Boe; we should try to negotiate, but this should be done by the Serrat, not by us. In that way we will be seen by the Var to be standing behind them, as observers in the negotiations, but with them if it comes to war.'

Mab smiled at Kanaka and said, 'Yes, I like that. My father would say it was a carrot and stick approach.'

Kanaka looked puzzled, but Boe laughed and said, 'Don't worry, Master Kanaka, I'll explain it to you when this is all over!'

Kanaka said, 'The first step is to arrange the meeting. It may be that the Var will refuse to negotiate in which case we will be at war with them.'

Mab replied, 'I have asked the Archangels to arrange a meeting with the three Serrat Queens today. We should all attend.'

Kanaka said, 'Mab, when you said this was urgent, I knew it was serious, but I didn't expect war with another universe! So, we have lunch and then travel with you to discuss the situation with the Serrat?'

Mab replied, 'Yes, I am sorry to drag you into this, but you must be involved in these discussions.'

Luticia said, 'Yes, this is our universe, and we will fight to protect it from these machines!'

Kanaka replied, 'Just so, Luticia!'

Mab and the other masters materialised beside the five Archangels and the four Serrat Queens. Mab made the introductions and said, 'We must consider this as a Council of War. However, our first action must be to seek a peaceful agreement with the Var, but I have to say that I consider this to be an unlikely outcome.'

Meshan said, 'Goddess, we have negotiated agreements with the Var on many occasions, but in every case, they have been short-lived. You do not understand them as we do. We are as nothing to them, and they consider us to be creatures entirely without value. We are not worthy of being party to an agreement with the Var. To them, any treaty they sign with us is utterly meaningless. They participate in the charade only if it serves to assist them in their goal of exterminating our species.'

Kanaka bowed to Meshan and said, 'Queen Meshan, why do the Var wish to exterminate your kind?'

Meshan replied, 'We are the Serrat; we are part of nature, and we live in harmony with it. The Var have rejected nature, their bodies are now of metal, their brains fused into machines. The Var are hideous, and we are beautiful. We remind them of what they once were, and for that, they despise us.'

Kanaka said, 'Are all of the Var part machines?'

Meshan replied, 'The leaders are linked to machine minds, but there are no visible connections. They share information and instructions, human mind to machine mind, in a way analogous to our psychic abilities but much slower and less efficient. But the Vard war machines are too powerful for us. We have tried to fight back, but the very concept of war is alien to us; our only hope of survival is to flee from them. They pursue us relentlessly and will not stop until we are no more. They will come for us here; we have brought this war upon you.'

Michael said, 'No, Queen Meshan, the Var have brought this war upon themselves. You and your people are innocents, and we are sworn to protect the innocent.'

Michael looked at Mab and said, 'The Goddess will not permit them.'

Mab held his stare and said, 'Michael is correct. The Var is an affront to the light; this cannot be allowed to continue. They will be given a choice, and if they choose badly, there will be no more Var.'

Uriel said, 'Mab, what do you mean?'

Mab looked at Uriel and said, 'Mother, the light is a harsh master.'

Uriel replied, 'No, you cannot do this!'

Mab looked at Kanaka, who said, 'Queen Meshan, Queen Gosshan, Queen Tenshan, Queen Cepshan, the situation at present is that we are effectively at war with the Var. However, we consider that a meeting should be arranged with the Var leaders to offer a negotiated agreement. This agreement would be based upon the Serrat initially living here peacefully and, at a defined future point in time, when your numbers are much greater, returning to repopulate your home worlds. This negotiation will be carried out by you, and we would like it to be in their home world. We will be there with you. If the Var accept the agreement, we will ensure that they adhere to its terms. If they reject the offer, our war status will be confirmed. As discussed, we consider it unlikely the Var will accept any negotiated agreement. In view of that, we would like you to pass all information that you have on the Var home world to us, particularly critical battle assets, their locations and capability, also details of the Vard machines and control ships.'

The Queens thought for a few moments, and then Tenshan said, 'We have some knowledge of the Var home world and their capabilities which we can pass to you. However, only Meshan will go with you to negotiate; we cannot risk the lives of our last remaining Queens.'

Kanaka nodded in agreement and said, 'We wish to have the meeting in their home world because if the agreement is rejected, we will attack them immediately and inflict significant damage. The Vard will pursue us as we travel back through the star, but the Angel host will be waiting for them. When the bulk of the Vard has been destroyed, the Goddess will then return to their home world, and the Var will be ended.'

There was silence for a few moments, and then Meshan said, 'Will it really work? Is our freedom so close after all these years?'

Mab said, 'Queen Meshan if the negotiations are unsuccessful, I will send you back here before we strike the Var. This is to ensure your safety and the future of your swarm. I also want you to understand that this is our war, not yours.'

Meshan replied, 'Thank you, Goddess; we are forever in your debt no matter the outcome.'

Michael said, 'Queen Tenshan has provided me with details of Varalian, their home planet.'

Mab looked up and said, 'They are here. A mothership with many hundreds of Vard. Michael Gabriel, go to them and arrange the negotiation. If they refuse, then we will fight them here. Go now.'

Michael and Gabriel vanished, appeared in the upper atmosphere and flew slowly towards the Var fleet. The mothership was similar in size to that destroyed by Mab but appeared to be more heavily armed with light-beam and projectile weapons.

A mechanical voice sounded in Michael's head. 'You have aided the Serrat. This is punishable by death. You will surrender immediately.'

Michael replied, 'The Serrat is innocent. We destroyed your war vessels because they were killing the innocent. The Serrat wish to discuss terms which would allow them to live in peace.'

The Var said, 'You have four Serrat Queens on the planet below. We will return them to their home planets.'

Michael replied, 'The four Queens are under our protection. Do you wish to negotiate with the Serrat, or do you wish to engage with us in another battle which you would lose?'

The Var said, 'We will discuss terms with the Serrat. Please bring the four Queens to us immediately.'

Michael replied, 'Queen Meshan will speak on behalf of the Serrat Queens. We will be present as observers only. The meeting will take place in your home world, Varalian.' There was a brief pause in the exchange, and then the mechanical voice said, 'Accepted, meeting details will be provided.' The Var mothership started to turn and accelerated towards the white star. The Vard fleet followed, each craft breaking away in a predetermined sequence.

Mab said, 'They intend to imprison us in the deepest, darkest dungeon on their home planet. Perfect!'

Michael replied, 'They must believe that they can imprison us. Otherwise, they would never have agreed to the terms.'

Mab said, 'Lucifer likes being imprisoned. Perhaps we should send him?'

Lucifer replied, 'I heard that! I will not be imprisoned again.'

Gabriel laughed and said, 'Is the Prince of darkness afraid of the dark?'

Lucifer replied, 'As you know, brother, I have always loved the darkness, but being imprisoned in darkness without the hope of light is quite different.'

Mab said, 'You three will accompany Queen Meshan. I will observe through her eyes. The host will be assembled and ready for battle along the exit route from the white star. The masters will support the host through mind space.'

Michael reassembled the War Council the following day when he had received details of the proposed negotiation from Varalian. Michael said, 'The information was sent on behalf of the Var High Command and signed by Commander of Battles, Pance. I am sending the details to you now. In summary, they are expecting all four Serrat Queens to be present together with two observers from our universe.

Mab replied, 'We have already agreed who we will send so I suggest we ignore that request.'

Michael nodded and continued 'They are saying that they will not accept any Serrat in their Universe now or in the future and that they will be responsible for controlling the pathway between two universes. They will base a mothership with Vard support in orbit around any planet occupied by the Serrat. Reparation will be made for the destruction of the Var mothership and the Vard vessels that protected the planet Boda in the Ashada system, and the responsible commander will be handed over to the Var for interrogation, trial and execution.'

Mab, looking at Michael, said, 'Who was our commander?'

Michael replied, 'Me?' Mab burst into laughter.

Kanaka said, 'Archangel Michael, I'm afraid you will have to get used to this.'

Mab said, 'Don't worry, Michael, we won't be handing you over. If they insist on someone, we will give them Lucifer.'

Lucifer looked at Mab with a wry smile on his face.

Uriel said, 'Mab, you are in one of your moods again. This is serious. If the negotiations fail, there will be a war, and many will die.'

Mab replied, 'Mother, I fully expect the negotiations to fail. The Var are committing genocide on the Serrat, and when that is complete, they will turn their attention to us and our universe. They are only having these negotiations because they think the four queens will be there, and they will be able to kill them and imprison us. The death of the four Queens will be the extinction of the Serrat. We will be kept alive for interrogation; they will drain the knowledge from us and store it in their machines. This knowledge will enable them to infiltrate our universe, and we will eventually share the same fate as the Serrat.'

Uriel said, 'Mab, you cannot know that. It may be that the Var are also searching for a peaceful outcome.'

Queen Meshan said, 'The Goddess understands. I did not think we would be able to convince you as to the nature of the Var. It took decades of our time, centuries even, for us to fully accept that the Var are truly evil. Their only interest is in torturing, killing and conquering other species. They have no emotions, no concept of compassion or empathy. There is no reasoning or treaty with them because we mean nothing to them.'

Mab said, 'Mother, I understand your feelings, but Queen Meshan is correct. When we were on the mothership at Boda you will remember that I entered the mind of Rogan, the Var Battle Commander. However, I went further. He was connected to his vessel but also to Varalian. I followed the artificial mind pathways back to Varalian. The source is a huge artificial mind known as the Master Controller. The Var have surrendered all decision-making to this machine. This is the reason there is no compassion, empathy, human reasoning or judgement. The Controller makes decisions based on billions of number sequences. It has no emotions, only logic. Over millennia it has developed complex algorithms that enable it to simulate the behaviour of a real mind. The Var are slaves to this master controller.'

Gabriel asked, 'Goddess, can this controller be destroyed and if so, what would be the consequences for the Var?'

Mab replied, 'A good question, Gabriel. It may be difficult to destroy it. The artificial mind is currently located in one place, but it can travel through the numerous pathways available to it should we attempt to destroy it. However, although it could escape, it would be diminished, as much of its extensive knowledge resources would no longer be available to it. As to the effect on the Var, I don't know what would happen. I imagine those more dependent on the Controller, the government and the military would be badly affected and perhaps even die.'

Uriel said, 'Mab, did you communicate with this controller?'

Mab replied, 'It was aware of my presence and tried to purge me from its mind. I retreated to Rogan, I didn't want to give it, or the Var, any advanced warning of our intentions or findings.'

Michael said, 'We should leave now. Otherwise, we will be late.'

Mab said, 'Uriel and I will accompany you until we reach the planet. We will watch the proceedings through Queen Meshan. Raphael will organise the host on my order; we leave in an hour or so and arrive late.'

Michael led the formation, closely followed by Gabriel, Lucifer and Queen Meshan, with Mab and Uriel at the rear. They flew through the white star and emerged from the black hole in the adjacent universe. The Archangels had thrown up a psychic shield, which Mab reinforced. When they escaped the pull of the black hole they accelerated apace and closed on Varalian, which was the second planet of the Vegin system. Mab and Uriel hung in the upper atmosphere while Michael led the group downwards toward the surface of the planet.

A machine voice sounded in Michael's mind: 'Please follow the guide to the reception bay.'

A drone appeared before them and accelerated rapidly. Michael followed the guide drone through a myriad of flyways, eventually entering a high-level reception bay in what was clearly a military facility. The group felt a powerful energy field blink out as they approached and then reinstated as they entered the facility. The bay was lined with huge soldiers who appeared to be humanoid but augmented with mechanical and optical implants. They carried heavy weapons and wore ornate metallic armour.

One of them stepped forward and said, 'You will follow me.' It led the group deeper into the facility. The soldier was truly enormous, much taller and more massive than the Archangels. His every step pounded on the metallic floor like thunder, and the group struggled to keep pace with him as he went deeper still into the heart of the building.

At last, they approached two huge doors which were guarded by four sentries who appeared to be even more massive than the soldier. Michael heard the soldier communicate with the guards, but he did not understand what was said.

Mab whispered, 'It is a machine code. He is handing you over to the Guards; you are no longer his responsibility.'

The Guards dismissed the soldier, and the huge doors opened slowly. Michael was surprised to see a meeting table with around ten humanoid forms already seated. They were each different in their own way, perhaps representing different races or clans of the Var.

At the head of the table, a figure appeared and said, 'Please be seated. Queen Meshan, you may find the floor area at the end of the table to be more comfortable. I am Varalian and seated before me are the leaders of my ten regional governments. Queen Meshan, you have come here today to negotiate terms, but the conditions set for this meeting have not been satisfied. Specifically, we required all four Serrat Queens to be present, but you alone have come.'

There was silence for a few moments, and then Queen Meshan said, 'I, Queen Meshan, speak for the four remaining Queens of the Serrat. Yes, only four of us remain when previously our Queens were numbered in the thousands. I have with me three observers named Michael, Gabriel and Lucifer, who are great warriors pledged to protect the innocent. Do you wish to hear our proposals?'

There was a further pause in the proceedings before Varalian replied, 'We will hear your proposals.'

Queen Meshan said, 'Currently, there are no Serrat that we know of in this universe. I, my three sisters and our swarms now occupy planets in the adjacent universe and live under the protection of the good people there, including those with me here today. We wish to continue living there in peace until our numbers recover and we are able, at some future point in time, to return to our home planets here and repopulate them. That is the basis of our proposal.'

Varalian replied, 'Your proposal is entirely unacceptable. You have already received our proposals. Do you reject them?'

Michael said, 'Yes, they are rejected in their entirety.'

Varalian replied, 'You are an observer here today; you have no other function in this meeting.'

Michael said, 'Yes, that is true. Queen Meshan may accept or reject your proposals. That is her prerogative. However, I speak for the Goddess Bellona. She will not accept the proposals, therefore, your point is irrelevant.'

Varalian replied, 'Goddess? We have conquered many civilisations with such religious beliefs, but their Gods never seem to appear, and we are always victorious!' There was loud laughter and rapping on the table from the regional government heads.

Michael replied, 'Nevertheless, your proposals have been rejected; even now, the Goddess watches you. She sees everything and expects you to accept Queen Meshan's proposal.'

Varalian said, 'I think not. This facility has a shield that cannot be breached. I do, however, see everything, and I don't see, and have never seen, any Goddess. Now, we will end this charade. Queen Meshan, you will be executed immediately; these observers will be interrogated and then executed. Guards!'

Queen Meshan vanished; a deafening alarm screamed into life, accompanied by a mechanical voice: 'Facility Breach! Facility Breach!'

Varalian said, 'Seal this chamber.'

Huge shutters of exotic material slammed down around every wall; artificial lights flickered to life and bathed the room in an eery glow akin to moonlight.

A regional government head, incredulous, said, 'Master, are we under attack!?'

Lucifer replied, 'You are not under attack. The Goddess approaches.'

Varalian said nothing but simply waited with a look of astonishment on his face. There was a loud thump on the door behind the shutter. Varalian smiled. But then the door shutter was struck a truly enormous blow. It buckled inwards but did not fully detach.

Varalian breathed, 'This is not possible, the energy required... it is not possible.'

The enormous shutter fell slowly inwards and settled gently onto the floor. Varalian saw a young woman standing in the doorway, and she was dressed in white apart from the leather sandals on her otherwise bare feet. Behind her was a sea of utter destruction, a scene of intense fighting; many soldiers and Guards lay dead, some torn apart with limbs ripped from their heavily armoured bodies. The young woman stood serenely; there was no blemish on her, no indication whatsoever that she had done anything more energetic than wander through a field of summer flowers.

She said, 'I am Bellona. May I come in?'

Varalian replied, 'Yes, of course.' Varalian searched billions of databanks in mere seconds, trying to find something that could explain what he was seeing, but nothing sufficed. Varalian said, 'What are you?' The three observers bowed deeply as she entered the room.

Mab looked at Michael, Gabriel and Lucifer and said, 'Queen Meshan has returned to her swarm. Uriel is with her; they await our return. I have decided to end these negotiations.' Mab looked at the ten leaders and said, 'You have allowed this machine to manage your affairs for eons. It has become a dictator, moulding the population into its own likeness of mechanical parts and energy circuits. You have betrayed your people and damned them into slavery. I will not allow this to continue.'

Varalian said, 'You have not answered my question!'

Mab turned her black eyes on the apparition and said, 'This is an abomination; it ends now.'

Michael said, 'Goddess, is there no other way?'

Mab replied, 'I have searched, there is none.'

Varalian said, 'What do you mean? You think you can kill me?'

Mab, still looking at Michael, said, 'I have already ordered the return of all Var and Vard spacecraft with immediate effect. The last of the stragglers are arriving even now.'

Varalian screamed, 'What are you doing!' Mab said, 'I had hoped you would accept our proposals, but clearly, you had no intentions of doing so. I now realise that this situation cannot be rectified. The people of Varalian are no longer human but mere drones tied to a malign artificial intelligence. Look at these so-called leaders; they have had no physical modifications, but their minds are blank because you have removed their ability to think. Now, they are also mere drones, just like the Vard. You will remain contained here on this planet whilst it is cleansed.'

Varalian said, 'You cannot contain me!'

Mab replied, 'It is already done and now you are dismissed.'

Varalian vanished, and the leaders simply sat and stared at each other.

Gabriel said, 'Goddess, what is your intention?'

Mab replied, 'Vegin will cleanse the planet; it will eventually recover, and life will return, but not for some time.'

Gabriel said, 'But the people, they will all be killed!'

Mab replied, 'Gabriel, you have not understood. There are no people. What was once the population is now seen in the Vard. This is now a machine world; the organs of the people have been used to create the machines that you see all around you. Varalian controls all of this, it is the controlling mind, and all others are drones or other forms of slaves. I cannot allow Varalian to escape the planet; with the last spacecraft now returned, it is trapped here. It needs a medium to travel through, but all are closed to it.'

Lucifer asked, 'There are no normal indigenous beings on this planet?'

Michael replied, 'No. I have also searched for the indigenous population. The Goddess uncovered what was left of them, their body parts used for machines.'

Gabriel said, 'Then it is truly an abomination!'

Mab replied, 'Yes, but this process was initiated by the population. Initially, mechanical implants were used when someone lost a limb or when an organ failed. Then they developed artificial intelligence as an aid to their technological activities. The direction of travel should have been clear to them, but they chose to carry on regardless until one morning, they awoke to find themselves slaves to the machines they helped create. But now we need to act fast, follow me.'

Mab led the Archangels along a maze of long corridors.

Lucifer said, 'Goddess, I see you met with a degree of resistance.'

Mab smiled at him and replied, 'Lucifer, I do believe you are developing a sense of humour.'

Gabriel said, 'Is that good, the Prince of Darkness having a sense of humour?'

Mab laughed and replied, 'That remains to be seen. Now with me!' as she launched herself into the air and soared upwards towards the upper atmosphere and out into the solar system.

Mab said, 'Varalian is the second planet of the system. The first planet is not habitable, so provided the flare does not reach the level of the third planet, the system will be unaffected.'

Mab and the Archangels hung in space above and behind Varalian as it moved through space. Mab said, 'Link minds, now focus with me on Vegin, go deep into the star. Now pull the gases towards us, pull harder, harder still!' Michael opened his eyes and saw an enormous solar flare rushing towards them.

Mab said, 'I'll throw up a shield when it reaches us; move back quickly!' The four figures moved backward rapidly, Mab still pulling on the gases as the flare wrapped itself around Varalian. She held the enormous flare in position for several minutes and then released her hold on the gases. The flare clung to the planet for a further few minutes, as if feeding greedily, before it reluctantly fell back to the surface of Vegin.

Mab reached out with her witch senses and said, 'Varalian is cleansed. We must now return to our own universe, come closer.' Mab focussed on Queen Meshan; the group vanished and reappeared beside the Queen.

Uriel wasted no time and said, 'Are we at war, or have they accepted our offer of peace?'

Michael looked at Mab, who nodded and said, 'The Var rejected our offer as Queen Meshan will, I am sure, confirm.'

Queen Meshan replied, 'Yes, as expected, the offer was rejected in its entirety, and I was sentenced to immediate execution. Fortunately, Goddess Bellona arrived and sent me back here to safety.'

Queen Gosshan said, 'Then the war continues, but this will be the last war, and I will commit all of my swarm; we cannot run any further.'

Michael said, 'There will be no need. The Var and the Vard are ended. Varalian was cleansed by the Goddess.' There was a stunned silence in the room.

Queen Meshan said, 'I don't understand. When you say they are ended, does this mean their military capability has been destroyed?'

Lucifer said, 'No, the entire planet and every living thing thereon has been incinerated. The Var and the Vard no longer exist; they have been purged from the universe.'

Uriel looked at Mab, who had a somewhat sheepish expression on her face, and said, 'Mab, please tell me that isn't true.'

Mab replied, 'Mother, it's not as bad as it sounds.

Michael explain it to her.'

Despite the circumstances, Kanaka was struggling not to laugh at Mab, who now had a naughty, childlike expression on her face.

Michael said, 'Uriel, what you do not understand is that there was no indigenous population on Varalian. The artificial intelligence, which called itself Varalian after the planet, had made use of the original population as spare parts for war machines. The planet itself had become a war machine that controlled drones to prosecute wars in pursuit of knowledge and wealth.' There was a period of awkward silence.

Mab said, 'Queens, I think it would be wise for you to stay here until your numbers recover before going back to your home planets. However, you may wish to visit just to ensure all is well. If so, please allow us to accompany you.'

Queen Meshan replied, 'Yes, Goddess, we would welcome that. I thank you on behalf of the Serrat for destroying the Var; you have rid the universe of great evil.'

Chapter Twenty-Five: Romans and Warlocks

It was late evening. Mab and Kanaka sat opposite each other in Kanaka's office, sipping a particularly good whisky.

Kanaka said, 'Lamm and Luticia have returned to their homes by horse. I think they both wanted time alone to think about what we have been doing in recent weeks. To ground themselves before they return to family and friends.'

Mab replied, 'Yes, I know exactly what you mean. I would love to go for a long ride, perhaps to visit Luticia and Fora and then head North through Deeping Forest.'

Kanaka replied, 'You could visit the ruins of the Palace!'

Mab laughed and said, 'That seems a very long time ago. But you have reminded me that I need to visit the northern covens and find the warlock Malphador.'

Kanaka replied, 'I heard it was he who commissioned the Balerak to kill Fora?'

Mab replied, 'No, the Balerak was commissioned to kill Luticia, but it thought to threaten Fora into administering a poison.'

Kanaka said, 'It doesn't feel like this Malphador issue is urgent. In fact, he almost certainly knows by now that the Balerak has been slain. So, if he has any sense he will be in hiding. The last time we made that journey, we didn't stop or even slow down to admire the scenery! To ride there now at a leisurely pace would be a real treat.'

There was a knock at the door; Boe's head appeared and said, 'Sorry to bother you.'

Mab ran to the door, hugged Master Boe and pulled him into the room. Master Paull walked in behind him.

Mab hugged Master Paull and said, 'Sorry, Master Paull, I didn't realise you were there. Please join us.'

Master Boe said, 'Thank you, Mab; we just wanted to remind Master Kanaka that we have a meeting first thing tomorrow morning to go through and sign-off the Guild accounts.'

Kanaka, with a glum expression on his face, replied, 'Yes, Master Boe, it is in my diary. How long will it take?'

Paul replied, 'It will be all morning, perhaps even into the afternoon.'

Mab said, 'I am sorry, masters, but you can have the morning only as Master Kanaka, and I are riding out at mid-day to complete unfinished business in the North.'

Boe said, 'Yes, of course, Mab, how long will you be gone?'

Mab replied, 'Could be a few days, depends how long it takes to find Malphador.'

Boe replied, 'Malphador, the warlock?'

Mab replied, 'Yes, do you know anything about him?'

Boe replied, 'He is something of a legend in the North. I came across his name when doing my research. Can I ask why you want to find him?'

Mab replied, 'He commissioned a Balerak to kill Luticia.'

Boe replied, 'That doesn't sound like the Malphador I know of. He would never do such a thing. How do you know it was Malphador who commissioned the Balerak?'

Mab said, 'Lucifer extracted the information from the Balerak just before he killed it.'

Boe replied, 'I guess the Balerak would not dare to lie to Lucifer but take care not to judge Malphador before discussing the situation with him.'

Mab said, 'Yes, Master Boe. We will take care.'

Boe said, 'Master Kanaka, I will let the stables know of your plans; horses and provisions will be ready for you both around lunchtime tomorrow.'

Kanaka smiled and said, 'Excellent!'

Mab left Kanaka's office and walked out into the cool night air. She felt good being back at the Guild again. She reached out and found Satta; she was up and moving around. Dassi was sleeping. Mab made her way to Amber House and knocked gently on the door of number 36.

Satta answered, 'Who is it?'

Mab replied, 'Satta, it's Mab. Can we talk?'

Satta opened the door, hugged Mab and said, 'Dassi is asleep, come in. Would you like tea?'

Mab replied, 'No thanks, I just wanted to ask you if you could travel with me to Yehuda early tomorrow morning. I have had discussions with Tiberius, and he has endorsed the changes we wanted, but I'm not sure the news will have reached Yehuda.'

Satta replied, 'Dassi will be in school, so as long as we are back before early evening, there should be no problem.'

Mab said, 'Great, let's meet in the dining area, have some breakfast and then visit Padwa.'

Mab made her way to the suite; as she climbed the stairs, she heard Cat's voice and laughter. The door was locked, but Mab opened it with a thought and walked into the room. Cat and Charly were there with two strangers. They ran to Mab and threw their arms around her.

Mab said, 'Sorry to burst in on you. Is everything alright?'

Charly said, 'These are friends of Gho; we decided to come back here for a few late-night drinks.'

Mab looked at the strangers and said, 'I don't recognise them. Are they students?'

Cat said, 'Well, not exactly, but Gho will vouch for them.'

Mab looked at the strangers, who were lounging on a sofa, and said, 'I am accustomed to people standing up or kneeling when I enter a room. What are your names?'

One of the strangers said, 'What's your name?'

Cat turned to Mab and said, 'Mab, I'm so sorry for this. The one on the right is Sedra, and the other one is Poger; they are just leaving.'

Mab reached out and found Gho, who was sleeping. He awoke with a start, and Mab pulled him towards her. He appeared in the room completely naked. Gho grabbed a cushion, used it to cover his modesty, and immediately bowed to Mab.

Mab said, 'Do you know these people?'

Gho looked at them and said, 'No, Mab, I have never seen them before.'

Mab replied, 'I am sorry to have interrupted your sleep.' Gho vanished and appeared back in his bed.

Mab said, 'Cat, where did you meet these two?'

Cat replied, 'We met them at Gho's birthday celebration. I thought Gho knew them.'

Mab turned to the strangers and said, 'You will tell me who you are and what you are doing here.' Mab's witch senses twitched; she scanned them and found that they had concealed weapons. The larger of the pair, Sedra, had two slender blades concealed in the lining of his trousers; the other, Poger, had a cudgel suspended inside his trouser leg. Mab mind messaged the Guards.

Sedra replied, 'Who we are is our business; we're leaving.'

Mab said, 'You will remain here until the Guards arrive.' Sedra and Poger found that they couldn't move. The Guards arrived promptly, and Mab said, 'These two are carrying weapons; they are to be imprisoned until I say they can be released.'

The Captain of the Guard said, 'Yes, Goddess, we will investigate this breach in security thoroughly.'

Mab nodded and said, 'Captain, please report your findings directly to me and to no one else.'

The Captain bowed and replied, 'Yes, of course Goddess.' He then ordered his men to escort the strangers to the cells.

Mab turned to Cat and Charly and said, 'What on earth do you think you are doing? You could be expelled from the Guild for this!'

Cat burst into tears, and Charly said, 'Mab, we have been so lonely and bored since we lost Izzy, and you haven't been around much.'

Mab replied, 'You must not allow outsiders onto the campus without permission. That is the rule, and it is there to protect everyone, including you. I have an early start tomorrow, so I'm going to bed. I suggest you do the same.'

Mab woke early, showered, dressed, hitched Onimaru onto her back, donned her white cape and, being careful not to wake Cat or Charly, walked out into the crisp morning air. She breathed the fresh, cold air deep into her lungs while controlling each inhale and exhale with the slow, smooth motion of her body. Then she thought of Tiberius, located him and entered his mind.

She said, 'Tiberius, it is I, Bellona. Are you in good spirits?'

Tiberius replied, 'Yes, Goddess. We have taken the first steps towards establishing this as a trading post. The clans have returned to their villages. We will leave two centurions; this will be a permanent trading encampment. The changes you required in Yehuda have been instructed, and the carrier bird returned late last night with Pilate's acknowledgment. I must now return to Rome.'

Mab replied, 'Excellent, I am on my way to Yehuda. If you find yourself in need of me, please call my name repeatedly in your mind. I will answer.'

Tiberius replied, 'Thank you, Goddess.' Mab headed for the dining area, and the kitchen staff were bringing out the food. Satta was already there and wore her High Priestess robe.

Mab waved to Satta as she approached, walked a bit more briskly to join her and said, 'Let's get our food now before everyone else arrives. I am so hungry!'

Satta laughed and replied, 'Mab, everyone knows that you are always hungry. It's all the travelling and fighting that you do, and it uses up your energy reserves!'

Mab piled her plate high with a bit of everything on offer, whereas Satta opted for a few pastries and a mug of hot coffee.

Satta said, 'When I first tasted this coffee drink, I thought it was truly awful. But now I love it; in fact, I couldn't do without it!'

Mab said, 'Yes, that's because it is addictive. But you are right, it was the same with me, although I am also addicted to white wine! I haven't contacted Padwa; I thought we would arrive unannounced and surprise him!'

When they had finished their breakfast, Mab took Satta's arm and focussed on Padwa. They materialised behind Padwa, who was seated at the head of a large table talking to some twenty or so people, including administrators, legionnaires, priests and local dignitaries.

Lucius pushed his chair back, bowed deeply and said, 'The Goddess has returned!' Everyone else followed his example.

Mab said, 'Padwa, apologies. I did not intend to disrupt your discussions. I instructed Tiberius to formalise the changes we discussed the last time I was here. Can you confirm that this has been done?'

Padwa replied, 'Yes, Goddess, that is the very reason for this meeting. The instruction from Tiberius was received by Pilate, who has confirmed that Lucius would take on the role of regional governor with immediate effect, reporting directly to Tiberius.

Lucius added, 'Goddess, we had assumed that Pilate would be here today, but no one knows where he is; we can only assume he has returned to Rome.'

Mab stared into space for a few moments and then said, 'No, he is not in Rome. Pilate carried a burden that could not be borne. He has taken his own life; he lies at the bottom of the Tiber.'

There was silence in the room. Lucius said, 'If I may ask Goddess. What burden would lead a man such as Pilate to kill himself? Surely not dismissal from his post or his return to Rome?'

Mab replied, 'No, Lucius, Pilate yearned to return to Rome. The burden he could not bear was the execution of the Prophet. He was merely a pawn in that, but he will be despised by billions. His name will endure through generations and become synonymous with the execution of the innocent.'

There was another uncomfortable silence in the room.

Mab looked around the Table, found Marcus and said, 'Marcus, your role is to protect the citizens of this region. I trust you will make the best use of the legions to achieve that?'

Marcus bowed and replied, 'Yes, Goddess, it will be done.'

Mab replied, 'You will need to help the legion commanders to understand their new role. If you need any assistance, please let me know.' Mab continued to stare at Marcus and then said, 'Lucius, when you travel to Rome you will need protection at all times. Marcus is to accompany you and remain by your side. This is my instruction, and it will not be gainsaid by any other. Is that understood?'

Lucius looked at Marcus and said, 'Yes, Goddess, of course, I understand.'

Mab then said to Ogan, the High Priest, 'Satta will be my link with the Priesthood; her mind is linked to mine, and she will continue her role as High Priestess working with you.'

Ogan nodded in assent.

Mab looked at Padwa and said, 'It seems that all is progressing as planned. Is there anything else that I should be aware of before Satta and I return to the Guild.'

Padwa said, 'No, Goddess. We have been searching for signs of daemon activity, but so far, we have not encountered any more of the creatures.'

Mab nodded and replied, 'Excellent. I must leave now. Satta come closer.'

Mab and Satta vanished and reappeared in the lost library.

Mab said, 'It seems that all is well in Yehuda. What do you think?'

Satta replied, 'Yes, I think I should make plans to return there with Dassi.'

Mab said, 'I will be away for the next few days. On my return we should go back with Dassi and stay overnight, she can meet her friends. Then take it from there?'

Satta hugged Mab and said, 'Yes, that would be great!' Mab walked back towards Amber House with Satta but then veered off towards the sports fields. She thought of Kanaka's favourite sword, kata, Lamu, and decided to execute it as fast and precise as possible. It was a long Kata, in excess of 50 individual moves depending on the interpretation. Lamu was, in effect, a battle simulation of one against multiple opponents. The kata defines the direction and nature of the attacks, but the response can be individually tailored, provided the moves are well-executed. Mab had never been an expert swordsman, but she had always been a formidable warrior, supplementing her sword skills with her psychic powers and martial arts skills. She mused on the fact that she no longer needed weapons to kill opponents, she could tear them limb from limb with a thought. Mab removed her cloak and stood perfectly still in the centre of the sports field. She slowed her breathing, waited patiently, lifted her heels off the ground and Onimaru flashed from the scabbard. Mab, on the balls of her feet, held the blade in the horizontal battle-ready position above her head. She held the position for a few seconds, then ran forward and executed four throat swipes, spun into the air and delivered two horizontal torso slices, one-handed and at full stretch. She then executed four high-side kicks and two roundhouse kicks in quick succession, all with blinding speed. She then paused in the battle-ready position. The kata continued; in some of the moves, Mab made herself unseen; in others, she used her psychic powers to levitate or spin around to execute strikes. She was entirely engaged in the battle, with virtual warriors, to the exclusion of everything else. She ended, as she started, in the battle-ready position, her sword and body as one and as still as a rock. She returned Onimaru to the scabbard and stood for a few moments, slowing her breathing and withdrawing from the intense focus of the battle. She turned around to find the entire Warrior School student population, together with Kanaka and Boe, watching in complete silence.

Kanaka broke the silence by clapping vigorously and then everyone else joined him and cheered their approval. Mab's face was beaded with sweat as she walked towards Kanaka.

Kanaka went to meet her, bowed and said, 'That was astonishing. It was as if you were in battle but with real, albeit invisible, opponents. Authentic, precise and blindingly fast; it was perfection.'

Kanaka turned to the audience and said, 'That was perfection. You will never see another perform Lamu with that degree of skill.'

Mab replied, 'Thank you, Master Kanaka. However, there is another who would execute Lamu differently but certainly with equal skill.'

Kanaka looked questioningly at Mab, who said, 'His name is Master Kanaka!' The audience laughed and roared their approval.

Kanaka smiled and said, 'Meet you in the stable block in, say, an hour?'

Mab replied, 'I'm so looking forward to sitting on a horse again!'

Mab was on her way back to the suite when she saw the Captain of the Guards walking towards her.

The captain bowed and said, 'Sorry to interrupt you, Goddess. I have concluded my investigation into the two unwanted guests, Sedra and Poger, found in your rooms. They are petty criminals well known to our security people, and they tend to prey on women who, for some reason, find them attractive. They arrived with a group of Gho's friends and must have remained on the campus looking for opportunities. We only checked the number in the group sanctioned by Gho, which tallied; we should have checked each individual. It was my mistake; it won't happen again. I would normally question all involved, but I thought I should seek your permission before questioning your roommates.'

Mab smiled at the captain and said, 'Thank you for your discretion. We all make mistakes, and I am sure it was not your mistake. There will be no need on this occasion to question Charly and Cat, and I will deal with them.'

The captain bowed and replied, 'Yes, Goddess. I am pleased that I could be of service to you.'

Mab beamed at the captain and said, 'Captain Joss, the next time you are doing a team event with the Guards, please invite me. I would like to understand more about the security function and the excellent work that you do.'

The captain was lost for words and could only blurt out, 'Yes, Goddess, I will do that! Thank you! Thank you!' When Mab reached the suite, neither Cat nor Charly were there. She showered and dressed in a light blouse, tight-fitting sports trousers and thick riding boots. She also wore a thick leather waistcoat and packed her robe. She fitted a couple of drinking flasks into her saddle bag together with some emergency food supplies. The stable would also pack food for the journey, but it was always best to have a reserve supply. She was just about to leave when Charly and Cat arrived.

Mab said, 'I'm just leaving. I will be back in two or three days.'

Charly said, 'Mab, I'm so sorry about what happened.'

Mab replied, 'It wasn't really your fault. They should not have been allowed onto the Campus. I have spoken to the Captain of the Guard. You will not be questioned; the matter is finished. But please be careful; those two are known criminals who exploit gullible young women.'

Cat looked at Charly and said, 'How could we have been so stupid!'

Charly said, 'Mab, thanks for helping us to get out of this mess.'

Mab opened her arms and said, 'Group hug?'

Charly and Cat ran to her, and they hugged for several minutes.

Mab said, 'Right, you two, I really do have to go now! When I get back, I promise we will go somewhere very special together.'

They waved goodbye as Mab ran down the stairs two at a time on her way to the stables.

Kanaka was checking what had been packed by way of provisions and said, 'Enough for a couple of nights, but I have brought a few extra things just in case we need it.'

Mab said, 'I did the same!' They rode out at a gallop. As they approached the main gate, Mab saw Captain Joss and waved to him; Joss raised his hand in acknowledgment. This created quite a stir amongst the guards; masters don't normally acknowledge guards, but for the Goddess to wave!

Kanaka said, 'I think he will be telling his grandchildren about that moment!'

Mab replied, 'There was an incident recently that made me realise I didn't know any of the guards. I asked Captain Joss to invite me when he next organises a team meeting. They do a crucially important job.'

Kanaka said, 'Yes, you are right. They are our first line of defence. I'll join you at the team meeting.'

They headed out and turned East in the direction of the Academy of White Witches and slowed to a canter.

Kanaka said, 'What's the plan?'

Mab replied, 'I thought we would head East and then turn North into Deeping Forest when we get close to the Academy. We follow that Trail all the way North and West almost to the palace district, and then we start our search for the northern covens and the warlock Malphador.'

Kanaka said, 'Do you think we should visit Luticia?'

Mab replied, 'You are thinking of the hospitality!'

Kanaka laughed and said, 'You mean you're not?'

Mab said, 'I admit it. But I was there fairly recently. I would really like to visit Lamm, but I've been so busy recently I just haven't had the opportunity. Likewise, with the Warrior School, I should be able to devote much more time to that now that a few urgent issues have been dealt with.'

Kanaka replied, 'We should arrange the next council meeting at Lamm's school. The recent meetings have been driven by events, which you understand more than I do, but these had to be addressed, and the Guild was the obvious venue. Regarding the Warrior School, we have managed to get by, but we all know that you have more important commitments. I have to say, though, that your demonstration of Lamu this morning was invaluable. Just watching you execute that kata in the space of a few minutes was worth months of teaching in the school.'

Mab said, 'I'm glad you liked it.'

Kanaka said, 'Suggest we stop for the night just inside the forest to avoid riding in poor light? We should be able to reach the palace district by midday tomorrow.'

Mab replied, 'Yes, that sounds good. Did you bring any alcohol with you?'

Kanaka replied, 'What a ridiculous question, of course I did. I brought a flask of my favourite whisky and a bottle of white wine, both courtesy of Alexei of the City.'

Mab burst out laughing and said, 'I brought exactly the same!'

Kanaka replied, 'I have a feeling that we won't remember too much about this trip!'

Tiberius rode in the second of his eight legions. He had already sent three rapidly moving light legions ahead with orders to remain outside of Rome until he arrived. History had taught Tiberius that the people of Rome were fickle, allegiances could change rapidly, and, most importantly, the Senate would rather have a pawn than an Emperor. Having three additional legions stationed just outside Rome helped to focus minds. Whatever the great scholars may say, Tiberius knew, as an indisputable fact, that the sword was, is, and always will be, more powerful than the pen. Tiberius watched as a rider approached at speed from the lead legion. He talked briefly with the legion commander and then rode furiously back to the front line.

The legion commander moved slowly towards Tiberius and said, 'Goths ahead, scouts report numbers equivalent to three or four of our legions. They occupy high ground and have been there for some time.'

Tiberius replied, 'They have been waiting for us?'

The commander said, 'Yes, no question. They must know of our encounter with the clans and concluded that we were defeated and limping back to Rome.'

Tiberius stared at his commander and said, 'Julius, take care with your words.'

Julius brought his fist to his chest, bowed and said, 'Emperor, forgive me, I meant no disrespect. Only that the Goths, in their error, believe us to be weak.'

Tiberius replied, 'Then we will exploit that error. Call a halt, and we make our stand here. We will draw them from the high ground, and you will assemble a weak front line that will break when they fully commit to the attack. Do you understand?'

Julius smiled and said, 'Yes, Emperor perfectly!'

The light was fading as Mab and Kanaka found the second Deeping Forest trail which left the eastern pathway and curved to the north and west.

Mab said, 'It's up there on the left.'

Kanaka replied, 'Let's ride into the forest a bit.' As they entered the trail Mab said, 'This brings back memories!'

Kanaka laughed and replied, 'I know; it wasn't so long ago that we rode from the Academy and took this trail to the palace. It just seems a long time ago!'

Mab said, 'Yes, but we had to turn back. Hopefully, that won't happen this time!' They found a narrow path leading off the trail, and it led to a small clearing beside a stream.

Mab said, 'This is perfect.'

Kanaka replied, 'Perfect for the horses, but we should camp under the trees.'

They left the horses on long ties, walked deeper into the tree cover and unpacked their provisions. It was a beautiful night, and as the sun slowly sank, they were bathed in moonlight. The only sound was the hooting and crying of night owls.

Kanaka whispered 'This is just wonderful, magical even. Perhaps this is an illusion, and you have cast a spell on me?'

Mab smiled and replied, 'You are right, it is magical. But this is a creation beyond my skills.' Mab shared out the fruit, cheese and bread and placed four small cups on the forest floor. She poured two small measures of single malt and two larger measures of wine.

Kanaka said, 'Just Perfect.' The two warriors finished their supper and sat back, sipping the whisky and reminiscing late into the night.

Kanaka laid out his groundsheet and said, 'I know I am going to sleep well tonight.'

Mab replied, 'I didn't bring a groundsheet, so I'll have to snuggle in with you.'

Kanaka said, 'Yes, please, you can keep my back warm.' Mab lay down and draped her arm around him, snuggled in and fell into a deep sleep.

Mab's eyes, triggered by her witch senses, snapped open. It was dawn; she levitated to a standing position several metres above the forest floor and reached out with her senses. Nothing obvious. The horses appeared calm. She entered the mind of her horse and looked around again, but nothing. Then, yes, a smell almost imperceptible, not sufficient to spook a horse, human but not human. Mab focussed her senses into a tight beam and scanned the area again. Four human-type shapes they were discernible by their body temperature, not quite matching the ambient in certain areas. Mab saw parts of heads and hands blinking in and out of her thermal vision. The shapes moved slowly through the forest in complete silence. A voice in her head said, 'High one, it is I, Amarok; you are in danger.'

Mab replied, 'Yes, I see them.'

Amarok replied, 'What they are, I do not know, but they smell of the Abyss.'

Mab said, 'Amarok, thank you for the warning. If you are close, then come to me; otherwise, stay clear and warn the packs to stay away from the creatures.'

Amarok replied, 'I am close, and I have already warned the packs.'

Mab mind linked with Lucifer and said, 'What are these?'

Lucifer replied, 'They are the Guardians. They exist to protect the Abyss from attack, and they are very capable.'

Mab said, 'Why would anyone want to attack the Abyss?'

Lucifer laughed and replied, 'Goddess, do I have to remind you?'

Mab said, 'Yes, well, I didn't attack the Abyss. I went there to rescue my mother.'

Lucifer replied, 'Goddess, would you like me to come and rescue you?'

Mab said, 'No, Lucifer, that will not be necessary. They are your people, and I just thought it would be polite to consult with you before I rip them apart.'

Lucifer appeared beside her and said, 'Goddess, may I intercede on their behalf?'

Mab smiled and replied, 'You may, but be quick about it; I'm on holiday today.'

Mab dropped to the floor of the Forest. Kanaka was awake, and Amarok was sitting beside him.

He said, 'Do we have company?'

Mab kissed Amarok and replied, 'Yes, Lucifer is dealing with it. Let's have breakfast.'

Kanaka laid out the provisions and said, 'If only we had some hot coffee.' Mab pulled two metal goblets from her saddle bag and unwrapped a ceramic bottle containing cold coffee. She poured it into the goblets and proceeded to heat the coffee with a beam of light.

Kanaka said, 'Amarok, do you see how the Goddess looks after her people!'

Amarok stared at Kanaka as if he had just committed heresy.

Mab said, 'Amarok, come sit with me.'

Amarok growled and said, 'They approach.'

Mab sat on the forest floor, resting her back on a nearby tree trunk. Kanaka handed her a goblet of coffee and some pastries.

Lucifer walked into the clearing. Amarok leapt to his feet and bowed low.

Mab and Kanaka remained seated and continued eating. Lucifer said, 'Goddess, these are Guardians of the Abyss. They are known to me. They have tracked you to this place with intent to kill you for the attack on the Abyss. I have spoken to them and explained the circumstances. Nevertheless, they wished to see you in person.' As Mab stood up, her clothes changed to a loose white robe and cape, her boots were replaced with open-toed leather sandals, and she wore a ring of white flowers in her hair.

Mab said, 'I am the Goddess Bellona; who are you?'

The lead Guardian said, 'We are Guardians of the Abyss. We have no other names.' Mab suddenly shifted in space and appeared instantaneously in front of the four. Their cloaking system was disabled, and they stood visible to all. They wore helmets with visors that completely covered their faces and full body armour that appeared to hug the contours of their bodies. All four carried huge swords, pikes and shields. Mab could sense the power in them, and they clearly had prodigious psychic abilities. She gently touched the lead Guardian with her forefinger; he gasped and staggered backward.

Mab said, 'You were human once, but now you are changed. Lucifer, what are they?'

Lucifer knelt before Mab and said, 'Goddess, they were indeed human once but have changed through the eons into what they are now, Guardians. They are not Balerak, and they are akin to elite legionnaires or special police; they are tasked with the defence of the Abyss.'

Mab replied, 'I imagine keeping order amongst the inhabitants would be their main role?'

Lucifer said, 'Yes, that is so Goddess.'

Mab looked at the four and said, 'Well, what do you want to say to me?'

The lead Guardian said, 'We are sorry, Goddess. We had no knowledge of the circumstances, only that you had attacked the

Abyss. We came here in response. The Lord Lucifer has advised that we are not required here and therefore we will return to the Abyss.'

Mab stared into space for several minutes, and there was complete silence.

She then said, 'John, Pierre, Anthony, Cheng. I have need of you and your brethren. John, can you assemble 100 of your kind?'

The lead Guardian looked at Lucifer, who nodded his assent, and said, 'John, yes, that was my name. It sounds strange; it has been so long since anyone called me by my name. I can assemble 100 of my kind, but for what purpose?'

Lucifer looked at John and said, 'Bellona is the Goddess of war.'

John replied, 'Goddess, we are ready to serve.'

Mab said, 'I will summon you when the time is right; be ready for battle.'

Lucifer said, 'Guardians, you are dismissed.' The guardians vanished. Lucifer looked at Mab and said, 'Are you expecting a battle?'

Mab replied, 'Yes, but not here.'

Lucifer said, 'I am available.'

Mab laughed and said, 'Lucifer, are you feeling left out?'

Lucifer replied, 'Yes, I am.'

Mab walked to him, reached up on her tip-toes, kissed him and said, 'I will summon you when the battle commences, but don't appear in that baby dragon form.'

Lucifer replied, 'What baby dragon form?'

Mab said, 'You know when you lived in the Abyss. You looked like a baby dragon. That's why I didn't kill you, and you looked so cute.'

Lucifer stared at her askance. Kanaka burst out laughing. Lucifer looked at him and said, 'I see; this is one of your Goddess jokes. Baby dragon, indeed. I am the Lord of Darkness.'

Mab went into a fit of laughter, threw her arms around him and said, 'Lucifer, you are the best! I will summon you, but come in your most ferocious form, whatever you consider that to be!'

Lucifer smiled, replied, 'I will Goddess' and vanished.

Mab turned back to Kanaka and Amarok and said, 'Now, more breakfast!'

Amarok said, 'I will leave you now, high-one. But I will scout ahead and give warning if necessary.'

Mab replied, 'Amarok, once again, thank you for your help.'

Amarok loped off into the depths of the forest.

Kanaka said, 'So, where is this trouble you are expecting?'

Mab replied, 'It's in the adjacent plane. Tiberius is travelling back to Rome from Germania, but his path is blocked by enemies. At present, he is discussing strategy with his commanders. The enemy has many more infantry than Tiberius thinks. They also occupy the high ground, have superior cavalry and are well-fed and rested. Tiberius will most likely be defeated. But, we need him to stay in power in view of the fragile situation in Yehuda. Therefore, we must intervene.'

Mab laid out fruit, cheese and bread and said, 'More coffee?'

Kanaka replied, 'Yes, please, but be careful we don't eat all our provisions in one sitting!'

A group of six Goths rode slowly from their hilltop encampment down towards the Roman legions and waited several hundred paces away from the front line. The commander of legions and the five legion commanders rode out to meet the Goth delegation. The Goths were fearsome. They wore animal skins but were also adorned with bones and skulls that appeared to be human. They reeked of sweat, smoke and excrement and wore heavy iron armour both on themselves and their horses; they were clearly veterans of many battles.

Julius, struggling not to retch, said, 'I am the commander of our five legions. Who are you, and what is your intention?'

The Goths leader said, 'I am Wallian; we are here to kill Romans; this day, I will have the head of Tiberius on my pike.'

Julius smiled and replied, 'I think not. History will know you as Wallian the fool, who thought he could defy the might of Rome but screamed like a girl when he was roasted alive by Tiberius. Now, get back to your filth. I cannot abide the stench any longer.'

Wallian reached for his sword and laughed as the legionnaires backed off. He then turned his horse, and the six rode furiously back to their encampment.

Julius and the five legion commanders returned to Tiberius's battle tent and said, 'There is no parley. They are here to kill everyone and take your head.'

Tiberius replied, 'What is your assessment of them?'

Julius said, 'There were six of them, which suggests six clan groups. My feeling is that our numbers are similar. The six leaders were clearly veterans, which suggests that this could be a difficult battle, especially with the terrain being in their favour.'

Tiberius said, 'As discussed, we form a weak front line; hopefully, we can draw their cavalry down from the high ground. We will send two legions to flank around the high ground East and West. When they commit to attacking our front line, the pincer will close behind them.'

Julius replied, 'What happens when their cavalry breaks our front line?'

Tiberius replied, 'The front line gives way. We have two legions waiting, arranged in a V formation. The open end of the V is the entrance to the killing area. We channel them in, and they will have no room to manoeuvre. The front line turns and closes the exit from the V. We kill them all.'

Julius said, 'Yes, that will work for the cavalry but what of their infantry?'

Tiberius replied, 'The flanking legions need to close quickly. It is important that the flanks attack their infantry as soon as possible after they send their cavalry towards us. We will hold our cavalry in reserve and release them only when we have theirs in the V-trap.'

Julius said, 'Yes, Emperor, it is an excellent strategy. We will work through the details and put the plan into action immediately.'

Tiberius poured himself a goblet of rich red wine and sat down to mull over the plan, its strengths and weaknesses. A voice in his head said, 'A good plan to defeat their cavalry, but I have scanned your enemy, and they outnumber you by two to one. They have superior cavalry but, in addition, far greater numbers of infantry. Your plan would succeed initially, but their infantry would overwhelm you.'

Tiberius replied, 'Goddess, are you able to lend assistance?'

Mab said, 'Follow the plan. When their infantry pours down the hill towards you, I will intervene.'

Tiberius smiled and replied, 'Thank you, Goddess.'

Tiberius went outside to check on progress. Julius walked towards him and whispered, 'Emperor, all is in order. The two flanking legions are now on their way, and the scouts left immediately. The front line is established, and we are currently looking at the positioning of the V-trap and piking the ground.'

Tiberius said, 'Julius, that is excellent. The scouts who reported the Goth numbers, are they known to you?'

Julius replied, 'No, they are not our scouts. They are locals who have had dealings with the enemy, buying and selling goods.'

Tiberius replied, 'So, the numbers they gave you are rough estimates?'

Julius replied, 'They told us their source was reliable, and they were certain of the numbers.'

Tiberius replied, 'They are wrong. The enemy is twice our number!'

Julius paused in shock and said, 'If that is true, our plan will fail!'

Tiberius replied, 'No, we follow the plan; the Goddess will intervene.'

Julius said, 'Are you sure?'

Tiberius said, 'She has spoken!'

Julius replied, 'Yes, Emperor. I will execute those responsible for the disinformation.'

Tiberius said, 'Interrogate and then execute. I want to know who paid them to provide the disinformation.'

Julius brought his fist to his chest and marched off, furious, to find the source of the disinformation.

The commander of the second legion, Maximus, brought the two locals, in iron shackles, to Julius and said, 'Commander, these provided the disinformation on the Goth numbers. As instructed, no one knows they are being held here under arrest.'

Julius looked at the two men, one old and the other young, and said, 'You will tell me who paid you to pass false information to us. If you lie to me, you and all your family members will be burned alive. Now speak!'

The older of the two said, 'Commander, we were told that if we were asked questions by anyone concerning the Goth numbers, we should say the equivalent of three Roman legions, which is roughly 10,000 legionnaires. We do not know the actual number.'

Julius replied, 'You have been to their encampment. What did you see?'

The older man replied, 'We went there to trade. This is my son; we live locally and have a farm. We were only allowed to enter the trade area, and it was not possible for us to see very much, although they did have many horses, I would say several hundred.'

Julius looked at the younger man, who was shaking with fear and said, 'This is your father?'

The young man stuttered, 'Yes, Lord, we are sorry if we have done wrong; it wasn't our intention.'

Julius said, 'Who else lives with you at the farm.'

The young man replied, 'My mother and two sisters.' Julius saw the older man frown at his son; he paused in thought and said, 'Max, escort these two back to their home. They are not to be harmed, they are innocent.'

Julius dropped to his knees and gasped as a warm feeling of wellness and hope suddenly washed through his consciousness.

Max said, 'Julius, are you alright?'

Julius replied, 'Yes, I just felt a bit strange.'

Julius made his way to the emperor's tent and said, 'I have questioned those responsible, a father and son who farm locally. They do not know the enemy numbers but were told by the Goths that they had the equivalent of three Roman legions.'

Tiberius replied, 'I trust you executed them in an appropriate manner?'

Julius paused and said, 'No, I told Maximus to escort them back home to their family.'

Tiberius turned, stared at him askance and said, 'You did what!'

Julius dropped to one knee and replied, 'Emperor, I can't explain it. I heard myself saying the words to Max, but it was as if I had no control over my own voice. Then, a wonderous feeling washed through me; my concerns and worries were swept away in an instant.'

Tiberius smiled and said, 'Julius, it is the Goddess. She is near and has favoured you with her presence.'

Kanaka smiled at Mab as they joined the main trail and said, 'You are absolutely sure that you have had enough breakfast?'

Mab laughed and replied, 'Now that you mention it, perhaps we should have an early lunch?'

Kanaka said, 'Lunch at the palace, or what is left of it, we should be there by midday. How long do you think it will take us to find the warlock?'

Mab replied, 'Malphador, not very long. I see him now, and he is awake in bed with two young witches who are sleeping. He is thinking about a meeting this afternoon, a meeting of the black covens of which he is the principal.'

Kanaka asked 'Is he a powerful witch?'

Mab looked at Kanaka, smiled and said, 'Yes, he is a powerful witch, but, unlike Morgana, he is also a fool.'

Kanaka asked, 'Do you intend to kill him?'

Mab replied, 'Yes, without doubt, he will be dead this day. The black covens are evil, and they sacrifice animals and children in their attempt to gain dark powers. They summon ancient daemons to do their bidding, but they have no understanding of what these creatures are or how to control them. Of course, as you know, they cannot control them. The daemon infestation we have been fighting originated from the black covens. They are fools, dabbling in matters that they don't understand.'

Kanaka said, 'I still feel bad about Morgana; I can't help thinking that she wasn't all bad.'

Mab said, 'She was also beautiful. Some men find it difficult to accept that a beautiful woman could be evil.'

Kanaka replied, 'I killed her; she was sleeping; I plunged my blade through her stomach. No matter how beautiful or evil she was, it was simply wrong.'

Mab said, 'You may remember that I stayed behind after you killed her? When you left, I plunged my blade through her chest just to make sure she was dead.'

Kanaka stared at her and said, 'Well, that makes me feel much better!'

They trotted on in silence for a few minutes, and then Mab smiled at Kanaka and said, 'She is not dead.'

Kanaka stopped, stared at Mab and said, 'How can she not be dead? We both killed her!'

Mab replied, 'I had intended to take her head, but she was so beautiful lying there, I couldn't do it. She has regenerated; I can sense her presence. She is still living in the Apartment, and I haven't made contact, I don't want to scare her. I promised Cat and Charly that I would take them to the city when we returned. If you come with me, we could meet with Alexei and Morgana. Perhaps we can come to some agreement with them regarding the narcotics business. It's now clear to me that no matter how many we kill, others will simply step into their place. We are damaging the supply side but the only way of solving the problem is to stop the demand.'

Kanaka replied, 'I don't think it's that simple. The people selling the stuff help to create the demand; perhaps we should attack the supply side at its source. I mean, the people making the stuff?'

Mab, moving her horse into a fast canter, said, 'It's complicated. That's why we should talk to Alexei and Morgana.'

Kanaka, keeping pace with Mab, replied, 'Yes, definitely worth a visit to Fat Joes!' The trail opened up, and Mab stepped up to a gallop.

Kanaka and Mab reached the Northern boundary of the forest on schedule and stopped for lunch. Kanaka said, 'I haven't been on a horse for some time, and I feel it!'

Mab replied, 'Yes, me too! Is it too early for wine?'

Kanaka replied, 'I'm still suffering from last night, but hot coffee with some bread and cheese would be good.'

Mab laid the food out and warmed up the remaining coffee. Mab suddenly looked up and said, 'Amarok?'

Mab stood up, closed her eyes and said, 'Amarok, I know you can hear me. I know where you are. I cannot hear you because the witches are blocking your mind. I am coming for you.'

Mab looked at Kanaka and said, 'We leave the horses here. The black witches have imprisoned Amarok.'

Kanaka replied, 'It is a trap. They know we are coming.'

Mab said, 'Yes, but nevertheless, we will go there. Master Kanaka, if Amarok has been hurt or killed, I will send you back here.'

Kanaka stared at Mab and then replied, 'Yes, Mab, I understand.' Kanaka unsaddled the horses, took them to water and put them on a long tether.

Mab said, 'They are in a large rock cavern in the foothills of the Blue Mountains.' Kanaka replied, 'That is a fair distance west of here. I think I know it, and I visited that area in my youth, rock climbing and exploring. The cavern system is known as the Devil's Retreat, and the climb up to the entrance is the Devil's Staircase.'

Mab took Kanaka's hand, entered his mind and said, 'Show me.' They materialised at the mouth of a large cave on a rock shelf surrounded by Deeping Forest. Mab said, 'If we climbed all the way to the top we would be able to see Cetha, but perhaps we do that on another day?'

Kanaka smiled and said, 'I could have done that in my youth, but now, at my age, I don't think so.'

Mab replied, 'Master Kanaka, you are not much older than me, and you are young for your age. I insist that we do this climb together!'

Kanaka laughed and said, 'Fine, but let's get through today first before we set a date!'

Mab and Kanaka walked into the mouth of the cave as the light faded, and several spheres of light formed before them and behind them. Mab said, 'Up ahead, lots of witches singing.'

Kanaka replied, 'Singing, surely not?'

Then Kanaka heard it and said, 'Mab, they are chanting. It is some kind of spell.'

Mab said, 'Let's have a look.'

They vanished and appeared in the shadows at the back of a huge cavern. Kanaka said, 'There must be a thousand witches here! The chant is affecting my mind; I need to get out of here.'

Mab said, 'Master Kanaka, remain calm, focus your mind entirely on one thing, something precious to you.' Mab vanished and reappeared in mid-air above the dais in the middle of the cave. She appeared in her white robe, open sandals and with flowers in her hair. The black witches continued to chant but were all now pointing at Mab who rotated slowly, smiling down at them. The chanting increased in tempo and volume, but Mab detected a level of urgency, panic even, in the timbre.

She reached out with her mind to all present and said, 'I thank you for your welcome. However, now YOU WILL BE SILENT!' The coercive power was such that the command had to be obeyed. Many witches were struck dumb, and others collapsed unconscious to the floor. Some managed to remain conscious and standing but with blood streaming from their ears, noses and eyes, but all were silent.' Mab lowered herself slowly down; a group of six warlocks were lying on the floor close to the dais. There was a thunderous rumble and crashing noise.

Mab said to all, 'I have sealed this cavern.'

She reached out and found Amarok, who materialised beside her, followed shortly by Kanaka.

Mab said, 'Amarok, have you been harmed?'

Amarok replied, 'No high-one, I am hungry and thirsty, but otherwise, I am fine.'

Mab looked at Kanaka and said, 'Master Kanaka, I will send you and Amarok back to the forest and the horses. I will join you shortly.'

Kanaka nodded.

Mab scanned the minds of the warlocks, looked directly at Malphador and said, 'You are the son of Malphador, also named Malphador. It was you who conspired to kill Principal Luticia and endangered the life of my friend. What do you have to say for yourself?'

Malphador Junior lifted himself onto all fours, struggled to stand and said, 'My father was a fool. I am now head of the covens.'

He feigned, turning away but then spun and threw a narrow silver blade directly at Mab's neck. The tip of the blade almost touched Mab's skin but stopped, hung in the air and then dropped to the floor.

Malphador found himself being lifted into the air and held before Mab, who said, 'You are evil and have no place in this world.'

Mab raised her arm, plucked Onimaru from the air and plunged the blade through his chest. She then withdrew Onimaru and decapitated him, allowing his body and head to fall to the floor with a dull thump. Mab rose up and, speaking to all, said, 'The covens here are finished. Magic and the Occult will only be practiced within the four magic schools of the South. Any witches here who wish to continue practicing must first relinquish evil and black magic. Those who wish to do so, move to my left.'

Mab estimated that around one-quarter of the witches had moved to her left, many removing their black robes. One of the warlocks shouted, 'What of those of us who want to carry on as before.' Mab replied, 'That is not permitted.'

She then said to all, 'Hear me, I am the Goddess Bellona. This is your last chance. I will not permit the teaching of evil and dabbling in daemonology. Many hundreds, if not thousands, of people, have been killed or had their lives stolen from them as a direct result of what you have been doing. It ends now!'

Mab waited patiently. A few more removed their black robes and ran across to join the others. Mab then turned to her left and said, 'You have chosen life and the light. I send you to the Academy of White Witches to work under the direction of Principal Luticia.'

The entire group of witches vanished. She then looked at the others and said, 'You have chosen death and the darkness. You will remain here until your life has expired.'

Mab looked up, pulled the roof of the cavern downwards and vanished as the remaining witches and warlocks were buried under the weight of the mountain.

Mab materialised beside Kanaka and Amarok. Many wolves were also there gathered close to Amarok.

Kanaka looked at Mab, who said, 'The covens are finished. Some were saved, but many died. But it is accomplished.'

Amarok said, 'High one, thank you for freeing me from that place of rock and cold.'

Mab replied, 'Amarok, go now, enjoy the forest and its fruits. Master Kanaka and I will stay here awhile and then head South.'

Amarok and his pack loped off into the depths of the forest.

Mab said, 'I saved the coffee from this morning, and we have plenty of provisions left.'

Kanaka smiled and replied, 'Let's sit down and enjoy what's left of our holiday.'

Mab laid out the food and warmed up the coffee, and Kanaka brought two small goblets and a bottle of single malt from his saddle bag. He poured two generous measures of the whisky and said, 'I think I need this more than you!'

Mab smiled and said, 'Were you worried about me?' Kanaka popped a piece of cheese in his mouth, took a sip of whisky and said, 'No, not at all; I knew you would be fine.'

Mab smiled and replied, 'So when the witches were chanting, I asked you to focus your mind on something precious to you. What did you think about?'

Kanaka replied, 'When I was a child, we had a dog. Her name was Sula. I thought of her and the times we shared together.'

Mab said, 'That's nice. You do know that I can read minds?'

Kanaka looked at Mab somewhat awkwardly and said, 'Yes?'

Mab leaned over, kissed him on both cheeks and said, 'Let's eat. This is becoming a working holiday!'

Kanaka said, 'More unfinished business?'

Mab replied, 'Yes, the Romans and the Goths. Would you like to see a real battle with cavalry, infantry, witches, angels and perhaps even a goddess?'

Kanaka laughed and replied, 'That is an offer that I cannot possibly refuse.'

Mab picked up a twig from the forest floor and, drawing on the ground, said, 'The Romans have five legions, two of which have been sent out to flank the enemy who occupy the high ground. That leaves three legions directly facing the Goths. The Romans originally thought that the Goths had the equivalent of three legions, but they actually had more than ten legions. They will first commit their cavalry, who not only outnumber the Roman cavalry but are also far superior warriors. The Goth cavalry will break the Roman front line and be closely followed by their infantry, who will sweep over the Romans by sheer weight of numbers. However, the Roman strategy is to draw the Goth cavalry down from the high ground and allow them to break through a weak front line. The Goths will then be channelled into a V-shaped killing area and be annihilated. However, this will only work if the Goth infantry can be slowed down as they follow their cavalry. The two Roman legions on the flanks will help but the Goth numbers are so great that my feeling is the Romans will be overrun.'

Kanaka replied, 'Yes, it is the sheer weight of the Goth numbers that is the problem. The Roman infantry will be massively outnumbered if the flanking legionnaires do not enter the battle promptly. I wouldn't want to be in the line facing that sea of Goth infantry pouring down the hill and knowing that their cavalry is behind me and could turn!'

Mab smiled at Kanaka and replied, 'That's exactly where we are going to be!'

Kanaka groaned and said, 'I wish I had kept my big mouth shut.'

When they had finished their lunch, Mab said, 'Let's take a quick look at the battlefield. We will go as eagles, but stay close to me, and there may be arrows!'

Kanaka and Mab vanished and appeared as eagles soaring high in the air above the battlefield. Kanaka said, 'The Goths have made many piles of tree trunks. These will be rolled down if the Romans try an infantry attack uphill.'

Mab replied, 'Yes, but that's not going to happen until the Goth infantry has been largely destroyed.' Mab said to Tiberius, 'The Goths intend to roll tree trunks downhill. You may need protective measures for the infantry. The flanks will be able to see and avoid the trees, but your front line and the legions in the V-trap could be damaged.'

Tiberius replied, 'Thank you, Goddess, we have seen this tactic many times before. We will stake out the ground as a precaution, but in this terrain, it is unlikely that the logs will reach the front line. They tend to veer off course and end up hampering their own infantry!'

Mab replied, 'Yes, I see what you mean. I can see your two flanking legions, and they are very well positioned to join the battle.'

Tiberius said, 'Goddess, it is the weight of numbers in their infantry that we are worried about.'

Mab replied, 'I understand, but your front line must not move forward to meet the enemy. I will need that space.'

Tiberius replied, 'Yes, Goddess, thank you for your help.'

Mab said, 'Tiberius, you must warn your legions that in this battle, they will see strange things and strange creatures. They must not be afraid; the strangers are here to help them defeat the enemy.'

Tiberius replied, 'Yes, Goddess, I will advise my legion commanders.'

Kanaka said, 'I have to admire the Romans, their battle strategy, the communications and line of command, the speed of mobilisation.'

Mab smiled and said, 'Yes, they are superb strategists and warriors.'

A voice in Mab's head said, 'Yes, sister, they should be. It was I who taught them!'

Mab said, 'Who are you?'

The voice said, 'Sister, you are not yet fully restored. I have longed for your return. Soon we will be together, Bellona and Minerva, reunited in love and glory!'

Mab, askance, said, 'You are my sister! Athena?'

Minerva replied, 'Yes, Bellona, I am. I know you have many questions but remain calm. We will meet soon, I promise.'

Kanaka said, 'Mab, are you alright; the battle is underway!' Mab looked down and saw the Goth cavalry racing downhill towards the Roman front line.

Mab said, 'Look at the speed. They will crash straight through the line!'

Kanaka said, 'Yes, but that's supposed to happen!' They watched as the Goth cavalry broke the Roman front line and funnelled into the V-trap, hacking and slashing at the Roman infantry.

Mab said, 'The V has held, it's working, the Goths are hemmed in, their horses can't turn.'

The Roman front line then closed the V and attacked the now stationary cavalry from behind. Roman archers were raining arrows down on the hapless Goths.

Kanaka said, 'It's a slaughter, but look, the Goth infantry are starting to move downhill!'

Mab said, 'Let's get down there!' The two great eagles plummeted downwards, landed in the middle of the battlefield and changed into human form. Kanaka looked at the thousands of ferocious Goth infantry racing downhill towards them and said, 'Mab, whatever you intend to do, please do it now!'

Mab laughed and replied, 'Master Kanaka, perhaps we could take them on alone?'

Kanaka stared at her with a grim expression on his face.

Mab said, 'Perhaps not. Lucifer, come to me and bring as many guards as you can!' There was no immediate reply. Mab looked at Kanaka and said, 'No response!' Dawn-breaker flashed into Kanaka's hand just as an intensely bright light expanded in the air before them. Several hundred Guardians appeared on the battlefield. Mab and Kanaka levitated upwards. Mab's mind linked to the Guardians and said, 'Stop the charge, slay the enemy.' The Guardians spread out into a two-deep line and walked slowly uphill to meet the hoard running at them. They drew their weapons: long swords, short swords and spears. When the Goths were within twenty or so paces, the Guardians launched a psychic wave of energy that hit the approaching enemy like a tsunami. Goths up to ten paces into the charge were killed instantly and dropped to the ground. Others further back were stunned and confused. This effectively created a wall of bodies, which brought the Goth charge almost to a halt. The Guardians continued their advance through the Goths, killing with ruthless precision.

After an hour or so, Kanaka said, 'The flanking legions are now attacking!'

Mab replied, 'This is turning into a slaughter.' A scream was heard from above. A huge black snake-like creature plummeted from the air and belched fire onto the Goths, incinerating hundreds with every breath. Mab looked down at the V-trap; the Roman line had closed the trap and the Goths were being utterly slaughtered. Mab saw a Roman cut the head of a terrified horse in order to bring the rider to the ground.

She said, 'Tiberius, the V-trap and flanking manoeuvres have served their purpose. Now stop the slaughter!'

Tiberius replied, 'Yes, Goddess, immediately.'

Tiberius sent runners to stop the legions in their tracks and to hold until for further orders.

Mab said, 'Lucifer, there has been enough killing.'

Lucifer replied, 'Yes, Goddess, would you like me to withdraw the Guardians?'

Mab said, 'Tell them to stop and hold in a ready but defensive posture.'

Kanaka said, 'The Goths are throwing down their weapons.'

Mab replied, 'They have been utterly decimated; not a single Guardian has been killed or injured.'

Mab said, 'Tiberius, we will bring the Goth leaders to your encampment.'

Tiberius replied, 'Goddess, I will make preparations to receive them.'

Mab and Kanaka materialised in the Goth encampment and walked towards what was clearly the Goth leader's battle tent. As they approached, any Goths that came too close dropped to the ground unconscious. Mab and Kanaka walked into the battle tent and found the Goth leaders arguing ferociously and drinking heavily. The place reeked of sweat and ale.

Mab created a powerful perfume of mixed herbs, cinnamon and citrus and said, 'I hope you don't mind, but this place really stinks. Do you ever wash?'

One of the clan leaders stood up, walked towards Mab and said, 'I will wash myself now with your blood.'

Mab leapt high into the air and kicked him in the throat. The huge Goth clutched his throat and, unable to breathe, dropped to the ground. Mab said, 'Your foolish friend is dying. You drunkards will come with me.'

Mab, Kanaka and the Goth leaders materialised in the Roman battlefield tent. Tiberius, Julius and the five legion commanders were present with swords drawn.

Mab said, 'You won't need swords. Put them away.' The Goth leaders were in a state of total confusion. Mab said, 'Sit down!' Everyone, other than Mab and Kanaka, immediately sat down.' Mab looked at the clan leaders and said, 'You have been defeated, but I will not have your people slaughtered while you sit in your tent and drink ale! I have paused the battle and brought you here to parley. Tiberius himself sits there. Make use of this short time for the good of your people!'

Wallian said, 'I am the clan's leader. We have been defeated, but not by Rome. Witchcraft is at play here. Nevertheless, defeat is defeat, and we cannot stand against the silver warriors and the fire-breathing creature. The Romans leave their lands and come here to rape our country. They kill or enslave our people, men, women and children. We gathered our clans together with the hope of destroying the tyrant Tiberius and freeing our people, but we are lost. Our Gods have deserted us.'

Mab stared at Wallian and said, 'I may have misjudged you. Who are your Gods?'

Wallian replied, 'Some of us pray to the Gods of the North. Others, me included, pray to the Greek Gods.'

Mab said, 'Which Greek God do you pray to?'

Wallian replied, 'Every morning, I pray to Athena, who is the Goddess of Battle Strategy and Wisdom.'

There was silence in the room. Mab said, 'Athena is my sister. I spoke to her from afar only this morning. The Romans know her as Minerva.'

Wallian stared askance at Mab and said, 'Who are you?' Mab's appearance changed; she stood in her white robe holding Onimaru in her right hand, and a silver whip hung from her left hip.

She said, 'I am Bellona, Goddess of War.'

Wallian's eyes widened, dropping to his knees he said, 'Goddess, please forgive me. I would never raise arms against Bellona or Minerva. I will take my life, but I beg mercy for my people.' The other clan leaders knelt beside Wallian with their heads bowed.

Mab replied, 'No, Wallian, you will not take your own life. You and Tiberius honour the Gods every day with your prayers, and we are well pleased. When, at last, I am reunited with my sister, you will see us side by side in all our glory.'

Tiberius said, 'Wallian, we worship the same Gods. This war between us must be ended. I will withdraw my legionnaires from the battlefield immediately. We have medics who will assist you with the wounded. I give you my word that there will be no more incursions into your country without agreement.'

Tiberius turned to Julius and said, 'Withdraw the legions!'

Mab said, 'The Gods want you to live in peace. Please, do not disappoint us!' Mab and Kanaka vanished and appeared beside their horses in Deeping Forest.

Mab said, 'Should we eat before we hit the trail?'

Kanaka replied, 'Yes, let us finish off the provisions. The horses need exercise, so we can stretch them out a bit and be back at the Guild before we lose the light.'

Mab and Kanaka reached the Guild before sundown as planned and had a late supper together in Kanaka's office.

Kanaka said, 'You must be looking forward to the reunion with your sister?'

Mab replied, 'Yes, she said I was not yet ready but that we would be reunited soon.'

Kanaka said, 'Yes, I suppose her definition of soon could run into centuries?'

Mab smiled and said, 'Maybe, but I think she really means soon as we understand it. As you know, my witch powers continue to accelerate, but there has been a marked change in the last few days.'

Kanaka replied, 'You mean levelling off to a steady state?'

Mab said, 'No the rate of change is increasing still. It's like a quickening to reach a destination, like a horse approaching the finishing line. But I fear what I may become at the finish. Minerva's voice sounded wonderfully human, but of course, I haven't met her in the physical sense.' Kanaka replied, 'Mab, I am sure it will all work out; just go with the flow for now.' Mab smiled and said, 'That is good advice. Before I go, Luticia wants to share the new students from the North with the other schools. I don't think she can cope with the numbers!'

Kanaka replied, 'A nice problem to have, provided they have funding, of course. We could certainly take on another twenty or so students, depending on their skills. The more advanced students could go into the Warrior School.'

Mab said, 'I'll let her know. The other issue is Morgana and Alexei. We need to reach some agreement with them regarding the narcotics business. Morgana could have taken that vile stuff to Yehuda or even here!' Kanaka replied, 'She could travel here?' Mab said, 'Yes, absolutely. My head tells me I should kill her, but my witch senses say otherwise. She has a role, a destiny that is not yet revealed to me.'

Kanaka replied, 'How could she survive two swords being driven through her?'

Mab said, 'I wasn't totally sure she would survive, but I wanted to test her. That's why I didn't take her head or incinerate her.'

Kanaka smiled and said, 'It was a fairly definitive test!'

Mab said, 'She recovered quickly. Morgana is certainly a powerful witch, cunning and intelligent; she and Alexei are well suited.'

Kanaka replied, 'Yes, they are both accomplished liars. But she is evil. Perhaps Lucifer may know something of her?'

Mab said, 'Yes, I will ask him. In the meantime, I'll ask Alexei to arrange a meeting at Fat Joe's for the day after tomorrow?'

Kanaka replied, 'That suits me. I suggest we get there early evening. Do you think it is safe to bring Charly and Cat?'

Mab said, 'I will ask Alexei to arrange something special for them, one of those club nights, whatever that means. If they get into trouble, which they almost certainly will, I'll rescue them.'

Kanaka laughed and said, 'Fine, but I did warn you!'

Mab made her way to the suite and found Charly and Cat drinking whisky. Mab said, 'Where did you get that?'

Cat said, 'Master Boe gave it to us, well, to you, actually. He said it was a bit too strong for him.'

Mab laughed and said, 'So he gave it to me, but you two thought to help yourselves?'

Charly said, 'Yes, of course! In this suite, we share everything. We see it as a sort of commune.'

Mab replied, 'Well, perhaps you could pour me a generous measure of our whisky?'

Cat did the honours and said, 'I hope you don't mind, Mab, we couldn't resist it.'

Mab smiled and said, 'The day after tomorrow, Master Kanaka and I are going to the city of the future for a meeting. I thought you might like to come with us. I will ask someone to show you around and take you to the entertainment places where you can eat, drink and enjoy yourselves?'

Charly jumped up, hugged Mab and said, 'Fantastic! What should we wear? What are the people like?'

Cat said, 'Will there be young men of our age? How do we get there?'

Mab said, 'Don't worry. Wear your usual clothes. I will make you sure your clothes fit in with the other young revellers. We will go there together; the journey will take only a few seconds.'

Charly and Cat hugged each other and then hugged Mab again.

Mab showered, lay back on her bed, closed her eyes and said, 'Lucifer?'

The response was immediate: 'Yes, Goddess.'

Mab said, 'Thank you for your help with the Goths; what was that form you took?

Lucifer replied, 'It was based on the Basilisk, a type of lizard. I added the fire breathing and the flying.'

Mab said, 'A dragon would have been better.'

Lucifer replied, 'Perhaps a large silver dragon?'

Mab said, 'Anyway, what do you know of the witch Morgana?'

Lucifer paused before replying, 'I have known Morgana for a long time. Goddess, if I may ask, what is your interest in her?'

Mab replied, 'I was thinking of killing her.' Lucifer was silent. Mab said, 'Lucifer, talk to me.'

Lucifer said, 'I once loved Morgana. She turned to the darkness when I was cast down. Do you see the irony, it was she who changed while I remained the same?'

Mab replied, 'Yes, Morgana changed because you fell into darkness, but your punishment was to remain the same while all around you became evil. But this means Morgana must be much older than I thought. I estimated her age as no more than one thousand years.'

Lucifer said, 'She undergoes a complete regeneration every thousand years, but she has lived for many millennia.'

Mab said, 'Lucifer, what is she?'

Lucifer replied, 'She is an immensely powerful witch, perhaps the first and last of her kind. Goddess, I do not have the right, but I ask you not to kill her.'

Mab said, 'You love her still?' Lucifer did not answer. Mab said, 'Lucifer, if you wish me to spare her, then of course I will do that. I am planning to see her soon, and I may call upon you to attend.'

Lucifer replied, 'Thank you, Goddess. I am not sure she would welcome my presence, but I will attend if required.' Mab closed her mind and fell into a deep sleep.

Minerva said, 'Sister, I feel the quickening in you. Soon we will be together.'

Mab replied, 'Are there others, like you and I?'

Minerva said, 'There are others but not like us. We are the true Gods. There are others who, in their ignorance, call themselves Gods, but they will come to know the error of their ways when we are reunited!'

Mab replied, 'Sister, come to me now.' A spot of bright light appeared above Mab. It elongated and widened. Minerva stepped through; she was tall, slim, athletic and muscular. She was also extraordinarily beautiful. Minerva wore an ankle-length robe of white silk. Her lustrous black hair was platted around her head and hung like a thick rope down her back. Mab, completely naked, levitated upwards from her bed until she was face to face with her and stared, in silence, into her black orb eyes.

Minerva moved her face closer, kissed Mab on the lips, held her tightly and whispered, 'Together again, my sister.'

Mab hugged Minerva more tightly and said, 'We were lovers, I remember.'

Minerva whispered, 'Yes, Bellona, but now I must go. I cannot maintain my presence here for long. But when you are ready, you will be able to come to me, and we will be reunited.' Minerva started to fade, but Mab pulled her back and held her. Minerva smiled and said, 'Even now, you are strong, but you must release me. You will know when the time is right.' Mab released Minerva, who slowly vanished until Mab was hugging only the air. Mab dropped down onto her bed and lay back smiling.

Chapter Twenty-Six: Unfinished Business

Kanaka sat in his office, thinking about the meeting with Morgana. How to face her, knowing that he pushed his blade slowly through her stomach. The expression on her face would never leave him. It was not accusatory but noble, dignified and forgiving. It made him feel petty and spiteful, everything that Morgana was not.

There was a knock at the door. Mab popped her head around and said, 'Master Kanaka, are you ready for us?'

Kanaka smiled and said, 'Mab, yes, of course.' Mab walked in with Cat and Charly, who were beyond excited.

Kanaka said, 'Have a seat. Can we go through the arrangements just to be sure we all know what to expect?'

Mab replied, 'Yes, Master Kanaka. We leave from here and arrive on the Haskins building roof. If everything looks normal, we will move to the adjacent alley and meet Morgana and Alexei in Fat Joe's bar area. We will have a couple of drinks there and then walk together to a local nightclub for dinner. Alexei has asked a couple of his friends to show Cat and Charly around the City.'

Kanaka said, 'And their safety is assured?'

Mab, looking at Cat and Charly, said, 'You will be perfectly safe. I will maintain my mind contact with you. This will enable you to communicate with the natives, and I will know immediately if you feel threatened or are in danger.'

Kanaka said, 'Will we need weapons?'

Mab replied, 'Weapons won't be necessary on this occasion. However, there is the important question of what Cat and Charly should wear?'

Kanaka said, 'Yes, absolutely, not to mention your own attire Mab.'

Mab replied, 'What do you mean, my attire.'

Kanaka said, 'The bars and nightclubs there will have dress codes for women. You, Charly and Cat will be expected to wear nice dresses, shiny shoes and groomed hair. Otherwise, they won't let you in.'

Mab said, 'What will you be wearing?'

Kanaka stood up and removed his robe. He sported a white shirt with a multi-coloured cravat, dark blue linen trousers with a snakeskin belt and, best of all, black highly polished pointed shoes.

Mab said, 'Where did you get all that stuff!?'

Cat and Charly applauded. Mab's appearance suddenly changed; she was wearing a white body-hugging short dress with black shoes, and her silver hair was platted around her head.

Kanaka said, 'That is perfect!'

Mab looked at Cat and Charly and said, 'What do you two want to wear?'

Cat replied, 'Mab, just like you, but a black dress.'

Mab replied, 'What about your hair?'

Cat replied, 'Could you do it the same as you but blonde?' Suddenly, Cat's appearance changed.

Charly said, 'I want the same dress but the colour of Master Kanaka's trousers. Shoes the same as Cat's and my hair jet black and platted down my back.'

Charly's appearance changed in accordance with her request.

Kanaka said, 'Mab, could you change this cravat to pure white?'

Mab rolled her eyes but obliged and said, 'If we are all happy with our appearance, perhaps we could set off?'

Charly replied, 'I'm not too sure about this shade of blue.' Mab stared at her.

Charly smiled and said, 'Only joking!'

The group appeared on the roof of the Haskins building. It was early evening, and there was a slight chill in the air. Kanaka and Mab wore their black robes and Charly and Cat grey student robes.

Mab reached out with her witch senses and said, 'Alexei and Morgana are already in Fat Joe's. I don't detect anything out of the ordinary.'

Cat started coughing.

Mab said, 'It's pollution in the air; you will get used to it in a few minutes.'

Mab moved the group to a dark alley opposite Fat Joe's and said, 'When the machines stop moving, we walk across.'

As they walked into Fat Joe's, their robes vanished. Morgana and Alexei were sitting at the far end of the bar area in a secluded corner. They stood up as Mab and Kanaka approached.

Alexei said, 'Mab, it is great to see you again.'

Mab simply stared at him, turned her gaze to Morgana, smiled and said, 'I trust you are well?'

Morgana replied, 'I am not fully regenerated, perhaps another month or so and I will be back to normal.'

Alexei said, 'Please, everyone sit down; I will order drinks.'

Mab said, 'Great, white wine for me, Charly and Cat.'

Alexei said, 'Charly, Cat, very pleased to meet you, I am Alexei.'

Charly and Cat nodded.

Kanaka said, 'I'll have a single malt, large measure.'

Alexei looked at Morgana, who simply nodded. When Alexei left, Mab said, 'I am pleased that you managed to regenerate.'

Morgana replied, 'Why did you not kill me?'

Mab said, 'I wanted to see if you could recover from two near-fatal injuries. I had intended to kill you tonight, but a good friend has pleaded your case. I am considering the matter. Alexei has lied to me on several occasions and colluded with the daemon ruler Samuel to assassinate me. Several attempts have been made on life. As you may know, my partner was assassinated by a Balerak under orders from Samuel. I should really kill Alexei now.'

Morgana replied, 'So, you are considering whether to kill Alexei and I. When will you come to your decision?'

Mab replied, 'This evening.'

Alexei arrived carrying a tray of drinks.

Cat looked at Morgana's drink and said, 'Morgana, if I may ask, what is that?'

Morgana smiled and said, 'It's a cocktail, which means that it is a drink with many different ingredients. This one is called a Pina Colada. Please try it.'

Cat looked at Mab, who nodded. Cat picked up the glass, took a gulp and said, 'This is wonderful! Charly, we must have a few of these!'

Morgana said, 'Pass it around. In this society, people drink and party a lot! The young women of today often try many different cocktails in a single night whereas the young men often drink ale or short spirits such as whisky.'

Alexei stood up and said, 'I'll order a few more.'

Kanaka said, 'It's a bit too sweet for me.'

Morgana said, 'Mab, what do you think?'

Mab waited until Alexei left to order more drinks and, looking at Morgana, said, 'Samael is dead, Azazel is dead, Azael is dead, and Mahazael is dead.'

Morgana stared askance at Mab. Mab said, 'Lucifer, come to me.'

Lucifer appeared, appropriately dressed in black. He stood like a titan, indomitable, his skin-tight clothes revealing his astonishingly toned athletic body.

Morgana immediately bowed and said, 'Lord Lucifer!'

Lucifer knelt before Mab and said, 'Goddess, how can I be of service?'

Mab said, 'You requested that I spare her life. I grant your wish, but only if you accept responsibility for overseeing her actions. Do you accept?'

Lucifer looked at Morgana and said, 'Yes, I accept.'

Mab looked at Morgana and said, 'Do you accept?'

Morgana smiled at Lucifer and replied, 'Yes, Goddess, I accept.'

Mab leaned over, kissed Lucifer on the cheek and said, 'Lucifer, there is no need for you to kneel in my presence.'

Lucifer smiled and replied, 'Thank you, Goddess, but I prefer to show respect for the light and gratitude for my redemption.'

Mab said, 'Very well. Now, please take Morgana somewhere nice and discuss how to keep her out of trouble. My house in Cetha is currently vacant.'

Morgana stood up but then knelt before Mab and said, 'Thank you, Goddess.'

Lucifer and Morgana vanished.

Alexei returned with four Pina Coladas and two double measures of single malt whisky.

Alexei said, 'Where is Morgana?'

Mab said, 'I have sent her on an errand. She may be gone for a few days.'

Alexei put the drinks down on the table and said, 'Mab, are you sure she is alright?'

Mab replied, 'Yes, of course. She is with a friend of mine. What are the arrangements for the rest of the evening?'

Alexei replied, 'You remember the nightclub I took you to previously? Well, we three are going there for dinner. The son of one of my friends will pick up Charly and Cat and take them to the latest hot-spot discotheque; he will be here soon. It was very difficult to get the tickets, so you two are very lucky girls!'

Charly said, 'What do we do when we get there?'

Alexei replied, 'You will love it. There is constant music and dancing, you can drink whatever you want, and of course, you may find a young man that you like and fall in love!'

Charly and Cat went into fits of laughter.

Alexei stood up, waved at someone and said, 'Josh is here now.'

Two young men approached the group, and they were both dressed in smart, open, necked shirts, tight-fitting trousers and highly polished shoes.

Josh, who had long blonde hair, said, 'Hi Alexei; you two must be Charly and Cat?'

Alexei replied, 'Yes, they have never been here before. So, you need to take special care of them. Stay close to them and make sure they have a good time.'

Josh replied, 'Yes, of course, Alexei, we will look after them. Charly, Cat, this is my best friend Mitch.'

Cat said, 'Hi, I'm Cat.'

Charly said, 'And I'm Charly.'

Mab said, 'And I'm Mab. If anything bad happens to Charly or Cat, you will die a horrible death.'

Josh and Mitch started to laugh but stopped when they saw the expression on Alexei's face.

Josh replied, 'Miss Mab, there is no need to worry. We will look after them, I promise.'

Charly said, 'Yes, don't worry, Miss Mab, we will be fine.'

Cat said, 'Miss Mab, what should I do if a boy wants to kiss me?'

Kanaka and Alexei started laughing.

Mab, also laughing, said, 'I'm sure you will think of something Cat!'

When Cat and Charly had left with their new friends, Mab said, 'It looks like I have four Pina Colada's to get through!'

Kanaka, sipping on his single malt, said, 'Alexei, did you ever meet the daemon Samael?'

Alexei, looking uncomfortable, replied, 'I worked for Robert Samael. He was a senior executive of the Haskins Corporation. Samael was responsible for the narcotics business, which was run under the cover of other legitimate businesses owned by Haskins.'

Mab said, 'What did you do for Samael?'

Alexei replied, 'Whatever he wanted.' Mab said, 'Hiring assassins?'

Alexei replied, 'Yes, I have on occasion hired assassins for Samael.'

Mab said, 'You sent three assassins to kill me.'

Alexei replied, 'Mab, I only found the assassins. I did not get involved in the mission or have any details of the targets. I brought the assassins to Samael, and he took over from that point.'

Mab said, 'I thought you were working for Morgana, but in fact, it was the other way around. Was it not?'

Alexei replied, 'We both worked for Samael. Morgana's role was foresight and protecting the executives. My role was, and is, fixing, which means making sure we get paid for the product and deterring competitors.'

Kanaka said, 'So you are still working for the Haskins Corporation?'

Alexei replied, 'Yes, I have taken Samael's place. I'm responsible for narcotics and the cover businesses.'

Mab said, 'Is Morgana still working for the Corporation?'

Alexei replied, 'Morgana works for Morgana. She has lost interest in the Haskins narcotics business. She had only just managed to recover from her wounds; she told me that she was moving on, leaving me and leaving this place. Normally, we would not allow anyone to exit the business, but with Haskins Senior and Junior both dead and Samael gone, there is nothing to prevent Morgana from walking away.'

Alexei continued, 'I don't know about you guys, but I am hungry. Should we make our way to the nightclub; it's only a short walk.

Kanaka looked at Mab and replied, 'I could do with some food.'

When they arrived at the club, the entertainment had already begun. A young black woman was singing. Mab was enthralled by the lyrics and the woman's beautiful melodic voice.

Alexei said, 'She is the resident soul singer; people travel a long way to see and hear her.'

Mab replied, 'Yes, she is a beautiful singer; her voice control is remarkable.'

Alexei said, 'Are you happy for me to order a selection of starters and food to share for the mains?'

Mab replied, 'Yes, Alexei, you order what you think is best. Master Kanaka and I can eat almost anything.'

When the food started to arrive, Alexei said, 'Mab, I have explained my role working with Haskins. It is a very lucrative job, and, frankly, I have no intentions of giving it up.'

Mab replied, 'Alexei, you will give it up. What you are doing is a great evil that cannot be allowed to continue. I know that others will come and take your place, but they will be dealt with. You can continue to work for Haskins, but you must not deal in narcotics.'

Alexei laughed and said, 'Without the revenue from narcotics, Haskins would run out of cash within a few months.'

Mab replied, 'Then the business is not worth saving.'

Alexei replied, 'Mab, I told you part of my job is deterrence. If anything happens to me, your two friends, Charly and Cat, will pay the price.'

Kanaka groaned and said, 'Alexei, you are a fool of the highest order!'

Mab replied, 'Charly and Cat are having a good time with Josh and Mitch. I see them now, and the club is very busy and very noisy.'

Alexei fiddled with his phone and said, 'They will be taken to a safe place. Nothing will happen to them if you cooperate.'

Mab looked at Kanaka and said, 'If he moves, kill him quietly. I'll be back soon, so look after my food.'

Mab vanished. She hung in the air unseen above the dance floor, looking down at Charly and Cat. She saw three burly men making their way through the crowd towards them. They pushed Josh and Mitch aside and escorted Charly and Cat away from the dance floor and upstairs to an office on the upper floor of the building. Josh and Mitch were following but were stopped from entering the office by two other men who were on guard.

Mab said to Charly and Cat, 'I am here, above you. Ask them why you have been brought here.'

Charly glanced upwards and then said, 'Why have you brought us here?'

The man behind the desk said, 'Do you know who I am?'

Charly said, 'No, who are you?'

He said, 'I'm Jonny Q. I own several clubs in this city, including this one. I am also a friend of Alexei Oblonsky, who wants you two put on ice.'

Cat said, 'He wants to freeze us!?'

Jonny stared at Cat, unsure how to respond and then said, 'I'll ask the questions. I need your names, addresses and phone numbers for you and your families.'

Cat, pointing up to the ceiling, said, 'Our Master is up there, and she will come down here and kick your butt if you don't let us go.'

Jonny glanced upwards, removed a pistol from a drawer, pointed it at Cat and said, 'Get writing!'

Mab manifested, dropped down onto the desk and said, 'Put that thing away.'

The three bodyguards collapsed to the floor unconscious. Jonny fired the pistol at Mab's chest. Mab watched the bullet approach and casually swatted it to the floor. She then leant forward, grabbed Jonny by the neck, lifted him one-handed high into the air and threw him across the room like a ragdoll. Jonny crashed through the wood-framed window and down onto the street below.

Mab turned to Charly and Cat and said, 'Josh and Mitch are outside. Would you like to go back to the dancefloor?'

Charly said, 'Yes, please!' Mab opened the office door, and the two guards dropped to the floor unconscious.

Mab said, 'There was a misunderstanding, all sorted now. Josh, Mitch, could you take the girls back to the dancing, please?'

Josh said, 'Yes, Miss Mab. Thanks for sorting things out.'

Mab went back into the office, piled the bodies up, locked the door from the inside, left the key in the lock and vanished.

Mab appeared back in her chair beside Kanaka and said, 'All is well. The girls are back on the dancefloor with Josh and Mitch. Everyone is fine and having a great time.'

Kanaka replied, 'At least you didn't have to kill anyone.'

Mab looked a bit sheepish and said, 'Well, everyone is having a good time apart from Jonny Q, the owner of the club. He could have hurt the girls, so I made him leave the room.'

Kanaka replied, 'You made him leave the room?' Mab said, 'I threw him out the window.'

Alexei said, 'Is he dead?' Mab replied, 'You should be more concerned about your own life. Why did you want to freeze Charly and Cat?'

Alexei replied, 'I have no idea what you are talking about.'

Mab said, 'Jonny Q said you wanted them put on ice.'

Alexei replied, 'That's a common expression; it means they are to be kept under strict supervision. What do you intend to do with me?'

Mab, tucking into her food, said, 'I thought I would obtain samples of the high-grade narcotics used in this city and trace the supply chains back to their origin, killing every person involved. I see traces of narcotics on your clothes, I see remnants of the humans you interact with, I see their faces, their locations, I see others through their eyes. I could enter their minds, kill them or coerce them into killing themselves or their families. I could pull them to me or place them on the moon that circles this planet. However, I have more important things on my mind at present than you and what happens in this place and time. So, you convince me as to why I should not kill you and everyone else involved in narcotics.'

Alexei thought for a few minutes and said, 'I don't think I can convince you, but wherever you find people, you will find drugs. You could eradicate narcotics in this city by killing many people and come back in a few months to find the problem remains. Also, many of these drugs are medicinal, but people misuse them and become addicted. It is not the drugs that are the problem, it is the people on both the supply and demand side. In many cases, it is greed and avarice. I guess I fall into that category, and in others, it is mental health issues that create the dependency. It is terrible to see young people deliberately experimenting with drugs. They think they are strong-willed and could never become addicted, but they are wrong and don't realise it until it is too late.'

Mab replied, 'So if I killed you now, others would take your place?'

Alexei said, 'Yes, that is so. And I suspect those who take my place would not perhaps be as understanding as I.'

Mab replied, 'Alexei, I will give you a few weeks to extract yourself from the narcotics industry. If, after that time has lapsed, you are still involved, then I will take your life, and all those involved in the enslavement of others will wish that they had not been born. Now leave me!'

Alexei walked out of the nightclub and didn't look back.

Mab looked at Kanaka and said, 'Do you think I was too harsh with Alexei?'

Kanaka replied, 'I thought what he said made sense. But he is in denial as to his role in the exploitation of the innocent. I expected you to kill him, and he certainly deserves it.'

Mab smiled and said, 'Yes, but I can kill him anytime. I want to see what he does, who else is involved.'

Kanaka said, 'That food was delicious!'

Mab laughed and replied, 'Yes, it is, but I can't wait much longer to see you dancing in the discotheque!'

Kanaka said, 'Sorry, but you will be waiting a very long time before you see that!'

Mab and Kanaka appeared on the dancefloor close to Charly and Cat. The music was so loud Kanaka thought his eardrums would burst. Mab picked up straight away that people were moving their bodies seemingly randomly but in time to the beat of the music. She started to emulate Charly and Cat who were too engrossed with Josh and Mitch to notice her arrival. Kanaka followed Mab's lead and moved with the music.

Mab moved into Kanaka's mind and said, 'This is really good, it feels liberating moving with the tempo of the music.' Suddenly the tempo increased markedly, multicoloured light beams flashed across the space and silver flakes were falling from above. People were now bouncing up and down, shouting, screaming, smiling and laughing. Mab and Kanaka joined in, astonished at the atmosphere that had been created.

Mab was losing herself in the music when her witch senses twitched. She reached out, it was a Balerak moving slowly, melding with the crowd expertly concealing its approach. Mab vanished, reappeared in Jonny Q's office and pulled the Balerak to her.

She said, 'Why are you here? Speak!'

The Balerak looked confused and said, 'I have come to kill Mabdelore Winter.'

Mab replied, 'I am the Goddess Bellona, also known as Mabdelore Winter. Name your client, or I will slay you where you stand.'

The Balerak smiled and said, 'Then you are my prey.' The expected wide spray of poison darts was released as the creature launched itself at Mab with a black short-sword held in a clawed hand. Mab was impressed with the speed of the creature but as it approached, she grabbed its sword hand and twisted the arm around. She then ripped the arm from its body, and there was a sickening tearing sound as the ligaments and sinews tore apart; yellow blood pulsed from the ruin that was the Balerak's shoulder. The creature howled in agony as Mab threw the arm, still clutching the short sword, to the floor. As the Balerak looked up at Mab, the poisoned darts, all of which struck the target, fell from her body.'

Mab said, 'Answer my question.' The Balerak was lifted up and hung in the air before Mab, who raised her hand and plucked Onimaru from the air.

The Balerak said, 'Oblonsky of the Haskins Corporation paid me.'

Mab thrust Onimaru through the creature's chest and then decapitated it as it fell to the floor. She then vanished and appeared beside Kanaka.

The music tempo had returned to normal. Kanaka said, 'Trouble?'

Mab replied, 'A Balerak, courtesy of Alexei. It must have been commissioned well before tonight. So, this was an expensive trap set by Alexei; he always intended to kill me.'

The music tempo soared once more, but to a new height of almost complete dancing frenzy, and then suddenly, it dropped to almost complete silence.

A digital voice said, 'Thank you all, hope you had fun, goodnight and stay safe.'

Kanaka looked at Mab and pointed to Charly and Cat, who were draped over Josh and Mitch.

Mab said, 'Why don't we walk back to Fat Joe's and have a couple of drinks?'

Kanaka nodded, and they headed for the exit.

Kanaka and Mab were sitting once more in the bar area of Fat Joe's, sipping generous measures of single malt whisky, when Joe approached them and said, 'Mab, it is good to see you again!'

Mab smiled up at him and replied, 'You too, Joe.'

Joe sat close to Mab and whispered, 'Haskins has put a price on your head. You are not safe here. There is a sniper on the roof of the building opposite.'

Mab replied, 'A sniper?'

Joe said, 'Mab, this is serious. They mean to kill you.'

Kanaka said, 'This sniper person has a projectile weapon?'

Joe replied, 'Yes! An expert marksman with the absolute best in high-velocity rifles!'

Kanaka took another sip and said, 'Mab, you are definitely attracting attention tonight.'

Mab looked at Joe and said, 'I guess the sniper only becomes dangerous when the weapon is fired?'

Joe replied, 'Jees, where do you guys come from. Mab, that guy is a professional; he will kill you. I don't understand why he didn't take you down on the way here?' Mab replied, 'He didn't see us.'

Joe stared at Mab and said, 'I like you, Mab. Let me sneak you out the back way and drive you out of town?'

Mab replied, 'Thanks, Joe. I'm really touched by your concern but there is nothing to worry about, and I don't want you getting into trouble for helping me.'

Just then, Charly and Cat arrived with Josh and Mitch.

They hugged Mab and said, 'That was the best time we have ever had!' Mab said, 'Well, I am sure there will be many more visits. Josh and Mitch may even want to visit you at the Guild if Master Kanaka agrees.'

Kanaka said, 'Yes, of course. Josh, Mitch, you would be most welcome, provided your parents are happy.'

Josh and Mitch thanked Kanaka, kissed Charly and Cat and said, 'Hopefully, we will see you soon.' Mab nodded to Kanaka, and they both stood up.

Mab kissed Joe on the cheek and said, 'Hopefully, I will get the chance to visit you again soon.'

Joe stood nervously at the door as the group walked outside. There was a loud scream and a dull thump.

Joe said, 'What was that!'

Kanaka said, 'It sounded just like someone falling off a nearby building?'

Mab led the group across the road and into the darkness, where they vanished from sight. Joe closed the doors, locked up for the night and dreamed of Mab winning her next cage fight.

Mab and Kanaka appeared in Kanaka's office, and Charly and Cat found themselves in the suite.

Kanaka poured two single malts and said, 'I guess Alexei is now the only loose end. But, even if you had killed him, I suspect you would continue to have assassins pursuing you in relation to the narcotics businesses.

Mab replied, 'Yes, I agree. However, Alexei suffered a serious brain haemorrhage last night, at around the same time the sniper fell from the roof of the Haskins building.'

Kanaka smiled grimly and said, 'When you say it like that, it sounds suspicious. The sniper is most definitely dead, but what of Alexei?'

Mab replied, 'Completely paralysed, he can't move or speak, but he is alive, and for that, he should be grateful.'

Kanaka said, 'Just so, Mabdelore.'

Chapter Twenty-Seven: The Ascension

Mab left Kanaka's office in the early hours of the morning. She chose to walk down the narrow spiral stairway; she felt the coolness radiating from the ancient rune-covered stone walls and thought back to when she first climbed this stairway with her Mum and Dad. Suddenly, she was back there looking down on herself and her parents, they were following Mona walking up the stairs. She saw herself look sideways at the walls and then upwards directly at her, clearly feeling uncomfortable. Mab's thoughts turned to her parents, Walim and Sopa and she went there, to her parent's home. The house was dark. Walim and Sopa were in bed and sleeping. Mab went to her room, lay on the bed, closed her eyes and entered a meditative state which lasted several hours. She then wound time back, first seeing herself as a child walking to school through Bluebell Wood, then Walim and Sopa signing her adoption forms, and then she saw Uriel wrapping her in a silk cloak, laying her in the warmest part of the church and instructing the priest. Mab went further back, and she was no longer an infant but a young woman standing in a group. Her hair was jet black, like polished obsidian. She wore a bright red cloak and an ornately decorated silver helm. Onimaru was sheathed at her right side, and a whip of light hung from her left hip. Her feet were bare.

The young woman looked at the others in the room and said, 'Leave me!' Mab started to feel uncomfortable, but the young woman turned, looked directly at her and said, 'There is a feeling of nausea when you meet yourself in the space-time continuum. It is a contradiction, an anomaly in the arrow of time which we can only sustain for a limited period.'

Mab said, 'You are me?'

The woman said, 'We are Bellona. I see that you have only just awoken. We, Gods, must go into the light and be reborn periodically. In two or three millennia, I will go back into the light and be reborn as you, Mabdelore Winter.'

Mab smiled and said, 'You are beautiful.'

Bellona laughed and replied, 'We are beautiful!'

Mab said, 'What of our family?'

Bellona said, 'There is no family; only Bellona and Minerva are of the Light. Those not of the Light fabricate complex stories to help explain our existence. The only other being of the Light was the Prophet, and he was created on Earth for a particular purpose which only he could fulfil.'

Mab replied, 'And the Angels?'

Bellona said, 'They serve the Light. Mabdelore, you must go. I am beginning to feel the effects of our proximity.'

Mab said, 'I will leave you now. Thank you, Bellona.' Mab returned to her own time and, withdrew back to her bedroom in Blant and fell into a deep sleep.

Mab woke when Sopa kissed her cheek. Sopa was sitting by her bedside. Mab said, 'That was the best sleep I have had for months!'

Sopa said, 'You must have arrived very late! It's lovely to see you, Mab. How about breakfast?'

Mab replied, 'Yes, please. I'll have a quick wash and see you downstairs in a few minutes!' Mab changed her appearance to be more in keeping with the locals. She wore a pair of brown riding trousers, polished black boots and a white silk blouse. She also changed her hair back to shoulder length and jet black in colour. As she came down the stairs, she spotted Walim and ran to embrace him.

Walim hugged Mab and said, 'We've missed you so much. It's great to see you again, and you are all grown-up!' Mab spent the whole day with Sopa and Walim, helping with chores around the farm. They sat down together for dinner late in the evening. Walim said, 'I guess you have been very busy with your role at the Guild.'

Mab replied, 'Yes, Dad, I have been very busy with that and other things.'

Sopa said, 'How is Izzy?'

Mab, with tears in her eyes, said, 'Izzy is dead, killed by an evil creature. I didn't get you involved as there was great danger. She is buried beside her parents at our home in Cetha.'

Walim said, 'You should have told us, Mab, we could have helped.'

Mab replied, 'No, Dad. You don't understand. The Guild has been fighting evil on several fronts. It is only now that we have been able to return to our work at the Guild. Izzy was killed by a creature from the Abyss because of me, and I should have been with her.'

Sopa said, 'It must have been terrible for you. Did the authorities manage to catch the creature?'

Mab replied, 'No, I killed it. But that is why you could not be involved; you would have become targets just like Izzy.'

Walim said, 'Yes, Mab, I understand.'

Mab entered their minds and said, 'I wanted to spend today with you because I will be going away for some time, I don't know how long. I'll try to visit when I can, but if you need me, if there is any trouble or problems, I want you to call me. Just shout out my name in your minds, and I will come to you.'

Walim looked at Sopa and said, 'That was the strangest thing!'

Mab said, 'I know who and what I am now. My real name is Bellona. When I was born, the Archangel Uriel was appointed to watch over and protect me. Uriel took me to the local church and instructed the Priests to have you adopt me. To me, you are my real Mum and Dad, my only Mum and Dad. This is my sister Minerva.' There was a flash of intense bright light, and Minerva appeared. She was dressed in a white silk robe with a red sash. Her skin was alabaster white and her hair lustrous black platted around her forehead and hung in a thick pigtail down her back. Her feet were bare, but she did not allow them to touch the floor. Sopa and Walim stood up and bowed to Minerva, unsure what to do or say. Mab then stood up, and as she did so, her appearance changed. Her hair was platted in a similar manner to Minerva's, and she wore a white silk robe. Mab hung in the air beside her sister. The likeness was striking, particularly the skin colour and the black orb eyes.

Sopa said, 'Yes, you are sisters, and you look beautiful together!'

Minerva smiled at Sopa who gasped as a feeling of warmth and well-being flooded through her body. Minerva turned to Mab and said, 'Sister, it is time; come with me.'

The two Goddesses vanished. Sopa turned to Walim, her eyes still wide and said, 'What does it mean?'

Walim replied, 'It means our daughter is a Goddess!'

Mab and Minerva appeared in the centre of a huge circular temple that had been sculpted rather than constructed. The floor and ceiling were of obsidian, and the seven columns were of white marble. The rocks flowed together at their interfaces as if they had been melded together with a great heat. The swirling effect of the black and white was beautiful and mesmerising. In the centre of the floor, seven seats, back to back, had been sculpted from white marble. The obsidian and the marble again flowed into each other at the interfaces, seemingly in a constant battle for dominance. Minerva pointed to one of the two widest columns, which were diametrically opposite each other. Mab saw her likeness sculpted into the stone. As she looked the figure of marble moved her head and smiled at her. She then looked at the other and saw Minerva smiling down at her.

Mab said, 'Who are the others?'

Minerva replied, 'The old Gods. Zeus, Hera, Aphrodite, Apollo and Ares. Only Minerva and Bellona remain, but now that you are reborn, we will suffice.'

Mab said, 'Suffice for what?'

Minerva replied, 'Sister, that is why you are here, to remember. Now sit, and we will begin.'

Mab took her seat and looked up at her image in the marble column. Minerva did the same and tilted her head back to touch Mab's. Mab realised that the seven seats had been sculpted for that very purpose. If all seven Gods were present, their heads would be in close proximity.

Minerva said, 'You must relax and open your mind. A huge volume of information and knowledge will be passed to you. Do not fight against it, and do not try to process or understand it during the transfer. The process is fast, but when complete, you will need to rest here for several hours. I will remain with you. Are you ready?'

Mab relaxed, brought her mind into a meditative state and said, 'Yes, I am ready.' Mab gasped at the volume of information that was being transferred, but she remained relaxed and allowed it to flow into her mind. She lost track of time and deliberately moved into a deep meditative state, aware and acknowledging the huge volume of information but not allowing it to distract her.

Minerva entered her mind and said, 'Sister, it is time to open your eyes.'

Mab woke and found Minerva gently stroking her hair.

Minerva said, 'It may take some time for you to assimilate the knowledge transfer. We can rest here for as long as you need.'

Mab smiled, wrapped her arms around Minerva and levitated upwards, pulling Minerva with her. Minerva laughed and leaned forward, kissing Mab passionately. Their arms and legs intertwined, and as they pulled each other tightly together, they were cocooned in an intense silver light.

Minerva whispered, 'What do you remember?'

Mab replied, 'Sister, I remember everything.'

Book Three

The Light and the Dark

Chapter Twenty-Eight: The Abyss

The consciousness that was Erebus glided through the gloom of the Abyss as a stream of space debris. This was his domain, it was vast, unfathomable, greater by countless orders of magnitude than that occupied by the light. Erebus existed long before the presence of the light; it was a primordial being and had no memory of its creation, only that it was and always will be. It was a master of the void, slaying anyone or anything that stood in its path. Its only allies were four clan leaders. In fact, Erebus and the clan leaders were entirely different in nature. Baydan led the most populous clan, who took the shape of large black scorpion-like creatures whereas clan Sladrin took the form of giant black snakes with cruel yellow eyes and carious fangs. Clans Dakigo and Humbra were bird-like in appearance, with hooked beaks, heavily scaled skin, and talons that could tear through the hardest of rock. The four clan leaders could take any desired shape or move through the void in spirit form; they feared no one but Erebus.

Erebus knew that the rate of change in the expansion of the light was slowing markedly. The light was thinning, becoming more diffuse. It would eventually be swallowed by the void and become nothing more than isolated remnants of its former self. But long before that, the clans would reclaim much of the space occupied by the light and be able to break through into new worlds. This time was approaching. The residents of the Abyss could sense the weakening, and soon, they would sate their hunger for the worlds of the light.

Erebus, incredulous at the arrogance of the light, said, 'Do they think they can invade our demesnes without incident? I, Erebus, born of the void, will no longer tolerate this outrage.'

Baydan responded, 'Erebus, we have allowed this to progress too far. We must act!'

Erebus replied, 'The time to act is indeed upon us. The five need to assemble.'

Baydan replied, 'Lord Erebus, come to us now.' Erebus brought its consciousness together, vanished and appeared beside the four leaders. Erebus took its preferred human form and stood like a giant amongst them.

It turned to the leaders and said, 'The light has now expanded to the point where it is thin enough for us to pass through, but without suitable hosts, we will be unable to remain.'

Sladrin hissed, 'Have I not said that the children of Chaos stand ready to assist us?'

Erebus stared at Sladrin and said, 'Have I not told you that these lords are not children of Chaos! I am the only child of Chaos in existence; do not speak of them in my presence!' Sladrin bowed his elongated head and slithered backward.

Humbra's soothing voice whispered, 'Erebus, our brother Sladrin meant no offense. These so-called children of the One are charlatans, but we may be able to make use of them. When they are no longer useful, perhaps you will allow me to feed on their corpses?'

Erebus smiled at Humbra, who moaned in pleasure, and said, 'Hum, it is good to hear your beautiful voice again.'

It then looked at Sladrin and said, 'Apologies, brother, let us conclude our discussions here before deciding on our next steps.' Sladrin bowed its head in acknowledgement.

Dakigo said, 'Erebus, we all feel the weakening and thinning of the light. It is slowing but nevertheless is still capturing more of our realm. What do you know of the gods of the light?'

Baydan laughed and said, 'I think you mean the god of the light? That would be Minerva. She is powerful, but the lords keep her under control.'

Erebus replied, 'Do not underestimate Minerva. She is extraordinarily powerful. I admit that I do not understand why she tolerates the lords, but do not make the mistake of thinking she is weak, that would be a grave error. Also, there is another.'

Baydan said, 'Another? I see Minerva, even now, but there is no other.'

Dakigo added, 'Yes, I also see and feel the presence of Minerva, she shines like a beacon, there is no other like her.'

Humbra laughed and replied, 'Perhaps you have taken a liking to her? Would you like to meet her face to face?' Dakigo smiled but said nothing.

Erebus said, 'You are both wrong; there is another. You cannot detect her because she conceals her presence, even from me.'

There was silence for several minutes, then Baydan said, 'I have reached out but cannot detect her. Erebus, how do you know this goddess exists if she cannot be detected?'

Erebus smiled and said, 'I didn't say I couldn't detect her. I said she conceals her presence. I know she exists because the space in which she exists is imperceptibly different from that around her. I surmise she favours the human female form because of the dimensions of that difference in space. If she is truly female, and I believe that she is, there is only one credible candidate, Minerva's sister, also a daughter of Juno.'

Baydan replied, 'Minerva has a sister?'

Erebus said, 'Yes, her name was Bellona. She was said to be the firstborn, but following the light war, she remained in obscurity. It was said she preferred the company of humans and animals to that of the gods.'

Humbra asked, 'This Bellona, was she present at the time of the light war?'

Erebus said, 'The war was fought across several planes and raged for millennia; many were slain. I, Erebus, the only true descendent of Chaos, survived the catastrophe. The gods of the light were also decimated. Some survived but were fatally injured, mentally and physically.

Minerva was thought to be the only god to have survived intact, and she was the most beautiful of all the gods of the light. Her sister, Bellona, became known as the lost god. Some said she was dead, others that she had become human, but she faded from our knowledge.'

Dakigo replied, 'Erebus, why then has this Bellona returned to her sister's side?'

Erebus said, 'Dakigo, that is indeed the most important question. I do not know the answer, but I know that she was not summoned by Minerva.'

Baydan replied, 'So, she has come of her own volition because she senses that the light is weakening?'

Erebus said, 'Yes, that is the most probable explanation.'

Dakigo replied, 'We have managed to keep Minerva at bay, surely this Bellona is no real threat to us and our plans?'

Erebus said, 'She is an unknown, and therefore we must consider her a threat. Hum asked about the light war. Yes, Bellona was there but I did not meet or see her in battle. However, a full battalion of my Alpha-Warriors assailed two of the now human planes, which were protected by Bellona. None of my clan returned from that conflict.'

Humbra replied, 'How were the soldiers of the light arrayed? They must have had superior numbers to defeat a full battalion of your alphas?'

Erebus replied, 'No, you misunderstand. There were no soldiers of the light, only Bellona. All fell before her.' There was a stunned silence.

Minerva sat in her usual seat at one end of an enormous stone meeting table, close to the summit of Raqus Mons on the planet Raqian in the Raamon system. The table had been formed by cutting away the solid rock of the mountain. It was created by master craftsmen of the long-forgotten old gods. Argaton was of Raqian, this was his home planet, and as a child he had climbed to the summit of Raqus Mons on several occasions. He discovered the table on the second ascent, and when he grew stronger, he made this his seat of power. Argaton was the most powerful of the lords of chaos and sat at the head of the table directly opposite Minerva with Seleran, Tabbar and Gorgat on his left and Mendan, Pelian and Castaran on his right. The lords were dressed in sky-blue robes of the finest silk and black shoes of soft leather. Minerva wore a white linen robe and open-toed sandals. Her hair was platted with white flowers. The lords created a psychic shield around the meeting area to provide a comfortable, sheltered environment.

Argaton opened the meeting by saying, 'Lords, we are assembled. There is much to discuss, but I wish to focus on three key issues. The first being the recent seemingly growing activity in the Abyss, the second being the crisis reported in the Vegin system and the third the reported activity in two of the human planes.' Argaton looked at Minerva and said, 'What do you know of the activity in the Abyss?'

Minerva replied, 'The dark gods are gathered together even now. They are watching and waiting. The skin between the light and the dark is now stretched to breaking point. Soon, they will break through; their hordes will first feast on the outer systems and move slowly inwards as the light fades. All will be consumed, and only we stand in their path.'

Tabbar replied, 'I have in the past contacted the god Sladrin. The dark gods are just like us, but they feel trapped by the light. I am sure they will be amenable to discussion for our mutual benefit.'

Argaton looked at Minerva, who replied, 'Tabbar, you are a fool. The Gods of the Abyss are nothing like us. Sladrin is pure evil. If you are lucky, it will rip you apart and feed you to its spawn. If you are unlucky, your death will be slow and agonising.'

Tabbar spat, 'It is you who are the fool!' as he leaped over the table and slapped Minerva across the face. Minerva did not flinch but simply stared at Argaton.

Argaton said, 'Tabbar, please return to your seat and apologise to the Goddess.'

Tabbar replied, 'Apologise, no, it is she who will apologise to me!' There was a blinding flash of light, and the lords shielded their eyes. A young woman appeared in the centre of the table. She wore tight-fitting sports leggings, a white blouse and stout brown riding boots. A long sword hung across her back, and her face was beaded with sweat.

Mab looked at Minerva and said, 'Apologies for my appearance. I was in sword practice, and I felt someone strike you.'

Minerva replied, 'It was nothing, sister, an unfortunate choice of words resulting in a minor physical assault. I am unharmed.'

Argaton said, 'Minerva perhaps you could introduce us to your friend who has arrived uninvited to our meeting?' Minerva said nothing. Mab turned, looked directly at Argaton and frowned. Argaton suddenly felt very weak. A trickle of blood escaped from his nose.

Mab said, 'Who struck my sister?'

Argaton, struggling to breathe, gasped, 'I will tell you nothing.' He then let out an agonising scream, as Mab's mind probe seared through his brain, and lapsed into unconsciousness.

Mab turned to Tabbar and said, 'You struck my sister. Why are you still alive?'

Tabbar said nothing but looked nervously towards

Minerva who said, 'Sister, I have a child, but I cannot be with him at all times.'

Mab reached out with her witch senses and said, 'Yes, I see him now. He is at play in one of my protected worlds.'

Minerva replied, 'Bellona, I hoped he would be safe there, but the lords also know where he is.'

Argaton, who had regained consciousness, said, 'That is correct, and you will continue to follow our instructions if you wish to see him grow and thrive.'

Onimaru flashed into Mab's hand as she spun around and sliced the head off Argaton. She then leapt into the air and brought Onimaru down on Tabbar's head, splitting him from head to crotch and destroying the ancient rock-formed seat, which exploded as the sentient blade ripped through it. The remaining lords leapt to their feet and rained psychic blasts of power on Mab, but nothing had any effect. Gorgat leapt onto the table, but Mab hit him with a backhanded slap that sent him tumbling onto the hard rock. Others tried to escape but found they were trapped within a sphere of power that enveloped the top of the mountain. Mab stamped her foot on the table and cried, 'Enough!' The massive rock table shattered, and the mountain itself seemed to lunge away from the force of the blow. Minerva watched and smiled.

The remaining lords stood together, shaking with fear and exhaustion.

Mab said, 'Sister, I can't imagine these petty lords being a threat to anyone. But if you feel they are a threat to your child, then I would be happy to slay them now.'

Minerva floated up to join Mab, kissed her and said, 'I had forgotten how effective your simple and direct ways could be.'

Minerva looked at the lords and said, 'Are you still a threat to my child? Would you like to die here in this place?'

Mendan said, 'No Goddess, I wish to support you in the good works that you do. Argaton was always our leader, and it was he who discovered the existence and location of your child and used that knowledge against you.'

Gorgat said, 'Goddess, I want you to know that I would never harm a child. I agree with my brother Mendan.' Castaran and Seleran nodded their agreement.

Pelian said, 'Never have I seen such raw power. Goddess Bellona, will you be joining us here?'

Pelian paused, hung her head, and then added, 'We have fallen into despair. We fight amongst ourselves.'

Mab could see that Pelian was pleading for help, the tears that had been building in her eyes had now broken free and were streaming down her face. The other lords hung their heads and remained silent. Mab looked at Pelian and smiled. Pelian looked up and gasped as a feeling of warmth and goodness suffused her body. Mab thought how beautiful Pelian looked at that moment. Her skin was paler than pale, her hair snow white, and her eyes sapphire blue. Curiously, her ears were pointed, which seemed to make her even more attractive.

Mab replied, 'I have come for a purpose that will be revealed in good time. I will not leave until my mission is completed. Yes, you are in despair and disarray, but this is not your doing. You are being watched and manipulated by those who seek to claim our worlds for their own. The proximity of these beings affects your thoughts and your consciousness; they sow the seeds of despair and hopelessness amongst you. Your leader, Argaton, and your fellow lord Tabbar were in collusion with them, against the will of the light.'

Pelian said, 'Who is this enemy? How do we combat them?'

Mab replied, 'You know who they are. But be calm. They cannot penetrate the shield I placed around this peak. And yet, I feel their malign presence everywhere in this place.'

Minerva said, 'Please, let us leave here together. We will go to my home and discuss matters further. Sister, are you able to carry the lords?'

Mab nodded, and Minerva vanished.

Mab looked at the lords and said, 'Come closer. It is a long journey.'

The lords gathered around Mab, and the group vanished.

Chapter Twenty-Nine: Palace of the Gods

Minerva said, 'This was the home of the old gods, but it now belongs to Bellona and I; we are the last of the old gods. The palace is situated at the top of Mount Olympus on a planet known as Earth, and we are in the third millennium after the birth of the Prophet. It is visible and accessible only by gods of the light and their guests.'

Castaran said, 'It is truly magnificent. How many rooms does it have?'

Minerva replied, 'The Palace is entirely self-sufficient; the number of rooms is always greater than that required.' The Palace was pristine. The walls and floors were made from different types and colours of polished stone. Minerva led them to a cloistered area with many columns. The centre of the area revealed an enormous column-free space with a table of thick ancient oak and chairs of stone, which were cushioned on the seat and the back with padded red velvet. As they walked through the cloisters, the columns swirled with every colour imaginable, and birds swooped around the columns, their songs seemingly in harmony with the changes in colour.

When they reached the table, Minerva gestured with her hand and said, 'Food and drink.' The table was instantly covered with platters of fruits, cold meats, cooked vegetables, and various types of bread.

Mab looked at Minerva who smiled and said, 'Wine?' several flagons of wine appeared on the table together with golden goblets.

Mab said, 'I'm impressed.'

Minerva said to the lords, 'My sister has a fondness for good wine.'

Mab replied, 'I'll let you know if it's good wine in a few moments!'

Minerva said to all, 'Please, be seated, eat and drink.'

The group gathered around one end of the huge table. Minerva sat at the head with Mab on her right. Mab poured herself a generous measure of white wine and took two large gulps. The lords went into fits of laughter. Mab looked around, somewhat surprised.

Minerva said, 'Sister, you drink wine as if you had just returned from the battlefield and narrowly escaped death!'

Mab laughed and said, 'In fairness, that is usually the case. I am sure the Lords will forgive my uncouth manners. However, I have to say that this wine is extraordinarily fine; I must take some home with me.'

Minerva said, 'The food and wine on this table are that of the old gods. If removed from this environment, it perishes.'

Mab, pouring herself another goblet of wine, replied, 'Well, in that case, I must drink my fill here!'

The lords raised their glasses.

Pelian said, 'I will drink my wine like the Goddess' She took two large gulps from her goblet and immediately went into a fit of violent coughing. The rest of the lords laughed loudly.

Seleran said, 'Pelian, that's what happens when you try to be a goddess!' Pelian's face went bright red.

Mab said, 'Pelian, you just need some practice. You and I will go out together and I will teach you how to be as uncouth as I when drinking fine wine!'

Pelian looked up at Mab and said, 'You would be my teacher?'

Minerva said, 'Sister, I think you meant to counsel Pelian only in the drinking of wine!'

There was an awkward silence around the table. Mab stared at Pelian for a few moments and said, 'No, sister, that is not what I meant. Pelian will be my student.'

Mab's stare then became a warm smile. Pelian stood up and, with a serious expression on her face, replied, 'It is a great honour, Goddess; I will not disappoint you.'

Minerva, changing the subject, said, 'We need to discuss what happened earlier this evening. Perhaps the lords could tell us what they know of the enemy?'

There was silence. Mab looked at Gorgat and said, 'Lord Gorgat, you may speak freely. This place is safe and secure.'

Gorgat relaxed back in his chair and said, 'Argaton and Tabbar were in contact with those who inhabit the Abyss. I confess that I was close to Tabbar. He told me that the Gods of the Abyss would soon cross over; the Raamon system, and Raqian in particular, was the intended location. My understanding is that location is optimal, but I do not understand the reasoning.'

Mendan said, 'Tabbar asked me on several occasions to help him find human hosts to assist the Gods of the Abyss in entering our world.'

Minerva said, 'The gods of the Abyss have crossed over into our plane?'

Mendan replied, 'Yes, Goddess, with the aid of human hosts.'

Minerva looked at Mab.

Mab shrugged and said, 'Seleran, Castaran, what do you know of this?'

Castaran replied, 'I only know what I was told by Argaton and Tabbar, the gods of the Abyss would soon breakthrough into our world. I know nothing of the use of human hosts.'

Seleran said, 'I also know nothing of this practice. But, as Pelian explained, we have been living in despair and fear knowing that the creatures of the Abyss would soon cross over.'

Mab said, 'On my home world we encountered problems with daemons of the Abyss crossing over. It was accomplished by the use of witches and priests summoning the daemon and then bringing the human host almost to the point of death by means of a herbal poison.'

Mendan replied, 'Goddess, we were told to administer to the hosts a potion which would allow the gods to occupy them. However, the hosts only lived for a short period, and when they perished, the gods returned to the darkness.'

Minerva said, 'How many humans have you killed by this means?'

Mendan replied, 'I would estimate around twenty. Please understand, Argaton told us that we had no choice in these matters. He said the gods of the Abyss were powerful beyond comprehension, and their instructions must be obeyed.'

Mab said, 'Please explain exactly how the possessions were accomplished.'

Mendan replied, 'We took the human hosts to a supposedly sacred cave deep in Raqus Mons. We administered the potion, placed the bodies on a slab of rock and returned to the surface. Argaton and Tabbar would wait at the entrance to the cave and escort the hosts bearing the gods of the Abyss to our palace. They were difficult to look upon. The presence of evil was palpable and the humans would usually perish within a few hours. We had to ensure that they had the very best food and drink and also young men and women; their appetite for all things was insatiable.'

Mab looked at Minerva and said, 'The creatures are able to cross without the aid of a witch or priest. The cave must lead to a location where the barrier between the Abyss and our worlds is particularly weak. We could easily close the cave, but I suspect there are other such locations.'

Minerva nodded and said, 'Mendan, what else do you know of these gods of the Abyss?' Mendan replied, 'Goddess, I know very little of them. Argaton mentioned Sladrin, but I don't know if that is one of them or perhaps a daemon. They were very careful not to reveal their names and would not be drawn on the subject.'

Mab said, 'Names are important. They are part of a daemon's very being and can be used as part of a conjuring, a binding or an exorcism. Daemons can be expelled by using their name against them, but I fear it will not be so easy with these gods.'

Minerva said, 'Bellona, they are five in number. Do you see them?'

Mab paused and said, 'Yes, I was aware of them the moment I arrived on Raqus Mons. That is why I placed a shield around the summit. They know I am here, but they cannot see me. Argaton's mind revealed the names Sladrin, Baydan, Dakigo, Humbra and Erebus. Argaton and Tabbar were in collusion with Sladrin, but Erebus is their leader.'

Minerva said, 'Erebus was in the light war. We thought all the primary dark powers had been slain, but Erebus survived.'

Castaran said, 'Perhaps it is not the original Erebus but another who has taken his name? The original Erebus was an ancient being who existed for eons before the arrival of the light. We lords pretend to be the children of Chaos, but Erebus really was descended from the One. At least, that is my understanding.'

Mab looked at Minerva and said, 'I will summon a friend of mine who has spent some time in the Abyss. He may be able to advise?'

Minerva nodded in agreement.

Mab said, 'Lucifer, come to me.' A few moments later, Lucifer manifested in the room. He was dressed in his usual skin-tight black top and trousers and black boots. His long black hair hung down over his shoulders and framed his face which was alabaster white.

Lucifer knelt and said, 'Goddess, how can I be of service?'

Mab smiled, kissed him on both cheeks and said, 'It is good to see you, Lucifer.'

Mab said, 'This is Lucifer Morningstar. He has spent a long time in the Abyss and is now an Archangel of the light. Lucifer, these are known as the lords of Chaos.'

Lucifer simply stared and said nothing.

Mab gestured and said, 'This is my sister, Minerva.' Lucifer walked towards her, bowed deeply and said, 'It is a very great honour to meet you, Goddess.'

Minerva replied, 'I have heard much about you, Lucifer. You are most welcome in our home. Please sit and enjoy the food and wine.'

Lucifer said, 'Thank you, Goddess, but I have already eaten. This is wonderful, and it reminds me of my own palace.'

Mab laughed and said, 'I can't imagine why.'

Lucifer smiled but said nothing.

Mab said, 'The five gods of the Abyss, what do you know of them?'

Lucifer replied, 'Goddess, I know they exist, but I have only encountered one of them. Mahaziel brought two of Sladrin's clan to my palace, and they took the form of great snakes. They wanted our assistance in the possession of humans and other creatures to enable them to leave the Abyss.'

Mab replied, 'What did you do?'

Lucifer replied, 'There was first a discussion, then a disagreement followed by threats. The two snakes were slain, but not without difficulty. Sometime later, Sladrin came. It moved through the palace unseen by our guards. I became aware of its presence only a few moments before it appeared in my room. It said it would slay me and all my followers if we failed to cooperate with them.'

Mab said, 'And?'

Lucifer said, 'I told it that if it didn't leave, I would have it skinned and feed its body to the hounds.'

Mab said, 'And?' Lucifer said, 'It attacked me.'

Mab said, 'Lucifer, can you please tell me the whole story without these continual pauses!'

Lucifer smiled. Minerva said, 'Is he always like this, so adorable?'

Mab replied, 'Yes, I'm afraid so.'

Lucifer, still smiling, bowed to Minerva, looked at Mab and said, 'Yes, of course, Goddess. I defended myself, but I could not defeat it. Sladrin is extraordinarily powerful. I summoned the Archdaemons, and together with the guards, we managed to drive it from the palace.'

Minerva said, 'We are trying to understand how powerful these creatures have become since the time of the light war. From what you say this Sladrin has prodigious psychic powers?'

Lucifer replied, 'Yes, most definitely.'

Minerva replied, 'What of Erebus?'

Lucifer replied, 'Erebus is their leader. That is all I know of it.'

Pelian said, 'Lord Lucifer, we are unable to enter the Abyss. Those who tried did not return. Argaton, our previous leader, told us that the Abyss would nullify our powers and that the environment was corrosive. Is this true?'

Lucifer looked at Mab, who said, 'Pelian is my new student. I will be her mentor and teacher.'

Lucifer looked back to Pelian, bowed and said, 'Pelian, you are honoured indeed. Your previous leader was correct; you would not survive for long in the Abyss. Many great warriors enter the Abyss of their own free will, usually to rescue friends or family members. As far as I am aware, only one has succeeded, the Goddess Bellona.' Lucifer's attention was suddenly elsewhere.

He turned to Mab and said, 'I must go immediately!'

Mab nodded, but as Lucifer left, he placed a single word in Mab's consciousness: 'Morgana.'

Mab looked at Minerva and said, 'I also must leave now, but I think we should meet with these gods of the Abyss. We cannot permit them to enter our realm; they are creatures of the void, and that is where they must remain.' Minerva nodded. Mab and Pelian vanished.

Minerva said, 'Lords, I will ask Bellona if Lucifer would be prepared to contact these Gods of the Abyss on our behalf. Remain careful and watchful, and report any relevant knowledge or findings to me immediately. This meeting is ended, you are dismissed.'

Mab and Pelian hung high in the air, hidden in mind-space.

Pelian said, 'Can they see us?'

Mab replied, 'Our bodies are shifted into mind-space; we cannot be seen although we may be detected. The woman in the black robe is Morgana, she is a powerful witch and a close friend of Lucifer. The creature that stands before them is a Balerak, it is an assassin from the Abyss.'

Pelian said, 'It must have been sent to kill the witch. Is that why Lord Lucifer left in such haste?'

Mab said, 'Yes, but something is amiss here. The Balerak is merely a host; it is Sladrin!'

Mab and Pelian floated slowly downwards and heard Lucifer saying, 'Morgana has already told you that she is no longer involved in trafficking humans for any purpose. If you require hosts, you must look elsewhere.' The Balerak said, 'The last time we met, I spared your life because I thought you could be useful. It seems I was wrong. If you cannot assist, I will slay you both. What is your decision?'

Morgana looked at Lucifer and said, 'You should not have come. Go now. I will discuss these matters further with Sladrin.'

The Balerak laughed and said, 'So touching, but I think not. If you refuse, you will both die here in agony.'

There was a flash of intense bright light, which extended to create a cut in space. Mab stepped through. She wore a white robe with a red sash, her sword was hitched high across her back, and a whip of light hung on her left side.

Lucifer and Morgana bowed, stepped back, and bent the knee.

Mab said, 'Lucifer, Morgana, please rise.'

The Balerak was about to talk when Mab turned her black orb eyes on it. It staggered backwards.

Mab said, 'I am Bellona. What are you doing here, Sladrin?'

Sladrin said, 'I came here to seek assistance.' Mab stared long and hard at Sladrin. The Balerak's face twisted in pain and exertion under her gaze.

She then said, 'You do not have my permission to be here. This realm is under my protection.'

The Balerak was in agony, and its angular head was visibly swelling and pulsing. It released a shower of poisoned darts, all of which dropped to the ground as they approached Mab. A whip of light lashed outwards, wrapped around the Baleraks neck and tightened.

Mab said, 'This creature has suffered enough. Now Sladrin, meet my friend Onimaru. The sword screamed as it swept from the scabbard; Mab pulled on the whip, and the Balerak was pulled off its feet and lunged toward her. Sladrin fled from the body as Onimaru drove through the creature's chest. Mab then struck the Balerak with the back of her hand; the creature was killed instantly and slowly slid from the sword to the ground. As Mab turned to look at Morgana, Pelian appeared by her side.

Mab said, 'Morgana, please explain why you were in conference with a creature from the Abyss. Is there no end to your foolishness?'

Morgana looked at Lucifer, who said nothing. She then replied, 'Yes, Goddess, it was foolish to meet with Sladrin, but to refuse would have been even more foolish.'

Mab paused and then replied, 'Yes, I see.'

Pelian said, 'Sladrin wanted human hosts, is that correct?'

Lucifer looked at Morgana and said, 'This is Pelian, one of the so-called 'Lords of Chaos,' she is being mentored by the Goddess.'

Morgana said, 'Pelian, what a beautiful name. Yes, you are correct. Sladrin wanted me to find human hosts. It must be important as it used a Balerak to enter our realm. They are expensive and difficult to source.'

Mab said, 'Lucifer, I think we should visit these Gods of the Abyss. What do you think?'

Lucifer replied, 'I would prefer to visit Fat Joe's.'

Mab burst into a fit of laughter. When she recovered enough to speak, she said, 'Morgana, what have you done to the Lord of Darkness!'

Morgana, also laughing, replied, 'The Abyss is the last place he would wish to visit, and we often go to Fat Joes for a drink.'

Mab said, 'I could do with another drink. Let's go there now.'

The group vanished and appeared on the roof of the Haskins building, adjacent to Fat Joe's Bar and Restaurant.

Mab said, 'Lucifer, you look fine, but we girls need to change our clothes.'

A few seconds later, Morgana, Pelian and Mab were dressed in short black dresses, polished shoes and warm overcoats. They moved to a shadowed lane at street level and walked across to Fat Joes.

Morgana led the group and was talking to a waiter, trying to arrange a table, when Joe walked into the bar area. When he saw Mab, he ran to her, hugged her tightly, kissed her on the cheek and said, 'Mab, where have you been? It's been so long since you were here last. Are you well?'

Mab laughed and said, 'Joe, it's great to be here, and yes, I am well. I think you know Morgana and her partner, Lucifer. This young lady here is Pelian, and I am mentoring her in warrior skills.'

Joe called a waiter over and said, 'These are my friends. Tonight, they can have anything they want, no charge.'

Morgana ordered cocktails for her and Lucifer and white wine for Mab and Pelian. Mab said to Morgana, 'The five gods of the Abyss, what do you know of them?'

Morgana replied, 'I only know of Sladrin. However, I have heard of Erebus, who is said to be a direct descendent of Chaos and is the most senior of the creatures. In previous times Sladrin has approached me regarding human hosts. However, more recently, it has used Argaton and Tabbar, so I'm not sure why it now wants my help.'

Pelian said, 'That's easy. The Goddess killed Argaton and Tabbar soon after meeting them.'

She then added in a hushed tone, 'They were disrespectful to her sister.' Lucifer almost laughed but then looked at Morgana and smiled. Morgana looked at Mab and said, 'Sister?'

Mab replied, 'Minerva.'

Morgana was lost in thought but then said, 'Are there others?'

Mab replied, 'No, my sister and I are the only survivors of the light war.'

Morgana said, 'Erebus must have participated in the light war?'

Mab said, 'Yes, but I did not meet it in battle. I did, however, slay many of its clans, which I am sure it will remember. I killed Argaton and Tabbar because they were in collusion with Sladrin. They also threatened to kill Minerva's child if she didn't follow their instructions. Of course, they were being manipulated by Sladrin.'

Joe arrived at the table and said, 'Mab, there is a fight on tonight. Will you be participating?'

Mab replied, 'No, not tonight. Perhaps at some point in the future, I will ask my student Pelian to enter, but she is not yet ready.'

Joe looked at Lucifer and said, 'What about you, sir? You have the warrior look about you; would you be willing to participate?'

Lucifer replied, 'No, I also am not yet ready.' Mab and Morgana went into fits of laughter.

Mab said, 'Joe, thanks, but we will watch on this occasion.'

Joe called a waiter and said, 'More drinks here.'

When Joe left, Lucifer said, 'Goddess, it may be that the gods of the Abyss have detected your presence and want to meet with you but cannot now find suitable hosts. Perhaps we should go there, but the gods will be much more powerful when in their own domain.'

Mab replied, 'Yes, that is true, but I think it is the only way. The alternative is to do nothing and wait for them to break through and lay waste to our worlds. I am not sure we are ready for another light war. Anyway, let's go downstairs and watch some fighting.'

The group sat in their usual elevated position at the rear of the room. The fighters were already limbering up in the cage, and the betting desk was open.

Pelian said, 'What is happening here?'

Morgana replied, 'This is known as a cage fight. Cage fights are illegal here, but the rewards can be life-changing, as can the injuries! Strictly speaking, no weapons are allowed, but competitors have been known to secrete them in their clothing. Injuries and deaths are common. The audience bet on who they expect to win; very large sums of currency are involved.'

Pelian whispered to Morgana, 'Are human females allowed to participate?'

Morgana said, 'I guess so, although the only female I have seen in the cage was the Goddess. She likes to practice the physical aspects of her warrior skills, and cage fighting is extremely physical.'

Joe said, 'Gents, Ladies, thank you for coming tonight; please remember betting closes very soon after the bell sounds. In the red corner, we have Johannes Keable, a current mixed martial arts champion and in the blue corner, Michael Burnet, ex-world kickboxing champion. The winner of tonight's fight will qualify for a quarter-final place in the all-comers Cage Fight Championship.'

Joe exited the cage, locked the steel mesh door, and sounded the bell. Morgana said, 'Goddess, who do you think will win?'

Mab replied, 'It's too close to call. Both fighters are of similar stature and their fighting styles seem very much alike. The guy in the red may have the edge, but it could go either way.'

The fighters circled each other, probing and testing their opponent's reactions. Burnet launched a flurry of high kicks that drove Keable back into the cage. Keable, with his back to the cage, dropped low and punched Burnet in the groin, but Burnet brought his knee up, rammed it into Keable's face and leapt away. Keable pushed himself upright; his nose was crushed, and his top lip had been punctured by broken teeth. He spat a mouthful of blood and tooth fragments onto the floor and slowly approached Burnet.

Burnet smiled and said, 'Just let me know when you've had enough.'

He then executed another series of high kicks at Keable, who backed off and once again found himself with his back to the cage. Burnet moved closer, launching body and head punches. Keable suddenly pushed off the cage, gripped him in a bearhug and spun him around against the cage. Keable released his grip slightly, brought his head back, and headbutted Burnet in the face. Burnet dropped to the floor, his features a pulp of blood, flesh and bone. Burnet groaned. Keable responded by grabbing his hair, twisting his head upwards and pounding his fist several times into the already ruined face. The blood-spattered both competitors and those seated close to the cage. Keable then kicked Burnet in the stomach and raised his arms in triumph.

Mab turned to Pelian, who was clearly appalled at what she was seeing, and said, 'These are fighters, not warriors. But there is a lesson here; do you know what it is?'

Pelian replied, 'Never fight anyone in a cage?'

Morgana and Lucifer burst into a fit of laughter.

Mab, also laughing, said, 'No, Pelian, that is not the lesson!' Morgana said, 'I'm beginning to smell the sweat and blood. Should we go back upstairs?'

The group made their way to the bar and ordered more drinks.

Pelian said, 'Goddess, what is the lesson I must understand?'

Mab replied, 'The two fighters were equally matched. Burnet was lucky; he delivered the first real blow with that knee to Keable's head, but after that, he was thinking of the next fight, of winning the championship. Keable did not give up. His mind was right there in the cage in the moment. That is how he won, but they were both sloppy fighters. You will be going to the warrior school at the Guild of Sorcerers to study under Master Kanaka. I know your psychic powers are already well-developed. I see that in you, but you need to learn how to fight and how to be a warrior.'

Pelian said, 'I had thought to surprise you with my psychic powers. I am not the strongest of the lords, but I am not the weakest. I had thought I would be studying under you?'

Mab replied, 'Yes, of course, you will be studying under me. I am the head of the warrior school. But Master Kanaka was, and is, my mentor. He will help to guide you in the ways of the warrior. You are by far the strongest of the lords, you just don't know it yet. That is why I chose to be your mentor and teacher.'

Pelian stared at Mab in astonishment and said, 'Thank you, it is a great honour.'

Lucifer said, 'Pelian, it is indeed a great honour, greater than you could possibly imagine.'

Pelian bowed and said, 'Thank you, Lord Lucifer.'

Morgana said, 'Goddess, we will take our leave now. Thank you once again for your help with Sladrin.'

Mab nodded. Lucifer said, 'Would you like me to contact Sladrin to arrange a meeting?'

Mab replied, 'I will discuss the matter with my sister. But my feeling is that you and I should meet with them.'

Morgana said, 'Goddess, it may make sense if I arrange the meeting in view of my previous involvement with them?' Mab stared thoughtfully at Morgana and then turned to

Lucifer and said, 'How would Michael and Gabriel be affected by the environment in the Abyss?'

Lucifer replied, 'For the purposes of a short meeting, they would be unaffected. However, if they were imprisoned for a prolonged period, they would eventually succumb.'

Mab replied, 'And yet you were unaffected?' Lucifer replied, 'I rejected the light and was cast down. Because of that, I adapted. However, Uriel could not and would not change. Those who serve the light cannot survive when it is removed from them unless they reject it utterly. I also would perish if I was imprisoned there again. I would choose that fate rather than to live without the light.'

Mab smiled and replied, 'Lucifer, I am sorry to bring back bad memories.'

Lucifer felt a wave of wellness, goodness, and joy flow through him.

He smiled at Mab and said, 'Thank you, Goddess.'

Pelian said, 'Goddess if you go to the Abyss, you too will be affected.'

Mab smiled at Pelian and replied, 'Does the light fear the dark? No, I am unaffected by the Abyss.'

Lucifer and Morgana knelt. Lucifer said, 'Goddess, we will await your instructions.' They both vanished.

Chapter Thirty: Warrior School

Masters Kanaka, Lamm and Luticia stood in the centre of the training room floor within the warrior school building, which was located on the Guild of Sorcerers campus. The warrior programme was funded jointly by the magic schools, with their Principals acting as the lead instructors. The school was founded by Kanaka, and it now boasted some sixty students with four of these being awarded warrior status and assisting with instruction of the novices. The subject matter included hand-to-hand combat, weapons of war, psychic enhancement, coercion, mind control and, integrity and morality. The younger students spent a mere ten percent of their time in warrior classes with the bulk of their studies being within the magic schools. The more senior students had already graduated from magic school and studied full-time within the warrior school.

The training room floor was divided into four quadrants, each supervised by an advanced student. Wooden swords were used for practice, these were made by skilled craftsmen to replicate the weight and balance of the various weapons in current usage. However, single-bladed swords were favoured by the warrior school. Kanaka screamed at one of the students to stop. He rushed over and took the sword from him. Kanaka held the sword in the ready position, horizontally above his head, and launched an attack on his opponent, driving her back with a flurry of vertical slices. Kanaka passed the sword back to the student and said, 'You need to concentrate on your opponent. Study her every movement, read her eyes, be ready, and when you attack, do it with all your strength, speed and conviction. These practice sessions are not a game! Your very life is at stake!'

The student bowed and said, 'Thank you, Master Kanaka. I will try harder.'

There was a sudden flash of bright light, and two figures appeared on the training room floor. There were gasps of astonishment, and all dropped to their knees, other than Master Kanaka, who bowed and opened his arms. Mab ran to embrace him. They hugged each other in silence.

Kanaka said, 'Mab, it has been a long time, too long.'

Mab replied, 'Yes, and we have much to discuss.'

Mab saw Lamm and Luticia and realised everyone was kneeling; she took Kanaka's hand and said, 'Please, everyone, rise.'

Mab then walked to Lamm and Luticia and embraced them.

Kanaka asked the students to relax and said, 'Master Winter has not been here for some time. But as you know, she has other responsibilities.'

There was muted laughter around the room.

Mab said, 'I know some of you, but for those of you I don't know, I am very pleased to meet you. I have come here to discuss urgent matters with the principals of the magic schools. This is Pelian. I am her mentor, and she will be studying here with you. I learned my sword skills from Master Kanaka, and I am keen to test myself against him once more. Unless, of course, he is unwilling to meet me in battle?' There was loud laughter and applause around the room.

Mab smiled at Kanaka and said, 'Well, Master, are you willing?'

Kanaka could barely contain his laughter but managed to say, 'Why yes, choose your weapon.'

Mab gestured with her right hand, and two wooden swords flew across the room, one to her and the other to Kanaka. Kanaka immediately took up the ready position. Mab held her sword horizontally above her head with one hand, her other hand open in front of her body. She then slowly circled Kanaka, who followed her only with his eyes. Mab suddenly ran at Kanaka, executing four vertical slices, which drove him back. On her last down stroke, Kanaka rushed forward, swiping his sword horizontally at full stretch. Mab leapt high into the air and spun over the wooden blade. As she hit the floor, she swept her sword across Kanaka's legs, but he was too fast. He did a backward flip and landed on his feet. Mab moved slowly towards him and attacked once again, but this time, Kanaka stood his ground. The swords smashed against each other, neither opponent giving any quarter. Mab suddenly threw her sword high into the air. Kanaka's down stroke came at blinding speed, but Mab was faster, she clapped her hands above her head and caught the blade. The sword snapped, and Mab kicked Kanaka in the chest, knocking him backwards. He caught her falling sword and resumed the ready position.

The students applauded wildly. Mab walked to Kanaka and embraced him.

Kanaka, still hugging Mab, laughed and said, 'I know you are all thinking that if these were real swords, my blade would not have snapped, but in this case, you would be wrong. I have witnessed the Goddess use the handclap against an opponent far more formidable than I, who wielded a demonic blade. But, this manoeuvre is not for you. It is much too dangerous even using the practice swords. I know of only a few sword masters capable of executing the handclap manoeuvre, but only one has used it successfully in battle, and she stands here beside me.'

Mab said, 'Master Kanaka is correct. My senses and reflexes are much enhanced, that is how I can carry out the handclap. I would like to ask you a question. Why do you think I threw my sword high into the air?' There was silence.

Pelian said, 'Goddess, was it to distract your opponent?'

Mab smiled at Pelian and said, 'Yes, Pelian, precisely. And was I successful?'

Pelian replied, 'No, Goddess. Master Kanaka's eyes were fixed on you at all times.'

Mab smiled warmly at Pelian, who gasped as a feeling of warmth swept through her body.

Mab said, 'Yes, most opponents would look upwards, follow the sword, but that would be a fatal error. Never let your eyes leave your opponent, even for an instant.' The students applauded.

Master Kanaka looked at Mab and said, 'So, Pelian will be a student here. We should really test her abilities. Can I assume that you have already done that?'

Mab said, 'She has highly developed psychic powers. The focus of her training should be on swordsmanship and weapons.'

Mab said, 'Who is the best student?'

Kanaka replied, 'That would be Birto.'

Mab replied, 'I have heard that name before.'

Lamm said, 'Yes, do you remember the story of the three students and a horse?'

Mab laughed and said, 'Yes, of course. I'm pleased to hear that he is now an advanced student!'

Lamm replied, 'The horse incident had a huge effect on him. He is now one of our best students and excels in warrior skills.'

Mab said, 'Master Kanaka, ask Birto to test Pelian. Birto will use a practice sword, and Pelian will be unarmed.'

Kanaka nodded. Mab mind linked with Pelian and said, 'Birto is an advanced student. He will have a practice sword. I want you to avoid contact with the sword using your speed and agility only.'

Pelian removed her robe. She wore tight-fitting leggings, a soft leather waistcoat and a white blouse. She kicked her boots off before walking onto the practice area. Mab smiled as she looked at Pelian, who appeared childlike in relation to Birto. While Kanaka was talking to Birto, Pelian turned, stared at Mab and smiled. Mab's heart melted. She knew she was falling in love with Pelian.

Mab mind linked and said, 'Keep those big eyes on your opponent, and don't worry, if he hurts you, I will kill him.'

Pelian laughed out loud. Birto stared at her askance and moved slowly forward, sword in hand. Pelian stood perfectly still and waited. Birto stopped a couple of paces from Pelian, and he was trying to assess her capability and looking for signs of concealed weapons. He feigned a move to the right, expecting a response, but Pelian did not move. Then he lunged forward, a diagonal swipe at Pelian's shoulder. Pelian stepped back, the tip of the sword almost touching her chest. Birto quickly leaped backwards, realising that he had over-committed. If Pelian was armed, he would most probably be dead. He moved closer and launched a series of vertical slices at Pelian. But she was moving so fast that he could not make contact; he switched to diagonal and horizontal slices, but she ducked under the first and leapt over the second. Birto was beginning to feel tired and somewhat humiliated. He threw the sword down and ran at Pelian, who dived to his left, kicked him lightly in the stomach and rolled to her feet. Birto moved slowly towards her once again with his fists ready and arms shielding his torso. Pelian waited with her fists raised. Birto moved in, throwing punches at Pelian's head and body, but none made contact. She moved around him with blinding speed, slapping and tapping but not hurting him.

Birto then started laughing and said, 'You are tickling me to death, I yield!'

Kanaka said, 'Thank you, Birto. Pelian, we will be pleased to have you here in the warrior school.'

Pelian replied, 'Thank you, Master Kanaka, and thank you, Birto, for allowing me to tickle you.'

Birto smiled and said, 'I enjoyed the experience.'

Mab went to Kanaka and said, 'Can we have a meeting of the Council tomorrow morning?'

Kanaka replied, 'Yes, I'll ask Lamm and Luticia if they will stay tonight. Perhaps we could have dinner together later this evening?'

Mab replied, 'Yes, perfect. I will bring Pelian. I should explain that she is one of the seven lords of chaos. It is possible, likely in fact, that there could be a war between the light and the dark. It is important that the lords of chaos align with the light. They have explored the multiverse to a much greater extent than any others. I will explain these matters further at the Council meeting. Is Master Boe available, his knowledge would be of great benefit?'

Kanaka replied, 'Yes, I am sure he will make himself available. Taggar's position at the Guild of Witches and Warlocks hasn't yet been filled, although their search for a new principal is ongoing.'

Mab replied, 'Understood. I will drop in to see Master Boe and ask him to arrange accommodation for Pelian.'

Kanaka replied, 'Don't worry, I will take Pelian with me now and make the necessary arrangements.'

Mab walked from the warrior school, made her way to the Guild main building and went downstairs to the lost library. She levitated upwards to the gallery, placed a sofa cushion on the table and sat in full lotus position before moving into a state of deep meditation. She woke refreshed several hours later and made her way to the suite she shared with her roommates, Cat and Charly. As she made her way up the stairs, she heard them talking and knew they were both there. She opened the door to find them trying various outfits, and clothes were thrown all over the room. When they saw Mab standing in the doorway, they ran to her and hugged her tightly.

Mab laughed and said, 'What are you two up to now?'

Charly said, 'We were preparing for your return and our next trip to Fat Joes!'

Mab replied, 'Yes, I think I may be able to fit that into my busy schedule. I guess Josh and Mitch may be missing you?'

Cat, laughing, said, 'Yes, and we have been missing them!'

Mab said, 'I'll see what I can do. I have urgent business that needs to be attended to first. But now I need to shower, change and have dinner with Master Kanaka.'

Mab showered, changed into her guild robe and knocked on Master Boe's door. There was no answer other than a low growl. Mab opened the door and popped her head around; Meldran leapt up and licked her face. Mab wrapped her arms around his huge neck and wrestled him to the ground. They were rolling around on the carpet together when Master Boe appeared from another room.

Boe laughed and said, 'Mab, I've just removed all the dog hairs from my robe; you will be covered in them!'

Mab got to her feet and said, 'It's great to see you again, Master Boe. Let me get rid of these hairs first.'

The dog hairs fell from her robe and gathered into a tight ball at her feet. Mab stepped over the hairball and hugged Master Boe.

Boe said, 'I hope you are keeping well if that's not an inappropriate question to ask a Goddess.'

Mab replied, 'I feel great now, but three hours of meditation followed by five minutes of wrestling with Meldran. What would you expect?!'

Boe laughed and said, 'Yes, I can see how that combination would be cathartic! Can I assume we are both going to the same dinner?'

Mab replied, 'Yes, there will be a council meeting tomorrow morning, but I want to discuss the issues informally first.' Boe, taking Mab's arm, said, 'Fine, lets enjoy the dinner first, though. Too much focus can lead to a lack of perspective.'

Mab smiled warmly at Boe, and he smiled back as he felt a wave of warmth and love wash slowly through him. When they arrived at Kanaka's office, the door was open and kitchen staff were bringing platters of food and a selection of wines. The masters were standing together with Pelian and turned to welcome Mab and Boe.

Pelian was wearing her sky-blue lord's robe, her long white hair hung loose over her shoulders, and her piercing blue eyes shone like sapphires. Mab struggled to take her eyes off her. The others in the room noticed there was an awkward silence.

Mab eventually looked at Kanaka and said, 'We have important matters to discuss.'

Kanaka said, 'Everyone, be seated, please help yourselves to food and drinks.'

Boe sat to Mab's left, and Pelian moved to Mab's right. They ate in silence for a few minutes until Luticia said, 'Mab, do you think you will have time to visit the Academy soon? It would be a real boost to the students.'

Mab replied, 'Yes, Luticia, I would love to, but a serious situation has developed that requires all of our attention.'

Kanaka said, 'Mab, perhaps now is the right time to summarise the nature of this crisis.'

Mab replied, 'Yes, Master Kanaka. This is indeed a crisis, but first, I need to explain as best I can the history and why we now find ourselves in this situation.' Kanaka nodded.

Mab said, 'The universe as we know it was created when the light appeared in the fabric of the void. The light multiplied and spread through the void, creating a great variety of constellations, solar systems, stars and planets. There are, in fact, multiple universes similar to ours but shifted in space and time. It is possible for beings from one universe to enter another. You will remember the Var and the Serrat who travelled from their universe to ours by means of a pathway through a white star. From our perspective, these universes were created by the light; it is the light that defines their existence. However, that perspective is incorrect. Before the light, the void existed as an infinite space where time as we know it did not exist.'

Boe said, 'Mab, surely that is a somewhat philosophical argument. For all intents and purposes, the light defines existence, and if there is no light, then, as you have said, there is no time and therefore no existence.'

Mab smiled and said, 'Master Boe, I would be forced to agree with you if not for one important fact.'

Boe replied, 'What would that be?'

Mab replied, 'The original inhabitants of the void are still there and very much alive.'

Boe replied, 'Are you saying these creatures existed before the light?'

Mab replied, 'Yes, millennia ago, there was a battle that raged across the multiverse. It was known as the light war; the light prevailed, but the cost was high. Only two of the light gods survived, Bellona and Minerva. I confess that I withdrew into obscurity, sickened by the blood on my hands. I assure you that you could not comprehend the devastation brought about by a war of the gods. Entire planets were split asunder, and the stars themselves trembled at the slaughter. In that war, I alone killed countless thousands of creatures.' Tears streamed down Mab's face.

Pelian put her arms around Mab and said, 'Goddess, it is enough for now.'

After a few minutes, Mab recovered her composure. Boe said, 'Mab, what became of the gods of the dark?'

Mab paused before saying, 'In truth, we do not know how many survived, but when I was on Raqus Mons, I detected five powerful beings in the near Abyss. These communicate on a regular basis. Four of these are clan leaders, and the fifth is Erebus, who is said to be a child of the original god Chaos.'

Kanaka said, 'But I thought Lucifer was Prince of the Abyss?'

Mab replied, 'Yes, as did I. But with Minerva restoring my memories, I now know the truth. Lucifer and his Archdaemons inhabited an insignificant part of the Abyss. Lucifer has encountered one of the Abyss gods, and its name was Sladrin. I had an opportunity to slay it, but it fled the host body before I could put Onimaru to the test.'

Lamm said, 'So what is the nature of this impending crisis? Has something changed?'

Mab replied, 'The light is dimming. As the constellations move apart, the starlight is spread more thinly. The creatures of the Abyss will soon be able to break through, and move between our star systems freely and harvest hosts from the outlying solar systems. They will then spread throughout the multiverse; this cannot be permitted.'

Luticia said, 'Are these gods like daemons?'

Mab replied, 'Yes, in some respects, but they are much more powerful. They are spirits who possess other creatures when they wish to experience life in the physical world. However, human hosts are fragile and cannot contain the gods for more than a few hours.

They, therefore, prefer to inhabit larger, more robust creatures and use humans to experience the pleasures that only other humans can provide.'

Pelian added, 'Young men and women coupled with copious amounts of alcohol would be their usual preference.'

Lamm said, 'Is it possible to prevent them breaking through?'

Mab replied, 'I think soon they may be able to inhabit Raqus. There is a particular location deep in Raqus Mons, which will very soon become an open doorway. Whether the Gods will be able to move further from the planet is another matter, but Raqus is only one of, what we must assume, many locations where the light is fading.'

Boe looked at Pelian and said, 'What role do the lords of chaos fulfil, and what do you know of these gods of the Abyss?'

Pelian replied, 'We are named the lords of chaos, but, unlike Erebus, we are not descended from the original god. We live at the extremity of the universe. Our stars are old and spread thin, and it feels like we are slowly being consumed by the void. We have travelled the multiverse seeking suitable planets, but they are surprisingly sparse. Also, we cannot carry more than a few people at any one time. Our leaders, Argaton and Tabbar, sought to build a relationship with the dark gods by supplying them with suitable hosts. At least, that is what we were told. We discovered only recently that our leaders were in collusion with the Abyss against the goddess Minerva. The return of Bellona and her reunion with Minerva has given us new hope.'

Luticia said, 'And what of your two leaders?'

Pelian replied, 'Both slain by Bellona within minutes of meeting her.'

Kanaka laughed and said, 'Why am I not surprised by that!'

Mab smiled and said, 'They were colluding with the Abyss to kill my sister and her child.'

Kanaka nodded, paused, and said, 'Thank you all for coming here tonight. Mab and Pelian, you have explained the gravity of the situation very clearly. We will need time to consider carefully what we have heard. It would make sense for all of you to attend the council meeting tomorrow morning, where we will take the necessary decisions and establish a forward plan of action.'

Mab and Pelian walked out into the campus grounds. There was a chill in the air, and both made good use of their hooded robes.

Pelian said, 'How long will we be staying here?'

Mab replied, 'I need you to develop your weapon skills, and this is the best place for you to learn. Kanaka is a master swordsman; if we go to war against the Abyss, you will need such skills.'

Pelian replied, 'I have always used my psychic powers for protection and attack. Is this not sufficient?'

Mab replied, 'No, it will not suffice. Master Kanaka has slain creatures with far greater psychic powers than he.'

Pelian replied, 'Will you be here?'

Mab stopped, turned to face her and said, 'Yes, I will be here as much as I can.'

Pelian replied, 'I have been given a room in the Sapphire block; Master Kanaka said, it was the room that you had before you married. I asked him about your wife, but he avoided the subject.'

Mab said, 'My wife's name was Izzy. She was killed by a Balerak commissioned by daemons. We had a room in the Guild building that we shared with two of our friends, Charly and Cat. I think you would really like them.' As they walked towards Sapphire, Pelian veered off into a shaded area.

Mab followed and said, 'What is it?'

Pelian replied, 'Come closer.' She then put her arms around Mab, kissed her slowly on the lips and whispered, 'Goddess, I want to be with you always.'

Mab smiled, returned the kiss and whispered, 'That would be wonderful. But first, you must become an expert swordsman.'

Pelian laughed and replied, 'Yes, I will do it for you!'

Mab pulled her close, kissed her and said, 'Time to go. I will collect you from your room in the morning and take you to breakfast. We will then go to the council meeting and hopefully make some progress.'

Pelian kissed Mab again and walked briskly towards Sapphire block.

Mab vanished and appeared in her room. She could sense that Cat and Charly had already retired. She stripped off, showered, and climbed into bed. She was about to fall asleep when her witch senses twitched. Her eyes flashed open, and a few seconds later, Pelian appeared in her room. She wore only a light silk gown, which she discarded, walked towards the bed, and climbed in.

Mab smiled and whispered, 'I thought for a moment that you weren't coming.'

Pelian smiled and replied, 'Well, arriving uninvited in the bed of a goddess is not a trivial matter!'

It was in the early hours of the morning when Mab's witch senses screamed in her head. She felt the blade enter the left side of her body. She stopped it immediately, but the poison it carried exploded into her body. She slowed time, levitated upwards and expelled the blade. Pelian was moving in slow-motion. Onimaru was already rocketing towards her; Pelian saw it and tried to spin out of its path. But the sword was faster. It penetrated the top of her chest close to the collarbone, slammed her against the wall and buried itself up to the hilt. Mab, writhing in pain, looked down at her.

Pelian said, 'I have killed you. That is certain.'

Mab replied, through gritted teeth, 'Why have you betrayed me?'

Pelian replied, 'You are a fool much like your sister. I am Baydan.'

Mab gagged as the poison spread through her but groaned. 'How can that be?'

Baydan laughed and spat, 'I use this child in many ways. I do not require consent! We will soon move freely amongst your people. We will supplant your leaders. Our clans will feast on an abundance of human flesh as I will feast on yours shortly.'

Mab said, 'Unfortunately for you, I am not so easily killed.'

The poison sprayed from the hole in Mab's side and ran down her thigh. It was putrid, and the stink made her gag.

Mab lifted her arm and pulled a huge silver sword from the air. Baydan started to struggle, and for the first time, it appeared to notice the sword that had pinned Pelian's body to the wall.

Mab said, 'That is my sword, Onimaru, slayer of daemons. This, however, is my mother's sword Durandal.'

Baydan stared at the sword and said, 'No, it cannot be. That sword and its twin were lost in the light war.'

Mab pressed the tip of the sword into Pelian's chest and smiled. Baydan started to panic. It tried to flee the body but realised it was pinned in place by Onimaru.

Mab said, 'Now, let us see whether Durandal will slay a god from the Abyss.'

Baydan gasped, 'If you kill me, you also kill Pelian.'

Mab laughed and said, 'Do you know who I am?'

Baydan, trying to remain calm, replied, 'You are the Goddess Bellona.'

Mab said, 'Do you know how many deaths I have on my hands?'

Baydan paused and said, 'No, I don't.'

Mab replied, 'Countless thousands. Do you think the death of this hapless child will affect me in any way whatsoever?'

Baydan was silent.

Mab said, 'You are an ancient but vile creature; you are not a god. And yes, the light has driven you from places you and your kind used to inhabit. But the void is infinite. The truth is that you covet life in the light and wish to sate yourselves with the blood of the innocent. This, I will not permit even if I must slay you and all of your brethren.' Mab lowered Durandal, pulled Onimaru from Pelian's body and said, 'Go now, tell Erebus that Minerva and I wish to discuss options for the future. But know this, Baydan, I am the Goddess of War, and war is my sole reason for being here.' Baydan fled from Pelian's body, which slumped to the floor. Mab placed her hand on the wound made by Onimaru, and a silver skin of light engulfed Pelian's body. She levitated Pelian, placed her back on the bed and lay down beside her.

Mab woke a few hours later and removed the skin of power that surrounded Pelian. She was conscious, and the wound had healed, but she was glancing furtively around the room. Mab said, 'I have placed a shield around this room. You may speak freely.'

Pelian looked up at Mab, tears in her eyes, and said, 'Goddess, I am sorry. I tried to resist, but it took control of my mind.'

Mab replied, 'When did it take control?'

Pelian replied, 'Shortly before it tried to kill you.'

Mab said, 'How was it able to enter your mind.'

Pelian, crying, replied, 'Goddess, I don't know how it is done, but Baydan is able to enter my mind whenever it chooses.'

Mab said, 'You should have told me of this!'

Pelian replied, 'I have told no one because I am ashamed. I am weak, but the others are able to resist possession. However, I am not strong enough. I know when it is present in my mind, but I can't do anything to prevent it. I allowed Baydan to enter my mind a long time ago. Argaton insisted that it only wanted to carry out some reconnaissance and that I would come to no harm. I was unconscious. I awoke in the cave on Raqus Mons, with Baydan in my mind, controlling my body. I do not wish to discuss the unspeakable things that ensued. But since that time, I have been unable to prevent him from using me.'

Mab looked thoughtfully at Pelian and said, 'Let's go for a walk and have an early breakfast. We will come back here before going to the council meeting.'

Mab walked with Pelian to sports fields and described the various fun events that took place throughout the year. She also explained the role of the four magic schools and how they competed for the most promising students but also worked together in times of need. The walk seemed to have the desired effect of calming Pelian. Mab said, 'This is foremost a place of learning; it is truly wonderful to be a student here. If we get time, I will show you my secret place where I go to meditate.'

Pelian smiled and said, 'Yes, it is beautiful. Everything is so bright and colourful! I am looking forward to developing my sword skills here. I just hope I don't let you down.'

Mab laughed and said, 'You won't be here all the time. As you know, we have things to do, and I will need you by my side.'

Pelian said, 'What about my problem? How will you be able to trust me?'

Mab put her finger to her mouth and said, 'Hush now, I always find that things look much brighter after breakfast.'

They walked into an empty dining area. The head chef rushed out when he saw Mab; he bowed and said, 'Goddess, you are somewhat early, but please be seated. The food is being placed now. Would you like some hot coffee while you wait?'

Mab replied, 'Yes, please, my student will have the same.' Mab looked at Pelian and said, 'You won't like the coffee when you first try it, but you will grow to love it!'

Pelian took a sip, screwed up her face, and said, 'Yes, you are right. I don't like it!'

Mab replied, 'As a good student, it is your duty to like both coffee and wine. Now, let's get some food.'

Following breakfast, Mab walked Pelian back to the suite, and Charly and Cat prepared to go to their first lecture.

Mab said, 'Pelian, this is Charly and Cat. Pelian is my student.'

Charly and Cat hugged Pelian and said they should all get together after classes.

Mab nodded and said, 'Pelian and I have some work to do now, but we will be back here later today.'

Mab asked Pelian to lie on the sofa and close her eyes. She kissed her on the forehead and said, 'I want to do a deep scan of your mind. You need to be awake, but you must remain calm.

Pelian replied, 'Yes, Goddess, I'll try.'

Mab mind linked with Pelian, and she started to probe gently through her thoughts and memories. When she reached the memories of Baydan, there was none that could explain what had happened, but there were many that Mab could barely bring herself to read. Pelian was not conscious when she entered the cave with Argaton, and when she regained consciousness, Baydan had already entered her mind. Mab said, 'It is exactly as you described. There is nothing in your memory or mind that explains how Baydan is able to control you. Something physical must have been done to you when you were unconscious.' Mab placed her hand on Pelian's stomach and moved it slowly over her body. She then pulled Pelian up to a sitting position and moved her hands over her back, chest, shoulders and neck. She then placed her hand on the back of her head and paused.

Pelian said, 'What is it? Have you found something?'

Mab replied, 'Yes, something has been placed in your head. I will remove it, but I need you to remain perfectly still.' Mab laid Pelian face down on the sofa and, with a gesture, placed her in a deep sleep. She then studied the organism that clung to Pelian's brain stem. She prodded it gently with a narrow beam of light. It moved and increased its grip on the brain. It was scorpion-like. Its long tail was wrapped around the brain stem while its claws were embedded into the surface of the brain. It seemed to feed from the blood vessels and, perhaps to some extent, the substance of the brain. Mab used a light beam to carefully sever the legs and tail of the creature. She pulled the body and head to her and placed the parts in a wine goblet. The thing was still alive; she placed a heavy book on top of the goblet just to be sure it couldn't escape. She then extracted the claws one by one and used the light beam to cut the tail into several pieces before removing it. She placed the various body parts in the goblet and rested her hand on Pelian's head.

Mab was revolted by what she had found. She thought about Baydan and reached out, her powerful senses penetrating deep into the Abyss. It was with the others, and they thought themselves safe there in the darkness. They thought that none could assail them. She moved into Baydan's mind and said, 'When we next meet, I will have your life for what you have done to Pelian.' She then withdrew, looked down at Pelian and carried out a thorough scan of her whole body.

Mab brought Pelian back to consciousness and said, 'How do you feel?'

Pelian replied, 'I have a headache and feel a bit dizzy, but otherwise, I am good. I can't explain it, but I feel something has changed. I feel lighter! Did you find something in my head?'

Mab said, 'Yes, I have removed it. She lifted the goblet and passed it to Pelian, who, upon seeing the creature, put her hand over her mouth and retched. Mab said, 'It was fixed to your brain. It must have been placed there by Baydan. It seems that this creature creates a link between Baydan's mind and yours. You were enslaved, but now you are free.'

Pelian burst into tears, threw her arms around Mab and said, 'I love you, I love you!'

Mab hugged her and said, 'Are you well enough to attend the council meeting?'

Pelian replied, 'Yes, I am fine.'

Mab said, 'Very well, bring your little friend in the goblet.'

Mab and Pelian arrived at Kanaka's office, knocked, and entered. The masters were already present. Mab poured herself a mug of hot coffee and looked at Pelian, who shook her head.

Mab said, 'Master Kanaka's coffee is even better than the breakfast coffee?'

Pelian smiled, her face glowing with love, and said, 'Yes, I will have some coffee.'

Kanaka looked at Lamm and winked. Luticia, noticing the exchange, looked at Pelian and said, 'How was your accommodation? Did you sleep well?'

Pelian simply smiled and nodded. Mab, returning with two mugs of coffee, said, 'Pelian spent the night in my room. There has been a serious development.'

Kanaka replied, 'Does it affect what we are about to discuss?'

Mab replied, 'Baydan, of the Abyss, took possession of Pelian last night and tried to kill me.' There was complete silence.

Kanaka looked at Mab's askance and said, 'How is that possible?'

Pelian said, 'It was my fault.'

Mab sat down, sipped her coffee, and said, 'The creature took possession of Pelian and stabbed me with a poisoned blade as I slept. I stopped the blade, but it discharged a large quantity of poison into my body, which I had to expel. I pinned Pelian's body to the wall with Onimaru, but of course, I could not slay the creature without killing Pelian, so I allowed it to leave.'

Lamm said, 'It would first have to travel here from the Abyss and then enter Pelian's mind without obtaining her consent. I had thought neither of these was possible?'

Pelian tipped the contents of the goblet onto the table and said, 'The Goddess found and removed this from my inside my head.' The body of the creature twitched.

Luticia said, 'It's horrible!'

Boe said, 'It appears to be a species of scorpion. Was it attached to the brain stem?'

Mab replied, 'Yes, Master Boe, it was. I think it was placed there many years ago when Pelian was told to host Baydan for a short time. She was unconscious when the creature was placed in her head.'

Boe said, 'I have come across something similar in my research, although I didn't believe it was really possible. The parasite picks up the brain message activity, and a powerful psychic can link through the parasite to the person. Can I take the body parts for further study?'

Mab nodded and said, 'We have to assume that our discussions yesterday were heard by Baydan, even though he may not have been present in Pelian's mind.'

Kanaka replied, 'Yes, that would be prudent.'

Lamm said, 'Did you learn anything from Baydan?'

Mab said, 'It said they would soon be able to move freely amongst us, that they would supplant our leaders and feast on our flesh!'

Kanaka replied, 'I guess that is a clear, albeit extremely worrying, strategy!'

Pelian, crying, said, 'I am sorry. I feel that I have brought this evil upon you.'

Kanaka replied softly, 'Pelian, you are a victim and a spectator in this. There is nothing that you could have done.' There was silence.

Mab said, 'This morning, I reached out, deep into the Abyss, and found Baydan. It is an ancient creature, it knows that it narrowly escaped death. It is afraid, perhaps for the first time in its existence, but thought itself safe in that place with the other gods. I went into its mind and told it that I would take its life for what it did to Pelian. It now knows that it is very far from safe and that I have vowed to kill it. Take some comfort from that.'

Pelian said, 'You reached into the Abyss? I did not think that was possible.'

Mab smiled and replied, 'It seems Baydan also thought that.'

Kanaka said, 'What seems clear is that we need to contain these creatures within the Abyss. Mab, you mentioned the five gods but what of the other creatures that live in that place?'

Mab replied, 'The gods have their clans, but we do not know their numbers or capabilities, nor do we know anything about the other creatures that live there.'

Boe said, 'I assume both sides do not wish to have another war. So, what do the gods of the Abyss really want?'

Pelian replied, 'They want to destroy the light and return the universe back into darkness. If the light cannot be extinguished, they will do the next best thing, kill all of the life that it created.'

Boe replied, 'But why?'

Pelian shrugged her shoulders but said nothing.

Mab said, 'Master Boe, only the gods of the Abyss can answer that question, but you may also ask why the light war was fought. I know we fought to defend ourselves against those we considered to be vile, evil and hateful. But the gods of the Abyss fought against the very presence of the light because they perceived it to be an ever-expanding invasion of their universe.'

Boe replied, 'We must do everything in our power to avoid another major war. Surely, if this Erebus creature lived at the time of the light war, it would concur?'

Mab smiled warmly at Boe and said, 'Master Boe, there is evil in the Abyss that cannot be rationalised by those of us who live in the light. The gods of the Abyss emanate despair and hopelessness and take pleasure in the suffering and torment of others. Baydan is guilty of unspeakable atrocities and horrors. I saw some of that in Pelian's mind and more when I entered the creature's mind. When Baydan said they would feast on our flesh, he meant that in the literal sense. They would rip babies from their mothers' arms or bellies and devour them before slaughtering the entire family. Master Kanaka is correct, and we cannot allow these creatures to escape the Abyss. The consequences would be catastrophic. However, the first step must be a parley with Erebus. We must understand their intentions and then plan for likely scenarios.'

Lamm replied, 'What do we think the worst-case scenario is?' Kanaka replied, 'I don't think we will know that until we have a better understanding of their intentions.'

Mab said, 'Exactly, but if there is to be a war, then it needs to be contained and preferably fought in their territory, which, of course, presents many problems. I must leave you now to speak with my sister, but it would be wise to prepare for war.'

Kanaka nodded. Mab hugged Pelian and vanished.

Chapter Thirty-One: Darkness Rising

Erebus lay back on a bed of rock within the heart of a meteor that raced through the everchanging currents of the Abyss. It brooded on the rapidly changing situation with the lords following the mysterious return of the goddess Bellona. It was averse to change ever since the light appeared. But there was something else. Something different that it could not quite bring into focus. Erebus relaxed and tried to clear its thoughts. There it was again, at the very edge of its consciousness, something important that could not be articulated. Erebus, in frustration, reached out to the clan leaders and said, 'Come to me!'

Humbra materialised immediately, followed soon after by Dakigo, Baydan and Sladrin. Erebus said, 'Sladrin, Baydan, my senses tell me that all is not well. Explain!' Humbra and Dakigo moved slowly away from the other two gods.

Sladrin said, 'In the absence of Argaton and Tabbar, I used a Balerak to meet in person with the witch Morgana to solicit suitable hosts for our meeting in the light. She was unwilling to help. I threatened her, but Lucifer Morningstar came to her assistance.'

Erebus replied, 'And you killed them both?'

Sladrin replied, 'I would have, but Bellona followed Morningstar. I barely escaped with my life.'

Erebus, staring at Sladrin, said, 'You barely escaped with your life! Did you even try to kill her?'

Sladrin said, 'Yes, Master, but in her own realm, she was too powerful to combat.'

There was a moment of silence before Erebus said, 'Describe her.'

Sladrin replied, 'She is small in stature; her skin and hair are white. Her hair was platted on both sides of her head, and she wore a white robe with a red sash. She carried a huge sword, hitched high on her back.'

Erebus said, 'Did she carry any other weapons?'

Sladrin replied, 'Yes, a whip of light hung on her left side. She ensnared the Balerak with that and drove her sword through its chest.'

Erebus hung his head and said, 'Yes, it is Bellona.'

Humbra said, 'Erebus, what does it mean?'

Erebus replied, 'Hum, I do not know.'

Baydan said, 'Master, I, too, have encountered Bellona.'

Erebus replied, 'And you too are still alive. At least that is positive, tell me!'

Baydan said, 'You may remember Pelian, one of the lords?'

Erebus replied, 'Yes, the young female?'

Baydan replied, 'I placed a scarp in her head so I could keep track of her activities. The Goddess has taken Pelian as a student and as a lover. I took control of Pelian and stabbed the Goddess as she slept. The blade barely entered her body before she brought it to a halt, but it was designed to deliver a massive dose of a deadly poison. It should have killed her instantly.'

Erebus replied, 'I assume it did not kill her?'

Baydan said, 'She groaned a bit, but her body expelled the poison. Pelian and I were pinned to the wall by her sword. The sword is sentient, I could feel it feeding on my essence, sapping my energy. I could not escape Pelian's body. The sword held me fast. I think she could have killed me, but instead, she told me to take a message to you.'

Erebus replied, 'What is the message; the exact words.'

Baydan said, 'Go now, tell Erebus that Minerva and I wish to discuss options for the future. But know this, Baydan, I am the Goddess of War, and war is my sole reason for being here.'

There was silence as Erebus considered the words. Baydan suddenly screamed in pain. Erebus looked at him and said, 'Calm yourself.'

Baydan replied, 'She entered my mind! She said she would take my life for what I did to Pelian!'

Sladrin said, 'That is not possible. She cannot reach us here in this place!'

Baydan replied, 'I tell you, a moment ago, she was in my mind!'

Erebus said, 'Enough! You have no conception as to what Bellona is and what she is capable of. Do not approach either of the Goddesses unless you have specific instructions from me. Is that clear?'

Dakigo said, 'Master, of course, we will follow your instructions. But why do you think Bellona has returned?'

Erebus replied, 'It is in her message. She is here to prosecute a war and we must make ready.'

Humbra said, 'Where does she imagine this war will be fought?'

Erebus replied, 'That will depend on both strategy and happenstance. I will be responsible for all interactions with the Goddesses. I need you to prepare your clans for war, both in the light and here in the Abyss. Now leave me!'

Mab appeared in the cloistered area in the Palace of the Gods. She knew Minerva was in the garden, but in eons past, the gods would never manifest close to each other, it was considered poor etiquette. Mab walked slowly through the Palace and out into the extensive gardens. Minerva was sitting naked in the shallows of what appeared to be a small lake that was fed by hot spring water. As Mab approached,

Minerva turned and said, 'Sister, would you like to join me?'

Mab smiled, her robe vanished, and she appeared beside Minerva in the lake. Mab said, 'This is beautiful. I wonder why I never visited this place in the past.'

Minerva laughed and replied, 'You were always a rebel, far too consumed with your love of humans and animals. That has always been the difference between us. I would be happy living here for eternity without a care for others, but you would not.'

Mab said, 'I would be happy living here, but not without a care for others.'

Minerva smiled and said, 'Is it war?'

Mab replied, 'We need to parley with Erebus, but yes, I believe it will be war.'

Minerva stood, her robe wrapping itself around her, and said, 'Where will this parley be held, in the Abyss?'

Mab replied, 'I had thought to have it in the Abyss but perhaps we should have it here in this palace?'

Minerva stared at Mab for a few moments and said, 'How long have you known?'

Mab replied, 'I know Erebus has been here; the rest is mere supposition. Sister, your affairs are my affairs and vice versa. If you have feelings for this creature, you must tell me.'

Minerva walked with Mab, in silence, to her room. Mab put her arm around her and pulled her close.

Minerva said, 'He is not a creature; he is an ancient being who is trying to defend a way of life that existed before the light. The clan leaders are monsters and vile in every respect, but Erebus is not of the clans. He is their leader because he is the strongest, and they are all he has left following the light war. I do not love him, but I do have great affection for him.'

Mab said, 'And yet he is able to travel here and enter this palace. How can that be?'

Minerva replied, 'He is extraordinarily powerful; he can hold himself here but only for a short time, and it greatly weakens him. He mind-links with me, and I permit him entrance to the palace.'

Mab said, 'Do you travel to the Abyss?'

Minerva replied, 'I have been there on a few occasions; I cannot sustain myself in that place for long.'

Mab said, 'Mind-link with him now; I wish to speak with him.'

Minerva stared at Mab and said, 'Very well, but remember that he is my friend.'

Minerva reached out, linked with Erebus and said, 'My sister wishes to speak with you.'

Erebus replied, 'It is nice to hear from you. I know your sister has returned.'

Mab said, 'Erebus, I have returned for a reason. I wish to discuss this with you and your so-called gods of the Abyss. If you refuse, then it will be war, and in that, I am well versed.'

Erebus replied, 'I do not take kindly to threats.'

Mab said, 'I do not make threats; I am stating facts.'

Erebus paused before saying, 'Where do you wish to meet?'

Mab replied, 'If you would be kind enough to host the meeting, we will come to you.'

Erebus replied, 'I think you will not find our environment to your liking. Your sister was quite ill following her last visit here.'

Mab replied, 'Minerva will not be attending in person but will communicate through me if needed; three friends of the light will accompany me, together with Pelian, one of the lords.'

Erebus said, 'I know of Pelian, and I apologise for Baydan's foolish attempt to kill you. I have told the clan leaders that all communications with you and Minerva will be through me.'

Mab replied, 'I suggest Baydan is not present at the meeting.'

Erebus said, 'I and my four clan leaders, including Baydan, will attend together with three of my alpha legion commanders. I am sure you will remember the latter?'

Mab replied, 'I remember their extraordinary courage and bravery, but I prefer to forget the rest.'

Erebus said, 'Yes, some things are too painful and must be forgotten if there is to be a future worth living.'

Mab paused before replying, 'Yes, I agree; Minerva will be in touch.'

Minerva said, 'Perhaps you will now agree that he is not a monster?'

Mab replied, 'I admit that he is not what I expected. But I will reserve judgement until after the meeting.'

Minerva said, 'At least you are referring to him as 'he' rather than 'it.' That is progress of sorts.'

Mab said, 'Could you agree with him on the meeting time and place?'

Minerva replied, 'Yes, of course. Now come here!'

Mab smiled and walked towards Minerva, who threw her arms around her and kissed her passionately.

Mab appeared on the Guild sports field; it was a cold morning with a hard ground frost. She was wrapped in her master's robe with Onimaru hitched high on her back. She knelt, bent forward, touched the ground with her forehead and then sat back in the full lotus position. She faced the rising sun and entered a deep meditative state. When she awoke, a large group of students was seated around her. Master Kanaka sat close to her, keeping her warm with his body heat. Fireballs floated around the group. She was wrapped in many robes and cloaks.

Mab said, 'Apologies, how long have I been here?'

Kanaka replied, 'You were discovered here yesterday morning by a fresher. We were afraid to wake you; we decided to keep you warm and wait for you to recover.'

Mab said, 'Thank you Master Kanaka.' A muffled sound came from beneath the many robes. Mab pulled them away, and Pelian's head appeared.

She looked up at Mab and said, 'Sorry, I fell asleep!'

The crowd applauded; Mab kissed her on the forehead and stood up, pulling Pelian to her feet at the same time.

Kanaka said, 'Let's get some hot food and coffee.'

Mab replied, 'Yes, please!'

Kanaka, Lamm and Pelian sat with Mab in a secluded part of the dining area and ate a hearty lunch.

Lamm said, 'We assumed you were in a deep meditation; Boe advised not to move you.'

Mab replied, 'Boe was right. I didn't expect to be under for so long.'

Kanaka said, 'Why didn't you go to the library?'

Mab paused and then replied, 'I had to face the sun. It is a special type of meditation where you focus on a particular issue and seek guidance or direction.'

Lamm said, 'Did it work?'

Mab replied, 'I don't know. Minerva has arranged a meeting with Erebus and the clan leaders, but it will be in the Abyss.'

Kanaka replied, 'Is that wise? Who will attend?'

Mab said, 'I will take three of the Archangels and also Pelian.'

Kanaka replied, 'Minerva will not be present?'

Mab said, 'No, we cannot both enter the Abyss. The risk of us both being killed is low, but the consequences are unacceptable. Therefore, my sister will remain in the palace and participate in the meeting through me.'

Pelian said, 'I have never been to the Abyss. Will Baydan be there?'

Mab looked at Pelian and said, 'You will be at my side. Baydan will be there, and when he looks into your eyes, he will see no fear.'

Pelian replied, 'Yes, goddess.'

Mab said, 'If the meeting is successful, there will be a follow-up to discuss and agree on the way forward. That will be held in the palace, and so the magic schools can be represented.'

Lamm said, 'What is the objective of the forthcoming meeting? What does success mean?'

Mab replied, 'Success means that war has been averted.'

Kanaka said, 'And if they refuse to negotiate?'

Mab replied, 'We can only hope they see reason; otherwise, it will be war, and many will die on both sides. This first meeting is, however to understand intentions and rationales. There will be no negotiations. That will only happen if the first meeting is successful.'

Kanaka nodded, looked at Lamm and said, 'Nevertheless, we should prepare for the worst and hope for the best.'

Mab said, 'I will visit Luticia tonight and explain the current situation and perhaps tomorrow I could visit the School of Psych and Sorcery?'

Lamm was clearly overjoyed and said, 'Yes, please and let me know when you will arrive. The students will be ecstatic!'

Mab smiled and said, 'Don't go to a lot of effort. I thought a nice lunch and a walk around the campus?'

Lamm replied, 'Perfect.'

Mab looked at Pelian and said, 'How are your sword skills developing?'

Pelian smiled and looked at Kanaka, who said, 'Her skills are truly extraordinary.'

Pelian looked at Mab and said, 'I never said I couldn't use a sword; it's just not my preference.'

Mab said, 'When I return, you will perform for me a flawless sword Kata. Master Kanaka knows which one, and following that, I will test you in battle.'

Pelian looked questioningly at Mab and replied, 'And what if I defeat you?'

Kanaka and Lamm burst into fits of laughter. Mab smiled at Pelian and said, 'Then perhaps you too will be a Goddess.' as she leaned over and kissed her cheek.

Mab made her way back to the suite; Cat was there but said Charly had gone back home to see her parents and would return in a couple of days. Mab hugged Cat and said, 'I've been very busy, but I haven't forgotten about us having a night out at Fat Joes. Perhaps when Charly gets back?'

Cat replied, 'That would be fantastic! It would really help Charly, and she's a bit down at the moment.'

Mab nodded and said, 'Let's wait until she gets back to the campus. I need a hot shower, and then I must go. I will be back in a couple of days.' As Mab showered, she reached out with her senses, found Charly and entered her mind. Charly and her mother were seated, but her father was standing and being questioned by a group of four, three of whom appeared to be ex-soldiers but the fourth wore a hooded robe and watched in silence from the shadows.

The leader of the group looked at Charly's father and said, 'So, this Mabdelore is a friend of your daughter's?'

Charly said, 'She is a Master of the Guild of Sorcerers, and she is my friend. My parents know nothing about her!'

The leader replied, 'We want to know the names of her parents and where they live. We will pay you in gold for the information. If you refuse to cooperate, then bad things will happen to your parents.'

He turned and punched Charly's father in the stomach. Charly's father doubled up in pain and dropped to his knees on the floor. Charly and her mother rushed to help him.'

There was a flash of intense white light, and Mab appeared in the room. The three ex-soldiers dropped to the floor unconscious. Mab stared at the figure in the shadows and said, 'You will remain exactly where you are!'

The figure laughed and replied, 'Witch, I have no intentions of going anywhere.'

Mab looked down at Charly and said, 'How is your father?'

Charly replied, 'Mab, thanks for coming. He is winded, but his breathing is under control now. He will be fine.'

Mab said, 'Take your father and mother to their bedroom and stay with them.'

When Charly and her parents left the room, Mab turned to the robed figure and said, 'Come here!' The stranger tried to resist, but the coercive power of the command was off the scale. The stranger walked lethargically towards the centre of the room and said, 'What are you?'

Mab replied, 'Silence! Remove your robe!' The robe fell to the floor to reveal a stunningly attractive young woman. She wore a protective waistcoat fashioned from the finest silver thread and of astonishing workmanship. Her hair was like polished obsidian and was braided down her back. Her eyes were piercing blue, and her ears pointed.

Mab stared at her and said, 'Pelian.'

The woman's eyes widened, and she replied, 'What do you know of Pelian!'

Mab paused and said, 'It is I who will ask the questions. Who are you, what are you doing in my friend's home, and why have you attacked her father?'

The stranger replied, 'I am of the Mevlen, my name is Gilian and I am the sister of Pelian. I have travelled the multiverse searching for her in vain. These humans told me of a powerful witch named Mabdelore, who was found as a child and adopted by human parents. I thought she could be Pelian as she was taken from us as an infant. I paid the humans in gold for their help in finding the witch Mabdelore or her parents. I did not intend any harm to this good family, and I am not familiar with the ways of humans.'

Mab replied, 'I am known by many names. Mabdelore Winter was my adopted name as an infant.'

Gilian's head dropped, and she said, 'So, another false trail. But where have you heard the name Pelian?'

Mab smiled, and Gilian gasped as a wave of warmth and hope flowed through her.

She dropped to her knees and said, 'Are you the Goddess Minerva?'

Mab replied, 'No, Minerva is my sister.'

Gilian stared askance and whispered, 'Bellona? The God Warrior, you are Bellona!?'

Mab smiled and said, 'Yes, I have returned to serve the light, should there be a need.'

Gilian replied, 'Then I may be able to offer my help and knowledge of the multiverse. I have seen much in my travels.'

Mab said, 'First, I will take you to your sister, and then we will talk.'

Mab lifted her up, and they vanished, taking the ex-soldiers with them. They reappeared just inside the Guild's main gates. Mab told the guards to lock the ex-soldiers in the cells. She then walked with Gilian towards the warrior school training facility.

As they walked, students and guards would stop and bow.

Mab said, 'Pelian should be here working hard on her swordsmanship.'

Gilian stopped and said, 'She may not recognise me, nor I her. She was taken as an infant, and I have been searching for her for many years since I came of age. I am not sure how she will react?'

Mab said, 'I think she will recognise you immediately. But I want this to be a surprise. Do you mind pulling your hood over?'

Gilian smiled and replied, 'Yes, Goddess, it will be a wonderful surprise for us both!'

Mab walked into the warrior school; Gilian veered off to the side of the practice areas and took a seat. Master Kanaka was holding Pelian, ensuring she was placing her body in the correct position to execute effective attack and defence moves. There was a sudden hush within the practice areas when Mab entered. Kanaka turned and saw her; Pelian watched as Mab walked slowly towards them.

Mab looked at Kanaka and then at Pelian and said, 'Is she ready.'

Kanaka said, 'No, but she will be ready in a few days. You have only been gone a few hours!'

Mab looked at Pelian and said, 'So, you are not ready?'

Pelian replied, 'Yes, I am ready!' as she jumped onto Mab and wrestled her to the ground. The students applauded furiously. Mab was on her back, lying on the floor laughing with Pelian sitting on her chest. Kanaka was leading the students in applause. A robed and hooded figure appeared beside Kanaka and said, 'Is this the way to treat a goddess?'

Mab lifted herself and Pelian to their feet and said, 'Pelian, this is someone I would like you to meet.' Gilian's robe fell to the floor as she looked into her sister's eyes. Pelian was transfixed, her mouth moved, but no sound came.

Gilian said, 'I am your sister, Gilian. I have searched the multiverse for you.'

Pelian stared at Gilian, studying every detail of her face, and said, 'Gilian, my sister?'

Mab said, 'You two have much to discuss. Gilian, I will return here tomorrow evening, Master Kanaka and I will then hear your story.' Mab nodded to Kanaka and vanished.

Kanaka said, 'Pelian, it would make sense if you shared your room with Gilian tonight. We will resume your training tomorrow morning. Gilian, I'm not sure what news you have brought, but do not discuss it with anyone until we meet with Mab tomorrow night.' Gilian nodded and embraced Pelian; the sisters walked in silence out of the warrior school and into the cool early evening air.

Mab appeared in Luticia's office within the Academy. She was seated at the head of a large table with her leadership team. Mab said, 'Luticia, apologies for interrupting your meeting. There is a matter of some urgency that I need to discuss with you.'

Luticia replied, 'Yes, of course. Everyone, please leave; we will resume this meeting tomorrow. All stood, bowed, and made their way to the door.

Mab smiled at Fora as she passed, mind linked with her and said, *'I will come to you later.'* Fora returned the smile and continued walking.

Luticia poured two coffees and gestured for Mab to sit.

Mab said, 'I need you to attend another meeting; it will be tomorrow evening in Master Kanaka's office. As you know, there is likely to be a war, and you need to prepare for it.'

Luticia replied, 'That was the very subject of the meeting I was just having.'

Mab replied, 'There has been another development. Pelian's sister, Gilian, is here on this plane. I came across her by accident when visiting a student and her parents. She is now at the Guild and hopefully brings good news. However, if it is as I suspect, then war will be inevitable.'

Luticia replied, 'Yes, of course, I will attend the meeting. Will you be staying for dinner?'

Mab replied, 'I thought I would spend some time with Fora; she is a very good cook, and then I need to visit Master Lamm.'

Luticia said, 'Mab, how much danger are we really in?'

Mab said, 'The situation is very serious. We need to put together a credible army to fight a war against opponents that we don't understand and are of unknown capability. Each of the magic schools will need to put forward their strongest adepts, masters and students.'

Luticia said, 'And if we fail?'

Mab stared at her askance and replied, 'We will not fail under any circumstances!'

Luticia swallowed hard and said, 'Yes, Goddess. I will begin the necessary preparations and report back tomorrow evening.'

Mab walked from the main building and across the market square. Cries of 'The White Witch' could be heard. The locals stopped and bowed low when she passed. The students of the academy bent the knee. Mab made her way to Fora's home, which was just off the square at the corner of two narrow streets. She knocked gently on the ancient wooden door.

Fora opened the door a crack wide and said, 'Who is it?'

Mab replied, 'You know who it is.'

Fora said, 'The goddess has returned?'

Mab laughed and said, 'Yes, the goddess has returned. Now let me in.'

Fora was about to reply when Mab's arms wrapped around her from behind. Fora turned, hugged Mab tightly, kissed her and said, 'You have been too busy to visit?'

Mab replied, 'No, I don't have much on at present.'

Fora laughed and kissed Mab's neck, cheeks and lips.

Mab said, 'How is Pip?'

Fora replied, 'She is fine. A friend is looking after her tonight. I explained to my friend that I had an unexpected visitor who could be very demanding.'

Mab smiled, kissed Fora and said, 'Before we get to my demands, have you had any more problems regarding your late husband's debts?'

Fora replied, 'No, I think the word has spread over the appearance of Lucifer.'

Mab said, 'What! You mean they fear Lucifer more than they fear me?'

Fora laughed so much she could barely speak but managed to say, 'Yes, he is huge and clearly a magnificent warrior. But you...'

Mab said, 'Yes?'

Fora went back into a fit of laughter.

Mab said, 'Right, time for bed and my list of demands.'

Lamm said, 'As you know, the Goddess has not visited our school before. It is important that she leaves with a good impression.'

Master Johans replied, 'This so-called goddess was a student at the GOS, was she not?'

Lamm replied, 'Johans, I am sure you, and everyone else at this meeting, knows of Mabdelore Winter and her background.'

Johans said, 'I know the story, but I know many stories, and most are nothing more than fantasy. Perhaps we should put her to the test?'

Lamm sighed and said, 'What test? What are you talking about Johans?'

Uvren said, 'There is an ancient tradition that any visitor who aspires to be acknowledged as a master of sorcery by this school may be challenged in combat by an existing master.'

Johans said, 'Yes, precisely, Master Uvren is correct.'

Lamm put his head in his hands and laughed.

Johans said, 'I do not think this is a laughing matter. The majority around this table have never met this so-called goddess, and yet we are expected to accept her as our leader!' There were some nods of approval.

Uvren said, 'You make a fair point, Johans, but who would challenge her?'

Johans replied, 'That is for us to decide, but I would be pleased to do so if all are agreeable.'

Uvren said, 'Johans, I think you misunderstand my meaning. In theory, I agree with the point you are making, but I have met the goddess. In practice, anyone who challenges her to a dual will surely die.'

Lamm said, 'Enough of this nonsense. Johans, you may challenge the goddess to a dual if you wish; it may provide some light entertainment for her, but it will be terminal for you.'

Master Sonder said, 'I also challenge this goddess; the reputation of the school is at stake. Master Lamm, she cannot go unchallenged.'

Master Etten said, 'I also challenge.'

Lamm's head dropped down into his hands once more.

Uvren said, 'Master Lamm, perhaps we could change this into a ceremony of sorts. The goddess is welcomed to the school and meets the challenge of the existing masters as required by tradition. You and I are reclused because she is known to us, and of course, we don't want to die; therefore, Masters Johans, Sonder and Etten will carry out the challenge.'

Lamm replied, 'Yes, that could work. Johans, I expect her to arrive mid-morning. Could you make the necessary arrangements? The entire student population should be invited to the event. But I warn you, if she feels under threat, she will kill all three of you.'

Johans laughed and said, 'I will make the necessary arrangements.'

Mab slept late and managed to extract herself from Fora without waking her. She mind-linked with Lamm and said, 'I will be with you shortly. Could I have breakfast when I arrive?'

Lamm laughed and said, 'Breakfast is no problem. However, I need to warn you of something. A few of the masters here have never met you, and they want to put you to the test. They are claiming this is an ancient school tradition, and Uvren has told me they are correct, but it has seldom, if ever, been used.'

Mab replied, 'What does it involve?'

Lamm replied, 'Basically, they will each have a go at trying to kill you.'

Mab replied, 'Sounds like a normal day then!'

Lamm laughed and said, 'The ringleader is Johans. I have a feeling he is planning something, so he will have some tricks to play.'

Mab asked, 'Am I allowed to kill them?'

Lamm said, 'In the case of Johans, yes, I think he has his own agenda. He was very unhappy when I was offered the principal role at the school, and he has been difficult ever since. The other two, Sonder and Etten, I think are genuine in that they see this as supporting the traditions of the school. But Mab, if you have to kill all three to protect yourself, then do so. And be careful with Johans, he may have others helping him. I'm sorry about all this. Would you like to postpone the visit until a more suitable time?'

Mab replied, 'No, I can see that you have had problems, but a hearty breakfast would be appreciated!'

Mab showered and dressed in her white robe with a red sash. Her hair was platted on both sides of her head, she carried a whip of light on her left hip and Onimaru was hitched high on her back. Her hooded black master's robe covered all with only the hilt and pommel of Onimaru visible above her left shoulder. Mab thought of Lamm, vanished and appeared by his side. He was seated together with the masters of the school; breakfast was already laid out on the table. All stood up to welcome her, but only Lamm and Uvren bowed deeply. Mab nodded to Lamm and Uvren and simply stared at the others.

There was an awkward silence; Lamm said, 'Please, Mab, take a seat.'

The other masters sat down, but Mab remained standing with Lamm and Uvren. She walked slowly to the chair. Her robe and sword vanished as she sat down.

Lamm and Uvren sat down. Lamm, clearly very upset, said, 'Please, Mab, help yourself.' Mab looked at him and could see the anguish in his expression. But she smiled, and a wave of calm and happiness flowed through Lamm. He gasped, his eyes filled with tears. Mab helped herself to the lavish breakfast in silence, only nodding occasionally to support Lamm.

When all had their fill, Johans said, 'I am sure Master Lamm has explained that any visiting master, who expects to be acknowledged as such by this school, must undergo a challenge.'

Mab looked disapprovingly at Johans, the way a teacher would with a naughty child. Johans struggled to breathe; small rivers of blood escaped his nose. He began to sweat profusely. But then Mab's attention was elsewhere, and she was looking through Johans to another place. There was a sudden flash of light; a golden giant appeared in the room, his eyes fixed only upon Mab.

Michael bowed, bent the knee and said, 'Goddess, I bring grim news in person.'

Mab said, 'Michael, you may speak freely.'

Michael said, 'The darkness rises; it is already present in the outer regions.'

Mab paused and said, 'And my suspicions regarding the Mevlen?'

Michael replied, 'You were correct, but she is extremely capable and dangerous.'

Mab replied, 'We will meet soon in the palace of the old gods with my sister. We will then decide on the best course of action.'

Mab paused before adding, 'Michael, we do not fear the dark. Go now, speak with Lucifer and Gabriel.'

Michael's grim expression faded. He smiled, nodded sharply, and vanished.

Lamm said, 'Mab, I can see that you have many important issues to deal with. Please don't feel you have to stay here any longer.'

Mab replied, 'Master Lamm, the slights I have experienced here are not of your making.' Mab turned to the three masters and said, 'What you do not understand is that when you insult me, you disrespect the light and that I will not tolerate. I therefore accept your challenge, but please take time now to speak to your families as you will not be returning home. Master Lamm, can I suggest we take the tour of the campus now? This will give your three colleagues the necessary time to prepare.'

Lamm replied, 'Yes, of course.'

Lamm walked Mab out of the main building and said, 'Are you really going to kill them?'

Mab laughed and said, 'If I receive an abject apology from them, then no, but Johans does intend to kill me. He has archers positioned on the roof of what looks like a sports stadium?'

Lamm replied, 'Yes, that is where the challenge is taking place, before the whole school. You read this from his mind?'

Mab said, 'Yes, but he is in league with others and what worries me is that I can see only fragments of them in his mind. Their presence has been erased, but not completely; it is strange. I think the darkness may have already reached this school.'

Lamm replied, 'Johans is an expert on herbs and poisons, so you should expect the arrows to be coated in something very nasty. Unfortunately, we don't have any serious security guards here. If I sent our caretakers, they would be killed; these assassins will be professionals.'

Mab said, 'Yes, they are professionals. They left traces of themselves on Johan's clothes. They are from the North, ex-soldiers now mercenaries. There are four of them in position on the roof of the stadium. I could kill them now and crush their minds, but we may be able to extract some information from them. Similarly, with Johans, I will scour his mind, but he won't survive the process.'

Lamm said, 'He is a traitor. What of Sonder and Etten?'

Mab replied, 'I could find nothing worrying in their minds. Johans is using them for his own purposes.'

Lamm took Mab to the accommodation blocks which were very similar to those at the Guild, although of more recent construction. They also visited the new sports centre, which was particularly impressive. The school had its own tradition of martial arts, and the students gave demonstrations of their abilities, including fixed kata-type routines and unarmed combat. Lamm explained that they did not teach the use of weapons in the school, but as an optional part of the curriculum, students were able to travel to the warrior school at the Guild if they so wished. When the demonstrations were completed, Lamm and Mab applauded enthusiastically.

A junior student approached Mab with a huge bunch of beautiful flowers, kneeled and said, 'Goddess Bellona, these are for you from the students of the school.'

Mab, clearly delighted and overcome, pulled the little boy close and kissed him on the cheek. She then stood up, thanked the students for their magnificent performances and said, 'I don't think I have ever received such a beautiful bouquet of flowers!'

As they left the sports centre, Lamm said, 'I must remember to bring you flowers more often!'

Mab, hugging the bouquet, replied, 'The truth is that I have never been given a bouquet of flowers. They are so beautiful. Where did you get them?'

Lamm said, 'We grow them here on the campus, mostly indoors but many also outside.'

As they approached the stadium, Mab said, 'It's huge and very old!'

Lamm replied, 'Yes, I think it was used in ancient times for something rather more serious than sport. I was thinking of pulling it down and making do with open fields, but it is really useful to have such a large, covered area.'

Mab said, 'Yes, I guess so, although it reminds me of Yehuda and the revolting games held there.'

They walked through an archway into the arena, and a huge roar of applause reverberated around the stadium.

Mab said, 'So, this is where everyone is! I wondered why the campus was so quiet.'

Lamm and Mab walked to the centre of the arena, where a group of masters was waiting.

Lamm looked at Johans and said, 'This is your challenge; please explain the rules.'

Master Uvren intervened and said, 'The rules state that by agreement, there can only be one challenger.'

Johans replied, 'Yes, I am the challenger.'

Sonder said, 'What of Etten and I?'

Uvren replied, 'It is not acceptable for the visitor to face three separate challenges; that would be grossly unfair.'

Mab said, 'Master Uvren, I do not have the time for three separate challenges; therefore, I will face all three at the same time.'

Uvren looked at Lamm, who nodded and said, 'Very well, but I wish it to be known that I do not agree with any of this nonsense. You, Johans, are not only a fool; you are also a disgrace to this school.'

Johans laughed and replied, 'And you, Uvren, are an old fool, now let's get on with this.'

Sonder and Etten unsheathed huge silver swords, and Mab could see immediately when they were much too heavy and poorly balanced. Johans walked to the edge of the arena and returned with a long, ornate spear that had silver barbs and razor-like blades at the tip. It was a fearsome weapon. Mab could see the poison sticking between the barbs; she looked closer and realised it was no ordinary spear. It was certainly enchanted, perhaps sentient.'

Johans smiled and said, 'Something wrong, goddess? Perhaps you thought us to be a bunch of country bumpkins incapable of combat. Well, it's too late for second thoughts.'

Mab stared upwards for a few moments and said, 'The archers you placed on the stadium roof, one of them was your brother?'

Johans looked at Mab and said, 'I don't know what you are talking about. What do you know of my brother?'

Mab said, 'He and the other three assassins are dead, their minds crushed. Now, Master Uvren, can you please ring the start bell.'

Lamm walked quickly to the edge of the arena, followed by Uvren and announced, 'Masters, students and adepts. This contest was claimed by Masters Johans, Sonder and Etten, who, under the rules and traditions of this school, claim the right to test any visitor wishing to be recognised as a master of the school. The Goddess Bellona has accepted the challenge and has agreed to face all three masters in combat to the death.' An eerie silence swept around the stadium; this was not what they expected.

Uvren said, 'The contest will commence upon the third strike of the bell.' Uvren struck the bell, but at the end of the second strike, five arrows were launched from within the stadium. Mab was aware immediately that the arrows took flight, the archers were experts, and all would strike home. Time slowed; Mab levitated high into the air, reached out to the archers and crushed their minds. The arrows fell harmlessly to the ground. Mab landed softly; as she did so, Sonder and Etten fell to the ground unconscious, leaving Johans standing alone, wielding his spear. The crowd leapt to their feet and applauded vigorously.

Johans moved towards Mab, stabbing at her with the barbed spear while launching psychic blasts that had little effect. Mab moved with astonishing speed, easily avoiding contact with the poisoned barbs. Johans rammed the staff forward, Mab spun around the barbed tip, grabbed the shaft, and struck it with her elbow. The spear bent but did not break. Mab leapt away, opened her right hand, and Onimaru screamed over her shoulder. She parried the next thrust and brought Onimaru down, and the sword bit deep into the spear shaft. Mab felt the power binding the spear snapping as the shaft severed; she spun around, grabbed Johans by the neck, lifted him off the ground and threw him backwards into the air and across the arena. Johans hit the ground awkwardly; he lay, groaning, with multiple injuries. Lamm walked to the bell, rang it three times and announced the challenge was satisfied. The crowd gave muted applause, clearly shocked by what they had seen. Lamm asked everyone to leave the stadium.

Mab waited until the crowd thinned and walked slowly towards Johans. She stared down at him and said, 'Tell me everything; this is your last chance.'

Johans spat blood at her and said, 'I will tell you nothing, Bitch!' Johan's broken body was lifted upright and slammed back hard against a thick wooden post.

Mab's mind probe seared into him; he screamed in agony, blood pouring from his nose and ears. Mab searched through his mind, reading, cutting and slashing layer upon layer, deeper and deeper, until there was nothing left.' Johans hung on the post, his eyes wide, saliva running from his mouth.

Mab turned to Lamm and, seeing the horror on his face, said, 'Master Lamm, this was necessary. It is as I suspected; he was in league with dark powers. We will discuss this later today at the Guild meeting.' She turned and hammered her fist into Johan's face, crushing his skull and killing him instantly; his ruined body dropped to the ground.

Mab picked up the spear, studied the barbed tip and said, 'Master Lamm, do you know where he obtained this weapon?'

Lamm, still in shock, replied, 'I will talk to the armoury; I have never seen it before.'

Uvren added, 'He kept it hidden until the last moment; perhaps that was deliberate?'

Mab replied, 'Yes, it was a named weapon, strengthened by a strange enchantment. I do not think it is of this plane. Master Lamm, if you agree, I will take it with me. Master Boe may be able to shed light on its origins.'

Lamm nodded and said, 'Mab, I am so sorry for all of this. I had hoped to impress you, but instead, I put you in jeopardy.'

Mab replied, 'Master Lamm, I was never in jeopardy. As for Johans, he was manipulated by others. Sonder and Etten will wake in a few minutes, but they have lost their powers. The archer assassins are all dead. I will travel to the Guild now, and I look forward to seeing you later.' Mab vanished and appeared in her bedroom at the Guild. She lay back on her bed, closed her eyes and went into a deep sleep.

Several hours later, Mab's eyes snapped open; Minerva appeared before her and said, 'Sister, what have you learned?'

Mab replied, 'I will know by mid-day tomorrow. I will come to you, and we will decide what must be done. There have been incursions and reports of fell creatures on outlying planets. Michael thinks this activity may not be related to Erebus; he may not even be aware that it is happening.'

Minerva nodded, opened her arms and said, 'Sister, you are weary.'

Mab embraced Minerva, and a burst of white light engulfed them. Mab could feel the power flowing into her, and she gasped with pleasure.

Chapter Thirty-Two: Council of War

Mab reached out and found Pelian. She and her sister were in the warrior school training facility. Mab changed into her white robe and pulled on her soft leather boots. As she dressed, her hair became as white as fresh snow; it set into a centre parting and hung short just above her shoulders. She walked downstairs and knocked on Boe's door, but there was no answer. She had intended to go straight to Kanaka's office but decided to drop into the warrior school. Mab vanished into mind space, entered the school and floated above the training floor. Pelian and Gilian were practicing with real swords.

They each held identical medium-length double-edged weapons, and Mab could tell that the blades were of an exotic material. She was impressed with their speed and agility as they took turns to attack each other. Gilian was clearly more experienced, and Mab could tell that she was holding back. However, what Pelian lacked in experience she made up by sheer effort; she was moving so fast that her sword was a blur. They were both breathing hard and sweating profusely when Mab materialised and dropped to the floor. Pelian ran to Mab and embraced her. Mab hugged and kissed her before walking with her to Gilian.

Mab said, 'Gilian, that was impressive; Pelian has learned much from you.'

Gilian replied, 'Thank you, goddess, but we have both learned much from Master Kanaka.'

Mab said, 'We have a meeting in Master Kanaka's office, so you two best get showered and changed. Tomorrow morning, we will practice together, and then Pelian, you will be put to the test, but I have to say I was very impressed by what I have just seen!'

Pelian smiled and said, 'Gilian is my sister; I had to be gentle with her.'

Mab said, 'So you are going to be rough with me?'

Pelian nodded solemnly.

Mab laughed and said, 'I am so looking forward to our battle!'

Kanaka paced around his desk while Lamm, Luticia and Boe helped themselves to the fine wine that he had ordered specially for Mab.

Lamm said, 'I could not believe what I was hearing when Johans challenged her to a duel.'

Kanaka replied, 'The difficulty is that she is not what she seems. But also, to be frank, your school is somewhat removed from what has been going on over recent years. You, of course, are very much aware, but unless they experience it themselves, it is irrelevant to their lives.'

Luticia nodded in agreement and said, 'Absolutely, I and my school were the enemy, and so Mab had to intervene. Now, every student knows her by sight, holds her in the very highest regard and treats her with the greatest respect, as, of course, do I.'

Boe said, 'Lamm, you need to get more of her time and organise some competitions or events.'

Lamm replied, 'Yes, I have been trying to do that, but she has been so busy recently. Also, I have had difficulty with the masters. They see me as an outsider, particularly Johans, who resisted almost every change I tried to make.'

Kanaka replied, 'Well, he won't be resisting now! Perhaps you should take this opportunity to do a clean sweep, get rid of the current masters and recruit a new team. We have a few advanced students, Gho, for example, who would welcome such an opportunity.'

Lamm replied, 'Yes, I will give that serious thought.'

Mab walked into the room and said, 'I hope you haven't finished the wine!'

Kanaka said, 'No danger of that; I have a generous stock!' They had a group hug and then took their seats.

Mab said, 'Master Lamm, I was thinking that I should visit you more often. Get to know the masters and the students. What do you think?'

Lamm replied, 'That would be much appreciated. Master Boe was only just saying the same thing and Master Kanaka suggested I change the leadership team, perhaps recruit some younger blood?'

Mab, raising a goblet of wine, replied, 'Yes, definitely. Johans is gone, and Sonder and Etten have no powers. You should be thinking about three new masters.'

Kanaka said, 'Mab, while we are waiting for Pelian and Gilian to arrive. What do you think is going on?'

Mab paused in thought and then said, 'I can tell you what I think, and fear is happening, but first, I need to hear from Gilian, and then I need to discuss it with my sister. I am sorry to be evasive, Master Kanaka, but we are on the precipice; loose talk could result in catastrophe.' There was silence around the table, which was interrupted by a knock at the door and Pelian's head appearing.

Master Kanaka said, 'Please come in, help yourself to the food and wine.' Gilian and Pelian sat down and immediately filled their plates with generous helpings of everything available.

Boe said, 'You two have the appetite of a goddess!'

Mab said, 'They have been training very hard. Pelian has threatened some rough treatment when we have our battle tomorrow.'

Kanaka laughed and said, 'I can't miss that. Boe, we need to invite the whole school!'

Boe nodded and replied, 'Perhaps we should have it on the sports field? It will be a bit chilly, but otherwise, the weather is set fine for tomorrow.'

Kanaka said, 'Perfect!'

Mab said, 'Yes, there will also be more room for me to escape Pelian's vicious attacks.'

Pelian laughed and replied, 'There will be no escape for you, goddess!'

Everyone laughed, but then Kanaka looked at Gilian and said, 'I understand you have some important knowledge to impart?'

Gilian looked at Mab, who nodded and said, 'My people are known as the Mevlen; we are not of this plane. We have three planets in our star system; we occupy the first and second of these. We are peace-loving but can defend ourselves if needed. I was with our military but left to search for my sister Pelian, who was taken from us when she was an infant. I travelled through many planes eventually reaching here, where I met the goddess. The darkness has grown somewhat, but it hasn't returned and is certainly not rising.

There is a degree of incursion, which is not unusual or excessive. For example, on my travels, I have encountered some creatures of the Abyss within the populations, but they are loners who are active only during the night. There is much scaremongering, although it is, of course, important to stay vigilant.'

Mab nodded and said, 'That is very good news indeed. So, you do not concur with the view that the darkness is rising in preparation for an invasion?'

Gilian replied, 'I have seen no evidence of that.'

Kanaka replied, 'Yes, this is very good news and calls for a celebration; fill your plates and goblets!'

The dinner lasted long into the night, driven by the party mood. Kanaka brought the event to an end by proposing yet another toast to the reunion of Pelian and Gilian. Mab stayed behind with Kanaka when the revellers made their way back to their respective accommodations.

Kanaka went to his drinks cabinet and retrieved a bottle of fine whisky.

Mab said, 'Is that what I think it is?'

Kanaka replied, 'Yes, courtesy of Fat Joe.'

Kanaka poured two generous measures and said, 'What Gilian said was a great relief to us all.'

Mab sipped the whisky, signed for silence and secrecy, and whispered, 'That creature is not Gilian.'

Kanaka stared in horror at Mab and replied, 'A daemon, I didn't detect anything?'

Mab said, 'No, it is not a daemon, and although it is from the Abyss, it is not from Erebus.'

Kanaka said, 'Then what is it?'

Mab replied, 'It is a dark god; Erebus is not the only power in the Abyss. I know this from the light war; we battled creatures who had no allegiance to anyone or anything but were driven only by their misplaced hatred of the light. The Abyss is quite literally chaos; there is no order and no enduring allegiances, but there is an infinite supply of creatures who despise the light.'

Kanaka said, 'But what of Gilian?'

Mab replied, 'I asked Michael to search for Gilian; he found her dead body on an adjacent plane. The dark god took her memories and her shape. It molded itself to create a perfect replica of Gilian and that is how Michael was able to find her body. The dark god's scent, her sweat, and her very cells are almost identical to that of Pelian. It is a powerful being; I believe it obtained information on Pelian from the lords and has come to kill my sister and me.'

Kanaka said, 'Mab if that thing harms you, I will intervene, so do not tell me otherwise!'

Mab smiled and replied, 'Tomorrow, when I test Pelian, I will also test the creature and try to kill it. You will need to keep the students well away from the fighting area. Also, it will most probably be able to read minds, so do nothing up until the point where I challenge it. Use the danger signal to alert the masters; do not use mind messaging. If things go badly wrong, the Archangels will join you to help save as many lives as possible. Michael and Lucifer will be in mind space watching the proceedings and only manifest if necessary.'

Kanaka nodded and said, 'We should try to get some sleep.'

Mab nodded, paused, and said, 'Master Kanaka, could you make sure Pelian doesn't do anything rash?'

Kanaka replied, 'I'll do my best!'

Mab slept late and woke refreshed. She wore her tight sports leggings with a thick leather waistcoat, high-length leather boots and leather gauntlets. She hitched Onimaru high on her back and made her way to the sports field. She always thought that killing was best done on an empty stomach. The entire sports field was cordoned off with bunting, and Mab thought this somewhat incongruous in view of what was about to happen; nevertheless, the fighting area was huge, so the spectators should be safe. The students were beginning to arrive and being shepherded by Lamm, Boe and Luticia. Boe approached Mab and said, 'You were correct; the barbed spear tip is not of this plane. It looks like silver, but it is an exotic alloy that I do not recognise.'

Mab replied, 'Could you give it back to Master Lamm and ask him to look into its origins?'

Boe nodded and walked off towards Lamm. Kanaka was working with Pelian, doing some last-minute coaching. Mab noticed

Gilian, who immediately looked in Mab's direction and waved. Mab nodded and looked back toward Pelian and Kanaka.

Kanaka left Pelian, walked to Mab and said, 'Are you ready?'

Mab nodded in reply, and Kanaka walked off to talk to Lamm, Luticia and Boe. Mab walked to the centre of the sports field, and Pelian ran to meet her. She could see immediately that something was wrong. Mab was tense, and she had never seen her like that. Pelian was about to speak when Mab reached behind and pushed the scabbard of Onimaru upwards and let it drop back down. An alert! Immediate danger, no mind communication. Pelian took a deep breath, looked into Mab's eyes and relaxed.

Mab smiled and said, in a loud voice, 'Well, are you ready to be tested?'

Pelian's face lit up, and she said, 'Yes, but I will not go easy with you!'

Kanaka had positioned the other masters around the fighting area, and as he walked towards Mab, he reached behind and touched the scabbard of Dawn-Breaker, giving the danger signal. As he walked, he glanced at each of the masters, and they understood the gravity of the situation! Kanaka announced, 'Today Pelian, a lord of chaos, will be tested for swordsmanship by Master Winter. Pelian glanced at Kanaka and knew immediately that he also was aware of the danger.

Mab whispered to Pelian, 'Keep your eyes on me and nothing else!'

Pelian nodded; Kanaka said, 'Mab when you are ready.' Onimaru screamed from the scabbard; at the same time, Mab's left foot kicked Pelian in the chest. Pelian fell backwards onto the ground but rolled sideways and somersaulted onto her feet, her silver sword drawn. The audience applauded; Mab smiled. Pelian launched a ferocious attack, her silver sword moving with blinding speed. Mab retreated apace, but she then dropped to the ground and kicked Pelian's legs from underneath her. Pelian changed sword hands in mid-flight, hit the ground with her right hand and cartwheeled back to her feet, the sword in her left hand slicing downwards, but Mab was already on her feet, Onimaru a blur as it moved through the air. Pelian retreated but maintained the pace, parrying everything that Mab threw at her; she then stopped and brought Mab's attack to a halt. They stood face to face, only a few paces from each other, their swords moving too fast to follow. But then Mab grabbed Pelian's sword arm at the wrist, threw Onimaru high into the air and cried, 'Enough!' Onimaru dropped directly into the scabbard. The audience roared; Pelian dropped her sword and threw her arms around Mab.

Kanaka approached and said, 'Pelian, very well done!' He then looked at Mab and said, 'What's the verdict.'

Mab replied, 'It was excellent; I saw all I needed to see in the first few seconds.'

She then looked at Pelian and said, 'Now, I want you to go with Master Kanaka and, no matter what happens, stay by his side. Do you understand?'

Pelian stared at Mab and knew something very bad was about to happen. She simply replied, 'Yes, I understand.' But

Mab said, 'Swear to me that you will stay by his side.'

Pelian paused and then said, 'I swear that I will not leave his side unless instructed by you.'

Mab looked at Kanaka and nodded. Kanaka walked to the edge of the sports field, Pelian beside him.

Mab walked in the opposite direction towards Luticia. As she approached the edge of the fighting area, Gilian turned to make her way toward Pelian. Mab called out, 'Gilian, it is now your turn to be tested.'

Gilian looked at Mab, smiled and said, 'So, you know who I am?'

Mab replied, 'I don't know who you are or what you are, but I do know that you killed Gilian. I can only assume that you are a shapeshifter?'

Gilian laughed and said, 'As you will soon discover, I am no mere shapeshifter.'

Mab replied, 'Then what are you?'

Gilian said, 'I am a god of the Abyss; I have always been and always will be.'

Mab replied, 'No, I am the goddess Bellona. I am of the light, and your life will end here.'

Mab soared backwards and upwards, and Gilian followed her at great speed. Mab raised her left hand, palm outwards and struck Gilian with a powerful psychic blast. Gilian was propelled backwards and tumbled from the air like a rag doll; she hit the ground hard but leapt back to her feet, seemingly unscathed. Mab dropped down to the middle of the fighting area and waited for Gilian, who approached slowly. Tentacles of dark power sprouted from Gillian and writhed through the air towards Mab, who felt them burn into her skin as they wrapped around her. She tried to break free, but they were too strong. Mab opened her right hand. Onimaru tumbled over her shoulder, slicing through the topmost tentacles. As Mab's hand grasped Onimaru, the tentacles retreated, freeing her arm; the blade powered through the tentacles, driving them back towards Gilian. Mab's hand went to her left hip, and a lash of white silver sliced through the air, passing through the tentacles like a hot knife through butter. The whip lashed Gilian across the face. Gilian screamed in agony. Mab lashed her again and again until she dropped to her knees. She then withdrew the whip, but Gilian vanished and appeared immediately in front of Mab. She held two long, thin iron blades in each hand. Mab grabbed hold of Gillian's neck with one hand and her arm with another. Gilian used her free arm to drive a blade deep into Mab's side. Mab's face twisted in pain, but she crushed Gilian's throat and ripped the arm from her body. Arterial blood sprayed from the ragged tear in Gilian's shoulder; muscle, flesh and bone dangled in a shower of red, which slowly diminished. Gillian dropped to her knees; Mab pulled the melee blade from her side and rammed it downwards through Gillian's skull, the point exiting from her crushed throat. She then kicked Gilian in the chest, knocking her onto her back. Her form began to change, first to an amorphous black mass and then to a vaguely human shape but with elongated limbs bearing vicious claws and a gaping mouth filled with carious fangs. The creature had bulbous frog-like eyes, and it stank of rotting flesh. It leapt upwards, wrapping its long legs and arms around Mab, pinning her arms to her sides, and sank its fangs into her shoulder. Mab groaned in pain and tried to break the creature's hold, but it was too strong. She let her head fall back and then rammed it forward, headbutting the creature's face. The blow stunned it, but it did not release its hold. The creature smiled, brought its face close to Mab's and bared its huge fangs. Mab closed her eyes as if in surrender; she felt the creature savouring the victory. She then opened her eyes; her black orbs were gone, and her eye sockets blazed silver light. Two narrow beams seared into and through the creature's head. It tried to escape, but Mab held it tightly and drilled ever deeper into its body. When she released the creature, it fell to the ground, badly injured but not dead. It changed shape once more, seemingly trying to find a form that would aid its escape. It rose up into the air in the form of a black cloud of matter. Mab raised her hand, the sky darkened and pointed at the creature. A bolt of lightning streaked across the sky and plummeted downwards, striking the black mass to the ground. The masters pushed the spectators further back, well away from the fighting area. Another more powerful lightning bolt streaked downwards and seared into the creature. Mab stood looking down at the creature as it changed back into human form, a small boy with blonde tousled hair, and pleaded to be set free. But Mab rained lightning bolts on the dark god until all that remained was an oily patch of foul-smelling blackness. Mab stared for a few moments before raising her hand and incinerating the remains with a broad beam of light.

Michael and Lucifer appeared at her side. Lucifer said, 'What was that thing?'

Mab replied, 'It was of the Abyss.'

Lucifer said, 'It bit you on the shoulder; you shouldn't have let that happen. It could lead to a nasty infection.'

Mab glanced up at Michael, who shook his head and laughed. Mab replied, 'Thank you, Lucifer; I will be sure to remember that the next time I do battle with a god of the Abyss.'

Kanaka arrived and said, 'Mab, are you injured?'

Mab replied, 'I have a couple of wounds, but they are almost healed.'

Michael said, 'Goddess, we will leave you now.'

Mab nodded, and Michael and Lucifer vanished. The rest of the masters arrived together with Pelian, who threw her arms around Mab and hugged her tightly. Mab said, 'I am sorry, but that creature killed your sister.'

Pelian replied, 'Master Kanaka has explained everything.'

Kanaka said, 'Why don't we have a late breakfast together?'

Mab replied, 'That would be perfect. I am absolutely starving!'

Mab, Pelian and the masters made their way to Kanaka's office, where breakfast had already been prepared.

Kanaka looked at Mab and said, 'I knew you wouldn't eat before the battle, and I figured if you didn't make it, then I would eat your share.'

Mab laughed and said, 'Well, thank you, Master Kanaka, but as you see, I did make it, and I intend to make the most of this wonderful spread!'

Lamm said, 'Mab, do you know what that creature was?'

Mab replied, 'It said it was a dark god of the Abyss. It was an ancient creature, perhaps the only one of its kind. I didn't want to kill it, but I had no other option.'

Luticia said, 'It had to be stopped; it killed Pelian's sister and would have killed many more innocent people.'

Mab nodded and replied, 'Yes, of course, but to kill such a creature, is that not also a crime? This is the reason I was sickened by the light war.'

Boe said, 'Yes, but that is the very nature of war. To be prepared to kill another without understanding their life story, to take everything from them, what they are and what they will be. It cannot be done without compassion or remorse.' There was a moment of silence.

Kanaka said, 'Master Boe, what you say is correct, and Mab has openly expressed her remorse for having to kill such a creature. However, whether we like it or not, and no matter where we may travel in the multiverse, all sentient creatures know that there is good and there is evil, all know the difference, and all are free to choose which path to follow.'

Lamm said, 'It is a circular argument which takes us back to the light and the dark as absolutes, but is there not a spectrum of positions between good and evil?'

A voice said, 'You will know them by their actions.' Minerva appeared in the room. The masters and Pelian all stood up and bowed.

Mab rose, embraced Minerva and said, 'I was about to visit you, but since you are here, please take a seat.'

Minerva replied, 'This place is not secure; we will go to the palace, bring your friends.'

Mab said, 'I haven't finished my breakfast!'

Minerva laughed and said, 'You will have a second breakfast with hot coffee and wine.'

Mab looked at Kanaka and said, 'We need to go with Minerva immediately.'

Kanaka laughed and said, 'Yes, I agree!'

The group appeared in the palace of the old gods. Mab said, 'Sister, Pelian and I must bathe. Will you join us?'

Minerva smiled and replied, 'I will join you shortly; I need to contact Erebus.'

The masters helped themselves to goblets of wine and wandered together around the extensive gardens. Mab and Pelian walked to the lake, and they kicked off their boots, and as they stepped into the water, their clothes disappeared. Pelian immediately submerged up to her neck and gasped as she felt the renewing effects of the water.

Mab said, 'It is wonderful, is it not?'

Pelian replied, 'Yes, and I see that your wounds have healed.'

She kissed Mab, and they both relaxed in the water. Minerva walked towards them, lowered herself into the lake and said, 'Erebus will be with us soon; he will be accompanied by Baydan and Sladrin.'

Mab replied, 'What have you told him?'

Minerva said, 'I have told him nothing, but he was very wary. He knows something has changed, most probably that creature you just killed.'

Mab replied, 'You were watching?'

Minerva said, 'No, but whatever that thing was, its death rang like a bell through mind space. I imagine it would have been even louder in the Abyss.'

Mab replied, 'It said it was of the Abyss. I didn't want to kill it, but I had no choice.'

Minerva said, 'They have arrived; I will allow them entry to the main hall.' Mab and Pelian walked from the lake, every drop of water running from their bodies. A red-sashed robe appeared on Mab and a blue hooded lord's robe on Pelian. They both wore sandals of soft brown leather.

Mab put her arm around Pelian and said, 'Be careful what you say.'

Pelian smiled and nodded.

The masters were waiting in the cloistered area close to the table in the main hall.

Kanaka, on seeing Mab and Pelian, said, 'You both look refreshed! How was the water?'

Mab replied, 'It was wonderful, you should try it! Erebus, Baydan and Sladrin have arrived. My sister has gone to bring them here.' Mab saw them approaching, and they had taken human form. Erebus was huge, heavily muscled and of a similar stature to Lucifer but not as lean or athletic in appearance. Sladrin was tall and thin, befitting his true reptilian form, whereas Baydan was short and squat but powerfully muscled. As they drew close, Mab could sense the tension in the air.

Minerva gestured in Mab's direction and said, 'This is my sister Bellona.'

Erebus stared into Mab's black eyes.

Mab held his stare, smiled and said, 'I am very pleased to meet you.'

There was a flash of light; Michael, Gabriel and Lucifer appeared behind Mab. Baydan and Sladrin flinched and stepped back.

Mab said, 'This is Michael, Gabriel and Lucifer, Archangels of the Light. Behind them, we have Master Kanaka, Master Boe, Master Lamm and Master Luticia. On my right is Pelian, recently of the so-called lords of chaos.'

Baydan leered at Pelian, who ignored the insult, but Mab said, 'You, Baydan, will take your eyes from her; otherwise, I will remove them from your head.' Baydan's eyes snapped to Mab's, but he could not hold her stare.

Minerva, with a grim smile on her face, said, 'Now, let us pretend we are civilised. Take a seat; we will eat together and perhaps even talk.'

When they sat food began to appear on the table. Kanaka realised that he only had to think about what he wanted, and it appeared. Rice, fish and fresh fruit appeared in front of him, together with a small ceramic cup of warm wine. He noticed that the other guests all had quite different tastes. Mab had cheese, fruits, rustic bread, smoked fish and a large goblet of ice-cold white wine. The guests from the Abyss ate large portions of roasted animal flesh and drank what appeared to be ale. The Archangels stood away from the table in silence but watched every movement.

Erebus looked at Mab and said, 'I know of you, Bellona, but I have never had the pleasure of meeting you. It is a great honour to be here with you and Minerva.'

Mab stared at him askance. His voice was like stone, deep and solid but also smooth and warm. It was a strange dichotomy, which made her feel somewhat uncomfortable. She replied, 'Thank you, Erebus; it is surprising that we have not met before. If we had, then perhaps things would have been different.'

Baydan, clearly uncomfortable by friendly banter, said, 'Goddess Bellona, it is said that unaided, you slew a full battalion of our alpha warriors. Is this truth or fanciful legend?'

Mab paused and replied, 'I have slain many; most deserved their fate, some did not.'

Baydan said, 'So it is a lie then?'

Michael stepped forward and, towering over Baydan, said, 'You will apologise to the Goddess.' Minerva looked at Michael and realised the gravity of the situation.

She turned to Baydan and cried, 'Apologise immediately!'

Baydan hesitated but then said, 'Goddess Bellona, I apologise; please excuse my clumsy words. I meant no disrespect.'

Mab nodded, Michael stepped back, and Erebus said, 'Baydan, your words were more than clumsy; they were extremely foolish.'

Mab looked at Lamm and said, 'Master Lamm, could you pass the spear tip to Erebus.'

Lamm removed the spear tip from his robe and passed it around the table to Erebus. Erebus turned it over, examining it closely. He then handed it to Sladrin and said, 'I don't recognise this; what do you think?'

Sladrin replied, 'It is certainly of the Abyss, perhaps from one of the more remote sects. Was it poisoned?'

Mab replied, 'Yes, a thick green substance, but that may have been sourced on our plane.'

Sladrin said, 'No, the poison is exuded from the spear itself.' He held it at arms-length, and suddenly, beads of a thick greenish substance accumulated on the barbs. Sladrin asked 'What happened to the shaft?'

Mab replied, 'My sword sliced through it; the spear was bound by an enchantment.'

Sladrin nodded and said, 'Yes, this spear is from the deep Abyss, possibly owned by a dark god. It is very valuable or was very valuable until it was unbound. The sword you hold must be very powerful; what did you call it?'

Mab plucked Onimaru from the air, black flames licked along the blade, and replied, 'This is Onimaru, slayer of daemons.'

Sladrin leapt back from the table. Erebus stared in astonishment and said, 'Where did you get that sword!?'

Mab replied, 'I was searching for a suitable weapon for Master Kanaka. It called to me, and I answered.'

Erebus said, 'I fear you do not know what you hold. It is....'

Mab interrupted him and said, 'Erebus, I know what I hold, and she knows what I am. I rescued her; she is bound to me, and I to her.'

Erebus stared at Mab for a few moments before replying, 'Your partnership is incongruous, to say the least, but it gives me some hope for the future.'

There was a period of silent eating before Pelian broke the mood by saying, 'Lord Sladrin, you mentioned a dark god; what is that?'

Sladrin looked at Erebus, who replied, 'The Abyss is vast, infinite; it hosts creatures that constantly surprise us. I am sure Lucifer will concur?'

Lucifer simply nodded but said nothing.

Erebus looked at Mab and said, 'However, I felt a disturbance in mind-space recently. It felt like a death, a dark singular power, dispersing back into the Abyss.'

Baydan, somewhat sheepishly, said, 'Lord Erebus, I sought help from the dark god Insheigra on how to recover Pelian. She agreed to help me in return for certain favours.'

Erebus said, 'Insheigra? Yes, I see it now; it was she who perished. But how?'

Mab replied, 'I killed her; it was unfortunate but necessary. She killed Pelian's sister, Gilian, and assumed her shape. She found me, and I her, by happenstance. I believed she was, in fact, Gilian and brought her to the Guild, where she was reunited with Pelian. But, sometime later, Michael found Gilian's body. I had thought she was a shapeshifter, but when I confronted her, she said she was a god of the Abyss. I didn't really care what she was but only that she killed Gilian and was a threat to Pelian and to the Guild.'

Baydan looked at Mab's askance and said, 'You killed Insheigra?'

Mab replied, 'Yes, and you, Baydan, are next on my list.'

Pelian laughed out loud; the others, including Erebus and Sladrin, smiled, but Mab did not smile or laugh. Minerva, seeing the expression on Mab's face, said, 'Baydan, what favours did you offer this dark god, and how was it able to enter our realm?'

Baydan replied, 'I offered her the opportunity to kill a goddess and, of course, to feed on the essence of Gilian of the Mevlen. I provided the initial host for the dark god, a human boy child. She found Gilian quickly from an item of Pelian's clothing, and thereafter, she took whatever form she needed.'

Baydan stopped talking, suddenly realising that in his enthusiasm, he had, perhaps, said too much. Erebus said, 'Baydan, you will go to your clan and await my return.' Baydan said nothing, stood up and vanished. Erebus looked at Minerva and said, 'I had no knowledge of this. I will deal with Baydan on my return.' He then turned to Pelian and said, 'I am sorry for the loss of your sister, Gilian, I will punish Baydan in my own way.'

Mab replied, 'You can do as you wish, but Baydan's life is forfeit for what he did to Pelian. I would have slain him here, but forbearance is required in this palace.'

Erebus said, 'You will not see him again; he will remain in the Abyss.' Mab replied, 'Then I will slay him in the Abyss. It matters nought to me where he dies.'

Minerva looked at Erebus and said, 'Should we discuss more important matters?' Erebus nodded his agreement.

Michael stepped forward and said, 'Certain planets in the outer systems are awash with creatures from the Abyss. We had initially thought these to be random incursions, but they are not. The creatures are being directed, there is discipline, and the planets involved may be considered strategically important should the objective be to occupy more populated systems. If this is permitted to continue, they will have access to a limitless supply of hosts which would threaten our home worlds and the future of all those who live in the light.'

Mab looked at Erebus and said, 'Do you expect us to believe that you have no knowledge of this?'

Erebus ignored Mab and, looking at Minerva, said, 'Perhaps you and I should discuss this another time when more rational minds are in the room?'

Mab stared balefully at Erebus, furious at the insult. Minerva glanced at Mab and saw that she was incandescent with rage. She looked back to Erebus and shook her head in despair. The Archangels staggered backwards away from the table, and the air around Mab bristled with power. Minerva also moved away but reached her hand out as if pleading for Mab to take it.

The masters retreated to the cloisters as the power field grew apace. Only Pelian remained seated by her side. Mab stood up, silver flames now licking around her body, lightning bolts streaked across the blue cloudless sky, and thunderclaps shook the palace to its very foundations. As she walked around the table towards Erebus, her eyes changed from deep black to silver. Erebus quickly realised that he had made a terrible error; he had never seen or felt such power.

Mab stared down at him and said, 'Do not mistake me for my sister! You will apologise immediately, or I will slay you here now.'

Erebus could barely speak or even think clearly; her very presence overwhelmed his senses. The palace rocked as if being shaken by the hand of an invisible giant. Erebus had to force each word out, 'I... apologise...Goddess.... an error...of judgement...on...my part.' Mab turned to walk back to her seat, and the storm subsided. Other than Pelian, everyone else had sought shelter.

Mab said, 'Where are you going? We are not finished here!' She took her seat, everyone else returned to their previous positions and remained silent. She then said, 'Erebus, what do you know of these incursions?'

Erebus replied, 'Goddess, I am aware of the growing activity in that area, but, in truth, it is of no interest to me. Please understand that the Abyss is my home, and I have no wish to leave it other than to visit this palace and be with Minerva. It may be that certain clans have decided to invade planets protected by the light. I do not know if it is a coordinated attack, but the Archangel says that it is, so it must be so.'

Minerva said, 'Erebus, can you find out what is happening?'

Erebus paused before replying, 'If you wish, I will go there, but it is not without risk even for me.'

Mab said, 'Lucifer will accompany you.'

Erebus nodded and replied, 'He would be most welcome.'

The three human-like figures sat in silence on stone chairs that surrounded the ruined table of rock at the summit of Raqus Mons. Erebus was dressed in a dark green shirt with matching trousers and wore a black cape of the finest silk, which matched his heavy black leather boots. His long silver hair hung over his shoulders, and his beard, also silver, was cut short. Humbra was tall and slender, and she was dressed in black tight-fitting sport-type leggings with a heavy brown leather waistcoat and boots. Her long black hair was platted in a thick rope that hung down her back. Sladrin lounged back in his chair, snake-like even when in human form. He was tall, slender, and dressed all in black with leather boots, tight-fitting trousers and a leather overcoat. His short hair and skin were as white as snow.

Erebus said, 'The lords will be here shortly; we need to know what they know.' The lords appeared just as Erebus stopped speaking.

Castaran said, 'Some of us have met before; I am Castaran, and my fellow lords are Seleran, Gorgat and Mendan. As you will know, Lord Erebus, Argaton and Tabbar were slain by the Goddess Bellona, who also took Pelian from us.' There was a flash of light, Lucifer appeared, he stood like a titan, indomitable as the surrounding rock.

Erebus gestured and replied, 'Sladrin and Humbra, and this is Lucifer, an Archangel of the light.'

Humbra was clearly dazzled by Lucifer, she could not take her eyes from him. Gorgat said, 'Lord Erebus, why is this Archangel here? We thought we had come here to discuss Minerva's sister and how to deal with her!'

Erebus looked at Lucifer, who said, 'No, we have come here to discuss the activity in the outer systems where creatures from the Abyss have occupied several planets. You will tell us what you know of this matter.'

Gorgat replied, 'Why should I tell you anything!' Lucifer smiled but said nothing.

Erebus said, 'Gorgat, you will tell us everything you know now!'

Gorgat blurted, 'Yes, of course, Lord Erebus. Clans of the deep Abyss have colonised two or three planets in the outer systems. I assume they are not here on Raqus because they know this is part of your domain. The indigenous populations on those planets provide ample hosts for the clans, and their numbers are now multiplying rapidly. My understanding is that dark gods of the Abyss are present, but I have not been there myself.'

Erebus said, 'These gods, do you know their names?'

Gorgat looked to Seleran, who said, 'Lord Erebus, the names given to us were Antobus, Mirablis, Insheigra, Infelice and Noticas. But please understand that we have not met or even seen any of these gods.'

Erebus looked to Humbra and Sladrin and said, 'Do you recognise any of the names?'

Humbra shrugged her shoulders, but Sladrin said, 'We know that Insheigra was slain recently by the goddess Bellona, but no, I don't recognise any of the other names.'

Gorgat said, 'I find it hard to believe Bellona could kill a god of the deep Abyss. What were the circumstances?'

Lucifer said, 'Insheigra killed Pelian's sister Gilian and replicated her body. The goddess found who she thought was Gilian and reunited her to Pelian. She soon realised her mistake and met Insheigra in battle. The contest did not last long. Insheigra was foolish in the extreme to challenge the Goddess.'

Erebus said, 'Lords, thank you for your help; you may leave now.'

But Gorgat replied, 'What of Pelian?'

Lucifer said, 'Pelian is favoured by the goddess; I advise that you stay away from her; she is with the goddess of her own free will.'

Castaran gestured with her right hand, and the lords vanished.

Erebus looked at Lucifer and said, 'I had assumed Bellona would be like her sister Minerva, as I thought she was at the time of the light war, but she is entirely different. I understand that she took you from the Abyss and reunited you with the other Archangels?'

Lucifer replied, 'She could have killed me, but instead, she brought me back into the light. For that, I will be eternally grateful to her.'

Humbra asked, 'She took you from the Abyss?'

Lucifer replied, 'The Goddess is unaffected by the Abyss. I was also foolish enough to battle with her, she defeated me with ease. She cast me down, ripped the black wings from my body, I lay before her dying, expecting the sword, but she lifted me up and redeemed me.'

Lucifer unfolded his enormous snow-white wings, Humbra gasped, and Erebus and Sladrin backed away. Lucifer smiled, and his wings retracted and vanished.

Humbra said, 'That was the most beautiful thing I have ever seen!'

Erebus said, 'Your wings are truly magnificent.'

Sladrin said, 'Control yourself, Hum, remember he is an Archangel!'

Erebus laughed and said, 'We have been here too long. Let us now visit these dark gods of the Abyss.'

Chapter Thirty-Three: The Dark God Noticas

Erebus led the group of four into the Abyss; they dropped into a rapidly flowing current and allowed themselves to be swept along with it. Lucifer rolled over onto his back and enjoyed the experience.

Humbra said, 'I think you are missing your home, Lucifer!'

Lucifer smiled and replied, 'I had forgotten how much I enjoyed riding the currents!'

Erebus said, 'Get ready to exit with me now!'

They propelled themselves off the current, hung in space for a few moments and then followed Erebus towards a point of dim light.

Erebus said, 'That is the Aardian system. There are two terrestrial planets, Aariet and Aafien, and these have been colonised by the gods.'

Lucifer said, 'How do you know that?'

Erebus replied, 'I sense two powerful beings, one on each of these planets.'

Lucifer reached out with his senses and said, 'Yes, there are many, but two, perhaps three, shine more brightly than the others. Do you know who they are?'

Erebus replied, 'No, but we can assume they are the gods mentioned by Seleran. Are you sure Insheigra is dead?'

Lucifer said, 'Of that, there is no doubt.'

Erebus said, 'I suggest we make our way to the god presence on Aariet. We will say we have become aware of their activity and simply wish to understand their intentions?'

Lucifer replied, 'We already know their intentions, and they will know that we know their intentions.'

Erebus said, 'Lucifer, this is politics. We are trying to get them to understand that they are on the wrong side of this issue, morally and from a military capability perspective. The objective is to reach a negotiated agreement.'

Lucifer replied, 'I don't think we should be negotiating. I am sure the goddess will expect them to leave and go back to the Abyss.'

Erebus, clearly somewhat frustrated, said, 'Yes, I am sure that is what she would expect. However, we don't want to be imprisoned on that planet, so let me do the talking. We are not committing to anything; the goddess can accept or reject our recommendations upon our safe return.'

Humbra added, 'Lucifer, let's just go there and see what happens?'

Lucifer replied, 'Yes, very well, but I am simply pointing out that we do not speak for the goddess; we are on a fact-finding mission only.'

Erebus rolled his eyes and said, 'Yes, fine we are all agreed on that.'

The group flew directly towards the Aardian system exiting the Abyss close to the planet Aariet. They hung in space for a few moments to locate the god presence and then rocketed downwards into the upper atmosphere of the planet. The group vanished and appeared in a huge open square. They were quickly surrounded by reptilian, heavily scaled creatures with sharp claws and razor-like teeth.

Humbra said, 'Carnivores, I suspect.'

Lucifer smiled and said, 'I expect so! Someone is approaching.'

Erebus replied, 'It is the god presence.'

The beasts parted as the god approached. It had the form of a tall, athletic male human. It was dressed in simple white linen trousers and a shirt with stout leather boots. It stared at the group and then, looking at Erebus, said, 'You are Erebus?'

Erebus replied, 'Yes, and this is Sladrin and Humbra of the Abyss. This is Lucifer; he has spent some time in the Abyss but is now an Archangel of the light. Who are you, and what are you doing here?'

The god said, 'I am Noticas. We are here to colonise this planet; there are many indigenous creatures that we can make use of as hosts or for sustenance. Moreover, this system is sufficiently remote from the light and allows an easy passing from the Abyss.'

Lucifer said, 'This planet is not yours.'

Noticas looked at Lucifer and said, 'You will remain here, Erebus, Sladrin and Humbra; you will come with me.'

Erebus replied, 'We will remain as a group; Lucifer is here to represent the goddess and will report our findings directly to her.'

Noticas laughed and said, 'I have no interest in humans or their angels or their petty gods. Nor do I have any objection to you remaining together, but I sense your friend Lucifer may not be comfortable with some aspects of our work here. I will give you a brief tour of our facility, and then perhaps we can discuss the future?'

Erebus nodded but was clearly feeling very uncomfortable; he looked at Lucifer and said, 'Are you sure you want to see this?' Lucifer grimaced but nodded in the affirmative.

The group followed Noticas to the edge of a huge crater that housed what appeared to be several hundred large stone buildings. The stone varied in colour from a pale orange to vivid red. The light was dim, and the ground dust dry.

Noticas said, 'The buildings are constructed from stone quarried from the surrounding hills. The roofs are made of wood and straw. The buildings on the far left are the food processing areas, and we keep a large stock of live creatures for fresh meat. The buildings to the right of those are the preparation areas where the creatures are slaughtered. The central buildings are where the craftsmen and other workers live and work to support colonisation. Moving further to the right, you will see the military facilities; they are extensive with most being underground. If you wish, we can walk around a few of the processing buildings?'

Noticas walked around the crater rim to a wide pathway that had been cut into the face of the crater wall and said, 'This is for the animals and to move materials; it is long and shallow. But, when in human form, I enjoy the sensation of walking.' They walked deeper into the crater, the heat increasing in intensity with every step.

When they reached the floor, it was almost unbearable, even for Lucifer, who said, 'I would like to see the live animals and how they are processed.'

Noticas replied, 'Yes, of course.' As they walked Lucifer noticed that the rock floor was polished smooth, presumably by the many unfortunate creatures that had been shepherded over it.

Lucifer said, 'How long have you been here?'

Noticas stopped, stared at Lucifer and said, 'Why do you ask?'

Lucifer replied, 'I have the feeling that you have been here a very long time.'

Noticas ignored the question and continued walking. The group arrived at the first of five large buildings; Noticas led them in through a side door. The smell was the first assault on the senses. Creatures of all sorts were crammed into metal pens, many barely alive. There was no separation of species other than animals and humans. There was no sound, no crying out for help, only silence. Lucifer was staggered by the helplessness, fear, despair and hopelessness that exuded not only from the humans but from all the animals.

He turned to Erebus and said, 'I have seen enough; I cannot remain here.'

Erebus nodded, but Noticas replied, 'You will remain here!'

Three huge guards appeared and encircled Lucifer, black tentacles wrapped around him, pinning his arms and legs.

Noticas said, 'Place him in a null chamber.'

The guards dragged Lucifer away; he struggled but could not break the tentacles that bound him.

Erebus said, 'This is unacceptable; you will release Lucifer immediately.'

But more guards appeared. Erebus blasted the guards back and vanished. Sladrin and Humbra tried to follow him, but they were too slow; Noticas pulled them back and ensnared them.

Sladrin said, 'You are a fool!'

Noticas replied, 'You align yourselves with an Archangel and a so-called goddess of the light. You are traitors! If Erebus returns, I will slay him!'

Sladrin said, 'You have imprisoned an Archangel; you use humans as hosts and consume them. She will come, and all of this will be destroyed.'

Noticas laughed and replied, 'Your so-called goddess is not interested in venturing far from her protected palace. But if she does come here, then I will feed on her with relish!'

Sladrin smiled and said, 'She has already slain Insheigra; you will be next.'

Noticas, askance, replied, 'Minerva killed Insheigra?'

Sladrin said, 'No, it was her older sister.'

Noticas stared at Sladrin, comprehension suddenly dawning, and replied, 'Bellona has returned?'

Sladrin, seeing the fear in his eyes, said, 'Yes, and you have imprisoned Lucifer. She will be arriving soon.'

Noticas replied, 'Thank you for the information. We will prepare an appropriate welcome.' Noticas looked at the guards and said, 'Take them to the null chambers immediately.'

Erebus entered the Abyss, fragmented into a stream of debris and rode a space current towards planet Earth and Minerva. He mind-linked with Minerva when he was close enough and explained what had happened.

Minerva said, 'What are you going to do?'

Erebus said, 'I will organise a rescue mission. But you should let your sister know. Lucifer was taken to a null chamber. I don't know what that is, but it won't be pleasant.'

Minerva replied, 'I will let her know now; please keep in touch.'

Mab was in discussions with Kanaka and the other masters when Minerva appeared. She knew immediately that something was wrong.

Minerva said, 'Erebus, Sladrin, Humbra and Lucifer went to the planet Aariet to investigate the growing activity there. They met a god of the Abyss named Noticas. Things were friendly initially, but they tried to separate Lucifer from the others. Erebus would not permit it, so they were taken as prisoners; only Erebus escaped. Erebus said Lucifer was taken to a null chamber, he doesn't know what that is or what happened to the others.'

Master Boe said, 'A null chamber is a containment where nothing can enter or exit. The prisoner is held in complete darkness and silence. It is likely to be protected by a powerful energy field.'

Mab stared upwards and reached out with her witch senses. Everyone else remained silent. Several minutes passed then Mab said, 'Lucifer, I can't hear you, but I know that you can hear me. Minerva has told me what happened. I am coming; you will be free soon.'

Mab stood up, and Michael and Gabriel appeared behind her; she looked at Minerva and said, 'There is no time; we must act now. Explain to Erebus.'

Mab, Michael and Gabriel appeared in the upper atmosphere of the planet Aariet. They hung there, reaching out with their senses.

Michael said, 'There are many underground tunnels; this has been long in the making.'

Mab nodded and said, 'They have been here for some time. Our priority here is to free Lucifer and the two clan leaders.'

Michael pointed and said, 'There, below the three tallest structures, a wide tunnel leading deep underground to a large void in the rock.'

Mab replied, 'Yes, they have tunneled downwards, making use of an existing fracture in the rock; the void is also a natural feature. There is an energy field around the void; perhaps the rock is unstable, but I see several other energy fields.'

Gabriel said, 'Perhaps the null chambers? They must be powerful to contain Lucifer.'

Mab focused for a few moments and said, 'Yes, Gabriel, you are right. The null chambers are machines, and the energy fields are very strong.'

Michael pointed to buildings around the edge of the crater and said, 'The god presence is there.'

Mab replied, 'I suggest that I go for the head of the snake while you two go underground?'

Gabriel replied, 'We may not be strong enough to free Lucifer. If you went underground, perhaps you could free Lucifer and return to assist us in slaying the god from the Abyss?'

Mab thought for a few minutes and said, 'No, we will go together to free Lucifer. That needs to be our top priority.' Mab paused for a few moments and said, 'Erebus is on his way here now with fifty of his alpha warriors. I have told him of our plans, and he will attack the head of the snake; we will aid him when we can.' Mab rocketed downwards, closely followed by the Archangels.

As they entered the lower atmosphere, they vanished and reappeared on the ground floor of one of the larger buildings. The air was fetid, it stank of animals, excrement and death.

Mab said, 'We don't have time to tarry here; we will return later.'

Gabriel pointed to a large square hole on the floor and said, 'That must be the tunnel entrance, ramping downwards under the adjacent structures and leading to the large void.' Mab and the two Archangels made their way down the stone ramp. Michael threw several balls of light into the air.

Mab said, 'The regular users of this path clearly don't require light.'

But soon, they began to see a dim glow in the distance. Michael dispensed with the balls of light and whispered, 'We are approaching the void.'

Mab said, 'Six human forms, all hosting daemons. Kill them quickly, keep one alive.'

Michael and Gabriel stormed into the room; their great swords flashed, and five bodies lay dead on the floor, black blood streaming from the lifeless corpses. Mab approached the remaining operative, Onimaru flashing into her hand, and said, 'You are Yakas; you will remove these energy fields and free our comrades.'

Yakas replied, 'You are a fool! The god Noticas will slay you.'

Michael looked at Mab and said, 'Erebus is here; they are attacking the god presence and its supporters.'

Mab pushed the tip of Onimaru into the daemon host's chest. Its eyes widened as it looked down at the sword. Mab said, 'My sword will consume your soul daemon; there will be no return to the Abyss for you.' Yakas tried to flee the human body, but Onimaru plunged through the host's chest. Yakas screamed in agony as his long life came to an end.

A series of coffin-like heavy metal chambers were laid on a wide shelf that had been carved out of the rock face. The chambers were surrounded by machines, wires, lights, large ducts and complex control systems. There was a constant humming sound. The weight of the rock above was almost palpable, giving the feeling of pressure and the need to escape from the space.

Mab said, 'We will need to revert to brute force to open these things!'

Gabriel pulled his great sword from the air and brought it down on the first chamber. The sword cut through the energy field but did not damage the chamber. Moreover, the energy field re-established itself.

Mab plunged her hand into the energy field and said, 'It is an artificial psychic shield generated by one of these other machines.'

Mab looked around at the many machines, pointed to one of the largest and said, 'That one, it generates and contains light, which is converted to create the energy fields.' Mab walked towards the machine and punched her fist deep into its innards; she then pulled her hand back, grasping a small ball of dull grey material. The machine shut down immediately, the alarm system sounded, and everything went black.

Michael threw up light balls and asked, 'Goddess, is that the heart of the machine?'

Mab replied, 'Yes, it is a special material. I will put it in a safe place.'

The grey ball vanished. Mab went to one of the null chambers, drew Onimaru and sliced the blade down into the metal. Onimaru cut through the top plate. Mab raised her fist and struck the plate a mighty blow, which buckled it down into the chamber space. She then grabbed the cut edge of the thick plate and peeled it back to reveal Lucifer's face.

Mab put her hand on his forehead and said, 'Lucifer, are you injured.'

Lucifer opened his eyes and realised that he was free. He vanished and reappeared beside the chamber. He said, 'I'm fine now. I shut myself down; I couldn't cope with being locked in that thing. We need to open the other chambers.' He plucked his huge black sword from the air and brought it down on the top of the adjacent chamber, cutting deep into the metal. Mab stepped forward and ripped the top of the chamber off to reveal Humbra.

She climbed out, fell to her knees, and said, 'Thank you for releasing me, Goddess.'

Mab put her hand on Humbra's head and said, 'You are welcome. Erebus is here and currently in a battle with Noticas; we must move quickly.'

Humbra replied, 'Sladrin is in the next chamber.' They opened all the chambers, but Sladrin was the only remaining prisoner. He fared less well than the others and struggled to remain standing.

Mab looked at Humbra and said, 'I will send Sladrin to Minerva; she will look after him until we return.'

Sladrin vanished. Mab said, 'We must go now to aid Erebus, come closer.'

Mab looked upwards and launched the group at enormous speed towards the roof of the void. An arrow-shaped energy field protected them as they powered through the rock and out into the open air above the crater. The floor of the crater collapsed downwards as they exited, filling the void spaces below and burying the null chamber machines.

They looked down on the scene below. The Alpha warriors were battling against huge reptiles, and their losses were mounting. Erebus was surrounded by twenty or so daemon hosts who were launching attacks while he was trying to combat the dark god. Mab said, 'Aid the Alpha warriors, slay those creatures. I will go to Erebus.' Mab hit the ground beside Erebus like a meteor; the shock wave rolled outwards, knocking the daemon hosts to the ground. Erebus was exhausted. Mab said, 'You have done enough; Sladrin is in a bad way; I sent him to Minerva. Go there now, no arguments!'

Erebus replied, 'Goddess, I am too old for this; I am grateful for your intervention. I will advise Minerva of the situation.' Erebus vanished.

Noticas laughed loudly and said, 'I was enjoying some sport with your grandfather, but it will be so much better with you!'

Mab turned baleful eyes upon Noticas and said, 'I am Bellona.'

The daemon hosts, who had only just managed to get to their feet, slowly backed away and turned to face Michael and Gabriel. Noticas had excellent senses, and he stared intently at Mab. Mab smiled and said, 'You see your death, but what else do you see?' Mab plucked Onimaru from the air; Noticas stared at the blade and then at Mab. Mab laughed and said, 'Poor Noticas, are you confused? Let me enlighten you.' Onimaru changed shape and took the form of a long black spear, fearsomely barbed at the tip. Mab threw Onimaru towards Noticas with blinding speed; Noticas started to vanish, but too late. The spear sliced deep into its chest. The creature tried to change its form, but Onimaru would not release it. Noticas lay on the ground, Onimaru still embedded in its chest. Mab looked down at it and said, 'Onimaru is feeding on you as you have fed on others. How does it feel?' Noticas could not speak; its very life force was being sucked from it by Onimaru. Mab blinked; two beams of light blasted from her eyes into Noticas. The creature screamed in agony for a few moments, and then there was silence. Mab pulled Onimaru from the body and threw it into the air. The spear changed back into the form of a sword and vanished. Mab incinerated what remained of Noticas.

The Archangels had slaughtered many of the reptilian hosts, their daemons retreating back into the Abyss.

Mab cried out, 'Enough! They are defeated.'

The fighting stopped, and the remaining reptilians fled.

Michael asked, 'Goddess, what of the dark god?'

Mab replied, 'It is slain.'

Humbra said, 'Where is Erebus.'

Mab replied, 'I sent Erebus to my sister. He was exhausted but not injured.'

Gabriel said, 'What do we do now?'

Mab replied, 'We go back into the crater to free the captive humans and animals.'

The group vanished and reappeared at the bottom of the crater. The central area had subsided, but the peripheral buildings were still intact. They went back to the large building that housed the access tunnel to the null chambers.

The group walked into the building through the main doors, past the access tunnel entrance and towards the animal pens. The pens were constructed from iron bars, probably the same iron used for the thick plate of the null chambers. They were on two levels and on both sides of the building. A continuous walkway was provided at the first-floor level with access stairways from the ground floor at both ends of the building.

Lucifer said, 'The silence is disturbing.'

Mab said, 'Yes, they are without hope. Open all the pens!' The ground-floor pens contained a mixture of native animals, including large ruminants but also carnivorous and omnivorous creatures, big cats and bears and a great variety of large reptiles. Mab imparted energy and hope to the animals together with an image of the route to the top of the crater. The animals ran from the building, all species making their way together towards freedom.

The upper floor cells contained humans; many of these were indigenous to the habitable planets in the Aardian system. Some were close to death; others could stand but were unable to walk more than a few steps. There were no toilet facilities; males and females alike defecated where they stood or lay. The smell was even more overpowering than in the animal pens. However, the final pen was large and housed four men and three women who were clearly well-fed. They had soft chairs and beds, well-stocked bookshelves and a separate toilet.

Mab said, 'Who are you?'

The leader of the group stepped forward and said, 'I am Doctor Jon Adams; this is my team of research scientists. We are prisoners here; you must leave this place; our captors have extraordinary powers.'

Mab stared at him askance and said, 'The creatures that imprisoned you are dead. Were you brought here from Earth?'

Dr. Adams replied, 'Yes, they made us design and construct the machines in this facility; we are kept here to ensure they continue to function. It is necessary for humans to have a skill. Those who don't, or cannot work due to injury or illness, suffer the same fate as the animals.'

Mab said, 'How long have you been here?'

Dr Adams replied, 'I don't really know, a long time, perhaps several earth years. We did not think we could possibly achieve what they expected, but they provided everything we requested. Who are you?'

Mab replied, 'Who we are is of no consequence. If you wish I will return you and your team to Earth, but I will not return you to your own time. You should know that many years have passed since you left that solar system.'

Dr Adams replied, 'You mean we have been gone more than a few years?'

Mab replied, 'A few years here would be almost one hundred years on your home planet. The time streams run at different rates; the average human life span is only seventy or eighty years. So, it is likely that everyone you knew on Earth will now be dead.'

Dr Adams thought for a moment and said, 'I will talk to the others.'

Mab said, 'The dark god Noticas has been slain; you will be safe here. Regarding the energy machine in the large void, where was the active material sourced?'

Dr Adams replied, 'Active material? Do you mean the core material?'

Mab replied, 'It was a small grey sphere held within the heart of the largest machine.'

Dr Adams turned to look at one of his colleagues who replied, 'I am Dr Susan Morrison. I think you are referring to the plutonium core; it was manufactured on Earth. We used this to power the facility and to create the special energy fields required around the null chambers and around the entire facility if required. Why do you ask?'

Mab said, 'I have removed it; it is unnatural and dangerous. I gave it to Aardian for save keeping.'

Dr Morrison replied, 'You removed it! How?'

Mab replied, 'I reached in and tore it from the machine. Do not be concerned; the light it emits cannot harm me. Help the others of your kind; I will return soon.'

The group of five made their way to the next building, where the animals and humans were slaughtered. It was too much for the Archangels who asked to be excused. Mab and Humbra continued and found two production lines, one for humans and the other for animals. The internal organs were removed and packaged separately. The heads, feet and hands of humans and animals were dehaired, crushed to a fine pulp and stored in large clay pots. The carcasses were then hung on metal hooks and moved by machine, human carcasses in one direction and animal carcasses in another. In the next building, the carcasses were cut into smaller pieces and packed into wooden boxes.

Mab said, 'Is it not strange how living creatures can be held captive in appalling conditions, be reduced in minutes to mere products and packed in pots and boxes to be eaten by other humans and animals? Is this not an abomination? Am I the only one who thinks this!?'

Humbra said nothing.

Mab said, 'I have seen enough. You go to Erebus and Sladrin. I will follow later.'

Humbra nodded but paused, knelt, and said, 'Goddess, I wish to serve you. I wish to serve the light, to exist in the light. Is it possible?'

Mab looked down at Humbra, her face beaming with pleasure, and said, 'Are you sure that is what you want?'

Humbra, tears streaming down her face, replied, 'I have never been more sure of anything in my life.'

Humbra gasped as a wave of goodness flowed through her body. Mab lifted Humbra up, kissed her and embraced her tightly. Humbra felt power pouring into her. Mab entered her mind, she almost lost consciousness, but then she was suddenly released and found herself somewhere else in space, she was facing Mab but surrounded by a light so intense that only Mab's face could be seen.

Mab said, 'You have been found worthy; I am Bellona, Goddess of the light, and you will be my acolyte. You will serve the light and do my bidding. Swear it now.'

Humbra smiled and said, 'I swear to serve the light and follow the bidding of Bellona, Goddess of the Light.'

There was another flash of bright light, and Humbra found herself once again in Mab's arms.

Mab whispered in her ear, 'You are now an angel of the light, you will be able to visit the Abyss, but you cannot remain there for protracted periods. You will be with me and the Archangels for all time. How do you feel?'

Tears of joy now flowed down Humbra's face as she said, 'I feel wonderful, thank you, Goddess, thank you!'

Mab gently pushed Humbra away and said, 'Let me look at you. Oh my!'

Humbra wore the body armour of an Archangel but in white and silver.

Mab said, 'Your sword?'

Humbra looked puzzled.

Mab said, 'Reach into the space behind the air and take your sword.' Humbra reached through the air and smiled as she felt the hilt of the sword. She pulled it free and gasped. It was a single-edged blade of the finest quality. The pommel, hilt and blade were fashioned as one piece. The blade was only slightly curved and was razor sharp. The grip was formed from runes embedded in the hilt.

Humbra said, 'It was made for me, light, strong and perfectly balanced!'

Mab stood smiling at Humbra as if waiting for something.

Humbra looked quizzically at Mab and said, 'Yes?'

Mab said, 'There is something else that I want to see.'

Humbra looked down at her feet and legs and then at her arms and chest and said, 'What?'

Mab said, 'The Wings!'

Humbra laughed and said, 'I don't have wings!'

Mab said, 'Shrug your shoulders!'

Humbra did as she was told, and two enormous snow-white wings unfolded behind her.

Mab said, 'They are huge and beautiful!'

Humbra threw her hands up into the air; the huge wings flexed and lifted her off the floor. She screamed with laughter and said, 'I can't wait to play with these things!'

Mab said, 'They are also fearsome weapons and can protect you from attack. Now, return to Minerva and wait for me. You can go directly to her; the palace will allow you to pass freely.'

Humbra bowed deeply and vanished.

Mab walked back to the pens and found the group of scientists helping the other humans. They had taken them to their toilet facilities, where they had fresh water and soap. They also had access to a very large larder of food and were spoon-feeding those who had no strength to eat.

Dr. Morrison walked to meet Mab and said, 'Most of these people are indigenous to this planet; a few are from neighbouring planets and were brought here as hosts to these spirit creatures but then discarded in favour of stronger hosts.'

Mab nodded and said, 'Where did the gods obtain the technology to construct the energy field machines?'

Dr Morrison replied, 'We are scientists, not engineers. We were assisted by one of the gods who had immense experience with machines and control systems. We never met him in person, but he appeared to us as a hologram and communicated detailed instructions by computer.'

Mab replied, 'What is a hologram?'

Dr Morrison replied, 'It is a virtual representation of something, a person, for example, it is generated by light.'

Mab nodded and said, 'Did this god have a name?'

Dr Morrison replied, 'Yes, he was known as the god Varalian.'

Mab grimaced.

Dr Morrison said, 'Do you know him?'

Mab replied, 'Yes, I thought I had killed it, but it appears I was wrong. I need everyone to be clear of this facility; I will destroy it before I return home.'

Dr Morrison replied, 'Where is home for you?'

Mab smiled and said, 'My home is on Earth, but my responsibilities span space and time.'

Dr Morrison replied, 'We have decided to stay here on this planet. In view of the time difference, it seems pointless to return to Earth. Perhaps we can make a new start here, a new Earth?'

Mab smiled and said, 'That is a good decision. You would not like Earth as it is today, too many machines!'

Dr Morrison replied, 'Thank you for freeing us.'

Mab walked out into the humid air and started to make her way toward the exit path from the crater. She thought a brisk walk would help to clear her head. The animals all seemed to have found their way out of the crater, but then she saw a lone bear. It was stumbling over the debris in the centre of the crater, seemingly lost. Mab entered her mind, the bear was badly dehydrated, and her long imprisonment had led to confusion. Mab calmed her and led her out of the crater. She used her witch senses to reach around the planet. She found a huge mountain forest with several rivers and streams. Mab and the bear vanished and appeared in the deep forest beside a freshwater stream. Mab sat on the riverbank as the bear drank her fill and frolicked in ice-cold water. The bear waded out of the river with a huge fish in her mouth and sat beside Mab, munching contentedly. Mab lay back, rested her head on the bear's side and fell into a deep sleep. When Mab woke, the bear had gone. She smiled, but then her witch senses alarmed. She leapt high into the air, spun around a nearby conifer tree and hung in the air, motionless, waiting.

Many soldiers approached; Mab could sense the presence of two gods. As they closed on her position, an energy field engulfed the area. It was spherical, half of the sphere being above ground and half below ground. The soldiers fanned out, encircling Mab's position. Mab estimated their number at around one hundred. She sensed the approach of the two gods; she dropped to the ground and sat at the foot of the tree. The two gods stopped within the forest, some fifty paces away and waited. Mab waited.

The gods eventually emerged from the cover of the trees and walked towards Mab, who remained seated. The first god had taken female form and wore black leggings and a heavy leather jacket buttoned tightly. She carried a huge black sword that hung from her right hip unscabbarded. The tip of the sword trailed behind her, a sloppy practice that Mab found particularly irritating. The other god took the form of a human male. He was tall, heavily muscled and wore thick brown leather trousers that matched his skin. He was bare from the waist upwards and carried two short silver swords.

He looked at Mab and laughed.

Mab remained sitting but stared at him and said, 'You are either very brave or very stupid.'

The first god said, 'He is Mirablis; he meant no slight against you. I am Infelice of the Abyss.'

Mab replied, 'What do you want?'

Infelice said, 'You killed Insheigra and Noticas. Do you expect us to accept this without consequence?'

Mab stood up, walked towards Infelice and said, 'You are in my domain without permission. That alone is sufficient for me to take your lives. You have also committed abomination with your treatment of humans and animals, and that I will not permit.'

Infelice replied, 'We, Mirablis and I, treat all living creatures with respect. But I accept there are some amongst us who see themselves as dark gods and superior to other sentient beings. This has led to the harsh treatment of humans, particularly possession, slavery and incarceration. We are not like Noticas; do not judge us in haste.'

Mirablis moved towards Mab with his blades at the ready, but Infelice stopped him with a glance and said, 'Put your blades away!'

Mab moved closer to Infelice and said, 'I hear what you say. However, this system is under my protection; you will leave and go back to where you belong; the alternative is death for all of you.'

Infelice was silent for a while but then bowed her head and replied, 'Goddess, we wish to live in the light; is that not also our right?'

Mab said, 'You are welcome to live in the light but not at the expense of other living creatures.'

Mirablis said, 'We are wasting our time; we should slay her now and be done with it!'

Infelice, wearily, replied, 'Mirablis, are you completely blind, look at her! We cannot slay her; we do not have the power.'

Mab gestured with her hand, and the energy field fell apart like wet tissue paper. She looked at Infelice and said, 'Take me to your encampment.'

Infelice turned to Mirablis and said, 'Go North, check all is well. I will take the goddess to our encampment.'

Just then, a huge bear leapt from the river, Mirablis brought both of his blades down with lightning speed, but they stopped dead a short distance above the bear's head. Mirablis pulled with all his might, but the blades were immutably locked as if embedded in solid rock.

Mab pulled Onimaru from the air and said, 'This bear is my friend; if you hurt her, you will answer to Onimaru.'

Instantly the point of Onimaru was at his throat. Mirablis felt the sword tugging at his mind, at his very being and knew immediately if it entered his body, it would consume him.

He looked pleadingly at Infelice, who said, 'Goddess, it was a misunderstanding. Mirablis thought the bear was attacking and sought to protect you.'

Onimaru vanished, and Mab said, 'I know, but I thought I would teach him a lesson.'

Infelice replied, 'What lesson would that be?'

Mab replied, 'Never kill a bear, especially if it is the friend of a goddess.'

Infelice laughed and said, 'Is this an old saying of wisdom, or did you just invent it?'

Mab smiled and replied, 'I think I am beginning to like you.'

Infelice said, 'That sounds reassuring.'

Mab grimaced and replied, 'Do not feel too reassured.' The two figures vanished and appeared in the middle of what appeared to be a small village. Human children were playing by the side of a stream, and dogs were barking excitedly.

Infelice said, 'We will go to my cabin; I have some nice cheese, made by the villagers, and wine which Mirablis acquired, probably stolen.'

The cabin was basic: a single bedstead pushed against one of the walls and covered with animal skins for warmth, a table, four chairs, several cabinets and a cold store, which was essentially a deep hole in the corner of the room, covered by a thick stone slab. Infelice gestured for Mab to take a seat. The heavy slab slid back as she approached; she reached down and retrieved a tall clay wine pot and a huge block of cheese wrapped in hessian. Infelice cut two thick slices of cheese and poured generous measures of wine into two wooden goblets.

Mab said, 'This is not what I expected.'

Infelice replied, 'I would like to say our other encampments are like this, but I'm afraid most are not.'

Mab said, 'Why is this different?'

Infelice replied, 'When I came to this planet, I travelled with Noticas. I took an immediate dislike to him. He set up the camp close to our point of arrival. I could not abide his presence and so I left with Mirablis. When I found this village, I decided that we would live in harmony with the people. It is we who would change, not the villagers. Our soldiers are volunteers from the outlying villages; they have sticks and pikes but no serious weapons. The villages need to be protected, not just from the indigenous carnivores but from other creatures of the Abyss. We came here to have a new life. The light here is sufficiently dim for us to live without having to take possession of other creatures, and yet, in comparison to the Abyss, it is a truly wonderful place.'

Mab said, 'Infelice, you are most welcome to live here in harmony with the people of this village. You have my thanks, my respect, and my protection.'

Infelice gasped as a wave of warmth and goodness washed over her.

Mab smiled and said, 'What you are doing here is a model for the future. If only others could see this and understand.'

Infelice replied, 'I agree, but this is very much an exception. I am not like others of the Abyss. I find the killing and possessing of other creatures abhorrent, but others revel in it. There are those in the Abyss who are greater than I. You must not allow them to enter your worlds; they would lay waste to them and slaughter your people. They are evil; do not let your understanding be confused by my actions and what you see here.'

Mab said, 'Yes, I understand.'

Infelice smiled and replied, 'We five, now three, are strong; that is why we are considered by many as gods. But, in the depths of the Abyss, there are creatures that are horribly powerful. They have no names that we know of, but they are the real gods of the Abyss.'

Mab said, 'You have met these gods?'

Infelice replied, 'When I was young and very foolish, I ventured deeper than I should have. It came as a black mist that took solid form as it drew closer. I could feel the energy being sucked from my body. It could have slain me, but it was distracted by something else, something unusual. It moved away at great speed. I used the last dregs of my strength to enter a rapidly flowing space current, which, fortunately, lifted me up. I exited and concealed my presence as best I could. I lay motionless for a very long time before I had enough strength to fully ascend. I never went back.'

Mab said, 'Would you go back with me?'

Infelice stared at Mab aghast and said, 'You cannot go there; the very environment would kill you even if you managed to evade the gods!'

Mab replied, 'I don't intend to evade them; I want to find them. The environment will not affect me.'

Infelice paused and said, 'I will go with you if you wish, but you must understand that these creatures are not like us; they do not reason. Their first instinct is to feed.'

Mab smiled and said, 'I will return soon; we will go to the deep Abyss and search for the gods! But now, I must go back and destroy the encampment of Noticas. The humans and animals held captive there should all now have departed. You may wish to contact them, help them even?'

Infelice nodded and said, 'Yes, we would welcome them here. I will come with you and seek them out.'

Mab nodded; they vanished and reappeared at the edge of the crater. Mab carried out a deep scan of the area and said, 'It is deserted.' She gazed upwards and then made a horizontal sweeping gesture with her hand. Mab and Infelice floated upwards, away from the crater. A bright light appeared in the sky. The meteor approached with astonishing speed and at a shallow angle. It impacted some distance away but gouged a huge trench across the land, completely obliterating the crater and everything in proximity to it. Water gushed into the enormous chasm from deep subterranean aquafers.

Infelice said, 'It is beautiful; the land here will soon be rich with vegetation; it will be unrecognisable!'

Mab smiled and said, 'I must go now; I will return, as promised.'

Chapter Thirty-Four: The Dark God Antobus

Mab appeared in the palace of the old gods. Minerva was there with Erebus; they stood up when Mab approached.

Minerva said, 'Sladrin has returned to the Abyss. Humbra left with Michael and Gabriel; I didn't know you could create angels?'

Mab smiled as she stripped off her clothes and said, 'Aariet is being looked after by Infelice; Noticas is dead.' Mab made her way to the lake and plunged into the healing waters.

A short time later, Minerva joined her and said, 'Erebus has returned to the Abyss.'

They sat in silence for a while before Minerva said, 'Your powers, are they still growing?'

Mab looked at Minerva and replied, 'You know the answer to that question, so why do you ask?'

Minerva put her arm around her and said, 'Sister, you have changed; you are not the same as you were before. Even Erebus has said as much.'

Mab replied, 'I didn't know Erebus in previous times, but I am the same as I ever was. I went into obscurity to avoid killing the innocent and to prevent an apocalypse.'

Minerva said, 'What do you mean apocalypse?'

Mab looked at Minerva and said, 'Had I not intervened, they would have destroyed everything, even time itself, in their deluded attempt to vanquish the enemy. It was a slaughter of staggering proportions on both sides. The old gods would have destroyed the multiverse; I could not permit that. I culled some of the most powerful gods on both sides. I then removed myself from the conflict.'

Minerva said, 'On both sides! What of our parents?'

Mab replied, 'Of them, I will not speak.'

They sat in silence again before Minerva said, 'So, will this enmity between the light and the dark ever come to an end?'

Mab replied, 'Yes, that is why I am here, to bring things to an end.'

Mab slept soundly and woke late the following morning. Minerva had left the palace, so Mab had a hearty breakfast alone but then thought of Infelice and appeared beside her in a forest clearing.

Infelice said, 'Mirablis has not returned from the North. No one knows where he is. The captain of the company said that he went off on his own to investigate an anomaly but never returned. They searched but found no sign of him.'

Mab replied, 'What kind of anomaly?'

Infelice shrugged her shoulders and said, 'They don't know. He must have sensed something.'

Mab said, 'Is the captain here?'

Infelice asked Mab to wait in her cabin and went off to find the captain. When she returned Mab had poured two goblets of wine and handed one to her.

Infelice smiled and said, 'This is Captain Yashin. He was the last person to see Mirablis.'

Mab said, 'You were born in this place?'

Yashin bowed and replied, 'Yes, Goddess, I have a small farm only a few minutes-walk from here.'

Mab said, 'I would like to see what you saw in the minutes before Mirablis disappeared. It may help us to find him. I need to enter your mind. I will be gentle, but you need to stay relaxed. Can you do that for me?'

Yashin looked at Infelice, who smiled and then looked back to Mab, nodding his assent. Mab entered his mind, and she saw Mirablis walking ahead of the company. He stopped and looked to his left. Yashin called a halt but walked forward to talk to Mirablis. Mirablis told Yashin to wait and walked off the trail into the forest. Mab felt and saw what Yashin experienced at that moment.

She withdrew from his mind and said, 'Thank you, captain, that will be all.' Yashin turned and walked away.

Mab turned to Infelice and said, 'The god presence on Aafien has taken him.'

Infelice said, 'Antobus was here? That is not possible; I would have sensed it.'

Mab replied, 'It concealed itself extremely well. It may have come to investigate the death of Noticas?'

Infelice paused in thought and said, 'I will go to Aafien and meet with Antobus.'

Mab replied, 'Would you like me to accompany you?'

Infelice replied, 'I think I should go alone.'

Mab said, 'Very well, but I will mind link with you periodically.'

Infelice smiled and replied, 'Is that concern I sense?'

Mab pulled her close, kissed her and said, 'No, but be careful. I will come to you if you need help.'

Infelice hugged Mab, kissed her and replied, 'That is good to know.'

Mab vanished and appeared beside Lamm, who was in discussions with masters Sonder, Etten and Uvren at the School of Psych and Sorcery. All stood and bowed to Mab.

Mab hugged and kissed Lamm and said, 'Please, be seated.'

Lamm said, 'We were discussing our leadership team. The death of that traitor Johans has brought things to a head. We need at least two additional masters, and I'm not sure we have any suitable candidates internally.'

Uvren added, 'In any case, we need some fresh blood. Someone who will raise our profile and excite our students, much as Mab did when she joined the GOS!'

Lamm laughed and said, 'Yes, that is exactly what we need another Mabdelore Winter!'

The masters all wrapped the table.

Mab poured herself a coffee and said, 'Actually, I think I can help you with that.'

The masters all stared at her in anticipation. Mab said, 'Pelian, my partner, would be an excellent candidate. She is a powerful witch and a lord of chaos. Her swordsmanship is second to none, or almost second to none!'

Lamm said, 'If Pelian would agree to become a master of our guild! That would be a tremendous boost for our students!'

Uvren replied, 'I agree; it also means we would see more of you, Mab!'

Mab smiled and said, 'Yes, absolutely. I would spend much of my time here with Pelian. I have two other suggested candidates, Gho and Birto, both known to master Lamm and currently with the GOS. My recommendation is that Masters Sonder and Etten take on more managerial and administrative duties working with you, Master Lamm, while Pelian, Gho and Birto engage with the students. Master Uvren you should carry on your excellent research work working with Master Boe across all the schools.'

Uvren nodded and said, 'Those are excellent suggestions!'

Lamm looked at the others and said, 'What say you?'

All the masters rapped the table to show their support.

Lamm said, 'We will invite Gho and Birto here for a formal interview, but Pelian's appointment could, and should, be done immediately.'

Sonder said, 'Yes, but we must have the ceremony. Goddess, when will you and Pelian next be here together?' Mab replied, 'I thought Master Lamm would organise a sumptuous dinner this evening; I will attend with my partner, and the ceremony will take place then?'

Lamm laughed and said, 'Short notice, but yes! That would be perfect. Luticia and Kanaka should be present.'

Mab smiled and replied, 'I will bring them with me. I'll leave you now and return this evening.' Mab vanished.

Etten said, 'This is a tremendous opportunity for the school, but we need to move quickly. When you think of the chaos surrounding the Guild of Witches and Warlocks because of their prevarication in appointing a new principal and their lack of engagement with the Goddess, their student numbers have all but collapsed, and yet they do nothing!'

Lamm replied, 'Etten, I am so pleased to hear you saying that. At last, I feel like we are working as a like-minded team. If, with Mab's help, we can attract Pelian, then hopefully, the other candidates will want to join us!'

Sonder said, 'Exciting times indeed!'

Mab appeared in Kanaka's office at the GOS and explained the situation in the outer solar systems to Kanaka. Kanaka asked, 'You trust this Infelice?' Mab replied, 'I do. She has taken permanent human form and left the Abyss because she wanted to change her life and not to change the lives of others.'

Kanaka said, 'And Antobus, what do you know of it?'

Mab replied, 'I know it is a dark god of the Abyss and that it is present on Aafien.'

Kanaka said, 'You could detect its presence?'

Mab replied, 'It only revealed its true self when it arrived on Aariet and took Mirablis. I am fully aware of it now, even though Aafien is shielded by Varalian!'

Kanaka said, 'Varalian! I thought it was killed when its home planet was cleansed?'

Mab replied, 'As did I, but it seems to have escaped. In any case I will await the return of Infelice before doing anything else.'

Kanaka nodded.

Mab said, 'On a more positive note. Would you like to join me for dinner tonight with Masters Lamm and Luticia?'

Kanaka replied, 'Yes! Absolutely. What's the occasion?'

Mab smiled and said, 'Pelian will be appointed a master of the School of Psych and Sorcery! I suggested it earlier today to Master Lamm.'

Kanaka replied, 'That is great news. Have you told Pelian?'

Mab said, 'No, it will be a surprise! I also mentioned Gho and Birto to Master Lamm as potential candidates?'

Kanaka nodded and said, 'Yes, they will, of course, be a loss to the Guild, but I had thought to promote Birto to a master position here in view of his role in the warrior school.'

Mab thought for a few moments and said, 'Yes, you are right Birto should remain here. Gho would be a better fit working with Master Lamm.'

Kanaka said, 'What about you?' Mab smiled and said, 'I will always remain a master of the Guild, and this will always be my home.'

Kanaka hugged Mab and said, 'I assume you will pick me up tonight?'

Mab replied, 'Yes, I'll drop you and Luticia off with Master Lamm and arrive a few minutes later with Pelian.'

Mab left Kanaka's office and walked slowly down the stone spiral staircase that she had used so many times as a student. She recognised every bump and crack in the stone, but the stairway felt strangely small, as if everything had shrunk around her. She thought of Izzy, and tears came to her eyes. A voice in her head said, 'Goddess, it is I, Morgana. I must speak with you.' Mab vanished and appeared beside Morgana, who was sitting on a large stone at the top of a hill overlooking a lake. Mab said, 'What is this place?'

Morgana smiled and replied, 'You feel it too?'

Mab reached out with her witch senses and replied, 'Yes, there is an ancient power here. It emanates from an artifact, a sword, buried deep in the ground beneath the lake. It is not of this planet. My senses tell me that it is not malevolent; it wishes to remain undisturbed.'

Morgana said, 'The lake is like a sheet of glass, is it not?'

Mab nodded. Morgana said, 'This area is known as Avalon, in legend, and in more modern times as Glastonbury. It will always be associated with magic and the occult.'

Mab said, 'Why did you summon me?'

Morgana replied, 'I come to this place and time regularly to meditate. A few moments ago, Antobus contacted me. It wanted me to pass a message to you in person. It told me that Mirablis and Infelice were imprisoned and would only be released if certain conditions were met.'

Mab stared at Morgana and said, 'What do you know of Antobus?'

Morgana's face drained of the little colour it possessed; she started to sweat profusely, blood trickled from her nose, and she struggled to form words. Mab removed her gaze and said, 'Apologies, tell me all you know of Antobus, but do it quickly!'

Morgana gasped with relief and replied, 'Thank you, Goddess. I have met Antobus on several occasions. It takes different forms sometimes appearing in spirit form, other times using large animals as a host. I met it only once when it took human form; that was on the planet Aafien.'

Mab said, 'When were you on Aafien?'

Morgana replied, 'A long time ago. I suspect Antobus retreated there shortly after the light war.'

Mab said, 'Why have you not mentioned this before?'

Morgana replied, 'I did not think it was relevant. Aafien is a long way from here, and Antobus wishes to live there undisturbed, a bit like that sword buried underneath the lake.'

Mab said, 'What of the indigenous population of Aafien?'

Morgana replied, 'I don't know if there was an indigenous population on that planet. When I was there, I saw a few small villages inhabited by human-like creatures, but I suspect they were brought in by Antobus. I know that the adjacent planet Aariet was inhabited. Noticas, Infelice and Mirablis arrived there much later; I don't know the current situation.'

Mab said, 'What conditions must be met for the release of Infelice and Mirablis?'

Morgana replied, 'Antobus insists that the Aardian system is now part of the Abyss and in his domain. Anyone or anything entering the system without permission will captured and summarily executed.'

Mab stared intently at Morgana for a few moments and said, 'Could you advise Antobus that I will be visiting Aafien soon and I expect Infelice and Mirablis to be in good health. When we meet, I will decide whether to allow it to return to the Abyss, that being the best of the options available to it. Now, I have an important dinner to attend.'

Morgana knelt and replied, 'Yes, Goddess.'

Mab vanished and appeared next to Pelian, who was with Charly and Cat drinking wine.

Charly and Cat embraced Mab, and Pelian joined them, forming a group hug.

Pelian said, 'Charly and Cat were telling me all about you when you were a student here!'

Mab replied, 'It wasn't so long ago.' Cat handed Mab a goblet of wine. Mab took a sip, and her appearance changed; she was now wearing a long white evening dress, her hair was platted tightly on both sides, and her master's robe hung loosely from her shoulders. Her boots were replaced with elegant, highly polished black shoes.

Charly said, 'Are we going out!'

Mab replied, 'Sorry Charly, Pelian and I are going to a dinner tonight, but I promise that as soon as I get some free time, we will all visit Fat Joe's, and I'll make sure your boyfriends are there!'

Cat said, 'Please make it soon, Mab!'

Mab smiled and replied, 'I'll do my best. Now, Pelian, you need an evening dress and some nice shoes, all black, I think.'

Pelian looked down and admired her new dress, which was similar to Mab's in design and fitted her perfectly. Her long snow-white hair hung loose down her back.

Pelian said, 'Should I wear my robe?'

Mab replied, 'No, you won't need it.'

Pelian said, 'What's the occasion?'

Mab smiled and said, 'It was arranged by Master Lamm; we are both invited and really should attend.'

Pelian looked at Charly and Cat and said, 'We will make up for it when we visit Fat Joes!'

Another group hug ensued until Mab said, 'We really must go; Masters Kanaka and Luticia are already there!'

Mab and Pelian appeared in the lobby entrance to the grand hall of the School of Psych and Sorcery.

Mab looked at Pelian and said, 'Ready?'

Pelian smiled. Mab took Pelian's hand, and they walked together into the grand hall. Pelian was astonished to see a phalanx of senior students arranged in two long diverging lines with the masters of the school waiting at the far end. Pelian looked at Mab and whispered, 'Are we getting married?'

Mab laughed but then pulled her close and said, 'No, not tonight. But I was thinking sometime soon?'

Pelian threw her arms around Mab and kissed her. The students and the masters cheered and applauded. As they walked towards the masters, a crier announced, 'The Goddess Bellona and Pelian, Lord of Chaos and elected Master of the School of Psych and Sorcery!'

Pelian looked up at Mab, her face beaming with pride and joy. The master's all bowed to Mab as she approached. Mab stopped and gently nudged Pelian forward. Master Lamm placed the black master's robe of the school on

Pelian's shoulders and said, 'Pelian, you have been elected a master of this ancient school. There will always be a home for you here, and we know that you will uphold the high standards of integrity and honour that the appointment demands.' Pelian replied, 'Master Lamm, masters and students of the school, I thank you for this great honour, which I am very pleased to accept.'

Cheers and applause followed. Master Lamm said, 'Masters, be seated!' The students left the hall, and the masters took their seats at one end of a huge oak dining table.

Master Lamm sat at the head of the table with Mab, Pelian and Luticia on his right and Kanaka, Uvren, Etten and Sonder on his left.

Lamm said, 'Pelian, we have accommodation here for you and your partner, of course! You will also be paid a stipend for your role here as a master. In return, we would like you to help train our students in warrior skills working between the School and the Guild. At present, our students need to travel to the Guild, which in many cases is not feasible. Your other teaching duties will be minimal as we recognise that you will be working with Mab in other endeavours.'

Pelian replied, 'Thank you, Master Lamm; I am looking forward to working with you and the other masters.'

Lamm lifted his goblet and said, 'To Pelian, Master of the School of Psych and Sorcery!'

All followed Lamm's toast with 'To Pelian!'

The food started to arrive, and it was a truly sumptuous banquet. Kanaka said, 'Lamm, this is an amazing spread of delicious food! I think I will need to up my game!'

Luticia said, 'I agree! Not that you need to up your game Master Kanaka! But this is a truly sumptuous banquet!'

Mab nodded and said, 'Master Lamm, thank you for this. It is fabulous!'

Lamm replied, 'It's nothing special; we eat like this all the time.'

There was much laughter, but then Kanaka said, 'Mab, have you heard anything from Infelice.'

Mab replied, 'She and Mirablis are being held captive by Antobus. I will go there soon to free them.'

Pelian said, 'Antobus is a dark god of the deep Abyss; it is feared even by those who inhabit that place. You must not go alone; I will come with you.'

Mab smiled, looked at the masters and said, 'I have good news. Pelian and I are to be married!'

The masters all stood and applauded. Kanaka hugged Mab and Pelian, as did Lamm and Luticia.

Kanaka said, 'Have you fixed a date?'

Pelian replied, 'No, but we want it to be soon.'

Lamm proposed another toast, 'To Mab and Pelian.'

The eating and drinking went on into the night until only Kanaka and Lamm remained with Mab and Pelian.

Kanaka said, 'Mab, you will need support if you intend to rescue Infelice and Mirablis. What can we do to help?'

Mab replied, 'Master Kanaka, I would like you, Master Lamm and Master Luticia to come with me to the meeting with Antobus. Pelian and the Archangels will remain close, observing but only intervening if needed. We will be in constant communication through mind-link. I will remove the energy field around the planet and that protecting the fortress.'

Kanaka replied, 'Fortress?'

Mab said, 'Yes, the creature has established itself as a sort of monarch that the lesser daemons are required to worship!'

Lamm said, 'King Antobus?' Mab laughed and replied, 'We will soon find out. I suggest we get a good night's sleep and visit Aafien tomorrow morning?'

Kanaka grimaced and said, 'How about tomorrow afternoon?'

Mab smiled and replied, 'Yes, you are probably right.'

Lamm said, 'Mab, can I ask a delicate question?'

Mab nodded.

Lamm said, 'Why do you need us there when you have Pelian and the Archangels?'

Mab replied, 'It's very simple. This war is primarily between humans and daemons. You must be there. The angels are protectors of the innocent. However, I cannot allow darkness to fall over Aafien, and it is an affront to Aardian. If necessary, I will destroy the planet.'

Lamm grimaced and said, 'Understood, let's hope it doesn't come to that!' Pelian looked at Mab and said, 'I will be by your side.' Mab smiled her acquiescence. Lamm said, 'Let's meet here tomorrow mid-morning for breakfast.' Mab nodded; she and Pelian vanished.

Kanaka said, 'This a very serious situation.'

Lamm replied, 'Could she really destroy the planet!?'

Kanaka said, 'I don't know; she said it was an option, so it must be possible. We need to keep calm to help reduce the tension. Hopefully, with Pelian being present she will be in a more amenable mood. Could you update Luticia?'

Lamm replied, 'Yes, I'll let her know. See you at breakfast.'

Kanaka leaned back in his chair, stretched his legs under the table and poured himself a generous goblet of red wine. In the corner of his eye, he saw an intense bright light that rapidly widened to a vertical cut in space. Minerva stepped into the room. Kanaka got to his feet and bowed deeply.

Minerva said, 'Kanaka, I will speak with you regarding Aafien and the confrontation with Antobus.'

Kanaka replied, 'Goddess, you should speak first with your sister.'

Minerva nodded and said, 'I have no secrets from my sister. However, a battle between Bellona and Antobus could result in massive collateral damage. Hundreds of thousands of innocent people could be killed.'

Kanaka replied, 'Then perhaps you should assist her?'

Minerva replied, 'I am no warrior, at least not in comparison to my sister. But also, one of us must survive to help preserve the light. We cannot take the risk that we are both killed.'

Kanaka said, 'You think this Antobus could kill your sister?'

Minerva replied, 'Antobus is very powerful. It is one of the ancients; it participated in the light war and survived. However, my sister's powers have increased beyond comprehension. If it is possible to kill it, then Bellona would be the one to do it.'

Kanaka said, 'What do you want of me?'

Minerva replied, 'You are not merely her mentor; she trusts your judgement implicitly. Are you willing to die for her?'

Kanaka, without hesitation, said, 'I would gladly give my life for her. I love her, and I will be at her side tomorrow for good or ill.'

Minerva walked to Kanaka, kissed him on the cheek and whispered, 'Council her. It is a mistake for Pelian to be present. She will be a distraction, and if she is injured or killed, the wrath of Bellona will be apocalyptic.'

Kanaka stared at Minerva and said, 'Yes, I understand what you are saying; I will consider the matter.'

Minerva smiled and vanished. Kanaka sighed, sat down, poured himself a top-up of red wine, and pondered on Minerva's words.

Kanaka woke early the following morning and made his way to the sports arena. He pulled Dawn-Breaker from the scabbard and assumed the ready position. He calmed his breathing and focused his mind, but a voice in his head said, 'What did she want?'

Kanaka groaned, sheathed Dawn-Breaker and said, 'I was just about to start a Kata!'

Mab replied, 'You will be doing the real thing this afternoon; why don't you join us for breakfast?'

Kanaka said, 'Your sister wanted me to convince you that Pelian should not be present at the confrontation this afternoon. And, having thought about it all night, I agree with her. I think Pelian should remain with the Archangels and only intervene if needed. She will be a huge distraction to you.'

Mab replied, 'I'm having hot coffee, rustic bread, eggs, muffins and all sorts here!'

Kanaka said, 'I'm on my way.' When Kanaka walked into the grand hall, he saw that Mab, Pelian, Lamm and Luticia were all having breakfast together.

Mab said, 'Master Kanaka, you look as if you have been up all night?'

Kanaka grimaced and helped himself to the buffet of food.

Mab turned to Pelian and said, 'Master Kanaka wishes you to remain with the Archangels; he thinks you could be a distraction during the negotiations.'

Pelian replied, 'Yes, I can understand that. If things go wrong, then I don't want you to be worrying about me.'

Mab looked at Kanaka and said, 'Pelian will join the Archangels; problem solved.'

Kanaka glanced at Lamm, who couldn't help laughing, and said, 'Great, I was awake most of the night worrying about it. But now the problem is solved in an instant.'

Mab replied, 'You should have mentioned it last night.' Kanaka rolled his eyes and drank copious amounts of hot coffee.

When they had all eaten their fill, Mab said, 'Let's make ready for battle; we will meet in the sports arena.'

When Mab and Pelian arrived, Kanaka, Lamm and Luticia were already there.

Mab said, 'As you know, we are visiting the planet Aafien, which has been occupied by the dark god Antobus and his followers. Antobus has imprisoned Mirablis and Infelice, both originally of the Abyss. Mirablis was taken by force from Aariet. Infelice went to have discussions with Antobus, and she, too, has been imprisoned. Antobus has been a resident of Aafien for a very long time; the planet is protected by an energy shield, as is the fortress. I expect there will be many inhabitants and many daemons. We know little of Antobus other than it is of the Abyss; it is an ancient creature, also we know that it participated in the light war. Our mission is to free Infelice and Mirablis, and also the indigenous population. The Archangels and Pelian will remain off-planet and only intervene if necessary. The energy shields are very powerful, Varalian has been aiding Antobus. I will bring the planet shield down, and we will land close to the fortress. We will approach the fortress openly and seek an audience with Antobus.'

Pelian said, 'Mab, I am sure you will be welcomed with open arms. However, while you are in the fortress, we will have no knowledge of the situation unless the local energy field is also brought down.'

Mab nodded and replied, 'I will bring it down before we enter the fortress; it may collapse when I take the planet-wide shield down. But, in any case, we will not enter the fortress unless the energy shield is down. Antobus may be adept at reading minds and thoughts, so be careful, do not let your mind wander, stay focused.'

The group vanished and appeared in the upper atmosphere of Aafien, where the Archangels were already assembled. Mab pointed to the shimmering energy field. Michael said, 'It is extraordinarily powerful. Do we know how it was created?'

Mab replied, 'It is the work of our old enemy Varalian. It is produced by machines which are powered by a special material that emits a type of light.'

Michael said, 'How do we destroy it?' Mab turned, pointed at the single visible star and said, 'Aardian will remove it. Stay close to me.'

Mab's open hand slowly closed, squeezed gently and released. Aardian pulsed. Mab repeated the action several times, Aardian pulsed in response. Mab then opened her hand wide and rapidly closed it to form a tight fist. Aardian flared wildly and expelled an enormous burst of electromagnetic radiation.

Mab said, 'The energy shield is down. Masters, follow me!' and rocketed downwards. The group was dragged along behind Mab, who flew low over the surface of the planet and landed in a dense woodland to the North side of the fortress.

Kanaka, breathing hard, said, 'That was fun!'

Mab replied, 'The fortress shield is also down. We should waste no time. Let's move!' Mab led the group to the edge of the forest; the fortress was huge with many entrances. Crowds of people were flocking through a huge gate, which was heavily guarded both at ground level and from the battlements above.

Luticia said, 'Perhaps we should seek another entrance?' They used the cover of the trees but only travelled a third of the way around the castle before the forest cover fell back. However, it was clear that they had found the main entrance due to the wide sweeping track, which was lined with wild cherry trees in blossom. The surrounding manicured gardens were beautiful and framed the enormous oak doors that led into the fortress.

Mab said, 'This is the formal entrance for dignitaries.'

Lamm said, 'Mab, you are a dignitary of the very highest order!'

Kanaka said, 'Absolutely, we are here to discuss important matters. So why skulk around in the forest? Let's knock on the door!'

Mab laughed and replied, 'Yes, I agree. Luticia, make your way over there and knock on the door.'

Luticia grimaced and said, 'I don't think so. I'm no dignitary, but I will be happy to stand behind you!'

Mab led the group out onto the blossom-covered track, and they walked slowly towards the entrance. As they got closer, guards appeared along the stone parapet. They held longbows and swords.

Kanaka walked forward and called out, 'We are here to meet with Antobus.'

The guard called back, 'Walk towards the gate; we will allow you entry.' A smaller door within one of the large doors opened, and as they stepped over the threshold, the guards surrounded them and marched them through a tunnel and into the fortress grounds. However, there was another wall with similar large doors before them. Cheering and Jeering could be heard from a large and raucous crowd.

Kanaka said, 'The fortress is double-walled.'

Mab turned to one of the guards, seized his mind, and said, 'What is happening on the other side of those doors.'

The guard screamed in pain and gasped, 'It is the games.'

Mab replied, 'Where is Antobus?'

The guard started to lose consciousness, but Mab said, 'You will answer me, or I will remove your head.'

The guard pointed to the doors and then collapsed to the floor. The other guards, who were immobilised, also dropped to the floor.

Kanaka said, 'That explains the huge crowds of people. Let's hope the games are less brutal than those we saw in Yehuda.'

Mab said, 'Antobus is at the far side of the arena. When we go through these doors, we will walk slowly towards it. Master Luticia immediately behind me, Master Kanaka to her left and Master Lamm to her right. Stay behind me, do not deviate; if anyone or anything gets too close push it back but remain in position. Keep your weapons sheathed and hidden unless you are attacked. Robes closed, hoods up. Understood?' The masters nodded and prepared themselves. Mab's shoulder-length hair platted back to the sides of her head, her heavy leather armour vanished and was replaced with a stunning white hooded robe and red waist sash. Mab walked to the inner doors, raised her arm and gestured with her left hand. A terrible screeching sound was heard as the doors started to buckle and suddenly exploded inwards into millions of fragments. Mab made the slightest movement with her right hand, and the millions of pieces of wood and dust froze in mid-air before dropping to the ground. The air was clear, and the crowd was silent.

Mab started to walk across the arena towards the dais. She could see Antobus and his acolytes, who seemed to be as shocked as the crowd. She stopped suddenly and threw her hood back. The arena was being used for animal fighting, and she saw several lions and bears. One of the bears was horribly injured, and the other two bears were running in different directions, frantically trying to escape.

Mab glanced at Kanaka and said, 'Remain here.'

She walked towards the lions and the injured bear. The lions lay down as she approached. Mab placed her hand on the bear and enveloped it in a silver skin of power. She walked back to Kanaka, and as she did so, the bears vanished. The crowd howled in protest. Mab continued as the crowd grew more raucous until she stood before Antobus.

Antobus said, 'Welcome to my home Bellona.'

Mab said, 'Infelice, Mirablis, give them to me now.'

Antobus paused before saying, 'And what will you give me in return?'

Mab turned, looked around the arena and said, 'I will give you and your followers a swift death.'

Her eyes flashed silver before returning to deep black orbs.

Antobus said, 'You threaten me?'

Mab replied, 'Return Infelice and Mirablis to me now. Otherwise, I will cleanse this planet, even if I must feed it to Aardian.'

Antobus replied, 'I am Antobus of the Abyss; you will leave now; otherwise, you will be staying here for a very long time.'

Mab paused as if in thought and said, 'You remind me of someone, Nasta? Surel? Abbadon? Kasta? Molochi? Tuchar?'

Antobus replied, 'Do not speak those names! These were great gods of the Abyss who gave their lives in the light war. You are not worthy to speak of them!'

Mab said, 'I will speak of them. They were filth; do you know what these so-called gods of the Abyss had in common?'

Antobus remained silent.

Mab said, 'They all fell under my sword. Yes, them and many more on both sides of the conflict until I was sated with their blood. And now I will slay you, Antobus and every daemon in this arena, and still, it will not be enough.'

Antobus screamed, 'Kill them all!' Antobus and his acolytes leapt towards Mab as the guards attacked from the flanks. Mab lifted her right hand and released an enormous psychic blast that propelled Antobus and his acolytes backwards. Antobus vanished and reappeared behind Mab, who soared upwards. Kanaka was scything through the guards, but Mab could see one of the acolytes heading directly for him and so translated to his side. Onimaru tumbled over her shoulder as she dropped low and swept the sword around in a wide arc, slicing the legs from the daemon. Black stinking blood sprayed from the leg stumps and fouled the earth. Mab looked up and saw the Archangels led by Pelian plummeting downwards towards the battle. The crowd was roaring and screaming at the same time, but most were trying to leave the arena only to find that the exits were barred by a powerful psychic shield.

The battle was frenetic; there seemed to be a never-ending stream of guards joining the fray. The numbers were such that only close-up fighting was possible. Mab concentrated on the acolytes, who, although smaller in number, were far more powerful than the guards. She caught sight of Antobus. Michael and Gabriel were driving him back, but their attack was frustrated by the sheer number of people in the arena and the dead and dying on the floor. Mab leapt into the air and landed immediately beside Michael but into the path of the black sword of Antobus. She was pushed hard from behind and found herself not only being trampled underfoot but being kicked, stabbed and slashed by the enemy around her. She blasted all around her away and rose upwards. Michael, Gabriel, Lucifer and Humbra were standing amid the carnage, ready to resume the battle. But something was wrong; they were in the ready position but not moving. Michael looked up at her; he had tears in his eyes. Mab stared at him askance and cried out, 'Pelian, where is Pelian!' It was the cry of a goddess in utter desolation; it brought the entire battle to a halt. Mab saw Pelian's trampled body behind Gabriel. She went to her and placed her hand gently on her head, but she then saw the wound. The black sword had cut deep into her skull. Kanaka knelt beside her, but he said nothing. No words were appropriate. Pelian vanished as Mab stood up, silver flame licking around her body.

Mab turned baleful eyes on Antobus. Everyone moved backward, clearing a large circle of the arena, which was nevertheless covered with the bodies of the dead and the dying. The stink of black blood was everywhere. Mab launched herself at Antobus and kicked it in the chest. The blow propelled Antobus backwards onto the ground. Mab landed on top of the creature and rained punches on its face. Her fists were a blur, and the blows were of staggering proportions; the ground shook violently. The deep bedrock below the arena screamed and fissured under the immensity of the impacts. Wide cracks raced across the floor of the arena.

Michael, with a grim smile, whispered, 'This is a catharsis, not a battle.' The structure of the arena began to collapse. Antobus started to change form; black tentacles sprung from its body and flickered upwards. Mab plucked Onimaru from the air and rammed it down through the black pulp that was now the face of Antobus. The creature screamed, the black tentacles retracted, and a great black snake began to take form. Mab leapt off the body and waited; the snake reared up, pulling Onimaru from the ground. Mab stared at the creature and said, 'Your true form at last, but you cannot escape; Onimaru holds you here. And now, you will know pain the like of which even you could not imagine.'

Mab turned to the Archangels and said, 'Leave me!' Michael, Gabriel and Humbra vanished immediately. Lucifer stood, indomitable, and said, 'I will remain by your side, Goddess.' The sky darkened, lightning bolts streaked through the blackness, and many threw themselves to the ground, cowering from the thunderclaps. A lightning bolt stabbed down and struck the great snake, which dropped to the ground, writhing in pain. But it suddenly reared up and lunged towards Mab. Its yellow slit eyes and carious fangs were fearsome to behold. Mab's appearance changed; she became a creature of pure light, she spread her arms wide, lightning bolts rained down and were channeled through her towards Antobus. The power increased to staggering proportions until Mab heard Kanaka's voice in her head. 'Mab, it is enough; pull back! pull back!' Mab lowered her arms and reigned in the power flowing through her body. She began to take human form and found herself standing at the bottom of a huge crater before the body of the giant snake, which was barely alive. Mab's hand went to her left hip, and a whip of light lashed out, scoring the great snake, which made no sound. Mab continued to lash the creature, the whip tearing deep into its flesh but evoking no response.

Lucifer appeared by her side and said, 'Goddess, please, enough.' The whip vanished; Mab raised her hands, and two broad beams of silver flame incinerated what was left of Antobus.

Lucifer said, 'Goddess, the death of the creature has released many from daemonic possession.'

Mab looked around; the crowd were kneeling and calling her name.

Lucifer said, 'You have set them free.'

Mab turned to Kanaka and said, 'And Master Kanaka has saved them, and this world, from my wrath.'

Kanaka bowed. Mab threw Onimaru into the air and said, 'Master Kanaka, we need to ensure no daemons remain here.'

Kanaka nodded, lifted his right arm, and Onimaru dropped into his hand.'

Mab said, 'Lucifer, we will free Infelice and Mirablis; I know where they are!'

Mab and Lucifer appeared in a deep underground vault. Lucifer created several balls of light which illuminated the space and said, 'It is as on Aariet.'

Mab nodded, pointed to one of the null chambers and said, 'Open it!' Lucifer brought his great sword down on the chamber and it bit clean through the top plate. Mab rammed her hand into the cut and ripped the entire top plate from the chamber. She then placed her hand on Infelice and poured energy into her.

Lucifer said, 'What of Mirablis?'

Mab replied, 'The other null chambers are empty; he must be imprisoned somewhere else.' Mab looked down at Infelice and gestured with her right hand; Infelice vanished.

Mab reached out with her witch senses and said, 'Mirablis is dead; follow me!' Mab and Lucifer walked past the null chambers and made their way down a long subterranean corridor; the temperature rose markedly as they went deeper into the rock. Eventually, they came to a large cavern, a river of lava flowed through a channel formed in the floor. There were many cells that had been created by excavating caves in the rock and fixing iron bars to seal the occupants inside.

Lucifer said, 'The cells have no doors; they have been imprisoned indefinitely.'

Mab pointed and said, 'No, not indefinitely; that is Mirablis.'

Lucifer looked and saw that Mirablis and several others had been staked to the rock face. Heavy iron spikes had been driven through their wrists and legs, pinning them to the wall. Their bodies had been horribly burned by ladling molten lava onto their skin. Iron pokers had been used to burn out their eyes and had been inserted into various body orifices. Mirablis was almost unrecognisable; lava had been used to burn away most of his face; his feet and hands were entirely consumed.

Lucifer said, 'Tortured to death.'

Mab said, 'But for what purpose?'

Lucifer shrugged his shoulders, pointed, and said, 'Perhaps they know.'

Two enormous creatures were making their way towards them. They seemed to be half human and half animal. Great horns protruded from their skulls, and their bodies were covered in thick brown fur. They were heavily armoured, and each carried a pike in one hand and an iron sword in the other.

Mab glanced in their direction and said, 'Lucifer, deal with them.'

Lucifer replied, 'Do you wish to speak with them first?'

Mab replied, 'No, I have had enough of this place.' Lucifer was upon them in a fraction of a second. His black sword cut the first guard in half, from head to crotch, and, on the return swipe, beheaded the second guard. Mab made a gesture with her right hand, and the bars were torn from the prison cells, ripping out huge lumps of rock. The prisoners staggered from their cells and out into the large cavern, but all were alive. Lucifer pointed to the way out and said, 'Go now, you are free!'

The prisoners began to flee, but one of them stopped and said, 'Sir, thank you for saving us. I was imprisoned by the god Antobus. He intends to spread his vile legions throughout the universe.'

Lucifer replied, 'Antobus is dead.'

The prisoner replied, 'I was told that it was not possible to kill such a being.'

Lucifer replied, 'The creature was slain by the Goddess Bellona, its body was incinerated on the floor of the arena above.'

Mab appeared at Lucifer's side, and the prisoner dropped to his knees. Mab said, 'Stand up, tell me who you are and what you know of Antobus and its plans.'

The prisoner stood up, but his head remained bowed. He said, 'My name is Gord; I don't know where I am; the stars have gone. I am from the planet Earth; the others were taken from different places. I think Antobus was collecting inhabitants from various planets.'

Mab replied, 'Where did you live on the planet Earth?'

Gord replied, 'I lived in Blant, a small village, with my parents. I went on an errand to the palace. When I reached the palace, I was imprisoned, then I found myself here. I don't know how long I have been here. I was questioned about Earth, the population and those that I knew. I answered all their questions, but they were never satisfied. I was brought down here only recently to be tortured.'

Mab was silent for a few moments and then said, 'Did they ask you about a girl named Mabdelore Winter?'

Gord replied, 'Why yes, they did ask about Mab and her friend Izzy. I told them that I had gone to school with them, but later, they had gone to the Guild of Sorcerers to study.'

Mab put her hand under Gord's chin and lifted his head. Gord stared into her eyes for a few moments, and tears began to pour down his face. Mab wrapped her arms around him and pulled him close.

Lucifer said, 'Goddess, I will assist Kanaka with the cleansing.'

Mab said, 'Gord, you are safe now. I will take you back home.'

Gord said, 'You are the Goddess?'

Mab smiled and replied, 'Yes, but you can still call me Mab! Now, walk with me.' Mab took his hand, and they walked together through the facility and out into the open air of the arena. Kanaka and the masters had the local population arranged in three long lines. Each person was checked by a master and released only if they did not host a daemon. Mab realised that Lucifer was correct; of the many hundreds that had been tested, only one had hosted a daemon which fled when the point of Onimaru touched the flesh of the host. As Mab and Gord walked, hand in hand, all bowed, and many kneeled.

When Mab reached Kanaka, she said, 'This is Gord, a school friend. When you are finished here, we can travel back home together.'

Kanaka nodded and said, 'Gord, there is food and water on the dais; please help yourself.'

Gord walked off in the direction of the dais.

Mab looked upwards and said, 'Sister, come to me.' There was an immediate flash of bright light, and Minerva hung in the air before Mab.

Mab said, 'Pelian?'

Minerva replied, 'She was gravely injured. Her recovery will be slow, and her powers and skills may be lost.'

Mab smiled and said, 'Thank you, sister. She lives, that is the very best news.' Tears of joy dropped from Mab's eyes as they contacted the ground; beautiful flowers sprouted from the barren soil and spread around her feet.

Minerva said, 'She remains unconscious; I will let you know when to come.'

Mab floated up and kissed her sister. Minerva smiled, returned the kiss, and vanished.

Mab looked at Lucifer and said, 'Varalian.'

Lucifer replied, 'Where?' Mab said, 'It thinks it can hide from me.'

Mab, followed by Lucifer, translated back to the null machines.

She stood staring at the machines for a few moments and then said, 'Varalian, I know you are here. I wish to speak with you.'

A mechanical voice replied, 'No, you wish to kill me, but you will not succeed.'

Mab immediately placed a spherical energy field around the entire room.

Varalian said, 'Nice try, but you can't stand there forever. I however, can wait here until the end of time if necessary.'

The sphere of energy rose upwards, taking everything and everyone inside with it. It melted everything it touched, including rock and soil. It emerged within the arena and paused in its upward ascent. Mab and Lucifer stepped out.

Mab said, 'Varalian, you cannot escape this energy field.'

Varalian replied, 'Then I will wait until it expires.'

Mab said, 'No, you will go to Aardian, where you will be consumed.'

The sphere rocketed upwards at enormous speed and disappeared into the light of Aardian.

Chapter Thirty-Five: Conspiracy Revealed

Mab sat with Kanaka, sipping a fine malt whisky.

Kanaka said, 'Have you been to see Pelian?'

Mab replied, 'No, she is still unconscious. It is important that she is not disturbed. Minerva is a skilled healer; she will let me know when to visit.'

Kanaka said, 'I hope she recovers, you deserve to have happiness once again in your life.'

Mab smiled and said, 'And so do you.'

Kanaka grimaced and replied, 'We have had this discussion before. I haven't met the right person.'

Mab said, 'Master Kanaka, I think I have found the right partner for you.'

Kanaka, bemused, replied, 'Oh really! Let me guess, is it Luticia?'

Mab laughed and said, 'No! It is not Luticia!'

Kanaka replied, 'Who is it?'

Mab said, 'Patience, you will meet her soon. But now I must go. I need to collect Gord from Cat and Charly and take him home.'

Mab appeared in her rooms and found Gord still chatting with Cat and Charly. Mab said, 'Gord, are you ready to go home?'

Gord replied, 'Yes, I can't wait to see my Mom and Dad, and my sisters!'

Mab said, 'I have returned you to your original Earth time stream. You have been away from your parents for less than a year. It may be best if you don't mention what happened?'

Gord replied, 'I'll say I was imprisoned somewhere in the North, and you rescued me.'

Mab said, 'Yes, that would be close enough to the truth!' Mab and Gord vanished and appeared in the garden of Gord's home in Blant. Mab watched as Gord knocked on the door and walked into the entrance hall. There was a great commotion, and the dogs were barking loudly amid the screams of joy from Gord's family. As Mab strolled down the garden path, her appearance changed. Her robe and trousers were replaced with a thick woolly jumper and tight-fitting sports pants. Her hair changed to a plaited pigtail that hung down her back. She laughed as she walked, thinking that she was quite the country girl out for a stroll in the gloaming. Mab turned off the main track and cut across the fields, eventually coming to her parents' home. She smiled as she clambered over the old wooden fence and laughed as she fell flat on her face. She stood up, her face and clothes covered in wet mud, then she heard her mom's voice. She was arguing with someone. Mab walked around to the front of the house and saw two burly men. Their voices were raised, and Mab's mother was on the verge of tears.

The nearest of the two men turned, looked at Mab, laughed, pointed and said, 'Let me guess, this is your daughter!'

Mab said, 'Silence!' The two men were struck dumb and completely immobilised. As Mab walked to her mother, the mud dropped from her clothes and her jumper was replaced with a blouse of the finest white silk. She embraced her mother and led her back into the house. Mab realised immediately that her dad had not been in the house for some time. She reached out with her witch senses and found his body in the local cemetery.

She whispered, 'When did he die?'

Her mom replied, 'A couple of weeks ago. It was an accident; he fell under the plough. It cut deep into his thigh, and he bled to death. I found him in the far field, late in the evening, he was cold.'

Mab said, 'Why didn't you come to the Guild?' Her mom replied, 'If I had found him earlier, I would have. But he was dead, and there didn't seem to be any point. I thought it best to wait for you to return.'

Mab was silent for a while and then said, 'Mom, I think you did the right thing.'

They sat holding each other for some time, and then Sopa said, 'I'll make us some tea and scones.'

Mab smiled in response. They sat together, sipping tea and eating warm fruit scones.

Sopa said, 'The men outside are here to collect money. It seems there is a land rent that we were unaware of, Walim was dealing with it.'

Mab replied, 'Mom, don't worry about that. Why don't you go to bed? I'll join you once I have spoken to the visitors.'

Sopa kissed Mab and made her way upstairs to her bedroom.

The door opened; the two men dropped to the ground.

Mab closed the door behind her and said, 'Get up!'

The men managed to stand, the first said, 'We are from the regional bank, you are going to regret treating us in this way.'

Mab's mind probe seared into the first man who screamed in agony. She released him, and another man appeared by his side. He was enormously fat and wore a red ceremonial coat with a chain of office around his neck. The fat man looked around and clearly didn't understand where he was.

He said, 'What is this. I was giving a speech!' When he saw Mab, he dropped to his knees and said, 'Goddess, how may I be of service?'

Mab replied, 'These two men work for you?'

The fat man looked up and replied, 'I am the regional mayor. I know these men; they work for the bank. Is there a problem?'

Mab said, 'If anyone else pursues my mother for money, for any reason whatsoever, I will remove every person associated with them, including colleagues, friends and family, and place them on a desert planet where they will remain for the rest of their lives. Do you understand?'

Before the mayor could answer, another man appeared beside him.

Mab said, 'You are the head of the bank?'

The man was dressed only in his night clothes and looked around him frantically, trying to decipher what was happening. He looked down at the mayor, then at Mab and immediately dropped to his knees.

He looked up at Mab hesitantly and said, 'Goddess, I am truly sorry for anything I have done wrong. Please forgive me?'

Mab replied, 'This is my mother's home and my mother's land. She owes you nothing. Now, you four can walk back home together and consider how fortunate you are to be alive. I am very disappointed in you, and I do not forget when I am slighted!'

The mayor said, 'Goddess, please forgive us. I promise we did not know of this practice. My colleague and I will ensure that this will never happen again.'

Mab replied, 'Then go, but know that I will judge you by your actions.'

Mab went back into the house and slammed the door behind her. Sopa was there; she had been listening.

Mab said, 'You didn't have to hear that.'

Sopa replied, 'I am glad I did listen. Now I know they won't be coming back!'

Mab said, 'How much money do you have?'

Sopa replied, 'I have only a little in the bank and a bit more in cash.'

Mab said, 'Let me see how much cash you have.'

Sopa returned with a small wooden box and emptied the contents onto the table. There were many copper and bronze coins, but only three gold coins. Mab picked up one of the gold coins and held it in her fist for several minutes. She then dropped five new gold coins into the box. She repeated the process until the box contained thirty-one gold coins.

Sopa picked one up, examined it and said, 'Is it real?'

Mab replied, 'Yes, they are solid gold, identical in every way to the original coin.'

Sopa laughed and said, 'I am rich!'

Mab replied, 'I will ask the Guild to transfer my monthly income to you. I have spent very little money since I joined the Guild! And, if I ever do need money, I will make it myself!'

Sopa said, 'There is no need to do that!'

Mab replied, 'Yes, there is! I want you to enjoy your retirement. You can't run this farm on your own. Why don't you turn it into a haven for wildlife? Let it look after itself?'

Sopa hugged Mab and said, 'Yes, you are right. I will do it!'

Mab said, 'I have a new love in my life. Her name is Pelian.'

Sopa replied, 'My darling, I am so happy for you!'

Mab said, 'We were fighting against evil creatures, she took a horrible blow that was meant for me. She pushed me aside, the black sword cut deep into her head.' Sopa put her hand over her mouth, aghast at what had happened.

Mab said, 'She is with Minerva, I think she will recover, but perhaps not completely.' Mab hung her head as the tears streamed from her eyes.

Sopa hugged Mab tightly and then said, 'What is that?'

Mab looked up, and they walked outside together. The entire sky flashed with lights of every colour. Every few seconds, a band of light would drop from the sky towards them.

Sopa said, 'It is the most beautiful thing I have ever seen!'

Mab turned and said, 'Look, fireflies!' The house was lit up by glowing spots of white light that danced to the rhythm of the lights in the sky.'

Mab lifted her right hand into the air and made a circular motion. The bands of light responded by swirling around. Mab laughed, and Sopa screamed with delight. Mab put her arm around Sopa and said, 'Don't be scared.' Mab levitated upwards high into the air until it seemed that they were alone with the lights.

Sopa said, 'Mab, I will never forget this moment.'

Mab said, 'It is a gift, from our birth star to you.'

Sopa looked at Mab and replied, 'A gift from the sun? It is surely the most beautiful of gifts.'

Mab replied, 'Yes, and it is a great honour to receive it.'

There was a flash of bright light, Minerva appeared beside them and said, 'Truly beautiful, your sun honours you, Bellona.'

Mab said, 'No, it is a gift to my mother for adopting me, protecting me and raising me to be what I am today.' The lights increased in intensity.

Minerva said, 'Yes, I see it now, it is for Sopa!' Tears of joy streamed down Sopa's face. They watched until the lights started to fade.

Minerva turned to Mab and said, 'Sister, Pelian has regained consciousness.'

Sopa said, 'Mab, you must go now!'

Mab returned Sopa to the farmhouse and appeared with Minerva in the palace of the old gods.

Minerva turned to Mab and said, 'I will bring her to you. Now, stay calm, this is the only palace we have. The last time you went into a rage, it was almost destroyed.'

Mab replied, 'I don't remember that?'

Minerva said, 'Yes, you do. Erebus slighted you. I thought you were about to slay him and bring the palace down around us!'

Mab wandered off through the cloisters and said nothing in response. She waited nervously, then she saw them approach. Minerva and Uriel were supporting Pelian, helping her to walk. Mab went to meet her but then stopped, her powerful senses reading every thought, every nuance of movement.

Minerva said, 'Pelian has not yet regained speech, but she understands everything. I could not have achieved even this without the help of Uriel.'

But the words drifted over Mab, who was focused intently on Pelian.

Mab said, 'Release her.'

Uriel started to object, but Minerva stopped her with a look.

Mab opened her arms and said, 'Come to me, my love.' Pelian walked slowly towards Mab and embraced her. The hair had been shaved from her head, and the large sword gash was an angry red.

Minerva said, 'It took a great deal of effort to combat the poison...'

Mab interrupted, 'Sister, Mother, thank you for everything you have done.' Mab slowly kissed Pelian's head along the line of the gash, and the redness disappeared.

Pelian gasped.

She then placed her hands on the sides of her head, stared intently into her deep blue eyes for several minutes, and said, 'I think we should go home?'

Pelian replied, 'Yes, my love. I have been lost without you.'

Mab smiled, her tears of joy dropping onto Pelian's face. Pelian's hair was instantly restored, and her face flushed red as a wave of goodness and health engulfed her. Mab kissed Pelian slowly on the lips, and the light surrounding them increased in intensity. Minerva and Uriel bathed in a wave of vitality that swept through the palace. Mab and Pelian vanished.

Mab woke late with Pelian in her arms; they had slept soundly together.

Pelian opened her eyes, beaming at Mab and said, 'Where are we?'

Mab replied, 'Have you forgotten that you are a master at the school of psych and sorcery?'

Pelian replied, 'I don't think I will be of much use to them. I have no powers; they are gone. Uriel said, the injury to my head must have damaged my brain.'

Mab replied, 'Your brain was not damaged, but it is in shock. Your powers are dormant, but I will release them, Mab pulled Pelian closer and said, 'Relax, I will enter your mind.' Pelian smiled and closed her eyes.

Mab said, 'It's a bit of a mess in here!'

Pelian replied, 'Don't make me laugh!'

Mab said, 'This might hurt a bit.'

Pelian could feel Mab pushing on something, like trying to turn a key in a stiff lock. Suddenly, it released, and Pelian felt a wave of power flowing into her mind.

Pelian said, 'Yes! It is done, I feel the power flowing back!'

Mab said, 'You are still a patient; you need to take things easy until you recover fully. Understood?'

Pelian said, 'When will we be getting married?'

Mab replied, 'As soon as possible. But we need to think about where you want to be married.'

Pelian said, 'Minerva told me about your father, I'm so sorry.'

Mab smiled and said, 'I will miss him. I wish I had spent more time with him and my mom.'

Pelian said, 'Perhaps our marriage could be in Blant where your mom lives, and the celebration dinner here or at the Guild.'

Mab smiled and replied, 'Nice thought, but I'm not sure that would work.'

Pelian said, 'I don't have a family, so don't expect many, or any, from my side.'

Mab replied, 'I think we should have the whole thing in the palace of the old gods.'

Pelian said, 'The palace! That would be magnificent!'

Mab replied, 'We need a father figure for you, I thought master Kanaka or perhaps Erebus! Yes, that would be fitting. Erebus could be the father figure, and Minerva your mother figure.'

Pelian said, 'Do you think they will agree to do it?' Mab said, 'Of course they will!'

Pelian replied, 'Well, that's my side sorted out! What about you?'

Mab said, 'Maybe Master Kanaka could be my father figure and Uriel my mother figure. Perhaps my Earth mom could walk with us down the aisle and perform the binding ceremony. But it needs more thought, let's agree that it will be in the palace and figure out the rest later.'

Mab and Pelian appeared in Lamm's office.

Lamm leapt to his feet, went to Pelian, embraced her gently, and said, 'How are you?'

Pelian replied, 'I am fine. I had the very best healers, the goddess Minerva, the Archangel Uriel and of course my wonderful partner.'

Mab said, 'Yes, but you need to rest, your wound has healed, but there was internal damage. Your powers need time to settle, so do not do anything that requires exertion or intense concentration.'

Pelian smiled and said, 'Yes, of course.'

Mab rolled her eyes, looked at Lamm and said, 'That means she will do precisely the opposite!'

Mab put her arms around Pelian, kissed her and said, 'I must leave now. I will return tonight; you need to rest. Master Lamm will make sure that you do so!'

Mab appeared on the planet Aariet, just outside the small village that Infelice had made her home. She took the form of an old man and was dressed in the apparel of a villager, wearing trousers of animal skin, a heavy leather waistcoat and stout boots. She wore a flat cap on her head and leaned on a gnarled wooden staff. She walked along a narrow track leading to the centre of the village. It was early morning; the villagers were busy tending crops and animals. Fires were being lit in preparation for breakfast. Mab caught sight of Infelice, who was with the village elders. They were seated on logs which had been arranged on the ground in the shape of a triangle, with three elders on each side. Mab strolled closer to the group and stood, leaning on her staff, overtly listening to the conversation.

One of the elders noticed her and said, 'Sir, you are a stranger to us, but you are welcome in our village. How can we help you?'

Mab replied, 'I would speak with your leader.'

Infelice stared at Mab and started to laugh.

Mab, shaking her staff in the air, said, 'You would make fun of an old man! I will smite you with my staff.'

Infelice laughed even harder.

The elder looked askance at Infelice and said, 'Do you know this man?'

Infelice stood, walked towards Mab, and embraced her. Mab's appearance changed. She was now the goddess Bellona, dressed in her characteristic white robe, red sash and open-toed sandals. Her white hair hung down to her shoulders. Onimaru was hitched high on her back, and a whip hung from her left hip.

Mab said, 'How are you? I trust my sister restored you to your present good health?'

Infelice smiled and replied, 'Yes, she allowed me to enter the sacred waters. It was magnificent, and I was healed in body and mind almost instantly. How is Pelian?'

Mab looked around and saw that all activity in the village had stopped; the villagers were kneeling. Mab said, 'Everyone, thank you. Please now stand up and go about your duties.'

Infelice whispered, 'Let's go to my cabin.'

As they walked, Mab said, 'Pelian is recovering albeit slowly.'

Infelice handed Mab a goblet of wine and placed a small block of white cheese on the table. Mab, tasting the cheese, said, 'Nice, very creamy!'

Infelice replied, 'I assume you haven't come here to sample my goat's cheese?'

Mab paused and said, 'Are you really happy here?'

Infelice stared at Mab and replied, 'I know you are up to something, but I also know there is no point in asking what it is. So, to answer your question. Yes, I am very happy here, although I guess I feel that I could, and should, contribute more.'

Mab replied, 'Contribute more?'

Infelice said, 'In the battle against slavery and to bring about peace for all living things.'

Mab replied, 'Yes, you are a powerful daemon even in human form, but you have retreated from the fight in order to live here in harmony with simple people. I would rather see you help us to protect all of the innocent. Also, it must be lonely for you living as a god amongst sheep.'

Infelice hung her head and said, 'Am I so transparent?'

Mab smiled, put her arms around Infelice, hugged her tightly and said, 'What you have done here is remarkable, but you don't have to be here all the time. The elders can lead the villagers, you can visit periodically to check all is well?'

Infelice sighed and said, 'What do you suggest?'

Mab replied, 'I would like you to help me, I have a position on a planet known as Earth. It is a small planet with a single star at the edge of a large galaxy. I am a master of the Guild of Sorcerers. There is a vacancy for another master. It would be your new home, you would help teach the students warfare, and assist them in developing their powers. You would meet many new gifted people!'

Infelice said, 'I would be your assistant?'

Mab replied, 'As a master of the school, you would report to Master Kanaka, as do I. However, we have other duties that include protecting humans, and other innocents, from evil across space and time.'

Infelice thought for a few moments and said, 'It sounds great, but there is a problem. I have never been to this planet Earth, and, although I have taken permanent human form, I am still a daemon. I would not survive there, particularly if it is part of a galaxy.'

Mab smiled and said, 'You will survive there, you bathed in the palace waters.'

Infelice stared at Mab and said, 'How long have you been planning this?'

Mab laughed and replied, 'Not very long, but the best is yet to come. I have found you a partner, he will be just perfect for you!'

Infelice's eyes widened. She was about to reply, but Mab vanished.

Mab appeared next to Pelian, who was in the school arena practicing with three of the most promising young students. The three students dropped to their knees immediately.

Mab hugged Pelian and said, 'You were supposed to be relaxing!'

Pelian replied, 'I am relaxing. Master Uvren assures me that these three are amongst the most promising students.'

Mab looked at the students and said, 'Please stand up.'

Two of the students were girls who were clearly very athletic; they had their heads bowed and did not look directly at Mab. The third was a rather skinny boy who was smaller and younger than the girls, but he stared directly at Mab. They were standing beside a pile of stone slabs.

Mab said, 'What are your names?'

The boy said, 'My name is Hassan.'

The first girl replied, 'Anikaa' and the second 'Moia'. Mab stared at the students for a few moments before turning to Pelian and saying, 'So, let me see what they can do.'

Anikaa approached the stone slabs and concentrated for a few moments. The top five slabs began to rise. She held the stones for several seconds, beads of sweat ran down her forehead, and then she gently lowered them.

Mab said, 'Well done, Anikaa!'

Pelian said, 'Moia, a sword kata.'

Moia carried out one of the more basic kata's, but she carried it out flawlessly, moving with speed and grace. When she had finished, Mab said, 'Moia, that was excellent!'

Pelian looked at the boy and said, 'Hassan, what would you like to do?'

Hassan replied, 'A fireball?'

Pelian smiled and winked at Mab.

Hassan cupped his hands in front of his chest. A ball of flame began to build, and it grew in both size and intensity. He released it suddenly; it rocketed across the arena and blasted a heavy practice log into thousands of pieces. Mab walked up behind Hassan, put her arms around him and said, 'That was very impressive! Do it again.'

Hassan tilted his head back and looked up, smiling at Mab.

Mab laughed and said, 'I can see you being a bundle of trouble!'

Hassan cupped his hands once more; the ball of flame started to form and grew in intensity.

Hassan was about to release it, but Mab said, 'No, it is not ready. Pour more energy into it, keep going until I tell you to stop.'

Hassan followed Mab's instructions until the ball of flame was white hot; he was struggling to contain it.

Mab said, 'Relax, it cannot harm you. Now take your eyes from it, look up at the target, and the heavy stone to the right of the practice logs. When you release the ball, I want you to stretch it into a spear shape and set it spinning by turning your hand. Do it!'

Hassan released the ball of flame and managed to stretch it into a short spear shape. Mab grabbed his right hand and twisted it clockwise. The spear spun on its axis, struck the target, and melted a circular hole almost entirely through the full thickness of the stone.' Hassan leapt into the air and ran across the arena towards the target.

Mab turned to Pelian and said, 'Three excellent students!

I think the GOS will have some stiff competition at the next inter-school sports event!'

Infelice slept soundly in her chosen human form for most of the night, dreaming of a new life on a distant planet known as Earth.

She awoke with a start when a voice in her mind said, 'You are of the Abyss, why do you disrespect your own kind?'

Infelice replied, 'I have taken human form and bathed in the sacred waters of the old gods. My life in the Abyss is now a memory, a bad memory which, if possible, I would expunge from my mind.'

The voice said, 'You know me.'

Infelice replied, 'Yes, you spared my life eons ago, but you planted your name on my consciousness before you left me.'

The voice said, 'You are of the Abyss, you belong to me, and I will now have you back to do my bidding.'

Infelice replied, 'I belong to no one, and I will not return to the Abyss.'

The voice said, 'Your brothers Antobus and Noticas are dead, and yet you still live. How can this be?'

Infelice replied, 'They were not my brothers, they meant nothing to me. Antobus imprisoned me, it was vile, I would have killed it myself if I had the opportunity. It tortured and killed my friend Mirablis!'

The voice said, 'And so you conspired with those of the light to kill Antobus and Noticas.'

Infelice replied, 'I conspired with no one. I was rescued from my imprisonment by the goddess Bellona, she killed both Antobus and Noticas.'

The voice was silent for several moments before saying, 'You witnessed the battle?'

Infelice replied, 'No, but it is said that Bellona slew them both with ease. My understanding is that she wishes to speak with those of the deep Abyss regarding the future.'

The voice said, 'This goddess has no future. If she dares to enter our demesnes, she will never return to the light; we will feast on her essence. I expect you to return to the Abyss without delay. Do not disappoint me!'

Mab woke early the following morning, nudged Pelian and said, 'I must go to Infelice. I am hoping she will be able to mediate between the light and the dark.'

Pelian replied, 'Please tell me that you are not going into the Abyss!'

Mab said, 'They cannot come to me, therefore I must go to them. Otherwise, this leakage of daemons will never be staunched.'

Pelian replied, 'I will come with you!'

Mab said, 'No, you have not fully recovered; in any case, you would not live long in that place. I will go with Infelice, she has unique knowledge of the deep Abyss and its inhabitants.'

Pelian replied, 'Do you trust her?'

Mab smiled and said, 'That is a very good question.'

Pelian replied, 'And what is your answer?'

Mab said, 'I do not know the answer, but I will soon find out.'

Pelian hugged Mab and said, 'Trust no one in that place, they are truly evil. Infelice may behave in unexpected ways when she returns to the Abyss; she may fall under the control of others.'

Mab whispered 'My love, you are wise beyond your years. But do not worry, if things go awry, I will summon help.'

Pelian replied, 'I do not think Erebus would come to your aid, even though he is enthralled with your sister. As for the others, they would not dare aid you against the gods of the Abyss. Where was Sladrin and his brothers when we were battling Antobus?'

Mab nodded and said, 'Yes, that is true, but help can come from unexpected places. In any case, you need to relax, remember no physical or mental exertion! I will return as soon as I can.'

Mab vanished and appeared beside Infelice, who was in her cabin preparing breakfast. Mab said, 'It seems I arrived just in time!'

Infelice hugged Mab and said, 'Yes, I have noticed that you tend to show up around mealtimes; take a seat.'

Infelice laid out two different cheeses, rustic breads, cold meats, goat's milk and wine.

Mab said, 'Perfect!'

Infelice replied, 'What of this new partner you have found for me on Earth?'

Mab smiled and said, 'You will meet him soon, after our return from the Abyss.'

Infelice sat down; she looked tired, worn down with worry.

Mab smiled, Infelice gasped, and slowly hung her head as a wave of wellness and hope washed through her body. Mab whispered, 'Is there something you wish to share?'

Infelice looked at Mab, she stared into those black orb eyes, and two small streams of tears flowed down her face. Mab reached across and held her hands.

Infelice said, 'I am unworthy. I lied to you about the creature I met in the Abyss. I know its name; it has a hold over me.'

Mab clenched her right hand. A sphere of argent power engulfed them. Mab said, 'It is known as Melchised, it is an ancient creature that dwells in the depths of the Abyss. There are four rulers of the infinite darkness, Melchised is not one of them.'

Infelice stared at Mab askance and whispered, 'How do you know this!?'

Mab said, 'You can speak freely. This energy sphere cannot be breached. What is the nature of the hold the creature has over you?'

Infelice replied, 'I met it only once; it is very powerful. I thought it would kill me, but it was distracted. It left its mark on me as it departed. It said that I was now its servant. When I left the Abyss, it told me to come to this planet rather than join Antobus, which was my original intention. I believe Antobus only spared me because it knew I was the property of Melchised.'

Mab said, 'What do you feel when the creature contacts you?'

Infelice replied, 'I feel revulsion. I can't not listen to what it says! How would you feel?'

Mab said, 'Can it take control of your body or make you harm living creatures?'

Infelice replied, 'No, at least I don't think so.'

Mab said, 'Do you mind if I examine you? I will need to enter your mind?'

Infelice replied, 'I am used to being violated, so why not!?'

Mab leaned over, kissed Infelice and said, 'I would never do such a thing. My partner suffered from a similar problem; the daemon was able to control her body, make her do things against her will. Something physical had been placed in her brain. I do not think that is the case with you, but it may be something more subtle.'

Infelice replied, 'Goddess, I am sorry. I have been dreaming of my new life on Earth, but Melchised has reminded me that I am not free to do as I wish. Please do whatever you can to help me!'

Mab placed her hands on Infelice's head and said, 'Remain calm, I will be gentle.'

Mab searched slowly through Infelice's memories and eventually found her memory of the meeting with Melchised. She looked through Infelice's eyes at Melchised, she could feel her fear of the creature. She saw it moving towards her, its hand outstretched, and words were spoken, but Mab did not understand what was said.

Mab withdrew from Infelice's mind and said, 'I found a partial memory, the creature approached you, placed its hand on your forehead and uttered a string of words.'

Infelice replied, 'I do not remember any of that!'

Mab said, 'It has placed an enduring enchantment upon you. Go to the far wall and face me.'

Mab faced Infelice and raised her left hand. Infelice was held in a vice-like grip; she could not move anything, even her eyes. Mab walked slowly towards her. Infelice felt a tension building in her mind.

Mab said, 'Remain calm, I have found the binding. I will break it, but it will be painful. Are you ready?'

Infelice simply stared back at Mab and then let off a terrible shriek as a searing pain sliced through her mind. She dropped to the floor unconscious. Mab lifted her up, placed her on the bed and carried out a thorough scan of her body. She then poured herself a goblet of wine and waited for Infelice to regain consciousness.

Infelice recovered quickly. She sat up in bed, placed her hands gently on her head and groaned.

Mab said, 'Sorry about the pain, the enchantment had been in place for a very long time.'

Infelice replied, 'I felt something break inside me, but apart from the headache, I feel good. I feel free!'

Mab sat beside Infelice and said, 'You are free. I gave you a thorough check, everything is now in good working order!'

Infelice hugged Mab and said, 'Thank you, Goddess.'

Mab said, 'I want to meet with Melchised and the others of its kind.'

Infelice replied, 'I know, and I also know you want me to go with you. But I can't go back there.'

Mab was silent for a few moments and then said, 'I understand. Don't worry, I will find someone else. Perhaps Lucifer or Humbra?'

Infelice was silent once again, but then said, 'No, I will go. I must help, I owe it to you and all those who lost their lives because of Antobus and Noticas. I should go alone in the first instance, as an emissary.'

Mab looked thoughtful and said, 'You will go with Erebus and Lucifer. Erebus is of the Abyss, Lucifer resided in the Abyss for eons before he came back into the light.'

Infelice replied, 'I have heard of Erebus; he is revered by many. It would certainly be worth having him present. I do not know Lucifer.'

Mab replied, 'Lucifer is an Archangel; it was he who helped me free you from the null chamber on Aafien.'

Infelice said, 'Then he has my thanks, I trust he is a skilled warrior?'

Mab smiled and said, 'Lucifer, come to me.'

Lucifer appeared immediately, bowed, and said, 'How can I be of service, Goddess?' Lucifer stood like a titan; his body perfection personified.

Infelice stared at Lucifer in astonishment and said, 'Lucifer, thank you for rescuing me from the null chamber.'

Lucifer merely nodded in response. Mab smiled at Infelice, turned to Lucifer and said, 'Infelice has agreed to travel back to the deep Abyss with a view to arranging a meeting with the rulers. I had thought to go myself, but, on reflection, perhaps you and Erebus should accompany her. I will follow proceedings through Infelice and intervene only if necessary.'

Lucifer looked at Infelice and said, 'When?'

Mab turned to Lucifer and said, 'I must leave! Contact Erebus. Go there as soon as possible. Keep me informed.'

Lucifer nodded; Mab vanished.

Lucifer said, 'I will explain the situation to Erebus, and we will both return here shortly. Will we need weapons?'

Infelice replied, 'No, weapons would be pointless.'

Lucifer nodded and vanished.

Mab appeared on the roof of the arena at the School of Psych and Sorcery. Pelian was standing in front of a small group of students. Master Lamm was making his way into the arena, walking towards the group. Gorgat and Mendan, of the Lords of Chaos, stood facing Pelian. Mab reached out searching for Seleran and Castaran; she found them on Raqus Mons.

Mab entered Pelian's mind and said, 'I am here, how are you feeling?'

Pelian smiled and replied, 'I am feeling good.'

Gorgat said, 'I trust that smile means you will be coming with us. If not, then I am afraid your students and masters will pay a heavy price.'

Mendan turned to Gorgat and said, 'She is here! I feel her presence.'

Gorgat looked around wildly, trying to locate Mab.

Mab replied to Pelian 'Yes, I feel it. You are much stronger. Show me!'

Pelian took two steps forward and leapt into the air. Onimaru appeared in her hand as she spun around with the sword at full stretch. The top of Mendan's head was completely severed, his body stood for several seconds before dropping to the ground, dark red blood pulsing onto the sand. Pelian stood in the ready position facing Gorgat, who, with blinding speed, drew two short swords and expertly cut the air in preparation for an attack.

Mab felt Pelian's confidence beginning to wane and said, 'Steady, use your powers to unbalance him. His blades are named, he thinks they will break your sword.'

Gorgat rushed Pelian with both of his blades, slicing through the air. Pelian waited in the ready position until he was almost upon her before lifting her left hand and releasing a focused blast of psychic power that struck Gorgat on the right thigh. Gorgat cried out in pain, dropped one of his swords, fell forward and rolled to a kneeling position, his left arm bringing his remaining short sword around in front of his chest in a wide horizontal arc. Pelian cartwheeled through the air, over the arc of Gorgat's sword, and swept Onimaru downwards, shattering the short sword into fragments. She landed perfectly and waited in the ready position.

Gorgat slowly pushed himself upwards and, glaring at Pelian, said, 'You...'

But he did not finish the sentence. Pelian moved so fast that the strike could not be seen. But time slowed for Mab. She saw Pelian stepping forward as she brought Onimaru down, slicing into Gorgat's head just above his right ear and exiting below his left armpit. His head and shoulder slid slowly from his torso before the two body parts separated and landed softly on the ground. Mab appeared beside Pelian, the students knelt, Lamm bowed, and Pelian smiled.

Mab looked down at the corpses, asked the students to stand and said, 'These are Mendan and Gorgat, traitors who colluded with the Abyss against the light. They were evil, do not pity them, think only of the many innocents they killed. Master Pelian, however, has just given us a lesson in swordsmanship that we will never forget!'

Mab looked at Pelian and started to applaud.

Lamm and the students joined in enthusiastically.

Pelian put her arms around Mab and hugged her tightly. The students applauded even more.

Erebus and Lucifer appeared beside Infelice in her cabin. Infelice bowed and said, 'It is an honour to meet you, Lord Erebus.'

Erebus replied, 'I thank you, but what reputation I have remaining will not aid us in the deep Abyss. I have seldom visited that place and suspect the creatures who dwell there are more likely to consider us as their next meal rather than as emissaries!'

Lucifer replied, 'The goddess thinks the god daemons Noticas and Antobus were released by the rulers in the deep Abyss. If there is another explanation for their presence in this solar system, we need to uncover it.'

Infelice said, 'Mirablis and I came of our own accord, but to integrate with those who live here in peace. Noticas and Antobus, however, came to conquer and enslave the indigenous populations. I suspect those of the deep Abyss are indeed behind this, but to what end I do not know.'

Lucifer added 'The god daemon that killed Gilian, Pelian's sister, was sent to kill the goddess. We do not know for sure if it was those of Abyss that sent her, but who else would do such a thing?'

Infelice said, 'I will lead you to the place where I first met one of the deep. We will wait in that location. If nothing happens, we will contact the goddess and ask for further instructions.'

The group flew upwards and out beyond the solar system into deep space. They entered the Abyss at a location favoured by Erebus and followed the seemingly chaotic currents, travelling ever deeper into the Abyss.

Infelice pulled free from a deep current and said, 'Stay together, we are directly above the target location. We drop straight down until I give the signal to stop.'

They fell still deeper into the Abyss until they reached an area of calm where Infelice signaled to stop.

Infelice said, 'Mind communication only.'

Lucifer said, 'I am used to the dark, but this is extraordinary.'

Erebus replied, 'Yes, I too have never been this deep. It is disconcerting to say the least.'

They waited in the deep for what seemed like an eternity until Erebus said, 'I think we should return and contact the goddess?'

Infelice was about to respond, but Lucifer said, 'They are here, all around us.'

A voice said, 'Infelice, you have returned and brought some gifts?'

Infelice replied, 'I have not returned. My colleagues and I are here on behalf of the Goddess Bellona. Erebus is of the Abyss, and Lucifer is an Archangel of the light. The Goddess wishes to meet with the rulers of the deep Abyss to discuss serious matters that have arisen due to incursions of god daemons into the multiverse.'

The voice said, 'What multiverse! We are of the Abyss, which is infinite. We care nothing for your petty universes and accursed light.'

Lucifer replied, 'And yet god daemons from this place have enslaved thousands and killed many others in our universe.'

The voice said, 'You try my patience, angel. You have had my response. Now you two will leave, Infelice will remain.'

Lucifer said, 'We are emissaries of the goddess; I can tell you that she will be most displeased by your refusal to meet. Indeed, she may consider that you are culpable for the enslavement and deaths of those under her protection. We three will leave now, together, and advise the goddess of your response.'

The voice laughed and replied, 'You think I fear your goddess. You will all remain here.'

Lucifer pulled a flaming sword from nowhere; it lit the surrounding area. They were circled by around twenty beings all dressed in black robes, with carious fangs and yellow slit eyes.

Suddenly, the circle of beings parted, and a huge creature, again dressed in black, approached. The beings all bowed their heads.

The creature said, 'I am known as Asteria, I and my three brothers are rulers of these demesnes. I heard your message; my brothers and I will meet with the Goddess Bellona. She may remember me from the time of the light war, when our paths crossed briefly. You may leave now, please pass our respects to the goddess and assure her that we wish to resolve any problems that we may have caused.'

Infelice replied, 'Asteria, thank you. I will pass your kind words to the goddess.'

Infelice led Lucifer and Erebus upwards, in silence, until they reached the powerful currents of the upper Abyss, where Erebus departed. Infelice and Lucifer followed the currents upwards and exited the Abyss close to Aardian.

Infelice said, 'We should report back to the goddess.'

Lucifer replied, 'I thought she was observing through you?'

Infelice said, 'No, she was not present.'

Lucifer said, 'I suggest you go to her. She will summon me if needed.'

Infelice replied, 'Lucifer, thank you. If you hadn't drawn your sword, the outcome may have been very different.'

Lucifer nodded and vanished.

Infelice reached out to Mab and said, 'Goddess, we have returned from the Abyss and bring news.'

Infelice suddenly vanished and appeared beside Mab. She was walking with two others.

Mab said, 'This is Infelice. Infelice, this is my partner Pelian, who has just given us a lesson in swordsmanship, and this is Master Lamm, who is the principal of this magic school.'

Infelice looked around her in astonishment, tears began to build in her eyes, she said, 'It is beautiful, everything is so bright and vibrant! The flowers, the buildings. It is overwhelming!'

Then she looked up at the sun, and tears flowed freely. Pelian went to her and hugged her tightly.

Mab said, 'Yes, it is beautiful. I'm afraid many of us who live here take it for granted!'

Infelice replied, 'Will I be staying here in this beautiful place?'

Master Lamm replied, 'You can stay here if you wish, but I think Mab has other plans for you. Why don't we have dinner together?'

Mab replied, 'Master Lamm, that would be lovely. Following that, I will take Infelice to the GOS to meet Master Kanaka.'

Pelian said, 'Infelice, you can come with Mab and me to freshen up before dinner.'

Mab and Pelian took Infelice to their new accommodation.

Mab said, 'Let's shower together, it will be quicker, and I am starving.'

Pelian laughed, looked at Infelice, and said, 'She is always starving!'

Infelice replied, 'Yes, I have noticed!'

Pelian said, 'Clothes off!'

Infelice replied, 'I must take my clothes off for this shower?'

Mab and Pelian laughed and said, 'Yes, you do!'

Mab gestured, and Infelice's clothes disappeared. She screamed, Mab and Pelian laughed and pulled her into the shower cabin.

The three stood huddled together. Pelian said, 'Are you ready?'

Infelice replied, 'Ready for what?'

Pelian pulled a wooden lever, and a torrent of ice-cold water was released into the cabin from above. Infelice screamed again, but her scream was drowned out by the torrent of water and the laughter of Mab and Pelian.

Mab threw a lump of soap towards Infelice and said, 'Use this, it's made with flower extracts.'

Mab and Pelian exited the shower and dried themselves with thick wool towels, but Infelice could not bring herself to leave. Mab had to pull her out.

Infelice said, 'I could stay in there forever.'

Pelian said, 'Don't worry about clothes, Mab has an extensive selection!'

Mab said, 'I think we should dress appropriately to celebrate the arrival of Infelice. How about black evening dresses?'

Mab gestured, and all three wore below-the-knee evening dresses and highly polished black shoes.

Pelian said, 'Hair?'

Mab gestured; they all had their usual styles, dried and positioned to perfection.

Mab said, 'Can we go now? My tummy is making strange noises!'

They vanished and appeared in the school's grand hall.

Master Lamm was already there together with Masters Uvren, Etten and Sonder. Lamm introduced them to Infelice. Students approached nervously with trays of drinks.

Mab recognised Moia and said, 'Moia, thank you. It's very nice to see you again!'

Moia was thrilled that Mab remembered her and received looks of admiration from the other students.

Master Lamm said, 'The dinner is about to be served. Please take a seat.'

The kitchen staff started to bring platters of cold meats of every description, breads, cheeses, fresh and dried fruits, smoked fish, herbs and spices, fresh milk and creams. The students acted as waiters and constantly topped up wine goblets.

Infelice said, 'This is wonderful, I have never seen so much tasty food in one place!'

Master Lamm said, 'Yes, we are very fortunate. Sometimes we need to be reminded of that!'

Master Sonder said, 'Infelice, I hope you don't mind me asking, if I understand things correctly, you were of the Abyss but now live in the light. What is it like to live in the Abyss?'

Infelice paused before saying, 'It was my home. I think in all worlds and societies, people love their home no matter the situation. Life in the Abyss is hard; food is sparse, and there are many predators and many dangers. We do not have families in the same sense as you. We are spawned and have no connection with our parents, but we do with our siblings. We have no specific gender, but when in human form, we choose our appearance. Life for me in the Abyss was better than for most. I was gifted, a god daemon, but

I decided to leave of my own accord. I made my home on Aariet with Mirablis, one of my followers. It is possible for us to survive where the light is dim, if we change into human form, but we must frequently regenerate in the Abyss, otherwise we perish.'

Uvren said, 'And do you need to return to the Abyss periodically?'

Infelice said, 'No, I have taken permanent human form, but I also bathed in the sacred waters in the palace of Bellona and Minerva. I have no wish to return to the Abyss, although I did so only a short time ago at the request of the goddess.' Mab said, 'And was your mission successful?'

Infelice said, 'I bring you a message. Do you wish to hear it now?'

Mab nodded.

Infelice said, 'Initially, we were met with a somewhat hostile welcome. The being that made its mark on me greeted us. It was vile; it rejected any possibility of a meeting with you. It ordered Erebus and Lucifer to depart, and me to remain. Lucifer drew a flaming sword, illuminating the dark. We were encircled by many strange daemons, but then another appeared. It was huge, and the others bowed as it entered the circle. Its name was...'

Mab interjected and said, 'Infelice, do not repeat its name here. Tell me what it said, and what was agreed.'

Infelice bowed and said, 'It said, it, and its three brothers were the rulers there and would meet with you. It thought that you may remember it from the light war where your paths had crossed briefly. It asked that we pass its respects to you and to assure you that they will resolve any problems that they may have caused.'

Mab paused in thought and said, 'The creature that marked you, what did it say in the presence of the ruler?'

Infelice replied, 'It said nothing.'

Mab said, 'And Erebus?'

Infelice replied, 'Lord Erebus said nothing in the meeting. However, in our preliminary discussions, he was reluctant to participate. Also, when we reached the target location, he wanted us to leave and report back to you. If not for Lucifer's intervention, we probably would have left prematurely.'

Mab said, 'If not for Lucifer, you may not have left at all. Anyway, your mission was a great success. Things are becoming clearer, and our forthcoming meeting with the rulers should be illuminating!'

The guests ate their fill; Mab thanked Lamm for the dinner, turned to Infelice and said, 'I will take you to your new home!'

Infelice thanked Lamm and hugged Pelian. Mab vanished, taking Infelice with her. They appeared in the office of Kanaka, who was in discussions with Boe.

Mab said, 'Excuse me, Master Kanaka, Master Boe, I have brought Infelice.'

Kanaka stood, embraced Infelice and said, 'I have heard much about you! It is good to meet you at last.'

Infelice replied, 'It is good to meet you too! This will be a new life for me, I am very grateful to you for offering me a position here.'

Boe said, 'Master Kanaka, would you like me to take Infelice to her accommodation?'

Kanaka replied, 'Yes, but could you return her here later? We have much to discuss.'

Boe nodded and left with Infelice. Kanaka turned to Mab and said, 'Is she a powerful daemon?'

Mab replied, 'She was a god daemon; she is extraordinary powerful. However, she has taken permanent human form and bathed in the sacred waters of the palace. So, I don't think we should refer to her as a daemon.'

Kanaka replied, 'Yes, she is certainly nothing like any daemon I have ever met!'

Mab said, 'She is beautiful, is she not?'

Kanaka stared at Mab, laughed, and said, 'Yes, she is.'

Mab paused, smiled, and said, 'Infelice and I must return to the Abyss to meet the rulers. I would like you to come with us, to represent humans.'

Kanaka replied, 'I was under the impression that humans could not survive in that place?'

Mab said, 'You will be safe in my aura. But you must stay close to me.'

Kanaka poured two large measures of single malt whisky, handed one to Mab and said, 'We have been battling daemons for a long time, but we never get to the root of the problem. I thought that when Mahaziel and his brothers were killed, we were free of them. But it seems that was only the beginning!'

Mab replied, 'Master Kanaka, we have been manipulated and used by masters of those arts. But we are getting closer to the truth.'

Kanaka said, 'Then this is a dangerous time.'

Mab grimaced and replied, 'Yes, precisely.'

There was a knock at the door, Boe popped his head round and said, 'I have brought Infelice back, I will leave you now. Meldran is rather unwell, so I don't want to leave him alone for too long.'

Mab said, 'Master Boe, please come in. I will bring Meldran here.'

Boe and Infelice entered the room, but Boe was clearly concerned and wanted to go back to Meldran. Mab reached out and found Meldran in Boe's room. She entered his mind and calmed him. She then pulled him to her. Meldran appeared on the floor beside Boe. His breathing was erratic, and every so often, he would moan softly.

Boe said, 'He has been like this for several weeks, he doesn't eat the way he used to, he is losing weight.'

Mab knelt beside Meldran and placed her hand on his side. She then ran her hands over his whole body, stopped close to his stomach and said, 'He has something in his stomach.'

Mab gestured with her right hand, and a fist-sized black mass appeared on the floor. Boe bent to pick it up, but

Infelice said, 'Stop! Do not touch it.'

Boe quickly pulled his hand back. The black mass started to move snail-like across the floor.

Boe said, 'What is that thing?'

Mab looked at Infelice, who said, 'It is the eyes and ears of the owner who is mind-linked to it. The owner can hear and see what the host sees and hears. It is usually placed in the victim's food. It grows inside the host, eventually killing it.'

Boe said, 'Why put it in Meldran's food!?'

Kanaka said, 'Boe, you often give Meldran scraps of your food; it was meant for you.'

Mab lifted her hand and incinerated the creature with a beam of light. Meldran leapt up and licked Mab's face.

Mab said, 'Meldran is feeling better already.'

Infelice said, 'Who would do such a thing?'

Mab replied, 'I think I know where it came from.'

Infelice looked at Mab and said, 'You know who is responsible?'

Mab nodded.

Kanaka said, 'Master Boe, I suggest you take Meldran back to your room. I think he needs some pampering!'

Boe replied, 'Yes, he does! Thank you, Mab.'

Boe left with Meldran, who was wagging his tail.

Kanaka looked at Mab and said, 'What do you think is going on?'

Mab replied, 'Master Kanaka, we will go back to the Abyss. That is where we will find the answers, but my senses tell me that the answers will not be to my liking.'

Infelice said, 'When do we return?'

Mab replied, 'We have breakfast here first thing tomorrow morning, and leave immediately following that.'

Kanaka said, 'In that case, I suggest we all get some sleep.' Mab nodded and vanished.

Kanaka poured a whisky and handed it to Infelice. Infelice sipped the whisky, smiled, and said, 'This is strong but nice!'

Kanaka laughed and said, 'It came from another time and place.'

Infelice replied, 'Time and place, words that have no meaning in the Abyss.'

Kanaka said, 'You will be appointed a master of this Guild. This will be your home for as long as you wish. All we ask in return is that you help our students to develop their full potential, not only regarding magical powers and warfare but also integrity and honesty. Of course, you will be working closely with Mab, protecting the innocent here and in many other places.'

Infelice nodded and said, 'It is a great honour, Master Kanaka, I am looking forward to my new life here.'

Kanaka smiled and said, 'We need gifted people. Mab told me that you possessed exceptional powers.'

Infelice replied, 'I have powers, but they are not sufficient to challenge the rulers of the deep Abyss.'

Kanaka said, 'Do you believe that these creatures would seek to harm us, perhaps take advantage of the meeting to do so?'

Infelice replied, 'You mean could it be a trap to lure the goddess into the Abyss and kill her?'

Kanaka nodded. Infelice said, 'I think it is unlikely. The ruler we met seemed genuine, and said it had met the goddess, albeit briefly, at the time of the light war. It seemed to possess human qualities of concern and integrity, which is very strange.'

Kanaka replied, 'It must have been difficult for you, going back there?'

Infelice said, 'Yes, it was very difficult. However, Lucifer and Erebus were with me, and I was there as an emissary of the Goddess. So, I felt no fear.'

Kanaka replied, 'Not even a little fear!?'

Infelice laughed and said, 'Perhaps a little!'

Kanaka said, 'I'll walk with you to your rooms. This is a very large campus; it is easy for newcomers to get lost!'

Infelice replied, 'I don't have that problem. I can vanish and reappear in any location I have visited previously. But I would like to walk with you.'

Kanaka nodded, and they made their way out of the main building. The sun was setting, and there was a slight chill in the air. Kanaka said, 'I asked Boe to put you in Emerald, that accommodation block has very spacious married quarters appropriate for a master.'

Infelice replied, 'Yes, my rooms are so spacious! I can't wait to have another shower!'

Kanaka said, 'Another shower?'

Infelice replied, 'Yes, I had my first shower earlier today with Pelian and the Goddess!'

Kanaka laughed and said, 'So, you showered together?'

Infelice replied, 'Why yes, it was wonderful. I will shower again tonight, perhaps you would like to join me.'

Kanaka laughed and said, 'Well, I would love to, but perhaps we should get to know each other a bit better?'

Infelice replied, 'We must know each other better before we shower together?'

Kanaka said, 'It is a custom that men and women do not have intimate relations until they know each other well.'

Infelice replied, 'I understand.'

Kanaka hugged Infelice, kissed her gently on the cheek and said, 'I am looking forward to getting to know you.'

Infelice smiled and said, 'So, how about that shower?' Kanaka replied, 'I thought you would never ask.'

They both laughed and disappeared into Emerald.'

The following morning Mab appeared in Kanaka's office, the breakfast was laid out, but neither he nor Infelice was there. She reached out and found him with Infelice.

She mind-messaged them both, '*Can I assume you are on your way here? Breakfast is waiting!*'

Kanaka replied, 'We will be there in a few moments.'

Mab poured herself a mug of coffee and started filling her plate with cheese, cold meat, dried fruits and rustic bread. The door opened, and Kanaka and Infelice tumbled in, looking somewhat disheveled.

Mab stared at Kanaka, smiled and said, 'Did you have a nice evening?'

Kanaka, looking somewhat sheepish, replied, 'Yes, we had a lovely evening.'

Infelice said, 'We showered together and then played with each other in bed! It was wonderful!'

Kanaka turned bright red. Mab burst out laughing and said, 'Infelice, what you do in bed should not be shared with others!'

Infelice replied, 'Sorry, I didn't know that.'

Mab hugged Infelice and whispered, 'I'm so pleased that you and Master Kanaka are together.'

Infelice replied, 'Goddess, thank you again for my new life.'

Mab smiled, Infelice gasped. When they finished breakfast, Mab called upon Lucifer, who appeared immediately, together with Morgana.

Lucifer said, 'Morgana brings you a message.'

Mab looked at Morgana, who said, 'The message is from Sladrin. He told me that the meeting with the rulers is a charade. They intend to kill you, but if that cannot be accomplished, they will imprison you deep in the Abyss for all time.'

Mab replied, 'Morgana, please thank Sladrin for this valuable information. You may go.'

Morgana glanced at Lucifer and vanished.

Mab turned to the others and said, 'Are you ready?'

The group appeared in the Abyss in the exact location of the previous meeting. They waited, shielded within a sphere of power. Mab pulled Kanaka closer to her, and the sphere of power vanished. They waited in complete darkness. Mab gestured with her right hand, and a groaning sound was heard. Mab lit the area, and a group of six creatures, robed in black, faced them. The leader was desperately clutching at its throat.

Mab released it and said, 'Kneel and be silent!'

All six of the creatures dropped to their knees.'

Lucifer said, 'A ruler approaches.'

The creature was huge but glided silently through the darkness towards the group. Mab dimmed her light.

The creature said, 'Goddess Bellona, it is a great honour to welcome you here to our demesnes. We have prepared food and drink for you and your party, please follow me.'

Mab led the group, following closely behind the huge figure of the ruler. They entered an enormous gash in what appeared to be a perfectly flat rock face that spread out in all directions. They arrived at a huge cavern. In the centre of the cavern, a table of polished granite had been sculpted from the rock; similarly, the chairs were part of the original rock that had been carved away to create the required forms. Five of the chairs were larger than the others and were clustered around the head of the table.

The creature sat there and said, 'Please be seated, my brothers will arrive soon.'

Mab sat at the opposite end of the table with the rest of the group.

Three huge figures appeared, and Mab stood up; the others followed her example.

The creature at the head of the table said, 'Please, be seated. I am known as Asteria, my three brothers are known as Panthaca, Soronica and Certinaca. We are the rulers of these demesnes.'

Mab said, 'I am Bellona, this is Archangel Lucifer and masters Infelice and Kanaka.'

We have come here to bring an end to the incursions of daemon kind into the light. These have resulted in many innocent deaths and countless thousands of humans being enslaved as daemon hosts.'

Asteria replied, 'We are not aware of these incursions.'

Mab simply stared at her.

Asteria replied, 'I remember you, goddess. I would not lie to you; I think you know this!'

Mab replied, 'I know you would not lie to me. However, I do not know your brothers or your subordinates.'

Soronica stood up and said, 'You dare make such accusations. We should slay you now!'

Mab smiled at Soronica and said, 'That would be a most unwise course of action.'

Asteria glared at Soronica and said, 'Be silent! You have not seen what I have seen!'

Soronica looked at Asteria and then at Mab and said, 'Apologies, I retract my words.'

Mab said, 'There is a conspiracy, your subordinates are involved. Those whom we met with earlier, bring them here.'

Panthaca nodded and said, 'They are being brought here now.'

Asteria said, 'What is the nature of this conspiracy?'

Mab replied, 'They seek to build new empires in the light where they can be rulers. My sister stood in their way, so they threatened her child and used that as leverage to bend her to their will. They were unaware of my existence; otherwise, they would have killed me when I was a child. When they found me, it was too late, my powers were released, and now I am fully restored.'

Asteria nodded and said, 'Had I known of this, perhaps I could have helped to protect you.'

Mab replied, 'I had no knowledge of who I was. I was adopted by a human couple who raised me as their daughter. This was done to protect me, the Archangel Uriel watched over me in my childhood, my memories were restored when I came of age.'

The six guards were brought before the rulers.

Mab pointed to the leader and said, 'You are in league with others to enslave the free people of the light. You will tell me who you are working with.'

The leader snarled, 'I am in league with no one!'

Asteria said, 'I hear the falsehood in your words. Speak the truth now, otherwise I will take your memories and end your life.'

The leader said nothing but one of his followers stepped forward, looked at Asteria and said, 'Great one, I will speak the truth. We were approached by those above. They told us of the deaths of Noticas, Antobus and Insheigra, three great gods of the Abyss who were slain by this goddess of the light. They also told us that Infelice, who stands before you now, was imprisoned and beguiled by the goddess.'

Mab replied, 'I killed Noticas and Antobus because they occupied worlds under my protection. They held many innocents captive, and many others were enslaved by daemonic possession. I killed Insheigra because it killed my partner's sister, Gilian, and sought to kill me.'

Infelice said, 'I lived in peace in a small village with my then partner Mirablis. The goddess discovered our presence but allowed us to remain and live in harmony with the villagers. Antobus came and took Mirablis; he was imprisoned. I went to Antobus and pleaded for his release, but I was imprisoned and Mirablis was tortured to his death. I had thought to end my life, but the goddess found me, set me free and gave me a new life.'

Mab turned to Asteria and said, 'I am wearying of this. I need to know who is involved in this conspiracy.'

Asteria turned to the leader of the six guards, a black tentacle speared outwards and embedded in its head. The creature screamed in agony as its mind was consumed.

Asteria said, 'Goddess, there are a few names, unknown to me, that were in direct contact with this guard. Baydan was the most frequent contact, followed by Sladrin and then Erebus. Do you know this Baydan?'

Mab smiled and said, 'It is as I thought. Thank you for your help, Asteria. I would now like to speak to you and your brothers in private.' Mab turned to Lucifer, Infelice and Kanaka and said, 'Return to the Guild. Lucifer, I will call you if needed.'

Mab followed the rulers into another much smaller living chamber.

Asteria said, 'The remaining guards will be punished, or would you wish something harsher?'

Mab replied, 'No, the leader was responsible and paid the price.'

Certinaca said, 'Goddess, I sense that you have something important that you wish to discuss?'

Mab replied, 'Yes, I do. Perhaps you should all sit down first.'

Panthaca poured generous measures of a liquor into five golden goblets and said, 'Drink first!'

Mab sipped on liquor, smiled and said, 'That is nice! What is it?'

Panthaca replied, 'You will be familiar with whisky, it is made from that, but we don't know its name.'

Mab said, 'A daemon drink!'

Panthaca made a strange noise that sounded a bit like a belly laugh, the others joined in.

Mab said, 'If you don't mind me asking, I notice that your rooms are designed for five, but there is always an unoccupied seat?'

Certinaca replied, 'Our sister was lost to us in the light war. Some say she was slain by you. Others say that, like you, she preferred obscurity to slaughter.'

Asteria said, 'We have searched the Abyss, sent emissaries across the multiverse, but there is no trace of her. We no longer search, but we continue to hope. Hope, a strange thing for a daemon, is it not?'

Mab replied, 'There is always hope,' as she pulled Onimaru from the ether. The sword hummed as it appeared, red and blue flames burst from the blade. The rulers leapt to their feet and stared in astonishment.

Mab said, 'This is Onimaru, slayer of daemons. Juno, my true mother, could not bring herself to slay your sister, so she bound her in this sword, condemning her to an eternity of killing her own kind. The justice of the gods, truly fitting is it not?'

Asteria said, 'Where did you find this?'

Mab replied, 'I was seeking a blade for Master Kanaka, my mentor and teacher. I found Onimaru in the tomb of an ancient emperor, but at the time, I didn't realise what it was. It is only recently that I detected the true nature of the presence within the blade and recognised the binding made by Juno.'

Certinaca said, 'We will break the binding and free our sister!'

Mab threw the sword to Asteria, who held it close and concentrated hard before saying, 'It is too strong, it cannot be done, it cannot be broken!'

Mab replied, 'I can't promise success, but I am willing to make the attempt. I promised the presence in the blade that I would return it to the Abyss, and that I would set it free if possible. What is its daemon name?'

There was silence. Mab said, 'I must have the daemon name to break the binding, otherwise there is no point in trying.'

Asteria said, 'Goddess, her true name is Tabatha.' The sword flared red and blue in response.

Mab said, 'Give it to me.'

Asteria passed Onimaru back to Mab, who placed the sword tip on the stone floor with the hilt resting on her tummy. She grasped Onimaru with both hands and focused her mind on the binding. She searched for a way in, a way to sever the invisible band of power wrapped around the sword that caged the daemon within. She dragged ancient chants from the depths of her memory and sang them to the sword, she swore in the name of Juno and the old gods, she cast sophisticated anti-binding spells, she poured power into the sword and tried to weaken the binding, but nothing was sufficient. Mab and the rulers sat in silence, despair and frustration etched on their faces.

Mab looked up and said, 'Sister, come to me.' An intense spot of light appeared and hovered over the table. The spot elongated to a vertical cut, and Minerva stepped through. Mab said, 'My sword, I wish to break Juno's binding and release the daemon trapped within. I have tried everything I can think of, but nothing has any effect.'

Minerva looked slowly around the room but then rested her eyes on the sword and said, 'Have you tried brute force? Our mother was known for her simple and direct approach to problems, much as you are. I suspect the binding was created such that no one, perhaps other than Jupiter, could overcome it.'

Mab said, 'So, what do you suggest?'

Minerva shrugged her shoulders and said, 'If all else has failed, break the sword?' Minerva promptly vanished.

Mab lifted Onimaru and rammed it point-first into the stone wall of the chamber, flat side upwards. She held the hilt gently with her right hand, lifted her left arm and struck the blade with an enormous blow. The entire rock structure shook violently under the impact. Mab grimaced and lifted her left arm again. This time, her arm was covered in shimmering silver light. Mab held her arm upwards for a few seconds and then brought it down, striking the blade a truly stupendous blow. The wall of the chamber split and partially collapsed, as the sword exploded and sprayed the room with fragments. Mab was blown backwards but managed to stay on her feet. The four rulers were knocked off their feet onto the floor and were trying to rise amid the dust and debris. As the dust settled, a black figure hovered in space before Mab. It was a beautiful woman, her skin the colour of polished obsidian.

The woman floated towards Mab and stared into her eyes before saying 'Am I free?'

Mab said, 'Yes, Tabatha, you are free. Your siblings are here to greet you.'

Five dark shadows flew upwards and embraced.

Asteria said, 'Goddess, we thank you for returning our sister to us, we are forever in your debt!'

Mab replied, 'I made a promise to Tabatha, I have now fulfilled my promise.'

Mab was about to leave when Tabatha appeared immediately in front of her, embraced her tightly and said, 'Goddess, call upon me whenever you are in need, I will be by your side again.'

Mab smiled warmly, kissed her, and vanished.

Mab appeared in Kanaka's office. The kitchen staff were delivering lunch.

Infelice pointed and said, 'I told you she would appear in time for food!'

Kanaka laughed and replied, 'Yes, you were right!'

Mab smiled and said, 'Master Kanaka, do you mind if Pelian joins us?'

Kanaka replied, 'No, of course not.'

Mab mind messaged Pelian, who appeared a few minutes later. They ate in silence, Mab being in a morose mood.

Kanaka said, 'Did your discussions with Asteria yield any fruit?'

Mab replied, 'Yes, in summary, it appears that Sladrin, Baydan and Erebus, aided by several guards of the deep Abyss, were attempting to follow the example set by Noticas and Antobus. But I suspect others, who remain in the shadows, may be involved.'

Kanaka said, 'Erebus? But what of....' His question trailed off, unsaid.

Mab replied, 'My sister?'

Kanaka said, 'Mab, I meant no offence, but perhaps you should discuss these matters with her?'

Mab replied, 'Master Kanaka, no offence taken. I will raise the subject of Erebus with her when the time is right.'

Infelice said, 'Erebus knows that you met with the rulers, that alone will give him cause for concern.'

Pelian said, 'But what would Erebus do, what can he do?'

Mab replied, 'Those are important questions, but the answers depend on those who sit behind him. Who are they? What is their capability?'

Kanaka nodded slowly and said, 'Where is Onimaru?'

Mab smiled and said, 'I released her into the Abyss. She is now reunited with her sisters.' Kanaka smiled grimly.

Chapter Thirty-Six: The Wrath of Bellona

Soronica lay back on his chair of rock, looked at Certinaca and said, 'We must kill her here, she will be much stronger in the light.'

Certinaca replied, 'I could not scan her, she is closed, but I could sense the power, the way she broke the binding to free Tabatha! I have never witnessed such a thing. I do not think we have the power to defeat her, even here in our demesnes.'

Soronica replied, 'We need to assassinate her. Clearly, we would be foolish to confront her in battle, although I do not rule that out. Yes, she is strong, but she could not defeat the two of us in combat.'

Certinaca said, 'Asteria knows more about her, and she was very careful not to upset her. Have you discussed this with Erebus?'

Soronica replied, 'Yes, I told him about our meeting with her. He is very worried; he thinks she knows that we are involved in the conspiracy. But what really worries him is that she knows for sure he is involved.'

Certinaca smiled but said, 'The demise of Noticas and Antobus is very concerning. If this goddess is not killed, then we may as well forget our plans. You need to push Erebus and his minions to make progress. If they can't, or won't, do the job themselves, then they must employ a professional assassin?!'

Soronica replied, 'I will talk to him.'

Mab and Pelian appeared on the summit of Raqus Mons.

Pelian said, 'They have gone.'

Mab said, 'No, they are in the cave system.'

Pelian said, 'Follow me, I know this place.' Pelian led Mab downwards to the narrow mouth of a cave and said, 'This is the entrance, it is where they took me to Baydan.'

Mab said, 'Baydan will soon be dead, as will Sladrin and Erebus. Humbra has confirmed that Dakigo was not involved in the conspiracy.'

Pelian nodded her head and walked into the cave system. They walked in silence until they heard voices.

Mab mind linked with Pelian and said, 'They will detect our presence soon, we will move into mind space and observe.'

Pelian found herself hanging in the air beside Mab but shifted to a place between the plains of existence. They were hovering above and behind Seleran and Castaran, who were talking to a black apparition that continually changed shape.

Mab said, 'It is Soronica, one of the rulers.'

The shape looked upwards directly at Mab and vanished. Mab and Pelian shifted back and dropped to the floor of the cave. The two lords spun around, but Mab closed her fist, and they dropped to their knees, clutching their throats.

Pelian said, 'Gorgat and Menden are dead. Tell us all you know, and we will allow you to live.'

Mab released her grip.

Seleran said, 'We will leave now. You do not know who you are dealing with!'

Mab walked towards Seleran, who had managed to stand, grabbed her by the throat and threw her hard against the wall of the cave. Seleran pulled her sword with lightning speed and sliced downwards. Mab clapped her hands together, above her head, catching the blade, which snapped and fragmented. She dropped the part-blade to the floor, pulled Seleran towards her and struck her a stupendous backhanded blow with her left hand. Seleran's head flew across the cave and was squashed to a pulp of white, red and grey on the adjacent wall.

Mab turned and looked balefully at Castaran, who said, 'I will tell you what I know!'

Pelian said, 'Who were you speaking to?'

Castaran said, 'It is of the deep Abyss, I do not know its name.'

Pelian replied, 'Then tell us what you do know.'

Castaran suddenly clutched his head and screamed in pain. Blood flowed from his nose and ears as he collapsed to the rock floor.

Mab bent over Castaran, placed her hand on his head and said, 'He has one of those creatures attached to his brain.'

Pelian said, 'Baydan!'

Mab nodded and said, 'We should go.'

Mab and Pelian appeared in the palace of the old gods. They made their way to the sacred waters, and their clothes disappeared as they approached.

They lay soaking in silence before Mab said, 'Sister, come to me.'

Minerva appeared in the cloistered area. She walked slowly towards the water and said, 'What brings you here, sister?'

Mab smiled and said, 'You know the answer to that question.'

Minerva replied, 'I would speak with you alone.'

Mab said, 'Is he here?'

Minerva said, 'No, do you wish me to call him?'

Mab replied, 'Yes, bring him here.'

Minerva turned and walked away.

Mab looked at Pelian and said, 'This is a very dangerous situation, let me do the talking.'

They left the waters and were dressed in white silk robes and soft brown sandals. Mab's hair was plaited on both sides while Pelian's hung loose down her back.

Mab and Pelian were having lunch when Minerva approached together with Erebus.

Minerva said, 'Would you mind if we joined you?'

Mab nodded but continued to eat in silence.

Eventually, Minerva said, 'You asked me to bring Erebus; he is waiting.'

Mab replied, 'You, and it, will wait until I am ready to speak to you.'

Erebus made to stand, but Minerva signed for him to stay seated. Pelian sat perfectly still, sipping a goblet of wine, trying not to look at anyone, especially Erebus.

When Mab finished her lunch, she turned to Erebus and said, 'You are in collusion, against the light, with one or more rulers of the deep Abyss, you were also involved with Noticas and Antobus. Do not deny it, I know it to be true.'

Erebus glanced at Minerva, whose face remained expressionless.

Mab looked at Minerva and said, 'Sister, it appears that your boy child does not exist. A very clever ruse, but my senses are now too well developed to be fooled by that.'

Minerva replied, 'I have been alone here for millennia, Erebus and I sought to bring about a conjoining of the light and the dark. The first step was to allow those of the Abyss an opportunity to live in the light. Noticas and Antobus were to be the first of many. Infelice and Mirablis were outsiders; they had no knowledge of our plans.'

Mab stared aghast at Minerva and said, 'So you aided the Abyss in the enslavement and killing of thousands of innocents?!'

Erebus replied, 'What of all the innocents slain in the light war?'

Mab ignored Erebus and, still looking at Minerva, said, 'You lied to me.'

The sky suddenly grew dark, and the palace and the mountain itself began to tremble.

Mab stood and added, 'You are enemies of the light; leave this palace now and never return.'

Minerva replied, 'We will leave, but this matter is not ended.'

Mab said, 'No, but you can be sure that it will be ended.'

Minerva and Erebus vanished.

Pelian placed her arm around Mab and asked, 'What does this mean?'

Mab replied, 'All is clear now. Minerva and Erebus are the hidden enemy, together with Soronica and perhaps other rulers of the Abyss.'

Pelian said, 'But Minerva and Erebus assisted us in many of our endeavours. How can they be the enemy?'

Mab replied, 'They appeared to assist us. Minerva is very clever; even as a child, she had the ability to use and manipulate others. She is a planner, a plotter who delights in conspiracy and strategy.'

Mab kissed Pelian and added, 'Whatever happens, if you need a place of safety, then come here. Minerva is now locked out of the palace.'

Pelian replied, 'We will be here together; this will be our home.'

Mab smiled, hugged Pelian, and they both vanished.

Soronica said, 'I saw her, and she saw me. There is no doubt. She knows that I am in league with the lords, and I suspect she will also know that Baydan was mind-linked to Castaran.'

Certinaca replied, 'No, it is supposition. There is no proof of our involvement in a conspiracy. In any case, why should you not have discussions with the lords? They are sources of valuable information.'

Soronica replied, 'I don't think Asteria will see it that way. She appears to be in awe of the goddess.'

Certinaca said, 'We have Minerva, she will follow instructions from Erebus, and he will follow instructions from us. The only mistake we made was agreeing to allow passage for those fools, Noticas and Antobus. We should have gone ourselves!'

Soronica replied, 'You know Asteria would never have permitted that. The real problem is Bellona; we need an end to her. I will talk to Erebus, the three of us together with Minerva could easily kill her.'

Certinaca nodded and said, 'Yes, that may be the best option.'

It was late evening, and Mab sat in Kanaka's office, sipping whisky, waiting for him to arrive. The door opened, Kanaka and Infelice walked in; Mab poured two additional measures of whisky.

Kanaka stared at Mab and said, 'I assume it is serious?'

Mab replied, 'Yes, Master Kanaka, it is very serious.'

Infelice said, 'Would you like me to leave?'

Mab replied, 'No, you should hear this.'

Kanaka and Infelice sat down. Mab said, 'The enemy includes Erebus, Baydan, Sladrin, several guards of the deep Abyss, Soronica, a ruler of the deep Abyss, and also my sister Minerva.'

Kanaka looked at Mab askance and said, 'Your sister! Are you sure?'

Mab nodded and replied, 'Yes, I am certain. I confronted her and Erebus. They admitted everything. I banished them from the palace; they are now in the Abyss.'

Infelice said, 'If you are sure Soronica is involved, perhaps you should discuss it with Asteria?'

Mab replied, 'Yes, I will do that, but we need to prepare for a potential war.'

Mab stared intensely at Infelice for a few moments. Infelice held her stare, but tears started to form in her eyes. Mab smiled warmly. Infelice gasped. Kanaka looked at Infelice quizzically, then looked back at Mab and said, 'I will summon Boe. I think he should be involved in this discussion.'

Mab nodded. Kanaka paused before saying, 'Minerva and Erebus supported our efforts against Noticas and Antobus, why would they do that if they were enemies?'

Infelice replied, 'Erebus cannot be trusted, those of the deep Abyss even less so. How much did they really support you in the battle with Noticas and Antobus?'

Mab nodded and said, 'The truth is they did not really support us. I should have seen through this whole charade much earlier, but she is my sister, so I was blind to it.'

Boe arrived and, catching the end of the conversation, said, 'The goddess Minerva is known for her skills in plotting and planning.'

Kanaka explained the situation to Boe, who sat back in his chair and listened intently.

Infelice said, 'Is it possible for Minerva to remain in the Abyss?'

Mab replied, 'I am not sure, but I can remain there, and she is there now, so I can only assume that she is unaffected by the environment.'

Boe said, 'This Soronica, are you sure he is the only ruler involved in the conspiracy?'

Mab replied, 'No, I am not sure. But I do not think Asteria is involved, and I know for sure that Tabatha is not involved.'

Boe replied, 'Then we have at least two important allies that need to be contacted.'

Mab replied, 'Yes, Master Boe, I will do that following this meeting.'

Kanaka said, 'The question is, what will Erebus and Minerva do next?'

There was silence for a few moments before Boe said, 'It is clear, they will try to assassinate Mab. She is the only significant obstacle to their plans succeeding. Yes, there will be problems for them in explaining their actions, but with Mab gone, these would be manageable.'

Kanaka said, 'We must make preparations, increase security.'

Boe said, 'Minerva knows Mab intimately. She, and they, know that Mab will be very difficult to kill. They will lure her to a place where the killing will be optimal for them, perhaps a meeting in the Abyss? The assassins will be powerful and be there in numbers. Perhaps Minerva and Soronica will be among them. They may possess special weapons, poisons, or other devices. Mab, you must never go anywhere alone, you need others to be with you, to protect you.' Boe's eyes were filling up.

Mab replied, 'Yes, Master Boe, do not worry, I will do as you say.'

Infelice said, 'Goddess, I will watch over you and fight by your side!'

Mab smiled warmly at Infelice and said, 'Thank you, Infelice, we are almost family. Please call me Mab.'

Infelice bowed and replied, 'Thank you, Mab. You know that I would gladly give my life for you.'

Kanaka hugged Infelice and said, 'Mab, we all feel the same. We will protect you, die for you if that is what it takes.'

Mab's eyes filled with tears as she said, 'Thank you all for your love and loyalty. I will contact Asteria, and following that, we will have a meeting with our allies to decide the way forward. Hopefully, we can avoid an all-out war, but we do need to prepare for it. Master Kanaka, could you brief Masters Lamm and Luticia?'

Kanaka nodded. Mab vanished and appeared in her bedroom, at the School of Psych and Sorcery, where Pelian was waiting for her.

Pelian said, 'Did you see Infelice?'

Mab replied, 'Yes, she was with Master Kanaka. I scanned her again and I am certain that she is genuine and was not involved in the conspiracy.'

Pelian replied, 'I'm so glad, I really like her!'

Mab replied, 'Me too!'

As Mab lay in bed, she moved her consciousness into mind-space and searched for Asteria. She found her in the place where she released Tabatha. Asteria was sitting alone, eating and reading an ancient parchment.

Mab whispered, 'Asteria, it is I, Bellona.'

Asteria looked around her almost in panic before saying, 'Where are you!'

Mab replied, 'I am at home, sleeping, with my partner. I must speak with you.'

Asteria replied, 'You can reach into the Abyss so easily! How is that possible?'

Mab replied, 'My powers continue to grow, I don't know the reason, but I sense it is because there is a likelihood of war.'

Asteria said, 'War? What do you mean? We have no intention of going to war with anyone.'

Mab replied, 'Erebus and my sister Minerva, with others, including Soronica, are involved. They seek to build empires on planets under my protection. Noticas and Antobus were but the first sojourn. I have banished Minerva from our palace; she is now living with Erebus in the Abyss.'

Asteria thought for a few moments and said, 'I will leave Erebus and Minerva to you, but I will look into the involvement of Soronica in this conspiracy.'

Mab replied, 'I think their first move will be to kill me. So be careful, you may also be a target or become a target.'

Asteria said, 'Thank you for the warning, I will take precautions. You know, when I first met you, I was little more than a child. You stood over me, splattered in blood; the dead were all around me. Do you remember what you said to me?'

Mab replied, 'No. I expunged much from my memory before I went into exile. I could not live with the slaughter.'

Asteria said, 'Then I will remind you. You said I was an innocent and would not be harmed, that only fools think a war can be won, and that in war everyone loses.'

Mab replied, 'Then I was wiser than I thought.'

Asteria said, 'We must prevent another war. That should be our priority.'

Mab replied, 'Agreed, but in order to do that, we must stay alive. Keep in touch!'

Mab pulled her consciousness back and fell into a deep sleep.

Asteria sat in her regular meeting with her three brothers and her recently found sister, Tabatha, who was still coming to terms with her freedom and being reunited with her siblings.

Panthaca looked at Asteria and said, 'Sister, you look tired. What is worrying you?'

Asteria said, 'The goddess Bellona contacted me following her visit. It seems her sister, Minerva, and Erebus are involved in a conspiracy to colonise protected worlds in the light.'

Soronica replied, 'Is this of any interest to us?'

Asteria stared hard at Soronica and said, 'She named others who were involved.'

Soronica was silent for a few moments, but then said, 'Yes, I am involved in assisting Erebus and Minerva. Have you forgotten Noticas, Antobus and Insheigra? We are entitled to live where we desire; why shouldn't we live in the light? You may fear this goddess, but I do not. The sooner she is dispatched, the better, and with the help of Minerva and Erebus, we will have access to many other worlds.'

Tabatha's head snapped around, and she said, 'You are a fool of the highest order if you think you can kill the goddess. She is powerful beyond your comprehension.'

Asteria said, 'Soronica, you have not seen the goddess in battle. I have seen her; Tabatha has seen her. The actions of Erebus and Minerva could lead to a second war with the light, I cannot permit that.'

Certinaca said, 'I am sorry, Asteria, I agree with Soronica. We cannot allow this goddess to dictate what we can and can't do!'

Panthaca said, 'We all heard the words of the goddess and of Infelice, they spoke the truth. It is we of the Abyss who have encroached on their worlds and killed or enslaved many of their people. I agree with Asteria, another war must be avoided at all costs.'

Asteria said, 'So, Soronica, Certinaca, you are outvoted, it is three against two. You will therefore desist from further interactions with Erebus and Minerva.'

Soronica glanced at Certinaca, then looked at Asteria and said, 'We cannot do that. We will leave these demesnes and support Erebus in his fight for freedom.'

Tabatha said, 'Then, brother, you will see me at the right hand of the goddess.'

Asteria said, 'Go! And do not return!' Soronica and Certinaca vanished.

Asteria said, 'It seems I have recovered my sister and lost two brothers in the blink of an eye.'

Panthaca replied, 'We can only hope they reflect on the situation and come to their senses.'

Tabatha said, 'No, they are suffused with greed and ambition. They see themselves as emperors ruling over worlds of countless enslaved subordinates. They are as deluded as Noticas and Antobus. But if they meet Bellona in battle, they will fall before her, that is certain, even they must realise that they cannot confront her. They will attempt assassination; we must warn her!'

Asteria replied, 'Tabatha, calm yourself. The goddess already suspects that. She warned me that I may also be a target. Panthaca, muster the guards, seek out any traitors or conspirators. I will remain in direct contact with the goddess. Tabatha, I want you to watch over and support the goddess. If an attempt on her life is made, it needs to be clear that we are with her, and not with Erebus and his rebels.'

Panthaca replied, 'I will also strengthen your personal guard.'

Asteria nodded and said, 'Stay in contact, report anything unusual.'

Panthaca and Tabatha vanished.

Pelian shook Mab awake and said, 'You need to get up!'

Mab replied, 'Is breakfast ready?'

Pelian said, 'No, it isn't! You are coming with me for early morning sword practice in the arena! The students will love it!'

Mab groaned and lifted herself out of bed. Pelian vanished. Mab looked around for something she could eat, groaned again, took a long shower, dressed and vanished. She appeared in the arena and found a scene of utter carnage. Three students were staked out on the floor of the arena. Their hands and feet had been nailed to the ground using metal stakes. They had already lost a lot of blood. Two other students had been torn apart, their limbs ripped off and thrown to the ground, their heads were mounted on metal spikes. Pelian was immobilised, wrapped in an iron chain. An iron band was fixed tightly around her neck and was connected to the chain. A huge creature held the other end of the chain in one hand and a black sword in its other hand. It resembled a large bull standing on hind legs; it had pointed black horns and a mouth full of tusks.

The creature said, 'I have been sent to end your life, petty goddess. Come and kneel before me, or perhaps you would like to watch as I feast on this tasty morsel.'

Mab watched every nuance as the creature stood holding Pelian. She realised the iron chain was enchanted and bound to the creature. She could see red marks around Pelian's neck where the iron burned her flesh. Mab walked slowly towards the creature; the creature raised its black sword. Mab stopped. The creature laughed. Mab's hand went to her left hip, a whip of light lashed outwards, severing the iron chain, simultaneously a psychic blast of power struck the creature on the chest, propelling it backwards across the arena. Mab gestured with her right hand, and Pelian and the three students vanished.

The creature bellowed with rage and charged across the arena towards Mab, who waited for it to arrive. The creature had intended to trample Mab into the earth, but realising she was simply waiting for it to reach her, it slowed and approached more cautiously.

Mab said, 'What are you and who sent you?' She could feel the creature trying to enter her mind, it was extraordinary powerful. A band of iron with a chain attached appeared around her neck. The creature hauled on the chain, but Mab did not move. Mab grabbed hold of the chain and dragged the creature slowly towards her. The creature raised its sword, Mab vanished, appeared immediately in front of it, and punched it in the throat. The creature dropped to its knees. Mab slipped her two index fingers between the iron band and her neck, stretched it, lifted it above her head and threw it to the ground. The creature was struggling to breath. Mab said, 'I was going to repeat the question, but to be honest, I don't care what you are or who sent you.'

Mab plucked her sword, Durandal, from the air and plunged it down through the back of the creature's skull. She then withdrew the sword and decapitated it in one fluid motion. She reached out to Master Lamm and pulled him to her. Lamm was aghast.

Mab said, 'I am sorry, Master Lamm. Two students have been killed, torn apart. Another three were staked to the ground but are still alive. Pelian was held in iron chains. I sent her and the students to heal in the waters of the palace. I will go there now to check all is well and return as soon as I can.'

Lamm nodded and said, 'I assume this was actually an attempt on your life?'

Mab replied, 'Yes, Baydan was involved. Pelian and I may need to move into the palace and work from there. It is too dangerous for students to be around us at present.'

Lamm nodded and said, 'Yes, I think that would be wise. I will make the necessary arrangements here.'

Mab vanished and appeared in the palace of the old gods.

Pelian was helping the third student to enter the sacred waters. Mab waited for her to finish and then called to her.

Pelian embraced Mab and, tearfully, said, 'I couldn't help them. As soon as I arrived in the arena, I had an iron band around my neck. I had no powers; I was completely helpless.'

Mab replied, 'Pure iron can have a nullifying effect on certain magical powers, but the iron band was also enchanted. I think it was a guard of sorts, sent out to drag offenders back to the Abyss.'

Pelian said, 'But the students, it tore them apart. They were innocents who couldn't fight back or even communicate with it!'

Mab replied, 'We must make this our home until matters are resolved. It is too dangerous for the masters and pupils with us living close to them. Stay here, watch over the students until I return.' Mab, incandescent with rage, flew upwards through the upper atmosphere and into space, her powerful senses reached out and located Baydan, who was in a particularly desolate part of the Abyss.

Mab entered the Abyss close to Baydan's location. She could see him in the distance, still in human form, standing on a high rocky shelf, shouting rallying cries to thousands of his minions, many of whom occupied the bodies of giant scorpions, others merely amorphous masses floating in space. Mab approached the huge crowd at enormous speed and swept broad beams of silver flame across them, incinerating everything in her path. She landed amid the chaos, some hundred or so paces from Baydan, who was high up on the rockface. Mab plucked two silver swords from the fetid air, Durandal and Eurandal, and meted out death and destruction the like of which had not been seen since the time of the light war. Her swords moved with blinding speed, and beams of light flashed from her eyes as she waded through the crowd. Periodically, she would blast attackers away to clear a pathway using psychic bursts of energy. She became a creature of death that knew only killing, and in that, she reached a state of utter perfection. Many hours later, she stopped, unrecognisable, layered in congealed blood, flesh and bone fragments, her twin swords dripping black. She did not feel tiredness, but only the warm glow she felt when performing a sword kata, feeling its beauty and precision. She looked around her at a sea of death, there was a strange silence, punctuated by an occasional groan somewhere in the distance. Mab looked up, Baydan was nowhere to be seen, but she knew he was there, in a cave, cowering with his close circle.

Mab translated up to the rock shelf and walked into the cave. Baydan was sitting with three others; they were all in human form. They stood up but made no attempt to defend themselves.

Mab said, 'You three will leave, Baydan, you will remain here.'

The three figures vanished immediately. Baydan moved to speak, but a whip of light wrapped around his neck and silenced his words.

Mab said, 'I warned you that I would take your life, for what you did to Pelian.'

Mab drove Durandal through Baydan's chest, pinning him to the rock face. She then decapitated him with Eurandal and incinerated the body. Mab leapt off the rock shelf and landed with a thump on the battlefield below. She reached out with her senses, and satisfied, she vanished and reappeared in the palace.

Pelian stared at her and said, 'Is that you under there? Where have you been?'

Mab smiled and said, 'I'll have a shower and then rest in the lake for a while. How are the students?'

Pelian said, 'Michael came, he helped me to return them to the school. They are fine, as am I!'

Mab replied, 'How long have I been away?'

Pelian said, 'Almost a whole day, in local time here on Earth.'

Mab frowned and made her way to the showers.

A few minutes later, Pelian joined Mab in the shower and said, 'That filth really stinks. What have you been doing? Draining a swamp?'

Mab laughed and replied, 'Yes, in a manner of speaking. I went to see Baydan.'

Pelian said, 'In the Abyss?'

Mab replied, 'Yes, you will be pleased to know that his head is no longer attached to his body.'

Pelian smiled, hugged Mab tightly and whispered 'Is he really dead?'

Mab replied, 'Yes, no doubt about it.'

Pelian kissed Mab passionately and said, 'Let's go to the lake and then to bed.'

Sladrin and Dakigo stood before Erebus, Minerva, Soronica and Certinaca.

Sladrin said, 'Seleran and Castaran were killed recently by Bellona on Raqus Mons. Now we have reports that our brother Baydan and his guards were killed here in the Abyss only a matter of hours ago. This goddess is waging war against us; she must be stopped!'

Soronica said, 'Were there witnesses to this killing?'

Sladrin replied, 'Yes, three of his command escaped.'

Erebus said, 'Bring them before us!'

Dakigo vanished and appeared some minutes later with three others.

Erebus said, 'You witnessed the killing of our brother Baydan? Why did you not intervene!?'

The guards remained silent, clearly wondering whether they would survive this interrogation.

Soronica said, 'Please, give us your account of what happened. You will not be harmed, but we must know the truth.'

The leader of the three guards stepped forward and said, 'We were hosting a rally of our clan. My two colleagues and I were in the eyrie together with Lord Baydan. The eyrie is a cave high up in the rock face overlooking our rally area. The goddess entered the eyrie, she told us to leave immediately and for Baydan to remain. We returned later, only burnt remains of Baydan and his possessions remained and the goddess had departed.'

Certinaca stared at the three guards and said, 'You did nothing to help him! How many of your clan attended the rally?

The guard leader replied, 'The entire clan was present and assembled on the plain below.'

Erebus said, 'If I remember correctly, your clan is some five thousand strong in warriors alone? Surely some could have gone to aid Baydan, or were they unaware of what was happening in the eyrie?'

The guard leader lowered his head and said, 'Lord Erebus, our clan includes seven thousand four hundred and eighty-five experienced warriors. But, with respect, you were not present. You did not see her; we did everything possible to protect our ruler.'

Erebus looked at the guard leader and said, 'I am missing something here. Why did the warriors on the plain not go to the aid of your ruler?'

The guard leader said, 'Because none survived, they all fell before her.'

There was a stunned silence before Soronica said, 'She used a weapon, or a poison to kill so many?'

The guard did not reply.

Erebus said, 'Answer the question!'

The guard leader said, 'The goddess used white flame from her eyes and two silver swords. She was both terrible and magnificent. Never have I witnessed such a thing.'

Minerva said, 'Baydan must have done something to provoke such an attack. My sister had an intense dislike of Baydan because of what he did to Pelian. She could have killed him at any time, but why this carnage, why kill his entire clan?' The guard leader looked uncomfortable.

Minerva said, 'You know more than you have told us. Speak!'

The guard leader said, 'We sent an assassin to kill the goddess and to drag Pelian back to the Abyss. It was a Balgoran, one of the old species and very powerful. Lord Baydan paid handsomely for the services of the creature.'

Minerva said, 'Do you know what happened?'

The guard replied, 'Not for sure. But our information sources tell us that the Balgoran killed several students at a school and captured Pelian. The goddess appeared and the Balgoran was slain.'

Minerva said, 'This creature killed children?!'

The guard replied, 'Balgorans feed on human flesh, the children would have been a good source of food. But I suspect it killed them to attract the attention of Pelian or of the Goddess.'

Minerva replied, 'So Baydan sanctioned the killing of children, the killing of Bellona and the chaining and capture of Bellona's partner. Now it all makes sense!'

Soronica said, 'Minerva, we did not know what Baydan was doing. But your sister must be captured or killed, otherwise our plans will not be realised.'

Minerva replied, 'Yes, there can be no future for us until that happens. However, we need to keep control of the situation; any attacks on Bellona, her partner or her friends need to be sanctioned by us!'

Erebus said, 'It will be done, Baydan was a fool, blinded by his obsession with Pelian. Guards, you are dismissed, report to Dakigo.'

The guards bowed and left.

Soronica looked at Minerva and said, 'I thought you had Bellona under control. You told us that you would deal with her in good time.'

Minerva replied, 'She is not as she was at the time of the light war. She is even more powerful, and her powers continue to grow. She expects a war, but I do not believe we should meet her on the battlefield. Assassination is our only hope.'

Certinaca said, 'No, I do not agree. We must meet her and her supporters on the battlefield and slay them all. We have many scores to settle.'

Erebus said, 'I think we should invite her here to talk, we then try to kill her. If that fails, then it must be war.'

Minerva replied, 'Many have tried to kill her and ended up dead!'

Sladrin said, 'That is true, goddess. However, if we lure her here and attack her together, then I am sure we could overcome her.'

Minerva replied, 'Perhaps, but she will not come here alone.'

Soronica said, 'I will contact her. We will invite her and others of her choice to meet with us. We should be more than sufficient to kill her. However, I do not think you should be involved with this, you and Dakigo should stay close and join the fray only if necessary.'

Minerva nodded.

Mab sat in the centre of the huge stone table in the palace of the old gods. On her left sat Masters Kanaka, Lamm, Boe, Luticia, Pelian, Infelice and also Morgana. On her right sat Archangels Michael, Gabriel, Lucifer, Uriel and Humbra. Mab explained the current situation, including Minerva's betrayal.

Lucifer said, 'Your sister has lost her mind.'

Mab replied, 'She was lonely, Erebus was there for her. Perhaps love is a form of madness? I would rather she choose a different partner, but it is her choice. However, she plots with Erebus and others against the light. Many attempts have been made on my life and I now know that Erebus, and by implication Minerva, were responsible.'

Uriel said, 'The recent attack, I understand the children were torn apart by a Balgoran? What kind of creature would kill innocent children?'

Tears streamed down Pelian's face as she replied, 'I could not help them, the creature tore them apart and staked others out on the ground.'

Mab put her arm around Pelian. Uriel looked at Mab and said, 'This Baydan deserved his fate.'

Mab nodded and replied, 'I killed him, and his clan, for what he did to Pelian and for the killing of innocents. If I had killed him earlier, the students could have been saved.'

Kanaka replied, 'Mab, that doesn't necessarily follow. You did your best and that is all anyone can ask.'

Lucifer said, 'You killed his clan also?'

Mab replied, 'Yes, they are all dead.'

Infelice said, 'Goddess, Baydan's clan numbers around seven thousand warriors. I am sure they cannot all be dead!'

Mab replied, 'I did not count the fallen, but I know that his entire clan now lie dead on the battlefield.'

Pelian stared askance at Mab but then smiled and said, 'My love, thank you. Baydan and his clan were vile.'

Lucifer had a grim smile on his face. Uriel simply stared into space and said nothing.

Lucifer broke the silence by saying, 'Goddess, forgive me, if there is a war, how do we deal with your sister?'

Mab stared at Lucifer and said, 'I have no answer to that question, but she will not die by my hand. I cannot kill my sister.'

There was a period of silence and reflection before Mab said, 'I have asked Asteria, Panthaca and Tabatha to join us. They are of the deep Abyss. I will admit them now.'

Three dark shapes began to take form above the centre of the table. A hollow, far-off voice said, 'Goddess, we will take human form and join you.' The three black clouds became three human figures, two female and one male. Asteria was the tallest of the three, Panthaca the shortest. Mab stood, and everyone else followed her example. To everyone's surprise, Tabatha leapt over the table and embraced Mab. Mab hugged her tightly and kissed her. Asteria said,

'I am Asteria of the Abyss, this is my sister Tabatha and my brother Panthaca. We are pleased to be here in this magnificent palace. However, we can only remain here for a short time.'

Mab introduced everyone else before saying 'Asteria, you will find that you can remain here for as long as you need. This is the palace of the old gods. If you are permitted entry, the palace will sustain your needs.'

Asteria replied, 'Goddess, that is wonderful!'

Mab said, 'Everyone, take your seats.' When all were seated she continued, 'Erebus, Minerva, Soronica, Certinaca, Sladrin and Dakigo are united against us. Morgana confirmed that clan Humbra was merged with clan Dakigo. Baydan and his clan no longer exist.'

Humbra said, 'Dakigo will do whatever he is told to do by Erebus.'

Morgana nodded and said, 'Yes, Sladrin told me that your clan is now under Dakigo. I think Sladrin is looking for a way out. The killing of Baydan and his entire clan has shaken him badly. He asked me if I could arrange a private meeting with you, Goddess, to discuss how he could help to avoid a war.'

Mab looked at Boe and said, 'Master Boe, what is your opinion of this proposal?'

Boe said, 'I think it could be an opportunity too good to miss.'

Mab smiled and replied, 'Yes, that was my thought also. But perhaps it could be a trap?'

Boe replied, 'For sure it is a trap.'

Mab looked at Morgana and said, 'Morgana, please arrange the meeting.'

Morgana replied, 'Yes, Goddess, it will be done.'

Asteria said, 'News of Baydan's demise reached us quickly, and it created quite a stir, especially in those who remember the light war. Soronica and Certinaca have aligned themselves with Erebus in their so-called war of freedom. This, of course, means that they would be free to do what they like, while many others are enslaved.'

Kanaka asked 'Will your two brothers be acting alone or will they have the support of others of the Abyss?'

Panthaca replied, 'A small number of our guards defected with our brothers, but they are insignificant. At present, our guards number around five thousand, although many of these are not highly trained in warfare. You must understand that countless billions of creatures inhabit our demesnes, but we have no real need to defend ourselves. However, we do not wage war on those who live in the light; the catastrophe of the light war is not forgotten.'

Mab replied, 'We also have not forgotten, but some, who played little or no role in it, choose to forget, and so history repeats itself.'

Asteria said, 'Yes, Goddess, that is so. However, if we eradicate the leaders, perhaps we can avoid an all-out war with millions of deaths.'

Mab grimaced and replied, 'That is exactly what I did to bring the light war to a conclusion, but only after millions had been slain. I do not wish to make that mistake again.'

Kanaka said, 'The question is which side in the conflict has the greater military capability?'

Boe replied, 'Yes, that is a valid question. But in this case, as Asteria pointed out, the focus should be on the leadership. The enemy outnumbers us, worst case, probably four or five to one. But if we compare the leadership teams, my feeling is that we have the advantage. So, I think this needs to remain focussed at the highest level, we cut the head from the snake. But it needs to be done quickly, before they have time to organise their campaign.'

Lucifer said, 'Goddess, the meeting with Sladrin is when they will try to kill you. As master Boe has said, this could, however, be an opportunity for us. They each know that they cannot kill you on their own; the many failed attempts on your life have proven that. Therefore, they will act together. Sladrin will be closest to you, so he will strike the first blow, or more likely try to poison you. He only needs to disable or even distract you for a few seconds before the others fall upon you. Of course, Sladrin will be committing suicide; he is not the smartest of daemons, as you will slay him in less than a second. However, he will have served his purpose.'

Mab laughed and said, 'Lucifer, thank you for that convincing analysis of how I will be killed. Perhaps you could now explain how I will be able to avoid being killed?'

There was laughter around the table.

Lucifer replied, 'Goddess, that is an important question. However, we need to know the location of the meeting. I suspect they will propose a location in the Abyss; if so, we should offer a neutral territory.'

Mab looked at Morgana and said, 'The summit of Raqus Mons on Raqian in the Raamon system. As soon as possible.'

Morgana nodded and vanished.

Mab added 'Morgana will confirm when and where the meeting will take place. We all need to be there and be prepared for battle. Now, I suggest we eat!'

A sumptuous spread of food appeared in front of Mab, who said, 'Think of your favourite meal!' Platters of food and drinks started to appear on the table.

Mab looked at Michael and said, 'You have not said much. Do you have concerns?'

Michael replied, 'No, the head must be cut from the snake. There is no other option. But what of Minerva, she is your sister?'

Mab said, 'Soronica and Certinaca are brothers to Asteria, Tabatha and Panthaca. What other options are available to us?'

Michael said, 'None, as far as I can see, but I wonder if Erebus is the key. It is an ancient, insidious creature. I feel its malevolence even here. It has slowly infected your sister over millennia and bent her to its will. Do you remember when Erebus slighted you here in this palace?'

Mab was staring at Michael intently, and all others stopped what they were doing to focus on the exchange.

Mab replied, 'Yes, I remember that I came close to killing him, but he apologised.'

Michael replied, 'No, he feigned fear. He slighted you deliberately, to provoke you and then to demonstrate that he was afraid of you. He is cunning; he wants to convince you that he is subordinate to your power, so he can remain in the shadows. He did the same thing when you attacked Noticas; he feigned fear and weakness. But he is neither afraid nor weak. He is evil beyond measure. I see it because that is my purpose, the reason I was made. To recognise evil.'

Mab turned slowly to Asteria and said, 'How long have you known Erebus?'

Asteria replied, 'As Michael has said, Erebus is an ancient creature, it existed long before the light war. It started to use the male

600

human form when visiting your sister. As you know, it rules over several clan leaders, but it seldom comes to our demesnes and always asks permission when it does come. It is held in high regard, but also feared throughout the Abyss.'

Mab turned back to Michael and said, 'Michael, thank you for your insight.'

Morgana stood before Sladrin, who said, 'The goddess must pay for what she did to clan Baydan.'

Morgana replied, 'Lord Sladrin, the goddess is willing to meet with you, but she fully expects an attempt on her life to be made. If you are anywhere near her when that happens, you will surely be as dead as Lord Baydan.'

Sladrin struck Morgana a powerful back-handed blow to her face, knocking her to the ground.'

Morgana lay still for several seconds but then slowly pushed herself upwards, first to a crouching position and then fully erect. She was bleeding profusely from her nose, which had been crushed, and from her mouth. Her jaw was at a peculiar angle, and white bone was protruding from her cheek. She gestured with her left hand, and Sladrin burst into flames and vanished. Morgana also vanished, returned to the palace and dropped to the floor.

Lucifer ran to her and picked her up as if she were an infant.

Mab said, 'Take her to the waters, quickly.'

Lucifer vanished, reappeared beside the lake and waded in, cradling Morgana in his powerful arms and lowered her slowly into the water. Morgana woke immediately and gasped in relief as the pain was washed away.

Lucifer sat holding her, but Morgana said, 'Lucifer, release me.'

Morgana sank slowly to the bottom of the lake.

Mab appeared beside Lucifer and said, 'She is fine, the waters will heal her completely, in body and mind.'

Lucifer replied, 'Yes, I feel its power. But to completely immerse in it! Could that be dangerous?'

Mab said, 'No, let her be. We need to make plans.'

Mab and Lucifer returned to the meeting area.

Mab said, 'I think we can safely assume that the meeting is not going to happen.'

Kanaka said, 'How is Morgana?'

Lucifer replied, 'She is well. The waters are healing her, it may take some time.'

Asteria said, 'Goddess, my brother Soronica wishes to speak with us. Can he enter the palace?'

Mab nodded. A black cloud formed above the meeting table.

Soronica said, 'Sladrin reported the incident with the witch Morgana. We apologise and hope that she will recover from her injuries.'

Asteria replied, 'What do you want?'

Soronica said, 'We want to meet with you, to reach a compromise, a war is in no one's interest.'

Asteria replied, 'We are willing to meet, but the location must be neutral territory.'

Soronica said, 'We had hoped to host the meeting, but I see your point. Where do you suggest we meet?'

Asteria looked at Mab, who said, 'The summit of Raqus Mons on Raqian, when Raamon is next at its zenith.'

Soronica replied, 'That would be acceptable to us. Who will represent you?'

Asteria again looked at Mab, who said, 'Asteria, Michael, Lucifer and I.'

Soronica replied, 'We will be represented by Erebus, Certinaca, Sladrin and me.' Mab replied, 'I require my sister to be present.' Soronica said, 'We will choose our own representatives.' Mab replied, 'Fine.' Soronica vanished.

Mab said, 'We need to move quickly. Michael and Gabriel, you will make ready the Angel host. Masters of the magic schools, you will muster all the senior students and adepts. Panthaca, you and Lucifer will ready the guards of the Abyss, and any other forces at your disposal. When the battle commences, which could be only minutes after the meeting begins, I will be the spear tip. Tabatha and Pelian will be on my right, Asteria and Lucifer will be on my left. Michael, Panthaca and Master Kanaka will decide when to commit our three commands unless instructed otherwise by me.'

Kanaka said, 'How much time do we have to prepare?'
Mab replied, 'Local time, mid-afternoon tomorrow.'

Chapter Thirty-Seven: War or Peace

Mab, Asteria, Michael and Lucifer hung in space directly above Raqus Mons.

Asteria said, 'There is an entrance to the Abyss within the mountain.'

Mab replied, 'Yes, that is where the lords used to meet with Baydan and Sladrin.'

Michael said, 'I sense movement around the top of the mountain and on the plain below.'

Mab nodded and said, 'They have arrived. It is time, follow me.'

Mab dropped down through the thin Raqian atmosphere and landed gently on the summit of Raqus Mons. Soronica was alone and stood some distance away. Mab's powerful senses swept across her before delving deep into the mountain.

She walked towards Soronica and said, 'I see you have brought Varalian with you. It seems that I will never be rid of that creature!'

Soronica replied, 'It is for my protection, until my colleagues arrive. Varalian will raise an energy shield around me should you choose to attack.'

Mab paused before saying, 'These are our terms. You will return to the Abyss, and my sister will be returned to me. There will only be one access route from the Abyss to the light. That will be controlled by Asteria and me. All the other known access points will be sealed.'

Soronica replied, 'That is not acceptable. We will colonise the local planets accessible to us, including this planet. It is our right to live wherever we wish.'

Mab replied, 'No, it is not. You can only survive here by enslaving others. I will not permit that.'

Soronica said, 'Then you will be destroyed!' and promptly vanished. A powerful cylindrical energy shield surged upwards from deep in the planet and enveloped Mab's group. Mab's senses screamed at her, she looked up and saw something falling rapidly towards her from space.'

Michael said, 'It is a weapon, we cannot escape, the energy field is too powerful. We must go downwards or upwards!'

Mab said, 'Remain here!' and rocketed upwards to meet the falling object. It was close to entering the open top of the energy field when Mab slammed into it. An intense white light spread out in every direction, closely followed by a pulse of electromagnetic radiation and a blast wave that shook the planet. The energy field was shredded, and the intense white light slowly diminished to reveal Mab hanging in space. Her head was back staring upwards at Raamon. Michael, Asteria and Lucifer appeared by her side. Mab looked down and pointed, a broad beam of white light burst from Raamon and seared downwards towards the planet. The light beam arrived within minutes and pierced Raqus Mons like a sharp knife through butter.

Mab said, 'Varalian's energy generator has been destroyed.'

The mountain rumbled, and a spout of red magma spewed from close to the summit.

Mab said, 'Now we must take the fight to the enemy.' Michael pointed and said, 'There is no need, they are assembled on the plain below!'

Erebus, Soronica, Certinaca, Sladrin and Minerva moved into sight around the foot of Raqus Mons. Their military power was arrayed behind them, the numbers were almost incalculable and consisted of creatures of every conceivable size and shape.

Asteria said, 'This has been long in the planning!'

Lucifer replied, 'They number around thirty thousand!'

Mab said, 'The numbers are irrelevant. We will slay them all if we must, but my sister is not to be harmed. Assume battle formation!'

Tabatha appeared on Mab's right. She was fearsome, like a caged panther about to be released on its prey. She wore a robe of the finest black silk and held a huge black sword that dripped venom. Pelian took position behind Tabatha. She wore her light blue lord's robe, and her silver sword was hitched on her back. Her piercing blue eyes were focused on Mab's every move. Asteria took position on Mab's left with Lucifer slightly behind her. Some five thousand guards of the deep Abyss were arranged immediately behind the head of the spear, led by Panthaca. Above these, a golden host of angels appeared, they were led by Archangels Michael, Gabriel, Uriel and Humbra. Their enormous wings were spread, and each held a huge golden sword. Immediately before Panthaca and behind the spear tip, some four hundred of Lucifer's palace guards appeared. They wore ornate helms with visors and carried a range of fearsome weapons.

Mab glanced at Lucifer and smiled.

Lucifer said, 'You may remember John, he is leading the guards, he insisted on being here.'

Mab nodded and replied, 'He is most welcome.'

Erebus and Soronica moved slowly forward, and Mab and Asteria moved to meet them. They stopped some thirty paces from each other. Erebus said, 'It is not too late, if you agree to our terms, you will have peace, if not, you will have war and destruction.'

Mab replied, 'We are not here to negotiate terms; that opportunity is now lost. We will meet you in battle here today. You and your entire force will be slain. Then we will have peace.'

Soronica replied, 'You would kill your own sister?'

Mab said, 'I am looking forward to killing you, Soronica. Now, I suggest you return to your hoard.'

Erebus said, 'You are heavily outnumbered, Goddess. I suggest you think again.'

Asteria replied, 'You are about to make the same mistake as Baydan. The numbers are irrelevant.'

Erebus turned and made his way back. Soronica looked at Asteria, tried to say something, but then turned and followed Erebus.

Erebus said, 'Sladrin, Dakigo, bring your forces forward.'

The black wave of daemons moved forward, parting when they reached Erebus and his cohort, akin to a black river flowing around a huge stone.'

Minerva said, 'Erebus, their front line is too strong, it needs to be broken!'

Erebus replied, 'It will be broken!'

Pelian looked at Mab and said, 'Snakes, scorpions, birds and humans. A strange mix of daemon hosts.'

Mab nodded, looked at Lucifer and said, 'Deploy your palace guards.'

The guards moved slowly forward in a two-line formation, the front line only a few paces ahead of the rear. The rear line was able to fire between the guards in the front line due to the lateral positioning.

Mab messaged Michael 'Wait until the guards engage their front line and then attack the flanks.'

Michael replied, 'I will attack their right flank and Gabriel their left.'

Mab messaged Panthaca 'Your legions must follow twenty paces behind the guards, kill anything that gets past them. If the guards fall, you will be the new front line.'

Panthaca replied, 'Understood, Goddess!'

Asteria pointed and said, 'Something is happening, their advance is slowing!'

Mab turned to Lucifer and said, 'Balgorans, they are making their way through the enemy ranks. Advise John to use maximum force as soon as they appear. If they cannot hold them, we will intervene immediately. We must hold our front line at all costs!'

Lucifer nodded.

A mouth appeared in the front wave of the black horde, and the fearsome creatures known as Balgorans spewed onto the battlefield. The enemy ranks roared their approval. Mab estimated around fifty Balgorans had entered the battle, many more than she had expected. The guards did not flinch; they continued to move forward with the same poise and precision, raising their weapons and firing bursts of energy at the approaching Balgorans. However, it was clear that the Balgorans were much too strong to be brought down by energy weapons alone. The Balgorans roared as the energy bursts from the guards simply dissipated on their heavy armour. The enemy ranks roared with them, cheering the Balgorans on. The guards stopped, the energy weapons were locked and carefully placed on the ground. The guards reached back, each removed two long silver swords that were concealed within their armour. The guards held their swords pointing upwards, elbows tight into their sides above each hip. As the Balgorans bore down on them, they took a step forward, thrust the swords forward and cried out 'Hia!' An enormous psychic pulse of energy swept towards the Balgorans, who were knocked to the ground. The guards were upon them immediately, their silver swords cutting the Balgorans to pieces. The Balgorans were slaughtered. The guards returned to their original formation, sheathed their swords, picked up their energy weapons and resumed their march towards the enemy. The enemy front line was in disarray, undecided whether to attack or retreat. Soronica and Certinaca appeared at the front and were attempting to calm the commanders.

Mab messaged Michael and said, 'Attack the flanks now!'

Lucifer messaged the guards and said, 'Attack their front line, maximum force!'

Lucifer's guards broke into a run towards the enemy front line, and they fired devastating energy rounds that penetrated deep into their ranks. Soronica went to support their front line, towards the left flank, which was collapsing under the pummelling it was receiving from the guards. However, he encountered Gabriel, who spun around and struck him with his right wing. Soronica hit the ground hard. He tried to rise, but as he looked upwards, Gabriel's golden sword pierced his throat and was driven deep into his chest. Certinaca screamed and raced towards Gabriel, but Asteria appeared immediately in front of him and said, 'Brother, this is your last chance. You will leave this place now and return to the Abyss, or I will take your life.'

Certinaca replied, 'No, sister, it is I who will take your life.'

Certinaca drew his sword to strike Asteria, but then gasped as a black blade was driven into his back and through his chest.

Tabatha said, 'Brother, you have paid with your life for your treachery.'

She pulled the blade from his body and decapitated him.

Mab and Pelian raced to the right flank of the enemy. Michael and the angel host were cutting through them with ease. The battlefield was awash with black, stinking blood, severed limbs, severed heads, mandibles, tails and every other conceivable body part of the enemy ranks. Meanwhile, the guards and Panthaca's legions were still wading relentlessly onwards, killing everything in their path. A black pike was thrust into Mab's shoulder. She groaned as she pulled the barbed tip from her flesh and expelled the poison that sought to pollute her blood.

Pelian cried out, 'Sladrin!'

Mab said, 'Leave him to me!' as she blasted several giant scorpions to pieces with a gesture. She leapt high into the air, Durandal appearing in her right hand, and landed within a few paces of Sladrin, who spun around with a short melee sword, which narrowly missed Mab's throat. Mab bent over backwards to avoid the blade but then leapt up and kicked Sladrin in the head. He went down but drew a combat knife and attacked Mab ferociously. Mab grabbed Sladrin's knife hand at the wrist and snapped the bone. She then ripped the entire arm from his body and threw it to the ground, black blood spraying over her. Sladrin started to fade in order to escape, unaffected by the massive loss of blood, but Mab drove Durandal downwards, through his skull, pinning him to the ground and killing him instantly. She then incinerated the body.

Michael messaged Mab 'Goddess, it is becoming a massacre. The bulk of the enemy forces are trying to leave the battlefield. Do you wish us to continue?'

Mab replied, 'Yes, the defeat needs to be absolute!'

Mab soared upwards, pulling Pelian with her. As they hovered above the battlefield, Mab messaged Kanaka, instructing him to stand down.

Pelian said, 'They are in retreat!'

Mab replied, 'Yes, but we need to finish this to ensure it never happens again.'

Pelian pointed and said, 'Look at Lucifer!'

Mab looked down and saw Lucifer wading through the enemy like a titan, slaying everything in his path. He wielded two long black swords and used them in concert, with deadly effect. His great wings folded and unfolded, protecting him from attack and breaking bones and carapaces alike. But Mab saw a dark cloud heading for Lucifer at great speed. She knew immediately that it was Erebus.

Mab vanished, appeared beside Lucifer and said, 'Erebus is approaching.'

Lucifer replied, 'Then we will slay him together!'

Mab smiled and vanished. She reappeared immediately in front of Erebus and blasted him backwards. The black cloud became Erebus in human form. Mab pointed to the summit of Raqus Mons and vanished.

Mab stood on an elevated but relatively flat area of rocky ground between two lava flows. Erebus appeared some twenty paces from her.

Mab said, 'Soronica, Certinaca and Sladrin are dead. Your legions are scattering. You have been defeated. What say you?'

Erebus replied, 'I say that you will be remembered as a petty goddess who thought to vanquish Erebus. You cannot kill me, but I will certainly kill you here today.'

Thick black tentacles sprouted from Erebus as he took his true form. The creature was huge with a bulbous head, cruel slits for eyes and a mouth filled with carious fangs. It moved through the air rapidly towards Mab, who responded by striking it with an enormous psychic blast. However, the creature seemed to lose and regain solidity at will, rendering the psychic energy ineffective. Mab soared upwards, holding her palms outwards, and narrow beams of silver light sliced through the creature. Erebus's face twisted in pain, but it did not slow.

Mab plummeted downwards, beams of light flashed from her eyes as she plucked Durandal from the air. She sliced and stabbed at the black mass, which was in a state of continuous flux. Durandal was a blur in Mab's hand, but what appeared to be solid body parts lost their solidity no matter how fast Durandal moved. Erebus's black tentacles wrapped around Mab, and although Durandal sliced through them, there were too many; Mab was being overwhelmed and rapidly becoming ensnared. But then she sensed the arrival of Michael and Lucifer, who commenced slicing through the creature. Mab regained some movement and, focusing on Michael, fought her way outwards, escaping the clutches of the creature which had grown to many times its original size. Mab's witch senses screamed; she vanished immediately and reappeared above Erebus. Minerva had tried to drive a sword through her from behind. She was now forcing Michael and Lucifer back, away from Erebus.

Mab stared down at her sister and said, 'Sister, enough!' Minerva looked up.

Lucifer plunged his sword through her stomach.

Mab gestured, and Lucifer and Minerva vanished.

Erebus roared and lashed Michael, who cried out in pain as the black whip gored his face. Mab soared upwards, pulling Michael with her. She looked upwards to Raamon, clenched her fist, and pointed at the black mass now approaching her. Raamon pulsed, a broad beam of white flame plummeted downwards. Mab and Michael continued their attack, but in the last few seconds, Mab translated, pulling Michael with her, as the searing beam of light reached Erebus. Erebus was engulfed entirely, but to Mab's astonishment, the darkness pushed the light upwards; the black tendrils writhed and battled for supremacy over the light. But Raamon was stronger, the light eventually mastering the darkness, driving it down, and drilling it into the surface of the planet. Mab gestured, and the beam of light vanished. Mab and Michael dropped to the ground and stood looking down at the creature, who was Erebus. It was lying at the bottom of a deep crater, writhing in pain.

Mab leapt to the bottom of the crater and said, 'It is dying.'

She raised her right arm and plunged Durandal into what appeared to be the head of the creature. This time, Durandal met solid matter; the creature lay still. Mab floated upwards and stood beside Michael at the edge of the crater. Michael asked 'Is it dead?'

Mab replied, 'Evil will always be amongst us. But, yes, Erebus is dead. This battle is over. I must go to my sister, stand everyone down and meet me at the Palace.'

Michael bowed, and Mab vanished.

Mab arrived at the Palace and made her way to the sacred waters.

Lucifer was cradling Minerva in his arms and said, 'Goddess, your sister is recovering.'

Mab waded into the lake and said, 'Lucifer, go back to the battlefield. I instructed Michael to order a standdown. The battle is over, but there may be a need for clean-up operations.'

Lucifer bowed and vanished. Mab looked down at

Minerva and said, 'Open your eyes.'

Minerva opened her eyes and said, 'Sister, I am sorry.'

Mab replied, 'Erebus is dead.'

Minerva shed tears but said nothing. Mab held her tightly for a while and said, 'Your mind has been poisoned. You will meld with me now. I will cleanse you.'

Minerva protested, tried to push Mab away. But Mab embraced her and soared upwards. Minerva resisted the meld, but Mab forced her way in, their minds conjoining, sharing every thought, every experience. Mab saw Minerva's weakness, millennia spent alone, her need for meaning in her life, for purpose, for a loving partner and the false hope of children. Mab realised that these were the levers Erebus used to poison her sister's mind. And, in that knowing, Minerva also recognised the truth. They held each other and shone like a newly born star high in the sky above Mount Olympus.

Mab and Minerva fell from the sky like a meteor, silver flame trailing behind them, and landed in the palace. Asteria, Tabatha, Panthaca, Michael, Lucifer, Uriel, Humbra, Infelice, and master's Kanaka, Lamm, Luticia and Pelian stood waiting, in silence, and bent the knee as Mab and Minerva approached. The goddesses stood, arms linked, flame still licking around their bodies. Mab said, 'My sister was sick, but now she is restored. Please rise, how long have you been waiting?

Michael replied, 'Goddess, it has been almost two days since you and your sister ascended, and we commenced this vigil.'

Mab said, 'Then we are all hungry and thirsty, let's eat!'

Mab embraced Pelian, and they held each other tightly.

Pelian whispered, 'I am starving!'

Mab said, 'Then we will see who can eat the most food!'

Pelian replied, 'I think I know the answer to that!'

Mab sat at the head of the table with Minerva to her left and Pelian on her right. Food began to appear on the table almost immediately; even the Archangels joined in the feast. Michael said, 'Goddess, Raqus is now free of daemons, we were able to expel many. Also, more hosts survived than those who died.'

Mab nodded and replied, 'What of the dead?'

Michael said, 'Incinerated in the lava flows.'

Minerva asked, 'And Erebus, what of his remains?'

Michael glanced at Mab before saying 'Goddess, his remains were at the bottom of a crater, they were left undisturbed. I placed a large stone over the grave. I would be happy to take you there if you wish.'

Minerva smiled and said, 'Thank you, Michael, but that will not be necessary.'

Chapter Thirty-Eight: The Wedding

The market square in the heart of the Academy of White Witches was particularly busy due to the seemingly never-ending victory celebrations. Principal Luticia had taken many of their best students to fight in a war far away, and all had returned safely. Fora walked amid the stalls searching for bargains and collecting fresh vegetables. She held a wicker basket in the crook of her arm. She was arguing with a vendor over the cost of a roll of cotton fabric. The vendor said, 'You are drinking my blood! I cannot drop my price any further! The vendor's eyes widened as Mab appeared at Fora's side. She was dressed in a white robe with a red sash and wore open-toed sandals of soft leather.

Mab put her arm around Fora and, looking at the vendor, said, 'What was the price of the cotton?'

The vendor bowed deeply and said, 'Goddess, I am hoping that Master Fora will accept this cotton as a free gift in view of her being one of my best customers.'

Fora laughed, handed the vendor a silver coin and said, 'This is a fair price.'

The vendor dropped to his knees and bowed his head.

Fora turned, hugged Mab and said, 'I hear congratulations are in order?'

Mab smiled and replied, 'Yes, that is why I am here, perhaps we should go to your home?'

The throng of the marketplace had gone, and there was complete silence. All in the market square were kneeling. Luticia came hurrying across the square and was somewhat breathless when she reached Mab and Fora.

She bowed deeply and said, 'Goddess, it is a great honour to have you here. Please, both of you, let me offer some refreshments.'

Mab replied, 'Luticia, yes, that would be most welcome. I am sorry to arrive unannounced.'

Luticia replied, 'You are always welcome, announced or otherwise.' Luticia called out to the crowd, 'Please now stand up. Three cheers for the Goddess Bellona!'

But the crowd stood and chanted 'The White Witch, The White Witch, The White Witch…'

Mab smiled and slowly opened her arms. White flower petals began to rain from the sky, but whenever touched, they disappeared. The crowd gasped in wonder, the children ran around laughing and screaming, trying to touch as many as possible before they reached the ground. Fora said, 'It is beautiful!'

Luticia led Mab and Fora to her office, where a spread of food was already arriving. Luticia said, 'I will be in the room next door, please let me know if you need anything.'

Mab nodded and said, 'Thank you, Luticia.' Mab poured hot coffee into two wooden cups and helped herself to rustic bread and cheese.

Fora said, 'I don't understand why you don't get fat! You are always eating!'

Mab smiled and replied, 'I'm a goddess, I can't get fat.'

Fora rolled her eyes.

Mab said, 'I'm getting married.'

Fora replied, 'Yes, I know! Who is the lucky girl?'

Mab replied, 'Her name is Pelian, she is the last of the so-called lords of chaos.'

Fora stared at Mab before saying, 'You love her, I can tell.'

Mab replied, 'Yes, I do love her, but I also love you. I want you to be maid of honour at my wedding.'

Fora was lost for words but managed to whisper, 'It is a very great honour. So, of course, I will do it, if you think I am worthy?'

Mab beamed at Fora, who gasped as a wave of wellbeing swept through her, and said, 'You are most definitely worthy. My sister Minerva will perform the marriage ceremony and represent the parent function for Pelian, who has no family. Master Kanaka, with my human mother, will represent the parent function for me. Pelian will have two maids of honour, Infelice and Tabatha. You and Uriel will be my maids of honour. The Archangels will be present as witnesses.'

Fora replied, 'Many of these are names of legend, are you sure you want me to do this?'

Mab said, 'Yes, I want my closest friends around me.'

Fora replied, 'Then yes. I would love to be there with you and Pelian. I need to think about what to wear!'

Mab laughed and said, 'No, the maids of honour will all be dressed in white silk, even Tabatha!'

Fora whispered, 'White silk, where will I find such a thing?' and then said, 'Who is Tabatha?'

Mab replied, 'You and Pip will collect your dresses when you arrive at the Palace, and they will be a perfect fit! You don't have to do anything. Tabatha is a very close friend of mine; I think she would prefer a black dress, but she will be wearing white!'

Fora said, 'I'm sure she wouldn't want to wear black at a wedding!'

Mab replied, 'She is a daemon from the deep Abyss.' Fora stared at Mab askance. Mab added 'She is also astonishingly beautiful, and I just know you will like her! Anyway, I am being summoned so I must leave.'

Mab appeared beside Michael and Gabriel, who hung in the atmosphere above the planet Raqus. Michael said, 'There has been a development.'

Mab replied, 'What do you mean?' Michael dropped downwards, followed by Gabriel and Mab, and landed on Raqus Mons, where the battle with Erebus took place.

Gabriel pointed to a large stone and said, 'The stone has been removed from the crater.'

Mab looked down into the crater and said, 'His remains have also gone!'

Michael said, 'But who could have removed the stone?'

Mab looked up and reached out with her witch senses, but could find no trace of Erebus. She looked at Michael and said, 'It may be that the creature still lives; evil can never be entirely eradicated.'

Michael replied, 'Yes, that is true, but we must not allow it to thrive.'

Mab nodded and said, 'Return the stone to the crater and do not speak of this to anyone else, especially my sister.'

Michael nodded and said, 'Understood.'

The palace was adorned with white flowers, perhaps for the first time in its existence. There was a tangible feeling of joy in the air as the guests started to arrive. Mab and Pelian stood in the master bedroom, which was enormous in its proportions. A huge circular bed was positioned in the middle of the room. It had been fashioned from the same stone as the floor and, as with all the other furniture, it seemed to have grown organically from it. The bed had many ornate, polished stone posts covered in runes, which seemed to be in a constant state of change. The curved half of the room had no visible external wall, but closer inspection revealed an almost transparent energy field that extended from the floor to the high, ornate ceiling above. The view was truly extraordinary.

Mab said, 'Welcome to the palace master bedroom, but we don't sleep here! There are many other smaller rooms in the palace that are more suitable. However, it is perfect as a dressing room.'

Minerva said, 'Bellona and I will be dressed in white silk only, as is the custom of the old gods. Pelian, have you decided on your dress?'

Pelian bowed and replied, 'Yes, I will be dressed as you and Bellona in silk only, but sky blue in colour and hooded in accordance with my Mevlen ancestors.' Minerva smiled and bowed her head slightly.

Mab said, 'Infelice, Tabatha. I think you should be in white silk also, but perhaps with a black sash?'

Infelice laughed and said, 'You mean we can't wear black dresses?'

Mab smiled and said, 'You can wear whatever you want!'

Tabatha replied, 'I prefer white silk!'

Infelice nodded her approval. Mab looked at Uriel, whose appearance changed to reveal a low-cut dress of white silk, tied at the waist with a golden sash. Her huge snow-white wings were folded over a rune-covered white cape, which was almost invisible against her dress. There were gasps of astonishment. Mab and Minerva both bowed to Uriel.

Mab said, 'Mother, you look beautiful.' Uriel smiled and bowed.

Fora said, 'Can Pip and I have wings too?'

Everyone laughed.

Mab said, 'Wings no. But you can have everything else!' Fora and Pip were suddenly dressed exactly like Uriel, minus the wings.

Sopa looked at Mab and said, 'What should I wear?'

Mab said, 'Mom, I think you should wear the same dress as Minerva. My dress is similar but with a few embellishments. Let's see how this looks.'

Mab gestured, and all were dressed in accordance with their wishes.

Soft music began to sound throughout the palace. Minerva and Sopa left the room and made their way to the chapel, where Kanaka was waiting for them, close to the front dais.

Minerva said, 'Do you have the rings?'

Kanaka reached into a secret pocket in his robe and pulled out a silver box. He opened the lid to reveal two rings, each resting on a cushion of velvet.

Minerva stared, Sopa gasped and whispered, 'They are so beautiful!'

Minerva said, 'They are more than beautiful. These are the rings of Juno and Jupiter; I had thought them lost. The white ring was Juno's and the blue Jupiter's; they were cut from the purest diamonds in the known universe by Juno herself.'

Kanaka said, 'They are beautiful, but I fear they will not fit!'

Minerva replied, 'They will fit, the question is whether they will accept the wearers! It is said that the rings of Juno may only be borne by those of pure heart.'

Kanaka replied, 'Then there will be no problem!'

Minerva said, 'Hopefully, but Bellona has slain many of both the light and the dark.'

The guests began to arrive at the Chapel. The Angel host appeared at the back of the room, and they were magnificent in their white and gold garments. Each had a golden sword held in a scabbard of purest white. The Archangels stood several paces behind the front ceremonial area, and behind them, the guests gathered, forming a wide aisle from the chapel door to the front dais. The Principals and Masters of the magic schools were present together with many senior students, including Charly and Cat. Asteria and Panthaca stood together and wore robes of black silk. Boe took up his allotted position at the front with his back to the dais. His role was to receive the brides as they entered the chapel, and present them to Minerva, Sopa and Kanaka.

A trumpet sounded to announce the arrival of the brides. The door of the chapel room swung open; Boe walked up the aisle to meet Pelian and Mab, who smiled at him as he approached. Mab put her arms around Boe, hugged him and kissed him on both cheeks. Boe was overcome; tears ran down his cheeks, but he turned and began the slow walk to the front dais. The music began to dim, but another sound began to take form. It was so beautiful that everyone stopped for a moment to listen. Mab and Pelian looked up to see figures of blazing light flying over them. The Archangels bowed their heads, and the Angel host bent the knee. Boe was transfixed.

Mab said, 'Master Boe, do not worry. It is the Seraphim; their presence here is a great honour.'

Boe continued his journey with Tabatha and Infelice walking behind Pelian, and Uriel and Fora behind Mab. Tabatha could not take her eyes or ears from the Seraphim and stared in wonder at them.

Boe arrived at the dais and passed the couple over to Minerva, who smiled and said, 'We are honoured indeed by the guests here today. Even the Seraphim are present! It is also a great honour for me to carry out this marriage ceremony for my only sister, Bellona, and her beautiful bride, Pelian. Please remove your head coverings.'

Mab and Pelian threw back their hoods of silk. Mab's hair was plated on both sides while Pelian's tumbled from the hood and flowed like a river of snow down to the small of her back.

Minerva opened her hands, and a band of golden fabric appeared.

She said, 'I, Minerva, ask you, Bellona and Pelian, to join your hands together before me to signify the conjoining of your lives from now and henceforth until your deaths.' Mab and Pelian reached out with their left hands, Pelian's resting on top of Mab's. Minerva wrapped the golden fabric around their hands and tied a loose knot. She gestured, and a thick slab of the purest marble floated before her.

Minerva said, 'Rest your bound hands on the stone.'

Pelian looked quizzically at Mab but followed her example. Minerva turned to Kanaka, who passed her the box bearing the rings. Minerva placed the unopened box on the stone. The Seraphim went wild, their singing and music bringing tears of joy from everyone in the room. They swept downwards around the two brides, but Mab stood perfectly still, and Pelian kept her eyes focused only on Mab.

Minerva gently lifted their hands and spread them apart on the stone without undoing the golden fabric. She then opened the ring box and took a step backwards to join Kanaka and Sopa. There was a sudden silence in the room, and the Seraphim hung in the air transfixed. Mab and Pelian stared at the rings of diamond, also transfixed. The white ring flared into life. It floated from the box and moved slowly to the centre of the stone. It rested there for a few seconds before moving quickly towards Mab's hand. Mab lifted her fingers off the stone, the ring paused for a few seconds and then slid onto her finger, fitting perfectly. Minerva looked at Mab and smiled. Pelian looked at the still dormant blue ring and then at Mab, tears building in her eyes. Mab was about to comfort her when there was a sudden flash of blue light. The ring lifted from the box and floated to the centre of the stone. It then moved towards Pelian, who now had tears of joy streaming down her face. The ring slid onto her finger and a burst of blue light coursed through Pelian and rose upwards, engulfing the entire room in a feeling of hope, goodness and wellness. The Seraphim bathed in the blue light, singing and laughing at the same time while swooping down around Pelian. The blue light then slowly shrank back into the ring.

Mab whispered, 'They love and celebrate your pure heart, as do I.'

Minerva said, 'Bellona, Pelian, please now kiss your bride.'

Pelian threw her arms around Mab, and they kissed slowly until Minerva said, 'The marriage ceremony is complete, now it is time for the celebration dinner!'

The dinner was lavish. Minerva had already placed many platters of food on the table, and of course, guests could eat and drink whatever they desired merely by thinking about it. Mab and Pelian were the centre of attention, and periodically, one of the guests would rise and propose a toast in their favour. As the day turned to evening, Minerva signalled to Mab, it was in a sign language that only they could understand. Mab stared for a long moment at her sister, tears appeared in her eyes as she signed her assent. Only Pelian, who was in conversation with Kanaka, noticed the exchange. She glanced at Mab, time slowed, she saw her pain and placed her hand on hers. Mab smiled reassuringly, and Pelian turned back to Kanaka. Minerva stood up, catching everyone's attention, and said, 'I would like to thank you all for coming here today, not only to celebrate the marriage of my sister Bellona but also to welcome the birth of a new goddess. The goddess Pelian!' The guests leapt to their feet and applauded vigorously.

Mab and Pelian stood up. Mab said, 'Yes, it is wonderful! Pelian was the reason the Seraphim were present. She was tested and confirmed as a goddess of the light.'

Minerva said, 'This is the end of an era. It has been a period of war, struggle and confusion. Now we are at the beginning of a new era of peace, hope and happiness. This was realised by the return of Bellona, and we must thank those who protected her, particularly Sopa and Walim, her human parents, but also Uriel and Master Kanaka and indeed many more who shepherded her through childhood and into adulthood.'

The guests all applauded. Then Minerva said, 'I must leave you now, to go back into the light. I will not see many of you again, but I know that one day I will once again be reunited with my sister.'

Mab smiled at Minerva, who faded and vanished.

Mab said, 'My sister was weary; she carried many burdens. But she will return, of that there is no doubt. Pelian and I will be here for you. Together, we won the war, but now we must win and secure the peace.'

Mab raised her goblet and said, 'A toast, to Peace, Happiness and Prosperity!'

All replied, 'Peace, Happiness and Prosperity!'

THE END

About the Author

David Martin was born in Glasgow and currently lives in rural Lincolnshire, England, with his wife Moira. He received his BSc degree from the University of Glasgow and was later awarded a PhD for fundamental research work in the field of engineering science. David has had a lifelong passion for science fiction and fantasy; his hobbies include long distance walking in Scotland and France.

www.ingramcontent.com/pod-product-compliance
Lightning Source LLC
Chambersburg PA
CBHW051128120626
46547CB00012B/711